THE DIVINE COMEDY
OF DANTE ALIGHIERI

THE DIVINE COMEDY
OF
DANTE ALIGHIERI

Edited and Translated by
ROBERT M. DURLING

Introduction and Notes by
RONALD L. MARTINEZ
AND ROBERT M. DURLING

Illustrations by
ROBERT TURNER

Volume 2
PURGATORIO

OXFORD
UNIVERSITY PRESS

OXFORD
UNIVERSITY PRESS

Oxford   New York
Auckland   Bangkok   Buenos Aires   Cape Town   Chennai
Dar es Salaam   Delhi   Hong Kong   Istanbul   Karachi   Kolkata
Kuala Lumpur   Madrid   Melbourne   Mexico City   Mumbai   Nairobi
São Paulo   Shanghai   Taipei   Tokyo   Toronto

Translations copyright © 2003 by Robert M. Durling
Introduction and Notes copyright © 2003 by Ronald L. Martinez and Robert M. Durling
Illustrations copyright © 2003 by Robert Turner

First published by Oxford University Press, Inc., 2003
First issued as an Oxford University Press paperback, 2004
198 Madison Avenue, New York, New York 10016

www.oup.com

Library of Congress Cataloging-in-Publication Data is available

ISBN 0-19-508741-0 (cloth)
ISBN 0-19-508745-3 (pbk.)

1 3 5 7 9 10 8 6 4 2
Printed in the United States of America
on acid-free paper

PREFACE

Since the submission of our *Inferno* for publication (1994) there has been an important renewal of discussion of the text of the *Comedy* in Lanza's (1995, 1997) and Sanguineti's (2001) critical editions: the first privileges the earliest Florentine manuscript, the Trivulziano (Milan, Trivulziano 1080), against Petrocchi's view of the northern tradition as superior, and the second argues for the unique authority of the Vatican's Urb. Lat. 366 (*Urb.*), from Urbino, on the basis of a collation of Barbi's famous 400 *loci critici* in the 600 existing manuscripts (at the time of this writing, the volume giving Sanguineti's detailed justification of his readings had not yet appeared). Both Lanza and Sanguineti adopt many readings rejected, rightly or wrongly, by the mainstream of modern editing.

The text presented here is a compromise; not persuaded of the exclusive authority of any manuscript (indeed, unwilling to exclude altogether the possible existence of author's variants), the editor has felt free to adopt readings from various branches of the stemma. Thus the text of our *Purgatorio* once again, in the main, follows Petrocchi's *La Commedia secondo l'antica vulgata* (1994), but the editor has departed from Petrocchi's readings in a number of cases, somewhat larger than in the previous volume, not without consideration of Lanza's and Sanguineti's readings (these departures are discussed under the rubric "Textual Variants," pages 627-29), and, as before, Petrocchi's punctuation has been lightened and American norms have been followed. The translation follows the same principles as that of the *Inferno* and has the same format, and the reader is referred to the Preface of that volume for discussion of its aims and those of the notes. As before, the numbers in the margins are those of the first Italian line of each terzina, and in the notes numbers always refer to the Italian text; *Vergil* refers to the historical person, *Virgil* to Dante's character.

One innovation in our notes to this volume is a section for each canto that we have dubbed *Inter cantica,* discussing the relation of the canto with the *Inferno* (we hope to include similar sections in our *Paradiso* volume). These *Inter cantica* are not exclusively discussions of the canto's relation to the similarly numbered canto in the *Inferno,* although that subject clearly deserves more attention than it has heretofore received; we have learned much from writing these notes: the self-referentiality of the *Comedy* is complex indeed.

Acknowledgments

We have again received generous help and encouragement from many friends and colleagues, and it is a pleasure to express our gratitude to them. In particular, Warren Ginsberg, Regina Psaki, and John A. Scott have commented in detail on extensive portions of the manuscript, Paul Alpers, the late Charles

T. Davis, and Nicholas J. Perella on the entirety of an earlier state of the translation. Nancy Vine Durling has caught many errors, typographical and otherwise, in our drafts, David L. Jones in the first printing. Père E.-H. Wéber, O.P., has given us kindly and helpful advice, reminding us that the interpretation of Aquinas, Albert, and other thirteenth-century thinkers remains subject to lively debate. Our debt to Albert R. Ascoli is once again profound, and our expression of gratitude to him in our first volume may be taken as applying to this one as well. Charles Lee, of McTek Enterprises, Berkeley, has given us invaluable help and computer first-aid. The staffs of the Bibliothèque Nationale de France (Sites François-Mitterrand and Richelieu), the Bibliothèque du Saulchoir (Paris), and the Doe and Bancroft Libraries at the University of California, Berkeley, have been unfailingly cordial and helpful. And once again the patience, forbearance, and active helpfulness of our wives, Nancy Vine Durling and Mary Therese Royal de Martinez, have been exemplary.

We again owe a great debt to the personnel at Oxford University Press, especially to Ruth Mannes, in charge of production of the volume.

The text of the *Purgatorio* is reprinted (with qualifications, as above) from *La Commedia secondo l'antica vulgata*, edited by Giorgio Petrocchi (sponsored by the Società Dantesca Italiana; copyright © 1994, Casa Editrice Le Lettere), with the kind permission of both sponsor and publisher.

As before, translations of biblical passages are from the Douay version of the Latin Vulgate, except as noted, and, unless otherwise identified, non-biblical translations are our own.

We record a deep sense of loss at the passing in 1998 of the great Dante scholar Charles T. Davis, a dear friend whose acute and kindly criticism and encouragement had long been of vital importance to us, as to many others. We dedicate this volume to his memory.

Berkeley   R.M.D.
Providence   R.L.M.
August 2002

CONTENTS

ADDITIONAL NOTES

MAPS

FIGURES

Italy, ca. 1300

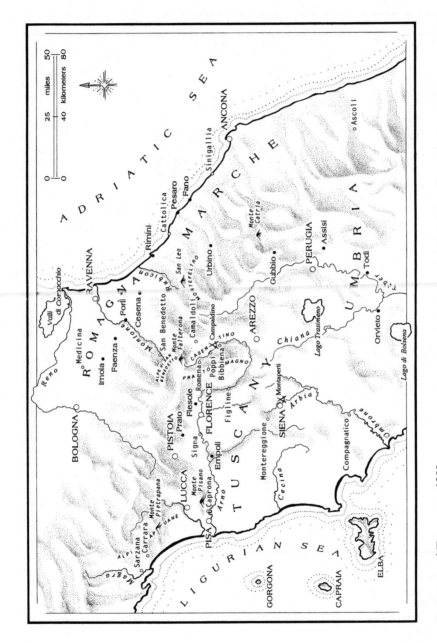

Romagna and Tuscany, ca. 1300

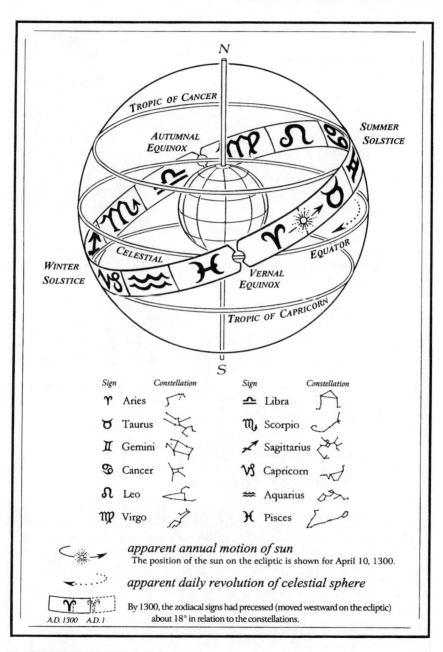

Sign		Constellation	Sign		Constellation
♈	Aries		♎	Libra	
♉	Taurus		♏	Scorpio	
♊	Gemini		♐	Sagittarius	
♋	Cancer		♑	Capricorn	
♌	Leo		♒	Aquarius	
♍	Virgo		♓	Pisces	

apparent annual motion of sun
The position of the sun on the ecliptic is shown for April 10, 1300.

apparent daily revolution of celestial sphere

By 1300, the zodiacal signs had precessed (moved westward on the ecliptic) about 18° in relation to the constellations.

A.D. 1300 A.D. 1

The Celestial Sphere and the Zodiac

The Earthly Paradise

The Lustful

The Gluttonous

The Avaricious and Prodigal

Purgatory   The Slothful

The Wrathful

The Envious

The Proud

The gate of Purgatory

Ante-Purgatory

The Late   ⎧ The Negligent Rulers
Repentant | The Unabsolved
           | The Indolent
           ⎨
           ⎩ The Excommunicate

The Structure of Dante's Purgatory

ABBREVIATIONS

Achill.	Statius, *Achilleid*
Acts	Acts of the Apostles
Aen.	Vergil, *Aeneid*
Apoc.	Apocalypse of Saint John
Cant.	Canticle of Canticles [Song of Songs]
CG	Aquinas, *Summa contra gentiles*
Chron.	Chronicles
Commentarii	Macrobius, *Commentarii in Somnium Scipionis*
Confessions	Augustine, *Confessions*
Consolation	Boethius, *Philosophiae Consolatio*
Conv.	Dante, *Convivio*
Cor.	Saint Paul's Epistles to the Corinthians
De civ. Dei	Augustine, *De civitate Dei*
De nom. div.	Pseudo-Dionysius, *De nominibus divinis*
De serm. Dom.	Augustine, *De sermone Domini in monte*
Deut.	Deuteronomy
DVE	Dante, *De vulgari eloquentia*
Eccles.	Ecclesiastes
Ecclus.	Ecclesiasticus
Ecl.	Vergil, *Eclogues*
ED	*Enciclopedia dantesca*
Eng.	English
Ep.	Dante, *Epistles*
Ep. mor.	Seneca, *Epistulae morales*
Eph.	Saint Paul's Epistle to the Ephesians
Etym.	Isidore of Seville, *Etymologies*
Ezek.	Ezekiel
Ex.	Exodus
Gal.	Saint Paul's Epistle to the Galatians
Gen.	Genesis
Geor.	Vergil, *Georgics*
Gr.	Greek
Heb.	Saint Paul's Epistle to the Hebrews
Inf.	*Inferno*
Is.	Isaiah
Jer.	Jeremiah
John	Gospel According to Saint John (with preceding numeral, Epistle of Saint John)
Jos.	Joshua
Jud.	Judges
Lam.	Lamentations of Jeremiah
Lat.	Latin
LDS	*Lectura Dantis Scaligera*

LDT	*Lectura Dantis Turicensis*
LDV	*Lectura Dantis Virginiana*
Luke	Gospel According to Saint Luke
Mal.	Malachi
Mark	Gospel According to Saint Mark
Matt.	Gospel According to Saint Matthew
Met.	Ovid, *Metamorphoses*
Mon.	Dante, *Monarchia*
NLD	*Nuove letture dantesche*
NT	New Testament
Num.	Numbers
Od.	Homer, *Odyssey*
OF	Old French
OT	Old Testament
Par.	*Paradiso*
Peter	Saint Peter's Epistles
Phar.	Lucan, *Pharsalia*
PL	Migne, *Patrologia . . . Latina*
Prov.	Proverbs
Ps.	Psalm(s)
Purg.	*Purgatorio*
Quaest.	Dante, *Quaestio de acqua et terra*
Raptus	Claudian, *De raptu Proserpinae*
Rom.	Saint Paul's Epistle to the Romans
Servius	*Servii grammatici . . . in Vergilii carmina commentarii*
SS	Cicero, *Somnium Scipionis*
ST	Aquinas, *Summa theologiae*
Theb.	Statius, *Thebaid*
Thess.	Saint Paul's Epistle to the Thessalonians
Tim.	Saint Paul's Epistles to Timothy
VN	Dante, *Vita nova*
Wisdom	Wisdom of Solomon
Zach.	Zachariah

Authors' names appearing in the notes without dates (e.g., "Singleton") refer to commentaries, listed in the Bibliography under "Editions and Commentaries on the *Divine Comedy*"; authors' names followed by dates (e.g., "Singleton 1966") refer to items listed in the Bibliography under "Modern Works." Primary sources are for the most part cited by author or abbreviated title (as above); references are to editions listed under "Works by Dante" and "Primary Texts."

Psalms are cited by the numbers of the Latin Vulgate, used by Dante; they differ from the numbers of the Hebrew Bible: Vulgate Psalm 9 is Hebrew Psalms 9 and 10; Vulgate Psalms 10-112 correspond to Hebrew Psalms 11-113; Vulgate Psalm 113 is Hebrew Psalms 114-115; Vulgate Psalms 114-115 are Hebrew Psalm 116; Vulgate Psalms 116-145 are Hebrew Psalms 117-146; Vulgate Psalms 146 and 147 are Hebrew Psalm 147; for Psalms 1-8 and 148-150 the numbers coincide.

THE DIVINE COMEDY
OF DANTE ALIGHIERI

INTRODUCTION

Dante seems to have completed and circulated the *Inferno* around 1314. Work on the *Purgatorio* was undoubtedly well under way by then, and it apparently continued without interruption, bringing this second cantica to completion within the next few years. These hypotheses, generally accepted today, are supported by the fact that the great majority of topical allusions in the *Purgatorio* refer to the years 1301-1308, a very small number to the events of 1312-1313, the years of the emperor Henry VII's unsuccessful effort to establish imperial authority in Italy, abruptly brought to a close by his illness and death; the background of the important political themes of the *Purgatorio* is discussed in the general Introduction (*Inferno* volume, pp. 4-15).

In many respects the *Purgatorio* is even more original and daring than the *Inferno*. The *Inferno* derives a number of its features from Vergil's Underworld, but the landscapes of the *Purgatorio* are virtually without precedent. Furthermore, the *Purgatorio* treats Christian theology with epoch-making freedom (the profound differences between Dante's representation of Purgatory and orthodox Christian views are discussed below); it voices a carefully thought-out, highly controversial political philosophy, with detailed consideration of important recent developments; it presents an elaborately developed theory of the nature, function, and history of poetry, integrated with an original interpretation of pagan Roman civilization as the preparation for the advent of Christianity, as well as a matchlessly insightful analysis of the human soul-body complex and the problematic of its integration; and, most surprising of all, it synthesizes all these public or general themes, as we may call them, with what is probably the most unusual personal love story in world literature, that of Dante's lifelong love for Beatrice, which motivates his entire other-world journey, leading, in a powerfully imagined climax that draws heavily on the biblical Apocalypse and other visionary literature, to reunion with the long-dead Beatrice in the Garden of Eden itself. The *Inferno* is the most accessible as well as the most sensational cantica of the *Divine Comedy*, but it is the *Purgatorio* that most fully reveals Dante's greatness as a poet.

The *Purgatorio* has a general outline parallel in many respects to that of the *Inferno*. After two preliminary cantos in each case, the ascent, replacing descent, begins through regions essentially separate from Purgatory proper: the Ante-Purgatory, original with Dante (for which he derived some suggestions from the episode on the banks of the Acheron and the encounter with Palinurus in *Aeneid* 6), in which late-repentant and other souls must wait before beginning active purgation (in extent—six cantos—though not in content, Ante-Purgatory corresponds to the infernal circles outside the City of Dis); Purgatory proper consists of seven circles, one for each of the Seven

Deadly Sins (more properly, Vices: see below), beginning with the most serious, thus being in a sense the inverse of Hell (in which the most serious sins are reached last, by descent); finally, purgation completed, the ascent reaches the Garden of Eden, imagined by Dante, in an unprecedented conception, as at the summit of the mountain of purgation (thus the symbol of earthly happiness is a place that corresponds with Cocytus, the lowest circle of Hell, and Satan).

Earthly happiness is the principal theme of this cantica, and each of the thematic concerns mentioned above is relevant to it. We cannot consider them all in detail in this introduction, particularly since they are best understood in context and in the sequence Dante fashioned for them (in addition to the Notes, we refer readers to the Additional Notes). Here we consider some general matters of background essential to understanding Dante's enterprise in this cantica: the background of the notion of Purgatory; ideas peculiar to Dante's conception of Purgatory (Original Sin; sin versus vice; the Mountain); and Dante's conception of allegory.

Purgation in the Afterlife. Many cultures—perhaps most—have imagined an afterlife involving the purification of the soul from the stains incurred in this life. In Antiquity, a particularly widespread version of this belief posited the reincarnation of the soul in successive lives that enabled it gradually to ascend toward ultimate freedom from the cycle of generation (or to descend into further punitive suffering); in Hinduism and other Oriental faiths this doctrine of karma is still very much alive. It was reportedly central to Pythagoras' thought and was voiced by Plato (*Phaedo, Republic* X, *Meno*), who posited a period of punishment and purification in a thousand-year interval between successive incarnations. Except for the *Timaeus*, however, Plato's dialogues were virtually unknown in the West during the Middle Ages, and the *Timaeus* was known only in part. Vergil's *Aeneid* was the vehicle through which some of these doctrines circulated.

Vergil's eclectic visionary eschatology sees the Underworld as a place of purgation from the infection of life in the body for all but the worst criminals. In Anchises' account:

> First, the sky and the earth and the flowing fields
> of the sea, and the shining globe of the moon and the Titanian sun,
> all these a spirit nourishes within, and, infused through these members,
> mind keeps driving the whole mass, and mingles with the great body.
> Thence is the race of men and of beasts and the life of flying things,
> and the monsters borne by the deep beneath its marbled surface.
> A fiery vigor and a heavenly origin dwells
> in those seeds, in so far as their harmful bodies do not slow them,
> their earthly limbs, their death-bound members weaken them.
> Hence they fear and desire, they grieve and rejoice,
> and they do not perceive the sky, closed up in darkness and a blind prison.
> Yes, and on the last day, when life departs,

not even then does every evil depart, nor entirely do
the plagues of the body disappear; it must be that deep down
many things have long hardened and grown into them strangely.
Therefore they are driven by punishments, and for old wrongs
they pay with sufferings: some are exposed empty,
suspended in the wind, others have their infected guilt
washed away under a vast torrent or burnt out with fire:
each of us undergoes his own death-spirits; afterwards we are sent
into broad Elysium, and a few remain in these happy fields
until the long day of the completed cycle of time
has cleansed the gathered decay, has left pure
the heavenly sense, the fire of simple air.
All these, when the wheel has turned for a thousand years,
the god calls forth in their long line to the Lethaean stream,
for they must return without memory to the convexity of the sky,
must begin once more to desire the life of bodies.

(*Aen.* 6.724-51)

Christians of course rejected the idea of reincarnation, as well as the idea that the body was the source of evil, but Vergil's richly poetic treatment of these themes strongly influenced their views of the afterlife, both because of the Latin Fathers' literary educations and because of the enormous prestige of the *Aeneid*.

Numerous passages in the Old and New Testaments fed the belief in what was to become known as Purgatory, although no scriptural passage explicitly asserts the existence of a place with such a name. But since Patristic times the Church had asserted its existence on the basis of statements regarding the efficacy of prayer for the dead, as well as from passages suggesting that if the Law was imperfectly obeyed in this life its obligations must be paid in the next (Matt. 5.17-26; 12.31-32). 1 Maccabees 2.12 and 41-46, concerning prayers offered on behalf of solders slain in battle while in sinful possession of pagan talismans, introduced the concept that was to justify paid masses and prayers to lessen the suffering of souls in the afterlife. The use in Matt. 5.25-26 of a monetary metaphor, speaking of a temporary punishment as repayment of a debt, encouraged the development of an "accountancy" of punishments; eventually it came to be thought that money, offered in the proper spirit, could in effect buy for the dead remission of their debt. Such a practice obviously left much scope for abuse (the Avignon papacy became notorious in this respect); in the early sixteenth century the selling of indulgences provoked the Protestant Reformation and led to the utter rejection of the doctrine of Purgatory by the Protestants.

A recent student of Purgatory, the historian Jacques Le Goff, argues that although existing as a concept since the early centuries of Christianity (discussed by Augustine and Jerome), Purgatory came into full existence only when the noun *purgatorium* [place of purgation] was coined, about 1170. For Le Goff, this linguistic manifestation accompanied an increase in the status of Purgatory due to a social need for a "middle" place, between Heaven and Hell, where the members of an increasingly influential and important "middle" class of merchants and bankers might find a place to atone for lives of avarice (sometimes of usury), bourgeois excesses of meat and drink, and spiritual neglect. The length of the purgatorial stays of this newly promoted class was increasingly drawn under the control of the newly centralized and bureaucratized Church promoted by the reforms of Pope Innocent III, and especially through the decrees of the fourth Lateran Council (1215), which were also crucial in advancing the dogmatic status of Purgatory. That the stay of souls in Purgatory might be mitigated or abrogated by suffrages—pious acts performed on the souls' behalf, such as masses for the dead—meant that the newly important and probably crowded place known as Purgatory was an opportunity to expand the scope of the Church's influence, as well as to increase its wealth.

Although Le Goff very much overstates the degree to which the Church's chronic financial need and its growing "accountancy" fostered the development of the theory of Purgatory, he draws attention to other roughly contemporaneous developments: institutional interest in the "inner life" of conscience (oral confession was made obligatory in 1215); prohibition of usury by Christians; the emergence of mechanically measured time (leading to the gradual shift from the traditional unequal hours to the equal hours of clock time). The doctrine of Purgatory (where "time is restored for time") does seem to have had strong appeal, especially for the wealthy and dynamic mercantile cities of Tuscany and northern Italy, where the arts of accounting were both the glory and the pitfall of prosperous burghers. It may well be that Dante's poem would have been inconceivable a century earlier, given the relatively unarticulated status of Purgatory before the twelfth century. Dante's Purgatory represents a marked advance in rendering the concept both concrete and systematic.

Dante's Purgatory: 1. Original Sin. Dante asserts unambiguously the doctrine that all humankind inherit Adam's sin and on account of it are relegated to Hell, except for those who are saved by faith in Christ. A clear statement is found in *Paradiso* 7:

    Per non soffrire a la virtù che vole   25
freno a suo prode, quell' uom che non nacque,
dannando sé, dannò tutta sua prole;
    onde l'umana specie inferma giacque   28
giù per secoli molti in grande errore,
fin ch'al Verbo di Dio discender piacque
    u' la natura, che dal suo fattore   31
s'era allungata, unì a sé in persona
con l'atto sol del suo etterno amore.

[25   By not enduring any rein upon the power that
wills, though for his good, that man who was not
born, in damning himself damned all his offspring;

28   therefore the human race lay weak for many
       centuries in great error, until it pleased the Word of
       God to descend
31   where he united with himself, in one Person, with
       the sole act of his eternal love, the nature that had
       gone far from its Creator.]

Before the coming of Christ, those who were eventually to be saved went after death to Limbo, the uppermost circle of Hell, to await his death and the Harrowing of Hell, after which they were led in triumph to Heaven (see *Inf.* 4.30-63, with notes); those Dante mentions are for the most part Old Testament figures (Adam, Eve, the patriarchs and prophets, etc.), although at least some pagans are included (*Purg.* 29.22-30; *Par.* 18.103-35; 20.100-138).

So far Dante's views agree with the overwhelming majority of Christian theologians of his own and earlier ages. Divergences of opinion begin, however, as soon as the question is raised of the exact effect on human nature of Adam's fall. There is a wide spectrum of opinion on this question in the Christian tradition before and after Dante. Augustine's contemporary Pelagius denied that sinfulness could be transmitted genetically or by inheritance and took such an optimistic view of human nature as to assert that human beings could merit salvation by the achievement of moral virtue — in other words, without divine help. These views led to a famous controversy, in the course of which Augustine intensified his already pessimistic conception of man's fallen nature, denying the possibility of knowing truth or of acting virtuously without Christ, a view that largely dominated the Latin theological tradition until the rediscovery of Aristotle. Dante's views, though their background has not been adequately investigated, seem to be among the most optimistic expressed during the entire Middle Ages.

That human nature suffered a wound [*vulneratio naturae*] when Adam fell is explicit in the passage from *Paradiso* 7 quoted above and seems to be the root idea in the grandiose myth of the Old Man of Crete of *Inf.* 14.94-120 (see notes there and *Inferno* Additional Note 5). But Dante's Limbo (*Inferno* 4) is populated by large throngs of persons who "did not sin" (*Inf.* 4.34); they lived blameless lives, and the only reason for their being confined to Limbo is their not having been baptized, or, if they lived before Christianity, their "not worshipping God as they should" (*Inf.* 4.33-42). In other words, whatever may have been the weakening of human nature that resulted from Adam's sin, it did not prevent non-Christians from living without voluntary sin or from achieving moral virtue.

This is a position repeatedly and explicitly attacked by Augustine in the course of his long campaign against Pelagius and his followers: "For if natural possibility, with free will, is sufficient unto itself both to know how to live well, and to do so, then Christ died to no purpose" (*De natura et gratia* 40; *PL* 44, 272). According to Augustine (whose position was ultimately based on St Paul's condemnation of paganism in Rom. 1.19-32), the *vulneratio naturae* so darkened man's mind and weakened his will that without God's special grace there is "a certain necessity of sinning": "Let man hear that there is a certain necessity of sinning, deriving from the wound in human nature, not from its creation, and that he may not be compelled by it, let him learn to say to God, *Deliver me from my necessities* [Ps. 24.17]" (*De natura et gratia* 76; *PL* 44, 286).

Aquinas, on the other hand, is much more optimistic, especially early in his career; he grants that unaided human nature is capable of carrying out God's commandments (since God would not command the impossible), though not of acquiring the theological virtues faith, hope, and charity, necessary for salvation and by definition the gift of grace (*In Librum II Sententiarum*, Dist. 28, Q. 1, A. 3). This is virtually identical with Dante's position (see *Purg.* 7.31-36 and the notes to Canto 16), except that Dante did not subscribe to as radical a distinction between "nature" and "grace" as was formulated by Aquinas.

Dante's Purgatory: 2. Sin and Vice. The assimilation of Aristotle's elaborate theories of natural moral virtue and vice, beginning in the twelfth century, accounts for the greater optimism of the Scholastics. The categories of *sin* and *vice*, though closely allied, are distinct, and the distinction is fundamental to the *Purgatorio*. *Sin* is action displeasing to God, contrary to God's law; by committing a sin, one becomes subject to the punishment of God's justice.

The term *vice* (Lat. *vitium*), on the other hand, refers to the idea of a flaw: a flaw in a diamond is a *vitium;* a tree that bears poor fruit is *vitiosus.* Just so, a *virtue* (Lat. *virtus*) is a power or perfection of a nature; precious stones have "virtue" in the sense of occult power; the bearing of good fruit is a "virtue," a power, of a tree. Applied to human beings, the terms *vice* and *virtue* may refer to weaknesses and strengths, inherited or not, whether of body or mind; characteristically, however, they refer to moral states. In the Aristotelian conception, vice is a tendency, usually reinforced by repeated acts, to act wrongly; virtue is a tendency, governed by reason and acquired by, and realized in, repeated action, to act rightly. It is important to see that *acting* on the inclination to act wrongly is what constitutes sin: without wrong action there is no voluntary sin; it would be most unusual, but one might possess a natural inclination toward gluttony, say, without ever giving in to it. In any case, both virtue and vice are *habits* (Lat. *habitus* [state or mode of being]) of the will.

It is here that the concepts of sin and vice intersect. For sin affects the nature of the sinner: it wounds him; as he repeats the sin, he becomes "hardened" to it. Adam's and Eve's transgression, in which their "lower" natures rebelled against their reason, or "higher" nature, began an inner war between impulse and reason, usually referred to as "concupiscence." In the traditional view, their sin was in part its own punishment, necessarily involving hardship, permanent conflict, and death, as well as subjecting them to God's anger. All the weaknesses of body and temperament which human beings inherit, including mortality, disease, and humoral imbalance, derive from Adam's and Eve's sin.

Both vice and virtue have gradations, in the Aristotelian systematizing of these concepts that dominated Scholastic views, depending on the degree to which the pattern of wrong behavior has become "connatural." The highest state was often referred to with the term *temperance* (drawing on Plato's usage): in this state the appetitive soul spontaneously follows the right rule present in reason. In a less perfect state, *continence*, the right rule is known by reason, which successfully restrains the rebellious appetite. Another step down is *incontinence*, in which reason knows the right rule but is unable to hold appetite back. In the worst state, *intemperance*, reason has forgotten the right rule and willingly follows the dictates of appetite: the order of the little state of man has been entirely subverted (see the notes to *Inferno* 5 and 11).

Aristotle and other classical thinkers doubted that the extremes of vice could ever be corrected; their analogy was with the growth of a tree: as the twig is bent, so the tree grows. But the less serious forms of vice could be corrected by a prolonged process of discipline, whereby one acquired the right understanding of the nature of vice and virtue and by repetition broke down the old habit and established the new habit of right behavior. The Christian conception of the cure of sin overlaps with the pagan view of the cure of vice; both realistically acknowledge the near impossibility of correcting many inherited defects of body or temperament. In the most conservative Christian view, stemming from Augustine, as long as one is alienated from God one's reason is incapable of truth and one's efforts at self-improvement must fail. In the more optimistic view of thirteenth-century Aristotelianism, natural human reason was not undermined by Original Sin (this is probably the explanation of the golden head of the Old Man of Crete, *Inf.* 14.94-120; see, in the *Inferno* volume, Additional Note 3), and therefore, in Dante's extremely optimistic view, moral virtue is attainable by its use (see Additional Note 6).

One must repent of one's sins and believe that Christ's death on the Cross paid the penalty demanded by justice. Ordinarily the sacrament of penance (confession) involved the priest's imposing some form of penance as a condition of absolution. When absolved, in the traditional terminology, one is in a *state of grace*, as opposed to a *state of sin*. Then, with the help of God's grace, one can expect to progress along the path of moral improvement. The forgiveness of sins does not remove the tendencies that originally drew one toward sin, including the inherited or acquired defects of temperament with which one is obliged to struggle. Augustine likens the state of sin to suffering from a sickness involving fever; when one's sins are forgiven, the fever passes and the disease is cured, but the weakness resulting from the illness remains, and there must be a period of convalescence. Another favorite analogy of his is with a wound: when sins are forgiven the weapon that made the wound is withdrawn, but the wound itself must then heal.

This is the logic that underlies Dante's conception of Purgatory. The souls who arrive on the shores of the mountain have repented their sins and have been forgiven—and they are actually now incapable of sinning, their state of grace is permanent. But most of them are still suffering from the effects of sin. In classical terms, they have brought their vices with them, and these must be corrected before they can rise to beatitude. The process of moral discipline that they must undergo is conceived partly in Aristotelian terms and is repeatedly compared to the training of falcons (see 14.143-51) or of horses (see the terminology of "spurs" and "reins," for instance, in 13.37-42)—an analogy that goes back at least as far as Plato's myth of the chariot of the soul in the *Phaedrus.*

These ideas constitute a transferring of the idea of moral discipline in this life to the next life, and this tropological or moral sense of the *Purgatorio* is easy to see. The traditional Catholic conception of Purgatory, however, is quite different. In it, although when one's sins are forgiven the eternal punishment for sin—damnation—has been forgiven, one is still subject to a temporal punishment. The logic is that of the traditional view that although a criminal may repent and be saved, he must still pay his debt to society. Inherent in the medieval conception of the sacrament of penance is that contrition and confession must be followed by satisfaction; absolution is always conditional upon the first two being sincere and the last being faithfully performed. Satisfaction is always conceived as the paying of a debt and the suffering of a penalty. In the traditional Catholic view, penance is a "good work" that results in the acquisition of "merit," which is "applied" to the "debt."

In the traditional Catholic view, then, Purgatory is the place where satisfaction, begun in this life, is completed. There is not a trace, in Aquinas' (or pseudo-Aquinas') elaborate discussion of Purgatory, of Dante's idea of Purgatory as a place of moral discipline; for the author of *ST Supplementum* it is exclusively a place of punishment, and the only punishment envisaged (following Scripture, e.g., Zach. 13.9, Mal. 3.2, 1 Cor. 3.13-15) is fire. Dante repeatedly draws on the traditional punitive conception of Purgatory (for instance, in *Purg.* 11.53), but his emphasis is radically different from the traditional one, according to which the idea of moral discipline is inapplicable to the afterlife, for the same reason that souls in Hell cannot repent: because one has freedom of choice only in this life.

Dante's Purgatory: 3. The Mountain of Purgatory. Among the most tormented questions regarding Purgatory during the thirteenth century was its location; the informed and judicious opinion of the major Scholastics (Aquinas and Bonaventura) did not close the question of whether it was nearer Hell or Paradise (most said near Hell; the number of these pessimists apparently grew during the thirteenth century) or whether purgation was carried out where the soul had sinned; this latter view was thought possible only in exceptional cases, but the view was tolerated, and remained popular (it is implicit in Boccaccio's *Decameron* 3.8, and possibly 5.8 as well). Popular traditions placed purgatorial places on the slopes of mountains and on islands (Mt. Etna in Sicily, for example, or Saint Patrick's Purgatory), and these views, as Graf and Nardi pointed out (see also Morgan 1991) were combined with learned speculation on the supposed scriptural situation of Eden in a remote South or East, thus—the Church Fathers had reasoned—

beyond the Oceans and the Equator, and on heights above the weather (thus nearly to the moon).

Such a distant, mountainous, and isolated location for the Earthly Paradise clearly had a decisive influence on the site that Dante has chosen for Purgatory in his poem. But it was evidently Dante's logical (and cosmological) habit of mind that placed Eden at the antipodes of Jerusalem (thus at the point of the globe opposite the place of Christ's crucifixion), so that the guilt of humankind and the act atoning for it would occur along a single axis. Such a situation also places Purgatory in the hemisphere Dante considered as metaphysically and morally "better" than the Northern hemisphere, according to Aristotle's famous demonstration that absolute Up (and therefore, for Dante, the direction toward God, from which Satan fell: *Inf.* 34.120-26) was South (a view reflected in early maps, a number of which placed South at the top; see Freccero 1959).

Dante intensively exploits the imagined geographical and physical site of his Purgatory. That Eden is surrounded by a wall of flame echoes an interpretation of Gen. 4.24 going back to Ambrose of Milan (Nardi 1966), according to which the fire of the cherub that prevents Adam and Eve from returning to Eden is the wall of fire surrounding Purgatory; in some other accounts, the wall of fire is the earth's torrid zone itself, blocking travel to the antipodes. Dante's high mountain alludes to a whole host of mountainous locations for important moments in salvation history, from the giving of the law on Mt. Sinai (C. Kaske 1972), to the temple mount and Mt. Zion in Jerusalem; to the mountains important in Christ's ministry, from the Sermon on the Mount (recalled in the mention of the Beatitudes, one on each terrace); to the Mount of Olives of the agony in the garden and the Ascension, the Mt. Tabor of the Transfiguration; to the mountain on the island of Patmos where John had the vision of the Apocalypse (all recalled in *Purgatorio* 29-33); and Mt. Carmel, traditionally the site of Ezekiel's vision. But there are classical sites too: the island of Delos, where Apollo and Diana were born, Mt. Parnassus (for Dante's mountain is both the habitat of poets and a place where poetry is seriously discussed), and Mt. Olympus (24.15; although the reference is a metaphor for Heaven) and the mountain of the Phoenix (21.46-54; see Lactantius, *De ave phoenice*, 123): all traditionally peaks so lofty they rose above the sphere of air and thus above weather. In placing his Purgatory halfway from the earth to the moon, so to speak— the moon was the boundary of the sublunar and the celestial, and thus between the world of mutability and that of the unchanging and perpetual— Dante neatly placed Purgatory on a kind of horizon between time and eternity, a place which corresponded uniquely well to the human species, as his platonizing anthropology insisted (see 25.61-63, with note). In this intermediate place the final preparations for entry into Heaven might be suitably performed.

A passage that greatly influenced the debate on Purgatory was 1 Cor. 3.10-15, where Paul speaks of a fire that will try the works of men. The passage is enigmatic and gave rise to many differing interpretations; some theologians seized on the mention of a fire that would try different kinds of works (represented by gold, silver, stone, clay, and straw) as an allegory defining how various sins (straw and clay) would be burned up by the refining fire of Purgatory, while good deeds (gold and silver) would emerge unscathed or purified. Dante reserves his sole use of purgatorial fire for lovers and poets: the poets Guido Guinizelli and Arnaut Daniel are among the lustful, the last group to be tried on the mountain. Fire had long been the element in which lovers professed to thrive, while the "refining fire" of the craftsman (from the potter to the sculptor) suited Dante's ideas regarding poets as artisans (Arnaut is a *fabbro*, a *smith* of words). The nature of Dante's fire, a material fire (because he, a living person, perceives it as hot) but no ordinary one (as it does not harm a hair of his head) represents the consensus of most late-thirteenth-century thinkers: for Dante, it comes at the end as a final trial, and in a sense sums up all the torments of Purgatory in that it at once tries, purges, and refines. The close juxtaposition of the fire of the seventh circle and the fountains of Eden, which remove memory of sin and restore memory of good, no doubt reflect a text much cited in discussions of Purgatory: Psalm 65.10-12, where purification is said to be accomplished by water and fire; in another sense, the text seems to suggest the whole exercise of the mountain, as the souls arrive by first crossing the ocean in a re-enactment of the Exodus (and so in a sense are tried by water) and conclude their stays with passage of the fire.

Dante's Allegory: Exodus. Explicit mention of the Exodus of the children of Israel from Egypt occurs in Canto 2, in the psalm sung by the souls in the angelic boat: "When Israel went out of Egypt, the house of Jacob from a barbarous people" (Psalm 113). This is an important moment in the poem, one in which basic patterns and structures of meaning are brought to the fore. As the attentive reader has grasped, the morning that opens the *Purgatorio* is Easter Sunday morning. Dante could expect his first readers, steeped in the rich symbolism of the Easter liturgy, to remember the *Exultet*, the proclamation of Easter during the Easter Vigil, just prior to the consecration of the Easter candle:

> For this is the paschal feastday, on which that true Lamb is killed, with whose blood the doorposts of the faithful are consecrated. This is the night in which you [God] first led forth our fathers, the children of Israel, out of Egypt and made them cross the Red Sea dryshod. This is the night which with the column of fire purged the darkness of sin. This is the night that returns to grace, today, all those who believe in Christ in the whole world, separated from the vices of the world and the stains of sin, and joins them to sanctity. This is the night in which, having shattered the bonds of death, Christ rose victorious from the dead.
>
> (*Liber usualis*)

In the *Exultet*, although the terms *figure* and *prefigure* are not used, the events of the Exodus—the Passover, the column of fire, the crossing of the Red

Sea—are celebrated as prefiguring, and as fulfilled by, the redemption of humanity (with its ramifications: freedom from sin, return to grace, ultimate ascent to Heaven) brought about by Christ's death and resurrection.

Although the correspondences are left implicit in Canto 2, they are clear enough: for the souls in the angelic boat, Egypt corresponds to the world of the living and of temptation, the Red Sea to death, and the Promised Land to Eden and/or Heaven. In the light of the whole story of the Exodus, the desert island of Purgatory corresponds to the Desert of Sinai, in which the Israelites wandered for forty years, where they received the Law at the hands of Moses, and from which, when all those who rebelled against the Law had died, they entered the Promised Land (this level of correspondence will be richly developed in the rest of the *Purgatorio;* see Singleton 1954 and 1957, Tucker 1960, Mazzotta 1979). As for the protagonist's own journey through Hell, although Hell is the place of those who remain enslaved to sin (thus in Egypt), there are many suggestions that it is to be seen as parallel to the Red Sea (cf. our note to *Inf.* 20.3, and "so cruel a sea," *Purg.* 1.3).

A convenient statement of the interrelation of the meanings of the Exodus is the discussion of allegory in the Epistle to Can Grande (*Epistle* 13), which exemplifies the traditional four senses of biblical exegesis from the opening of Psalm 113 (although the Epistle is of disputed authorship [see Hollander 1994, Kelly 1994], this passage illuminates some of the modes of signifying of the *Comedy,* but it should not be supposed to exclude others):

> One must know that the sense of this work is not simple, rather it can be called polysemous, having several senses; for the first sense is what is conveyed by the letter, another is what is conveyed by the things signified by the letter. And the first is called literal, the second either allegorical or moral or anagogical. This mode of treatment can be made clear by considering it in these verses: "When Israel came out of Egypt, the house of Jacob from a barbarous people." For if we look to the letter alone, the Exodus of the children of Israel from Egypt in the time of Moses is signified to us; if to the allegory, our redemption wrought by Christ is signified to us; if to the moral sense, the conversion of the soul from the grief and wretchedness of sin to the state of grace is signified to us; if to the anagogical, the passage of the holy soul from the servitude of this corruption to the freedom of eternal glory. And although these mystical senses are called by various names, generally all of them can be called allegorical, since they are different from the literal or historical.

While it is no doubt true that the codification of the theory of the four senses was a relatively late development, and that in practice medieval biblical exegesis was more flexible and less systematic than is often supposed (see Lubac 1964, Lieberknecht 1999), still the four senses represent an unavoidable set of fundamental types of reference. The four senses of the Exodus set forth in the Epistle are the founding narratives of medieval Christian belief.

They concern the single most important event of the Jewish prehistory of the faith; the central event of the faith; the effect for each individual in this life; the passage of each soul to the next life. Each implies all the others; all have the same or a closely parallel structure; and together they articulate a causal sequence.

Any singing of Psalm 113 (or of any psalm) is necessarily situated at some point in this causal sequence, normally on earth, in the present, with "those who believe in Christ" and are presumably "returned to grace." The meaning of the structure does not change if one imagines the psalm sung at some other moment, for instance by souls in an angelic boat, situated at a moment in which "the passage of the holy soul from the servitude of this corruption to the freedom of eternal glory" is taking place. (The entire structure of the medieval liturgy in fact asserts a figural relation to biblical events of each moment of the Church year.)

The singing of the souls in the angelic boat, then, takes place in a literal situation that corresponds to the anagogical sense of the psalm set forth in the Epistle. Dante clearly understood that the interdependence of the four narratives permitted any one of them to be treated as a literal sense evoking one or more of the others. Thus, leaving the singing out of consideration, the literal sense here is the arrival of the souls on the shores of Purgatory; the allegorical sense is "our redemption wrought by Christ" (in which the Exodus itself, as preparing it, would also be included); the moral sense is an initial freeing of the individual soul, in this life, from the bondage of sin, facing the process of moral discipline that will overcome the inclination to sin (see Additional Note 6); and, since our literal sense is an early stage in the soul's passage from this life to glory, the anagogical sense refers to the final completion of the soul's passage to glory.

Since for the Middle Ages the paradigmatic narratives present the basic patterns both of God's action in history and of all human experience, a moment's reflection will show that in medieval terms it was virtually impossible to invent a narrative which did *not* embody one or another of these patterns, either *in bono* or *in malo*. It is well known that the Middle Ages interpreted pagan myths as distorted versions of biblical truth (Rahner 1945). Thus Hercules and Theseus were thought of as types of Christ (for Hercules in the *Inferno*, see Miller 1984; for Theseus, see Stock 1971); the *Ovide moralisé* interpreted Apollo's crowning himself with the laurel (in the myth of Apollo and Daphne, *Metamorphoses* 1) as signifying Christ's taking on of the flesh of the Virgin Mary, Pyramus' suicide (*Metamorphoses* 4) as signifying Christ's death on the Cross.

Thus the notion that in the Middle Ages only "factual" historical events could be invested with theologically allegorical significance is untrue. Furthermore, Singleton's repeated claim that the *Comedy* is unique as a fiction imitating the modes of figural allegory is simply mistaken. One need look no further than the Arthurian material, such as the works of Robert de Boron (see Bogdanow 1996) or the Vulgate *Queste del saint Graal*, which is filled with fictitious events that fictitious religious hermits interpret as if they were historical events figurally related to other fictitious events or, indeed, to biblical ones (see *Queste* pp. 35-40, 67-70, 74-78, 94-103, and passim). And in the famous, often misinterpreted discussion of allegory in *Convivio* 2.1, after pointing out that his canzone has a fictitious literal sense, Dante also claims that it does have both moral and anagogical senses (see Scott 1990, 1994).

As Dante understood, the structure of mutual implication of his system of belief, as of his poetic text, exists independently of its truth, which is always a matter of faith (see *Par.* 24.82-111, with notes). Therefore other fictions can be brought into the powerful matrix of these associations, as when in the *Comedy* Dante gives Virgil a role parallel to that of Moses in the Exodus, or invents a dream that reflects the figural structure of the entire poem (see *Purg.* 9.13-33, with notes), or turns Charon and his boat, a myth or poetic fiction lifted from a pagan poet, into a figural anticipation of his own (fictitious) angelic boat, on the pattern of the relation between Old Law (Old Testament, retribution, Hell) and New Law (New Testament, forgiveness, Purgatory and Paradise), or, within the *Inferno* itself, Dante invents punishments that echo Christ's crucifixion or resurrection—which is the same as saying that their allegorical sense is "our redemption wrought by Christ" (see, in the *Inferno* volume, Additional Note 16).

The status of pagan myth—especially Vergilian and Ovidian myth—is of course centrally important for Dante; for him it represented the crystallized wisdom of the ancient world. One of his most original achievements is the way the entire *Aeneid* is drawn into this signifying matrix, as prefiguring, in the history of poetry, the *Comedy* itself. Thus the extraordinary freedom of Dante's poetic imagination and of his manipulation of traditional modes of allegory utterly transcends any rigid formula. Indeed, Dante heralds the manneristic age of the fourteenth and fifteenth centuries, in which sacred truths were to be played with in unprecedented ways. He had learned from the *Aeneid* that figural relations, fictitious or not (such as, in the *Aeneid,* those between Aeneas and Augustus, or Dido and Cleopatra) are the stuff and structure of poetry. The figural/metaphorical coherence of medieval Catholicism, as Dante saw it, was, in the strictest sense, poetic.

Suggested Introductory Readings on the Purgatorio

Carroll, John S. 1971. *Prisoners of Hope. An Exposition of Dante's Purgatorio* (Reprint of 1904 edition). Port Washington, N.Y.: Kennikat Press.

Lectura Dantis Virginiana. 1993. *Dante's Purgatorio: Introductory Readings.* Charlottesville: University of Virginia Press.

Scott, John A. 1996. *Dante's Political Purgatory.* Philadelphia: University of Pennsylvania Press.

Singleton, Charles S. 1957. *Dante Studies II: Journey to Beatrice.* Cambridge, Mass.: Harvard University Press.

Other recommended readings, including general ones, are listed in the *Inferno* volume, pp. 23-24.

PURGATORIO

CANTO 1

Per correr miglior acque alza le vele   1
omai la navicella del mio ingegno,
che lascia dietro a sé mar sì crudele,
   e canterò di quel secondo regno   4
dove l'umano spirito si purga
e di salire al ciel diventa degno.
   Ma qui la morta poesì resurga,   7
o sante Muse, poi che vostro sono,
e qui Calïopè alquanto surga,
   seguitando il mio canto con quel suono   10
di cui le Piche misere sentiro
lo colpo tal, che disperar perdono.
   Dolce color d'orïental zaffiro   13
che s'accoglieva nel sereno aspetto
del mezzo, puro infino al primo giro,
   a li occhi miei ricominciò diletto,   16
tosto ch'io usci' fuor de l'aura morta
che m'avea contristati li occhi e 'l petto.
   Lo bel pianeto che d'amar conforta   19
faceva tutto rider l'orïente,
velando i Pesci, ch'erano in sua scorta.
   I' mi volsi a man destra e puosi mente   22
a l'altro polo, e vidi quattro stelle
non viste mai fuor ch'a la prima gente.
   Goder pareva 'l ciel di lor fiammelle: 25
Oh settentrïonal vedovo sito,
poi che privato se' di mirar quelle!
   Com' io da loro sguardo fui partito,   28
un poco me volgendo a l'altro polo,
là onde 'l Carro già era sparito,

CANTO 1

Proposition and invocation—dawn on the island of Purgatory—the four stars—Cato of Utica—the pilgrim washed and girt with a rush

1   To run through better waters the little ship of my wit now hoists its sails, leaving behind it a sea so cruel,

4   and I will sing of that second realm where the human spirit purges itself and becomes worthy to ascend to Heaven.

7   But here let dead poetry rise up again, O holy Muses, since I am yours, and here let Calliope arise somewhat,

10   accompanying my song with that sound of which the wretched Magpies so felt the blow that they despaired of pardon.

13   The sweet color of eastern sapphire, gathering in the cloudless aspect of the air, pure to the first circle,

16   began to delight my eyes again, as soon as I came forth from the dead air that had weighed my eyes and breast with sorrow.

19   The lovely planet that strengthens us to love was causing all the east to laugh, veiling the Fish, which were her escort.

22   I turned to the right and considered the other pole, and I saw four stars never seen except by the first people.

25   The sky seemed to rejoice in their flames: Oh northern site, widowed because deprived of gazing on those!

28   When I had left their gaze, turning somewhat toward the other pole, from which the Wain had already disappeared,

vidi presso di me un veglio solo,   31
degno di tanta reverenza in vista
che più non dee a padre alcun figliuolo.

    Lunga la barba e di pel bianco mista   34
portava, a' suoi capelli simigliante,
de' quai cadeva al petto doppia lista.

    Li raggi de le quattro luci sante   37
fregiavan sì la sua faccia di lume,
ch'i' 'l vedea come 'l sol fosse davante.

    "Chi siete voi che contro al cieco fiume   40
fuggita avete la pregione etterna?"
diss' el, movendo quelle oneste piume.

    "Chi v'ha guidati, o che vi fu lucerna,   43
uscendo fuor de la profonda notte
che sempre nera fa la valle inferna?

    Son le leggi d'abisso così rotte?   46
o è mutato in ciel novo consiglio,
che, dannati, venite a le mie grotte?"

    Lo duca mio allor mi diè di piglio,   49
e con parole e con mani e con cenni
reverenti mi fé le gambe e 'l ciglio.

    Poscia rispuose lui: "Da me non venni: 52
donna scese del ciel, per li cui prieghi
de la mia compagnia costui sovvenni.

    Ma da ch'è tuo voler che più si spieghi   55
di nostra condizion com' ell' è vera,
esser non puote il mio che a te si nieghi.

    Questi non vide mai l'ultima sera;   58
ma per la sua follia le fu sì presso
che molto poco tempo a volger era.

    Sì com' io dissi, fui mandato ad esso   61
per lui campare; e non li era altra via
che questa per la quale i' mi son messo.

    Mostrata ho lui tutta la gente ria,   64
e ora intendo mostrar quelli spirti
che purgan sé sotto la tua balìa.

    Com' io l'ho tratto saria lungo a dirti;   67
de l'alto scende virtù che m'aiuta
conducerlo a vederti e a udirti.

31   I saw close by me a solitary old man, worthy, by his appearance, of so much reverence that never son owed father more.

34   Long was his beard and mixed with white hair, similar to the hairs of his head, which fell to his breast in two strands.

37   The rays of the four holy lights so adorned his face with brightness that I saw him as if the sun had been before him.

40   "Who are you that up the blind river have fled the eternal prison?" he said, moving those reverend plumes.

43   "Who has guided you, or what has been your lantern, coming forth from the deep night that makes the valley of Hell forever black?

46   Can the laws of the abyss be broken, then? or has some new counsel been adopted in Heaven, that although damned you come to my cliffs?"

49   My leader then lay hold on me and, with words and hands and gestures, made reverent my legs and brow.

52   Then he replied: "I have not come on my own: a lady came down from Heaven, because of whose entreaties I have helped this man with my company.

55   But since it is your will that our condition be further set forth as it truly is, it cannot be my will to refuse you.

58   This man never saw his last evening; but through his folly he was so near it that not much time remained to turn.

61   As I have said, I was sent to rescue him; and there was no other way than this by which I have come.

64   I have shown him all the wicked people, and now I intend to show those spirits who are purifying themselves under your care.

67   How I have led him would be long to tell you; from on high descends a power that helps me bring him to see you and hear you.

Or ti piaccia gradir la sua venuta: 70
libertà va cercando, ch'è sì cara,
come sa chi per lei vita rifiuta.

Tu 'l sai, ché non ti fu per lei amara   73
in Utica la morte, ove lasciasti
la vesta ch'al gran dì sarà sì chiara.

Non son li editti etterni per noi guasti,   76
ché questi vive e Minòs me non lega,
ma son del cerchio ove son li occhi casti

di Marzia tua, che 'n vista ancor ti priega,   79
o santo petto, che per tua la tegni:
per lo suo amore adunque a noi ti piega.

Lasciane andar per li tuoi sette regni;   82
grazie riporterò di te a lei,
se d'esser mentovato là giù degni."

"Marzïa piacque tanto a li occhi miei   85
mentre ch'i' fu' di là," diss' elli allora,
"che quante grazie volse da me, fei.

Or che di là dal mal fiume dimora,   88
più muover non mi può, per quella legge
che fatta fu quando me n'usci' fora.

Ma se donna del ciel ti move e regge,   91
come tu di', non c'è mestier lusinghe:
bastisi ben che per lei mi richegge.

Va dunque, e fa che tu costui ricinghe   94
d'un giunco schietto, e che li lavi 'l viso
sì ch'ogne sucidume quindi stinghe;

ché non si converria, l'occhio sorpriso   97
d'alcuna nebbia, andar dinanzi al primo
ministro, ch'è di quei di paradiso.

Questa isoletta intorno ad imo ad imo,   100
là giù colà dove la batte l'onda,
porta di giunchi sovra 'l molle limo:

null'altra pianta che facesse fronda   103
o indurasse vi puote aver vita,
però ch'a le percosse non seconda.

Poscia non sia di qua vostra reddita;   106
lo sol vi mosterrà, che surge omai,
prendere il monte a più lieve salita."

70   Now may it please you to favor his coming: he seeks freedom, which is so precious, as one knows who rejects life for her sake.

73   You know it; for to you, because of her, death was not bitter in Utica, where you left the raiment that will be so bright on the great day.

76   The eternal edicts have not been broken by us, for he is alive, and me Minos does not bind; for I am from the circle that holds the chaste eyes

79   of your Marcia, who still seems to beg you, O holy breast, to consider her your own: for love of her, then, incline towards us.

82   Permit us to go through your seven realms; I will take back kind greetings from you to her, if you deign to be mentioned down there."

85   "Marcia so pleased my eyes when I was back there," he said then, "that whatever kindness she wished from me, I did.

88   Now that she dwells beyond the evil river, she can move me no longer, according to the law that was made when I came forth from there.

91   But if a lady from Heaven moves and governs you, as you say, no flatteries are needed: let it be enough that you ask me for her sake.

94   Go then, and see that you gird this man with a smooth rush and wash his face so as to remove all grime;

97   for it would not be fitting, were his eye shadowed by any cloud, to go before the first minister, who is one of those from Paradise.

100   This island, all around its very base, down there where the surf beats on it, bears rushes upon its soft mud:

103   no other plant that bears leaves or hardens can have life there, because it would not yield with the blows.

106   Afterwards, do not return this way; the sun will show you, for it is rising now, where to take the mountain by an easier ascent."

Così sparì; e io sù mi levai   109
sanza parlare, e tutto mi ritrassi
al duca mio, e li occhi a lui drizzai.

El cominciò: "Figliuol, segui i miei passi: 112
volgianci in dietro, ché di qua dichina
questa pianura a' suoi termini bassi."

L'alba vinceva l'ora mattutina,   115
che fuggia innanzi, sì che di lontano
conobbi il tremolar de la marina.

Noi andavam per lo solingo piano   118
com' om che torna a la perduta strada,
che 'nfino ad essa li pare ire in vano.

Quando noi fummo là 've la rugiada   121
pugna col sole, per essere in parte
dove, ad orezza, poco si dirada,

ambo le mani in su l'erbetta sparte   124
soavemente 'l mio maestro pose:
ond' io, che fui accorto di sua arte,

porsi ver' lui le guance lagrimose;   127
ivi mi fece tutto discoverto
quel color che l'inferno mi nascose.

Venimmo poi in sul lito diserto,   130
che mai non vide navicar sue acque
omo che di tornar sia poscia esperto.

Quivi mi cinse sì com' altrui piacque: 133
oh maraviglia! ché qual elli scelse
l'umile pianta, cotal si rinacque

subitamente là onde l'avelse.   136

109   With that he disappeared; and I rose up without speaking and drew all close to my leader and turned my eyes to him.

112   He began: "Son, follow my steps: let us turn back, for from here this plain slants down to its low boundaries."

115   The dawn was overcoming the morning hour, which fled before it, so that from afar I recognized the trembling of the waters.

118   We were going along the lonely plain like one returning to the lost path and, until he reaches it, feels he walks in vain.

121   When we were where the dew resists the sun, being in a place where it evaporates but little in the breeze,

124   both his hands, spreading them, my master gently placed on the tender grass: and I, aware of his intention,

127   offered him my tear-stained cheeks; there he uncovered all that color of mine which Hell had hidden.

130   Then we came on to the deserted shore, which never saw any man sail its waters who afterwards experienced return.

133   There he girded me as it pleased another: Oh wonder! for as he plucked the humble plant,

136   it was suddenly reborn, identical, where he had uprooted it.

NOTES

1-12. To run through . . . despaired of pardon: The cantica begins with traditional formulas of narrative exordium: announcement of subject-matter (1-6), invocation of the Muses (7-12). In *Inferno* these were postponed to Canto 2.

1-3. To run through . . . sea so cruel: The traditional topos of composition as a voyage, used in *Conv.* 2.1.1, extensively developed in the *Paradiso* (e.g., *Par.* 2.1-18). As a topic of exordium, *Geor.* 2.39-41: "inceptumque una *decurre* laborem / . . . pelagoque volans da vela patenti" [*run through* with me the labor begun . . . spread the sails, flying over the open sea] may have suggested Dante's "correre" [run through], for "little boat" cf. Propertius 3.3.23: "non est ingenii cumba gravanda tui" [do not overload the little boat of your wit]. Cf. lines 130-32.

2-3. a sea so cruel: Hell, where the damned are "submerged" (cf. *Inf.* 20.3); for the figurative "sea of this world," see *Inter cantica* below and the note to 2.46-48.

4-6. and I will sing . . . ascend to Heaven: The proposition, identifying Purgatory as the subject of the cantica. Periphrasis is traditional in epic propositions; cf. "Arms and the man I sing, who first" etc., *Aen.* 1.1 ff. For the important theological concepts mentioned here, see Introduction, pp. 6-10.

7-12. But here let . . . despaired of pardon: This invocation alludes to Ovid's account (*Met.* 5.294-678) of the contest between the Muses and the daughters of Pierus (the Pierides), who, still defiant after losing (Ovid does not refer to their feeling despair), were turned into magpies. The presumptuous Pierides slandered the gods; Calliope sang of Proserpina, carried off to the underworld by Dis, Ceres' search for her, and Jupiter's compassion; the theme is closely related to the loss and recovery of Eden (see 28.49-51). Cf. the references to Arachne (*Inf.* 17.14-18) and Marsyas (*Par.* 1.19-22), also losers of artistic contests, punished for their presumption.

7. let dead poetry rise up again: All beauty, except the terrible beauty of God's justice, is banished from Hell, thus poetry is dead there (for the "dead writing" of *Inf.* 3.1-9, see *Inf.* 8.127, with note). The theme of forgiveness and rebirth is announced by resurrecting poetry itself, whose nature is a major theme of the cantica. Cf. *Inf.* 32.1-12.

8. O holy Muses: The Muses are now securely enlisted in the service of Christianity; compare *Inf.* 2.7-9, with notes.

8-9. and here let Calliope arise somewhat: Calliope is the Muse of epic poetry. See *Met.* 5. 338-39: "Calliope arises [*surgit*], her flowing hair gathered with ivy . . ." Cf. *Aen.* 9.525: "Goddesses, and you, Calliope, I pray, breathe into me as

I sing." Calliope is to rise only "somewhat" because Dante's style and themes will rise still higher for the *Paradiso* (Buti).

8. I am yours: Cf. Horace, *Odes* 3.4 (also addressed to Calliope), lines 21-22: "I am yours [*vester*], Muses, yours, and as yours I climb the arduous Sabine hills" (Chiavacci Leonardi).

13-30. The sweet color . . . already disappeared: The lines fulfill the final verse of the *Inferno* with the first full view of the sky since *Inf.* 1.37-40 (cf. *Inf.* 3.85); the pilgrim has the posture that distinguishes man from the beasts (*Met.* 1.82-86; *Timaeus* 47); see *Inter cantica* below. He has emerged from the underworld facing east.

13-21. The sweet color . . . her escort: The rebirth of poetry is now enacted with the evocation of the beauty of the heavens, whose changing color is the chief indicator of the passage of time (Gen. 1.14-19; cf. Ps. 8.4, 18.1-7). Unlike Hell (cf. *Inf.* 3.29), Purgatory exists in time, and time governs the purging of souls. Note the emphasis on process in "s'accoglieva" [was gathering] and the rising of Venus.

13. eastern sapphire: The color of the eastern sky just before dawn: the pilgrim is facing east. In his lapidary Marbod of Rennes describes sapphire as "similar to the pure sky," adding "it frees those in prison . . . and touched to chains, releases them" (Chiavacci Leonardi). The Virgin Mary is a "sapphire" at *Par.* 23.101.

15. the air, pure to the first circle: Dante's term *mezzo* [lit., medium] refers to Aristotle's theory of vision, according to which light is propagated instantaneously in its medium, the diaphanous; here, the air, clear of any mist or vapor. The "first circle" is the horizon; it is the "first" celestial circle because it can be at least approximately perceived (the others, such as the meridian and the Equator, must be imagined). Cf. 4.70-72, with note, Additional Note 3.

19-21. The lovely planet . . . her escort: Venus rising veils with its brightness the stars of Pisces, the sign that rises before Aries (as usual, Dante does not clearly distinguish between signs and constellations; see the figure on p. xiii). In April, 1300 Venus was in fact the evening star. The best explanation of Dante's error, which has occasioned much discussion, is that he used the famous almanac of Prophatius, which labels the positions of Venus confusingly (Boffitto/Melzi 1908). Dante's astrology will be more fully discussed in our *Paradiso* volume.

22-23. I turned to the right . . . the other pole: The pilgrim turns toward the south, where the southern celestial pole is visible, the pilgrim and Virgil are now in the southern hemisphere; see figs. 1 and 2 and *Inf.* 34.106-26.

23-24. I saw four stars . . . first people: This invented constellation, invisible to all save Adam and Eve in the Earthly Paradise and thus very close to the pole, is not the Southern Cross (never seen by Dante, though visible up to 20° N. lat.). It will be identified in 29.121-32 and 31.106-109 as representing the four cardinal virtues, justice, temperance, prudence, and fortitude (cf. lines 37-39 and 8.88-93).

25-26. Oh northern site ... gazing on those: The hemisphere of land (mainly northern) is "widowed" primarily because humanity is banished from Eden and deprived of the original justice of mankind, symbolized by the four stars (for the tropes of marriage and widowhood, see *Inf.* 19.2-4); in one sense the *Purgatorio* is an extended "Lament for Eden" (Singleton 1957, Martinez 1997).

29-30. turning somewhat . . . disappeared: At the latitude of Purgatory as Dante conceives it, the Wain (Big Dipper), located between Dec. 43° and 63° N., would be visible for several hours during the April night; now it has set. The northern celestial pole is of course visible only north of the Equator.

31-109. I saw close by ... he disappeared: Almost half the canto is taken up by the encounter with the guardian of Purgatory, who appears without warning (cf. the note to line 109); once satisfied that the pair's presence is authorized, he instructs them how to proceed. Not identified until line 84, this is Marcus Porcius Cato (grandson of Cato the Censor), whom Dante repeatedly cites as the chief example of Roman virtue and an analogue of God (*Conv.* 4.28.16; *Mon.* 2.5.15-16); the principal source of his conception is the portrait of Cato in Lucan's *Pharsalia* (2.234-391 and 9.253-618). Unwilling to survive the destruction of republican liberty in the civil war that established the Empire, Cato committed suicide at Utica (North Africa); see Additional Note 1. As supervisor of the reestablishment of justice, Cato is a figure of Moses, the law-giver (see the Introduction and the note to lines 34-36).

31-39. I saw close by me . . . before him: The encounter before dawn draws on that of Mary Magdalene with the risen Christ (John 20.14-17); cf. lines 88-90.

34-36. Long was his beard . . . two strands: Note that the "two strands" are identified (by the plural *quai*) as capelli [hairs of the head], an addition to Lucan's description (*Phars.* 2.372-78); the touch recalls representations of Moses and other Patriarchs (e.g., in the Florentine Baptistery; see Schreckenberg 1996).

37-39. The rays . . . been before him: The lighting of Cato's face by the four stars no doubt signifies that he possessed the cardinal virtues in a superlative degree. Some commentators implausibly take line 39 to mean "as if the sun were before me," i.e., as if Cato were as bright as the sun; this would make line 75 pointless (see the note to 8.25-36).

40-48. Who are you ... to my cliffs: Note Cato's insistence, taking up 5½ out of 9 lines, on the darkness and eternity of Hell; see *Inter cantica* below.

40-41. the blind river . . . the eternal prison: "Blind" because subterranean, this is the stream (perhaps deriving from Lethe, cf. *Purg.* 28.121-33, with notes) that the wayfarers have ascended (*Inf.* 34.127-39); for Hell as a prison see the notes on line 13 and *Inf.* 10.58, as well as *Inter cantica* below.

42. those reverend plumes: Cato's long beard. For the beard as male plumage, see *Inf.* 20.40-45 (of Tiresias) and *Purg.* 31.61-69, with notes.

43-44. Who has guided you . . . your lantern: Virgil will answer this question by adducing Beatrice's request and divine help (lines 52-54), but the "lantern" has been Virgil himself. In classical Latin *lucerna* meant properly an oil lamp, but the Gospels use it to mean "candle" or generically "light" (Matt. 5.15, Luke 11.33-34); the metaphor will be important later (8.112-14, where the mention of wax implies a candle; 22.61-69, which seems to require a lantern).

46. Can the laws . . . be broken: Cato imagines that the travelers have broken the law binding them to specific places of punishment (cf. the note on line 77).

48. my cliffs: Cato at last explicitly asserts his authority over this realm (see line 66).

49-51. My leader then . . . my legs and brow: That is, Virgil has the pilgrim kneel and bow his head; he takes hold of him (for the expression, cf. *Inf.* 22.73), speaks, pushes him downward, and also gestures: measures of the reverence owed to Cato (lines 32-33), whom Virgil can identify (revealing new dimensions of knowledge in this realm; cf. lines 66, 68, 75).

52-84. Then he replied . . . mentioned down there: After briefly indicating the nature of his own authority (lines 52-54), Virgil makes a little oration (technically a *suasoria*), constructed on traditional rhetorical lines: proem (lines 55-57), narration (lines 58-69), request (lines 72), peroration (lines 73-84). He answers all three of Cato's questions, in order.

52. I have not come on my own: A close echo of *Inf.* 10.61 (the pilgrim to another father figure): "Da me stesso non vegno" [I do not come on my own].

58-69. This man never saw . . . and hear you: Virgil's narration recapitulates the events of the *Inferno*, with special reference to Canto 2; see *Inter cantica* below.

58. his last evening: A trope for "his last day": the pilgrim is still alive.

65-66. those spirits . . . under your care: The idea of Cato as the supervisor of the reestablishment of justice in the soul seems to have been suggested by *Aen.* 8.670 (part of the description of the underworld on Aeneas' shield): "and the just, off by themselves, and Cato giving laws to them." See 2.120-23, with notes, and Additional Note 1.

67-69. How I have . . . and hear you: A *praeteritio* [naming of what is omitted] and restatement of the initial summary (lines 52-54).

68-69. from on high . . . and hear you: These lines assert continuous divine help and account for the new dimensions of Virgil's knowledge.

70-72. Now may it please . . . for her sake: Statement of the pilgrim's purpose and direct request that Cato further it, the point of the entire little speech. The pilgrim seeks freedom of the will from sin and its compulsions (Rom. 6-7; see Introduction, p. 14 and Additional Note 1; cf. the note to lines 88-90).

73-75. You know it . . . so bright on the great day: Virgil appeals to Cato's love of liberty, to which he attributes his suicide; he foresees (cf. *Inf.* 4.53, with note) that at the Last Judgment (the "great day") Cato's resurrected body will be particularly glorious (Dante regarded Cato's death as sacrificial, analogous to Christ's; see *Mon.* 2.5.15; this view stems from the expiatory prayer Lucan attributes to Cato, *Phars.* 2.312-13); see Additional Note 1.

76-84. The eternal edicts . . . mentioned down there: Virgil's answer to Cato's third question (lines 46-48) leads into his peroration, which both restates the request (line 82) and makes an extended appeal to what he supposes will be Cato's emotions about his wife, Marcia.

77. me Minos does not bind: Since Limbo is the circle above the entrance where Minos hears the souls' sins and assigns their punishments (*Inf.* 5.1-15), Virgil is free to move about (cf. *Inf.* 9.16-30).

78-79. the chaste eyes of your Marcia: In a famous instance of Stoic "generosity," Cato divorced Marcia and commanded her to marry his friend Hortensius, who was in love with her; she obeyed, but, when widowed, begged to return to Cato, who accepted her (though excluding conjugal relations). "Your Marcia" alludes to Marcia's wish to have "Catonis Marcia" [Cato's Marcia] inscribed on her tomb (cf. *Purg.* 8.79-81). In *Conv.* 4.28.11-19, Dante translates Lucan's version of Marcia's request (*Phars.* 2.338-49) as an allegory of the return of the noble soul to God in old age. Though inapplicable to Marcia here, the return to God is the basic theme of both *Purgatorio* and *Paradiso*.

79-82. who still seems . . . incline towards us: Virgil's description of Marcia attributes to her a fixed, emblematic attitude similar to others in Limbo (e.g., *Inf.* 4.123, 131-35). His "incline" echoes Lucan's "hae flexere virum voces" [these words made the man bend] (*Phars.* 2.350).

80. holy breast: Translates Lucan's "sacrum pectus," used of Cato (*Phars.* 9.255).

82. your seven realms: The first indication of the arrangement of Purgatory, with clear indication of Cato's authority over it.

82-84. I will take back . . . mentioned down there: Although Virgil identifies Cato's office and the fact that he is saved, his appeal to Cato's love for Marcia reveals that his understanding has a limit (cf 19.133-38, with notes), as Cato's reply will show.

85-108. Marcia so pleased . . . easier ascent: Cato's reply acknowledges his former love for Marcia, which no can longer move him, but accepts the authority of Beatrice; he directs Virgil to cleanse and gird the pilgrim.

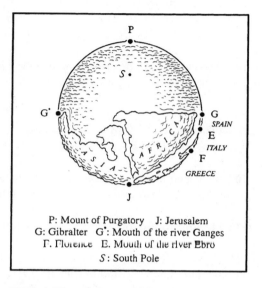

P: Mount of Purgatory   J: Jerusalem
G: Gibralter   G˙: Mouth of the river Ganges
F: Florence   E: Mouth of the river Ebro
S: South Pole

Figure 1. The relative positions of Gibraltar, Jerusalem, the Ganges, and Purgatory.

88-90. Now that she dwells . . . when I came forth: The reference is to the "new law" of grace and forgiveness (Rom. 8.2: "For the law of the spirit of life, in Christ Jesus, hath delivered me from the law of sin and of death"; cf. also Rom. 7.1-4). Cato left Limbo at the Harrowing of Hell (see *Inf.* 4.46-63, with notes). For "she can move me no longer," cf. Beatrice's "your misery does not touch me [*non mi tange*]" (*Inf.* 2.92): both phrases echo the risen Christ's words to Mary Magdalene: "Noli me tangere" [Do not touch me] (John 20.17). Echoes of the Resurrection of Christ (it is Easter Sunday) will be frequent; see 3.109-11.

88. the evil river: The Acheron, called by Vergil "amnem severam" [the stern river] (*Aen.* 6.374; see Brugnoli 1993), cf. *Inf.* 3.70-81, 14.115-16.

92-93. no flatteries . . . for her sake: Virgil's elaborate classical rhetoric is rebuked.

94-108. Go then . . . easier ascent: Cato addresses Virgil, not the pilgrim, with his instructions, elaborately phrased (the lines on the girding surround those on the washing; both actions are derived from liturgical practices; see the notes on lines 118-20 and 127-29). The pilgrim will confront the angel at the gate of Purgatory in Canto 9.

94-95. a smooth rush: The pilgrim's long robe (cf *Inf.* 15.24, 16.8-9) has been ungirt since his knotted belt was used to lure Geryon (*Inf.* 16.103-14; see *Inter cantica* below).

100-102. This island . . . its soft mud: The first and only panoramic description of the island, associating its rushes with those of the Red Sea.

103-105. no other plant . . . with the blows: Softness and flexibility are associated with humility, and the rush has many scriptural associations (e.g., the small ark woven of papyrus for Moses, as well as the rushes among which it was found: Ex. 2.3-5; Rashi gives OF *jonc* [rush] as the equivalent of the term for papyrus).

106. Afterwards, do not return this way: There may be an echo of the Gospel narrative of the Magi (Matt. 2.12: "they went back another way into their country").

106-108. the sun . . . an easier ascent: See *Inf.* 1.17-18, with note, and cf. 4.55-75, 13.13-21, also with notes.

109. With that he disappeared: Cato's sudden appearances and disappearances recall those of Christ in the resurrection narratives (e.g., Luke 24.31, 36, 51).

112-14. Son, follow my steps . . . to its low boundaries: Girding with the rush requires a descent; see *Inter cantica* below.

115-16. The dawn . . . fled before it: "Ora mattutina" [morning hour] refers to the last canonical hour of the night that, personified, flees the light (Buti, Sapegno). It. *ora* has also been taken as the breeze [*aura*] preceding the dawn (cf. the note to lines 1-2), possibly associated with line 117.

116-17. from afar . . . trembling of the waters: A "naturalistic" detail (of the ripples on the surface of the ocean visible in the rising sun); see *Aen.* 7.9: "splendet tremulo sub lumine pontus" [the deep shines beneath the trembling light], of the moonlight; derived from this are Claudian's lines on dawn (*Raptus* 2.2-3: "nondum pura dies; tremulis vibratur in undis / ardor" [day was not yet full; the light flashed from the trembling waters].

118-20. We were going . . . walks in vain: A reminder that the journey through Hell was a detour from the direct path up the mountain (*Inf.* 1.91-93). The note of haste recalls the "hastening to be washed" (by baptism) of catechumens (see Augustine, *In Iohannis Evangelium, PL* 35,1714; cf. *PL* 40, 202).

127-29. offered . . . had hidden: Hell had not only begrimed his face, it had also turned him pale (cf. 2.122-123 with note, for purgation as the removal of scurf). This washing puts a seal on the parallel between the journey through Hell and baptism (see previous note and Singleton 1954, 1957).

130-32. Then we came . . . pleased another: These lines are a clear reference to Ulysses' voyage and shipwreck (*Inf.* 26.133-42); see *Inter cantica* below. For presumption punished, cf. lines 7-12, with notes.

133. as it pleased another: A literal echo of *Inf.* 26.141: "another" is Cato here, but, of course, also God, as in Ulysses' speech.

135-36. reborn . . . had uprooted it: The rebirth of the rush alludes to that of the talismanic golden bough (*Aen.* 6.143-44): "primo *avulso* non deficit alter / aureus, et simili frondescit virga metallo" [when one branch is *uprooted* another appears, golden, and its stem bears leaves of the same metal]. Carroll notes that Aeneas reaches up, Virgil, here, down. According to the *Golden Legend* the sea-rush furnished Christ's crown of thorns.

Inter cantica. One of the most striking aspects of the *Comedy,* which will be explored under this rubric, is its system of recall of the earlier cantiche, often in the form of parallels between similarly numbered cantos, sometimes even between similarly numbered lines. In *Purgatorio* 1 and 2, in addition to the explicit references to the *Inferno*, important in the transition between the cantiche, establishing the new atmosphere of hope and natural beauty, repeatedly contrasted with that of Hell (see the notes to lines 2-3, 7, 40-41, 127-29), there are less explicit but fundamentally important parallels, within a governing parallelism of situation; for the first time since the opening of the *Inferno,* we are on the surface of the earth, and in an important sense the mountain of Purgatory is the same as the mountain of *Inferno* 1 (see the note to *Inf.* 1.13); *Pur.* 1.118-20 calls attention to the fact. The ascent will represent salvation and the attainment of moral freedom and autonomy. At the beginning of the poem the pilgrim is blocked; he cannot ascend but must undergo the penitential journey through Hell that reveals the nature of sin and his own kinship with the damned. At the beginning of the *Purgatorio* he has turned away from evil and has gained the initial humility that is required for the ascent; he is in a sense reborn (see the note to lines 127-29).

As the action begins just before dawn, we are beside the sea at the foot of a mountain that the pilgrim intends to ascend. In *Inferno* 1, we have: A. upward gaze: the mountain lit by the rising sun (16-18); B. the pilgrim turns back to gaze at the (metaphorical) sea (22-27); C. he begins to climb but is blocked (28-54) and D. driven back down the slope (55-60); E. he sees Virgil and appeals to him (61-90); F. Virgil prescribes the journey to the other world (91-120); G. Virgil explains his damnation (121-29); H. the descent into Hell begins (136). In a different order and with vastly different significance, these elements recur in *Purgatorio* 1: I. (cf. A). upward gaze (no sight of the mountain, but full expanse of sky); II. the view is blocked (cf. C) by Cato, another classical figure, III. to whom Virgil appeals (cf. E), IV. referring to Cato's salvation (cf. G); V. Cato prescribes their path (cf. F); VI. as the pilgrim and Virgil descend to the shore he sees the trembling of the sea (cf. D, H). His descent is no longer a danger, and the view of the open sea is no longer the horrified gaze of the newly shipwrecked (VI vs. B). Finally, in lines 130-32 both the metaphorical shipwreck of *Inferno* 1 and the literal shipwreck of Ulysses are recalled (note that lines 131, 133, and 135 use the same rhymes—in two cases the same words and in one case an entire phrase—as are used of Ulysses' shipwreck in *Inf.* 26.136, 139, and 141).

CANTO 2

Già era 'l sole a l'orizzonte giunto   1
lo cui meridïan cerchio coverchia
Ierusalèm col suo più alto punto,

   e la notte, che opposita a lui cerchia,   4
uscia di Gange fuor con le Bilance,
che le caggion di man quando soverchia,

   sì che le bianche e le vermiglie guance,   7
là dov' i' era, de la bella Aurora
per troppa etate divenivan rance.

   Noi eravam lunghesso mare ancora,   10
come gente che pensa a suo cammino,
che va col cuore e col corpo dimora.

   Ed ecco, qual, sul presso del mattino,   13
per li grossi vapor Marte rosseggia
giù nel ponente sovra 'l suol marino:

   cotal m'apparve—s'io ancor lo veggia—   16
un lume per lo mar venir sì ratto
che 'l muover suo nessun volar pareggia.

   Dal qual com' io un poco ebbi ritratto   19
l'occhio per domandar lo duca mio,
rividil più lucente e maggior fatto.

   Poi d'ogne lato ad esso m'appario   22
un non sapeva che bianco, e di sotto
a poco a poco un altro a lui uscìo.

   Lo mio maestro ancor non facea motto,   25
mentre che i primi bianchi apparver ali;
allor che ben conobbe il galeotto,

   gridò: "Fa, fa che le ginocchia cali.   28
Ecco l'angel di Dio: piega le mani;
omai vedrai di sì fatti officiali.

CANTO 2

Sunrise—the angelic boat with the souls—Casella and his singing—
Cato's rebuke

1   Already the sun had reached that horizon whose
meridian circle covers Jerusalem with its highest
point,

4   and Night, circling opposite him, was coming
forth from Ganges with the Scales, which fall from
her hands when she predominates,

7   so that the white and rosy cheeks of lovely
Aurora, there where I was, were becoming orange
with advancing age.

10   We were still alongside the sea, like people
thinking about their path, who go with the heart
and with the body remain.

13   And behold, as when near the morning Mars
shines red through the heavy vapors, low in the
West, over the surface of the sea:

16   such appeared to me—so may I see it again!—a
light coming across the sea so rapidly that no flight
equals its motion.

19   After I had a little withdrawn my eye from it to
question my leader, I saw it again, grown brighter
and larger.

22   Then on each side of it appeared I knew not
what whiteness, and below it, little by little,
another whiteness came forth.

25   My master still did not say a word, while the
first white things showed themselves to be wings;
then, when he had recognized the oarsman,

28   he cried: "See, see that you bend your knees.
Behold the angel of God: fold your hands;
henceforth you will see such ministers.

Vedi che sdegna li argomenti umani,   31
sì che remo non vuol né altro velo
che l'ali sue, tra liti sì lontani.

Vedi come l'ha dritte verso 'l cielo,   34
trattando l'aere con l'etterne penne,
che non si mutan come mortal pelo."

Poi, come più e più verso noi venne   37
l'uccel divino, più chiaro appariva,
per che l'occhio da presso nol sostenne,

ma chinail giuso; e quei sen venne a riva   40
con un vasello snelletto e leggero
tanto che l'acqua nulla ne 'nghiottiva.

Da poppa stava il celestial nocchiero,   43
tal che parea beato per descripto;
e più di cento spirti entro sediero.

"In exitu Isräel de Aegypto"   46
cantavan tutti insieme ad una voce
con quanto di quel salmo è poscia scripto.

Poi fece il segno lor di santa croce,   49
ond' ei si gittar tutti in su la piaggia:
ed el sen gì, come venne, veloce.

La turba che rimase lì, selvaggia   52
parea del loco, rimirando intorno
come colui che nove cose assaggia.

Da tutte parti saettava il giorno   55
lo sol, ch'avea con le saette conte
di mezzo 'l ciel cacciato Capricorno,

quando la nova gente alzò la fronte   58
ver' noi, dicendo a noi: "Se voi sapete,
mostratene la via di gire al monte."

E Virgilio rispuose: "Voi credete   61
forse che siamo esperti d'esto loco;
ma noi siam peregrin come voi siete.

Dianzi venimmo, innanzi a voi un poco,   64
per altra via, che fu sì aspra e forte,
che lo salire omai ne parrà gioco."

L'anime, che si fuor di me accorte,   67
per lo spirare, ch'i' era ancor vivo,
maravigliando diventaro smorte.

31   See how he disdains all human means, so that he needs no oars nor any sail but his wings, between shores so distant.

34   See how he has them stretched toward the sky, beating the air with his eternal feathers, that do not change like mortal hairs."

37   Then, as the divine bird came closer and closer to us, it grew brighter, so that my eyes could not sustain it up close,

40   but I lowered them; and he came to shore with a vessel so swift and light that the waters engulfed none of it.

43   At the stern stood the angelic pilot, who seemed to have blessedness inscribed on him; and more than a hundred spirits were sitting within.

46   "*In exitu Israel de Aegypto,*" they were singing all together with one voice, with as much of that psalm as is written thereafter.

49   Then he made the sign to them of the holy cross; at which they all threw themselves on the beach; and he went away as quickly as he had come.

52   The crowd that remained there seemed strange to the place, looking around as one does who assays new things.

55   In every direction the sun was shooting daylight, and with his unerring arrows he had driven Capricorn from the midst of the sky,

58   when the new people lifted their brows toward us, saying: "If you know, show us the way to reach the mountain."

61   And Virgil replied: "You believe perhaps that we know this place, but we are strangers here, as you are.

64   We arrived just now, a little before you, by a different way that was so harsh and steep that climbing now will seem like play to us."

67   The souls, who had perceived by my breathing that I was still alive, became pale with wonder.

E come a messagger che porta ulivo   70
tragge la gente per udir novelle,
e di calcar nessun si mostra schivo,

    così al viso mio s'affisar quelle   73
anime fortunate tutte quante,
quasi oblïando d'ire a farsi belle.

    Io vidi una di lor trarresi avante   76
per abbracciarmi, con sì grande affetto
che mosse me a far lo somigliante.

    Ohi ombre vane, fuor che ne l'aspetto!   79
tre volte dietro a lei le mani avvinsi,
e tante mi tornai con esse al petto.

    Di maraviglia, credo, mi dipinsi;   82
per che l'ombra sorrise e si ritrasse,
e io, seguendo lei, oltre mi pinsi.

    Soavemente disse ch'io posasse;   85
allor conobbi chi era, e pregai
che per parlarmi un poco s'arrestasse.

    Rispuosemi: "Così com' io t'amai   88
nel mortal corpo, così t'amo sciolta:
però m'arresto; ma tu perché vai?"

    "Casella mio, per tornar altra volta   91
là dov' io son, fo io questo vïaggio,"
diss' io; "ma a te com' è tanta ora tolta?"

    Ed elli a me: "Nessun m'è fatto oltraggio,   94
se quei che leva quando e cui li piace,
più volte m'ha negato esto passaggio;

    ché di giusto voler lo suo si face: 97
veramente da tre mesi elli ha tolto
chi ha voluto intrar, con tutta pace.

    Ond' io, ch'era ora a la marina vòlto   100
dove l'acqua di Tevero s'insala,
benignamente fu' da lui ricolto.

    A quella foce ha elli or dritta l'ala,   103
però che sempre quivi si ricoglie
qual verso Acheronte non si cala."

    E io: "Se nuova legge non ti toglie   106
memoria o uso a l'amoroso canto
che mi solea quetar tutte mie voglie,

70   And, as around a messenger bearing an olive branch people draw close to hear the news, and no one seems shy of crowding:

73   so those fortunate souls stared at my face, all of them, almost forgetting to go to make themselves beautiful.

76   I saw one of them draw forward to embrace me, with affection so great that it moved me to do the same.

79   Oh empty shades, except in appearance! three times I clasped my hands behind that shade, and as many times I drew them back to my breast.

82   Wonder, I believe, was painted on my face, at which the shade smiled and drew back, and I, following it, moved forward.

85   Gently it told me to stand still; then I knew who it was, and I begged it to stop a little to speak with me.

88   It replied: "Just as I loved you in the mortal body, so do I love you when loosed from it; therefore I stop; but why do you come here?"

91   "My Casella, to return another time to where I am do I go on this journey," I said; "but how is it that so much time been taken from you?"

94   And he to me: "No outrage has been done me, if he who takes aboard when and whom he will, several times has barred me from this passage;

97   for his will derives from a just will: indeed, for three months he has taken whoever has wished to enter, all peacefully.

100   Thus I, who had returned just now to the waters where the Tiber becomes salt, was graciously gathered in by him.

103   Back to that river mouth he has now directed his wing, because always all gather there who do not descend to Acheron."

106   And I: "If a new law has not taken from you the memory or habit of the amorous singing that used to quiet all my desires,

di ciò ti piaccia consolare alquanto   109
l'anima mia, che, con la sua persona
venendo qui, è affannata tanto!"

"Amor che ne la mente mi ragiona"   112
cominciò elli allor sì dolcemente,
che la dolcezza ancor dentro mi suona.

Lo mio maestro e io e quella gente   115
ch'eran con lui parevan sì contenti,
come a nessun toccasse altro la mente.

Noi eravam tutti fissi e attenti   118
a le sue note; ed ecco il veglio onesto
gridando: "Che è ciò, spiriti lenti?

Qual negligenza, quale stare è questo?   121
Correte al monte a spogliarvi lo scoglio
ch'esser non lascia a voi Dio manifesto."

Come quando, cogliendo biade o loglio,   124
li colombi adunati a la pastura,
queti, sanza mostrar l'usato orgoglio,

se cosa appare ond' elli abbian paura,   127
subitamente lasciano star l'esca,
perch' assaliti son da maggior cura:

così vid' io quella masnada fresca   130
lasciar lo canto e fuggir ver' la costa,
com' om che va, né sa dove rïesca;

né la nostra partita fu men tosta.   133

109   let it please you to console my soul a little in that way, for, coming here with its body, it is so wearied!"

112   "Love that discourses with me in my mind," he began then, so sweetly that the sweetness still sounds within me.

115   My master and I and those people that were with him seemed as contented as if nothing else touched anyone's mind.

118   We were all fixed and attentive to his notes; and here was the venerable old man, crying: "What is this, laggard spirits?

121   What negligence, what standing still is this? Run to the mountain to shed the slough that keeps God from being manifest to you."

124   As when, gleaning oats or tares, doves have gathered to feed quietly, without showing their usual pride,

127   if something appears that they fear, they suddenly abandon the food, because assailed by a greater care:

130   so I saw that fresh band leave the singing and flee toward the cliffs, as one does who goes without knowing where he will arrive;

133   nor was our own departure less sudden.

1-9. Already the sun . . . advancing age: The first three lines refer to sunset as seen from Jerusalem: the meridian circle of any point on the earth passes through the North and South Poles and directly overhead (through the zenith); since any given point has a single horizon, the meridian circle can also be spoken of as being the horizon's as well, since only one of its points is crossed by the meridian.

In lines 4-6, Night is imagined as a point circling opposite the sun (cf. *Met.* 4.92): thus when the sun sets for Jerusalem (over Gibraltar; see Fig. 1), Night simultaneously rises from the Ganges. Since the sun is in Aries, Night is thought of as being opposite, in Libra (the Scales); the Scales are said to fall from Night's hands when the sun enters Libra because Libra no longer appears in the night sky. Jerusalem and Purgatory, being antipodal, share the same horizon: from Purgatory, the Ganges is 90° to the west, Gibraltar 90° to the east. Seen from

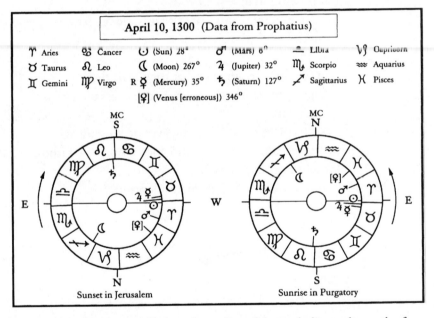

Figure 2. The Ecliptic, projected on the surface of the earth, lies to the south of any point north of the Tropic of Cancer; the sun crosses the meridian when it is due south of such a point. Thus horoscopes for the Northern Hemisphere show south (the *medium coeli* [midpoint of the heavens], noon) at the top of the chart: looking south, east is to the left, west to the right. In the same way, in the Southern Hemisphere, the Ecliptic lies to the north of any point south of the Tropic of Capricorn; the sun crosses the meridian when it is due north of such a point. Thus horoscopes for the Southern Hemisphere show north (the *medium coeli* [midpoint of the heavens], noon) at the top of the chart: looking north, east is to the right, west to the left. See also the diagram on page xiii.

Purgatory, then, the sun rises from Gibraltar and sets over the Ganges (see *Inf.* 34.90-139). See also fig. 2.

Lines 7-9 mean that the white and then rosy color of first dawn is changing to bright orange as the sun begins to appear (see the note to 1.13-27). For Aurora, goddess of the dawn, see also 9.1-6, 19.1-6, 27.109-14.

13-51. And behold . . . as he had come: The arrival of the angelic boat bringing souls to be purified. For its relation to Charon's boat, see *Inter cantica* below; for connections with the romance motif of magic boats, see Picone in *LDT* and 1996.

13-15. near the morning . . . surface of the sea: As Dante says in *Conv.* 2.14.21, Mars appears redder when seen through thick vapors.

19-26. After I had . . . to be wings: Dante realistically both notes the increase in size of the approaching vessel and draws on the fact that when a ship is first seen only its sails are visible, until "little by little" the hull appears ("another whiteness," lines 23-24).

25-27. My master . . . recognized the oarsman: Like the pilgrim, Virgil must infer the identity of the pilot; his knowledge is still limited.

44. who seemed to have blessedness inscribed on him: That is, his blessedness was legible in his face and bearing (cf. 10.40-45, with notes). For the interesting textual variant here, see Textual Variants, p. 627.

46-48. In exitu Israel de Aegypto [When Israel went out of Egypt] **. . . written thereafter:** The souls are singing Psalm 113, early recognized as consisting of two distinct poems: the first (eight verses long) is on the miracles of the Exodus and the entry into the Promised Land, the second (eighteen verses long) is mainly an attack on idol-worship. In insisting that the souls sang all of the psalm, Dante perhaps wishes to call attention to the ending of the second poem: "The dead shall not praise thee, O Lord: nor any of them that go down to hell. But we that live bless the Lord: from this time now and forever." (Compare *Inf.* 3.103-105; *Purg.* 12.112-14; see Scott 2004). The first eight verses of the psalm read:

> When Israel went out of Egypt, the house of Jacob from a barbarous people: Judea was made his sanctuary, Israel his dominion. The sea beheld and fled; Jordan was turned back. The mountains skipped like rams, and the hills like the lambs of the flock. What ailed thee, O thou sea, that thou didst flee: and thou, O Jordan, that thou wast turned back? Ye mountains, that ye skipped like rams, and ye hills, like lambs of the flock? At the presence of the Lord the earth was moved, at the presence of the God of Jacob: Who turned the rock into pools of water, and the stony hill into fountains of waters.

For the fundamental importance of the Exodus to the allegory of the *Comedy*, see Introduction, pp. 12-15.

This is the first of many instances in the *Purgatorio* of singing based on the liturgy of the Church. All of this psalm was traditionally sung in the vesper service on Sundays; according to the opening of the canto, the time in Jerusalem is that of vespers. Presumably the souls are singing the more elaborate psalmody customary on Easter Sunday.

52-54. The crowd . . . new things: This first group of souls seems to belong to no particular category other than that of new arrivals: recently released from the body and from the world, in a sense reborn, uncertain of the way, about which they inquire in lines 59-60. Other groups will be more definitely categorized.

56-57. with his unerring . . . midst of the sky: The metaphor draws on the mythological figure of Apollo the archer. Since the sun is in Aries, at sunrise the "midst of the sky" (the *medium coeli*, where the ecliptic crosses the meridan, not, as some commentators suppose, the zenith) is occupied by the sign Capricorn, 90° west of the sun, driven away because no longer visible or because supplanted at the meridian by the next sign, Aquarius (Gizzi 1974).

63. we are strangers here, as you are: Virgil and the pilgrim are as tentative as the new souls. Italian *peregrino* adds to the meanings of Lat. *peregrinus* [away from one's own fields, a traveler or foreigner] the specifically Christian meaning of *pilgrim*. Mahrt 2001 observes that the psalm tone used uniquely for "In exitu" was known as the "tonus peregrinus" [wandering tone] because, uniquely again, the second hemistich of each verse was sung on a different pitch from the first, always a step higher (note the theme of ascent).

67-68. The souls . . . still alive: The first instance in the *Purgatorio* of the major motif of the presence of the pilgrim's body.

70-71. a messenger . . . crowding: The custom was still alive in Dante's day that a messenger bringing good news would carry an olive branch: Sapegno cites Villani 12.105, Chiavacci Leonardi the *Cronaca bolognese*. (There are Vergilian precedents as well—*Aen.* 8.115 and 11.100—both involving embassies.)

75. almost forgetting: This will be Cato's rebuke (lines 120-23).

76-119. I saw one of them . . . to his notes: A much-discussed encounter (see Additional Note 2). Although there is a reference in an early musical manuscript to a Casella, perhaps a composer, and perhaps Dante's friend, nothing more is known of him. Most of the early commentators say Dante's Casella was Florentine.

79-81. Oh empty shades . . . to my breast: Based on *Aen.* 6.792-94 (also, verbatim, in *Aen.* 2.700-702):

Three times I tried to throw my arms around her neck:
three times in vain her image, grasped, slipped through my hands,
like the light winds, most like the swiftness of dreams.

94-105. No outrage . . . descend to Acheron: No explanation for the angel's refusal is given, except obedience to God's just will (line 97; see next note). Lines 100-101 imply that Casella had wandered for several months away from the mouth of the Tiber (see map, p. xiii), where, we now learn, all souls not condemned to Hell congregate to embark.

98-99. for three months . . . all peacefully: In February 1300, Boniface VIII proclaimed 1300 (retroactively to Christmas) as a Jubilee or Holy Year (apparently the first in history), with plenary indulgence (i.e., release from all time in Purgatory) to those who came to Rome and visited the basilicas of Saint Peter and Saint Paul a specified number of times (see the note to *Inf.* 18.28-33). The chronology of Casella's death and wanderings is intentionally vague, but lines 94-96 mean that his desire to board the angelic boat had been repeatedly denied before Christmas, "three months" earlier, when Boniface VIII's proclamation took effect. For the implications of this passage and Dante's view of indulgences, see Additional Note 2.

106-107. If a new law . . . amorous singing: The phrase "new law" alludes to Cato's statement in 1.89-90; as Dante expects his readers to understand, this is saint Paul's New Law of forgiveness of sins and freedom from their bondage.

107. amorous singing: Italian *amoroso* is much broader in meaning than English *amorous*; *il canto amoroso* can mean, also, "singing about love," and "lovely singing."

112-17. Love that discourses . . . anyone's mind: The commentators draw the parallel with the description of the power of music in *Conv.* 2.14.24 (itself deriving from a tradition going back to Plato): "Music draws to itself human spirits, which are principally vapors arising from the heart, so that they almost cease from every operation; so whole is the soul when it hears it that all the powers [of the soul] run, as it were, to the sensitive spirit that receives the sound"; cf. 4.1-12, with notes.

112. Love that discourses with me in my mind: The first line of a canzone ("Amor che ne la mente mi ragiona") apparently written after 1293 but before 1300. It was later included in Book 3 (1304?) of the unfinished *Convivio*. The choice of this canzone here has puzzled the commentators; some hold that it represents a repudiation of the view of philosophy taken in the *Convivio*. Whether the historical Casella actually composed music for any of Dante's canzoni is unknown, but no musical settings of poems by Dante have survived from his lifetime—in fact no Italian settings of canzoni have survived from this period (Monterosso 1970).

119-23. here was . . . manifest to you: Cato explicitly rebukes the souls for neglecting the task of purifying themselves, for indulging in pleasant delay. The souls in Purgatory can no longer sin (and, within the terms of the vision, the same must be true of the pilgrim). Again, see Additional Note 2.

122. to shed the slough .. manifest to you: The image is that of a snake's skin, to be shed or sloughed, and derives from Colossians 3.1-2, 9-10:

> Mind the things that are above, not the things that are upon the earth . . .
> stripping yourselves [*expoliantes*, the etymon of *spogliarvi*] of the old man
> with his deeds, And putting on the new, him who is renewed into knowledge.

The "old man" refers to the principle of fleshliness, which stands as an obstacle to the direct knowledge of God (see Pertile 1995 and *Tesoretto* 2655 in Contini 1960). Cato's dispelling the group's attention to poetry draws on Philosophy's driving away of the Muses of elegy in *Consolation* 1. Pr. 1. The complex meanings of *scoglio* are discussed in Additional Note 13.

124-29. As when, gleaning . . . a greater care: The rapt attention of the group (lines 116-19) to the sweetness of Casella's song is compared to the feeding of doves. The metaphor of pleasure in poetry as feeding occurs in the passage of the *Consolatio* mentioned above. Shoaf 1975 discusses biblical commentaries that identify the dove as a type of negligence.

Inter cantica. Central to the *Purgatorio*, as to the *Inferno,* are the meetings or interviews with the souls of the dead; especially important are those personally known to the pilgrim (e.g., in the *Inferno*, Francesca in Canto 5 and Brunetto Latini in Canto 15). Casella is the first acquaintance met in the *Purgatorio*, and the choice was no doubt carefully considered. That he is a close friend contributes to the central theme of reconciliation and contrasts strongly with most of the encounters in Hell (especially in lower Hell: Vanni Fucci in *Inferno* 24-25, Bocca degli Abati in *Inferno* 32).

This canto continues the elaborate parallelism with the opening cantos of the *Inferno* begun in Canto 1. Line 10, involving the pilgrim's desire to climb the mountain and his inability to do so, refers to *Inf.* 1.28-54. The angelic boat and its pilot offer a sharply focused contrast with Charon and his boat (*Inf.* 3.82-117; note also the contrast with the angel of *Inf.* 9.80-84): the angelic boat approaches from the horizon; Charon's comes from across Acheron (*Inf.* 3.82). Charon has lost his former wings (he is a fallen angel) and rows with an oar: the angel "needs no oars nor any sail." In *Inferno* 3 the souls enter Charon's boat at individual beckonings; they curse their birth and all its circumstances, then go off to their punishments: in *Purgatorio* 2 the souls are singing of God's action in history (especially the Exodus) while still in the boat; they leave the boat as the angel signs them with the Cross; lines 100-105 tell us that as the damned congregate on the near shore of Acheron (*Inf.* 3.107-108, 121-27), so the saved gather at the mouth of the Tiber. The angelic boat is clearly the "lighter vessel" that Charon says must carry the pilgrim (*Inf.* 3.93). Both the angel and Charon are called *nocchieri* [pilots or oarsmen]; the angel is white with purity and blessedness, Charon with age; both are compared with fire. Other parallels include bird imagery (*Inf.* 3.115-16; *Purg.* 2.34-39); verbal parallels include *gittare* [to throw] (*Inf.* 3.116; *Purg.* 2.50), *pelo* [hair] (*Inf.* 3.83; *Purg.* 2.36).

The ending of the canto provides a further parallel with Charon. Cato's rebuke (lines 120-23) is closely related to Charon's "Guai a voi, anime prave! / Non isperate mai veder lo cielo . . ." [Woe to you, wicked souls! Never hope to see the sky] (*Inf.* 3.84-85). Practically identical in rhythm is "Che è ciò, spiriti lenti" [What is this, laggard spirits]; the passages are also linked by the motif of sight, in *Inferno* of the sky (which declares the glory of God, Psalm 5) in *Purgatorio* of God himself.

The placement of the various elements in these parallels is reversed: Cato's rebuke, at the end of the canto, parallels Charon's opening threat; the angelic boat carries the souls to us, Charon's away from us; Charon beckons to the souls before they enter his boat, the angel signs them before they leave his boat. The reversal helps emphasize that the parallels contrast a pattern *in malo* (i.e., with a clearly negative meaning) with one *in bono*.

Thus the parallels with *Inferno* 3 operate on a number of levels; perhaps most important, they help establish the differences between the place of damnation and despair and that of forgiveness and hope, which derives ultimately from the difference between the Old Law, the law of exact retribution, embodied by Hell, and the New Law, the law of love and forgiveness. Thus, as the Old Law prefigures the New Law, so within the *Comedy* Charon prefigures both the angelic boatman and Cato. The infernal is always a parody of the good.

Other references to the *Inferno* include the general parallel, also inverted, of the angelic boat with Ulysses' ship (*Inf.* 26.124-42, especially 133-42), already alluded to in 1.130-32, with prominent mention, as here, of such parts of ships as oars—compared with wings (*Inf.* 26.125)—and poop (*Inf.* 26.124, 140). The pilgrim's weariness, mentioned in line 111, is parallel with that in *Inf.* 1.22-28, and both include the term *affannata* [wearied, laboring]. Freccero (1973) and Barolini (1984) observe a number of parallels with *Inferno* 5 involving the relation of the protagonists to lyric love poetry.

CANTO 3

Avvegna che la subitana fuga   1
dispergesse color per la campagna,
rivolti al monte ove ragion ne fruga,

i' mi ristrinsi a la fida compagna: 4
e come sare' io sanza lui corso?
chi m'avria tratto su per la montagna?

El mi parea da sé stesso rimorso: 7
o dignitosa coscïenza e netta,
come t'è picciol fallo amaro morso!

Quando li piedi suoi lasciar la fretta   10
che l'onestade ad ogn' atto dismaga,
la mente mia, che prima era ristretta,

lo 'ntento rallargò, sì come vaga,   13
e diedi 'l viso mio incontr' al poggio
che 'nverso 'l ciel più alto si dislaga.

Lo sol, che dietro fiammeggiava roggio,   16
rotto m'era dinanzi a la figura
ch'avëa in me de' suoi raggi l'appoggio.

Io mi volsi dallato, con paura   19
d'essere abbandonato, quand' io vidi
solo dinanzi a me la terra oscura;

e 'l mio conforto: "Perché pur diffidi?"   22
a dir mi cominciò tutto rivolto.
"Non credi tu me teco e ch'io ti guidi?

Vespero è già colà dov' è sepolto   25
lo corpo dentro al quale io facea ombra;
Napoli l'ha, e da Brandizio è tolto.

Ora, se innanzi a me nulla s'aombra,   28
non ti maravigliar più che d'i cieli,
che l'uno a l'altro raggio non ingombra.

CANTO 3

*Haste—the pilgrim's shadow—the foot of the mountain—the
excommunicated—Manfred*

1   Although their sudden flight had scattered
those souls over the plain, turning them back to
the mountain where reason probes us,

4   I drew closer to my faithful companion: and
how could I have run without him? who would
have led me up the mountain?

7   He appeared to be reproaching himself: O
worthy clear conscience, how bitter a bite to you is
even a little fault!

10   When his feet left off the haste that robs every
action of its dignity, my mind, until then reined in,

13   broadened its attention in its eagerness, and I
looked toward the hill that higher than all others
unlakes itself toward the sky.

16   The sun, flaming ruddy behind us, was broken
before me in the shape of its rays' resting on me.

19   I turned to the side, afraid that I had been
abandoned, when I saw the ground darkened only
in front of me;

22   and my strength: "Why do you distrust?" he
began to say, turned fully toward me. "Do you not
believe that I am with you and guiding you?

25   It is already vespers there at the tomb of the
body within which I cast a shadow; Naples has it,
from Brindisi it has been taken.

28   Now if in front of me no shadow falls, do not
marvel more than at the heavens, which give no
obstacle to each other's rays.

A sofferir tormenti, caldi e geli   31
simili corpi la Virtù dispone
che, come fa, non vuol ch'a noi si sveli.

   Matto è chi spera che nostra ragione   34
possa trascorrer la infinita via
che tiene una sustanza in tre persone.

   State contenti, umana gente, al *quia*;   37
ché se potuto aveste veder tutto,
mestier non era parturir Maria;

   e disïar vedeste sanza frutto   40
tai che sarebbe lor disio quetato,
ch'etternalmente è dato lor per lutto:

   io dico d'Aristotile e di Plato   43
e di molt' altri"; e qui chinò la fronte,
e più non disse, e rimase turbato.

   Noi divenimmo intanto a piè del monte;   46
quivi trovammo la roccia sì erta
che 'ndarno vi sarien le gambe pronte.

   Tra Lerice e Turbìa la più diserta,   49
la più rotta ruina è una scala,
verso di quella, agevole e aperta.

   "Or chi sa da qual man la costa cala,"   52
disse 'l maestro mio fermando 'l passo,
"sì che possa salir chi va sanz' ala?"

   E mentre ch'e' tenendo 'l viso basso   55
essaminava del cammin la mente,
e io mirava suso intorno al sasso,

   da man sinistra m'apparì una gente   58
d'anime, che movieno i piè ver' noi,
e non pareva, sì venïan lente.

   "Leva," diss' io, "maestro, li occhi tuoi: 61
ecco di qua chi ne darà consiglio,
se tu da te medesmo aver nol puoi."

   Guardò allora, e con libero piglio   64
rispuose: "Andiamo in là, ch'ei vegnon piano;
e tu ferma la spene, dolce figlio."

   Ancora era quel popol di lontano,   67
i' dico dopo i nostri mille passi,
quanto un buon gittator trarria con mano,

31   Such bodies are disposed to suffer torments, heat, and freezings by the Power that does not wish its ways to be unveiled to us.

34   He is mad who hopes that our reason can traverse the infinite way taken by one Substance in three Persons.

37   Be content, human people, with the *quia*; for if you had been able to see everything, there was no need for Mary to give birth;

40   and you have seen those yearning fruitlessly whose desire would be stilled, which is given them eternally for their grief:

43   I speak of Aristotle and Plato and many others"; and here he bent his brow and said no more, and remained troubled.

46   We arrived meanwhile at the foot of the mountain; there we found the rock so steep that in vain would legs be agile on it.

49   Between Lerici and Turbìa the wildest, the most broken landslide is a stairway open and easy, next to this one.

52   "Now who knows on which side the slope is less steep," said my master, staying his steps, "so that one who goes without wings can climb it?"

55   And as he, looking down, was examining his mind about the way, and I was looking upward around the rocks,

58   on the left hand I saw a band of souls who were moving their feet toward us without seeming to, so slowly were they coming.

61   "Raise," I said, "master, your eyes: behold over here those who will give us counsel, if you cannot have it from yourself."

64   He looked then, and with a confident air replied, "Let us go over there, for they are approaching slowly; and you, bolster your hope, dear son."

67   Those people were still distant, even after we had walked a thousand paces, as far as a good thrower could reach by his unaided hand,

quando si strinser tutti ai duri massi   70
de l'alta ripa e stetter fermi e stretti,
com' a guardar chi va dubbiando stassi.

   "O ben finiti, o già spiriti eletti,"   73
Virgilio incominciò, "per quella pace
ch'i' credo per voi tutti s'aspetti,

   ditene dove la montagna giace   76
sì che possibil sia l'andare in suso;
ché perder tempo a chi più sa più spiace."

   Come le pecorelle escon del chiuso   79
a una, a due, a tre, e l'altre stanno
timidette, atterrando l'occhio e 'l muso,

   e ciò che fa la prima, e l'altre fanno,   82
addossandosi a lei, s'ella s'arresta,
semplici e quete, e lo 'mperché non sanno:

   sì vid' io muovere a venir la testa   85
di quella mandra fortunata allotta,
pudica in faccia e ne l'andare onesta.

   Come color dinanzi vider rotta   88
la luce in terra da mio destro canto,
sì che l'ombra era di me a la grotta,

   restaro e trasser sé in dietro alquanto,   91
e tutti li altri che venieno appresso,
non sappiendo 'l perché, fenno altrettanto.

   "Sanza vostra domanda io vi confesso   94
che questo è corpo uman che voi vedete,
per che 'l lume del sole in terra è fesso.

   Non vi maravigliate, ma credete   97
che non sanza virtù che da ciel vegna
cerchi di soverchiar questa parete."

   Così 'l maestro; e quella gente degna   100
"Tornate," disse, "intrate innanzi dunque,"
coi dossi de le man faccendo insegna.

   E un di loro incominciò: "Chiunque   103
tu se', così andando, volgi 'l viso:
pon mente se di là mi vedesti unque."

   Io mi volsi ver' lui e guardail fiso: 106
biondo era e bello e di gentile aspetto,
ma l'un de' cigli un colpo avea diviso.

70   when they all shrank back against the hard
masses of the high bank and stood still, crowded
together, as those who walk in fear do in order to
gaze.

73   "O happy dead, O spirits already chosen," Virgil
began, "for the sake of that peace which I believe
you all await,

76   tell us where the mountain slopes so that it is
possible to climb it; for losing time displeases most
those who know most."

79   As the little sheep come forth from the fold by
ones, by twos, by threes, and the rest stand timid,
their eyes and muzzles to the ground,

82   and what the first one does the others do,
pressing up against it if it stops, simple and quiet,
and they know not why:

85   so I saw the head of that fortunate flock move to
come forward then, shamefast in face and modest
in walk.

88   When those in front saw that the light on my
right side was broken, so that the shadow extended
from me to the cliff,

91   they stopped and drew back somewhat, and all
the others that were coming after, without
knowing why, did the same.

94   "Without your asking, I confess to you that this
is a human body you see, by which the light of the
sun is split upon the ground.

97   Do not marvel, but believe that not without
power that comes from Heaven does he seek to
surmount this wall."

100   So my master; and that worthy folk: "Turn
back," they said, "walk on ahead of us, therefore,"
making a sign to us with the backs of their hands.

103   And one of them began: "Whoever you are, as
we walk turn your eyes to me: consider if you have
ever seen me back there."

106   I turned toward him and looked at him closely:
he was blond and handsome and of noble appearance,
but a sword-blow had divided one of his brows.

Quand' io mi fui umilmente disdetto   109
d'averlo visto mai, el disse: "Or vedi,"
e mostrommi una piaga a sommo 'l petto.

   Poi sorridendo disse: "Io son Manfredi,   112
nepote di Costanza imperadrice;
ond' io ti priego che, quando tu riedi,

   vadi a mia bella figlia, genitrice   115
de l'onor di Cicilia e d'Aragona,
e dichi 'l vero a lei, s'altro si dice.

   Poscia ch'io ebbi rotta la persona   118
di due punte mortali, io mi rendei
piangendo a quei che volontier perdona.

   Orribil furon li peccati miei;   121
ma la Bontà infinita ha sì gran braccia
che prende ciò che si rivolge a lei.

   Se 'l pastor di Cosenza, che a la caccia   124
di me fu messo per Clemente allora,
avesse in Dio ben letta questa faccia,

   l'ossa del corpo mio sarieno ancora   127
in co del ponte presso a Benevento,
sotto la guardia de la grave mora.

   Or le bagna la pioggia e move il vento   130
di fuor dal Regno, quasi lungo 'l Verde,
dov' e' le trasmutò a lume spento.

   Per lor maladizion sì non si perde   133
che non possa tornar, l'etterno amore,
mentre che la speranza ha fior del verde.

   Vero è che quale in contumacia more   136
di Santa Chiesa, ancor ch'al fin si penta,
star li convien da questa ripa in fore,

   per ognun tempo ch'elli è stato, trenta,   139
in sua presunzïon, se tal decreto
più corto per buon prieghi non diventa.

   Vedi oggimai se tu mi puoi far lieto,   142
revelando a la mia buona Costanza
come m'hai visto, e anco esto divieto;

   ché qui per quei di là molto s'avanza."   145

109   When I had humbly denied ever having seen him, he said: "Now see," and showed me a wound high on his breast.

112   Then, smiling, he said: "I am Manfred, grandson of the Empress Constance; and so I beg you, when you return,

115   go to my lovely daughter, mother of the honor of Sicily and Aragon, and tell her the truth, if something else is being said.

118   After I had my body broken by two mortal thrusts, I gave myself up, weeping, to him who gladly pardons.

121   Horrible were my sins; but the infinite Goodness has such open arms that it takes whatever turns to it.

124   If the shepherd of Cosenza, who had been sent by Clement to hunt me then, had read this face aright in God,

127   the bones of my body would still be at the head of the bridge near Benevento, under the protection of the heavy cairn.

130   Now the rain bathes and the wind drives them outside the Kingdom, near the Verde, where he transferred them with candles extinguished.

133   By their curse no one so loses the eternal love that it cannot be regained, as long as hope has any touch of green.

136   It is true that whoever dies in contumacy of Holy Church, though he repent at the end, must remain outside this cliff,

139   for every time that he persisted in rebellion, thirty times, if that decree is not shortened by good prayers.

142   Now see whether you can gladden me, revealing to my good Constance how you have seen me, and also this exclusion;

145   for here we gain much from those back there."

NOTES

1-45. Although . . . remained troubled: This first section of the canto, which takes the travelers to the very foot of the mountain, emphasizes Virgil's limitations in the light of Christian truth (cf 1.49-51, 66, 68-69, 73-75), but his loss of dignity in lines 10-11 is tempered by insistence on his fidelity as a guide.

3. where reason probes us: Note the parallel with *Inf.* 30.70 (Master Adam on his punishment); here the image is that of a surgeon probing a wound (cf. 25.139), introducing a system of references to wounds, cutting, splitting, breaking, that will extend into the next cantos.

7-9. He appeared . . . a little fault: Virgil is very close here to being a personification of conscience. Note the play on the etymology of *rimorso* [reproached, also remorse], which derives from *rimordere* [to bite again, or from behind].

10-11. the haste . . . its dignity: It. *dismagare* [to weaken, to dismay, to enchant] is a borrowing from OF *esmaier,* apparently going back to a Germanic root **magan* [to be able]; cf. its use in 10.106, 19.20.

12-15. my mind . . . toward the sky: As conscience relaxes its self-reproaches, the mind is freed for the first direct view of the mountain. Described by Ulysses (*Inf.* 26.133-35) as the highest he had ever seen, the mountain rises far above all meteorological disturbances of the atmosphere (see 21.40-54, 28.97-114).

16-45. The sun . . . remained troubled: The sun, which rose at 2.1, is now high enough to cast shadows. Although the shades cast no shadows, lines 31-33 make it clear that their apparent bodies are not mere illusions but are capable of feeling pain and, presumably, pleasure. The contribution of the body to the process of purgation is a major theme of the cantica; see Additional Note 6.

16-17. The sun . . . was broken: The pilgrim's body interrupts the sunshine. Note the terminology of violence in *rotto* [broken] and *fesso* [split], which culminate in Manfred's account of his death (see especially lines 108, 118-19, with notes).

19-21. I turned . . . in front of me: The intensity of the pilgrim's surprise and fear at the absence of a shadow helps prepare for the reactions of the shades to the presence of his. It also provides a strong sense of physical presence (including the reader's memory of the sun on his own back). The fleshly error of the bishop (lines 124-29) is parallel to this one.

22-45. and my strength . . . remained troubled: Virgil's long speech begins as a reassurance of his presence in spite of his lack of a shadow, but it moves, seemingly by association, through the topics of his loss of his natural body (lines 25-

27), the analogy of his airy body with the heavenly spheres (lines 28-30), and the impenetrable mystery of God's provision of it (lines 31-36). At this point the speech becomes a sermon against the presumptuousness of human reason, concluding with the eternal frustration of "Aristotle and Plato and many others" (obviously including Virgil himself), who must eternally yearn for the knowledge of God that is denied them, and Virgil "remained troubled" (lines 37-45). All this from his lack of a shadow! A shadow has been cast over Virgil that lasts until they reach the foot of the cliff (line 46). See the note to lines 94-99.

22-24. Why do you . . . guiding you: Although the point here is that Virgil is present without a natural body, there are echoes of the words of the risen Christ to Thomas (John 20.27: "and be not faithless, but believing") and others (Matt. 28.20: "and behold I am with you all days"; cf. Luke 24.39, John 20.20).

25-27. It is already vespers . . . it has been taken: Vergil died at Brindisi, on the heel of Italy, when returning from Greece; his body was transferred to Naples at the order of Augustus. Compare Vergil's epitaph (preserved in Donatus's biography): "Mantua me genuit; Calabri rapuere; tenet nunc Parthenope" [Mantua begot me, the Calabrians carried me off (i.e., I died in Calabria); Parthenopea (Naples) holds me now]. Vergil's supposed tomb in Naples attracted literary pilgrims in the Middle Ages; Boccaccio sets scenes of his *Filocolo* (c. 1336) there. For other echoes of the epitaph, see 5.134 and 6.72-75, with notes, and Additional Note 4.

28-30. Now if in front of me . . . each other's rays: Virgil compares the translucent shades to the celestial spheres: although material, these do not interrupt light.

31-33. Such bodies . . . unveiled to us: Virgil here asserts that the nature of the shades' airy bodies is not accessible to reason; later in the cantica, however, he seems to have a better understanding, though deferring to Statius (25.22-108).

32-44. the Power . . . many others: His assertion of the limits on his understanding leads Virgil, the personification of human reason, to proclaim the utter transcendence and mystery of God's power.

34-36. He is mad . . . in three Persons: See Is. 55.8, Rom. 11.33. The reason for Virgil's ability to cite the orthodox doctrine of the Trinity (one Substance, the Godhead, in three equal Persons: Father, Son, Holy Spirit; the classic discussion is Augustine's *De trinitate*) is especially difficult to discern.

37-44. Be content . . . many others: *Quia* [that, conjunction], used in biblical and Scholastic Latin to introduce direct quotations, acquired, when used as a substantive, the meaning "the matter of fact," "the fact [that]." The *quia* with which human beings should be content is the mere fact that things are as they are; they should not suppose they can know or understand what is beyond them (cf. *Quaest*. 77: "Let men desist, therefore, let them desist from searching into what is beyond them"). Even the highest human reason, as in Aristotle, Plato, and Virgil himself, falls short of understanding God. For the eternal yearning of the ancient philosophers, see *Inf*. 4.34-42, with notes. This is one of the more noteworthy moments setting forth the pathos inherent in Dante's conception of Virgil.

46-145. We arrived . . . those back there: Almost two thirds of the canto take place at the foot of the cliff, including Virgil's puzzlement as to the correct path (lines 46-57) and the encounter with the group of shades who instruct them (lines 58-102), which culminates in the encounter with Manfred (lines 103-45).

46-48. We arrived . . . agile on it: The mountain has at first the appearance of an unsurmountable wall (cf. line 99). Lerici and Turbìa (modern Le Turbie) mark the two ends of the coast of Liguria: Lerici is just north of La Spezia (Tuscany), Turbìa east of Nice. Their steep coastlines plunge into the sea but provide some pathway with their landslides. The difficulty of passage of these places was well known to travelers between Italy and France. Here there is no access; for landslides, see *Inf*. 12.1-12 and *Inferno* Additional Note 16.

52-66. Now who knows . . . your hope, dear son: The contrast between Virgil, seeking the path inwardly, and the pilgrim, alert to his external surroundings, is pronounced; close again to personification allegory, it emphasizes the usefulness of the body and the senses. When Virgil and the pilgrim turn left to face the shades, they face south and the mountain is to their right, to the west.

67-102. Those people . . . of their hands: There are three phases to the interaction with the group of shades as a whole: 1) after gradual approach, the shades shrink back, presumably at their first sight of the travelers, and are ceremoniously addressed by Virgil (lines 67-78); 2) the shades resume their approach until they notice the pilgrim's shadow, whereupon Virgil acknowledges the presence of his living body (lines 79-99); 3) the shades answer Virgil's question.

67-69. Those people . . . unaided hand: After walking for about a mile (Lat. *mille passuum* [a thousand paces]), the shades are a long stone's-throw away: perhaps 25 or 30 yards.

73-78. O happy dead . . . who know most: Virgil owes his prompt awareness of the presence of the shades to the pilgrim's alertness; without him Virgil would have lost a good deal of time, the shades are walking so slowly.

73. O happy . . . chosen: Contrasting strongly with the picture of the frustrated longing of the pre-Christian philosophers (lines 40-44), this first address of a group of shades on the mountain sets the style for those that follow (see 13.85-87, 19.76-78).

74-75. for the sake . . . all await: These lines are a formula of conjuration and do not modify *chosen* (line 73).

79-87. As the little sheep . . . modest in walk: The tentativeness is characteristic of the souls in the lower Ante-Purgatory (cf. 2.58-75). As we infer from lines 133-41, this group consists of souls who died while excommunicated; contumacious in life, they are now humbled. The image of the faithful as sheep is biblical (Ps. 22, Is. 40.11; the saved are sheep separated from the goats in Matt. 25.32).

88-99. When those in front . . . surmount this wall: The second instance (for the first, see 2.67-69; and cf. the note to lines 16-45 above) of the recurrent motif of the shades' amazement at the presence of the pilgrim's body, most frequently associated with their perception of his shadow (see 5.1-9, 25-36; 8.58-66; 13.142-47; 23.111-14; 26.7-15).

88-91. When those in front . . . back somewhat: See the note to lines 94-99 and Additional Note 13.

88-90. the light . . . to the cliff: Note the echo of line 17 in *rotta* [broken], again applied to the sunlight; the pilgrim's shadow reaches all the way to the cliff (line 90): undoubtedly an intended parallel with fact that the pilgrim's noticing Virgil's lack of a shadow occasioned talk lasting from line 16 to the foot of the cliff (line 46). See the next note.

94-99. Without your asking . . . surmount this wall: After *rotto* (line 17) and *rotta* (line 88), the light is now called *fesso* [split], in close proximity to the term *parete* [wall]. For the implicit references here to Ovid's tale of Pyramus and Thisbe, see Additional Note 13.

102. making a sign . . . of their hands: What for English-speakers is a beckoning to approach was for Dante, and still is in Italy and many parts of Europe, a sign to move away (or a wave goodbye); the palm of the hand invites approach.

103-45. And one of them . . . those back there: The final third of the canto is devoted to the encounter with Manfred (1232-1266), the natural son of the emperor Frederick II of Hohenstaufen. After the death of his father in 1250, and during the absence of the Emperor's legitimate heir, Conrad, Manfred was regent of the so-called Kingdom [*Regno*], which included southern Italy and Sicily; after Conrad's death, he assumed the same role during the minority of the Emperor's grandson Conradin, and was crowned king after rumors of Conradin's death in Germany. Manfred's efforts to consolidate Hohenstaufen power on the peninsula led to his excommunication by the pope, who in 1266 enlisted Charles of Anjou (the brother of Louis IX of France) against him. Betrayed by his Apulian barons, Manfred was defeated and killed at Benevento on February 26, 1266, and Charles established the Angevin dynasty in the Kingdom.

Although he accepted the Guelph propaganda that Frederick II was damned as an Epicurean (see the note on *Inf.* 10.119), Dante repeatedly expressed admiration for his and Manfred's political and cultural achievements; they surrounded themselves with a brilliant court of intellectuals and writers, fostering the earliest courtly poetry in Italian (see *DVE* 1.12.4, *Purg.* 24.49-63, with notes). The vivid evocation of the violence besetting Italy in the thirteenth century will continue in Cantos 5-7.

103-104. And one of them . . . as we walk: Dante's efficiently implied stage directions have brought the entire group of shades up to the travelers and now indicate that all are now walking as directed in lines 101-102.

103-105. Whoever . . . back there: Manfred's opening speech expresses his awareness of having been a public figure known to many who were unknown to him. Dante, of course, was not a year old when Manfred was killed.

107-108: he was blond . . . of his brows: Manfred was famous for his beauty and gallantry. Gmelin quotes the thirteenth-century chronicler Saba Malaspina: "He was blond, of agreeable face and pleasing aspect, ruddy of cheek, entirely white-skinned, of medium height" (perhaps also recalling I Kings 16,12: "Now he was ruddy [usually so translated, though Lat. *rufus* means "red-headed"] and beautiful to behold, and of a comely face," of David when anointed by Samuel).

108. but a sword-blow . . . of his brows: Dante's "un colpo avea diviso" [a blow had divided] does not specify the weapon. *Diviso* [divided] is a close equivalent of *fesso* [split]: see the notes to lines 94-99 and 110-12.

109-10. When I had . . . seen him: The humility of the pilgrim's reply expresses his instinctive recognition of Manfred's kingliness. Presumably he would have used the respectful *voi* form (see the note to *Inf.* 10.49-51).

110-12. Now see . . . I am Manfred: The pilgrim has just denied ever having seen Manfred before, and this displaying of wounds is probably not meant as a means of identification (see *Inter cantica* below), though it is true that Manfred's wounds were much discussed by the chroniclers, albeit inconsistently. Rather, the display associates Manfred with the risen Christ (it is Easter Sunday; see 1.88-90 and 3.22-24, with notes), who repeatedly shows his wounds to his disciples (e.g., Luke 24.40, John 24.20: they are the proof of the identity of his resurrected body with his living one, and of his not being a mere phantom, as "doubting Thomas" had feared; cf. *Par.* 11.106-108). Manfred's mysterious smile greatly enhances the effect. None of the many other shades we encounter who died violently (see 5.52-136) is said to retain his wounds or is given such a gesture. There is a strong suggestion of martyrdom (for the parallel between annointed kings and Christ, see Kantorowicz 1957): like Christ, Manfred was vilified and persecuted by the high priests (cf. *Inf.* 109-23) and betrayed by friends. It is clear from the chronicle of Saba Malaspina, Guelph though he is, that such a view circulated in Ghibelline circles; he describes the discovery of Manfred's dead body by surviving followers: "Alas, alas, the Lamb has been killed, our King, our leader, our Lord, who elected to die with his people rather than to live without them."

112-45. I am Manfred . . . those back there: Manfred's speech expresses his concern that his daughter understand that he repented at the moment of death and is saved (lines 114-23). This leads to criticism of the official position of the Church, represented by the bishop of Cosenza (lines 124-32), and to the penalty that the excommunicated must suffer (lines 133-41). The speech ends on the hope that when his daughter learns that her prayers can help him, his time of waiting will be shortened (lines 142-45).

This speech introduces a major recurrent theme, the power of the prayers of the living to help the souls in Purgatory, central especially to Cantos 5 and 23. That this theme is introduced by the figure of Manfred, contrasting the importance of the loving prayers of intimates with the mistaken views of the corrupt institutional hierarchy, is part of Dante's anti-papal polemic (see Aurigemma 1965). The largeness of the divine mercy is sharply contrasted, too, with the vengefulness of the clergy. As usual, Dante accepts the distinction between the official authority of the clergy and their personal qualities (see *Inferno* 19 and *Purgatorio* 19, with notes); their blindness does not invalidate the excommunication. The same distinction is operative in relation to the sanctity of the office of annointed king and the imperfections of the man, whose sins were "horrible."

112-16. Then, smiling . . . Sicily and Aragon: Manfred was the grandson of Constance, daughter of Roger II of Sicily and wife of Henry VI of Hohenstaufen and mother of Frederick II; she appears in *Par.* 3.109-20. The second Constance, named in line 143, was Manfred's daughter by Beatrice of Savoy; she died in 1302. Married to Pedro III of Aragon (d. 1285; see 7.112-17), she bore him Alfonso (king of Aragon 1285-1291, the "honor of Aragon," praised in 7.115-17), James (King of Sicily 1285-1295) and Frederick (king of Sicily 1296-1337); they are denounced in 7.118-20; referring to them, "honor" can only refer to the dignity of the kingship itself. Manfred omits mention of his father.

117. tell her the truth . . . being said: The assumption here is that the Church's claim that Manfred died unrepentant, and therefore damned, was widely accepted, even by his daughter (she had become a Franciscan nun when widowed).

118-19. After I had . . . mortal thrusts: The chroniclers differ on Manfred's wounds: eye, throat, and chest are mentioned. Dante's blows to head and breast attack the chief bodily seats of pride and rebelliousness; compare *Inf.* 10.35-36. Note the presence of the motivic *rotta* (see the note to lines 94-99): the splitting of Manfred's bodily wall lets in the light (cf. 5.25-26 and 97-102, *Inf.* 33.27; Additional Note 13).

119-23. I gave myself . . . turns to it: Dante seems to have been aware of reports of Manfred's dying conversion (the first surviving written one dates from the 1330s); he is supposed to have exclaimed, "God have mercy on me, a sinner" (citing Luke 18.13). As the commentators point out, Dante's complex view of Manfred does not minimize his sins; the emphasis is rather on God's eagerness to forgive (see Ezek. 33.11, John 6.37, 1 Tim. 2.4). That the outstretched arms of the crucified Christ expressed the desire to embrace all sinners was a commonplace that appears frequently, as in the *Golden Legend* and (significantly, given the crusade preached against Manfred) crusade songs. Cf. 5.106-107.

124-32. If the shepherd . . . candles extinguished: Charles of Anjou had Manfred honorably buried (but not with Church rites) under a cairn of stones (cf. 2 Kings 18.17) at the head of the bridge over the Calore near Benevento (see map, p. xiii). At the order of pope Clement IV, it is said, the bishop of Cosenza exhumed the body and cast it out of the Kingdom, over its northern boundary (the river Verde—the Garigliano on our map). The inverted, unlit candles, derived from the ceremony of anathema, may be Dante's addition; but so may be the entire account. Note the irony of the "shepherd" being turned into a hunter of one of the lambs (line 79). This casting out of Manfred's body is contrasted with the honors paid by Augustus to Vergil's, alluded to in lines 25-27, and see next note.

124-26. If the shepherd . . . aright in God: The reference of the term *face* [*faccia*] is uncertain. The most probable is to God's compassionate desire to save the sinner; the commentators cite *Mon.* 3.15.14: "They [misguided electors] do not discern the face of God's decree" (this could mean "the face decreed by God," i.e., that of the true emperor). Manfred's own face, as well as various tropes (e.g., a page of the Bible) have been proposed as the referent here. In any case, the target is the lack of spiritual insight and compassion of the hierarchy. (See the note to lines 19-21.)

130-31. Now the rain . . . drives them: As the commentators point out, there is an important parallel with Vergil's Palinurus (*Aen.* 6.337-84, especially line 362: "nunc me fluctus habet versantque in litore venti" [now the flood has me and the winds drive me along the shore]; see the notes to 5.89-129, and Additional Note 4. In his *De cura pro mortuis gerenda* Augustine cites Palinurus as exemplifying the pagan superstition, debunked by Christianity, that the unburied are barred from crossing the Styx to their rest (cf. *City of God* 1.12-13): Dante's point as to the irrelevance of burial to salvation is Augustinian.

133-35. By their curse . . . touch of green: That even excommunication does not exclude saving grace was standard doctrine, but Dante's view of the serious nature of even an unjust decree of excommunication (cf. the note to lines 112-45: the validity of a rite is unaffected by the personal nature of the performer) is indicated by this penalty; Manfred was excommunicated in 1255, the arithmetic here would have him wait 330 years (cf. 4.131-32). Green is, of course, the color that signifies hope; Manfred is reported to have especially favored green clothing.

Inter cantica. There are a number of parallels between the excommunicated and the trimmers and neutral angels of *Inferno* 3; both groups are excluded: note the verbal parallels (*caccia*, *Purg.* 3.124; *caccianli*, *Inf.* 3.40); but Manfred was a figure of heroic nobility (see *DVE* 1.12.4), while the trimmers "lived without infamy and without praise" (*Inf.* 3.35-36). Manfred's exclusion is of course only temporary; his salvation is assured, thanks to the "touch of green" of his hope (3.135; see also 3.66), while the dark writing on the Gate of Hell (*Inf.* 3.1-9) commands despair: "Abandon all hope you who enter."

Although the principal parallel to Charon's boat is in *Purgatorio* 2 (see *Inter cantica* there), the solidarity and shyness of the elect, especially in lines 79-81, where they are like sheep (for Christ as the good shepherd, see John 10.1-16), is meant to recall the despairing separateness of the damned souls and their merciless pilot in *Inf.* 3.112-17:

> As in autumn the leaves remove themselves one
> after the other, until the branch sees all its raiment on
> the ground
> so the evil seed of Adam throw themselves from
> that shore one by one, when beckoned to, each like a
> falcon to its lure.

Parallel to the liminal position of the neutrals, inside the Gate of Hell but above the infernal torments, is the liminal position of the souls in the Ante-Purgatory, richly developed in Cantos 2-8.

Manfred's officially decreed damnation but actual salvation recall the inverse situation of Guido da Montefeltro in *Inferno* 27, he died shriven but in fact damned; he, too, is included among the paired fathers and sons, the first damned, the second saved: see the *Inter cantica* to Canto 5.

The evocation of the battle of Benevento and the death of Manfred recalls *Inf.* 28.1-21, which imagine that the ninth bolgia contains more terrifying wounds than were produced by all the wars on "the travailed earth of Apulia," including Benevento (the betrayal of Manfred is referred to in lines 16-17) and Tagliacozzo, where the sixteen-year-old Conradino was captured (lines 17-18), to be beheaded at Naples. That Manfred's wounds are understood as emblematic by Dante is confirmed by the symbolism of the punishment of the sowers of discord; compare especially Bertran de Born (*Inf.* 28.118-42): in Dante's eyes, Manfred was the legitimate head of the body politic, his killing a crime (cf. *Purg.* 20.67-68).

CANTO 4

Quando per dilettanze, o ver per doglie,
che alcuna virtù nostra comprenda
l'anima bene ad essa si raccoglie,

par ch'a nulla potenza più intenda;
e questo è contra quello error che crede
ch'un'anima sovr' altra in noi s'accenda.

E però, quando s'ode cosa o vede
che tegna forte a sé l'anima volta,
vassene 'l tempo e l'uom non se n'avvede;

ch'altra potenza è quella che l'ascolta,
e altra è quella c'ha l'anima intera:
questa è quasi legata e quella è sciolta.

Di ciò ebb' io esperïenza vera,
udendo quello spirto e ammirando;
ché ben cinquanta gradi salito era

lo sole, e io non m'era accorto, quando
venimmo ove quell' anime ad una
gridaro a noi: "Qui è vostro dimando."

Maggiore aperta molte volte impruna
con una forcatella di sue spine
l'uom de la villa quando l'uva imbruna,

che non era la calla onde salìne
lo duca mio, e io appresso, soli,
come da noi la schiera si partìne.

Vassi in Sanleo e discendesi in Noli,
montasi su in Bismantova e 'n Cacume
con esso i piè, ma qui convien ch'om voli,

dico con l'ale snelle e con le piume
del gran disio, di retro a quel condotto
che speranza mi dava e facea lume.

CANTO 4

The weary climb—a ledge—the sun is to the north—explanation—
Belacqua and the negligent

1   When because of pleasures, or else pains, that some
     faculty of ours may grasp, the soul focuses sharply
     upon that,

4   it seems to heed no other power; and this is again
     the error that believes one soul is kindled over anoth
     in us.

7   And therefore, when we hear or see something th
     holds the soul strongly turned to it, time passes and
     do not notice its passage;

10   for one is the power that listens to time, and ano
     that which now occupies the whole soul: the lat
     bound, as it were, the first unbound.

13   Of this I had true experience, hearing that spi
     marveling, for a full fifty degrees

16   the sun had mounted, and I had not perceiv
     when we came to where those souls, as one, c
     us: "Here is what you asked."

19   A larger opening is often filled up by the fa
     with a forkful of his thorns, when the grape

22   than was that passageway up which my lea
     climbed, and I after him, the two of us alone,
     crowd had left us.

25   One can go up to Sanleo and descend to
     can climb to Bismantova or up the Cacume
     feet, but here one must fly,

28   I mean with the swift wings and the pini
     desire, following that guide who gave me
     light.

Noi salavam per entro 'l sasso rotto,   31
e d'ogne lato ne stringea lo stremo,
e piedi e man volea il suol di sotto.

Poi che noi fummo in su l'orlo suppremo   34
de l'alta ripa, a la scoperta piaggia,
"Maestro mio," diss' io, "che via faremo?"

Ed elli a me: "Nessun tuo passo caggia;   37
pur su al monte dietro a me acquista,
fin che n'appaia alcuna scorta saggia."

Lo sommo er' alto che vincea la vista,   40
e la costa superba più assai
che da mezzo quadrante a centro lista.

Io era lasso, quando cominciai: 43
"O dolce padre, volgiti e rimira
com' io rimango sol, se non restai."

"Figliuol mio," disse, "infin quivi ti tira,"   46
additandomi un balzo poco in sùe
che da quel lato il poggio tutto gira.

Sì mi spronaron le parole sue   49
ch'i' mi sforzai carpando appresso lui,
tanto che 'l cinghio sotto i piè mi fue.

A seder ci ponemmo ivi, ambedui   52
vòlti a levante ond' eravam saliti,
ché suole a riguardar giovare altrui.

Li occhi prima drizzai ai bassi liti;   55
poscia li alzai al sole, e ammirava
che da sinistra n'eravam feriti.

Ben s'avvide il poeta ch'ïo stava   58
stupido tutto al carro de la luce,
ove tra noi e Aquilone intrava.

Ond' elli a me: "Se Castore e Poluce   61
fossero in compagnia di quello specchio
che sù e giù del suo lume conduce,

tu vedresti il Zodïaco rubecchio   64
ancora a l'Orse più stretto rotare,
se non uscisse fuor del cammin vecchio.

Come ciò sia, se 'l vuoi poter pensare,   67
dentro raccolto imagina Sïòn
con questo monte in su la terra stare

31   We were climbing within the broken rock, and on either side the banks hemmed us in, and the ground beneath us required both feet and hands.

34   When we were on the upper rim of the high bank, on the open slope, "My master," I said, "what way shall we take?"

37   And he to me: "Let no step of yours go downward; still following me, gain on the mountain, until there appear to us some wise guide."

40   The summit was so high it vanquished sight, and the slope was much haughtier than a line from mid-quadrant to center.

43   I was weary, when I began: "O sweet father, turn and look back at how I am left alone, if you do not stop."

46   "My son," he said, "pull yourself up that far," pointing to a ledge a little further up, which girdled all that side of the mountain.

49   His words so spurred me that I forced myself, crawling on hands and knees after him, until the circling ledge was beneath my feet.

52   We sat down there, both turned to the east, whence we had climbed, for it usually does one good to look back.

55   First I directed my eyes to the low shores; then I raised them to the sun, and I was amazed that it struck us from the left.

58   The poet well saw that I was lost in wonder at the chariot of the sun, where it came between us and Aquilon.

61   Wherefore he said to me: "If Castor and Pollux accompanied that mirror that leads its light both north and south,

64   you would see the ruddy Zodiac wheel even closer to the Bears, as long as it did not abandon its old path.

67   How that can be, if you want to be able to conceive it, turning inward imagine that Zion and this mountain stand on the earth

sì ch'amendue hanno un solo orizzòn   70
e diversi emisperi; onde la strada
che mal non seppe carreggiar Fetòn,

   vedrai come a costui convien che vada   73
da l'un, quando a colui da l'altro fianco,
se lo 'ntelletto tuo ben chiaro bada."

   "Certo, maestro mio," diss' io, "unquanco   76
non vid' io chiaro sì com' io discerno,
là dove mio ingegno parea manco,

   che 'l mezzo cerchio del moto superno,   79
che si chiama Equatore in alcun' arte,
e che sempre riman tra 'l sole e 'l verno,

   per la ragion che di', quinci si parte   82
verso settentrïon, quanto li Ebrei
vedevan lui verso la calda parte.

   Ma se a te piace, volontier saprei   85
quanto avemo ad andar; chè 'l poggio sale
più che salir non posson li occhi miei."

   Ed elli a me: "Questa montagna è tale   88
che sempre al cominciar di sotto è grave;
e quant' om più va sù, e men fa male.

   Però, quand' ella ti parrà soave   91
tanto che sù andar ti fia leggero
com' a seconda giù andar per nave,

   allor sarai al fin d'esto sentiero;   94
quivi di riposar l'affanno aspetta.
Più non rispondo, e questo so per vero."

   E com' elli ebbe sua parola detta,   97
una voce di presso sonò: "Forse
che di sedere in pria avrai distretta!"

   Al suon di lei ciascun di noi si torse,   100
e vedemmo a mancina un gran petrone
del qual né io né ei prima s'accorse.

   Là ci traemmo; e ivi eran persone   103
che si stavano a l'ombra dietro al sasso
come l'uom per negghienza a star si pone.

   E un di lor, che mi sembiava lasso,   106
sedeva e abbracciava le ginocchia,
tenendo 'l viso giù tra esse basso.

70   in such a way that the two have a single horizon and different hemispheres; thus the road along which Phaëthon could not drive the chariot, to his hurt,

73   you will see must go first on one side and then on the other side of that horizon, if your intellect pays clear attention."

76   "Certainly, my master," said I, "never have I seen so clearly as I now discern, there where my wit had seemed lacking,

79   that the middle circle of the daily rotation, which is called Equator in science, and which always stands between the sun and winter,

82   for the reason you give is as far from here toward the north, as the Hebrews saw it toward the hot region.

85   But if it pleases you, I would gladly know how far we have to go; for the mountain rises farther than my eyes can."

88   And he to me: "This mountain is such that it is always more difficult at the bottom, at the beginning; and the further up one goes, the less it gives pain.

91   Thus, when it shall seem so easy to you that going up will be like floating downstream in a boat,

94   then you will be at the end of this path; wait to rest your weariness there. I answer no further, but this I know for truth."

97   And when he had spoken this word a voice from nearby sounded: "Perhaps you will be obliged to sit before then!"

100   At the sound of it both of us turned, and we saw to the left a great boulder that neither he nor I had noticed previously.

103   We drew near; and there were persons in the shade behind the rock, in postures people take for negligence.

106   And one of them, who seemed weary, was sitting embracing his knees, holding his face down low between them.

"O dolce segnor mio," diss'io, "adocchia 109
colui che mostra sé più negligente
che se Pigrizia fosse sua serocchia."

Allor si volse a noi e puose mente, 112
movendo 'l viso pur su per la coscia,
e disse: "Or va tu sù, che se' valente!"

Conobbi allor chi era, e quella angoscia 115
che m'avacciava un poco ancor la lena
non m'impedì l'andare a lui; e poscia

ch'a lui fu' giunto, alzò la testa a pena, 118
dicendo: "Hai ben veduto come 'l sole
da l'omero sinistro il carro mena?"

Li atti suoi pigri e le corte parole 121
mosser le labbra mie un poco a riso;
poi cominciai: "Belacqua, a me non dole

di te omai; ma dimmi: perché assiso 124
quiritto se'? attendi tu iscorta,
o pur lo modo usato t'ha ripriso?"

Ed elli: "O frate, andar in sù che porta? 127
ché non mi lascerebbe ire a' martìri
l'angel di Dio che siede in su la porta.

Prima convien che tanto il ciel m'aggiri 130
di fuor da essa quanto fece in vita,
per ch'io 'ndugiai al fine i buon sospiri,

se orazïone in prima non m'aita 133
che surga sù di cuor che in grazia viva:
l'altra che val, che 'n ciel non è udita?"

E già il poeta innanzi mi saliva 136
e dicea: "Vienne omai: vedi ch'è tocco
meridïan dal sole, e a la riva

cuopre la notte già col piè Morrocco." 139

109   "O my sweet lord," said I, "look at that fellow: he appears more negligent than if Laziness were his sister."

112   Then he turned to us and gave us his attention, shifting his face up a bit along his thigh, and said: "Now you go on up, you are so vigorous!"

115   Then I knew who he was, and the pain that made my breath still come somewhat quickly did not prevent my going to him, and when

118   I reached him, he barely raised his head, saying: "Have you seen clearly how the sun drives his chariot over our left shoulder?"

121   His lazy movements and his brief words moved my lips to smile a little; then I began: "Belacqua, now I do not grieve

124   for you any longer; but tell me: why are you sitting just here? are you waiting for a guide, or have your old habits claimed you again?"

127   And he: "O brother, what good would climbing do? for the angel of God sitting on the threshold would not let me go in to the torments.

130   First it is necessary for the heavens to turn around me outside here as long as they did in my life, since I delayed my good sighs until the end,

133   unless prayer help me first, which must rise up from a heart that lives in grace: what good is any other, since it is not heard in Heaven?"

136   And already the poet was climbing ahead of me and saying: "Come along now: see, the meridian is touched by the sun, and on the shore of ocean

139   night already covers Morocco with its foot."

NOTES

1-18. When because . . . what you asked: The idea that the unitary soul possesses an array of faculties or powers directed toward specific objects (e.g., sensation, desire, judgment) is central to Aristotelian Scholasticism. This passage is confusing because the metaphor of binding, occupying, and loosing is used of the entire soul in lines 3 and 8, and then later of the separate faculties (lines 10-12), but the basic point is clear: the pilgrim has not noticed the passage of time between 3.103, when he began listening to Manfred, and his arrival at the opening, and this is direct experience of the unity of the soul, for if it were multiple he could have "listened" both to Manfred and to time; instead, his soul has been engrossed (line 11) by Manfred, and his capacity to observe the passage of time has remained unutilized ("unbound," line 12). This passage is an important contribution to the central theme of the *Purgatorio*: the unity of the soul and the problem of integrating the entire soul-body complex around its fundamental goals. See the note to 2.112-17.

5-6. and this is against . . . over another in us: Dante's target here would seem to be Plato, for whom the intellect, the animal soul, and the vegetative soul had separate physical locations (respectively brain, heart, and liver). Dante knew of Plato's conception from Aristotle's refutation (*De anima*, Book 2). In his discussion of the unity of the soul (*ST* 1a q. 76 a. 3), which Dante must have read, Aquinas mentions only Plato and Aristotle as representing the two positions, and offers a similar argument against the Platonic position: "One operation of the soul, if it is intense, can impede others. This would not occur unless the principle of its activity were in essence single."

10-12. for one is . . . the first unbound: The "power that listens to time" (unnamed, perhaps the *vis aestimativa* [judgment]) is a different power of the soul from the one that now engrosses (*ha* [lit., has, possesses]) the entire soul; this latter power (in the *intentio* [bending] toward Manfred) is "bound" because dedicated to Manfred, and the first (the power that listens to time) is "unbound" because unfocussed on its object (the feminine singulars in lines 11-12—*altra, questa, quella*—all have *potenza* [power] as antecedent; the syntax excludes their referring to *anima* [soul]). For other explanations see Barbi 1975, Pézard.

15-16. a full fifty . . . had mounted: Since the sun moves across the sky some 15° per hour, some 3 hours, 20 minutes have elapsed; it is now about 9:20 A.M. Thus the sun has moved more than halfway from dawn (due east) to noon (due north).

19-51. A larger opening . . . beneath my feet: The first part of the climb up the mountain, to be resumed in 5.1, first within the cloven rock (lines 19-33), then on the "open slope" (lines 34-51).

19-33. A larger opening . . . feet and hands: Initially the climb takes place within a narrow cleft; progress up the mountain will alternate what might be called internal and external passages.

19-23. A larger opening . . . my leader climbed: The opening filled by the peasant is in a hedge, the traditional protective border of vineyards. The ostensibly homely comparison is rich with biblical resonances: Cant. 2.15, Is. 5.1-7, Mark 12.1-12. In Jesus' parables the grape harvest (cf. "when the grape darkens") is a figure for the Day of Judgment (e.g., Matt. 20.1-12, 21.33-40). For the narrowness, cf. Matt. 7.14, "How narrow is the gate and strait the way that leadeth to life." For clefts in the rock, see Is. 2.10: "Enter into the rock and hide thee in the dust, for fear of the Lord" (cf. Jer. 48.28, Cant. 2.14).

25-26. Sanleo . . . Noli . . . Bismantova . . . Cacume: These are actual localities reachable on foot, though laboriously: Sanleo is a hilltop fortress near Urbino; Noli a sea-level city on the Ligurian coast, approached by a stairway cut in the cliff; Bismantova is uncertain; Cacume a peak near Anagni (cf. 20.85-93).

27-30. here one must fly . . . hope and light: Cf. 3.46-51. Note the correlation of physical and moral effort, as well as the early reference to the Neoplatonic wings of the soul (see *Inferno* Additional Note 6), only fully grown toward the end of the cantica (see 27.121-23). For light and hope, see *Inf.* 1.37-43, with note.

34-51. When we were . . . beneath my feet: The second phase of the climb, on the outer surface, where the slope is steeper than 45° (lines 40-42), also divided: a) climbed erect (lines 34-45); b) climbed on hands and knees (lines 46-51).

36-39. My master . . . some wise guide: See lines 29-30: the pilgrim shows his reliance on Virgil's guidance.

41-42. and the slope . . . mid-quadrant to center: A quadrant of a circle is a quarter of its circumference; a line from mid-quadrant to center makes an angle of 45°. The ancestor of trigonometry lies behind this terminology: tables giving the ratios of radii and chords of the circle had been used by astronomers since Ptolemy.

46-51. My son . . . beneath my feet: As in *Inf.* 24.43-57, an even more emphatic passage, Virgil's urgings reawaken the pilgrim's energies.

47-48. a ledge . . . side of the mountain: The implication is that the ledge extends only partly around the mountain, unlike the ledges within Purgatory proper, which entirely encircle it.

52-139. We sat down . . . with its foot: Almost two thirds of the canto are devoted to this pause on the ledge, which has two main parts: a) discussion with Virgil; b) encounter with Belacqua.

52-96. We sat down . . . know for truth: The discussion with Virgil concerns two topics: a) the changed perspective on the motions of the sun resulting from the change of hemispheres (lines 52-84); b) the nature of the mountain (lines 85-96).

52-84. We sat down . . . the hot region: Looking back toward the East, the pilgrim is surprised to see the sun to his left (toward Aquilo, the north wind), instead of to his right (see fig. 2). This leads to an explanation by Virgil, further enlarged on by the pilgrim.

55-57. First I directed . . . from the left: The pilgrim's surprise has been well prepared: at this season, only when the sun has risen significantly above the horizon could its position toward the North become evident. Since the sun is to the travelers' left, their shadows fall to their right; cf. *Phars.* 3.247-48: "And you, O Arabs, visit a clime unknown to you, amazed that the shadows of the groves do not fall to the left," cited by Piero di Dante; cf. also *Phars.* 9.538-39 (where Lucan confuses the Tropic of Cancer with the Equator).

61-66. Wherefore he said . . . its old path: Divested of its metaphors, this passage means: if it were May or June, you would see the sun wheeling even further toward the North. Castor and Pollux are the Twins of Gemini, through which the sun moves in May and June; the Bears are Ursa Major and Ursa Minor; the sun is a "mirror" because it reflects or refracts God's creative power; in its annual motion, it moves along the ecliptic (its "old path") both North and South of the Equator. The "wheeling" of the "ruddy Zodiac" (i.e., the part of the Zodiac heated by the sun) refers to the fact that as the sun moves north along the ecliptic the arc it describes across the sky each day reaches further north at noon.

67-75. How that can be . . . clear attention: The kind of mental exercise now enjoined by Virgil is confusing to moderns, but traditional instruction in astronomy made extensive use of it; see Sacrobosco's *De sphaero,* which enumerates eleven circles to be visualized (Grant 1974); cf. the similar instance in *Conv.* 3.5.8-21. The reader has been prepared for this passage by 2.1-6, which require the same act of visualization of Jerusalem and Purgatory with their common horizon.

71-72. the road. . . drive the chariot: This is the Ecliptic; for the myth of Phaëthon, see *Inf.* 17.106-108, with notes, and *Inferno* Additional Note 6. This is the central one of five references to the sun and the Ecliptic/Zodiac in the canto. See Additional Note 3.

76-84. Certainly, my master . . . the hot region: The pilgrim demonstrates his mastery of the mental image proposed by Virgil by complicating it further, requiring us to add the Equator

79-84. the middle circle . . . the hot region: That is, Purgatory lies as far south of the equator as Jerusalem does to the north, but the idea is phrased in terms of the points of view of the inhabitants of Jerusalem (the Hebrews) and of Purgatory. The "hot region" is the Tropical Zone.

79-81. the middle circle . . . sun and winter: The celestial Equator is meant, 90° from the North and South Poles, around which the diurnal revolution of the heavens takes place (see *Conv.* 2.3.13-15). It is between the sun and winter: when the sun is to the south of the Equator (as at the winter solstice) it is winter in the northern hemisphere, and vice versa.

80. in science: The Italian may also mean "in certain treatises."

85-96. But if it pleases . . . know for truth: The pilgrim changes the subject with a question that implies the allegorical dimension of the mountain, already strongly suggested in lines 27-29, 43-51; as Benvenuto observes, the summit of the mountain reaches beyond sight because the achievement of virtue leads to Heaven. See the next note.

88-96. And he to me . . . know for truth: Virgil's description represents the translation into literal terms of the traditional allegory of the mountain of virtue, which goes back at least as far as Hesiod (*Works and Days* 287-92). Though it is unlikely that Dante knew Silius Italicus (see Delz/Dunstan 1976), his lines have parallels with *Punica* 15.102-109 (a close translation of Hesiod); the speaker is Virtue:

> casta mihi domus et celso stant colle penates
> ardua saxoso perducit semita clivo.
> asper principio—neque enim mihi fallere mos est—
> prosequitur labor . . . mox celsus ab alto
> infra te cernes hominum genus.
> [My chaste dwelling and my Penates stand on a high mountain,
> a steep path leads to them up the rocky slope.
> Harsh at the beginning—for I do not deceive—
> is the labor to be done . . . soon raised on high
> you will see the rest of mankind below you.]

(On the connection with the "choice of Hercules," see Panofsky 1999.)

91-94. Thus, when it . . . end of this path: This striking image is to be connected with a system of river imagery; see 13.85-90 with notes. Chiavacci Leonardi cites Serravalle on *Eth. Nich.* 2.3.165: "Therefore Aristotle says in the second *Nichomachean*: the sign of having acquired virtue is that [virtuous] action is pleasurable."

96. I answer . . . know for truth: Virgil has not answered the pilgrim's question; perhaps we are to infer that he understands the problem of the acquisition of virtue but not the ultimate crowning by grace (see 28.55-57, with note).

97-139. And when he . . . with its foot: The discussion is now interrupted by Belacqua (identified in line 123), and the rest of the canto is devoted to this new encounter.

98-99. Perhaps . . . before then: Belacqua's sarcastic remark reveals that he has been listening to the conversation between the travelers all along (cf. lines 119-20, with note); the moment he chooses for intervention allows him to emphasize the disparity between Virgil's optimistic representations and the exhaustion of the pilgrim, who in lines 115-17 is still somewhat out of breath. Belacqua thus reveals the cast of mind that made him negligent, amply demonstrated in the rest of the interview. In all his speeches Belacqua addresses only the pilgrim, using the familiar *tu* form; he never takes notice of Virgil.

100-105. At the sound . . . for negligence: As we will learn in lines 130-32, this group represents a second category of late repentants, the negligent. Most medieval thinkers considered negligence to be an aspect of sloth, on which see Cantos 17-19 (and see Aquinas' nuanced discussion in *ST* 2a 2ae q. 35 a. 3). That the souls are sitting in the shade as noon approaches (line 138) may suggest that in life they were prey to the "noonday demon" of inactive melancholy.

106-35. And one of them . . . heard in Heaven: The encounter with Belacqua is conspicuous in the *Comedy* for its humor, though it is far from unique (other instances: *Inf.* 23.127-48, *Purg.* 22.19-27). The identity of this shade seems well established; according to the Anonimo Fiorentino, he was a lute-maker who lived near Dante, with whom Dante had close relations, and who replied to Dante's reproaches about his laziness by quoting Aristotle (*Phys.* 7.3.247b): "Sitting in quietness makes the soul wise," to which Dante replied, "Certainly if sitting makes one wise, no one has ever been wiser than you." Archival evidence places his death in 1302 (Chiavacci Leonardi). Belacqua provides a kind of parody of the contemplative life, of which an important part is study of the heavens.

106-11. And one of them . . . were his sister: Belacqua's posture is one traditionally attributed to the slothful; the commentators cite the sloth sonnet among Fazio degli Uberti's sonnets on the seven capital vices. Belacqua is so lazy—the trait of laziness so permeates his body—that he seems to have a genetic similarity to the very personification of laziness. It should be remembered that such traits of temperament were thought hereditary. On Dante's use of personification, see Additional Note 7.

112-17. Then he turned . . . going to him: Up to this point Belacqua has not even troubled to look at the travelers; perhaps he has recognized the pilgrim by his voice (cf. 23.43-45). Belacqua's mocking rejoinder to being called the brother of Laziness is meant to remind the pilgrim of how tired he has claimed to be, but the pilgrim's concern for Belacqua, whom he now recognizes, overcomes his lack of breath.

119-20. Have you seen . . . left shoulder: These lines, which echo the pilgrim's terminology in line 72, show that Belacqua has been listening to the entire conversation on the ledge, presumably waiting for a good opening.

123-26. Belacqua, now . . . claimed you again: The pilgrim is assured that Belacqua is not among the reprobate and therefore need not be mourned; his further questions both lead to clarifications about this group of souls and allow Belacqua further colloquial enactment of his laziness: the episode is a little masterpiece of comic characterization. Note the parallel questions and answers in lines 127-29 and 135.

136-39. And already . . . with its foot: The pressure of the zeal Belacqua mocks is now renewed, and we are again reminded of the passage of time: it is noon (thus 2½ hours have elapsed in this canto), and the urgency is increased by the mention of night (the sun has set in Morocco). This passage may have contributed to Archibald MacLeish's powerful "You, Andrew Marvel"; see especially lines 2-4:

> And here upon earth's noonward height
> To feel the always coming on
> The always rising of the night.

Inter cantica. In light of the Aristotelian tag regarding the way to wisdom, Belacqua's sitting (4.52, 99, 107, 124, even 129) suggests a burlesque of philosophical leisure and of the solemn ancient philosophers in Limbo. We recall Aristotle "sitting among a philosophical company" (*Inf.* 4.132). Belacqua's banter with the pilgrim contrasts with the ceremoniousness of Limbo (*Inf.* 4.79-81), while the slowness of his glance (4.108) parodies the "slow, grave eyes" of the philosophers (*Inf.* 4.112). All is not drollery, however; in the previous canto, Virgil's exhortation of the pilgrim ("bolster your hope," 3.66, 4.29-30) may remind us that the pagans are "without hope" *(Inf.* 4.42), and the grief of Aristotle and Plato (3.40-45) is part of the same system.

Prominent early in the *Purgatorio* (see 1.130-35 and note), references to Ulysses occur also in Canto 4: the height of the mountain (4.40, 87) recalls *Inf.* 26.134-35; in contrast to the "mad flight" westward (*Inf.* 26.124-25), the wayfarers look to the East (4.52-54) on a journey that is no less a flight (4.27-29), using wings equally metaphorical (*Inf.* 26.125; 4.29-30). The pattern is confirmed by mention of Morocco, both Ulysses' last sight of land and the last shore touched by the sunlight as the night moves westward (cf. *Inf.* 26.104, 4.139). The parallel drawn between Ulysses' voyage and Elijah's ascent (*Inf.* 26.36) may also be applied to the solar chariot (*carro della luce*) misgoverned by Phaëthon (4.59, 72). In both cases, of course, the tenor of the comparison is the pilgrim's upward flight: sanctioned, like Elijah's, by the divine will.

CANTO 5

Io era già da quell' ombre partito   1
e seguitava l'orme del mio duca,
quando di retro a me, drizzando 'l dito,

   una gridò: "Ve' che non par che luca   4
lo raggio da sinistra a quel di sotto,
e come vivo par che si conduca!"

   Li occhi rivolsi al suon di questo motto,   7
e vidile guardar per maraviglia
pur me, pur me, e 'l lume ch'era rotto.

   "Perché l'animo tuo tanto s'impiglia,"   10
disse 'l maestro, "che l'andare allenti?
che ti fa ciò che quivi si pispiglia?

   Vien dietro a me, e lascia dir le genti: 13
sta come torre ferma, che non crolla
già mai la cima per soffiar di venti;

   ché sempre l'omo in cui pensier rampolla   16
sovra pensier, da sé dilunga il segno,
perché la foga l'un de l'altro insolla."

   Che potea io ridir, se non "Io vegno"?   19
Dissilo, alquanto del color consperso
che fa l'uom di perdon talvolta degno.

   E 'ntanto per la costa di traverso   22
venivan genti innanzi a noi un poco,
cantando "*Miserere*" a verso a verso.

   Quando s'accorser ch'i' non dava loco   25
per lo mio corpo al trapassar d'i raggi,
mutar lor canto in un "oh!" lungo e roco;

   e due di lor, in forma di messaggi,   28
corsero incontr' a noi e dimandarne:
"Di vostra condizion fatene saggi."

CANTO 5

1   I had already left those shades and was following
the footsteps of my leader, when one behind me,
pointing with his finger,

4   cried out: "See how the rays seem not to shine
to the left of the one below, and how he seems to
walk as if alive!"

7   I turned my eyes to the sound of these words,
and I saw them gazing in wonder at me, at me and
the light that was broken.

10   "Why is your soul so entangling itself," said my
master, "that you slow your pace? What do you
care what they are whispering there?

13   Come after me, and let the people talk: be like a
strong tower whose top never falls, however hard
the winds may blow.

16   for always the man in whom one care sprouts
above the other makes his target more distant,
because the impulse of the one weakens the other."

19   What could I reply, if not "I am coming"? I said
it, somewhat sprinkled over with that color that at
times makes one worthy of pardon.

22   And now across the slope there came people a
little above us, singing "*Miserere*" verse by verse.

25   When they perceived that my body gave no way
for the rays to pass through, they changed their
song into an "Oh!" long and hoarse;

28   and two of them, like messengers, ran to meet
us and asked: "Inform us of your condition."

E 'l mio maestro: "Voi potete andarne   31
e ritrarre a color che vi mandaro
che 'l corpo di costui è vera carne.

Se per veder la sua ombra restaro,   34
com' io avviso, assai è lor risposto:
fàccianli onore, ed esser può lor caro."

Vapori accesi non vid' io sì tosto   37
di prima notte mai fender sereno,
né, sol calando, nuvole d'agosto,

che color non tornasser suso in meno;   40
e, giunti là, con li altri a noi dier volta
come schiera che scorre sanza freno.

"Questa gente che preme a noi è molta,   43
e vegnonti a pregar," disse 'l poeta:
"però pur va, e in andando ascolta."

"O anima che vai per esser lieta   46
con quelle membra con le quai nascesti,"
venian gridando, "un poco il passo queta.

Guarda s'alcun di noi unqua vedesti,   49
sì che di lui di là novella porti:
deh, perché vai? deh, perché non t'arresti?

Noi fummo tutti già per forza morti,   52
e peccatori infino a l'ultima ora;
quivi lume del ciel ne fece accorti,

sì che, pentendo e perdonando, fora   55
di vita uscimmo a Dio pacificati,
che del disio di sé veder n'accora."

E io: "Perché ne' vostri visi guati,   58
non riconosco alcun; ma s'a voi piace
cosa ch'io possa, spiriti ben nati,

voi dite, e io farò per quella pace   61
che, dietro a' piedi di sì fatta guida,
di mondo in mondo cercar mi si face."

E uno incominciò: "Ciascun si fida   64
del beneficio tuo sanza giurarlo,
pur che 'l voler nonpossa non ricida.

Ond' io, che solo innanzi a li altri parlo,   67
ti priego, se mai vedi quel paese
che siede tra Romagna e quel di Carlo,

31   And my master: "You can go back and say to those who sent you that this man's body is real flesh.

34   If they stopped because they saw his shadow, as I suppose, that is a sufficient reply: let them do him honor, and it can be advantageous to them."

37   I have never seen flaming vapors in early night rend the clear sky or the clouds in August at sunset, as swiftly

40   as those two went back up; and, once there, with the others they turned to us like a squadron that gallops unreined.

43   "These people who are crowding on us are many, and they are coming to beg from you," said the poet: "therefore walk on, and listen while walking."

46   "O soul who go to be happy in the limbs with which you were born," they cried as they came, "halt your steps a little.

49   Look if you ever saw any of us, so that you can take news of him back there: Ah, why are you walking? Ah, why do you not stop?

52   We were all killed violently, sinners until the last hour; then light from heaven awakened us,

55   so that, repenting and forgiving, we came forth from life at peace with God, who pierces our hearts with the desire to see him."

58   And I: "Though I stare at your faces, I recognize none; but if anything I can do can please you, well-born spirits,

61   tell me, and I will do it, by that peace which, following the feet of this guide, from world to world makes me seek itself."

64   And one began: "Each of us trusts your good offices without your swearing, as long as your will is not cut off by inability.

67   And so I, speaking alone before the others, beg, if ever you see the land that sits between Romagna and Charles's realm,

che tu mi sie d'i tuoi prieghi cortese   70
in Fano, sì che ben per me s'adori
pur ch'i' possa purgar le gravi offese.

    Quindi fu' io; ma li profondi fóri   73
ond' uscì 'l sangue in sul quale io sedea,
fatti mi fuoro in grembo a li Antenori,

    là dov' io più sicuro esser credea: 76
quel da Esti il fé far, che m'avea in ira
assai più là che dritto non volea.

    Ma s'io fosse fuggito inver' la Mira   79
quando fu' sovragiunto ad Orïaco,
ancor sarei di là dove si spira.

    Corsi al palude, e le cannucce e 'l braco   82
m'impigliar sì ch'i' caddi; e lì vid' io
de le mie vene farsi in terra laco."

    Poi disse un altro: "Deh, se quel disio   85
si compia che ti tragge a l'alto monte,
con buona pïetate aiuta il mio!

    Io fui di Montefeltro, io son Bonconte.   88
Giovanna o altri non ha di me cura,
per ch'io vo tra costor con bassa fronte."

    E io a lui: "Qual forza o qual ventura   91
ti travïò sì fuor di Campaldino
che non si seppe mai tua sepultura?"

    "Oh!" rispuos' elli, "a piè del Casentino   94
traversa un'acqua c'ha nome l'Archiano,
che sovra l'Ermo nasce in Apennino.

    Là 've 'l vocabol suo diventa vano   97
arriva' io forato ne la gola,
fuggendo a piede e sanguinando il piano.

    Quivi perdei la vista, e la parola   100
nel nome di Maria fini'; e quivi
caddi e rimase la mia carne sola.

    Io dirò vero, e tu 'l ridì tra ' vivi: 103
l'angel di Dio mi prese, e quel d'inferno
gridava: 'O tu del ciel, perché mi privi?

    Tu te ne porti di costui l'etterno   106
per una lagrimetta che 'l mi toglie:
ma io farò de l'altro altro governo!'

70   that in your courtesy you beg those in Fano to
pray well for me, so that I may purge my grave
offenses.

73   I was from there; but the deep holes through
which my heart's blood poured out, were given me
in the bosom of the Antenori,

76   where I believed I was safest: he of Este had it
done, angered with me far beyond what justice
allowed.

79   But if I had fled toward Mira, when they
overtook me at Oriago, I would still be back there
where people breathe.

82   I ran to the swamp, and the reeds and the mud
entangled me so that I fell; and there I saw a pool
form on the ground from my veins."

85   Then another said: "Ah, so may the desire be
fulfilled that draws you to the high mountain, with
good pity help mine!

88   I was from Montefeltro, I am Buonconte.
Neither Giovanna nor any other takes care for me,
so I go with lowered brow among these people."

91   And I to him: "What force or chance carried you
away from Campaldino, so that your burial place
was never known?"

94   "Oh!" he replied, "the foot of the Casentino is
crossed by a torrent that is called the Archiano,
born above the Hermitage in the Appenines.

97   There where its name becomes empty I arrived,
pierced in the throat, fleeing on foot, and
bloodying the plain.

100   There I lost sight, and speech in the name of
Mary I ended; and there I fell, and only my flesh
remained.

103   I will tell the truth, and do you retell it among
the living: the angel of God took me, but the one
from Hell cried: 'O you from Heaven, why do you
deprive me?

106   You carry off the eternal part of him because of a
little teardrop that takes him from me: but I will
govern the other otherwise!'

Ben sai come ne l'aere si raccoglie 109
quell' umido vapor che in acqua riede
tosto che sale dove 'l freddo il coglie.

Giunse quel mal voler che pur mal chiede 112
con lo 'ntelletto, e mosse il fummo e 'l vento
per la virtù che sua natura diede.

Indi la valle, come 'l dì fu spento, 115
da Pratomagno al gran giogo coperse
di nebbia, e 'l ciel di sopra fece intento

sì che 'l pregno aere in acqua si converse, 118
la pioggia cadde, e a' fossati venne
di lei ciò che la terra non sofferse;

e come ai rivi grandi si convenne, 121
ver' lo fiume real tanto veloce
si ruinò, che nulla la ritenne.

Lo corpo mio gelato in su la foce 124
trovò l'Archian rubesto, e quel sospinse
ne l'Arno, e sciolse al mio petto la croce

ch'i' fe' di me quando 'l dolor mi vinse. 127
Voltòmmi per le ripe e per lo fondo;
poi di sua preda mi coperse e cinse."

"Deh, quando tu sarai tornato al mondo 130
e riposato de la lunga via,"
seguitò 'l terzo spirito al secondo,

"ricorditi di me, che son la Pia; 133
Siena mi fé, disfecemi Maremma:
salsi colui che 'nnanellata pria

disposando m'avea con la sua gemma." 136

109   You know how the wet vapor gathers in the air
and turns back into water as soon as it rises to
where the cold grasps it.

112   That evil will, desiring always evil, took counsel
with its intellect and moved the vapor and the
wind by the power its nature gave it.

115   And, as soon as day was spent, it covered all the
valley with fog, from Pratomagno to the great
yoke, and thickened the sky above it

118   so that the pregnant air turned to water, the rain
fell, and into the ditches came what the earth did
not accept;

121   and when it came together in the great streams
the water rushed so rapidly toward the royal river
that nothing held it back.

124   My body, now cold, the violent Archiano found
just at its mouth and drove it into the Arno and
loosed at my breast the cross

127   that I made of myself when the agony
vanquished me. It whirled me along the banks and
along the bottom; then with its spoils it covered
and girded me."

130   "Ah, when you are returned to the world and are
rested from the long journey," a third spirit
continued after the second,

133   "remember me: I am Pia; Siena made me,
Maremma unmade me: he knows it within himself
who earlier, wedding me,

136   had given me his ring and gem."

NOTES

1-9. I had already . . . that was broken: There is humor in the souls of the negligent being startled out of their torpor (and cf. line 27); the shadow was not visible in the shade (4.103), but now the pilgrim is in the sunlight. The materiality and fragility of the body are principal themes of this canto.

9. at me . . . was broken: Italian *pur me* is more emphatic than "at me," but less so than "only at me," or "still at me." Some early commentators took it as a confession of vaingloriousness, though Virgil's rebuke (lines 10-18) does not mention that vice. For *lume rotto* [broken light], see 3.17, 88-89, 94-99, with notes.

10-18. Why is your soul . . . weakens the other: Once under way (4.136-39), the pilgrim should not be affected by the shades' remarks.

22-136. And now across the slope . . . his ring and gem: The rest of the canto relates the encounter with a third category of souls, the late repentant who died by violence (lines 52-57). After the preliminaries (lines 22-45), the focus is on three individuals, two prominent public figures and a woman whose identity is uncertain. All three accounts conspicuously mention the places of birth and death, and all, especially the first two, emphasize the validity of even the briefest instant of true repentance. The first and third take place in low, swampy regions (near Venice and in southern Tuscany), the second among the mountains of the upper Arno valley, the Casentino (there is a certain analogy in this order with the mountain of Purgatory itself, its base surrounded by rushes: 1.94-99, 133-36).

22-42. And now . . . that gallops unreined: Contrasting with other groups, these souls are not passive or uncertain; they take swift initiatives and freely express their amazement and curiosity. The metaphor of galloping cavalry looks forward to line 52 and sets off the absence of horses in the first two accounts.

24. singing *"Miserere"* verse by verse: This is probably Psalm 50, the most important of the penitential psalms, sung every morning in the prayer service of Lauds (see Additional Note 2), rather than Ps. 55 or 56, which begin with the same word (cf. *Inf.* 1.65), but note the violent enemies in Ps. 56. "Verse by verse" probably indicates that the souls are singing the entire psalm, perhaps antiphonally. This is the first instance of liturgical song since Canto 2 (see 2.46-48, with note); it will become increasingly frequent.

27. an "Oh!" long and hoarse: Note the frequency of brief interjections in this canto (lines 27, 51, 85, 94, 130), and see below, *Inter cantica*.

37-39. I have never seen . . . as swiftly: Like most commentators, we take "flaming vapors . . . rending" to govern both "the clear sky" and "clouds," referring in the first case to meteors, in the second to lightning, both explained in

Aristotle's *Meteorologica* as caused by particles of fire ("vapors") in the atmosphere (see also *Inf.* 14.35). Some early commentators took *sol calando* [setting sun] as a second grammatical subject: "nor a setting sun [rending] clouds of August"; others take the clouds themselves as swift.

49-50. Look if you . . . back there: Note the parallel with 3.104-110.

48-57. halt . . . desire to see him: The urgency expressed by these souls, like their singing the *Miserere*, marks a considerable advance in confidence over the souls met earlier (see 2.75, 3.70-72, 3.79-94, 4.103-45, with notes).

52. We were all killed violently: As Singleton points out, the Italian *già* here "distributes the time referred to: 'we were slain, each in his own time.' Without the 'già' there might somehow be the suggestion that all were slain at . . . the same time."

55. repenting and forgiving: Both are necessary presuppositions of the souls' narratives (see Matt. 5-7, especially 5.43-48 , 7.1-5).

58-59. And I: Though . . . recognize none: Picone in *LDT* observes that Dante had certainly known both Iacopo and Buonconte, who will soon speak; his inability to recognize them implies that they are somehow transfigured.

64-84. And one began . . . from my veins: Though unnamed, this first speaker can be identified, for his murder was a public scandal. Iacopo del Cassero (pronounced Càssero), ca. 1260-98, a prominent nobleman of Fano (see map, p. xii), in 1288 commanded the Fano contingent against Arezzo (Dante participated in the campaigns). Podestà of Rimini in 1294, of Bologna in 1296, he opposed Azzo VIII of Este's ambitions. Named podestà of Milan in 1298, he traveled by sea to Venice and then toward Padua, avoiding Azzo's lands, but at Oriago he was overtaken by Azzo's assassins. See Fallani 1976.

66. as long as . . . inability: Note the metaphor of cutting, wounding.

68-69. the land . . . and Charles's realm: For Romagna, see the map on p. xii. Charles is Charles II of Anjou, ruler of the kingdom of Naples. The region Iacopo indicates, then, includes Umbria, Lazio, and the Marche.

71-72. those in Fano . . . grave offenses: Like Manfred and Buonconte, Iacopo asks for prayers from intimates in order to begin his purgation.

74. my heart's blood poured out: Literally, "the blood where my soul throned poured out." The thought derives from Aristotle's doctrine that the heart was the reservoir of blood and the seat of the rational soul (hence *sedea* [throned]); the metaphor of the heart as the "acropolis" of the body is Aristotle's (*On the Parts of Animals* 3.7). When the heart's blood is lost, the body dies (for this physiology in Dante, see Durling 1981a). Cf. *Theb.* 9.346 (of a spear): "animae tota in penetralia sedit" [the point rested in the inner chamber of his soul]. Iacopo's name, *Cassero*, derived from a noun meaning "citadel" or "keep," may have suggested—or his example may have been chosen for—this microcosmic imagery.

75-76. in the bosom . . . I was safest: Iacopo's confidence was probably founded on some official safe-conduct, but he was in Paduan territory: referring to the Paduans as "Antenori" is a reminder of the tradition that Padua had been founded by Antenor, said in medieval retellings to have betrayed Troy to the Greeks. Note the recurrent imagery of the human breast.

79-84. But if I had fled . . . from my veins: From Oriago Iacopo apparently fled south, into the marsh beside the Venetian Lagoon, instead of westward, where safety lay. Overtaken, he watches his blood pour out onto the mud (*palude* is properly a body of stagnant water, *laco* a "lake"). Cf. "the fury and the mire of human veins" (Yeats, "Byzantium"). See the note to line 97. Picone in *LDT* finds parallels between Dante's phrasing and Iacopo's epitaph in Fano (cf. the note to 3.25-27).

85-129. Then another . . . and girded me: The second speaker is Buonconte da Montefeltro (line 88), son of Guido da Montefeltro (see *Inferno* 27). Born ca. 1250, Buonconte also became a prominent condottiere for the Ghibellines, particularly in the struggle over Arezzo; he was killed in the battle of Campaldino (June 1289), which established Guelf—and eventually Florentine—supremacy in Tuscany. Note the parallels with Manfred (3.112-45).

In his *Life of Dante*, Leonardo Bruni quotes a letter of Dante's, now lost), relating his participation in the battle of Campaldino as a *feditore* [striker, i.e., in shock cavalry], and his experience of "great fear" in it, perhaps reflected in his account of Buonconte's death (see also *Inf.* 21.94-96, with note, and *Inferno* Additional Note 9). Dante repeatedly visited the Casentino during his exile, particularly in 1307-1308 and 1311; from there he wrote several Latin epistles, as well as his famous canzone "Amor, da che convien ch'io pur mi doglia" [Love, since I must indeed suffer].

88. I was . . . I am Buonconte: Born in Montefeltro, the mountainous region just over the Passo dei Mandrioli from Poppi, Bibbiena, and the plain of Campaldino, Buonconte would normally have succeeded his father as Count of Montefeltro. Note the contrast in verb tenses: preterite for his status in life, present for his eternal identity.

89. Giovanna . . . other: His wife and other relatives. Buonconte's sadness at being forgotten by the living is part of the parallel with Palinurus (*Aen.* 6.336-84); see the next two notes.

91-93. And I . . . never known: The lines echo Aeneas to Palinurus (*Aen.* 6.341-42): "quis te, Palinure, deorum / eripuit nobis medioque sub aequore mersit?" [Which of the gods, Palinurus, carried you off from us and drowned you in the midst of the deep?]. Note the parallels with Manfred; cf. the note on 3.130-31.

94-129. Oh, he replied . . . and girded me: Buonconte's narrative is Dante's invention, but it has a factual basis in the disappearance of Buonconte's body and in the storm itself, reported by other sources (see Roddewig 1985). Here, as in 6.28-48, Dante is concerned to refute what the Sybil tells Palinurus: that it is useless to pray to change one's fate; cf. the closely related 3.130-31, with note, and Additional Note 4.

94-99. the foot of the Casentino . . . bloodying the plain: The main source of the Archiano is near the Eremo [Hermitage] above Camaldoli. *In Apennino* [in the Apennines] here refers to the so-called Giogana, on which both Camaldoli and the Eremo are located. Campaldino is the plain between the Giogana and Pratomagno (see map, p. xii, and cf. line 116); the Archiano crosses it and flows into the Arno (and then is no longer called Archiano) between Poppi and Bibbiena, several miles from the battlefield. *Traversa* [crosses] can mean "pours forth" as well as "crosses": Buonconte is also doing both.

97. where its name becomes empty: Note the recurrent parallel between the veins of the earth and of the human body: where the Archiano pours into the Arno, Buonconte's veins pour themselves out; his name, too, becomes empty, and the Arno carries off what is left of him, along with the Archiano (see the notes to lines 74 and 79-84).

98-99. pierced . . . bloodying the plain: *Forato* [pierced] derives from *foro* [hole], used of Iacopo del Cassero's wounds (line 73); the trail of blood recalls the "pool" of line 85; cf. the notes to 3.94-99, 108.

100-102. There I lost . . . flesh remained: For the punctuation here, see "Textual Variants," p. 627. In our view the lines relate a progression typical of death by loss of blood: sight is lost before speech, speech before balance and motion of the limbs (higher functions go first). Buonconte's power of speech leaves him as he is saying the name of Mary: the last sound he utters is apparently "Ma . . ." [But . . .]. The washing away of Buonconte's body involves also a reference to baptism, which washes away the "Old Man" (Rom. 6.6, Eph. 4.22, Colossians 3.9). *Theb.* 9.349-50 provided a suggestion: "ultimus ille sonus moribundo emersit ab ore, / 'Mater!'" [This last sound came forth from his dying mouth: "Mother!"]. Cf. also the river Ismenus' revenge for this killing, a great swelling of his waters (*Theb.* 9.404-521).

104-108. The angel of God . . . other otherwise: The widespread medieval theme of the contest between an angel (or saint) and a devil for the possession of the soul (or body) of the dying goes back to ancient tradition: "When Michael the archangel, disputing with the devil, contended about the body of Moses, he durst not bring against him the judgment of railing speech" (Jude 9; cf. the silence of Dante's angel; according to Deut. 34.6, Moses' burial place was never known). The dispute was a frequent subject of visual art from early times (a regular feature of scenes of the Last Judgment shows the archangel Michael and the devil on opposite sides of the scales that weigh the souls, e.g., at Torcello, Amiens,

Bourges, Tournus); examples of the dispute at the moment of death are in Hughes 1968: the Traini Triumph of Death (Pisa), the Rohan Hours, and others; see also Garnier 1982 fig. 23. See *Inter cantica* below.

106-108. You carry off . . . otherwise: The devil's rhetoric, as Momigliano observed, turns the individual into abstract terms, *l'eterno* [the eternal] (what is eternal) and *l'altro* [the other] (what is merely temporal, the body). It becomes particularly scornful in "per una lagrimetta" [because of a little teardrop], and in the paranomasia in line 108, "altro altro" [other other].

112-13. That evil will . . . intellect: The meaning here has been debated. We take *con lo 'ntelletto* to depend on *giunse*, with *voler* as grammatical subject.

114. the power its nature gave it: Ancient tradition, both Jewish and pagan, associated demons with the air. The devil is "the prince of the powers of the air" (Eph. 2.2); the early Fathers (e.g., Augustine *De Genesi ad litteram* 3.10) often followed the Neoplatonic belief (known from Apuleius, see Gersh 1986) that "murky air" was a place of punishment for the demons. Aquinas (*ST* 1a q. 64 a.4) asserted that both good and evil angels could "condense clouds into rain, and [do] similar acts" (*ST* 1a q. 112 a. 2).

115-16. all the valley . . . to the great yoke: The valley is that of Campaldino, the "great yoke" the Giogana; cf. *Aen.* 5.19-20.

122-26. the water rushed . . . into the Arno: Cf. *Aen.* 6.355-56, spoken by Palinurus: "Notus . . . vexit me violentus aqua" [the violent south wind drove me through the water]. The pilgrim himself will refer to Palinurus in 6.30.

122. the royal river: The Arno.

126-27. the cross . . . vanquished me: Buonconte's very last action is to cross his arms on his breast, signifying acceptance of death in imitation of the crucifixion (see Barasch 1987).

130-36. Ah, when . . . ring and gem: The last of the three speakers is a woman about whom nothing certain is known, except that she was born in Siena and was killed (line 52) in the Maremma, the swampy region in southwestern Tuscany (see map, p. xii, and *Inf.* 13.1-9), presumably by her husband (lines 135-36), said by the early commentators to have been a minor lord, Nello Pannocchieschi; according to some he killed her for infidelity, according to others, in order to remarry (see *Inter cantica* below). Pia's name recalls Vergil's epithet for Aeneas, *pius* [devoted, compassionate]; her imagining the pilgrim's resting from his journey gives respite from the violence of the other narratives.

130-33. Ah, when . . . remember me: Note the parallel with the words of the "good thief" to Christ on the Cross: "Domine, memento mei, cum veneris in regnum tuum" [Lord, remember me, when you shall have come into your kingdom] (Luke 23.42).

133. I am Pia: The Italian definite article *la* before the name contributes an untranslatable shade of intimacy.

134. Siena . . . unmade me: Note the parallels with Vergil's famous epitaph (see the note to 3.25-27), and see *Inter cantica* below; see also the note to *Inf.* 1.70.

Inter cantica. Like *Inferno* 5, this canto ends with the pilgrim's encounter with a woman murdered by her husband; the parallel strengthens the suggestion that Pia, like Francesca, was adulterous. The storm in the Casentino also offers a parallel with *Inferno* 5, but here the souls are no longer caught in the whirlwind. On the contrary, both Pia's calm (after the storm) and the emphatically dramatized fact that the demon's storm affects only Buonconte's body, are signs of these souls' transcendence of earthly turbulence (they are "pacificati" [pacified], line 56). For the relation of the passions to the four elements—of which three (air, water, earth) figure in these accounts—see the note to *Inf.* 11.70-75.

The storm of *Purgatorio* 5 is to be connected also with *Inferno* 6; note the parallel between Pia's play on "fe' disfece" [made unmade] (line 133), preterites, and Ciacco's past participles of the same verbs, "disfatto, fatto" *Inf.* 6.42, whose violence is similar to that of the demon's "altro altro" [other other] (*Purg.* 5.108).

In its evocation of the mountains and rivers of the Casentino, with the castles of the Conti Guidi at Romena and Poppi (not explicitly named, but conspicuous landmarks), *Purgatorio* 5 recalls Master Adam's memories (*Inf.* 30.64-75), which also draw the parallel between the veins of the earth and the human body and involve the theme of baptism (see the notes to *Inf.* 30.64-75 and *Purg.* 5.74, 97). *Inf.* 28.73-81 relates another murder by a tyrant of the region.

The most striking connection of this canto with the *Inferno*, however, is between Buonconte's narrative and that of Guido da Montefeltro (*Inferno* 27). The two passages are the only instances in the *Comedy* of the struggle for the soul at death, and they form an elaborate diptych: a father and son; one carefully preparing for death, the other dying in battle; one lost because of backsliding, the other saved by last-minute repentance; one confused and divided, the other compressing his entire being into a tear. In one case the devil is triumphant; in the other defeated, but in both he is scornful; in both cases only the devil speaks, in fact the devil's words and actions are a main focus. There are parallel double constructions in the devils' words: *Inf.* 27.114, "non portar, non mi far torto" [Do not carry off, do not wrong me]; *Purg.* 5.106-107, "perché mi privi? Tu te ne porti" [Why do you deprive me? You carry off] (*portar* figures in both, cf. the devil of *Inf.* 21.29-45). The correlation of condemned father and saved son has roots both in the Bible (the rebellious Israelites must die in the desert; their children enter the Promised Land: Num. 14.20-33) and Arthurian romance (the *Queste del saint Graal* has the backsliding Lancelot blocked from the vision of the Grail, reserved for his son Galahad). Other cases in the *Comedy* also carry thematic weight associated with the Pauline "Old Man." Some are literal (Frederick II and Manfred, Ugolino and Nino Visconti; see *Inter cantica* to Cantos 3 and 8), but perhaps the most important is metaphorical: Brunetto Latini (*Inferno* 15) and Virgil are damned, but their metaphorical son is saved.

CANTO 6

Quando si parte il gioco de la zara,　　　　　　1
colui che perde si riman dolente,
repetendo le volte, e tristo impara;

　con l'altro se ne va tutta la gente;　　　　　4
qual va dinanzi, e qual di dietro il prende,
e qual dallato li si reca a mente;

　el non s'arresta, e questo e quello intende;　7
a cui porge la man, più non fa pressa,
e così da la calca sì difende.

　Tal era io in quella turba spessa:　　　　　10
volgendo a loro, e qua e là, la faccia
e promettendo, mi sciogliea da essa.

　Quiv' era l'Aretin che da le braccia　　　　13
fiere di Ghin di Tacco ebbe la morte,
e l'altro ch'annegò correndo in caccia.

　Quivi pregava con le mani sporte　　　　　16
Federigo Novello, e quel da Pisa
che fé parer lo buon Marzucco forte.

　Vidi conte Orso e l'anima divisa　　　　　19
dal corpo suo per astio e per inveggia,
com' e' dicea, non per colpa commisa:

　Pier da la Broccia dico; e qui proveggia,　　22
mentr' è di qua, la donna di Brabante
sì che però non sia di peggior greggia.

　Come libero fui da tutte quante　　　　　25
quell' ombre, che pregar pur ch'altri prieghi
sì che s'avacci lor divenir sante,

　io cominciai: "El par che tu mi nieghi,　　28
o luce mia, espresso in alcun testo,
che decreto del Cielo orazion pieghi;

CANTO 6

Other late repentants—Can prayer affect God's judgments?—late afternoon—Sordello of Mantua—denunciation of Italy, the emperor, and Florence

1   When the game of hazard breaks up, the one who has lost stays behind grieving, repeating the throws, and sadly learns;

4   with the winner all the people go off; this one goes in front, this one pesters him from behind, the one alongside begs to be remembered;

7   the winner does not stop, but listens to this one and that one; those to whom he stretches out his hand press no more upon him, and thus he defends himself from the crowding.

10   Such was I in that thick crowd: turning my face to them on this side and that and making promises, I loosed myself from them.

13   There was the Aretine who at the fierce hands of Ghino di Tacco met his death, and the other who drowned while running with the hunt.

16   There Federigo Novello begged with hands outstretched, and he of Pisa who showed the strength of the good Marzucco.

19   I saw Count Orso and the soul divided from his body by spite and envy, as he said, and not for any crime committed,

22   Pierre de la Brosse, I mean; and let the lady of Brabant take care, while she is over here, not to belong to a worse flock because of it.

25   When I was free of all those souls, who were still praying to have others pray for them to hasten their becoming holy,

28   I began: "It seems, O my light, that in a certain text you expressly deny that prayer can bend the decree of Heaven;

e questa gente prega pur di questo: 31
sarebbe dunque loro speme vana,
o non m'è 'l detto tuo ben manifesto?"

    Ed elli a me: "La mia scrittura è piana,   34
e la speranza di costor non falla,
se ben si guarda con la mente sana,

    ché cima di giudicio non s'avvalla   37
perché foco d'amor compia in un punto
ciò che de' sodisfar chi qui s'astalla;

    e là dov' io fermai cotesto punto   40
non s'ammendava, per pregar, difetto,
perché 'l priego da Dio era disgiunto.

    Veramente a così alto sospetto   43
non ti fermar, se quella nol ti dice
che lume fia tra 'l vero e lo 'ntelletto.

    Non so se 'ntendi; io dico di Beatrice: 46
tu la vedrai di sopra, in su la vetta
di questo monte, ridere e felice."

    E io: "Segnore, andiamo a maggior fretta, 49
ché già non m'affatico come dianzi,
e vedi omai che 'l poggio l'ombra getta."

    "Noi anderem con questo giorno innanzi,"   52
rispuose, "quanto più potremo omai;
ma 'l fatto è d'altra forma che non stanzi.

    Prima che sie là sù, tornar vedrai   55
colui che già si cuopre de la costa,
sì che ' suoi raggi tu romper non fai.

    Ma vedi là un'anima che, posta   58
sola soletta, inverso noi riguarda:
quella ne 'nsegnerà la via più tosta."

    Venimmo a lei: o anima lombarda,   61
come ti stavi altera e disdegnosa
e nel mover de li occhi onesta e tarda!

    Ella non ci dicëa alcuna cosa,   64
ma lasciavane gir, solo sguardando,
a guisa di leon quando si posa.

    Pur Virgilio si trasse a lei, pregando   67
che ne mostrasse la miglior salita;
e quella non rispuose al suo dimando,

31   and these people pray for just that: would their
hope, then, be in vain, or is your saying not fully
manifest to me?"

34   And he to me: "My writing is plain, and their
hope is not deceived, if one looks well with sound
mind,

37   for the summit of justice is not lowered though
the fire of love fulfill in an instant what those who
are stationed here must satisfy;

40   and where I fixed this point, defect was not
amended by praying, because prayer was disjoined
from God.

43   However, do not desist from such a deep doubt
until she tells you, she who will be a light between
the truth and your intellect.

46   I don't know if you understand; I mean Beatrice:
you will see her above, on the summit of this
mountain, smiling and happy."

49   And I: "Lord, let us go with greater haste, for I
am not laboring as much as before, and you see
that now the mountain is casting a shadow."

52   "We will go forward in this daylight," he replied,
"as long as we still can; but the fact is of another
form than you suppose.

55   Before you are up there, you will see him return
who already is hidden behind the slope so that you
do not break his rays.

58   But see there a soul who, sitting all alone, is
looking toward us: that one will teach us the
quickest way."

61   We came up to it: O Lombard soul, how
proudly and disdainfully you were holding
yourself, and how worthy and slow was the
moving of your eyes!

64   The soul said nothing to us, but was letting us
go by, only gazing, in the manner of a lion when it
couches.

67   Still Virgil drew near to it, begging that it show
us the best upward path; and it did not reply to his
question,

ma di nostro paese e de la vita 70
ci 'nchiese; e 'l dolce duca incominciava:
"Mantoa . . ." e l'ombra, tutta in sé romita,

surse ver' lui del loco ove pria stava, 73
dicendo: "O Mantoano, io son Sordello
de la tua terra!" e l'un l'altro abbracciava.

Ahi serva Italia, di dolore ostello, 76
nave sanza nocchiere in gran tempesta,
non donna di province, ma bordello!

Quell' anima gentil fu così presta, 79
sol per lo dolce suon de la sua terra,
di fare al cittadin suo quivi festa;

e ora in te non stanno sanza guerra 82
li vivi tuoi, e l'un l'altro si rode
di quei ch'un muro e una fossa serra!

Cerca, misera, intorno de le prode 85
le tue marine, e poi ti guarda in seno,
s'alcuna parte in te di pace gode.

Che val perché ti racconciasse il freno 88
Iustinïano, se la sella è vòta?
Sanz' esso fora la vergogna meno.

Ahi gente che dovresti esser devota 91
e lasciar seder Cesare in la sella,
se bene intendi ciò che Dio ti nota,

guarda come esta fiera è fatta fella 94
per non esser corretta da li sproni,
poi che ponesti mano a la predella.

O Alberto tedesco, ch'abbandoni 97
costei ch'è fatta indomita e selvaggia,
e dovresti inforcar li suoi arcioni,

giusto giudicio da le stelle caggia 100
sovra 'l tuo sangue, e sia novo e aperto,
tal che 'l tuo successor temenza n'aggia!

Ch'avete tu e 'l tuo padre sofferto, 103
per cupidigia di costà distretti,
che 'l giardin de lo 'mperio sia diserto.

Vieni a veder Montecchi e Cappelletti, 106
Monaldi e Filippeschi, uom sanza cura:
color già tristi, e questi con sospetti!

70   but asked us of our city and our life; and my
sweet leader began: "Mantua . . ." and the shade,
all gathered in itself,

73   rose toward him from the place where it had
been, saying, "O Mantuan, I am Sordello from
your city!" and each embraced the other.

76   Ah, slavish Italy, dwelling of grief, ship without
a pilot in a great storm, not a ruler of provinces,
but a whore!

79   That noble soul was so quick, merely for the
sweet sound of his city, to make much of his
fellow-citizen there;

82   and now in you the living are not without war,
and of those whom one wall and one moat lock in,
each gnaws at the other!

85   Search, wretched one, the waters around your
shores, and then look into your bosom, whether
any part of you enjoys peace.

88   What does it profit that Justinian fitted you with
the bridle, if the saddle is empty? Without the
bridle the shame would be less.

91   Ah, people who should be devoted and permit
Caesar to sit in the saddle, if you attend to God's
words to you,

94   see how this beast has become savage, not being
governed by the spurs, ever since you seized the
reins.

97   O German Albert, who abandon her, so that she
becomes untamed and wild, while you should
mount between her saddle-bows,

100   may just judgment fall from the stars onto your
blood, and let it be strange and public, so that your
successor may fear it!

103   For you and your father, held fast by your greed
for things up there, have suffered the garden of the
empire to be laid waste.

106   Come and see the Montecchi and Cappelletti,
the Monaldi and Filippeschi, heedless man: those
already wretched, and these fearful!

Vien, crudel, vieni, e vedi la pressura   109
d'i tuoi gentili, e cura lor magagne;
e vedrai Santafior com'è oscura!

Vieni a veder la tua Roma che piagne   112
vedova e sola, e dì e notte chiama:
"Cesare mio, perché non m'accompagne?"

Vieni a veder la gente quanto s'ama!   115
E se nulla di noi pietà ti move,
a vergognarti vien de la tua fama.

E se licito m'è, o sommo Giove,   118
che fosti in terra per noi crucifisso,
son li giusti occhi tuoi rivolti altrove?

O è preparazion che ne l'abisso   121
del tuo consiglio fai per alcun bene
in tutto de l'accorger nostro scisso?

Ché le città d'Italia tutte piene   124
son di tiranni, e un Marcel diventa
ogne villan che parteggiando viene.

Fiorenza mia, ben puoi esser contenta   127
di questa digression, che non ti tocca,
mercé del popol tuo che si argomenta.

Molti han giustizia in cuore, e tardi scocca   130
per non venir sanza consiglio a l'arco;
ma il popol tuo l'ha in sommo de la bocca.

Molti rifiutan lo comune incarco;   133
ma il popol tuo solicito risponde
sanza chiamare, e grida: "I' mi sobbarco!"

Or ti fa lieta, ché tu hai ben onde: 136
tu ricca, tu con pace e tu con senno!
S'io dico 'l ver, l'effetto nol nasconde.

Atene e Lacedèmona, che fenno   139
l'antiche leggi e furon sì civili,
fecero al viver bene un picciol cenno

verso di te, che fai tanto sottili   142
provedimenti, ch'a mezzo novembre
non giugne quel che tu d'ottobre fili.

109   Come, cruel one, come, and see the distress of
your nobles, and care for their ills; and you will see
how Santafiora is darkened!

112   Come and see your Rome, which weeps
widowed and alone, and day and night calls out:
"My Caesar, why do you not keep me company?"

115   Come and see how the people love each other!
And if no pity for us moves you, come to be
ashamed at your reputation.

118   And if it is permitted me, O highest Jove, who
were crucified on earth for us, are your just eyes
turned elsewhere?

121   Or is it a preparation that in the abyss of your
counsel you are making, for some good utterly
severed from our perception?

124   For the cities of Italy are all filled with tyrants,
and every peasant who joins a faction becomes a
Marcellus.

127   My Florence, well can you be pleased with this
digression, which does not touch you, thanks to
your people, who are so keen.

130   Many have justice in their hearts but loose the
arrow late, so as not to come to the bow without
counsel; but your people have it ready on their
lips.

133   Many refuse communal burdens; but your
solicitous people reply without being asked, and
shout: "I'll take it on!"

136   Now be glad, for you surely have cause: you
rich, you at peace, you with wisdom! If I speak the
truth, the results do not hide it.

139   Athens and Lacedaemon, which made the
ancient laws and were so civilized, made but a little
gesture toward right living

142   next to you, who make so many subtle provi-
sions, that what you spin in October does not
reach to mid-November.

Quante volte, del tempo che rimembre,   145
legge, moneta, officio e costume
hai tu mutato, e rinovate membre!
    E se ben ti ricordi e vedi lume,   148
vedrai te somigliante a quella inferma
che non può trovar posa in su le piume,
    ma con dar volta suo dolore scherma.   151

145 How many times, in the period that you remember, have you changed laws, coins, offices, and customs, and renewed your members!

148 And if you take stock of yourself and can see the light, you will see that you resemble that sick woman who cannot find rest on her mattress,

151   but shields her pain by tossing and turning.

NOTES

1-12. When the game . . . myself from them: The canto opens with an elaborate simile, comparing the pilgrim to a winner at dice surrounded by friends begging for money. The game of *zara* (from Arabic *zahr* [face of a die?], from which also Eng. *hazard*), is described in the *Book of Games* of Alfonso X, the Wise; played with three dice, it had complicated rules, hence the puzzlement of the loser.

13-24. There was the Aretine . . . because of it: Three terzine listing two supplicants each, four identified by periphrases, and followed by a fourth terzina expanding the last periphrasis; some of the identifications are uncertain. This catalog of mostly Tuscan victims of clan warfare, civil faction, and court intrigue prepares for the lament-invective that occupies the second half of the canto. Note the frequency of forms of *pregare* [to pray] and related terms.

13-15. the Aretine . . . with the hunt: The Aretine is Benincasa da Laterina (near Arezzo), a judge who as he sat on the bench in Rome was beheaded by the highwayman Ghino di Tacco (see *Decameron* 10.2) because he had sentenced two of Ghino's kinsmen to death. The second is possibly Guccio de' Tarlati, of Pietramala near Arezzo, drowned while pursuing, or pursued by, enemies (said to be the Bostoli, after the battle of Campaldino; see 5.93 and notes).

16-18. Federigo Novello . . . Marzucco: Federigo Novello of the Conti Guidi, son of Guido Novello, was killed in 1289 or 1291, while aiding the Tarlati against the Guelf Bostoli of Arezzo; "he of Pisa" is presumably the son of Marzucco da Scornigliano: the early commentators differ on whether Marzucco avenged his son (Lana, Ottimo), forgave the murderer (Buti), or braved Count Ugolino to obtain his body (Benvenuto). Marzucco (d. 1296) became a Franciscan in the convent of Santa Croce, where Dante could have known him.

16-17. begged with hands outstretched: See *Aen.* 6.313-14, of shades "holding out their hands in their love of the further shore" (of Acheron).

19. Count Orso: The son of Napoleone of Mangona, Orso was murdered by his cousin Alberto to avenge Alberto's father (see *Inf.* 32.41-57).

19-24. the soul divided . . . because of it: Pierre de la Brosse had become the chamberlain of Philip III (the Bold) of France (1270-1285) when he was arrested, condemned by an assembly of nobles, and hanged in June, 1278. He had accused the queen, Marie of Brabant, Philip's second wife, of poisoning Philip's son by his first wife, Isabella of Aragon, to clear the way to the throne for her own son, the future Philip the Fair (see 7.109 and note). It was rumored that Marie had forged letters implicating Pierre in plots against Philip.

28-48. I began . . . smiling and happy: The series of requests for prayers that began with Manfred's (see 3.130-31 and 5.91-93, with notes) here receives an important theoretical clarification. The "text" the pilgrim remembers relates that when the unburied Palinurus begs Aeneas to help him across the Styx, the Sybil rebukes him (*Aen.* 6.373-76): "Whence does this evil desire come upon you, O Palinurus? . . . Cease to hope that the decrees of the gods can be changed by praying!" (for other revisionist references to Vergil's works, see *Inf.* 13.48, 20.113-14; *Purg.* 22.37-42 and 70-72, 30.21, with notes).

34-42. My writing . . . disjoined from God: Virgil's reply generalizes Belacqua's remark (4.134-35): what the Sybil said to Palinurus was valid, for before the coming of Christ God was impervious to pagan prayers (for Dante's theory of the Atonement, see *Paradiso* 7). However, *Inf.* 4.37-38 seem to hold out the possibility that some pagans prayed efficaciously.

37-39. for the summit . . . must satisfy: The principle here is closely analogous to that of the Atonement, in which Love vicariously satisfies the demands of Justice (see Aurigemma 1965). Vergil's *flecti* [to be changed, bent], which implies as its opposite the idea that the gods' decrees are *fixed* or *rigid*, suggests to Dante's biblical sensibility the metaphorics of the mountain: the *top* [*cima*] (cf. *vetta* [peak], line 47) is not lowered (*non s'avvalla* [literally, does not become a valley]). Behind these metaphors the presence of Is. 40.4 is palpable: "Every valley shall be exalted and every mountain and hill made low, and the crooked straight and the rough places plain [*planas*]" (cf. line 34). Love can exalt humility and make the way flat for those who must ascend.

43-48. However, do not . . . smiling and happy: Virgil's mention of Beatrice indicates that the explanation can only be fully grasped in a context transfigured by love (the pilgrim's love for Beatrice will illuminate his understanding); cf. *Inf.* 10.130-32. For the "three lights" behind such passages, see Singleton 1957.

49-51. And I: Lord . . . a shadow: The evocation of Beatrice's smile renews the pilgrim's eagerness; his reference to the shadow of the mountain expresses his sense of the need for haste. For the gradual easing of the difficulty, see 4.85-96. For the shadow, cf. *Ecl.* 1.83: "maioresque cadunt altis de montibus umbrae" [lengthening shadows fall from the high mountains].

52-57. We will go . . . break his rays: Virgil sees that the pilgrim expects to reach the summit before night; he points out that the ascent will take more than one day, for the pilgrim will see the sun rise again. The disappearance of the pilgrim's shadow within the shadow of the mountain (lines 51, 56-57), which explains the shades' later supposing that the pilgrim is also a shade, begins a long transition to the coming of night in Canto 9. It was noon at the end of Canto 4; presumably it is now past mid-afternoon. Again the motivic *rompere* [to break], of the light, for the pilgrim's shadow.

58-151. But see . . . tossing and turning: After the recall of his own canzone in Canto 2, Dante's anthology of poets continues; in fact two thirds of the canto are devoted to the meeting with Sordello and the invective against Italy that it triggers. Sordello's prominence in Cantos 6-8 has occasioned much debate; in the *Convivio* and the *DVE* Dante seems to have had him in mind in his bitter condemnation of those who turned their backs on the Italian vernacular (*Conv.* 1.11.1: "To the perpetual infamy and discrediting of the wicked men who commend foreign vernaculars and look down upon their own . . ."; *DVE* 1.15.2: "Sordello . . . though such an eloquent man, abandoned his paternal vernacular not only in writing poetry but in his every use of language"). In Canto 6 we have the striking image of his solitary, dignified meditation, suddenly broken, when he hears Virgil's Mantuan accent, by his outburst of love for his native city; as Scott 1996 points out, this is a comment on the real Sordello's having participated in and profited from Charles of Anjou's invasion of Italy. As Scott and Perugi 1983 (cf. also Perugi in *LDT*) argue, Sordello's tribute to Virgil as having developed the potentialities of Latin (7.16-19) is precisely the reverse of Sordello's actual position, for he turned his back on the possibilities of Italian, abandoning, as Dante saw it, a great historic opportunity (just as Rudolph and Albert of Hapsburg turned their backs on the need to assert their authority in Italy). It is Dante who will fulfill the potentialities of his paternal vernacular, just as he takes over the role of social critic and true patriot.

58-75. But see there . . . embraced the other: Born of impoverished nobility at Goito near Mantua, Sordello gained notice as a troubador writing love poems (*cansos*), political satires (*sirventes*), and poetic debates (*tensos*), exclusively in Provençal; his most famous poems are the lament for the death of Blacaz (d. 1236; see 7.91-136, with notes), and the *Ensenhamen d'onor* [Instruction of Honor]. He early involved himself in scandal by abducting, at the behest of her brothers and possibly for her own safety, Cunizza da Romano (see *Par.* 9.31-33), the wife of his then lord Riccardo di San Bonifazio, the ruler of Verona; a liaison with the lady was rumored (1226). Sordello escaped to Provence (see previous note). He was dead by 1269. Dante's portrait of him reflects the knowledge that Sordello was an intimate and highly valued counselor of both Raymond Berenguer IV, Count of Provence, who knighted him, and Charles of Anjou, who married Raymond's daughter and granted Sordello fiefs in northern and southern Italy, as we know from surviving documents (Boni 1954, 1970).

58-60. But see . . . quickest way: For Sordello's abstraction and solitude (line 58), see Lam. 3.28: "sedebit solitarius et tacebit" [he shall sit solitary, and hold his peace]. He seems clearly distinguished from the late-repentant souls who died by violence, although some commentators see him as one of them (Baldelli 1997). Note the parallel with Virgil's "Vedi là Farinata" (*Inf.* 10.32), another context involving the vernacular and a shade who had made war on his native land.

61. O Lombard soul: The narrator's exclamation suggests that the act of narration arouses the feelings felt during the journey (see *Inf.* 1.4-7, with note); thus the apostrophe of Sordello also prepares for the long outburst just ahead.

63. worthy and slow: So also of the philosophers in Limbo (4.112; see *Inter cantica* below). The commentators cite Aristotle's *Nichomachean Ethics* 4.3: "The accepted view of the magnanimous man is that his gait is measured, his voice deep, his speech unhurried."

66. in the manner . . . it couches: Lions, said in bestiaries to spare the weak, were emblems of magnanimity; see Gen. 49.9 (Jacob to Judah): "Requiescens accubuisti ut leo" [Resting you couched as a lion]. The comparison evokes also carved lions protecting sacred spaces (e.g., the Florentine Marzocco); cf. 7.53-54.

70. asked of our city and our life: For the first time since Cato's challenge (1.40), the travelers are being asked to identify themselves. For this topic, see 14.13, with note; lines 76-151 can be seen as one kind of answer.

72. all gathered in itself: The phrase describes Sordello's attitude before hearing Virgil. For the mournful mood of the valley, see 7.82, 93, 107-108, 136, 8.1-6 .

72-75. Mantua . . . from your city: Benvenuto, reading the variant *Mantua*, saw Virgil as beginning to quote his epitaph, already echoed several times (3.27, 5.133-134), and most critics have followed him in printing the Latin form; but Virgil has a "Lombard" accent (see *Inf.* 22.97-99 and 27.21-22, with notes, the note on line 72 in "Textual Variants," p. 627, and the note to 7.16-17). In line 75 Sordello will echo the "suono" [sound] (see also the note to lines 79-81); his answer is also perhaps meant to evoke his Provençal biography, which begins: "Lo Sordels si fo de Mantoana" [Sordello was from the territory of Mantua]; cf. *Inf.* 2.58, with note.

76-151. Ah, slavish Italy . . . tossing and turning: An outburst unparalleled in the *Comedy* for length, vehemence, and rhetorical elaboration. Perugi 1983 analyzes its combination of Provençal genres (funeral plaint [*planh*]—see 7.94-126 and 8.124-32, with notes—and political invective [*sirventes*]), both exploited by Sordello, and their mediation by medieval Latin handbooks of rhetoric, as well as by crusading literature (newly stimulated by the fall of Acre in 1291; cf. *Inferno* 27.87-90). The application by medieval exegetes of the Ciceronian categories of complaint and invective (*conquaestio, indignatio*) to the Book of Lamentations also contributes (Martinez 1997). The passage had great influence on the emergence of a nationalistic concept of Italy and on patriotic poetry in the Renaissance and Risorgimento (Petrarch, Ariosto, Leopardi, and others).

The invective is a series of apostrophes: of personified Italy (lines 76-90); of the clergy (lines 91-96); of the (uncrowned) emperor Albert of Hapsburg (lines 97-117); climactically, of God (lines 118-26); finally, of Florence (lines 127-51). Within this sequence there is a wealth of variation: we find comparisons, periphrases, descriptions, antitheses, and other "colors" of rhetoric, including puns and *exclamatio* ("Ah, slavish"), *conduplicatio* ("Come, come"), *dubitatio* ("are your just eyes . . ."). In lines 76-78 Italy is first a dwelling, then the ship of state in a storm, finally a human figure combining the biblical and the Vergilian, but the metonymy of *bordello* [brothel] (the dwelling used for its inhabitant, "whore") maintains the motif of *containers* and helps support the more literally geographic references of lines 82-87.

After reaching a first high point with the direct appeal to God, the tone seems to relax in line 127, but the transition to bitter scorn and sarcasm provides even greater intensity. One of the elements in this increased tension is the renewal of the technique of contrast: when the apostrophe is directed at Florence, an anaphoric series (lines 130-44) compares Florence with her neighbors and even with Athens and Sparta; and the whole concludes with the analogy of the sick woman, like the personification with which the "digression" began.

76-78. Ah, slavish Italy . . . but a whore: Dante's borrowings from Lam. 1.1 ("Domina gentium, princeps provinciarum facta est sub tributo" [The queen over the nations, the ruler of provinces is made a tributary, our translation]; see the note to lines 112-14) and other biblical passages (e.g., Is. 1.21: "quomodo facta est meretrix civitas fidelis, plena iudicii" [how is the faithful city, that was full of judgment, become a harlot]) are influenced by vernacular laments and polemics that also echo them. Rome's status as ruler over provinces figures in the glosses to Justinian's code as well as in Manfred's oration to the Romans of 1263.

77. ship . . . in a great storm: The ship of state is an image that goes back to antiquity (e.g., Horace, *Odes* 1.14; see Additional Note 4). Laments on the Holy Land, crusade songs, and attacks on the papacy frequently use the figure of the *navicula Petri*, the ship of the Church, in stormy seas (Perugi 1983); cf. 32.129, *Ep.* 6.3.

79-81. for the sweet sound of his city: Virgil and Sordello are united by Mantuan accents and love for their birthplace (cf. 7.18, with note), in contrast to the violence suffered by the souls at the beginning of the canto. That the peace of nations begins with the peace of citizens is a commonplace, based on Aristotle's *Politics* (1.2; 1252) and Augustine's *City of God* 19.16 (cf. *Conv.* 4.4.1-4).

83-84. whom one wall . . . gnaws at the other: For the echo of Ugolino gnawing on the nape of Archbishop Ruggieri, see *Inter cantica* below and the note to *Inf.* 10.52-72.

88-89. What does it profit . . . saddle is empty: The Roman emperor Justinian (482-565 A.D.) ordered the compilation of Roman law (see lines 139-40, *Par.* 6.10-12, with notes): law is the "bridle" on human behavior, its enforcement the function of the emperor. The horse is riderless: no emperor had attempted to deal with Italy since Frederick II (cf. *Inf.* 10.119 and 13.58-68 ; *Conv.* 4.3.6).

88-99. the bridle . . . saddle-bows: Bridle, saddle (lines 89, 92), reins (line 96) and saddle-bows evoke the image of the emperor as the rightful rider of the "untamed and wild" (line 98) horse that is Italy (in *Conv.* 4.9.10 the emperor is the "rider of the human will"; cf. *Ep.* 6.12, 22-23). The image brings into focus a fundamental metaphor of the entire cantica: rational control over impulse is like the governing of horses and falcons (which must be trained) and the steering of chariots and ships; cf. 14.142-51 and Additional Note 4.

91-93. Ah, people . . . words to you: Dante addresses the clergy, especially the papacy and its apologists, who disregard Christ's words, "render unto Caesar the things that are Caesar's" (Luke 20.25), usurping temporal power (see line 96 and 16.97-114, with notes; cf. *Mon.* 3.12.5-7, *Ep.* 5.17, 27).

97-102. O German Albert . . . may fear it: Dante now addresses the elected (but uncrowned) emperor, Albert of Hapsburg, son of Rudolf of Hapsburg. As Holy Roman Emperor, Albert is the bridegroom (*sponsus*) of the Empire and of Italy, as well as the rightful "rider" of the "untamed beast." Albert has abandoned his bride to humiliation, slavery, and violence (see Lam. 1.11; *Ep.* 5.5-6; "Tre donne," 9-12). Albert is addressed as if alive at the time of writing, though he died in 1308 (after having been elected emperor in 1298); see next note.

100-102. may just judgment. . . may fear it: This threat must have been written after the death (1307) of Albert's son and heir, perhaps after Albert's murder by his cousin John of Swabia on May 1, 1308. Whether it reflects knowledge of the death in Italy (1313) of Albert's successor as emperor, Henry VII, on whom Dante had pinned all his political hopes, is debated.

103-105. held fast . . . laid waste: The neglect of Italy is blamed on the covetousness of Rudolf and Albert of Hapsburg: the greed that Dante saw as the worst vice of humanity (cf. *Ep.* 11.15, 26; *Purg.* 20.10-15; Scott 1996). The language ("distretti" [held fast], line 104) echoes a *sirventes* by Sordello, on worthless rulers: "tan los *destreing* nonfes e cobeitatz" [idleness and greed so hold them fast].

105. garden of the empire: Italy, "noblest region of Europe" (*Mon.* 2.3.16, 2.6.10).

106-17. Come and see . . . reputation: The four central terzine of the 75 lines of the invective. Marked by anaphora and repetition, they call on Albert to witness the harm caused by his neglect: "come and see" appears five times, "come" by itself a sixth time; as in this sixth canto the emperor is named six times, and six cities are named (as in the invective as a whole there are six apostrophes, including Rome's appeal to Caesar; cf. 14.55-66, 20.70-93, 32.106-60). This passage derives a number of features, including the appeal to shame, from Jupiter's message reproaching Aeneas for neglecting his duty in Italy (*Aen.* 4.272-76; cf. *Ep.* 7.17):

106-107. Montecchi . . . Filippeschi: All four of these family names had become shorthand for political factions in the civil struggles between Guelphs and

Ghibellines that intersected local rivalries. The Montecchi or Monticoli of Verona had led the Ghibelline supporters of Ezzelino III da Romano (see *Inf.* 12.109-10, with note); by 1291 Verona was ruled by the Della Scala family, who would be Dante's patrons. The Cappelletti stand for the Guelph faction in Cremona. The Monaldi and Filippeschi, respectively Guelph and Ghibelline, were violent rivals for control of Orvieto; because imperial authority is absent, the former are extinct, the latter in jeopardy (line 108).

109-10. the distress of your nobles: Dante's "pressura" [distress] echoes Luke 21.25: "there shall be great distress [*pressura*] in the land," part of a version of the "Little Apocalypse" (cf. Matt. 23-24; Luke 19.40-44), in which Christ laments the future destruction of Jerusalem.

111. Santafiora is darkened: The town of Santafiora belonged to the Ghibelline Aldobrandeschi family (Dante treats them among the proud; see 11.52-79, with notes) until conquered by the Sienese.

112-14. Come and see your Rome ... My Caesar: See the note to lines 76-78; Lam. 1.9 and 1.16 are also relevant. The image of Rome widowed of her bridegroom, the pope or the emperor (or both), was frequent in controversial literature and in vernacular laments (see *Ep.* 11.21). Lamentations was chanted at Matins during the last three days of Holy Week, to express the grief (and guilt) of Jerusalem at the Crucifixion (see line 119); thus the emperor, who figures Christ as the bridegroom, also figures Christ in his tragic absence (see *Ep.* 5.5, Martinez 1997).

115. Come and see ... love each other: The embrace of Sordello and Virgil sharpens the bitter sarcasm.

118-23. And if it is permitted ... our perception: Perugi cites Geoffroy de Vinsauf's *Poetria nova,* line 412: "Si fas est, accuso Deum" [If it is permitted, I accuse God], a particularly good testimony to Dante's grounding in the rhetorical treatises; cf. Ps. 43.24, Lam. 5.20: "Why wilt thou forget us forever?"

121-22. the abyss of your counsel: One of the first appearances in the *Comedy* of the recurrent metaphor of God as an ocean unfathomable by angels or men; cf. Ps. 35.7: "Thy judgments are a great deep[abyssus multa]."

125-26. every peasant ... Marcellus: That is, supposes himself a hero or great leader. Most commentators take "Marcellus" to refer to Marcus Claudius Marcellus, one of Caesar's enemies (*Phars.* 1.313).

127-51. My Florence ... tossing and turning: The bitter end of the invective, now identified as a "digression." Note the gradation from "your city" (Sordello to Virgil, line 75), to "My Caesar" (Rome to the emperor, line 114) and "My

Florence" (line 127): rather than tempering the poet's ferocity, the possessive intensifies it (cf. *Conv.* 1.3.3-4).

130-32. Many have justice . . . on their lips: With the obvious suggestion that what is always on their lips is not in their hearts.

133-35. Many refuse . . . I'll take it on: Again, the obvious suggestion is that they hope to profit from public office.

137. You rich . . . you with wisdom: The ironically praised Florentine peace, wisdom, and prosperity contrast with Italy's servitude and Rome's solitude; cf. also the lists of Florentine vices in *Inf.* 6.74-75, 15.61-75, and 26.1–10.

139-41. Athens and Lacedaemon . . . a little gesture: In Justinian's *Institutes* 1.2.10 these two cities are identified as the founders of common and statutory law respectively: "And the civil law appears not inelegantly to be of two kinds. For it has its origins in the institutions of . . . Athens and Sparta . . . on the whole, the Spartans committed to memory that which was observed as law while the Athenians obeyed ordinances which were set down as legislation." Dante satirizes the Florentine claim to be a new Athens (see *Par.* 17.46-48, with note).

143-47. what you spin . . . your members: Referring to the change in executive councils [*signorie*] between October and November 1301; see *Inf.* 24.142-50. Line 147 refers to the expulsion of citizens, "members" of the civic body), including Dante (cf. the note to *Inf.* 24.144, *Inferno* Additional Note 9).

149-51. you will see . . . tossing and turning: Like the gluttons in *Inf.* 6.20-21. See *Confessions* 6.16, "it [Augustine's soul] turned and turned again upon its back and sides and belly, but all places were hard to it, for you [God] alone are rest" [tr. Ryan].

See the *Inter cantica* after Canto 7.

CANTO 7

Poscia che l'accoglienze oneste e liete   1
furo iterate tre e quattro volte,
Sordel si trasse e disse: "Voi chi siete?"

"Anzi che a questo monte fosser volte   4
l'anime degne di salire a Dio,
fur l'ossa mie per Ottavian sepolte.

Io son Virgilio, e per null' altro rio   7
lo ciel perdei che per non aver fé."
Così rispuose allora il duca mio.

Qual è colui che cosa innanzi sé   10
súbita vede ond' e' si maraviglia,
che crede e non, dicendo: "Ella è, non è . . .":

tal parve quelli; e poi chinò le ciglia   13
e umilmente ritornò ver' lui,
e abbracciòl là 've 'l minor s'appiglia.

"O gloria d'i Latin," disse, "per cui   16
mostrò ciò che potea la lingua nostra,
o pregio etterno del loco ond' io fui,

qual merito o qual grazia mi ti mostra?   19
S'io son d'udir le tue parole degno,
dimmi se vien d'inferno, e di qual chiostra."

"Per tutt' i cerchi del dolente regno,"   22
rispuose lui, "son io di qua venuto;
virtù del ciel mi mosse, e con lei vegno.

Non per far, ma per non fare ho perduto   25
a veder l'alto Sol che tu disiri
e che fu tardi per me conosciuto.

Luogo è là giù non tristo di martìri,   28
ma di tenebre solo, ove i lamenti
non suonan come guai, ma son sospiri.

CANTO 7

*Virgil identified to Sordello—inability of souls to climb at night—the
Valley of the Princes involved in earthly cares*

1   After the virtuous, glad welcomes had been
repeated three and four times, Sordello drew back
and said: "Who are you two?"

4   "Before souls worthy to rise to God were turned
to this mountain, my bones were buried by
Octavian.

7   I am Virgil, and for no other crime did I lose
Heaven than for not having faith." Thus my
leader replied then.

10   As one does who suddenly sees before him a
thing that makes him marvel, who both believes
and does not, saying: "It is, it is not . . .":

13   so did that other appear; and then he bent his
brow and, humbly turning toward Virgil,
embraced him where the lesser takes hold.

16   "O glory of the Italians," he said, "through
whom our language showed its power, O eternal
honor of the place I was from,

19   what merit or what grace shows you to me? If I
am worthy to hear your words, tell me if you come
from Hell, and from what cloister."

22   "Through all the circles of the grieving
kingdom," he replied, "have I come here; a power
from Heaven moved me, and by it I come.

25   Not for doing, but for not doing, have I lost the
sight of the high Sun that you desire and that I
knew too late.

28   There is a place down there, not saddened by
torments but only by darkness, where the laments
do not sound as shrieks but are sighs.

Quivi sto io coi pargoli innocenti   31
dai denti morsi de la morte avante
che fosser da l'umana colpa essenti;

  quivi sto io con quei che le tre sante   34
virtù non si vestiro, e sanza vizio
conobber l'altre e seguir tutte quante.

  Ma se tu sai e puoi, alcuno indizio   37
dà noi per che venir possiam più tosto
là dove Purgatorio ha dritto inizio."

  Rispuose: "Loco certo non c'è posto;   40
licito m'è andar suso e intorno;
per quanto ir posso, a guida mi t'accosto.

  Ma vedi già come dichina il giorno,   43
e andar sù di notte non si puote;
però è buon pensar di bel soggiorno.

  Anime sono a destra qua remote;   46
se mi consenti, io ti merrò ad esse,
e non sanza diletto ti fier note."

  "Com' è ciò?" fu risposto. "Chi volesse   49
salir di notte, fora elli impedito
d'altrui, o non sarria ché non potesse?"

  E 'l buon Sordello in terra fregò 'l dito,   52
dicendo: "Vedi? sola questa riga
non varcheresti dopo 'l sol partito:

  non però ch'altra cosa desse briga,   55
che la notturna tenebra, ad ir suso;
quella col nonpoder la voglia intriga.

  Ben si poria con lei tornare in giuso   58
e passeggiar la costa intorno errando,
mentre che l'orizzonte il dì tien chiuso."

  Allora il mio segnor, quasi ammirando,   61
"Menane," disse, "dunque là 've dici
ch'aver si può diletto dimorando."

  Poco allungati c'eravam di lici,   64
quand' io m'accorsi che 'l monte era scemo,
a guisa che i vallon li sceman quici.

  "Colà," disse quell' ombra, "n'anderemo   67
dove la costa face di sé grembo,
e là il novo giorno attenderemo."

31   There I dwell with the innocent little ones
devoured by the teeth of death before they could
be exempted from human sin;

34   there I dwell with those who were not clothed
with the three holy virtues, but without vice knew
the others and followed all of them.

37   But if you know and can tell us, give us some
sign by which we may arrive more quickly where
Purgatory has its true beginning."

40   He replied: "No fixed abode is given us; I am
permitted to go up and around; as far as I may go, I
will be a guide at your side.

43   But see how the day declines already, and we
cannot ascend by night; therefore it is well to think
of a pleasant resting-place.

46   There are souls hidden here on the right; if you
consent, I will lead you to them, and not without
pleasure will they be made known to you."

49   "How is that?" was replied. "One who wished to
climb at night, would he be prevented by another,
or would he be unable?"

52   And good Sordello drew his finger along the
ground, saying: "See? not even this line would you
cross, after the sun has gone down:

55   not because anything fought to prevent you
from climbing, other than the darkness of night,
which shackles the will with inability.

58   One could of course descend and walk
wandering along the shore, while the horizon
holds the day closed up."

61   Then my lord, as if marveling: "Lead us then,"
he said, "to where you say it will be so pleasant to
sojourn."

64   We had walked but a little distance from there
when I perceived that the mountain fell back, as
valleys hollow them here.

67   "Over there," said that shade, "will we go, where
the slope makes a bosom, and there we will await
the new day."

Tra erto e piano era un sentiero schembo   70
che ne condusse in fianco de la lacca,
là dove più ch'a mezzo muore il lembo.

Oro e argento fine, cocco e biacca,   73
indaco, legno lucido e sereno,
fresco smeraldo in l'ora che si fiacca,

da l'erba e da li fior, dentr' a quel seno   76
posti, ciascun saria di color vinto,
come dal suo maggiore è vinto il meno.

Non avea pur natura ivi dipinto,   79
ma di soavità di mille odori
vi facea uno incognito e indistinto.

"*Salve, Regina*" in sul verde e 'n su' fiori   82
quindi seder cantando anime vidi,
che per la valle non parean di fuori.

"Prima che 'l poco sole omai s'annidi,"   85
cominciò 'l Mantoan che ci avea vòlti,
"tra color non vogliate ch'io vi guidi.

Di questo balzo meglio li atti e ' volti   88
conoscerete voi di tutti quanti,
che ne la lama giù tra essi accolti.

Colui che più siede alto e fa sembianti   91
d'aver negletto ciò che far dovea,
e che non move bocca a li altrui canti,

Rodolfo imperador fu, che potea   94
sanar le piaghe c'hanno Italia morta,
sì che tardi per altri si ricrea.

L'altro, che ne la vista lui conforta,   97
resse la terra dove l'acqua nasce
che Molta in Albia, e Albia in mar ne porta:

Ottacchero ebbe nome, e ne le fasce   100
fu meglio assai che Vincislao suo figlio
barbuto, cui lussuria e ozio pasce.

E quel nasetto che stretto a consiglio   103
par con colui c'ha sì benigno aspetto,
morì fuggendo e disfiorando il giglio:

guardate là come si batte il petto!   106
L'altro vedete c'ha fatto a la guancia
de la sua palma, sospirando, letto.

70   Between steep and flat, a slanting path led us to
the flank of the depression, where the bank more
than half disappears.

73   Gold and fine silver, cochineal and white lead,
Indian amber bright and clear, fresh emerald at the
instant it is split,

76   each would be surpassed in color by the grass
and flowers placed within that fold, as the lesser is
surpassed by the greater.

79   Nature had not only painted there, but of the
sweetness of a thousand odors made a single one,
unknown and fully blended.

82   "*Salve, Regina*" I saw souls singing, seated on the
green and the flowers, who had not been visible
from outside the valley.

85   "Before the little sun remaining goes to its nest,"
began the Mantuan who had guided us, "do not
wish me to lead you among them.

88   From this rise you will better know all their
gestures and faces than if received down in the glen
among them.

91   He who is seated highest and wears the
expression of one who neglected what he should
have done, and does not move his lips to the
others' singing,

94   was the emperor Rudolph, who could have
healed the wounds that have killed Italy, and it will
be long before any other revives her.

97   The next, who seems to be comforting him,
ruled the land where the water is born that the
Moldau carries to the Elbe, the Elbe to the sea:

100   Ottakar was his name, and even in swaddling
clothes he was better than Wenceslaus his son
when bearded, whom lust and idleness feed.

103   And that small-nosed one, who seems close in
council with that other who appears so benign,
died fleeing and deflowering the lily:

106   look there how he beats his breast! See the next,
who has sighing made of his palm a bed for his
cheek.

Padre e suocero son del mal di Francia: 109
sanno la vita sua viziata e lorda,
e quindi viene il duol che sì li lancia.
    Quel che par sì membruto e che s'accorda,   112
cantando, con colui dal maschio naso,
d'ogne valor portò cinta la corda;
    e se re dopo lui fosse rimaso   115
lo giovanetto che retro a lui siede,
ben andava il valor di vaso in vaso,
    che non si puote dir de l'altre rede: 118
Iacomo e Federigo hanno i reami;
del retaggio miglior nessun possiede.
    Rade volte risurge per li rami   121
l'umana probitate, e questo vole
quei che la dà, perché da lui si chiami.
    Anche al nasuto vanno mie parole   124
non men ch'a l'altro, Pier, che con lui canta,
onde Puglia e Proenza già si dole.
    Tant' è del seme suo minor la pianta   127
quanto, più che Beatrice e Margherita,
Costanza di marito ancor si vanta.
    Vedete il re de la semplice vita   130
seder là solo, Arrigo d'Inghilterra:
questi ha ne' rami suoi migliore uscita.
    Quel che più basso tra costor s'atterra,   133
guardando in suso, è Guiglielmo marchese,
per cui e Alessandria e la sua guerra
    fa pianger Monferrato e Canavese."   136

109   They are the father and father-in-law of the plague of France: they know his vicious, filthy life, and thence comes the grief that pierces them so.

112   The one that seems so muscular and harmonizes, singing, with the one with the manly nose, was girt with the belt of all knightly worth,

115   and if the young boy who sits behind him could have remained king after him, his worth would have descended well from vessel to vessel,

118   which cannot be said of his other heirs: James and Frederick have the kingdoms now; the better heritage no one possesses.

121   Seldom does human probity rise up through the branches, and this is willed by him who gives it, that it may be attributed to him.

124   My words touch him of the nose no less than the other, Peter, who is singing with him, for whom Puglia and Provence already grieve.

127   The plant is as much inferior to its seed, as Constance can still boast of a better husband than Beatrice or Margaret can.

130   See the king who lived simply, sitting alone there, Harry of England: he has better issue in his branches.

133   The one who lower down sits on the ground among them, looking up, is the marquis William, for whom Alexandria and its war

136   make Monferrato and Canavese weep."

NOTES

1-36. After the virtuous . . . all of them: About a quarter of the canto is devoted to the identification of Virgil, including Sordello's tribute.

1-3. After the virtuous . . . Who are you two?: The narrative resumes as if no digression had taken place after Virgil's and Sordello's embrace. "Three and four times" echoes attempted embraces at *Aen.* 2.791-94 and 6.700-702; see *Purg.* 2.76-81 and Martinez 1995. Sordello's meeting with Virgil is the first high point in the cantica so far.

4-6. Before souls . . . Octavian: Cf. Virgil's account of himself in *Inf.* 1.67-74 and his reference to the transfer of his body to Naples in *Purg.* 3.25-27. Lines 4-5 remind us that the souls of the blessed were still in Limbo when Virgil died (*Inf.* 4.46-63). Mention of Virgil's burial renews the association with Palinurus; see Additional Note 4.

7. I am Virgil: Note the parallels with Manfred's, Buonconte's, Pia's, and Sordello's naming of themselves (3.112, 5.88 and 133, 6.74). This is the first occasion in the cantica of Virgil's name being spoken aloud.

7-8. for no other . . . not having faith: This is more precise than Virgil's other statements about his damnation (*Inf.* 1.125, 4.37-39). See Additional Note 14.

10-19. As one does who . . . shows you to me: Cf. Luke 24.41-43, where the risen Christ shows the Apostles that his flesh is real, "but . . . they yet believed not, and wondered for joy."

15. embraced him . . . takes hold: That is, around the knees or feet, in a gesture of reverence that recognizes Virgil as "our greatest Muse" (*Par.* 15.26). See the meeting of Statius and Virgil (*Purg.* 21.124-36) and *Ep.* 7.6.

16-17. O glory . . . showed its power: Sordello is essentially crediting the historical Vergil, not without justice, with having created literary Latin. Dante evidently considered the historical Vergil's spoken Latin to have been close to the Italian of Dante's day and, like it, characterized by many local dialects. See the note to 6.58-151.

21. tell me if you . . . what cloister: Compare Cato's question, 1.40-48, and 9.85-86; see also 21.62 and 26.128-129, with notes. For the "cloisters" of Malebolge see *Inf.* 29.40; for those of Heaven, besides 26.128, see *Par.* 3.107.

22-36. Through all the circles . . . all of them: Virgil amplifies lines 7-9, again recalling the unbaptized infants and virtuous pagans in Limbo (cf. 1.76-81, *Inf.* 4.25-42). The mention of the sorrowful sighing of Limbo (lines 22, 28-30), as of his lack of faith as "not doing," relates Virgil to the princes sighing for their negligence.

37-63. But if you know . . . pleasant to sojourn: Virgil returns to his intention in approaching Sordello (6.58-60), to ask where Purgatory proper begins. In answer, Sordello offers to guide them, but suggests they find a resting-place for the night: this leads to the statement of an important principle: upward progress is only possible during the day. This passage, like following ones, derives in part from the visit of Aeneas and the Sybil to the Elysian Fields (especially *Aen*. 6.637-81); see the next note and the note to lines 61-136.

40-42. No fixed abode . . . I will be a guide: See *Aen*. 6.673-76: "Nulli certa domus" [None have fixed dwellings], said by Musaeus, who offers to be their guide (cf. lines 46-47, note to lines 61-136). Note the echo of *Inf*. 1.113.

43. But see . . . declines already: This line is based on Luke 24.29: "Mane nobiscum, quoniam advesperascit et *inclinata est iam dies*" [Stay with us, for it grows late and *the day already declines*: our translation], words of disciples to the risen (but unrecognized) Christ on the road to Emmaus (cf. lines 10-19).

46-48. There are souls . . . known to you: The first mention of the "Valley of the Princes," which will occupy the second half of the canto. That the souls are removed, or hidden [*remote*], also anticipates the Vergilian pattern of the Valley (and cf. the note to 1.65-66).

49-59. How is that . . . day closed up: Although Virgil has informed the pilgrim that the ascent will require several days (6.52-57) and seems to imply that it requires daylight, here he seems surprised at Sordello's line 44. The principle links the progress of souls on the mountain to the sun, their "guide" (see 13.16-21, *Inf*. 1.17-18); without the sun, their movement can be lateral or downward only. Compare John 12.35, "ambulate dum lucem habebitis" [walk whilst you have the light]. The restriction applies to all the souls on the mountain, including the pilgrim, unlike the restraints on Manfred, Belacqua, and others; cf. 17.70-75, 21.61-69, with notes.

52-54. And good Sordello . . . has gone down: Sordello's gesture is strongly reminiscent of Christ's in John 8.1-20, though there is little thematic relation; it is appropriate to Sordello as an "ethical" poet setting limits for kings and princes.

61-136. Then my lord . . . Canavese weep: The elaborate transition completed, the three enter on a sloping path (cf. *Inf*. 2.142). Note the allusiveness, in lines 61-90, to *Aen*. 6.676-81:

> "hoc superate iugum, et facile iam tramite sistam."
> dixit, et ante tulit gressum, camposque nitentis
> desuper ostentat; dehinc summa cacumina linquunt.

> At pater Anchises penitus convalle virenti
> inclusas animas superumque ad limen ituras
> lustrabat . . .

> ["Climb this hill, and I will soon set you on an easy path."
> He spoke and walked before them, pointing out the shining
> fields from above: then they went down from the summit.
>   And father Anchises was surveying the souls enclosed
> deep in a green valley, soon to return to the upper light.]

(Cf. *Aen.* 6.703-704: "in valle reducta / seclusum nemus" [in the hidden valley a secluded grove].) Dante drew on Vergil's Elysian Fields also for the Noble Castle in Limbo (see especially *Inf.* 4.111-20) and will again for the Earthly Paradise.

65-68. the mountain . . . makes a bosom: The mountain acquires a maternal aspect and will prove to be protected by the Virgin Mary (see line 82 and 8.37-39); contrast the treacherous "bosom [*grembo*] of the Antenori" (5.75) and the afflicted "bosom" [*seno*] of Italy (6.85-86). "The bosom of Abraham" ("sinus Abrahae") of Luke 16.23 was traditionally thought of as similar to Purgatory (see *Inf.* 30.62-63).

73-75. Gold . . . emerald at the instant it is split: The catalog of colors adopts the manner of the lyric *plazer* [list of pleasing things], such as Cavalcanti's "Biltà di donna" (cf. line 8, "oro, argento, azzurro 'n ornamenti" [gold, silver, lapis lazuli in ornaments]). Gold and silver leaf, cochineal (insects dried and clustered like berries, Gr. *kókkos*), white lead, and smaragdus (real emerald does not fade when split) were all used in pigments. The punctuation and sense of line 74 are uncertain: "indaco legno" might be ebony (from India); or "indaco," followed by a comma, the dye indigo, and the rest of the line "polished wood."

82. *Salve Regina*: As becomes clear in Canto 8, the souls are remembering the Compline service, the last prayer service of the daily Office, which includes the Marian antiphon "Salve regina," all of which has pointed relevance to their situation (the text of the antiphon, and an outline of Compline are in Additional Note 5). The petition that Mary turn her eyes on her votaries ("Salve regina," line 7) anticipates her intervention in the next canto (and resonates with 6.120).

88-89. From this rise . . . gestures and faces: In Vergil's Elysium, both Musaeus and Anchises point out shades from prominences; see the note to lines 61-136, and *Aen.* 6.754-55: Aeneas "tumulum capit unde omnis longo ordine posset / adversos legere et venientum discere vultus" [climbs a mound from which all of them, in their long order, he can see as they come, and read and learn their faces]. D'Ovidio 1906 noted parallels with Anchises' enumeration of the future Romans, in which Caesar and Pompey, future enemies, are "of one accord" before birth (*Aen.* 6.827). Here the enemies are reconciled after death.

91-136. He who is seated . . . Canavese weep: The commentators identify this passage as drawing on the lament (*planh*) for Blacaz attributed to Sordello, an invitation to a series of feckless princes to eat Blacaz' heart so as to gain courage: Dante combines Roman and Provençal models. Dante imitates the hierarchy of Sordello's poem, for he begins with the highest (emperor) and descends through kings and a marquess; the rank determines also their seating. Dante adds the pairing of former enemies, now sitting and singing together. In the *planh*,

Figure 3. Melancholy.

each ruler receives a mere half-stanza; here the allotment of space follows hierarchy. Dante's princes, regretful of their negligence and misgovernment, in some cases of baneful offspring, are united in melancholy (see fig. 3).

91-94. He who is seated. . . emperor Rudolph: Rudolph of Hapsburg (1218-1291), who, though elected emperor in 1273 in preference to Ottakar of Bohemia, never came to Italy to be crowned. Only Rudolph (for Albert, see 6.97-102) is taxed here with failure in his secular role; his guilt is greatest because of his responsibility for establishing world peace, especially in "the garden of the Empire": this echoes Sordello's "all wickedness springs from the greatest, then descends by degrees to the least" (Boni 1954). Italy "wounded" echoes 6.109-11, while lines 96 ("tardi per altri si ricrea" [it will be long before anyone revives her]) and 120 (*retaggio* [heritage]), key terms for Dante, echo terms framing Sordello's poem (*jamais si revenha*, 6, *deseretaz*, 38).

97-100. The next . . . Ottakar was his name: Dante describes Ottakar's kingdom in terms of the course of the Moldau, which joins the Elbe near Prague. King of Bohemia 1253-1278, Ottakar did not recognize the claim of Rudolph, who twice defeated him in battles, killing him in the second (Aug. 26, 1278). Ottakar now comforts his adversary, whose melancholy silences him during the "Salve regina."

101-102. better than Wenceslaus . . . lust and idleness: Wenceslaus II succeeded Ottakar and was son-in-law to the emperor Rudolph; he ruled Bohemia from 1278 to 1305 (see *Par.* 19.125). Dante's invective against Wenceslaus follows traditional models. The idea of degenerate offspring, absent from Sordello's poem, now becomes the main theme.

103-106. that small-nosed one . . . beats his breast: Philip III the Bold of France (1245-1285), beating his breast in the ritual gesture. He became king in

1270, the son and successor of Louis IX and nephew of Charles of Anjou (line 113). His son by Isabella, daughter of James I of Aragon, became Philip IV, the Fair (line 102). After Charles of Anjou's loss of Sicily to the Aragonese in 1282 (the "Sicilian vespers"; see *Par.* 8.73-75), Philip III made war on Pedro III of Aragon. Although he captured Gerona, his fleet was destroyed in 1285 by Ruggiero di Luria, Pedro's admiral, and Philip withdrew to die of fever at Perpignan. "Marring the lily" of the French royal coat of arms may refer to defeat, to the loss of Sicily, or to both: Dante's *disfiorando* [deflowering] echoes both Sordello's coinages and Guittone d'Arezzo's *disfiorata* [deflowered], of the Florentine lily, in his laments for Guelph defeats (see 6.127 and notes).

104. that other who appears so benign: As lines 109-11 will indicate, this is Henry I the Fat, King of Navarre 1270-1274, brother and successor of Thibault II of Navarre (*Inf.* 22.52), further described in lines 107-108. Since his daughter Jeanne married Philip IV, he is the father-in-law of the "plague of France" (line 109). His benign appearance is perhaps the result of his long stay in the Valley, since he was famed as irascible.

107-108. See the next . . . sighing: Henry has the posture of sorrow and inertia associated in medieval treatises with melancholy; cf. fig. 3 and Belacqua (4.106-11; cf. "Tre donne," 120-21, and Martinez 1995). Henry laments his failings and their effects, especially through his son-in-law Philip the Fair (see line 111). This group rates nine lines, focusing on the figure Dante considered the most destructive.

109. the plague of France: Philip the IV, the Fair, succeeded Philip the Bold; he was the elder brother of Charles of Valois, who carried out the coup d'état that led to Dante's exile. In the *Comedy* he receives harsh criticism (cf. *Inf.* 19.87, *Purg.* 20.85-93, *Par.* 19.118-20; also *Purg.* 32.152-53) for his violence, lack of scruples, and greed. The phrase *il mal francese* came to mean syphilis only in 1502, after Charles VIII of France invaded Naples.

110-11. they know his . . . pierces them so: Pietro di Dante and others take the failing of the princes to be neglect of their salvation, and only secondarily neglect of their God-given responsibility to rule (see 8.120, regarding Currado Malaspina); we see the two themes as closely related.

112-114. The one that seems . . . knightly worth: Pedro III of Aragon, king from 1276-1285. His marriage in 1262 to Costance, daughter of King Manfred (3.115-16), gave him claim to the Sicilian crown, obtained after the "Sicilian Vespers" of 1282 (*Par.* 8.73-75). Despite Charles of Anjou's efforts, Pedro held the island until 1285, the year of his death. For the "belt of valor," referring to knighthood and its virtues (cf. *Inf.* 16.106), see Is. 11.5; Prov. 31.17 (of Wisdom): "she hath girded her loins with strength."

113. the one with the manly nose: This is Charles of Anjou, the son of Louis VIII of France and Blanche of Castile and the brother of Louis IX. Born in 1226, Charles married Beatrice of Provence in 1246, becoming count of Provence, and after her death in 1267 his marriage to Margaret of Burgundy further increased his domains (for these acquisitions, see *Purg.* 20.61-66 and notes). He became king of Naples and Sicily after he defeated Manfred and Conradino in 1266-1267 (see *Inf.* 28.16,17, with notes). Charles died in January, 1285. Although he shaped Dante's world, he is referred to only by his nose (also in line 124).

116. the young boy: Probably Pedro, last-born son of Pedro III of Aragon; he never assumed the throne.

117. his worth . . . from vessel to vessel: "From vessel to vessel" echoes Jer. 48.11: "and hath not been poured out from vessel to vessel"; Jeremiah announces the coming desolation of fertile Moab, morally unregenerate. For other genealogical trees, see 14.100-123, with notes.

119-20. James and Frederick . . . no one possesses: Mentioned by Manfred (3.116) as "the honors of Sicily and Aragon," James II the Just, king of Sicily from 1295 to 1295 and of Aragon from 1291 to 1327, was the second son of Pedro III, on whose death in 1285 his eldest son, Alfonso, became king of Aragon, while James succeeded to the crown of Sicily. On Alfonso's death in 1291, James succeeded him in Aragon, leaving Sicily to his younger brother Frederick. In 1295, however, ignoring his brother's claims, James ceded Sicily to Charles II of Naples, whose daughter Blanche he married. The Sicilians renounced their allegiance to James and acclaimed Frederick as their king (1296). Charles and James went to war against Frederick, but in 1299 James withdrew his troops, and in 1302 Frederick was confirmed in his tenure. James died in 1327.

120. the better heritage: Virtue, as opposed to land. Mourning for a lost feudal heritage of valor and probity is at the heart of Cantos 5-7; for Dante's analysis of the duties of nobility, see *Conv.* 4.10-19.

121-23. Seldom does . . . to him: In *Conv.* 4.20.5-7 Dante explains that "the divine seed [of nobility] falls not upon the race, that is the stock, but falls upon individuals . . . the stock does not ennoble individuals, but individuals ennoble the stock." See also James 1.17: "Every good gift and every perfect gift is from above, coming down from the Father of lights."

121. rise . . . the branches: Implicit is a genealogical tree which, as typical in Dante's time, shows ancestors at the root (cf. *Par.* 15.88-89; 17.13), descendants in the branches. The most influential medieval one is the frequently represented Tree of Jesse, showing the descent of the Virgin Mary from Jesse and his son David (see Is.11.1: "And there shall come forth a rod out of the root of Jesse, and a flower shall rise up out of his root"; cf. Matt. 1.1-17). Genealogy and the decline of the feudal families are fundamental themes of the *Purgatorio* (cf. 14.88-123 and notes; 16.106-29 and notes).

126. for whom Puglia and Provence already grieve: Dante turns from the grief of the princes to that of the regions their descendants misgovern (lines 126 and 136). Puglia and Provence lament the rule of Charles II, degenerate son of Charles of Anjou, as hereditary king of Naples (*Apulia, Puglia*) and count of Provence (*Proenza*). Not crowned until 1289 because imprisoned in Spain, he died in May, 1309. He is referred to, always negatively, at *Purg.* 5.69, *Par.* 19.127; *Conv.* 4.6.20, and *DVE* 1.12.5.

127-29. The plant is . . . Beatrice or Margaret: Grandgent untangles the statement of proportions: the plant (the son, Charles II) is as much inferior to Charles I, the father, as Charles I was to Peter III; and to the same extent that Costance boasts of her husband (Peter) more than Beatrice and Margaret boast of theirs (Charles, who married them both). The conundrum suggests relations of merit might be charted, like the differentia of Aristotelian logic, on stem-diagrams.

130-32. See the king who . . . in his branches: Henry III, who succeeded his father John and reigned for 56 years (1216-1272). He married Eleanor, another daughter of Raymond Berenger IV, count of Provence. Because of his longevity, Henry III is the one king Dante's verses share with Sordello's *planh* for Blacatz. Henry's "simple life" could refer to a lack of pomp but also to lack of wit; the chroniclers say little good of him (the term may reflect Sordello's word *nualhos* [good-for-nothing]). Henry sits alone, as did Sordello when first perceived.

133-36. who lower down sits . . . Monferrato and Canavese weep: William VII ("Longsword") of Monferrato, marquis from 1254 to 1292, took advantage of the discord in the Lombard cities to subject them to his rule. Allied to Charles of Anjou during his first descent into Italy (1265), William opposed him after the death of Manfred, when Charles attempted to subdue Lombardy. After initial success in reducing the rebellious cities, William was captured attacking Alessandria in 1290; he died in 1292, after being exhibited in an iron cage. To avenge him his son John I attacked Alessandria, but aided by Matteo Visconti the citizens invaded Monferrato instead, occupying several towns.

136. Monferrato and Canavese weep: Monferrato, between the Po and the Ligurian Apennines, and Canavese, between the Pennine and Grian Alps and the Po, formed William's marquisate. The canto ends regretting lost Imperial authority.

Inter cantica (Cantos 6-7). In juxtaposition with the embrace of Virgil and Sordello, Dante's image of civic hatred at 6.83 evokes the tense exchange of the pilgrim and Ciacco (cf. esp. *Inf.* 6.49-63), also Ugolino's gnawing of Ruggieri (*Inf.* 33.127-32); the echo anchors several other references: to Ugolino and

Cocytus (for Count Orso, of the Alberti of Mangona [cf. *Inf.* 32.41-57] and Marzucco Scornigliani, see 6.13-24 and note) in Cantos 6-8 (at 8.52-54 we find Ugolino's grandson and former enemy, Judge Nino Visconti).

The Valley of Princes, a *grembo* or "lap" in the mountain, where the edge [*lembo*] dies away, evokes the *limbo* of *Inf.* 4.45, which Virgil also evokes explicitly (*Purg.* 7.28-30); the account of the valley as a pleasance in 7.29-81 also echoes the "green enamel" of Limbo (*Inf.* 4.118; and cf. *Purg.* 8.114, of Eden). Both the valley and Limbo contain poets and poetry: in addition to Sordello's meeting with Virgil and the imitation of the Provençal plaint, souls sing the Marian antiphon "Salve regina" (7.82, 112) and the hymn "Te lucis ante" (8.13); in Limbo the wayfarer meets the "lovely school" (4.94), including Homer, "sovereign poet" (4.88).

After the encounter of Virgil and Sordello, the prospect and enumeration of the princes (7. 91-136) including faces and gestures (7.88-90), and the meetings with Nino and Currado Malaspina (8.52-54, 112-20), echo the viewing of poets, heroes, and philosophers in Limbo (*Inf.* 4.81-96, 121-29, 130-44); for Vergilian influences here, see lines 40-42, 65-69, 73-81, 88-89, and notes.

In *Inferno* 5-7 the turnings of Fortune's wheel, implicit in the first two cantos (see 5.64-66, 6.67-72), become explicit in the third (7.77-96, Fortune as a planetary angel of mutability). This pattern recurs in *Purgatorio* 5-7. Florence the spinner of changeable legislation (6 144-47) and the game of *zara* (7.1-6) suggest mutability and luck, but Fortune is also the fortune of war (*Purg.* 5.91-93 and 6.13-18) and of the sea (tempest, 6.77; see *Inf.* 7.22 and note, Charybdis). Fortune's "sphere," her wheel, is attested in *Purgatorio* 7 in the listing of the princes from highest to lowest (7.91-136) and by the difficult "ascent" of virtue through the genealogical tree (7.121, 132). Where opposed grasping and wasting emit an infernal cacophony (*Inf.* 7.30-33), choral singing in the valley (*Purg.* 7.112) testifies that rivalries springing from disparate fortunes have been overcome.

CANTO 8

Era già l'ora che volge il disio   1
ai navicanti e 'ntenerisce il core,
lo dì c'han detto ai dolci amici addio,

e che lo novo peregrin d'amore   4
punge, se ode squilla di lontano
che paia il giorno pianger che si more,

quand' io incominciai a render vano   7
l'udire e a mirare una de l'alme
surta, che l'ascoltar chiedea con mano.

Ella giunse e levò ambo le palme,   10
ficcando li occhi verso l'orïente,
come dicesse a Dio: "D'altro non calme."

"Te lucis ante" sì devotamente   13
le uscìo di bocca e con sì dolci note
che fece me a me uscir di mente,

e l'altre poi dolcemente e devote   16
seguitar lei per tutto l'inno intero,
avendo li occhi a le superne rote.

Aguzza qui, lettor, ben li occhi al vero,   19
ché 'l velo è ora ben tanto sottile,
certo, che 'l trapassar dentro è leggero.

Io vidi quello essercito gentile   22
tacito poscia riguardare in sùe,
quasi aspettando, palido e umìle,

e vidi uscir de l'alto e scender giùe   25
due angeli con due spade affocate,
tronche e private de le punte sue.

Verdi come fogliette pur mo nate   28
erano in veste, che da verdi penne
percosse traean dietro e ventilate.

CANTO 8

1   It was already the hour that turns back the desire of seafarers and softens their hearts, on the day they have said farewell to their sweet friends,

4   the hour that pierces the new pilgrim with love, if he hears a bell far off that seems to mourn the dying day,

7   when I began to empty out my hearing and to gaze at one of the souls, risen to its feet, who with its hand asked all to listen.

10   It joined and raised both palms, sending its gaze toward the east, as if to say to God: "I care for nothing else."

13   "*Te lucis ante*" came forth from its mouth so devoutly and with such sweet tones that it rapt me from awareness of myself,

16   and the others then sweetly and devoutly followed it through all the rest of the hymn, their eyes turned toward the supernal wheels.

19   Sharpen here, reader, your eyes to the truth, for the veil is now surely so fine that passing within is easy.

22   Then I saw that noble army silently gaze upward, as if waiting, pale and humble,

25   and I saw two angels come forth from on high and fly down, bearing two fiery swords, broken off and deprived of their points.

28   As green as newborn leaves were their robes, which, struck and fanned by green feathers, trailed behind.

L'un poco sovra noi a star si venne,   31
e l'altro scese in l'opposita sponda,
sì che la gente in mezzo si contenne.

Ben discernëa in lor la testa bionda,   34
ma ne la faccia l'occhio si smarria,
come virtù ch'a troppo si confonda.

"Ambo vegnon del grembo di Maria,"   37
disse Sordello, "a guardia de la valle,
per lo serpente che verrà vie via."

Ond' io, che non sapeva per qual calle,   40
mi volsi intorno, e stretto m'accostai,
tutto gelato, a le fidate spalle.

E Sordello anco: "Or avvalliamo omai   43
tra le grandi ombre, e parleremo ad esse;
grazïoso fia lor vedervi assai."

Solo tre passi credo ch'i' scendesse,   46
e fui di sotto, e vidi un che mirava
pur me, come conoscer mi volesse.

Temp' era già che l'aere s'annerava,   49
ma non sì che tra li occhi suoi e ' miei
non dichiarisse ciò che pria serrava.

Ver' me si fece, e io ver' lui mi fei: 52
giudice Nin gentil, quanto mi piacque
quando ti vidi non esser tra ' rei!

Nullo bel salutar tra noi si tacque;   55
poi dimandò: "Quant' è che tu venisti
a piè del monte per le lontane acque?"

"Oh!" diss' io lui, "per entro i luoghi tristi   58
venni stamane, e sono in prima vita,
ancor che l'altra, sì andando, acquisti."

E come fu la mia risposta udita,   61
Sordello ed elli in dietro si raccolse,
come gente di sùbito smarrita.

L'uno a Virgilio e l'altro a un si volse   64
che sedea lì, gridando: "Sù, Currado!
Vieni a veder che Dio per grazia volse!"

Poi, vòlto a me: "Per quel singular grado   67
che tu dei a colui che sì nasconde
lo suo primo *perché* che non li è guado,

31   One came to stand a little above us, and the other descended to the opposite bank, so that the people were contained between them.

34   I saw clearly their blond heads, but my eye was dazzled by their faces, as a faculty is confounded by excess.

37   "Both come from Mary's bosom," said Sordello, "to guard the valley, because of the serpent that will come along soon."

40   At which I, who did not know by what path, turned about all chilled, and drew close to the faithful shoulders.

43   And Sordello again: "Now let us go down into the valley among the great shades, and we will speak to them; it will be a great grace for them to see you."

46   Only three steps, I think, did I go down, and I was below, when I saw one who kept staring at me as if he wished to recognize me.

49   It was the time already when the air was becoming dark, but not so that between his eyes and mine it did not reveal what earlier it had hidden.

52   He started toward me, and I toward him: noble judge Nino, how I rejoiced to see that you are not among the damned!

55   No happy greeting was held back between us; then he asked: "How long is it since you came to the foot of the mountain across the distant waters?"

58   "Oh!" I said to him, "coming through the grim places I arrived this morning, and I am in my first life, though I am acquiring the second by this journey."

61   And when my reply was understood, Sordello and he drew back, like folk suddenly dismayed.

64   One turned to Virgil and the other to a soul sitting nearby, crying, "Up, Conrad! Come see what a grace God has willed."

67   Then, turning to me: "By the singular gratitude you owe to him who so hides his first *because* that there is no ford to it,

quando sarai di là da le larghe onde,   70
dì a Giovanna mia che per me chiami
là dove a li 'nnocenti si risponde.

Non credo che la sua madre più m'ami,   73
poscia che trasmutò le bianche bende,
le quai convien che, misera, ancora brami.

Per lei assai di lieve si comprende   76
quanto in femmina foco d'amor dura,
se l'occhio o 'l tatto spesso non l'accende.

Non le farà sì bella sepultura   79
la vipera che ' Melanesi accampa,
com' avria fatto il gallo di Gallura."

Così dicea, segnato de la stampa   82
nel suo aspetto di quel dritto zelo
che misuratamente in core avvampa.

Li occhi miei ghiotti andavan pur al cielo,   85
pur là dove le stelle son più tarde,
sì come rota più presso a lo stelo.

E 'l duca mio: "Figliuol, che là sù guarde?"   88
E io a lui: "A quelle tre facelle
di che 'l polo di qua tutto quanto arde."

Ond' elli a me: "Le quattro chiare stelle   91
che vedevi staman, son di là basse,
e queste son salite ov' eran quelle."

Com' ei parlava, e Sordello a sé il trasse,   94
dicendo: "Vedi là 'l nostro avversaro,"
e drizzò il dito perché 'n là guardasse.

Da quella parte onde non ha riparo   97
la picciola vallea, era una biscia,
forse qual diede ad Eva il cibo amaro.

Tra l'erba e ' fior venìa la mala striscia,   100
volgendo ad ora ad or la testa, e 'l dosso
leccando come bestia che si liscia.

Io non vidi, e però dicer non posso,   103
come mosser li astor celestïali,
ma vidi ben e l'uno e l'altro mosso.

Sentendo fender l'aere a le verdi ali,   106
fuggì 'l serpente, e li angeli dier volta,
suso a le poste rivolando iguali.

70   when you are back beyond the wide waves, tell
my Giovanna to call out for me to the place where
innocents are answered.

73   I do not believe her mother loves me any more,
since she gave up the white fillets, which,
wretched, she will yearn for again.

76   Through her one readily understands how long
the fire of love lasts in a female, if sight or touch
do not frequently kindle it.

79   The viper under which the Milanese pitch camp
will not adorn her tomb as much as the cock of
Galluria would have done."

82   So he spoke, his face stamped with the rightful
zeal that flames temperately in the heart.

85   My greedy eyes were still seeking the sky,
especially where the stars are slowest, like a wheel
closest to the axle.

88   And my leader said to me: "Son, what are you
staring at up there?" And I to him: "At those three
little torches with which the pole here is all
aflame."

91   Then he to me: "The four bright stars that you
saw this morning are low over there, and these
have gone up where those were."

94   As he was speaking, Sordello drew him closer,
saying: "See there our adversary," and he pointed
where he should look.

97   On the side where the little valley has no barrier,
there was a snake, perhaps like the one that gave
Eve the bitter food.

100   Among the grass and the flowers came the evil
slither, now and again turning its head and licking
its back like a beast that smooths itself.

103   I did not see, and therefore cannot say, how the
two celestial hawks began to move, but I clearly
saw them both in motion.

106   Hearing their green wings cleave the air, the
serpent fled, and the angels turned, flying paired
back up to their posts.

L'ombra che s'era al giudice raccolta 109
quando chiamò, per tutto quello assalto
punto non fu da me guardare sciolta.

"Se la lucerna che ti mena in alto 112
truovi nel tuo arbitrio tanta cera
quant' è mestiere infino al sommo smalto,"

cominciò ella, "se novella vera 115
di Val di Magra o di parte vicina
sai, dillo a me, che già grande là era.

Fui chiamato Currado Malaspina; 118
non son l'antico, ma di lui discesi;
a' miei portai l'amor che qui raffina."

"Oh!" diss' io lui, "per li vostri paesi 121
già mai non fui; ma dove si dimora
per tutta Europa ch'ei non sien palesi?

La fama che la vostra casa onora, 124
grida i segnori e grida la contrada,
sì che ne sa chi non vi fu ancora;

e io vi giuro, s'io di sopra vada, 127
che vostra gente onrata non si sfregia
del pregio de la borsa e de la spada.

Uso e natura sì la privilegia 130
che, perché il capo reo il mondo torca,
sola va dritta e 'l mal cammin dispregia."

Ed elli: "Or va, ché 'l sol non si ricorca 133
sette volte nel letto che 'l Montone
con tutti e quattro i piè cuopre e inforca,

che cotesta cortese oppinïone 136
ti fia chiavata in mezzo de la testa
con maggior chiovi che d'altrui sermone,

se corso di giudicio non s'arresta." 139

109   The shade that had drawn near the judge when he called, through that whole assault had not left off gazing at me.

112   "So may the lamp that leads you on high find sufficient fuel in your free will to take you to the flowering summit,"

115   it began, "if you know any true tidings of Val di Magra or any nearby place, tell me, for I was once powerful there.

118   I was called Conrad Malaspina; not the ancient one, but from him descended; I bore my people the love that is here refined."

121   "Oh," said I to him, "I have never been through your lands; but where in all Europe does anyone dwell where they are not celebrated?

124   The fame that honors your house is loud among lords and in the countryside, so that he knows of it who has never been there;

127   and I swear to you, so may I go above, that your honored people have not been stripped of the worth of purse and sword.

130   Custom and nature so privilege them that, even though the wicked head of the world lead it astray, they alone walk erect and scorn the path of evil."

133   And he: "Believe so: the sun will not lie down seven times in the bed that the Ram covers and straddles with all four feet,

136   before that courteous opinion will be fixed in the center of your head with larger nails than the speech of others,

139   if the course of judgment is not stayed."

NOTES

1-9. It was already ... asked all to listen:
One of the most famous canto-openings in
the poem, a periphrastic indication of the
hour: twilight on the pilgrim's first day on
the island of Purgatory. Cantos 7 and 8 round
out the themes that have dominated the first
day: new arrival, disorientation, nostalgia for
home and the body, exile.

1-6. It was ... dying day: The seafarers are
probably not thought of as on the deep;
mooring close to shore—even disembark-
ing for the night—was more typical of the

Figure 4. Guardian Angels.

Mediterranean in this period. The two groups affected by twilight—seafarers
and pilgrims on land—correspond both to the protagonist and to the new arriv-
als of Canto 2. The mention of seafarers [*navicanti*] also recalls the image of Italy
as a ship [*nave*] in peril (6.75).

5-6. a bell ... the dying day: This line inspired the opening of Thomas Gray's
"Elegy in a Country Churchyard": "The curfew tolls the knell of dying day."

5. a bell far off: The nature of the bell, whether of a church or convent, is not
specified. As Gmelin notes, the sunset Ave Maria bell (the "Angelus") was not yet
widespread at this date; Dante is thinking of the Compline bell.

7-8. to empty out my hearing and to gaze: To give my attention to what I was
seeing (the soul that has stood up), rather than to Sordello's words, which pass
unnoticed (cf 4.1-12).

10. joined and raised both palms: This posture, erect with the palms joined
and lifted above the head, is one of those illustrated in the treatise on prayer
attributed to Peter the Chanter (12th century), where it is said to express "the
tension of the heart toward God" (Trexler 1987), as well as in the handbook
attributed to saint Dominick (see Boyle 1996a, Schmitt 1990). See Ps. 133.2: "In
the nights lift up your hands to the holy places" (part of the Compline service;
see below). Note also the contrast with the seated kings.

11. toward the east: Toward the sunrise; traditionally Christians prayed facing
east, hence the orientation of churches.

13-18. *Te lucis* ante ... supernal wheels: "Te lucis ante terminum" [To you
before the end of day] is the traditional Compline hymn (text and ttranslation in
Additional Note 5). The intoning of the hymn by one soul, after which the others

join in, reflects monastic practice, though the souls are not performing but remembering Compline (but see McCracken 1993). The hymn begs for protection during the night, especially against sexual dreams ("ne polluantur corpora" [lest our bodies be polluted]). The souls do not sleep, only the pilgrim; nor can they sin.

19-21. Sharpen here . . . is easy: The first of seven apostrophes of the reader in the *Purgatorio* (the others are: 9.70-72, 10.106-11, 17.1-9, 29.97-105, 31.124-26, 36.136-41; see Gmelin 1951). The "veil" is the fictional narrative; the "truth" is discernible through the veil, as the understanding "passes within": the familiar medieval dichotomy of external "integument" and internal "nucleus" of meaning. The commentators differ as to whether the meaning is particularly easy to grasp here or requires a special sharpening of the mind. See *Inter cantica* below.

22-108. Then I saw . . . to their posts: The episode of the angels, in two parts, alternating with the dialogues (lines 46-84 and 109-39) is probably what is meant by the "veil" in line 20. It is a little *sacra rappresentazione* [sacred drama] or miracle play, enacting the theme of the Compline service (see Additional Note 2), drawing especially on Ps. 90.4 and 11-13:

> He will overshadow thee with his shoulders: and under his wings thou shalt trust. His truth shall compass thee with a shield: thou shalt not be afraid of the terror of the night. . . . For he hath given his angels charge over thee: to keep thee in all thy ways. . . . Thou shalt walk upon the asp and the basilisk: and thou shalt trample under foot the lion and the dragon.

Dante would have been alert to the fact that "all thy ways" [*omnibus viis tuis*] comprehends the several forms of travel mentioned in lines 1-9. An important implication is that the pilgrim's destiny (like that of Nino's daughter and wife, see lines 71-81) is in the hands of God's Providence.

22-24. Then I saw . . . pale and humble: Like the other souls the pilgrim has met so far, those in the Valley of Princes have not yet begun the active process of purgation and still carry with them the inclinations that will later be corrected; they suffer anxieties no longer felt by the souls actively purging themselves. (Allegorically, souls in this life should rely on God's help, always granted.)

25-36. two angels . . . confounded by excess: The first angels to appear since the angelic boatman of Canto 2; like him they are assigned a specific function, they guard the Valley (we are left to wonder whether all the Ante-Purgatory is guarded in this way), and like his, their brightness is too great for mortal vision, but while in Canto 2 the angel's entire form was too bright for the pilgrim (2.37-39), here he can discern all but their faces. (For the other angels in the *Purgatorio* see the note to 27.58-60.)

   The angels frame the group of souls between them, as if on a stage. Their fiery swords recall the angel set to guard Eden in Gen. 3.24; Güntert in *LDT* explores the episode as an inversion of the expulsion of Adam and Eve from Eden (and see next note). The blunted swords have been variously explained (they are merely for defence; this is not the principal fight with the serpent; etc.); for the early commentators the blunted tip signified God's mercy, the sharp edge his justice.

37. Mary's bosom: An expression calqued on "Abraham's bosom" (Luke 16.22). Here it refers to Heaven and to the loving intercession of the Virgin (see the text of "Salve Regina" in Additional Note 5; the correlation Mary-Eve underlies the action. The Valley of the Princes is itself a "bosom" (see the note on 7.65-69).

40-42. At which I . . . shoulders: The pilgrim shares the souls' fears. Like the mention of wings, the mention of shoulders echoes Psalm 90.

43-45. And Sordello . . . to see you: Answering both the pilgrim's fear and providing a transition to the next part of the canto.

46-84. Only three steps . . . in the heart: Nino (short for Ugolino) Visconti, ca. 1264-1294, was the son of a daughter of Count Ugolino (*Inf.* 32-33; see *Inter cantica* below, and the note to *Inf.* 33.13-18); he was judge (chief magistrate) of Galluria in Sardinia under the Hohenstaufens (see the note to *Inf.* 22.81-87) and was associated with Ugolino in the government of Pisa, fleeing when his grandfather joined the Ghibellines. After the death of Ugolino, it was Nino who lodged complaint against the Archbishop Ruggeri. Nino was frequently in Florence; however, this passage is the only record of the friendship with Dante. Like Manfred and Buonconte, Nino is the son/grandson of a father/grandfather who is damned (a similar pattern governs Dante's view of his widow and daughter).

49. It was the time . . . had hidden: A renewed indication of the time, roughly a third of the way into the canto, and part of the transition to the new section; cf. lines 86-87, with note.

56-57. How long . . . distant waters: Like Sordello (and cf. 5.1-9), Nino does not see the pilgrim's shadow and therefore supposes him a shade; cf. lines 61-63.

57. to the foot . . . waters: Nino imagines the pilgrim to have arrived in the angelic boat of Canto 2. The evocation of vast spaces recalls Pia in 5.131.

60. the second: The second life is, of course, that in Heaven, as the second death (*Inf.* 1.117) is damnation.

65-66. Up, Conrad . . . God has willed: We learn in line 109 that Conrad does come to Nino's side in answer to his call.

68-69. him . . . no ford to it: The ocean imagery again (cf. 6.121-22, with note). God's "first *because*" is his fundamental reason or motive (see Is. 40.28: "neither is there any searching out of his wisdom"). See "Textual Variants," page 627.

71. my Giovanna: Nino Visconti's only child (1291-1339?), who in 1308 married Rizzardo da Camino, lord of Treviso (see *Par.* 9.49-51, with note); after he was assassinated (in 1312), penniless, she took refuge in Florence; the city provided her with a pension. In 1300 she was nine years old.

71-72. to call out . . . are answered: To pray to Heaven for him.

73-84. her mother . . . in the heart: Nino's wife was Beatrice, daughter of the notorious Obizzo III d'Este (see *Inf.* 12.111-12, 18.55-57); in 1300, she married the Ghibelline ruler of Milan, Galeazzo Visconti (d. 1324), thus renouncing the white fillets of a widow; she would regret them because when her husband lost Milan in 1302 they became poverty-stricken. She was able to return to Milan only when her son Azzo was recalled in 1328.

76-81. Through her . . . would have done: The arms of the Milan Visconti were a red viper swallowing a blue Saracen; those of the Pisa Visconti a cock (the families were not related). In the Middle Ages, when women remarried, although the marriage was still considered a sacrament, the nuptial blessing was not pronounced (women were thought to remarry because of self-indulgence). Thus (lines 79-81) it would have been more honor to Beatrice to have remained faithful to Nino's memory (cf. Dido's "breaking faith with the ashes" of her first husband, *Inf.* 5.62). When Beatrice died (1334), both viper and cock were carved on her tomb.

82-84. stamped . . . in the heart: Nino's words seem less temperate to us than to Dante. The striking phrase "his face stamped with" derives from minting: the soul stamps form on the body as if on a coin (cf. 10.43-45).

86-87. where the stars . . . to the axle: The pilgrim's attention being drawn to the now visible stars provides a further indication of the falling of night. His eyes seek the (southern) celestial pole, near which the rotation of the stars is slowest.

89-93. At those three . . . where those were: The three stars that have risen in the place of the four seen in 1.22-25 obviously symbolize the three theological virtues (faith, hope, and love), as the four represent the cardinal virtues (the symbolism is reiterated in 31.106). Although the distinction is not to be pressed, the two passages, with 7.52-60, associate the active life with day, the contemplative life with night. Lana and Buti take the replacement as historical: the classical era of moral virtue is succeeded by the Christian era of grace.

Dante's concern is symbolic in these passages, and they do involve some astronomical legerdemain, if not impossibility. The pilgrim and Virgil are imagined as on the eastern slope of the mountain (see the note to 4.53), and thus the pole is to the right. Some commentators unthinkingly take the words "di là basse" [low over there] to mean "below the horizon." But if the two groups of stars are near the southern celestial pole ("closest to the axle," line 87), both should be above the horizon: like the Septentrion, they would never set, as long as they were within 32 degrees of the pole (at 32° latitude, the pole is 32° above the horizon). Other commentators suppose that the mountain is blocking the view of the four stars of the morning; this is a possible explanation.

94-108. Sordello ... to their posts: The second part of the *sacra rappresentazione* (see note to lines 22-108). Attention is abruptly shifted from the tranquil stars to the threatening, though harmless-seeming serpent.

94. Sordello drew him closer: Compare the pilgrim's movement in line 42.

95. our adversary: *Avversaro* literally translates the NT *diabolus*; see the note to *Inf.* 8.115.

97-102: On the side ... smooths itself: There is a suggestion that the angels are needed because of the exposure of the eastern side of the valley.

99. perhaps like ... the bitter food: The note of uncertainty here is vital to the dreamlike quality of the episode: the uncanniness of the tempter lies partly in the ambiguity of its appearance. Dante frequently refers to the Fall as due primarily to Eve (see especially 29.22-30, with notes); the opposition between the Virgin and Eve that underlies this canto has now been made explicit.

100. Among the grass and the flowers: The *locus amoenus* of the valley is linked with Eden (cf. line 14). Flowers and grass as hiding places of snakes are of course proverbial; cf. *Ecl.* 3.92-93: "You boys who are gathering flowers and young strawberries close to the ground, the cold snake (flee it!) is hiding in the grass."

100. the evil slither: A trope: the name of the action (or its result, as if the snake were leaving a trail) for the actor. The serpent's glancing about and preening contribute to the uncanniness; for looking about, cf. 32.150, with note.

103-108. I did not see ... to their posts: The serpent is routed by the mere sound of the angels' wings (cf. lines 29-30). They return to their posts with equal flight (at the same speed), a touch that emphasizes their imperturbable vigilance. Their moving from and returning to their posts also parallels their coming forth from Heaven and their eventual return there.

103-105. I did not ... clearly ... in motion: The motion began before the pilgrim turned away from the serpent to see the angels' reactions (cf. lines 34-36).

104. celestial hawks: Compare 2.38: "the divine bird." The term *astore* [hawk] derives from Lat. *accipitorem*, used in the Middle Ages for short-winged, long-tailed, low-flying hawks used in hunting (but distinct from falcons). According to the Ottimo, *astori* have a particular enmity toward snakes. The imagery of hawking/falconry was associated with the fallen angels in the *Inferno* (see the note on *Inf.* 17.127-32); the hawks also look forward to the eagle of Canto 9.

109-39. The shade . . . is not stayed: The numerous and powerful Malaspina family controlled Lunigiana, a somewhat vaguely defined region centering on the Val di Magra (line 116), the broad valley of the river Magra, on the border between Lombardy and Tuscany, flowing into the sea between Lérici and Carrara (see map on p. xii); they were often in conflict with the bishops of Luni. In the context of the family divisions and enmities Dante so frequently deplores, the Malaspinas are notable for their solidarity. Conrad II, dying without male children, in 1294 left his territories to his brothers and uncles; in 1296 Franceschino Malaspina di Mulazzo (see below) signed an agreement with his cousins to do likewise. Not much more is known about Conrad II; he may have fought against Nino Visconti.

111. had not left off gazing at me: The fixity of Conrad's gaze, motivated by his eagerness to have news of his home, expresses his attachment to earthly affairs (cf. line 120). Cf. Farinata, who for similar reasons remains immobile and fixed on the pilgrim during an interruption (*Inf.* 10.73-76); see *Inter cantica* below.

112-14. So may the lamp . . . flowering summit: The term *lucerna* refers properly to an oil-lamp. Its use here has commonly been explained as referring to illumination by God's grace (following the Ottimo), and such a meaning is not to be excluded. But considering the metaphor of the lantern in connection with Virgil's guidance (see especially 22.64-69), it should probably be taken as a reference to him. In either case, the flame of the light that guides the pilgrim must be maintained by the effort of the will.

The "flowering summit," of course, is the Earthly Paradise at the top of the mountain. "Al sommo smalto" means literally "on the highest enamel," i.e., "the enamel at the summit": for enamel as referring to grass and flowers, see *Inf.* 4.118 and *Purg.* 7.73-78.

115-17. if you know . . . tell me: Unlike Nino, Conrad seems not to know of recent events regarding his family (cf. lines 73-84 and *Inf.* 10.94-108).

119. not the ancient one . . . descended: Conrad I, Conrad II's grandfather, was a principal architect of the family's fortunes; he married Costanza, a natural daughter of the emperor Frederick II, and left four sons, including Conrad II's father.

121-39. Oh, said I . . . is not stayed: The canto concludes with one of the two most fervent tributes to a noble family found in the poem (the other is to the Della Scala family, rulers of Verona, in *Par.* 17.70-93). Dante's relations with the Malaspinas are known only in part. In 1306 Franceschino di Mulazzo named Dante as the representative of the family in peace negotiations (successful, in the event) with the bishop of Luni. In 1307 or '08, from the Casentino, Dante addressed his Epistle IV to Moroello Malaspina (probably the lord of Giovagallo, not the Moroello of *Inf.* 24.145), speaking warmly of Moroello's recent hospitality and the liberal atmosphere of his court.

121-32. Oh, said I . . . the path of evil: This speech implies that in 1300 (before his exile) Dante had not yet visited Lunigiana, although he knew of the family's fame.

127-29. and I swear . . . purse and sword: The "honor of purse and sword" refers to the chief chivalric virtues prized by Dante (and Boccaccio), liberality and valor.

130-32. Custom and nature . . . path of evil: "Custom" (the family's traditions) and "nature" (actual personal qualities) guarantee that the family is not led astray by the ill government that plagues the world (cf. 16.82-105). "Torca" [twist] is used in a kind of zeugma, meaning both "lead astray" (on the "evil path") and "cause to be twisted in body" (not "walking erect"); cf. 23.126.

131, 137. head of the world, center of your head: The Ram is also involved in this head imagery: in "melothesia" (correlation of the signs of the Zodiac with the human body), Aries governs the head.

133-39. And he . . . judgment is not stayed: The sun is in Aries in the spring; thus in less than seven years the pilgrim will know by direct experience ("larger nails than the speech of others") how true his opinion of the Malaspinas is: this is a veiled prophecy of Dante's *exile*, hence the force of the expression. The chronology is corroborated by surviving documents.

133. Believe so: The Italian "or va" [now go] has no idiomatic equivalent in English. Both here and in 24.82 (where it again introduces a prophecy) it implies corroboration.

139. if the course of judgment is not stayed: If the decree of God's Providence is not changed.

Inter cantica. Like *Inferno* 5-7, *Purgatorio* 6-8 include a catalog of misfortunes and frequently refer, though at a submerged level, to the imagery of Fortune's Wheel. More conspicuously, both *Inferno* 8-9 and *Purgatorio* 8-9 form transitions between major divisions of the other world: *Inferno* 8-9 from the circles of the incontinent to the City of Dis and the sins of malice, *Purgatorio* 8-9 from Ante-Purgatory to Purgatory proper (and in both cases the tenth cantos are involved). There are obvious parallels between incontinence, in which there is no specific intent to harm others, and negligence and late repentance, as well as between the theme of specific evil will toward others (City of Dis) and the focussed effort to master the will (Purgatory proper). Both the City of Dis and Purgatory have gates, are surrounded by walls, and are guarded by angels; both require divine assistance for entry.

The contested entry into Dis in *Inferno* 8-9 has three phases: 1. After an initial parley with the devils, the gate is shut in Virgil's face (*Inf.* 8.82-117), and the pair must wait. 2. While waiting, Virgil has an extraordinary moment of prophetic vision, quickly lost (*Inf.* 8.118-30, 9.1-15), and tells of his earlier descent (9.16-33); the pilgrim's attention is abruptly drawn to the Furies on the battlements, soon joined by the Medusa (9.34-63). 3. The angelic messenger foreseen in *Inf.* 8.130 opens the gate with a little wand; Virgil and the pilgrim enter (*Inf.* 9.64-106). These three phases all have counterparts in *Purgatorio* 8-9; here we will discuss those involving *Purgatorio* 8 (for 9, see *Inter cantica* there).

It is primarily the first, and partly the second, of the three infernal phases that find counterparts in *Purgatorio* 8; naturally the parallels invert the infernal terms. While in Hell "more than a thousand" fallen angels speak with Virgil and temporarily block entrance into Dis, in the *Purgatorio* only two heavenly angels block the "adversary" from entering the Valley of Princes, and Virgil and the pilgrim are inside, not outside. In both cases the exclusion is not definitive: the heavenly angels must continue to stand guard, and the serpent will return; but of course in both cases the ultimate defeat of Hell is guaranteed. The obvious contrasts between the glorious angels and the devils and Furies hardly need comment (the color green figures importantly in both, with very different meanings; cf. *Inf.* 9.40, *Purg.* 8.28-30 and 106).

Purgatorio 8, with part of 9, corresponds also to the second phase of the infernal episode, the waiting: all the souls in the Valley of Princes must wait for Purgatory to be opened to them, and the pilgrim must rest through the night. The visit of the serpent thus corresponds to the arrival on the battlements of the Furies and Medusa (the relative spatial positions are reversed). The nature of the threat is left unspecified in both cases: in *Inferno* 9 it is the very sight of the Medusa; Virgil turns the pilgrim about and covers his eyes with two sets of hands; in *Purgatorio* 8, too, there is emphasis on the theme of sight (see 8.35-36, 85-87, 95-104), but the mere sight of the serpent is not damaging. Both threats are emphatically marked by addresses to the reader (*Inf.* 9.61-63, *Purg.* 8.19-21), both of which use the imagery of veil and inner truth. As in the *Inferno,* too, the eighth and ninth cantos hold the first two apostrophes of the reader in each cantica (see *Inf.* 8.94-96 and *Purg.* 9.70-72). There are also parallels of detail: both eighth cantos give the term *avversaro* prominence (*Inf.* 8.115, *Purg.* 8.95); in both episodes an unexpected sight draws the pilgrim's eyes upward while a companion is speaking (*Inf.* 9.34-36, *Purg.* 8.85-87). Finally, several touches in connection with Conrad Malaspina recall Farinata degli Uberti (see the notes to lines 111 and 119) of *Inferno* 10.

A number of parallels exist with other parts of the *Inferno* in this canto. The most important is the connection of Nino Visconti with Count Ugolino (see note to 46-84), the last instance in the Ante-Purgatory of the recurrent pattern discussed in the *Inter cantica* to Cantos 3 and 5. Others are pointed out in the notes to lines 100, 104, 112-14. A last system of references to the *Inferno* involves the *sacra rappresentazione* as such. For *Inferno* 21-22, with this canto and *Purgatorio* 29-33, constitute the most elaborate sets of reference in the *Comedy* to the theater of Dante's time, especially the miracle plays. Critics are agreed on the presence, self-consciousness, and importance of these references, but a full understanding of them will probably never be possible; for medieval Italy we have nothing like the great wealth of information in the work of Karl Young and others on medieval English drama.

CANTO 9

La concubina di Titone antico   1
già s'imbiancava al balco d'orïente,
fuor de le braccia del suo dolce amico;

di gemme la sua fronte era lucente,   4
poste in figura del freddo animale
che con la coda percuote la gente;

e la notte, de' passi con che sale,   7
fatti avea due nel loco ov' eravamo,
e 'l terzo già chinava in giuso l'ale;

quand' io, che meco avea di quel d'Adamo,   10
vinto dal sonno, in su l'erba inchinai
là 've già tutti e cinque sedavamo.

Ne l'ora che comincia i tristi lai   13
la rondinella presso a la mattina,
forse a memoria de' suo' primi guai,

e che la mente nostra, peregrina   16
più da la carne e men da' pensier presa,
a le sue visïon quasi è divina,

in sogno mi parea veder sospesa   19
un'aguglia nel ciel con penne d'oro,
con l'ali aperte e a calare intesa,

ed esser mi parea là dove fuoro   22
abbandonati i suoi da Ganimede,
quando fu ratto al sommo consistoro.

Fra me pensava: "Forse questa fiede   25
pur qui per uso, e forse d'altro loco
disdegna di portarne suso in piede."

Poi mi parea che, poi rotata un poco,   28
terribil come fólgor discendesse
e me rapisse suso infino al foco.

CANTO 9

1   The concubine of ancient Tithonus was already
turning white on the eastern balcony, having left
the arms of her sweet lover;

4   with gems her forehead was shining, set in the
shape of the cold animal that strikes people with its
tail;

7   and night, in the place where we were, had made
two of the steps with which it ascends, and the
third was already lowering its wing;

10   when I, who had with me something of Adam,
overcome by sleep, reclined on the grass where all
five of us were sitting.

13   In the hour near morning when the swallow
begins her sad lays, perhaps in memory of her first
woes,

16   and when our mind, journeying further from
the flesh and less taken by its cares, is almost a
diviner in its visions,

19   in dream I seemed to see an eagle hovering in
the sky, with golden feathers and open wings,
intent to stoop,

22   and I seemed to be where his people were
abandoned by Ganymede, when he was carried off
to the highest consistory.

25   I was thinking to myself: "Perhaps by custom
the eagle strikes only here, and perhaps it disdains
to carry prey off in its claws from elsewhere."

28   Then it seemed to me that, having wheeled a
little, it descended terrible as lightning, and carried
me off, up as far as the fire.

Ivi parea che ella e io ardesse,   31
e sì lo 'ncendio imaginato cosse
che convenne che 'l sonno si rompesse.

  Non altrimenti Achille si riscosse,   34
li occhi svegliati rivolgendo in giro
e non sappiendo là dove si fosse,

  quando la madre da Chirón a Schiro   37
trafuggò lui dormendo in le sue braccia,
là onde poi li Greci il dipartiro,

  che mi scoss' io, sì come da la faccia   40
mi fuggì 'l sonno, e diventa' ismorto,
come fa l'uom che spaventato agghiaccia.

  Dallato m'era solo il mio conforto,   43
e 'l sole er' alto già più che due ore,
e 'l viso m'era a la marina torto.

  "Non aver tema," disse il mio segnore;   46
"fatti sicur, ché noi semo a buon punto;
non stringer, ma rallarga ogne vigore.

  Tu se' omai al Purgatorio giunto: 49
vedi là il balzo che 'l chiude dintorno,
vedi l'entrata là 've par digiunto.

  Dianzi, ne l'alba che procede al giorno,   52
quando l'anima tua dentro dormia
sovra li fiori ond' è là giù addorno,

  venne una donna, e disse: 'I' son Lucia;   55
lasciatemi pigliar costui che dorme:
sì l'agevolerò per la sua via.'

  Sordel rimase e l'altre genti forme;   58
ella ti tolse e, come 'l dì fu chiaro,
sen venne suso, e io per le sue orme.

  Qui ti posò, ma pria mi dimostraro   61
li occhi suoi belli quella intrata aperta;
poi ella e 'l sonno ad una se n'andaro."

  A guisa d'uom che 'n dubbio si raccerta   64
e che muta in conforto sua paura
poi che la verità li è discoperta,

  mi cambia' io; e come sanza cura   67
vide me 'l duca mio, su per lo balzo
si mosse, e io di rietro inver' l'altura.

31   There it seemed that it and I burned, and the imagined fire was so hot that my sleep had to break.

34   Not otherwise did Achilles shake himself, turning his awakened eyes about in a circle, not knowing where he was,

37   when his mother fled with him sleeping in her arms from Chiron to Skyros, whence the Greeks later took him away,

40   than I shook myself, as soon as sleep fled from my face, and turned pale, as one does who freezes in terror.

43   At my side was only my strength, and the sun was already more than two hours high, and my eyes were turned toward the waters.

46   "Have no fear," said my lord; "be assured, for we are at a good point; do not pull back, but give free rein to every strength.

49   You have now reached Purgatory: see there the bank that encloses it around, see the entrance there, where the bank seems divided.

52   Earlier, in the dawn that precedes the day, when your soul was asleep within you on the flowers that adorn the earth down there,

55   a lady came, and she said: 'I am Lucia; let me take up this sleeper: so will I ease him on his way.'

58   Sordello stayed behind, and the other noble forms; she took you and, when the day was bright, came on up here, and I in her footsteps.

61   Here she put you down, but first her lovely eyes showed me that open entrance; then she and your sleep went away at the same moment."

64   As one does who is reassured in his doubt and changes his fear into strength when the truth is revealed to him,

67   so I changed; and when my leader saw me without care, up the bank he started, and I after him, toward the height.

Lettor, tu vedi ben com' io innalzo   70
la mia matera, e però con più arte
non ti maravigliar s' io la rincalzo.

   Noi ci appressammo, ed eravamo in parte   73
che là dove pareami prima rotto,
pur come un fesso che muro diparte,

   vidi una porta, e tre gradi di sotto   76
per gire ad essa, di color diversi,
e un portier ch'ancor non facea motto.

   E come l'occhio più e più v'apersi,   79
vidil seder sovra 'l grado sovrano,
tal ne la faccia ch'io non lo soffersi;

   e una spada nuda avëa in mano,   82
che reflettëa i raggi sì ver' noi,
ch'io dirizzava spesso il viso in vano.

   "Dite costinci: che volete voi?"   85
cominciò elli a dire, "ov' è la scorta?
Guardate che 'l venir sù non vi nòi."

   "Donna del ciel, di queste cose accorta,"   88
rispuose 'l mio maestro a lui, "pur dianzi
ne disse: 'Andate là: quivi è la porta.'"

   "Ed ella i passi vostri in bene avanzi,"   91
ricominciò il cortese portinaio:
"Venite dunque a' nostri gradi innanzi."

   Là ne venimmo; e lo scaglion primaio   94
bianco marmo era, sì pulito e terso
ch'io mi specchiai in esso qual io paio.

   Era il secondo tinto più che perso,   97
d'una petrina ruvida e arsiccia,
crepata per lo lungo e per traverso.

   Lo terzo, che di sopra s'ammassiccia,   100
porfido mi parea, sì fiammeggiante
come sangue che fuor di vena spiccia.

   Sovra questo tenëa ambo le piante   103
l'angel di Dio, sedendo in su la soglia
che mi sembiava pietra di diamante.

   Per li tre gradi sù di buona voglia   106
mi trasse il duca mio, dicendo: "Chiedi
umilemente che 'l serrame scioglia."

70   Reader, you see well how I am elevating my matter, and therefore do not marvel if with more art I bolster it.

73   We drew near until, where there had first seemed to me to be a break, like a crack that divides a wall,

76   I now saw a door, with three steps below approaching it, of different colors, and a gate-keeper who spoke no word as yet.

79   And as I opened my eyes more and more at the sight, I saw that he was sitting over the topmost step, so bright of face that I could not endure it;

82   and he had a naked sword in his hand, which so reflected the sunbeams toward us that I often directed my eyes in vain.

85   "Speak from there: what do you wish?" he began to say, "Where is your escort? Beware lest coming up be harmful to you."

88   "A lady from Heaven, wise in these things," my master answered him, "just now said to us: 'Go there: there is the gate.'"

91   "And may she advance your steps in goodness," began again the courteous gate-keeper: "Come forward therefore to our stairs."

94   There we came; and the first step was white marble, so polished and shining that I was mirrored in it just as I appear.

97   The second was darker than purple, made of a rough, dry stone, cracked both lengthwise and across.

100   The third, which weighs the others down, seemed of porphyry to me, as flaming as blood spurting from a vein.

103   On this one the angel of God had both his feet, sitting on the threshold, which seemed to me a stone of diamond.

106   Up the three steps with good will my leader drew me, saying: "Ask humbly that he open the lock."

Divoto mi gittai a' santi piedi;   109
misericordia chiesi e ch'el m'aprisse,
ma pria nel petto tre volte mi diedi.

Sette *P* ne la fronte mi descrisse   112
col punton de la spada, e: "Fa che lavi,
quando se' dentro, queste piaghe," disse.

Cenere, o terra che secca si cavi,   115
d'un color fora col suo vestimento;
e di sotto da quel trasse due chiavi.

L'una era d'oro e l'altra era d'argento;   118
pria con la bianca e poscia con la gialla
fece a la porta sì ch'i' fu' contento.

"Quandunque l'una d'este chiavi falla,   121
che non si volga dritta per la toppa,"
diss' elli a noi, "non s'apre questa calla.

Più cara è l'una; ma l'altra vuol troppa   124
d'arte e d'ingegno avanti che diserri,
perch' ella è quella che 'l nodo digroppa.

Da Pier le tegno; e dissemi ch'i' erri   127
anzi ad aprir ch'a tenerla serrata,
pur che la gente a' piedi mi s'atterri."

Poi pinse l'uscio a la porta sacrata,   130
dicendo: "Intrate; ma facciovi accorti
che di fuor torna chi 'n dietro si guata."

E quando fuor ne' cardini distorti   133
li spigoli di quella regge sacra,
che di metallo son sonanti e forti,

non rugghiò sì né si mostrò sì acra   136
Tarpëa, come tolto le fu il buono
Metello, per che poi rimase macra.

Io mi rivolsi attento al primo tuono,   139
e "*Te deum laudamus*" mi parea
udire in voce mista al dolce suono.

Tale imagine a punto mi rendea   142
ciò ch'io udiva, qual prender si suole
quando a cantar con organi si stea,

ch'or sì or no s'intendon le parole.   145

109   Devoutly I threw myself at his holy feet; I begged that he have mercy and open to me, but first three times I struck my breast.

112   Seven *P*s he inscribed upon my forehead with the point of his sword, and: "See that you wash these wounds, when you are within," he said.

115   Ashes, or earth dug up dry, would be of one color with his garment; and from beneath it he drew forth two keys.

118   One was of gold and the other of silver; first with the white and then with the yellow he unlocked the gate, so that I was content.

121   "Whenever either of these keys fails, so that it does not turn correctly in the lock," he said to us, "this passage will not open.

124   One is more precious; but the other requires much art and wit before it unlocks, because it is the one that untangles the knot.

127   From Peter I have them; and he told me to err rather in opening than in keeping closed, as long as the people kneel before me."

130   Then he pushed open the door of the blessed gate, saying: "Enter; but I warn you that whoever looks back must return outside."

133   And when the pins turned in the hinges of that sacred palace, pins made of strong, resonant metal,

136   Tarpeia did not roar so nor seem so harsh when the good Metellus was taken from it, so that later it was left lean.

139   I turned attentive to the first thunderclap, and I seemed to hear voices, singing "*Te Deum laudamus,*" blended with the sweet sound.

142   The image rendered in what I heard was exactly what one perceives when there is singing with an organ

145   so that now one understands the words, now not.

NOTES

1-9. The concubine . . . with which it ascends: There is general agreement about lines 7-9; the steps with which night rises (as always, conceived as a point circling opposite the sun; see 2.1-9, with notes) are the hours between sunset (about 6 P.M.) and midnight: thus it is about 9 P.M. on the mountain. Early commentators (Lana) took lines 1-6 to refer to moonrise: sunrise (Aurora) being Tithonus' wife (for the myth, see note to lines 1-3), moonrise would be his lover. Some modern commentators argue that since no ancient source mentions any infidelity of Tithonus, lines 1-6 must refer to sunrise as seen from Italy, and they point out that at 9 P.M. in Purgatory it would be 6 A.M. in Italy, and Scorpio must be understood as in the western sky (Chiavacci Leonardi; see Cornish in Stewart/Cornish 2000).

It seems not to have been noticed that on *either* hypothesis (i.e., whether the "concubine" is sun-dawn or moon-dawn), Scorpio would dominate the eastern sky at 9 P.M., seen from the antipodes of Jerusalem. Furthermore, as Moore 1887 noted, three days after being full the moon would indeed be about to rise at 9 P.M. It is therefore less strained and considerably more vivid to take the "gems [on] her forehead" of line 4 as referring to the stars that immediately precede the rising moon. The argument that Dante would never invent an unprecedented figure is a mere prejudice. From Italy both the moon and the stars of Scorpio would have been visible crossing the sky from 9 P.M. on (the moon would in fact have obscured the stars), and the absurdity of the stars being on Aurora's "forehead" as seen from Italy ought to be obvious. But the motivation of the obscurity remains to be explained: does Dante describe moonrise because of the dream that follows? That the moon focused the influence of the superior stars and planets made it crucial for dream interpretation (Gregory 1992).

1-3. The concubine . . . her sweet lover: According to the myth, the goddess of the dawn fell in love with Tithonus (a prince of Troy); her request that the gods make him immortal was granted, but since she forgot to request eternal youth for him, he grew ever older; hence "antico" [ancient], line 1 (one version of the myth has him shriveling to a grasshopper); Tennyson's "Tithonus" is a particularly fine treatment of it. For the classical narrative formulae Dante has in mind, see *Aen*. 4.584-85: "And now Aurora first scattered new light across the lands, leaving Tithonus' saffron couch," and *Geor.* 1.447.

5-6. set in the shape . . . with its tail: The early commentators were surely correct in identifying this as the constellation Scorpio. Some supporters of the sun-dawn interpretation argue that the reference is to Pisces (as in 1.19-21), but fish are not said to strike people with their tails (cf. *Inf.* 17.25-27).

7-9. and night . . . lowering its wing: Picone in *LDT* notes a parallel with the first sonnet of the *VN* (and cf. "lucente" [shining]).

10-11. something of Adam . . . on the grass: The pilgrim's mortality and the resulting need for sleep are results of Adam's Fall; since Hell is timeless, there was no need for sleep there. The very grass recalls the pilgrim's mortality (Is. 40.6 "All flesh is grass"; cf. James 1.9-11, cited in the note to 11.115-17).

13-33. In the hour . . . had to break: The first of the pilgrim's three dreams on the mountain; it is the most encompassing and the most cryptic of the three.

13-18. In the hour . . . in its visions: Belief in the divinatory truth of early-morning dreams was ancient (e.g., Ovid, *Heroides* 19. 195-96: "near the dawn . . . when true dreams are wont to be seen") and is a medieval commonplace; see Adelard of Bath: "in dreams the soul, as it is in some way then freer from the irritations of the senses, focuses its sight and sometimes apprehends the truth about the future or a resemblance of it; it is least deceived under the dawn" (cf. 17.13-18, *Ep.* 6.24). *Conv.* 2.8.13 asserts that dreaming (consciousness free of the body) proves the immortality of the soul.

13-15. the swallow begins . . . her first woes: In *Met.* 6.424-674, Philomela is raped by Tereus, her sister Procne's husband; he cuts out her tongue and secretly imprisons her, but she weaves a tapestry depicting the crime and sends it to her sister. Freeing Philomela, the furious Procne kills and cooks her son Itys and feeds him to his father. Informed of this by both women (in fact Philomela triumphantly shows him his son's head), Tereus pursues them sword in hand, but all three become birds, Tereus a hoopoe. Since Servius Procne is the swallow, Philomela (whose name means "lover of song") the nightingale. In *Ecl.* 6.78-81 Vergil seems to identify the nightingale as Procne, but there is no reason to suppose that Dante followed him (see the note to 17.18-19). Cf. also *Geor.* 4.511-15, whence Dante derived "sad lays": "miserabile carmen . . . moestis . . . questibus" [wretched song . . . sad complaints].

19-20. an eagle hovering in the sky: Gregory the Great, *Moralia in Job* (*PL* 76.623-30) writes: "In holy scripture the eagle . . . sometimes designates the subtle intelligence of the saints, or the swift flight downward of the incarnate God and his sudden reascent to the heights . . . the word eagle can also figure earthly power, as is said in Ezekiel the prophet" (Ezek. 17.3: see the note to 32.112-114). In the same passage, Gregory observes that the emblem of John the Evangelist is the eagle (see 29.92-93 and notes), and he adds: "let us consider how sublime an eagle was Paul, who flew up to the third heaven, and heard words it is not lawful for a man to utter [2 Cor. 12.4]." For the eagle compared to epic poets, see lines 70-73. The imperial eagle of Rome is also implicated here (see 10.80-81 and note); in *Ep.* 5.11, "the sublime eagle descending like lightning" refers to the emperor Henry VII.

22-27. I seemed to be . . . from elsewhere: Ganymede, the son of Tros (for whom Troy was named), while hunting on Mt. Ida, near Troy, was seized by Zeus (who had taken the shape of an eagle) to be his cupbearer on Olympus ("the highest consistory"). From antiquity on the story was allegorized as the ascent of the soul to Heaven, but this did not purge its original violent eroticism (Barkan 1994). *Aen.* 5.252-55 and *Theb.* 1.548 are reticent; only Ovid (*Met.* 10.155-61) mentions the sexual ardor of Zeus. The dreamer's supposing that he is on Mt. Ida assimilates it to both the mountain of Purgatory and that of *Inferno* 1; see the note to *Inf.* 1.13.

28-30. having wheeled a little . . . as far as the fire: The archetypal "descent from heaven" of the divine power (see also 12.27, 32.108-11 and notes). See Is. 58.14 [I will lift thee up above the high places of the earth]; also Exod. 19.4. The dream suggests: the pilgrim's moral renewal through the mysterious violence of grace; his election as apologist of the providential role of empire; and the poetic buttressing of *Purgatorio* itself.

31-33. There it seemed . . . had to break: Three references to burning in as many lines suggest that "the fire" may be both the destination of the flight and the sensation that wakens the dreamer. "Burning" is ambiguous both grammatically and narratively (in the Italian, the verb is in the singular, and the pronoun referring to *aguglia* [eagle] is feminine; both the grammar and the mythical reference suggest an embrace). Bestiary lore about eagles was often based on Ps. 102.5 ("their youth shall be renewed like the eagle's"). Cf. Brunetto Latini, *Trésor*, 1.145: "Know that the eagle . . . renews itself and puts aside its old age. And most say that it flies to so high a place near the heat of the sun that its feathers burn, and the fire takes away all the dimness of its eyes, and then it allows itself to fall into a fountain where it bathes three times, and then is as young as at the beginning" (cf. Deut. 32.10-11, Is. 40.31).
   No student of Dante should fail to read the delicious parody of this dream, with its garrulous eagle, in Chaucer's *House of Fame*, Book 2 (and see the notes by Fyler, in Chaucer 1987; also Schless 1984).

34-42. Not otherwise . . . freezes in terror: Dante's simile derives from Statius (the events are summarized in the note to *Inf.* 26.61-62), *Achill.* 247-50:

> when the boy, his sleep disturbed, feels the day
> filtering into his open eyes. First the air amazes him:
> what's this place, these waves, where is Pelion? All is changed
> and all unknown; he hesitates even to recognize his mother.

44-45. the sun was already . . . toward the waters: An implied warming of the pilgrim's body by the sun is perhaps connected with the burning in the dream. His surprise at the sight of the sea reflects his changed location; he is looking east, as at 4.52-53; the rising sun would have struck his face (see 27.133, 30.25-27 and 32.18 and notes).

46-48. Have no fear . . . every strength: Virgil's words echo "Nolite timere," used by the angels (Nativity: Luke 2.10; Resurrection: Matt. 28.5), and by the resurrected Christ (Luke 24.36; Apoc. 1.17), cf. *Purg.* 20.133-35, 21.78. The terms *reining* and *exerting* name the major focuses of Purgatory proper: restraining vice and practicing virtue (cf. 13.37-42 and 18.64-67, with notes).

49. You have now reached Purgatory: The self-confidence Virgil encourages results in part from the progress just made; cf. 27.127-42 and notes.

50-51. see the entrance . . . the bank seems divided: The description of the opening alludes once again to Matt. 7.14 (see the note to 4.19-24); the allusion to the crack in the wall of *Met.* 4.65-66 becomes clearer in lines 74-75. For the "eye of the needle," see 10.16, with note.

52-63. Earlier, in the dawn . . . at the same moment: Virgil now relates the "real" events that took place during the "imagined" events of the pilgrim's dream. Virgil's account also presents a gradual and maternal intervention (cf. the reference to Thetis) rather than a violent, masculine one. Lucia's arrival corresponds to the beginning of the dream (lines 13-14, 52), but Virgil minimizes the disjunction of soul and body ("your soul was asleep within you," line 53; cf. lines 16-17), feminizes the agent of grace (Lucy vs. the eagle) as well as the means of carrying the pilgrim (bosom vs. claws); rather than being shattered, the dream concludes with Lucia and sleep departing as one. In the use of classical allusion in the canto, there is movement from the archaic and terrible (rape, mutilation, and cannibalism in the Philomela story; the violence and arbitrariness of Jupiter toward Ganymede) to the epic and (for Dante) historical life of Achilles, to Virgil's immediate, benign account. The myth of Ganymede mediates the extremes by including both erotic violence and sublime elevation.

The commentators tend to suppose that Virgil's account is to be taken as the last word; as Chiavacci Leonardi puts it, "In these lines Virgil explains Dante's dream, which thus in fact [*sic*] represented a real event, . . . Lucia carrying Dante to the Gate." But the range of reference of the dream is much broader than that: 1. Lucia carries the pilgrim from the Valley of Princes (Mt. Ida) to the beginning of Purgatory (the fire); 2. Virgil (the eagle among epic poets and the singer of the Roman eagle) will lead Dante from the mountainside of *Inferno* 1 through the fire of the last circle of Purgatory (for Dante this of course corresponds to the establishment of law, the preparation of humanity by the Roman Empire for the coming of Christ); 3. God's grace takes the pilgrim from the mountainside of *Inferno* 1 all the way to the Empyrean [heaven of fire] at the end of the poem. The dream thus represents a powerful condensation of the entire poem, and this condensation itself is also the subject of the dream.

64-69. As one does who . . . toward the height: Thus imitating Lucia and Virgil just before (line 60). On the importance of "following," see 22.62-63 and 24.58-59, with notes.

70-72. Reader . . . with more art I bolster it: The second address to the reader (cf. 8.19-21) in the *Purgatorio* and ninth in the *Comedy* (see 17.1 and note), dividing the canto exactly in half (cf. 4.70-72 and 17.70-72, with notes; Durling/Martinez 1990); here the upward motion in the dream is distinguished from the upward progress resumed after lines 91-93, subjective from objective ascent (mediated by Virgil's interpretation of the dream). The pilgrim's confidence, at this stage of the journey, accompanies the poet's claim of loftier subject matter more elaborately treated (see 1.9 and note). Like the eagle, the epic voice soars aloft (*Inf.* 4.95-96, and *DVE* 2.4.10-11, where it is an "aquila astripeta" [star-seeking eagle], echoing *Aen.* 6.129-131 and *Ecl.* 9.36).

73-75. We drew near . . . divides a wall: The reference to the tale of Pyramus and Thisbe could hardly be more pointed; see the notes to 3.94-99, Additional Note 13.

76-78. I now saw . . . spoke no word: The third mention of the entrance, gate or door; there will be several more. This second half of the canto is the "door" or threshold of Purgatory proper. Some memories of the gate into the garden in the *Romance of the Rose* seem to be operative here, but the main reference is of course to saint Peter's Gate (*Inf.* 1.134: "la porta di san Pietro").

81. so bright of face . . . not endure it: So of the angels in the Valley of Princes (8.35-36).

82-83. a naked sword . . . reflected the sunbeams: Sword and keys (lines 117-129) are the attributes of saints Paul and Peter respectively; see 29.140, with notes, and Apoc. 1.16. The bright sword, its brilliance suggesting its spiritual nature, recalls the flaming and whirling sword [*flammeum gladium atque versatilem*] of the Cherub guarding Eden in Gen. 3.24 (lines 83-84 seem to correspond to the whirling); this was often taken in the Middle Ages to be a circle of fire around Purgatory (see Introduction, pp. 10-12, and 27.7-12, with notes; for exclusion, see 4.128-129).

85-87. Speak from there . . . be harmful to you: The angelic doorkeeper questions the wayfarers, as did previous guardians (Minos, *Inf.* 5.19-20; Chiron, *Inf.* 12.63, and Cato, *Purg.* 1.40-48).

91-93. may she advance . . . to our stairs: The verses join the pilgrim's path to the steps leading to the threshold. The plural ("our steps") emphasizes the public use of the passage, in contrast to the privacy of the dream. Like the infernal custodians, this gatekeeper is tractable after Lucy is mentioned, just as Virgil's account of her descent tempers the imagery of the dream.

95-102. white marble . . . spurting from a vein: The three lower steps have caused much discussion. Commentators ancient and recent have treated the episode as an allegory of the sacrament of penance, which begins with the conviction of sin (self-knowledge, line 96), continues with oral confession and the expression of remorse (contrition [being entirely broken], lines 98-99), followed by the absolution of the priest, which promises the forgiveness, conditional on performance of the penance imposed (which must express charity: the red of sacrificial blood, lines 101-102). Armour's 1983a arguments against the traditional view rest on the notion that Dante adheres to the narrow orthodox conception of the sacraments and of Purgatory, and seem to us to miss the tropological dimension that refers to this life (see our Introduction, pp. 5-7).

102. blood spurting from a vein: See the previous note, and Additional Note 13.

107-10: Ask humbly . . . open to me: A clear allusion to the ritual kneeling before the priest in confession. Beating the breast is the ritual gesture of contrition, normally accompanied by the words: "Mea culpa, mea culpa, mea maxima culpa" [By my fault, by my fault, by my most grievous fault]. The passage enacts Matt. 7.7: "Ask, and it shall be given you; seek, and ye shall find; knock, and it shall be opened to you."

112-14. Seven *P*s he inscribed . . . when you are within: The *P*s have been taken to stand for *Peccatum* [sin], *Plaga* [wound], and *Penitentia* [penitence] (these are all more or less equivalent). One *P* will be erased on each terrace. For the *vulneratio naturae* and the debt of satisfaction, see Introduction, pp. 7-10. The engraving of the *P*s marks the soul's advance to active purgation (as opposed to the passive waiting of Ante-Purgatory; they are perhaps meant to recall the letter Tau ("signa Tau super frontes") marked on the foreheads of the elect (cf. Ezek. 9.2-6 and Apoc. 7.2-14; Sarolli 1971).

115. Ashes, or earth dug up dry: Like a religious habit, the gatekeeper's garment signifies penitence (like the cross of ashes drawn on the forehead on Ash Wednesday). It also resembles haircloth, the garment of mourning. To become worthy of Eden, all must mourn; see Ezek. 9.4: only those who "sigh and mourn" over Jerusalem receive the mark of salvation (see previous note).

117-27. he drew forth . . . I have them: These are the keys entrusted by Christ to Peter (Matt. 16.19) and of which Boniface brags in *Inf.* 27.103-105; they are usually interpreted as discretion and power (i.e., deciding the fitness of penitents, and opening to them the kingdom of Heaven). On the charge to be lenient, see Matt. 18.21-22. The emphasis on the gate and its opening is striking: some twenty words in fourteen lines. See *Inter cantica* below.

130-32. Then he pushed . . . must return outside: Commentators cite Gen. 19.26 (Lot's wife), Luke 9.62: "no man putting his hand to the plough, and looking back, is fit for the kingdom of God," and *De civ. Dei* 16.30, as well as the myth of Orpheus, who loses Eurydice by looking back at her.

133-45. And when the pins . . . the words, now not: Most commentators assume the singing in lines 139-41 to be distinct from the sound of the door, but the notion that the singing is the sound of the hinges (Barbi 1934) ought not to be discarded, as Dante draws a veil of indistinctness over the whole passage (lines 140, 145). Modulation from harsh to sweet balances the change of tragedy into song at the beginning of the canto.

136-38. Tarpeia . . . was left lean: *Phars.* 3.153-68 narrates how Lucius Caecilius Metellus, custodian of the public treasury (Temple of Saturn) at the foot of the Tarpeian rock, resisted Julius Caesar's attempt to loot it, but was forced away:

> Metellus pulled aside, the temple was at once thrown open.
> Then the Tarpeian rock resounded, and a great noise
> Witnesses the opening of the doors
> . . . shameful theft despoils the temple,
> And then for the first time Rome was poorer than Caesar.

The allusion emphasizes the rarity and difficulty of the passage of the gate, and echoes distantly the beating down of the gates of Hell, as narrated in the apocryphal Gospel of Nicodemus (see *Inf.* 9.64-72, with note).

140. *Te deum laudamus* [You, God, we praise]: One of the oldest hymns of the Church, said to have been sung spontaneously by Ambrose and Augustine at the latter's baptism; habitually sung, Buti reports, when novices leave the world and enter a religious order, as well as on occasions of public rejoicing. The hymn enumerates the praises of God from the angels through the martyrs and the whole Church (1-10), concluding with petitions for God's mercy (22-29); at its heart (11-20) is direct address of the Trinity and especially of Christ, in his Incarnation, Atonement, and Judgment.

142-45. The image . . . the words, now not: Most critics hold that Dante refers to singing accompanied by an organ, in which distinguishing the words is proverbially difficult. Fallani argues that Dante's "organi" refers to *organa,* the early form of polyphony.

Inter cantica. The canto echoes the transition of *Inferno* 8-9, notably with the reiteration of a double appeal to the reader, as at *Inf.* 8.94-96 and 9.61-63, in 8.19-21 and 9.70-72: they are arranged chiastically, those at *Inf.* 9.63 and *Purg.* 8.19, the means, inviting the reader's interpretation, the other two, the extremes, steering an emotional response ("think, reader, if I became weak"; "do not marvel"). The addresses frame the transitions that furnish the narrative content of the cantos, and the text features terms related to gates, doors, and stairs, as well as verbs for entry and passage (for the steps, see lines 94-105 and notes): between lines 9.62 and 9.131 we find "door" or "gate" four times (9.76, 86, 120, 130), but also "entrance," "crack," "keyhole," (9.62, 75, 123), as well as related terms such as doorman (*portier,* 9.78), lock (*serrame,* 9.108) and keys (*chiavi,* 9.111); note also the terms "open," "closed," and "enter" (*aprisse,* 9.110, *serrata,* 9.128, *intrate,* 9.131). Compare "gate" and *"sanza serrame"* [lit. "without locks"] at *Inf.* 8.125-26 (of the gate of Hell, 3.10-12) and "door" at 9.89, as well as "opened" at 8.130 and 9.90 and "entrance" at 8.81; forms of "enter" are at 8.90 and 9.106. The parallels are dynamic as well, the *Inferno* narrating the descent of the angelic messenger (8.128-130) and Virgil's previous "descent" to the *più basso loco* (9.17, 28, "lowest place"), the *Purgatorio* the raising up (*suso*) of the pilgrim by the eagle and Lucy (9.29, 9.60) to what will be, ultimately, the "highest [*sommo*] consistory," (9.24, 27).

The notion of elevation, at once narrative and stylistic, emerges in the second address to the reader, where the poet speaks of "raising up" his subject (*innalzo*). See notes to lines 70-73. At a deeper level, *Inferno* 8-9, one of the most complex transitions of the *Inferno*, with its approach to Dis, failure of Virgil, and descent of the *messo* [messenger], stages the poem's layering of allegorical levels and its workings as a journey of interpretation (see "Allegory" in Lansing 2000).

The three steps (lines 94-105) form one of the great transitions on the way from Hell to Paradise along a continuous ladder or stairway (see *Inferno* Introduction and Additional Note 8). From this viewpoint, the sequence white-black-red-white recalls and reorders the white-red-black of Lucifer's faces in *Inferno* 34, referring to the maturation of mulberries—turned red by Pyramus' spurting blood—from off-white to red to black, and there taken as a sign of Lucifer's negative "maturation," i.e., corruption (Freccero 1965). But the Ovidian tale that explains the darkening of the mulberry was also taken *in bono* to refer to Christ's blood, in which the blessed are washed white (Apoc. 7.14). The sequence is thus from white to black, innocence to sin, then to red, the blood of redemption, and back to white again, the adamantine threshold of the church, its authority and efficacy resting upon the merits of the Passion. Thus the steps recapitulate salvation history from Adam to Christ.

Figure 5. The Annunciation.

CANTO 10

Poi fummo dentro al soglio de la porta,   1
che 'l mal amor de l'anime disusa
perché fa parer dritta la via torta,

    sonando la senti' esser richiusa;   4
e s'io avesse li occhi vòlti ad essa,
qual fora stata al fallo degna scusa?

    Noi salavam per una pietra fessa   7
che si moveva e d'una e d'altra parte
sì come l'onda che fugge e s'appressa.

    "Qui si conviene usare un poco d'arte,"   10
cominciò 'l duca mio, "in accostarsi
or quinci, or quindi al lato che si parte."

    E questo fece i nostri passi scarsi   13
tanto che pria lo scemo de la luna
rigiunse al letto suo per ricorcarsi

    che noi fossimo fuor di quella cruna.   16
Ma quando fummo liberi e aperti,
sù dove il monte in dietro si rauna,

    ïo stancato e amendue incerti   19
di nostra via, restammo in su un piano
solingo più che strade per diserti.

    Da la sua sponda, ove confina il vano,   22
al piè de l'alta ripa che pur sale,
misurrebbe in tre volte un corpo umano;

    e quanto l'occhio mio potea trar d'ale,   25
or dal sinistro e or dal destro fianco,
questa cornice mi parea cotale.

    Là sù non eran mossi i piè nostri anco,   28
quand' io conobbi quella ripa intorno
che, dritta, di salita aveva manco,

CANTO 10

Ascent to the first terrace, of pride—carved examples of humility—the souls of the proud, bearing heavy stones

1   When we were within the threshold of the gate,
in disuse because of human souls' evil love, which
makes the twisted way seem straight,

4   I heard it being closed again, resounding; and if I
had turned back my eyes to it, what would have
been a worthy excuse for the fault?

7   We were climbing up through a cleft rock that
moved from side to side like the wave that flees
and then approaches.

10   "Here we must use a little skill," began my
leader, "clinging to the side that recedes, now here,
now there."

13   And this made our steps so slow that the hollow
moon reached its bed to lie down again

16   before we came forth from that needle's eye.
But when we were free of it and in the open, up
where the mountain gathers itself back,

19   I weary, and both uncertain of our path, we
came to a halt on a plain lonelier than roads
through desert places.

22   From its edge, where it borders on the
emptiness, to the foot of the high bank that keeps
on rising, a human body would measure three
lengths;

25   and as far as my eye could wing its flight, now
on the left, now on the right side, this ledge
seemed unvaried.

28   We had not yet moved our feet up there, when I
saw that the inner bank, which, rising straight up,
permitted no ascent,

esser di marmo candido e addorno   31
d'intagli sì, che non pur Policleto
ma la Natura lì avrebbe scorno.

    L'angel che venne in terra col decreto   34
de la molt' anni lagrimata pace,
ch'aperse il ciel del suo lungo divieto,

    dinanzi a noi pareva sì verace   37
quivi intagliato in un atto soave,
che non sembiava imagine che tace.

    Giurato si saria ch'el dicesse *"Ave!"*   40
perché iv' era imaginata quella
ch'ad aprir l'alto Amor volse la chiave,

    e avea in atto impressa esta favella   43
"Ecce ancilla Deï," propriamente
come figura in cera si suggella.

    "Non tener pur ad un loco la mente,"   46
disse 'l dolce maestro, che m'avea
da quella parte onde 'l cuore ha la gente.

    Per ch'i' mi mossi col viso, e vedea   49
di retro da Maria, da quella costa
onde m'era colui che mi movea,

    un'altra storia ne la roccia imposta;   52
per ch'io varcai Virgilio, e fe'mi presso,
acciò che fosse a li occhi miei disposta.

    Era intagliato lì nel marmo stesso   55
lo carro e ' buoi, traendo l'arca santa,
per che si teme officio non commesso.

    Dinanzi parea gente; e tutta quanta,   58
partita in sette cori, a' due mie' sensi
faceva dir l'un: "No," l'altro: "Sì, canta."

    Similemente al fummo de li 'ncensi   61
che v'era imaginato, li occhi e 'l naso
e al sì e al no discordi fensi.

    Lì precedeva al benedetto vaso,   64
trescando alzato, l'umile salmista,
e più e men che re era in quel caso.

    Di contra, effigïata ad una vista   67
d'un gran palazzo, Micòl ammirava
sì come donna dispettosa e trista.

31   was of white marble and adorned with such carvings that not only Polyclitus but even Nature would be put to scorn there.

34   The angel who came to earth with the decree of peace, for many years bewailed with tears, which opened Heaven after its long prohibition,

37   appeared before us so truly, carved there in his gentle bearing, that he did not seem a silent image.

40   One would have sworn that he was saying, "*Ave!*" for imaged there was she who turned the key to open the high Love,

43   and in her bearing was stamped this speech: "*Ecce ancilla Dei*," exactly as a figure is sealed in wax.

46   "Do not fix your mind on one place alone," said my sweet master, who had me on the side where people have their hearts.

49   Therefore I turned my eyes, and I saw behind Mary, on the side where he was who was prompting me,

52   another story carved in the rock; therefore I crossed beyond Virgil and drew near it, so that it would be wholly before my eyes.

55   There in the very marble was carved the wagon and the oxen drawing the holy Ark, because of which people fear offices not appointed.

58   Before it appeared people; and all of them, divided into seven choruses, made one of my two senses say: "No," the other: "Yes, they are singing."

61   Just so the smoke of the incense imaged there made eyes and nose discordant as to yes and no.

64   There, preceding the holy vessel, leaping with his robes girt up, was the humble Psalmist, and he was both more and less than king on that occasion.

67   Opposite, portrayed at a window of a great palace, Michal was gazing out like a disdainful, wicked woman.

I' mossi i piè del loco dov' io stava,   70
per avvisar da presso un'altra istoria
che di dietro a Micòl mi biancheggiava.

Quiv' era storïata l'alta gloria   73
del roman principato, il cui valore
mosse Gregorio a la sua gran vittoria:

i' dico di Traiano imperadore;   76
e una vedovella li era al freno,
di lagrime atteggiata e di dolore.

Intorno a lui parea calcato e pieno   79
di cavalieri, e l'aguglie ne l'oro
sovr' essi in vista al vento si movieno.

La miserella intra tutti costoro   82
pareva dir: "Segnor, fammi vendetta
di mio figliuol ch'è morto, ond' io m'accoro!"—

ed elli a lei rispondere: "Or aspetta   85
tanto ch'i' torni"—e quella: "Segnor mio,"
come persona in cui dolor s'affretta,

"se tu non torni?"—ed ei: "Chi fia dov' io,   88
la ti farà"—ed ella: "L'altrui bene
a te che fia, se 'l tuo metti in oblio?"—

ond' elli: "Or ti conforta; ch'ei convene   91
ch'i' solva il mio dovere anzi ch'i' mova:
giustizia vuole e pietà mi ritene."

Colui che mai non vide cosa nova   94
produsse esto visibile parlare,
novello a noi perché qui non si trova.

Mentr' io mi dilettava di guardare   97
l'imagini di tante umilitadi,
e per lo fabbro loro a veder care,

"Ecco di qua, ma fanno i passi radi,"   100
mormorava il poeta, "molte genti:
questi ne 'nvïeranno a li alti gradi."

Li occhi miei, ch'a mirare eran contenti   103
per veder novitadi, ond' e' son vaghi,
volgendosi ver' lui non furon lenti.

Non vo' però, lettor, che tu ti smaghi   106
di buon proponimento per udire
come Dio vuol che 'l debito si paghi.

70   I moved my feet from the place where I was standing, so as to see up close another story that shone white for me from behind Michal.

73   There was pictured the high glory of the Roman prince whose worth inspired Gregory to his great victory:

76   I mean of the emperor Trajan; and a poor widow woman was at his bridle, in an attitude of tears and grief.

79   Around him appeared a great crowding of horsemen, and above them the eagles in the gold seemed to be moving in the wind.

82   The wretched woman, among all these, seemed to be saying: "Lord, avenge my son who has been killed, so that I am broken-hearted!"—

85   and he to be replying: "Now wait until I return" —and she: "My lord," as a person speaks in whom sorrow is urgent,

88   "if you do not return?"—and he: "Whoever will be in my place will do it for you"—and she: "What will another's good be to you, if you forget your own?"—

91   then he: "Now be comforted; for it is fitting that I fulfill my duty before I move: justice demands it and compassion holds me here."

94   He in whose sight nothing is new produced this visible speech, novel to us because it is not found here.

97   While I was delighting to see the images of so many humilities, precious to see also because of their maker,

100   "Behold on this side, but their steps are slow," murmured my poet, "many people: these will send us to the ascending steps."

103   My eyes, content to gaze in order to see new things, which they desire, were not slow in turning toward him.

106   But I do not wish you, reader, to be dismayed in your good intention, when you hear how God wills that the debt be paid.

Non attender la forma del martìre: 109
pensa la succession, pensa ch'al peggio
oltre la gran sentenza non può ire.

  Io cominciai: "Maestro, quel ch'io veggio   112
muovere a noi, non mi sembian persone,
e non so che, sì nel veder vaneggio."

  Ed elli a me: "La grave condizione   115
di lor tormento a terra li rannicchia,
sì che ' miei occhi pria n'ebber tencione.

  Ma guarda fiso là, e disviticchia   118
col viso quel che vien sotto a quei sassi:
già scorger puoi come ciascun si picchia."

  O superbi cristian, miseri lassi,   121
che, de la vista de la mente infermi,
fidanza avete ne' retrosi passi,

  non v'accorgete voi che noi siam vermi   124
nati a formar l'angelica farfalla
che vola a la giustizia sanza schermi?

  Di che l'animo vostro in alto galla,   127
poi siete quasi antomata in difetto,
sì come vermo in cui formazion falla?

  Come per sostentar solaio o tetto   130
per mensola talvolta una figura
si vede giugner le ginocchia al petto,

  la qual fa del non ver vera rancura   133
nascere 'n chi la vede: così fatti
vid' io color, quando puosi ben cura.

  Vero è che più e meno eran contratti   136
secondo ch'avien più e meno a dosso,
e qual più pazïenza avea ne li atti

  piangendo parea dicer: "Più non posso."   139

109   Do not regard the form of the suffering: think what follows it, think that at worst it cannot go beyond the great Judgment.

112   I began: "Master, what I see moving toward us do not seem to be persons, and I know not what, my sight is so confused."

115   And he to me: "The heavy condition of their torment buckles them toward the earth, so that my eyes at first had to struggle.

118   But gaze fixedly there, and disentangle with your eyes what comes under those stones: already you can make out how each is beating his breast."

121   O proud Christians, weary wretches, who, weak in mental vision, put your faith in backward steps,

124   do you not perceive that we are worms born to form the angelic butterfly that flies to justice without a shield?

127   Why is it that your spirit floats on high, since you are like defective insects, like worms in whom formation is lacking?

130   As to support a ceiling or a roof we sometimes see for corbel a figure that touches knees to breast,

133   so that what is not real causes real discomfort to be born in whoever sees it: so I saw them to be, when I looked carefully.

136   It is true that they were more and less compressed according as they had more and less upon their backs, and he whose bearing showed the most patience

139   weeping seemed to say: "I can bear no more."

NOTES

1-4. When we were . . . resounding: The loud closing of the gate recalls the sounds of its opening (9.133-46) and reinforces the solemnity.

2-3. in disuse . . . seem straight: The rarity of souls entering Purgatory is a recurrent lament (cf. 9.137-38, with note, 12.95-96, and the note to line 16).

3. the twisted way: Cf. *Inf.* 1.3, "the straight way." The process of purgation will be described in terms of unwinding and untwisting: "climbing and turning about the mountain that straightens [those] whom the world twisted" (23.125-26; cf. Is. 40.4, in the note to lines 20-21).

5-6. if I had turned . . . for the fault: Cf. 9.131-32, also based on Luke 9.62: "No man putting his hand to the plough, and looking back, is fit for the kingdom of God." Cf. *Inf.* 15.13-15, with note.

7-16. We were climbing . . . that needle's eye: Some have supposed the rock to be literally moving, others that the two sides of the cleft alternately diverge and converge. But the entire cleft is to be understood as changing direction, and that it is a *cruna* [needle's eye] excludes divergence of the walls: the way is narrow, steep, and crooked.

14-16. the hollow moon . . . needle's eye: Cf. the note to 9.1-9. In 9.43 the sun was more than two hours high (about 8 A.M.). The waning moon, four or five days past full (according to *Inf.* 20.128, the moon was full Thursday night; it is now Monday), would rise at this season at about 10 P.M. and would set at about 10 A.M.: the wayfarers reach the terrace after 10 A.M. Note the echoes of *Inf.* 15.19-21.

16. that needle's eye: Matt. 19.24: "It is easier for a camel to pass through the eye of a needle than for a rich man to enter the kingdom of Heaven" (and cf. *Inf.* 15.21); as so often, Dante has in mind Matt. 7.14 (see the note to 4.19-24).

18. where the mountain gathers itself back: By attributing conscious agency to the mountain, the trope emphasizes the difference of this ledge from anything humanly fashioned.

20-21. a plain . . . desert places: Is. 40.3-4 (quoted in Matt. 3.3, Mark 1.3, Luke 3.4-6, John 1.23): "The voice of one crying in the *desert*: prepare ye the *way* of the Lord, make straight in the *wilderness* [*solitudine*] the paths of our God" (italics indicate words echoed by Dante); cf. also the note to 6.37-39.

28-99. We had not . . . because of their maker: The examples in Purgatory proper are drawn from NT, OT, pagan history; the first example of the virtues is always the Virgin. For their function, see Additional Notes 6 and 12. The theme of humility has close parallels in the three panels. All three juxtapose a woman with a monarch: in the case of the first, with the messenger of the monarch; in two cases the monarch's humility is the focus; in two the woman's humility and virtue win the monarch to relent. All three of the panels seem audible, an effect that is gradually intensified. For the political implications, see *Inter cantica* below.

29-30. inner bank . . . no ascent: The carvings are vertical both because they must be seen by the crouching souls and because in them humility is being exalted, while pride is trodden underfoot (in Canto 12); see Additional Note 6. (The text is confused here; see "Textual Variants," p. 628.)

31-32. not only Polyclitus but even Nature: Nature as imitating God, man as imitating Nature. With Phidias, Polyclitus (fifth century B.C.) was the most famous sculptor of antiquity; Dante knew of him from Cicero and other ancient authors, as well as from medieval sources. This passage is an early form of a favorite Renaissance topos: the rivalry between art and nature (cf. *Inf.* 11.97-111).

34-45. The angel . . . sealed in wax: The first panel draws on Luke 1.26-38:

> And the angel [Gabriel], being come in, said unto her: Hail [*Ave*], full of grace, the Lord is with thee: blessed art thou among women . . . And the angel said to her: Fear not, Mary, for thou hast found grace with God. Behold thou shalt conceive in thy womb, and shalt bring forth a son . . . And Mary said to the angel: How shall this be done, because I know not man? And the angel, answering, said to her: The Holy Ghost shall come upon thee, and the power of the most High shall overshadow thee . . . And Mary said: Behold the handmaid of the Lord [*Ecce ancilla Domini*]; be it done to me according to thy word. And the angel departed from her.

(The angel also informs Mary that her cousin Elizabeth is pregnant with the child that will become John the Baptist.) The phrases Dante quotes enclose the entire incident, from the angel's "Ave" to Mary's final acquiescence.

34-40. The angel . . . *Ave*: The angel is the first figure described (and the only non-human in the three scenes), so as to emphasize God's taking the initiative (the idea is explicit in 11.7-9); the order, from left to right, reflects the usual placing of the angel and Mary in medieval art (see fig. 5). That the figures do not seem silent is offered as the highest possible praise.

34-36. the decree . . . long prohibition: The scene is introduced by a statement of its place in history. The "decree of peace" is that of the Incarnation, imagined as issued in the court of "that Emperor on high" (*Inf.* 1.124; cf. *Conv.* 4.5.3). It will reconcile man and God, estranged by Adam and Eve's sin (a long tradition noted that "Ave" reverses "Eva"); humanity has yearned for this peace for many years, has wept at its absence. For "the long prohibition" see *Inf.* 4.47-60, *Purg.* 6.28-42 with notes.

41-45. for imaged . . . sealed in wax: The Virgin "turned the key to open the high [i.e., God's] Love," because of her perfection, including her humility. For the keys, cf. *Inf.* 13.58-61 and *Purg.* 9.118-29, with notes.

43-45. in her bearing . . . sealed in wax: The Virgin's "*Ecce ancilla Domini*," which implies the rest of her speech in Luke 1.38, expresses a humility so complete that it permeates her bearing. For Dante the Virgin was without sin; the doctrine of the Immaculate Conception (i.e., that the Virgin was conceived by her parents without inheriting Original Sin) was widely held in the Middle Ages, though not promulgated until the nineteenth century: her soul imposes its form on her body as completely as if her body were wax (see 25.37-108, with notes).

47-53. on the side . . . beyond Virgil: At first the pilgrim is to Virgil's left; he looks to the right, sees the next carving, and passes beyond Virgil, who is finally to the pilgrim's left.

55-69. There . . . wicked woman: The second scene is also historically significant, for King David's transporting of the Ark of the Covenant to Jerusalem sealed the union of the northern and southern tribes under the single monarchy. The founding of the unified kingdom was in Dante's eyes parallel to the founding of Rome; in *Conv.* 4.5.6 he claims that David was born when Aeneas arrived in Italy (an idea derived from Latini's *Trésor*: Scott 1972); thus David is linked to Trajan.

> And David danced [Lat. *saltabat*] with all his might before the Lord: and David was girt with a linen ephod. And when the ark of the Lord was come into the city of David, Michal the daughter of Saul, looking out through a window, saw David leaping and dancing before the Lord: and she despised [Lat. *despexit*] him in her heart (2 Sam. 6.13-16).

56-57. the wagon . . . not appointed: An ox-drawn wagon was built for the Ark. On the road to Jerusalem, the oxen strayed, and Uzzah steadied the Ark with his hand; for his presumption (line 57) he was struck dead (1 Chron. 13.9). Dante defends himself against this parallel and a similar charge in *Ep.* 11.5.

58-63. all of them . . . yes and no: Although the sense of hearing says the choruses are not audible ("No"), the eyes say they are ("Yes"). Note the progression: two individuals in the first carving, seven choruses in this one. The same disagreement occurs between the eyes and the sense of smell.

64-66. There, preceding . . . that occasion: "The *trescone* is a lively, jumping dance (see *Inf.* 14.40)" (Singleton). Dante is translating the Vulgate's *saltabat* [was dancing or leaping]. The Psalmist (David) was less than king in setting aside his dignity, more than king in his humility and ecstasy.

67-69. Opposite . . . wicked woman: Dante's "dispettosa" [scornful] adapts the Vulgate's *despexit* (both verbs imply *looking down on*). Michal's scorn is vivid in 2 Sam. 6.20-23:

And Michal the daughter of Saul coming out to meet David, said: How glorious was the king of Israel today, uncovering himself before the handmaids of his servants, and was naked, as if one of the buffoons should be naked. And David said to Michal: Before the Lord . . . I will both play and make myself meaner than I have done: . . . and with the handmaids of whom thou speakest, I shall appear more glorious. Therefore Michal the daughter of Saul had no child to the day of her death.

(David was "naked" because he had girt up his long skirts in order to dance.) Dante has thought carefully about the connections between these texts, noticing the contrast between the barren Michal and Mary (cf. "handmaid" [*ancilla*] in both).

67. Opposite: As we learn from line 72 ("behind Michal"), the figure of Michal is at the right side of the carving.

72. shone white for me: Again the emphasis (as in line 55) on the whiteness of the marble; cf 9.2, of the dawn.

73-93. There was pictured . . . holds me here: The third scene is the famous story of the emperor Trajan and the widow, which appears in the various lives of Gregory the Great (see Colgrave 1968) and in other texts that Dante knew, such as the *Golden Legend* and John of Salisbury's *Policraticus*. According to the legend, the pope was impressed by a sculpture in the Forum of Trajan depicting a charitable action of the emperor; he prayed so fervently for Trajan's salvation that Trajan was brought back to life long enough to embrace faith in Christ (Dante refers to the story also in *Par.* 20.43-48 and 100-117). (The legend may refer to Trajan's Column, misread, and Dante may have the column in mind; see Vickers 1983.)

73-74. the high glory . . . prince: The phrase refers both to the pomp surrounding the emperor and to his humility, his higher glory: he ranks the claims of justice and mercy (line 93) above pomp.

79-81. Around him . . . in the wind: Trajan led many military campaigns in person. Dante's evocation of the crowded scene may allude to the crowded scenes characteristic of Giovanni Pisano (see Ayrton 1969).

80-81. the eagles . . . in the wind: Dante imagines the imperial eagles as figured on golden banners; flags were in fact a European borrowing from Islam: the eagles of the Roman legions were castings atop standards.

83-93. Lord, avenge . . . holds me here: The story had been retold many times: it is impossible to determine which of the many versions Dante used. In the *Fiore e vita di filosafi*, a Tuscan translation (after 1264) of parts of Vincent of Beauvais' *Speculum historiale*, it reads:

A widow came and grasped his foot, and tenderly weeping begged and required him to do justice on those that had killed a son of hers, who had been most virtuous and without fault. And he spoke and said to her: I will satisfy you when I return.—And she said: And if you do not return?—And he replied: My successor will satisfy you.—And she said: How do I know that? And supposing he does, what good will it do you if that other man does good? You owe it to me, and according to your works will you be rewarded. It is fraud not to wish to give someone what is owed him. Your successor will have his own responsibilities toward those who receive injury. Another's justice does not relieve your obligation; and your successor will be fortunate if he carries out his own (Segre and Marti 1959).

Note that Dante places the widow at Trajan's bridle; cf. 6.91-99, 13.37 and 42.

91-93. Now be comforted . . . holds me here: The emperor's humility is expressed by his submitting to justice and duty, as well as by his compassion for the importunate widow. The representative of God's power in the political realm, Trajan embodies the two principles of God's dealings with man, justice and mercy (see *Par.* 7.103-20, 19.13).

94-96. He in whose . . . found here: God, the "ancient of days," is the author of these carvings with their "visible speech": renewed insistence that the imagined dialogue derives from sight alone. Note the association of novelty with artistic excellence (see Additional Note 7).

97-99. While I . . . their maker: The pilgrim's delight in the carvings stems both from the beauty of the virtue represented and the beauty of the representation itself, which requires that one love the artist (cf. 26.112-14, with note): another idea directly applicable to human art.

100. on this side: Since Virgil is on the pilgrim's left (lines 47-54), the souls are approaching from that side; they are circling the mountain counterclockwise. This means that they will see the carvings in the same order as the pilgrim.

106-11. But I do not . . . great Judgment: The third address to the reader (see the note to 8.19-26), suggesting that the punishment will be very severe; it is one of the principal passages in which Dante writes of the temporal punishment for sin as a debt [*debito*] to be paid.

110-11. at worst . . . great Judgment: After the Resurrection of the Dead and the ensuing Last Judgment, Purgatory will be abolished.

112-17. Master, what . . . had to struggle: The difficulty of perceiving, experienced here by both the pilgrim and Virgil, contrasts sharply with the clarity of the carvings, to which no ambiguity is attached (cf. line 122).

115-20. The heavy condition . . . his breast: The souls are bent under stones, ritually beating their breasts (see the note to 9.108-10). This seems a better reading than that God's justice is beating the souls metaphorically.

121-29. O proud Christians . . . is lacking: The denunciation of the proud as blind to the goal of human existence, which requires radical change from earthly values, makes explicit a central motif of the *Comedy*: spiritual change as metamorphosis. The analogy is with insects, whose first phase (*vermo* [worm], lines 124 and 129) is defective, lacking form. On man as worm, Singleton quotes Job 25.6, Ps. 21.7, and Augustine *In Ioannem* 1.13: "All men born of the flesh, what are they but worms? And of them he makes angels." Cf. Augustine's *De serm. Dom.* 1.12: "that change into angelic form that is promised after this life." Dante's brilliant adaptation of the attraction of the moth to the flame has the angelic butterfly survive the fire (cf. 9.28-33). In Hell (*Inf.* 7.53-54; 24.99-111; 25.49-66 and 91-138; 30.49-57; 34.34-36), metamorphoses go downward; now they will go upward.

130-35. As to support . . . looked carefully: The penitent souls are compared to corbels and capitals in the shape of crouching figures, called "Telamones," common in Romanesque and Gothic buildings (see fig. 6). Note the emphasis on empathic response to the "feigned discomfort" (see Additional Note 7).

138. whose bearing showed the most patience: There has been dispute over whether *pazienza* should be taken to mean "patience" (even the most patient of the souls seemed at the limit of his strength) or suffering (the souls apparently suffering the most seemed at the limit of their strength). The former seems more likely. The translation of gesture into words is parallel with lines 37-45.

Inter cantica. The terrace of pride corresponds to the circle of heretics (*Inf.* 9.109–11.115), the first within the walls of Dis. There are many parallels, including the unexpected absence of visible figures on first entrance, after the exciting events of previous cantos (*Inf.* 9.109-15; *Purg.* 10.19-27). Farinata's obstinate pride is contrasted with the vertically aligned examples of humility (from the foot of Farinata's sarcophagus, the pilgrim looks up at him: *Inf.* 10.40), as well as with the bent-over figures of the penitents. Farinata's bearing expresses his "cervice superba" [proud neck] (*Purg.* 11.54); he seems to have Hell "in gran dispitto" [in great disdain] (*Inf.* 10.36): Michal is "dispettosa" [disdainful] (*Purg.* 10.68). If *Inferno* 9-10 are dominated by the image of the sarcophagi of the heretics, the penitent proud have escaped confinement, and it is as if they carry the stones that almost trapped them (cf. the motif of enclosure in *Inferno* 32 and 33, and see the note to *Inf.* 32.22-25 and the *Inter cantica* to *Purgatorio* 11, 12, and 19).

The parallels with *Inferno* 10 involve the political theme that has dominated the Ante-Purgatorio: Dante viewed the pride of the magnates as a major cause of civil wars and resistance to imperial authority; meditation on the relation between the Roman Empire and the ancestry of Christ (David, whom Dante thought contemporary with Aeneas) is part of the learning of political humility.

CANTO 11

"O padre nostro che ne' cieli stai,   1
non circunscritto, ma per più amore
ch'ai primi effetti di là sù hai,

    laudato sia 'l tuo nome e 'l tuo valore   4
da ogne creatura, com' è degno
di render grazie al tuo dolce vapore.

    Vegna ver' noi la pace del tuo regno,   7
ché noi ad essa non potem da noi,
s'ella non vien, con tutto nostro ingegno.

    Come del suo voler li angeli tuoi   10
fan sacrificio a te, cantando *osanna,*
così facciano li uomini de' suoi.

    Dà oggi a noi la cotidiana manna,   13
sanza la qual per questo aspro diserto
a retro va chi più di gir s'affanna.

    E come noi lo mal ch'avem sofferto   16
perdoniamo a ciascuno, e tu perdona
benigno, e non guardar lo nostro merto.

    Nostra virtù, che di legger s'adona,   19
non spermentar con l'antico avversaro,
ma libera da lui che sì la sprona.

    Quest' ultima preghiera, segnor caro,   22
già non si fa per noi, ché non bisogna,
ma per color che dietro a noi restaro."

    Così a sé e noi buona ramogna   25
quell' ombre orando, andavan sotto 'l pondo,
simile a quel che talvolta si sogna,

    disparmente angosciate tutte a tondo   28
e lasse su per la prima cornice,
purgando la caligine del mondo.

CANTO 11

1   "O our Father who are in the heavens, not circumscribed, but because of the greater love you bear those first effects up there,

4   praised be your Name and your Power by every creature, for it is fitting to give thanks to your sweet Spirit.

7   Let the peace of your kingdom come to us, for we cannot attain to it by ourselves, if it does not come, with all our wit.

10   As the angels sacrifice their wills to you, singing *Hosanna*, so let men do with theirs.

13   Give us this day our daily manna, without which in this harsh wilderness he goes backwards who most strives forward.

16   And as we forgive all others for the evil we have suffered, do you forgive us lovingly, and do not regard our merit.

19   Our strength, which is easily subdued, do not tempt with the ancient adversary, but free it from him who spurs it so.

22   This last prayer, dear Lord, we do not make for ourselves, since there is no need, but for those who have stayed behind."

25   Thus begging good progress for themselves and for us, those shades walked bearing burdens like those we sometimes dream of,

28   variously anguished and weary, all of them, around and around on the first ledge, purging the dark mists of the world.

Se di là sempre ben per noi si dice,   31
da qua che dire e far per lor si puote
da quei c'hanno al voler buona radice?

   Ben si de' loro atar lavar le note   34
che portar quinci, sì che mondi e lievi
possano uscire a le stellate ruote.

   "Deh, se giustizia e pietà vi disgrievi   37
tosto sì che possiate muover l'ala,
che secondo il disio vostro vi lievi,

   mostrate da qual mano inver' la scala   40
si va più corto; e se c'è più d'un varco,
quel ne 'nsegnate che men erto cala,

   ché questi che vien meco, per lo 'ncarco   43
de la carne d'Adamo onde si veste,
al montar sù, contra sua voglia, è parco."

   Le lor parole che rendero a queste   46
che dette avea colui cu' io seguiva
non fur da cui venisser manifeste,

   ma fu detto: "A man destra per la riva   49
con noi venite, e troverete il passo
possibile a salir persona viva.

   E s'io non fossi impedito dal sasso   52
che la cervice mia superba doma,
onde portar convienmi il viso basso,

   cotesti, ch'ancor vive e non si noma,   55
guardere' io, per veder s'i' 'l conosco
e per farlo pietoso a questa soma.

   Io fui latino e nato d'un gran Tosco: 58
Guiglielmo Aldobrandesco fu mio padre;
non so se 'l nome suo già mai fu vosco.

   L'antico sangue e l'opere leggiadre   61
d'i miei maggior me fer sì arrogante
che, non pensando a la comune madre,

   ogn' uomo ebbi in despetto tanto avante   64
ch'io ne mori', come i Sanesi sanno,
e sallo in Campagnatico ogne fante.

   Io sono Omberto; e non pur a me danno   67
superbia fe', ché tutti miei consorti
ha ella tratti seco nel malanno.

31   If there they always call blessings on us, back here what can be said and done for them, by those who have their will securely rooted?

34   Surely we must help them wash away the marks they took hence, so that, cleansed and light, they can go forth to the starry wheels.

37   "Ah, so may justice and mercy soon unburden you and let you move your wings, and may they lift you according to your desire,

40   show us on what hand the stairway can be found most quickly; and if there is more than one crossing, teach us which has the gentler slope;

43   for he who comes with me, because of the burden of Adam's flesh that clothes him, against his will is slow to climb."

46   The words with which they answered these spoken by my leader came from a source not manifest,

49   but this was said: "Come with us to the right along the bank, and you will find a pass possible for a living person to climb.

52   And were I not impeded by the stone that tames my proud neck, so that I must keep my eyes turned down,

55   I would look at this man who is still alive and is unnamed, to see if I know him and to make him have pity on this burden.

58   I was Italian, born of a great Tuscan: Guglielmo Aldobrandesco was my father; I know not if his name was ever known to you.

61   The ancient blood and noble works of my ancestors made me so arrogant that, forgetting our common mother,

64   I looked down on every man so much that I died for it, as the Sienese know, and every child in Campagnatico knows it.

67   I am Omberto; and pride has harmed not only me, for all my consorts it has drawn into misfortune.

   E qui convien ch'io questo peso porti   70
per lei, tanto che a Dio si sodisfaccia,
poi ch'io nol fe' tra ' vivi, qui tra ' morti."

   Ascoltando chinai in giù la faccia;   73
e un di lor, non questi che parlava,
si torse sotto il peso che li 'mpaccia

   e videmi e conobbemi e chiamava,   76
tenendo li occhi con fatica fisi
a me che tutto chin con loro andava.

   "Oh!" diss' io lui, "non se' tu Oderisi,   79
l'onor d'Agobbio e l'onor di quell'arte
ch'alluminar chiamata è in Parisi?"

   "Frate," diss' elli, "più ridon le carte   82
che pennelleggia Franco Bolognese;
l'onore è tutto or suo, e mio in parte.

   Ben non sare' io stato sì cortese   85
mentre ch'io vissi, per lo gran disio
de l'eccellenza ove mio core intese.

   Di tal superbia qui si paga il fio;   88
e ancor non sarei qui, se non fosse
che, possendo peccar, mi volsi a Dio.

   Oh vana gloria de l'umane posse!   91
com' poco verde in su la cima dura,
se non è giunta da l'etati grosse!

   Credette Cimabue ne la pittura   94
tener lo campo, e ora ha Giotto il grido,
sì che la fama di colui è scura.

   Così ha tolto l'uno a l'altro Guido   97
la gloria de la lingua, e forse è nato
chi l'uno e l'altro caccerà del nido.

   Non è il mondan romore altro ch'un fiato   100
di vento, ch'or vien quinci e or vien quindi,
e muta nome perché muta lato.

   Che voce avrai tu più, se vecchia scindi   103
da te la carne, che se fossi morto
anzi che tu lasciassi il 'pappo' e 'l 'dindi,'

70   And because of it I must bear this weight here
among the dead until God is satisfied, since I did
not do it among the living."

73   Listening, I bent down my face; and one of
them, not the one who was speaking, twisted
under the weight that hampers them,

76   and saw me and knew me and was calling,
struggling to keep his eyes on me as all bent over I
walked along with them.

79   "Oh!" I said to him, "Are you not Oderisi, the
honor of Gubbio, and the honor of that art called
illumination in Paris?"

82   "Brother," he said, "the pages touched by
Franco of Bologna's brush, laugh more; the honor
is now all his, and mine in part.

85   I would certainly not have been so generous
while I lived, because of the great desire of
supremacy that my heart was intent on.

88   Here we pay the toll for such pride: and I would
not be here yet, were it not that while still able to
sin I turned to God.

91   Oh vain glory of human powers! how briefly it
stays green at the summit, if it is not followed by
cruder ages!

94   Cimabue believed he held the field in painting,
and now Giotto has the cry, so that the fame of the
first is darkened.

97   Just so, one Guido has taken from the other the
glory of our language, and perhaps he is born who
will drive both of them from the nest.

100   The clamor of the world is nothing but a breath
of wind that comes now from here and now from
there, and changes names because it changes
directions.

103   What more acclaim will you have if you strip off
your flesh when it is old, than if you had died
before you left off saying 'pappo' and 'dindi,'

pria che passin mill' anni? ch'è più corto   106
spazio a l'etterno ch'un muover di ciglia
al cerchio che più tardi in cielo è torto.

  Colui che del cammin sì poco piglia   109
dinanzi a me Toscana sonò tutta;
e ora a pena in Siena sen pispiglia,

  ond' era sire quando fu distrutta   112
la rabbia fiorentina, che superba
fu a quel tempo sì com' ora è putta.

  La vostra nominanza è color d'erba   115
che viene e va, e quei la discolora
per cui ella esce de la terra acerba."

  E io a lui: "Tuo vero dir m'incora   118
bona umiltà, e gran tumor m'appiani;
ma chi è quei di cui tu parlavi ora?"

  "Quelli è," rispuose, "Provenzan Salvani,   121
ed è qui perché fu presuntüoso
a recar Siena tutta a le sue mani.

  Ito è così e va, sanza riposo,   124
poi che morì; cotal moneta rende
a sodisfar chi è di là troppo oso."

  E io: "Se quello spirito ch'attende,   127
pria che si penta, l'orlo de la vita
là giù dimora e qua sù non ascende,

  se buona orazïon lui non aita,   130
prima che passi tempo quanto visse,
come fu la venuta lui largita?"

  "Quando vivea più glorïoso," disse,   133
"liberamente nel Campo di Siena,
ogne vergogna diposta, s'affisse;

  e lì, per trar l'amico suo di pena   136
ch'e' sostenea ne la prigion di Carlo,
si condusse a tremar per ogne vena.

  Più non dirò, e scuro so che parlo,   139
ma poco tempo andrà, che ' tuoi vicini
faranno sì che tu potrai chiosarlo.

  Quest'opera li tolse quei confini."   142

106   before a thousand years have passed? which is a briefer space compared with eternity than the blinking of an eye to the circle that turns slowest in the sky.

109   He who takes such short steps in front of me, all Tuscany resounded with; now they hardly whisper of him in Siena,

112   where he was master when the Florentine rage was destroyed, as proud in that time as now it is whorish.

115   Your renown is the color of grass that comes and goes, and he makes it fade who brings it unripe out of the earth."

118   And I to him: "Your true words instill good humility in my heart, and you reduce a great swelling in me; but who is he of whom you spoke just now?"

121   "He is," he replied, "Provenzano Salvani; and he is here because he presumed to bring all Siena into his own hands.

124   He has walked like that, and still walks, without rest, since he died; this is the coin which must be paid by whoever presumed too much back there."

127   And I: "If a spirit that delays, before repenting, until the very rim of life, must stay down there and not come up here,

130   if good prayer does not help it, for as long a time as it lived, how was he allowed to come here?"

133   "When he was living in greatest glory," he replied, "freely, in the Campo at Siena, laying aside all shame, he took his stand;

136   and there, to free his friend from the punishment he was suffering in Charles's prison, he brought himself to tremble in every vein.

139   I will say no more, and I know my saying is obscure; but not much time will pass before your neighbors will act so that you can gloss it.

142   This deed set him free from those confines."

NOTES

1-24. O our Father . . . stayed behind: An expanded paraphrase of the Lord's Prayer (Matt. 6.9-13), of which the classic discussion is Augustine's *De serm. Dom.* 2.15-39, along with his *Epistle* 130 (they are the only authorities Aquinas cites in *ST* 2a 2ae, q. 83, a. 9). For Augustine it includes everything prayer may rightly ask (*Ep.* 130): "If you run through all the words of the [biblical] prayers, you will find nothing, I think, that is not contained and completed in the Lord's Prayer. Thus it is permitted to use these or other words, as long as we say the same things when we pray; but it must not be permitted to say different things." The exegetes follow Augustine in distinguishing seven petitions in the prayer, the first three valid eternally, the last four only in this life. He saw it as a particular remedy against pride (*De serm. Dom.* 2.16): "Here rich men and those of noble birth in the eyes of the world are admonished, once they have become Christians, not to act proudly toward the poor and those of common birth; for all together address God as *our Father*: which they cannot truthfully and devoutly do unless they know each other to be brothers" (cf. *Ep.* 130. 23).

Paraphrases were authorized by Augustine's "these or other words"; for Italian examples, see Monaci/Arese 1955, No. 67, De Luca 1951. Dante's stresses the respects in which the Lord's Prayer enjoins humility, most of them going back to Augustine (see Additional Note 6).

1-3. O our Father . . . effects up there: Paraphrasing "Our Father which art in Heaven" (Matt. 6.9).

2. not circumscribed: God's being "in the heavens" is not to be taken as limiting him (cf. *Par.* 14.30); the observation appears in Augustine's *De serm. Dom.*

2-3. because . . . effects up there: That God loves the angels more than man (cf. *Par.* 1.3-4) is not in Augustine's or Thomas' discussions of Matt. 6.9. The angels were the first things created; in Augustine's reading of Gen. 1.1: "heaven" refers to the angels, "earth" to all else.

4-6. praised . . . sweet Spirit: Cf. "hallowed be thy name" (Matt. 6.9). All the persons of the Trinity ("your Name," "Power," and "Spirit") are addressed. Dante is drawing on Psalm 148, which calls on all creation to praise God, perhaps also on St. Francis of Assisi's "Cantico di frate Sole."

6. it is fitting to give thanks: The Preface of the Mass, just before the Canon, begins: "Truly it is fitting and just, equitable and healthgiving, always to give thanks to you . . ." (cf. 2 Thess. 1.3).

7-9. Let the peace . . . all our wit: Cf. "thy kingdom come [adveniat]" (Matt. 6.10). Dante's interpretation of the prefix *ad* on the verb also follows Augustine's reading of the verse (cf. *Mon.* 3.16.7).

9. with all our wit: The phrase seems aimed at the problem of pride in artistic genius, for which *ingegno* [wit] is Dante's normal word.

10-12. As the angels . . . with theirs: Cf. "thy will be done, as in heaven so on earth" (Matt. 6.10). The sacrifice of individual will is central; like Augustine, Dante is thinking of Matt. 26.39: "My father, if it be possible, let this chalice pass from me. Nevertheless, not as I will, but as thou wilt."

13-15. Give us . . . strives forward: Cf. "Give us this day our superessential bread" (Matt. 6.11), conflated with Luke 11.3 ("our daily bread"). Following Augustine, the exegetes saw three kinds of "bread" in this verse: physical food, spiritual nourishment in general, the Eucharist. For the souls in Purgatory, the first meaning applies, renewing the analogy with the Desert of Sinai (see note to 10.20-21); for manna, see Ex. 16.13-21, 31-35; John 6.30-40.

15. he goes backward . . . strives forward: Self-willed striving goes backward; cf. 10.123.

16-18. as we forgive . . . our merit: Cf. "and forgive us our debts, as we forgive our debtors" (Matt. 6.12), again with a reversal of the order (drawing on Matt. 6.14-15).

18. do not regard our merit: Their sins have already been forgiven, and only this last part of the terzina is strictly applicable to these souls: they are begging for imputed merit, as opposed to what is properly their own (satisfaction does depend on merit).

19-21. Our strength . . . spurs it so: Cf. "and lead us not into temptation, but deliver us from [the evil one]" (Matt. 6.13). These two petitions were regarded as one in the traditional exegesis. Augustine interprets "lead us not into" as "let us not be overcome by"; Dante gives it a weaker meaning. Augustine discusses temptation in *De serm. Dom.* 2: the devil is permitted to tempt us so that our strength may be perfected.

20-21. with the ancient . . . free it from him: Rheinfelder 1966 observed that this reading of Matt. 6.13 is unusual: in the West it was customary to take *malo* as neuter, "evil"; Dante here takes it as masculine: "the evil one," as was usual in the Greek church.

22-26. This last prayer . . . and for us: Some commentators take "this last prayer" to refer to the last four petitions (those in lines 13-21), applicable exclusively to this life. But the reference is to lines 19-21: "prayer" is singular, and lines 13-18 are adapted to Purgatory. "Those . . . behind" are the living, perhaps also those in Ante-Purgatory. These lines state a position contrary to the usual one (as in *ST* 2a 2ae, q. 83, a. 11 ad 3), which denied that souls in Purgatory pray for the living.

25. progress: The derivation and meaning of *ramogna* are uncertain. We follow Buti and Benvenuto, who derive it from *ramo* [oar].

26-27. bearing burdens . . . dream of: The nightmare of suffocation by a great weight, known as *incubus.*

30. dark mists: *Caligine* means both "darkness" and "mist": pride darkens understanding; cf. 10.121-22.

31-36. If there . . . starry wheels: Rounding out this first section of the canto, Dante states the traditional responsibility of the living to help the souls in Purgatory. He adds gratitude as a motive (see the note to lines 22-26). Mention of the stars invokes the entire cosmos and the ascent to Paradise.

33. those who . . . securely rooted: Those whose wills are rooted in God's will, those in a state of grace; cf. 4.133-34, 8.71-72.

37-45. Ah, so may . . . slow to climb: Virgil appeals to the souls' desire to complete their purgation, contrasting their penance with the idea of flight (cf. "light," line 35).

37. justice and mercy: The unvarying principles of God's actions, see the note on 10.91-93.

43-44. the burden of Adam's flesh: The phrase connects the pilgrim with these bearers of weights: he is one "carrying about his mortality" (see Additional Note 6). For Adam, cf. 9.10-11.

46-72. The words . . . among the living: This first speaker is Omberto Aldobrandeschi (line 59); the pilgrim cannot see who is speaking (lines 48 and 53-54). Why it is Omberto who answers is not stated, but his words show his desire to be pitied and helped by the living (lines 56-57).

49-50. Come with us to the right: The regular direction of circling the mountain, opposite to that in Hell, where turns are to the left (except in *Inf.* 9.132).

52-54. were I not . . . turned down: The weight on Omberto prevents him from even turning his head; the implication is that he cannot see the examples of humility yet, only those of pride punished (12.16-69). Here and in lines 70-72, Omberto speaks of his burden as imposed; he uses the language of *satisfaction* (paying the temporal penalty for sin); see the note on 12.1.

56-57. to see . . . this burden: In these and the following lines it is clear that although he is struggling with it Omberto has not progressed very far in overcoming his pride.

58-60. I was . . . known to you: Guglielmo Aldobrandeschi (d. 1254) was descended from a powerful family who dominated large domains in the Maremma; they were allied with Florence against Siena, other Ghibelline cities, and the emperor Frederick II. Guglielmo was so famous that Omberto has been suspected of false modesty in line 60.

61-69. The ancient blood . . . into misfortune: Omberto exemplifies pride in noble birth. There are conflicting accounts of his death in 1259 in Campagnatico (see map, p. xii), at the hands of the Sienese: that he was suffocated in his bed by hired assassins, that he fought singlehandedly in the public square until his horse was killed under him.

63. our common mother: This is of course Eve. "When Adam delved and Eve span / Who was then the gentleman?" Social classes arose long after. That we all descend from Eve is here adduced as a reason for humility, of course.

66. every child: *Fante* can mean both "child" and "footsoldier"; we take the line to mean that Omberto's story is told to children in Campagnatico as a warning against pride.

70-72. because of it . . . among the living: The terminology of satisfaction; see the note to lines 52-54.

73-142. Listening, I bent . . . those confines: The interview with Oderisi occupies almost half the canto; Oderisi and Provenzano Salvani, whom Oderisi points out, are instances of pride in artistic achievement and political power, respectively. Dante especially shares the first of these, but we can infer from the enmity his political career aroused that he was no stranger to the latter (see 13.133-38).

73-78. Listening, I bent . . . along with them: Lines 73 and 78 emphasize the pilgrim's adoption of the bodily posture of the pentitents and his going "along with them": to some extent he shares the penance. Note the intensity of Oderisi's effort to see the pilgrim: he can turn his head, therefore, unlike Omberto, he can see the examples of humility if his desire to do so is strong enough.

79-81. Oh! I said . . . in Paris: The pilgrim recognizes Oderisi (active in the late 1260s and early '70s, d. 1299), a leading manuscript illuminator, like Franco Bolognese; Dante apparently knew him well (cf. Oderisi's "frate" [brother], line 82). He seems to have been active in Bologna, where Dante probably met him.

81. that art . . . in Paris: The pilgrim uses the French term (*enluminer*) rather than the Italian (*miniare*, from *minio* [cinnabar], a red pigment), thus introducing the idea of light.

82-84. Brother . . . mine in part: Oderisi pays a generous tribute to Franco of Bologna, apparently a younger man (cf. "or" [now] and the note to lines 91-99). Since miniaturists rarely signed their works, their identification is often hypothetical; art historians disagree about both attributions to them and their differences in style (Longhi 1950, Bottari 1967, Fallani 1971 and 1976).

82-83. the pages . . . laugh more: The *illuminations* cause the pages to *laugh*: cf. *Conv.* 3.8.11: "what is laughter except a flashing of the delight of the soul, that is, a light appearing externally as it is internally?" (cf. *Par.* 1.142-44).

84. the honor . . . mine in part: Oderisi's use of *honor* echoes the pilgrim's (lines 80-81). His inability to entirely relinquish his own glory finds delicious expression, after his humble granting of "all the honor" to Franco. The Ottimo slyly observes that Oderisi's part is "a very small one, we are to understand."

85-90. I would . . . turned to God: The term "excellence" should be understood to mean "superiority." Oderisi says he repented "while still able to sin," early enough for him to avoid the stay in Ante-Purgatory of those who repent at death, like Provenzano Salvani (see lines 127-32).

88. Here we pay the toll: Oderisi has identified the structure of pride (see 17.115-17) but still uses the penal terminology.

91-99. Oh vain glory . . . from the nest: Oderisi's meditation springs naturally from the memory of his former reputation. Besides expressing Dante's interest in art (cf. *VN* 35) and his friendly relations with artists, it evokes the excitement and competitive striving of the extraordinary outburst of creative energies in Northern Italy during Dante's lifetime. That Franco Bolognese and Giotto are objectively superior to their predecessors is explicit in one case and implied in the other; thus the passage gives early voice to the idea of progress in the arts (the theme of Vasari's *Lives of the Artists*, 1550-68, which mentions both Oderisi and Franco). The burgeoning itself, Oderisi says, guarantees that the renown of each wave will be obscured by the next, and the cycle is exemplified in two famous painters and two leading poets. These last two will be surpassed by a third (no doubt Dante himself).

91-92. how briefly . . . at the summit: How soon the leaves at the top of the tree (or the tip of the branch; see *Inf.* 13.44) fade and wither, to be followed by others (cf. lines 115-17, with note). The metaphor suggests that the cycle takes about a generation, roughly the age difference among the examples. Fallani 1981 cites Eccles. 1.4, 6, 11: "One generation passeth away, and another generation cometh: but the earth standeth for ever . . . the wind goeth forward surveying all places round about, and returneth to his circuits . . . There is no remembrance of former things."

92. if it is not followed by cruder ages: Such as the period following Rome's flowering in the Augustan and Silver periods, followed by the "Dark Ages." Dante anticipates the Renaissance periodizing of history.

94-95. Cimabue . . . in painting: Cimabue supposed that he had achieved supremacy (he was said to be arrogant); note the military metaphor of holding the field. The Florentine Giovanni (or Cenni) di Pepo, nicknamed Cimabue (ca. 1240–ca. 1302), was the first to follow the newer, more flexible style evolving in Byzantium; he was Giotto's teacher. His Crucifix, in the Uffizi Gallery in Florence, was severely damaged in the flood of 1966. Vasari relates that Cimabue's epitaph in Santa Maria Novella read:

> Credidit ut Cimabos picturae castra tenere:
> sic tenuit vivens, nunc tenet astra poli.
> [Just as Cimabue thought he held the fort in painting:
> so he did, when alive, and now he holds (i.e., inhabits) the stars of the pole.]

95-96. now Giotto . . . is darkened: For his naturalness and dramatic expressiveness, Giotto di Bondone dal Colle (born near Florence ca. 1266, died in Florence in 1337) is recognized as the founder of Tuscan painting, especially in his fresco cycles in Assisi, Padua, and Florence. According to Benvenuto, Dante and Giotto were friends (a fresco portrait of Dante in the Bargello in Florence may have been by Giotto, and Dante seems to have been in Padua while Giotto was working there). The lines imply, of course, that Giotto's glory, too, will pass.

97-99. Just so . . . from the nest: The same rapid succession takes place in poetry as in art.

97-98. one Guido . . . of our language: Guido Cavalcanti has taken from Guido Guinizelli the glory of being the foremost poet in Italian. On Guido Guinizelli, see 26.73-135, with notes.

97. one Guido from the other: Some scholars (most recently, Stefanini 1996) argue that the first Guido is Guittone d'Arezzo, the second Guido Guinizelli; but 26.124-26 attribute Guittone's renown to readers' bad judgment, which does not seem relevant here; for a thorough discussion, see Del Sal 1989.

98-99 perhaps he is born . . . from the nest: Virtually all commentators take these lines as a reference to the future triumph of Dante's poetry: his fame will eclipse that of both the Guidos. And indeed it has. One should remember, however, that this is said penitentially: Dante's glory will fade like that of his predecessors (but cf. *Par.* 17.118-20). The metaphor of driving rivals from the nest invokes the idea of exile, and lines 139-41 refer to Dante's own exile (for this knot of themes see *Inter cantica* below); on the relation of these lines to Dante's feelings of guilt toward Cavalcanti, see Durling 2001a.

99. both of them: Stefanini 1996 argues that this phrase refers to practitioners of the two arts, painting and poetry, meaning that a new painter will obscure Giotto and a new poet Guido.

100-102. The clamor . . . changes directions: What the world shouts is mere breath, like the wind, which is always changing and is Boreas from the north, Zephyr from the west. For fame as empty breath, cf. *Consolation* 2. pr. 7 "populares auras inanesque rumores" [the winds and empty noises of the mob]; cf. the note to lines 91-92.

103-108. What more acclaim . . . in the sky: The topos of the brevity of human life in comparison with the Great Year (see note to line 108), or with eternity itself, and the consequent littleness of fame, is ancient. The passage commonly cited from *Consolation* 2 pr. 7, is itself based on Cicero's *Dream of Scipio* 7.1-5 and Macrobius' *Commentarii* 2.11.14.

105. before . . . pappo and dindi: That is, before leaving early childhood: *pappo* (cf. Eng. *pap*) was baby talk for food, *dindi* (from *denaro*) for money.

108. the circle . . . in the sky: The sphere of the fixed stars, which, Dante says in *Conv.* 2.14.11, "has an almost imperceptible motion, turning from west to east one degree every hundred years" (360 degrees in 36,000 years), the Great Year of Platonic tradition (today the cycle of precession is calculated at 26,000 years).

109-14. He who takes . . . it is whorish: Oderisi now points out a soul moving particularly slowly just ahead of him. This is Provenzano Salvani, who never speaks, though he no doubt listens. We thus turn to pride in political power and influence. Although the explicit focus is the penance of individuals, this theme includes the pride of cities (cf. *Inf.* 7.67-96), such as that of Florence, destroyed at Montaperti (1260; see *Inter cantica* below).

115-17. Your renown . . . out of the earth: The language and thought are biblical, e.g., James 1.9-11: "For the sun rose with a burning heat, and parched the grass, and the flower thereof fell off . . . so also shall the rich man fade away in his ways" (cf. Is. 40.6-7). Dante's "he . . . by whom it comes unripe out of the earth" is both the sun and God.

118-19. Your true words . . . swelling in me: The pilgrim acknowledges that his tendency to pride is great. The classic locus on pride as swelling is 1 Cor. 13.4-5: "Charity . . . is not puffed up; is not ambitious, seeketh not her own . . ."

121-23. He is . . . his own hands: Provenzano Salvani (ca. 1220-1269) rose to dictatorial power in republican Siena. He was the leader of the expansion in which Omberto Aldobrandeschi's territories were annexed, and after Montaperti he was a chief advocate of the razing of Florence (*Inf.* 10.32, 83-93, with notes). He was captured and beheaded by the Florentines during the battle of Colle Val d'Elsa. See 13.106-39.

125-26. this is the coin . . . back there: Penance as a debt to be paid: a particularly clear economic metaphor.

133-42. When he was living . . . those confines: According to the early commentators, a close friend of Provenzano Salvani's was captured by Charles of Anjou at Tagliacozzo (1268), the last stand of the Italian Ghibellines. Charles is said to have demanded 10,000 florins for the friend's life, to be paid within a brief period; Salvani raised the money by wearing sackcloth and begging.

138. to tremble in every vein: With shame and with the effort to master his habitual pride. The veins tremble when the heart communicates its own tremors to them (cf. *Inf.* 1.20, with note). By this "deed" (*opera* [work done]) Salvani gained "merit" (*mercede*; cf. *Inf.* 4.34), applied to his obligation in Ante-Purgatory. There is an imitation of Christ implicit in Provenzano's action: he freed another with his veins (cf. 23.75)

139-41. I will say . . . can gloss it: When Dante is exiled, he will have to beg for his bread and will understand the humiliation that Salvani underwent. The hostility that will exile Dante is implicitly contrasted with the generosity of Salvani's neighbors.

Inter cantica. This canto continues the parallels with the *Inferno* gateway cantos. Here the parallels involve principally the infernal circle of the heretics: there, too, we saw examples of the types of pride featured here: Farinata degli Uberti (pride of noble birth and political power), Cavalcante (pride in his son's "high genius"). In *Purgatorio* 11 we find two other protagonists of the political struggles of the mid-thirteenth century: the Ghibelline Salvani and the Guelph Aldobrandeschi, with direct references to Montaperti (*Purg.* 11.112-14; *Inf.* 10.85-87), and implicitly to the dispute at Empoli in which the Florentine Farinata and the Sienese Salvani opposed each other (we can now see that in *Inf.* 10.89-93 Dante has Salvani specifically in mind). Although more vengeful at Empoli than Farinata, Salvani yet repented and was saved. Dante, too, is a victim of this political tradition, and the two cantos include similarly couched prophecies of his exile (*Inf.* 10.79-81, *Purg.* 11.139-41), emphasizing that personal experience will give Dante new insight into what others have suffered.

The pride of artistic genius is also a major focus of both cantos, and in both a central concern is the troubling figure of Guido Cavalcanti, Dante's "first friend" and chief poetic rival, some ten years his elder (see *Inf.* 10.52-72, with notes); in both cantos Dante is said to surpass Guido: in *Inferno* 10 in grace, in *Purgatorio* 11 in poetry. And in both there are suggestions that Dante's desire to surpass Guido had a disturbing, even fratricidal dimension: there is a knot of unresolved guilt in Dante (see the notes to *Inferno* 10). Guido's exile, as well as Dante's, is at stake in Oderisi's foretelling of Dante's poetic victory with the terminogy of exile: he "will drive both Guidos from the nest." (For further discussion, see Durling 1981b, 2001a.)

Figure 6. A Telamon.

CANTO 12

Di pari, come buoi che vanno a giogo,   1
m'andava io con quell' anima carca,
fin che 'l sofferse il dolce pedagogo.

Ma quando disse: "Lascia lui e varca;   4
ché qui è buon con la vela e coi remi,
quantunque può, ciascun pinger sua barca,"

dritto sì come andar vuolsi rife'mi   7
con la persona, avvegna che i pensieri
mi rimanessero e chinati e scemi.

Io m'era mosso, e seguia volontieri   10
del mio maestro i passi, e amendue
già mostravam com' eravam leggeri;

ed el mi disse: "Volgi li occhi in giùe: 13
buon ti sarà, per tranquillar la via,
veder lo letto de le piante tue."

Come, perché di lor memoria sia,   16
sovra i sepolti le tombe terragne
portan segnato quel ch'elli eran pria,

onde lì molte volte si ripiagne   19
per la puntura de la rimembranza,
che solo a' pii dà de le calcagne:

sì vid' io lì—ma di miglior sembianza   22
secondo l'artificio—figurato
quanto per via di fuor del monte avanza.

Vedea colui che fu nobil creato   25
più ch'altra creatura, giù dal cielo
folgoreggiando scender, da l'un lato.

Vedëa Brïareo, fitto dal telo   28
celestïal, giacer da l'altra parte
grave a la terra per lo mortal gelo.

CANTO 12

First terrace, continued: carved examples of pride cast down—the angel, erasure of one P, a Beatitude—climb

1   Side by side, like oxen under a yoke, I was walking along with that burdened soul, as long as my sweet tutor allowed it.

4   But when he said: "Leave him and pass on; for here it is good that each propel his bark with sail and oars, as much as he can,"

7   I stood erect in body, as one should be to walk, although in thought I remained bent over and humbled.

10   I had moved on, and gladly followed my master's steps, and we were both already showing how light we were;

13   and he said to me: "Turn your eyes downward: it will be good for you, to smooth your path, to see the bed where the soles of your feet are resting."

16   As, over the buried dead, to preserve their memory, the tombs in a pavement are signed with what they were in life,

19   so that often we weep again because of the pricking of memory, which drives its spurs only into the devoted:

22   so I saw carvings there—but of better appearance, thanks to the workmanship—over all that projects from the mountain as a path.

25   I saw him who was created nobler than all creatures, falling like a thunderbolt down from Heaven, on one side.

28   I saw Briareus, pierced by the celestial bolt, lying heavy on the earth in the frost of death, on the other side.

Vedea Timbreo, vedea Pallade e Marte,　　　　31
armati ancora, intorno al padre loro,
mirar le membra d'i Giganti sparte.

Vedea Nembròt a piè del gran lavoro,　　　　34
quasi smarrito, e riguardar le genti
che 'n Sennaàr con lui superbi fuoro.

O Nïobè, con che occhi dolenti　　　　37
vedea io te segnata in su la strada,
tra sette e sette tuoi figliuoli spenti!

O Saùl, come in su la propria spada　　　　40
quivi parevi morto in Gelboè,
che poi non sentì pioggia né rugiada!

O folle Aragne, sì vedea io te　　　　43
già mezza ragna, trista in su li stracci
de l'opera che mal per te si fé!

O Roboàm, già non par che minacci　　　　46
quivi 'l tuo segno, ma pien di spavento:
nel porta un carro, sanza ch'altri il cacci.

Mostrava ancor lo duro pavimento　　　　49
come Almeon a sua madre fé caro
parer lo sventurato addornamento.

Mostrava come i figli si gittaro　　　　52
sovra Sennacherìb dentro dal tempio
e come, morto lui, quivi il lasciaro.

Mostrava la ruina e 'l crudo scempio　　　　55
che fé Tamiri, quando disse a Ciro:
"Sangue sitisti, e io di sangue t'empio."

Mostrava come in rotta si fuggiro　　　　58
li Assiri poi che fu morto Oloferne,
e anche le reliquie del martiro.

Vedeva Troia in cenere e in caverne:　　　　61
o Ilïòn, come te basso e vile
mostrava il segno che lì si discerne!

Qual di pennel fu maestro o di stile　　　　64
che ritraesse l'ombre e ' tratti ch'ivi
mirar farieno uno ingegno sottile?

Morti li morti e i vivi parean vivi:　　　　67
non vide mei di me chi vide il vero
quant' io calcai, fin che chinato givi.

31   I saw Thymbraeus, I saw Pallas and Mars, still in armor, around their father, gazing at the scattered limbs of the Giants.

34   I saw Nimrod at the foot of his great work, almost dazed, gazing at the people who had been proud with him in Shinar.

37   O Niobe, with what grieving eyes did I see you carved in the surface of the road, amid seven and seven of your dead children!

40   O Saul, how you appeared, killing yourself on your own sword in Gilboa, which thereafter felt neither rain nor dew!

43   O mad Arachne, so I saw you, already half a spider, sitting wretched on the shreds of the work you made to your own ruin!

46   O Rehoboam, your image there no longer seems menacing but full of terror: a chariot carries it off without anyone pursuing.

49   Shown also by the hard pavement was how Alcmaeon made the unlucky ornament seem costly to his mother.

52   It showed how his sons fell upon Sennacherib in the temple, and how, when he was dead, they left him there.

55   It showed the ruin and the cruel slaughter done by Thamyris, when she said to Cyrus: "You have thirsted for blood, and with blood I fill you."

58   It showed how the Assyrians fled in a rout when Holofernes was killed, and also what remained from the murder.

61   I saw Troy in ashes and cavernous ruins: O Ilion, how low and vile the carving seen there showed you to be!

64   What master of the brush or stylus could portray the shadings and the outlines there, which would cause a subtle wit to marvel?

67   Dead seemed the dead, and the living living: one who saw the true event did not see better than I all that I trod upon, while I walked bent over.

Or superbite, e via col viso altero,   70
figliuoli d'Eva: e non chinate il volto
sì che veggiate il vostro mal sentero!

Più era già per noi del monte vòlto,   73
e del cammin del sole assai più speso,
che non stimava l'animo non sciolto,

quando colui che sempre innanzi atteso   76
andava, cominciò: "Drizza la testa;
non è più tempo di gir sì sospeso.

Vedi colà un angel che s'appresta   79
per venir verso noi, vedi che torna
dal servigio del dì l'ancella sesta.

Di reverenza il viso e li atti addorna,   82
sì che i diletti lo 'nvïarci in suso;
pensa che questo dì mai non raggiorna!"

Io era ben del suo ammonir uso   85
pur di non perder tempo, sì che 'n quella
materia non potea parlarmi chiuso.

A noi venìa la creatura bella,   88
biancovestito e ne la faccia quale
par tremolando mattutina stella.

Le braccia aperse, e indi aperse l'ale;   91
disse: "Venite: qui son presso i gradi,
e agevolemente omai si sale.

A questo invito vegnon molto radi: 94
o gente umana, per volar sù nata,
perché a poco vento così cadi?"

Menocci ove la roccia era tagliata;   97
quivi mi batté l'ali per la fronte;
poi mi promise sicura l'andata.

Come a man destra, per salire al monte   100
dove siede la chiesa che soggioga
la ben guidata sopra Rubaconte,

si rompe del montar l'ardita foga   103
per le scalee che si fero ad etade
ch'era sicuro il quaderno e la doga:

così s'allenta la ripa che cade   106
quivi ben ratta da l'altro girone;
ma quinci e quindi l'alta pietra rade.

70   Now assert your pride, and stride on with haughty brow, you sons of Eve: and do not lower your eyes to see your evil path!

73   We had circled more of the mountain, and used up much more of the sun's path, than my spirit, all absorbed, supposed,

76   when he, who walked always intent on what was ahead, began: "Raise your head; it is no longer time to walk so bent over.

79   See there an angel preparing to come toward us, see how the sixth handmaid returns from serving the day.

82   Adorn your face and actions with reverence, so that he may be pleased to send us upward; think that this day will never dawn again!"

85   I was quite used to his admonitions never to lose time, so that on that subject his speech could not be obscure to me.

88   Toward us came the lovely creature, clothed in white and in face like the trembling morning star.

91   He opened his arms and then he opened his wings; he said: "Come: near here are the steps, and the climb now is easy.

94   To this invitation they very rarely come: O human race, born to fly upward, why do you fall at so little wind?"

97   He led us to where the rock was cut; there he struck my forehead with his wings, then promised me safe passage.

100   As on the right hand, to climb the hill where the church sits that dominates the well-guided city above Rubaconte,

103   the fierce thrust of the slope is broken by the stairway made in an age when the record book and the measure were still secure:

106   so is the bank made easier that falls steep from the next terrace; but on this side and on that the high rock closes in.

Noi volgendo ivi le nostre persone, 109
"Beati pauperes spiritu!" voci
cantaron sì che nol diria sermone.

Ahi quanto son diverse quelle foci 112
da l'infernali! ché quivi per canti
s'entra, e là giù per lamenti feroci.

Già montavam su per li scaglion santi 115
ed esser mi parea troppo più lieve
che per lo pian non mi parea davanti.

Ond' io: "Maestro, dì, qual cosa greve 118
levata s'è da me, che nulla quasi
per me fatica, andando, si riceve?"

Rispuose: "Quando i *P* che son rimasi 121
ancor nel volto tuo, presso che stinti,
saranno, come l'un, del tutto rasi,

fier li tuoi piè dal buon voler sì vinti 124
che non pur non fatica sentiranno,
ma fia diletto loro esser sù pinti."

Allor fec' io come color che vanno 127
con cosa in capo non da lor saputa,
se non che ' cenni altrui sospecciar fanno,

per che la mano ad accertar s'aiuta, 130
e cerca e truova e quello officio adempie
che non si può fornir per la veduta:

e con le dita de la destra scempie 133
trovai pur sei le lettere che 'ncise
quel da le chiavi a me sovra le tempie,

a che guardando, il mio duca sorrise. 136

109   As we were turning into it, voices sang: *"Beati pauperes spiritu!"* in a way that speech cannot describe.

112   Ah, how different are these passageways from those in Hell! for here one enters with singing, down there with fierce laments.

115   Already we were mounting the sacred steps, and I seemed to be much lighter than I had been before, on the level ground.

118   So I: "Master, say, what heavy thing has been lifted from me, so that while going up I feel almost no exertion?"

121   He replied: "When the *P*s that still remain on your forehead, almost effaced, are, like the first, entirely gone,

124   then your feet will be so vanquished by your good will that not only will they feel no labor, but it will be a delight to them to be urged upward."

127   Then I did as those do who go about with something on their head unknown to them, except that the signs made by others make them suspect,

130   so that their hand tries to make certain, and seeks and finds and carries out the task that sight cannot perform:

133   and with the fingers of my right hand I found diminished and but six the letters that he of the keys had engraved above my temples,

136   and, watching this, my leader smiled.

NOTES

1-9. Side by side . . . humbled: Virgil interrupts the pilgrim's dialogue with Oderisi: their needs are different, and each must progress in his own way. The suggestion of 11.73-78 is now explicit (for the question of the vicarious nature of the pilgrim's purgation, see Additional Note 7).

1. like oxen under a yoke: The OT metaphor of the yoke (cf. also 11.52-53) is used mostly for enslavement, but Lam. 1.14 uses it of the weight of guilt. In the NT the key passage is Matt. 11.28-30: "Come to me, all you who labor, and are burdened, and I will refresh you. Take up my yoke upon you, and learn of me, because I am meek, and humble of heart: and you shall find rest for your souls."

5. sail and oars: For the nautical metaphor, see 1.1-3, 11.25, and 24.3, with notes. On *sail,* see "Textual Variants," p. 628.

7-9. I stood erect . . . humbled: These lines encapsulate some of the principles of the purgative process; see Additional Note 6. What might be called introjection is described as the retention in mental attitude of the bodily attitude imitated from the penitents. Oderisi's words have been equally important, of course. *Humbled* translates *scemi* [emptied, lessened], implying a former swelling (cf. 11.119, 12.133-34).

10-75. I had moved . . . supposed: The first main division of the canto, the description of the carvings of pride punished, is 54 lines long, as opposed to 83 lines for the examples of humility (10.17-99), and is introduced by six lines (12.10-15), as opposed to twelve (10.17-28).

12. how light we were: The pilgrim's practice of humility is having its effect (cf. lines 115-26).

13-15. Turn your eyes . . . resting: More instruction in humility. *Per tranquillar la via* [literally, to make your way tranquil] seems odd to us, in connection with the scenes of destruction to follow; note the related metaphor of the *floor* as the *bed* of the soles of the feet (the tomb will be the bed of the entire body, of course). Treading things down is traditional for superiority to them; cf. *Par.* 22.128-29, drawing on *Geor.* 2.475-92, especially 490-92:

> felix qui potuit rerum cognoscere causas
> atque metus omnis et inexorabile fatum
> subiecit pedibus strepitumque Acherontis avari.
> [Happy he who has been able to learn the causes of things
> and has placed under his feet all fears and inexorable
> fate and the clamor of greedy Acheron.]

As opposed to the proud Stoic/Epicurean supe-
riority Vergil urged, for Dante only true hu-
mility can actually rise above fear and death.

16-24. As, over the buried . . . as a path: Tomb
slabs set in the floors of churches were com-
mon in the Middle Ages; they often bore bas-
relief effigies of the buried, their coats of arms,
and inscriptions. Some twenty (all but one later
than Dante's death) are visible in the crypt—
originally the floor of Santa Reparata, the old
cathedral of Florence—beneath the nave of
Santa Maria del Fiore (see Morozzi 1987), many
also in Santa Croce. Dante may have been aware
that tomb sculpture portraying the buried was
a relatively recent phenomenon in Italy (since
1272: Bauch 1976), although common in north-
ern Europe for at least a century and a half. See
fig. 7. For the tomb as bed, see *Inf.* 10.78.

18. are signed: See the note to 14.7-9. Here
Dante is referring primarily, but not exclusively,
to bas-relief sculptures. Today many such in-
scriptions, and even the sculptures, have been
worn away.

22-23. carvings . . . over all: Literally, "that all
. . . was carved (or figured)."

Figure 7. A tomb slab.

25-72. I saw . . . evil path: The passage directly concerned with the carvings
occupies 15 terzine (45 lines): 13 of enumeration, and 2 of general description

25-63. I saw . . . showed you to be: In the first twelve terzine, four begin with
the word *vedea* [I saw] (lines 25-36); four with the word *O* (lines 37-48); four
with the word *mostrava* [it showed] (lines 49-60); in the last terzina the succes-
sive lines begin with *vedea, O, mostrava*. The inital letters form the word *VOM*
[man], spelled out five times (see also the note to lines 64-69); they are thus a
form of acrostic, related to the alphabetical acrostics of Lamentations, most elabo-
rate in Chapter 3, where each letter begins a verse three times; such texts must be
parsed both horizontally and vertically (cf. line 13, "Turn your eyes downward").
The examples here are drawn alternately from the Bible and classical myth and
history: Satan (25-27); Briareus and the Giants (28-33); Nimrod (34-36); Niobe
(37-39); Saul (40-42); Arachne (43-45); Rehoboam (46-48); Eriphyle (49-51);
Sennacherib (52-54); Cyrus (55-57); Holofernes (58-60); Troy (61-63). Parodi
argued that the three groups were differentiated: the first four being rebels directly

against God, the next four foolishly self-destructive, the last tyrannical. Commentators observe that the events are represented as in progress and, pointing out the emphatic references in each terzina to seeing: the beginning of understanding man is *seeing* his fall.

25-27. him who was created . . . on one side: A locus classicus on pride is Isaiah's "Burden of Babylon" [*onus Babylonis*] on the fallen king (Is. 13-14), taken by Christians to refer to Satan (see *Inf.* 34.28-60, with notes); see especially Is. 14.12-15: "How art thou fallen from heaven, O Lucifer, who didst rise in the morning? how art thou fallen to the earth . . . And thou saidst in thy heart: I will ascend into heaven, I will exalt my throne above the stars of God . . . I will be like the most High. But yet thou shalt be brought down to hell, into the depth of the pit." For the use of "burden" [Lat. *onus*] as a title for prophecies of destruction, see also Is. 15.1, 17.1, 19.1, 21.1, 22.1, 23.1. For "folgoreggiando" [ablaze like lightning] see Luke 10.18.

28-33. Briareus . . . limbs of the Giants: The defeat of the Giants (cf. *Met.* 1.151-62) is the only example in this canto to occupy two terzine. In *Inferno* 31, the pilgrim saw three of the Giants (Nimrod, Ephialtes, and Antaeus), and heard of the others; for Briareus, see *Inf.* 31.97-105. The passage derives details from *Theb.* 2.595-601.

30. heavy on the earth: See 11.43, with note.

31-32. Thymbraeus . . . their father: Apollo (called Thymbraeus after a Trojan shrine), Athena, and Mars around Jupiter, without whose thunderbolts, according to the myth, they would have lost the battle.

34-36. Nimrod . . . Shinar: For Nimrod, the Tower of Babel in Shinar, and Dante's unusual conception of the confusion of tongues (Gen. 10.9-10, 11.1-9), see *Inf.* 31.46-81, with notes. Nimrod is dazed because no one can understand him, nor he them.

37-39. O Niobe . . . dead children: In her pride Niobe boasts that her seven sons and seven daughters makes her superior to Latona (mother of only two, Apollo and Diana); at Latona's behest Apollo and Diana slay them along with her husband; Niobe becomes a stone dripping tears (*Met.* 6.142-312).

37-38. with what grieving eyes . . . carved: The ambiguity in the translation follows the Italian: the primary meaning is that Niobe's eyes are grieving.

40-42. O Saul . . . rain nor dew: Defeated on Mount Gilboa in a battle in which three of his sons were killed, Saul fell on his sword (1 Sam. 31.1-6); in his grief David cursed Mount Gilboa (2 Sam. 1.21): "Ye mountains of Gelboe, let neither dew nor rain come upon you, neither be they fields of firstfruits: for there was cast away . . . the shield of Saul." In the *Glossa Ordinaria* (PL 113, 563), "they say" [*ferunt*] that the curse was fulfilled. Dante echoes David's curse in *Ep.* 6.11, threatening the rebellious Florentines with destruction.

43-45. O mad Arachne . . . to your own ruin: Arachne, who challenged Athene to a tapestry-weaving contest and perhaps surpassed her, was turned by the goddess into a spider (*Met.* 6.1-145, immediately before the story of Niobe); this is the central example of the series: the presumptuous artist (and as a weaver, Arachne worked vertical and horizontal threads). Cf. 10.28-99 and *Inf.* 17.14-18.

46-48. O Rehoboam . . . pursuing: This example alone does not end with death but with ignominious flight. Rehoboam's arrogance (as Solomon's son and successor) caused the definitive rejection of the House of David by the northern tribes (1 Kings 12.18-19; see the note to 10.55-69).

49-51. how Alcmaeon . . . to his mother: In *Theb.* 2.265-305 and 4.187-212, to gain the necklace made by Vulcan for the goddess Harmonia, Eriphyle betrays the hiding place of her husband, the seer Amphiaraus (see the notes to *Inf.* 20.31-36 and 33), so that he must fight at Thebes, where he dies. Although in *Par.* 4.103 Beatrice says that Amphiaraus asked Alcmaeon to avenge him, in *Thebaid* 7 it is to Apollo that he entrusts the revenge he foresees his son will take. "Sventurato addornamento" [unlucky ornament] translates *Theb.* 2.265-66: "infaustos . . . ornatus."

52-54. his sons . . . left him there: Sennacherib, king of Assyria (704-631 B.C.), besieged Jerusalem in 701. Some modern scholars doubt the story of the sudden destruction of his army at a later siege of Jerusalem, which, according to 2 Kings 19.35-37 and Is. 37.36-38, led to his murder; but see McNeill 1976.

55-57. the ruin . . . I fill you: Dante read of the death of Cyrus II the Great, founder of the Persian Empire (? - 530 B.C.) and destroyer of the Babylonian, in Orosius. Thamyris was a queen of the Scythians whose son Cyrus had murdered when a hostage. After capturing Cyrus in battle, she is said to have cast his head into a bladder full of blood, with the words Dante quotes. Cyrus had permitted the Jews to return to Jerusalem and rebuild the Temple.

58-60. the Assyrians . . . from the murder: The almost certainly fictitious story of the beheading of the drunken Assyrian general Holofernes by the Jewish widow he had hoped to seduce, and the rout of his army, demoralized by the discovery of his corpse, is told in the apocryphal Book of Judith.

60. what remained from the murder: Commentators have been divided as to whether Dante is referring to Holofernes' head, carried off by Judith (Judith 13.10-19) or to discovery of his body (Judith 14.1-7). We incline to the latter as *left behind*, *reliquie* [remains] (cf. line 54).

61-63. Troy . . . showed you to be: The destruction of Troy (*Aeneid* 2; see 10.28-99) is the climax of the entire series of examples; the lines draw on *Met.* 15.422-25:

magna fuit censuque virisque,
perque decem potuit tantum dare sanguinis annos,
nunc humilis veteres tantummodo Troia ruinas
et pro divitiis tumulos ostendit avorum.
[it was great in wealth and men, and through ten years could give so
much blood, now, leveled, Troy shows only ancient ruins and, instead of
wealth, the tombs of her ancestors.]

Cf. *Aen.*3.2-3: "ceciditque superbum / Ilium et omnis humo fumat Neptunia
Troia" [proud Ilium has fallen and all Neptunian Troy lies smoking on the ground]
(Scott in *LDT*). Just as the acrostic is recapitulated in this final terzina, the ex-
ample of Troy sums up all the others, especially those which for Dante involve
major turning points in history; it is not merely the pride of individuals that is
targeted (see the note to 11.109-14).

64-69. What master . . . bent over: This conclusion emphasizes the superlative
realism (*enargeia*) of the representations even more explicitly than Canto 10.

64-66. What master . . . to marvel: The most gifted human artist, though
possessing the most subtle *ingegno* [wit or genius], would be incapable even of
copying these carvings adequately.

67. Dead seemed . . . living: The reader is invited to consider what the signs of
death and life would be in the represented bodies.

68-69. one who . . . bent over: Seeing pride truly and treading it down requires
the bowed head of humility and mourning. The pilgrim keeps this posture until
line 78.

70-72. Now assert . . . your evil path: Again the emphasis on bodily posture as
expressive of spiritual states. The evil end to which pride leads is visible every-
where, since "your evil path" is on the earth (cf. lines 28-30): "Dust thou art and
unto dust shalt thou return" (Gen. 3.19). cf. 10.121-29.

73-136. We had circled . . . my leader smiled: The second half of the canto,
the concluding ritual of the purgation, derived from the priestly absolution in
the sacrament of Penance (see the notes to 9.95-127).

74. used up . . . the sun's path: If, as suggested in the note to 10.14-16, the
travelers reached the terrace of pride soon after 10 A.M., and it is now noon (lines
80-81, with note), they have spent about two hours there. For the pilgrim's for-
getting of time, cf. 4.16 (where more than three hours elapse). The rest of the
day is probably thought of as evenly divided between the next two terraces; the
travelers reach the fourth terrace (17.70-78), a little after 6 P.M.

76-84. he, who . . . dawn again: Virgil is close to a personification of Reason/
Prudence here (the term *prudentia* [prudence] is a contraction of *providentia* [fore-
sight]): he judges when to end the pilgrim's penances, announces the approach

of the angel, tells the time, enjoins appropriate conduct, and concludes with the exhortation not to waste time.

80-81. the sixth handmaid ... the day: The sixth of the personified Hours has completed her task.

85-87. I was ... obscure to me: For Virgil on the use of time, see, e.g., *Inf.* 4.22 and 34.96; *Purg.* 3.78. *Raggiornare* [to dawn again] seems to be a coinage of Dante's.

88-99. Toward us ... safe passage: On each terrace the last event is the encounter with the angel, who invites the travelers to climb and brushes the pilgrim's forehead with his wings, effacing one of the *P*s.

88-90. Toward us ... morning star: The first of the angels within Purgatory proper; cf. the notes on earlier angels, 2.58-51, 8.25-26, and 9.79-132.

89. clothed in white: In the Gospels angels appear clad in white only after the Resurrection (see Matt. 28.2-3, Mark 16.5, Luke 24.4, John 20.12); white is worn by the blessed, including angels, in the Apocalypse (e.g., 6.11, 7.9, 15.10, 19.14).

89-90. in face ... morning star: For the brightness of the angels' faces, cf. 2.39, 8.34-36, 9.81, and Matt. 28.3, Apoc. 10.1. The morning star is an established term of comparison for the lady's beauty in the Dolce Stil Nuovo (see Guinizelli's sonnets "Vedut' ho la lucente stella diana" and "Io voglio del ver la mia donna laudare"); cf. also Apoc. 22.16: "I am the bright and morning star" (said by Christ), which alludes to Is. 14.12 (see note to lines 25-27).

91. He opened ... wings: The opened arms recall those of Christ, as in 3.122-23; the opening of the wings provides a powerful intensification.

92-93. Come ... now is easy: See the note to line 1, citing Matt. 11.28-30; for the invitation, cf. Matt. 25.34, Apoc. 22.17.

94-96. To this invitation ... little wind: The lament of 10.2-3 (cf. 10.16, with note), now put in the mouth of the angel; it picks up the insect metaphors of 10.121-29, and the "wind" recalls the theme of pride as swelling (11.119).

100-136. As on the right ... my leader smiled: The remainder of the canto is devoted to the climb to the next terrace. The passageway is still a narrow cleft, as in 10.7-18, but now it is a stairway.

100-105. As on the right ... still secure: The stairway to the next terrace is compared to the one leading from Porta S. Miniato in Florence up the steep hill toward San Miniato al Monte, the "church that dominates" Florence, begun soon after 1018 and finished around 1200. This is not the stairway that exists today, which was built in the sixteenth century (see fig. 8). Florence is sarcastically called "well guided" (cf. the denunciation of 6.127-51). The Rubaconte was the bridge (later called the Ponte alle Grazie) named after Rubaconte da Mandella, the podestà under whom it was begun in 1237 (see Additional Note 8).

104-105. made in an age . . . still secure: The stairway was built in an age when Florence was still governed honestly. The lines refer to famous scandals. In 1299 the official record book of the city (the *quaderno* [register]) was tampered with to erase testimony against one of the priors; the culprits were heavily fined (Compagni, *Cronica,* 1, 19). In 1283 one of the noble Chiaramonte family, in charge of the salt monopoly, greatly profited from selling with a dishonest measure, made

Figure 8. The stairway to San Miniato in Dante's day.

by omitting one of the narrow *doghe* [barrel-staves] required by law. Benvenuto says that he was beheaded; the Anonimo, who gives the fullest account, says ambiguously that his punishment was "heavy and shameful." In *Par.* 16.105 Dante alludes to the shame still felt by the Chiaramonte family.

110. *Beati pauperes spiritu*: As the travelers begin to leave each terrace, one of the Beatitudes that open the Sermon on the Mount (Matt. 5.3-12) is sung or recited (see 15.38 [Matt. 5.7], 17.68-69 [Matt. 5.9], 19.50 [Matt. 5.5], 22.5-6 [Matt. 5.6], 24.151-54 [Matt. 5.6], 27.8 [Matt. 5.8]). "Beati pauperes spiritu quia illorum est regnum coelorum" [Blessed are the poor in spirit, for theirs is the kingdom of heaven] (Matt. 5.3) is the first, traditionally taken (see Augustine, *De serm. Dom.* 1) to refer to humility.

110-11. voices sang: In 15.38, too, we are told that the Beatitude "was sung behind us," but not by whom; in the other cases the angel pronounces the Beatitude, in four out of five cases merely speaking it, but in the last he sings it (27.8). It has become customary, in the wake of D'Ovidio and Sapegno, to suppose that since in five cases the Beatitude is said or sung by the (single) angel, it must be so for the other two. This is arbitrary. The text gives "voices sang," and so more than one voice was singing. A single voice might seem anticlimactic after 9.142-45; Dante may well have wished the completion of the initial and most difficult purgation to involve special solemnity and 15.38 to provide transition.

112-14. Ah, how different . . . fierce laments: To this first climb between levels within Purgatory proper, the closest parallel is probably the first such transition in Hell, *Inf.* 5.1-3:

> Così discesi del cerchio primaio
> giù nel secondo, che men loco cinghia
> e tanto più dolor che punge a guaio.
> [Thus I descended from the first circle down to the
> second, which encloses a smaller space, but so much
> more suffering that it goads the souls to shriek.]

Cf. *Inf.* 3.22-24, 13.15, 14.27, 29.36-43, etc. See *Inter cantica* below.

115-36. Already . . . my leader smiled: The final event in the purgation of pride is the experience of its effect, the lifting of weight and the erasing of one of the *P*s inscribed by the angel in 9.112-14. Since pride is the "root" and "mother" of vice, its purgation lessens the soul's tendencies toward other vices; therefore the six remaining *P*s are "almost effaced."

115-17. Already . . . on the level ground: See lines 10-12.

121-26. He replied . . . urged upward: This passage is a companion piece to 4.88-95: there, in connection with the first heavy exertion of climbing, Virgil expressed the expected ease of ascent with the image of a boat floating downstream; here, in the first post-purgative ascent, the terminology is that of a transformed relation between soul and body (see note to 10.43-45).

133-34. with the fingers . . . the letters: There is disagreement on the meaning here of *scempie* (from Latin *simplex* [simple]). Most take it to mean "spread out," referring to the fingers; Buti took it to mean "alone," i.e., without other assistance. We follow Porena in taking it to modify *lettere* [letters]; that is, there are now only six letters, and those that remain are "almost effaced" (line 122); cf. *scemi* in line 9.

136. watching this, my leader smiled: Virgil's smile expresses both affectionate humor and satisfaction at the success of the purgation.

Inter cantica. Lines 112-14 compare the "passageways" of Purgatory and Hell; the parallel extends far beyond the contrast between singing and laments (for instance the blessings of the Beatitudes are correlated with the cursing and blaspheming in Hell, as in *Inf.* 3.103-104). Dante's term *foci* [narrow outlets or inlets] derives from Latin *fauces* [throat]; in Italian the original literal sense was largely forgotten, but not by Dante, who remembers *Aen.* 6.201: "they came to the throat of foul-smelling Avernus," an allusion to the traditional body analogy (see *Inferno*, Additional Note 2). Hell swallows its victims, Purgatory frees them.

With the carvings of pride punished (led by Satan, reminding us especially of his fall from Heaven [*Inf.* 34.121-26]), compared with floor tombs, we have another reminder of the sarcophagi of the heretics: Cantos 11 and 12 have seen the stones of pride move from the backs of the penitents, ultimately to be trodden underfoot.

CANTO 13

Noi eravamo al sommo de la scala,   1
dove secondamente si risega
lo monte che salendo altrui dismala.

Ivi così una cornice lega   4
dintorno il poggio come la primaia,
se non che l'arco suo più tosto piega.

Ombra non li è né segno che si paia: 7
parsi la ripa e parsi la via schietta
col livido color de la petraia.

"Se qui per dimandar gente s'aspetta,"   10
ragionava il poeta, "io temo forse
che troppo avrà d'indugio nostra eletta."

Poi fisamente al sole li occhi porse;   13
fece del destro lato a muover centro,
e la sinistra parte di sé torse.

"O dolce lume a cui fidanza i' entro   16
per lo novo cammin, tu ne conduci,"
dicea, "come condur si vuol quinc' entro.

Tu scaldi il mondo, tu sovr' esso luci: 19
s'altra ragione in contrario non ponta,
esser dien sempre li tuoi raggi duci."

Quanto di qua per un migliaio si conta,   22
tanto di là eravam noi già iti,
con poco tempo, per la voglia pronta;

e verso noi volar furon sentiti,   25
non però visti, spiriti parlando
a la mensa d'amor cortesi inviti.

La prima voce che passò volando   28
"Vinum non habent!" altamente disse
e dietro a noi l'andò reïterando.

CANTO 13

Second terrace, of envy: examples of compassion—the souls of the envious, their eyes sewn shut—Sapia

1   We were at the summit of the stairway, where the mountain that cures ills by climbing is cut back a second time.

4   There a ledge binds the slope about, like the first, except that its arc bends sooner.

7   No shade is there, nor any sign to be seen: the bank and the road appear bare, with only the livid color of the rock.

10   "If we wait here for people to ask," spoke my poet, "I fear that perhaps our choice will be too much delayed."

13   Then he looked fixedly at the sun; he made his right side a center for his moving, and he turned his left side.

16   "O sweet light in whose trust I enter on the new path, do you guide us," he was saying, "in the way one should go here.

19   You warm the world, you shine above it: if some other reason does not weigh more, your rays should always lead us."

22   As far as counts as a mile here, so far had we walked from there, in little time, for our wills were eager,

25   when flying toward us were heard, but not seen, spirits speaking courteous invitations to the table of love.

28   The first voice that flew past said loudly: "*Vinum non habent!*" and behind us went repeating it.

E prima che del tutto non si udisse   31
per allungarsi, un altra "I' sono Oreste!"
passò gridando, e anco non s'affisse.

  "Oh!" diss' io, "padre, che voci son queste?"   34
E com' io domandai, ecco la terza
dicendo: "Amate da cui male aveste!"

  E 'l buon maestro: "Questo cinghio sferza   37
la colpa de la invidia, e però sono
tratte d'amor le corde de la ferza.

  Lo fren vuol esser del contrario suono;   40
credo che l'udirai, per mio avviso,
prima che giunghi al passo del perdono.

  Ma ficca li occhi per l'aere ben fiso,   43
e vedrai gente innanzi a noi sedersi,
e ciascun è lungo la grotta assiso."

  Allora più che prima li occhi apersi;   46
guarda'mi innanzi e vidi ombre con manti
al color de la pietra non diversi.

  E poi che fummo un poco più avanti,   49
udia gridar: "Maria, ora per noi!"
gridar "Michele!" e "Pietro!" e "Tutti santi!"

  Non credo che per terra vada ancoi   52
omo sì duro che non fosse punto
per compassion di quel ch'i' vidi poi,

  ché, quando fui sì presso di lor giunto   55
che li atti loro a me venivan certi,
per li occhi fui di grave dolor munto.

  Di vil ciliccio mi parean coperti,   58
e l'un sofferia l'altro con la spalla,
e tutti da la ripa eran sofferti.

  Così li ciechi a cui la roba falla   61
stanno a' perdoni a chieder lor bisogna,
e l'uno il capo sopra a l'altro avvalla

  perché 'n altrui pietà tosto si pogna,   64
non pur per lo sonar de le parole
ma per la vista, che non meno agogna.

  E come a li orbi non approda il sole,   67
così a l'ombre quivi ond' io parlo ora
luce del ciel di sé largir non vole:

31   And before it had become entirely inaudible in the distance, another passed, crying: "I am Orestes!" and it, too, did not stop.

34   "Oh!" I said, "father, what voices are these?" and as I asked, behold the third, saying: "Love those from whom you have had evil!"

37   And my good master: "This circle whips the guilt of envy, and therefore the cords of the whip are braided of love.

40   The bridle needs to be of the opposite sound: I believe, from what I perceive, that you will hear it before you reach the pass of pardon.

43   But probe the air fixedly with your eyes, and you will see people sitting ahead of us, and each is sitting alongside the cliff."

46   Then, more than before, I opened my eyes; I looked ahead and saw shades wearing cloaks not different in color from the rock.

49   And when we we had gone a little further, I heard them crying: "Mary, pray for us!" crying: "Michael!" and "Peter!" and "All saints!"

52   I do not think anyone walks the earth today so hardened that he would not be pierced with compassion at what I saw next,

55   for, when I had come so close to them that I could see their bearing clearly, my eyes were milked of heavy grieving.

58   They seemed clothed in base haircloth, and each suffered the other to lean against his shoulder, and the cliff suffered them all.

61   Thus the blind who lack substance stand at Pardons to beg for their needs, and one leans his head on the other

64   so that pity may quickly be instilled, not only by the sound of their words but by the sight, which is no lesser spur.

67   And as the sun does not reach the blind, so to the shades there of whom I speak now the light of heaven does not grant itself:

ché a tutti un fil di ferro i cigli fóra   70
e cusce, sì come a sparvier selvaggio
si fa però che queto non dimora.

   A me pareva, andando, fare oltraggio   73
veggendo altrui, non essendo veduto:
per ch'io mi volsi al mio consiglio saggio.

   Ben sapev' ei che volea dir lo muto,   76
e però non attese mia dimanda
ma disse: "Parla, e sie breve e arguto."

   Virgilio mi venìa da quella banda   79
de la cornice onde cader si puote,
perché da nulla sponda s'inghirlanda;

   da l'altra parte m'eran le divote   82
ombre, che per l'orribile costura
premevan sì che bagnavan le gote.

   Volsimi a loro, e: "O gente sicura,"   85
incominciai, "di veder l'alto Lume
che 'l disio vostro solo ha in sua cura,

   se tosto grazia resolva le schiume   88
di vostra coscïenza, sì che chiaro
per essa scenda de la mente il fiume,

   ditemi, ché mi fia grazioso e caro,   91
s'anima è qui tra voi che sia latina,
e forse lei sarà buon s'i' l'apparo."

   "O frate mio, ciascuna è cittadina   94
d'una vera città; ma tu vuo' dire
che vivesse in Italia peregrina."

   Questo mi parve per risposta udire   97
più innanzi alquanto che là dov' io stava,
ond' io mi feci ancor più là sentire.

   Tra l'altre vidi un'ombra ch'aspettava   100
in vista; e se volesse alcun dir "Come?"
lo mento a guisa d'orbo in sù levava.

   "Spirto," diss' io, "che per salir ti dome,   103
se tu se' quelli che mi rispondesti,
fammiti conto o per luogo o per nome."

   "Io fui sanese," rispuose, "e con questi   106
altri rimendo qui la vita ria,
lagrimando a colui che sé ne presti.

70   for each had his eyelids pierced and sewn by an iron wire, as we do to a wild sparrowhawk because it will not be still.

73   It seemed to me as I walked that I was transgressing in seeing others, not being seen: so I turned to my wise counsellor.

76   Well he knew what the mute wished to say, and so he did not wait for my question but said: "Speak, and be brief and to the point."

79   Virgil was walking with me on the side of the ledge where one can fall, since it is not garlanded with any bank;

82   on my other side were the devout shades, who through the horrible sutures pressed tears that bathed their cheeks.

85   I turned to them and began: "O people sure of seeing the deep Light that is the sole concern of your desire,

88   so may grace quickly dissolve the scum from your conscience, that the river of the mind may be clear descending through it,

91   tell me, for it will be gracious and dear to me, if there is a soul here among you who is Italian; and perhaps it will be good for it that I learn."

94   "O my brother, each of us is citizen of one true city; but you mean to say 'who lived in Italy as a pilgrim.'"

97   I seemed to hear this in reply from somewhat ahead of where I was standing, and so I made myself heard again further along.

100   Among the others I saw a shade that looked as if it were waiting; and if someone were to say "How so?" it was raising its chin as the blind do.

103   "Spirit," I said, "who are mastering yourself so as to ascend, if you are the one who answered me, make yourself known to me by place or by name."

106   "I was Sienese," it replied, "and with these others here I repair my wicked life, weeping to him so that he may grant himself to us.

Savia non fui, avvegna che Sapìa   109
fossi chiamata, e fui de l'altrui danni
più lieta assai che di ventura mia.

E perché tu non creda ch'io t'inganni,   112
odi s'i' fui, com' io ti dico, folle,
già discendendo l'arco d'i miei anni.

Eran li cittadin miei presso a Colle   115
in campo giunti co' loro avversari,
e io pregava Iddio di quel ch'e' volle.

Rotti fuor quivi e vòlti ne li amari   118
passi di fuga; e veggendo la caccia,
letizia presi a tutte altre dispari,

tanto ch'io volsi in sù l'ardita faccia,   121
gridando a Dio: 'Omai più non ti temo!'
come fé 'l merlo per poca bonaccia.

Pace volli con Dio in su lo stremo   124
de la mia vita, e ancor non sarebbe
lo mio dover per penitenza scemo,

se ciò non fosse ch'a memoria m'ebbe   127
Pier Pettinaio in sue sante orazioni,
a cui di me per caritate increbbe.

Ma tu chi se', che nostre condizioni   130
vai dimandando, e porti li occhi sciolti,
sì com' io credo, e spirando ragioni?"

"Li occhi," diss' io, "mi fieno ancor qui tolti,   133
ma picciol tempo, ché poca è l'offesa
fatta per esser con invidia vòlti.

Troppa è più la paura ond' è sospesa   136
l'anima mia del tormento di sotto,
che già lo 'ncarco di là giù mi pesa."

Ed ella a me: "Chi t'ha dunque condotto   139
qua sù tra noi, se giù ritornar credi?"
E io: "Costui ch'è meco e non fa motto.

E vivo sono; e però mi richiedi,   142
spirito eletto, se tu vuo' ch'i' mova
di là per te ancor li mortai piedi."

109   I was not wise, although Sapia was my name, and I rejoiced at others' harms much more than at my own good luck.

112   And lest you believe that I deceive you, hear if I was mad, as I tell you, when the arc of my years was already descending.

115   My fellow-citizens were joined with their enemies in the field at Colle, and I prayed God to do what he then willed to do.

118   They were routed there and turned in the bitter steps of flight; and seeing them hunted down, I took joy from it greater than all other joys,

121   so that I turned my bold face upwards, shouting to God: 'Now I fear you no more!' as the blackbird did for a little sunshine.

124   I wished peace with God at the end of my life, and my debt would not yet be canceled by penance,

127   were it not that Piero the comb-seller remembered me in his holy prayers, having pity on me in his charity.

130   But who are you, who go asking our condition and have your eyes unsewn, I believe, and breathe as you speak?"

133   "My eyes," I said, "will be taken from me here, but for a short time only, for they have offended little by being turned with envy.

136   Much greater is the fear that holds my soul in suspense for the torment below, and already the burden down there weighs on me."

139   And she to me: "Who then has led you up here among us, if you expect to go back down?" And I: "This one who is with me and does not speak a word.

142   And I am alive; and therefore, chosen spirit, ask me, if you would have me move my still living feet for you back there."

"Oh, questa è a udir sì cosa nuova,"   145
rispuose, "che gran segno è che Dio t'ami;
però col priego tuo talor mi giova.

E cheggioti per quel che tu più brami,   148
se mai calchi la terra di Toscana,
che a' miei propinqui tu ben mi rinfami.

Tu li vedrai tra quella gente vana   151
che spera in Talamone, e perderagli
più di speranza ch'a trovar la Diana;

    ma più vi perderanno li ammiragli."   154

145   "Oh, this is such a strange new thing to hear," she replied, "that it is a great sign that God loves you; therefore with your prayers help me from time to time.

148   And I beg you by what you most desire, if ever you tread the soil of Tuscany, restore my good fame among my relatives.

151   You will see them among that vain people who place their hopes in Talamone and will lose more hope in it than in seeking the Diana,

154   but the admirals will lose even more."

NOTES

1-24. We were . . . wills were eager: Initial description of the entirely bare and apparently empty second terrace, and Virgil's choice of direction.

3. cures ills: *Dismala* (coined by Dante; cf. 3.15, with note) might be rendered "disevils"; it is much less jarring in Italian than in English. Cf. 10.2-3.

7-9. No shade . . . of the rock: As in 10.20-21, the ledge recalls a desert (see our Introduction, p. 12 and Additional Note 6). Both nouns in line 7 are ambiguous. *Ombra* [shade] can refer to souls, shadows, or images (cf. 12.65). *Segno* [sign] was used in the senses we give to *sign* in English (including "miracle": see the note to lines 29-30), and was also, in both Latin and Italian, a common word for "statue" (see the note on 14.139); it can naturally be taken to refer to the absence of sculptures, but its extended meaning looks forward to the inability of the envious to see (cf. the note to lines 58-66).

9. the livid color of the rock: The color of lead or of bruises, generally described as dark blue or purple, is the color typical of envy (Lat. *livor* means both "livid color" and "envy"). Dante derived this detail from Ovid's account of the transformation of Aglauros (see the note to 14.139), and there is a relation between the vice and the rock that is parallel to the relation between them on the previous terrace. Pride and envy both spring from Lucifer: see Wisdom 2.23-25: "For God created man incorruptible . . . but by the envy of the Devil death came into the world" (and cf. *Inf.* 1.111). Dante links them here (see lines 133-38), as in *Inf.* 6.74-75 and *Par.* 9.128-29.

10-21. If we wait . . . always lead us: On the terrace of pride, the travelers are confronted with the carvings; the interval before the appearance of the penitents is filled by examining the images, during which the travelers move toward the right, later accompanying the penitents in that direction. It is possible that Virgil is inferring the immobility of the envious from the nature of their vice; the emphasis on following the sun here may seem gratuitous, but see lines 16-21 and 36 and note.

14-15. he made his right . . . left side: With his right side fixed, Virgil wheels his left side around it (that is, he turns to the right), perhaps an allegory of reason dominating impulse (cf. *Inf.* 1.30, with note). The travelers' turn to the right once more makes their motion around the terrace counter-clockwise.

16-21. O sweet light . . . always lead us: Virgil's invocation to the sun initiates an insistence on the analogy between visible and spiritual light that pervades the central cantos of the cantica and thus of the entire poem (see 15.1-33, 64-72; 16.106-108; 17.13-18; 18.10-12, 76-81; 19.1-15). For the analogy between the sun and God, see the note on *Inf.* 1.17-18 and *Conv.* 3.12.6-9, a passage that has many points of contact with this one and where both light (wisdom) and heat (love) are involved (and cf. *Consolation* 5 m. 2). Love was frequently compared to the sun in thirteenth-century treatises; cf. the notes to line 35-36. For the sunlight as *dolce* [sweet], cf. *Inf.* 10.69 and note, also Eccles. 11.7.

22-42. As far as counts . . . the pass of pardon: As the travelers walk, voices pass them loudly pronouncing (Dante may have Prov. 8.1 in mind here) phrases originally uttered out of compassionate love by the examples to be imitated (for the Scholastics' elaboration of the correlation of vices with corrective virtues—Chaucer's *Parson's Tale* is an example—see Wenzel 1984).

25-27. flying toward us . . . table of love: After the intensely visual presentation of the examples of humility exalted and pride punished on the first terrace, those on the terrace of envy are exclusively auditory; the reasons are soon apparent. Note the correlation of the clockwise motion (around the terrace) of the invisible spirits with the directionality of the pilgrim's contemplation of the examples on the first terrace.

27. the table of love: Mention of the table involves the Eucharist, but the sacrament is itself a figure of the more perfect union with Christ that is expected in Heaven, where the blessed partake of the "bread of the angels" (identified by Dante with Wisdom, i.e., Christ as the Logos; see *Conv.* 1.1.1-7, *Par.* 2.10-12, with note). The eucharistic suggestion is continued in the first example: the miracle of Cana (wine) was interpreted to prefigure the Crucifixion and thus the Eucharist.

Because the antidote to envy is love, the greatest of the virtues, closely identified with God himself (1 Cor. 13.13; John 3.16; 1 John 4.16), Dante's examples echo its supreme expression, the redemptive sacrifice of Christ. See also Prov. 9.2: "Wisdom hath . . . slain her victims, mingled her wine, and set forth her table. She hath sent her maids to invite to the tower, and to the walls of the city: Whosoever is a little one, let him come to me. And to the unwise she said: Come, eat my bread, and drink the wine which I have mingled for you."

28-30. The first voice . . . repeating it: The first voice quotes the Virgin Mary's words to Christ at the wedding in Cana (cf. 22.40-42), John 2.1-12; see especially verses 3, 5-11:

> And the wine failing, the mother of Jesus said to him: They have no wine [*Vinum non habent*] . . . Now there were set there six waterpots of stone, according to the manner of the purifying of the Jews, containing two or three measures apiece. Jesus saith to them: Fill the waterpots with water. And they filled them up to the brim. And Jesus saith to them: Draw out now, and carry to the chief steward of the feast. And when the chief steward had tasted the water made wine . . . [he] calleth the bridegroom, and saith to him: Every man at first setteth forth good wine, and when men have well drunk, then that which is worse. But thou hast kept the good wine until now.

This is Christ's first miracle ("initium signorum" [beginning of miracles], John 2.11), said by the exegetes to be his sanctification of marriage as a sacrament; Christ himself is the "bridegroom," the spouse of the Church. The miraculous wine was taken as symbolizing Christ, whose coming in the sixth age (cf. the six urns) signified the transformation of Old Testament prophecies (the water) into the fulfillment of the New Testament (the wine, with eucharistic implications), thus from "insipidity" to "sapidity" (see Sapia, below).

30. went repeating it: Thus only the single phrase is spoken, without any more of the passage; the penitents must reconstruct the incident for themselves.

32-33. another passed . . . did not stop: Orestes (the son of Agamemnon) and his friend Pylades were captured by the tyrant of Tauris, who wished to put Orestes to death but did not know him; the friends vie to save each other, each claiming to be Orestes (cf. John 15.13: "Greater love than this no man hath, that a man lay down his life for his friends," of Christ). Dante knew the story from Cicero's *De amicitia* and *De finibus,* perhaps also from Ovid's *Ex Ponto.*

34-35. Oh! I said . . . behold the third: The speed with which the voices pass is conveyed by their rapid succession, as in lines 31-32.

36. Love those . . . had evil: In all the examples of virtues on the terraces of Purgatory, this is the only case of quotation or paraphrase of the words of Jesus; like the Beatitudes and the Lord's Prayer, they are from the Sermon on the Mount (Matt. 5-7); see Matt. 5.43-45:

> You have heard that it hath been said, Thou shalt love thy neighbor, and hate thy enemy. But I say to you, Love your enemies: do good to them that hate you: and pray for those that persecute and calumniate you: That you may be the children of your Father who is in heaven, who maketh his sun to rise upon the good and bad, and raineth upon the just and the unjust.

37-42. This circle whips . . . pass of pardon: Virgil here invokes the analogy of the acquisition of virtue with the training/governing of horses (whip, bridle), one of the fundamental motifs of the cantica. Note the parallel with the image of Italy as a horse allowed, by the neglect of its rider the emperor, to become wild and ungovernable (6.88-99); the image of the spur, a variant of the whip, appears in line 95.

38-39. the cords . . . braided of love: The metaphor is exact, as whips were braided from leather thongs: here each strand is one example (Singleton), and the braiding is the logical and thematic linking of them.

40-42. The bridle . . . the pass of pardon: The reference is to 14.130-41. For the bridle of law (the prescription of penalties for wrong action as deterrents), cf.

6.88-90. The "pass of pardon" is of course the transition to the next terrace (15.1-39); but cf. line 62.

43-72. But probe the air . . . will not be still: The shades of the envious are now introduced: immobile, leaning against the cliff and each other, blinded by having their eyelids sewn shut with iron wires. The idea of this penance derives directly from the traditional etymology of the term *invidere* [to envy] as made up of *in-* (privative) and *videre* [to see]; Uguccione of Pisa's dictionary entry reads: "invideo tibi, idest non video, idest non fero videre te bene agentem" [I envy you, that is I do not see you, that is I cannot bear to see you doing well]. Carroll cites Matt. 6.23: "if thine eye be evil, thy body is full of darkness." Dante also has in mind Ovid's personified Envy, *Met.* 2.775-78: "Pallor in ore sedet, macies in corpore toto, / nusquam recta acies, livent rubigine dentes" [her face pale, her whole body wasted, her gaze never direct, her teeth dark with rust] (see *Inter cantica* below).

43. But probe . . . with your eyes: The shades are difficult to distinguish from the livid rock because of the identical color of their garments; their blending with it is a distant parallel with the carvings below, which were resplendently white (see the note to 14.139). The emphasis on the pilgrim's probing eyes (cf. *Inf.* 4.10-12, 9.73-75), here and in lines 73-75, contrasts with the forced blindness of the souls (hence line 46).

49-51. And when we . . . All saints: Changing perception is again correlated with motion in space. The brief invocations cried out by the souls are parallel to the reciting of the paraphrased Lord's Prayer by the proud; they derive from the litany of all saints (recited most elaborately at the Easter vigil, after the baptism of the catechumens), appealing to the Virgin Mary, the archangel Michael, saint Peter, and then, repeatedly, all the saints.

52-57. I do not think . . . heavy grieving: The pilgrim's compassion makes his tears flow copiously; cf. lines 133-35. These lines draw on a traditional topos; compare *Aen.* 2.6-8:

> quis talia fando
> Myrmidonum Dolopumve aut duri miles Ulixi
> temperet a lacrimis?
> [Who of the Myrmidons
> or Dolopians, or what soldier of hard Ulysses, speaking
> of such things, could hold himself back from tears?]

and, in the "Stabat mater" (attributed to the Franciscan Iacopone da Todi):

> Who is the man who would not weep [non fleret]
> were he the mother of Christ to see
> in such suffering?

Compare also Lam. 1.12 and *Inf.* 33.40-42, and see *Inter cantica* below.

58-60. They seemed clothed . . . suffered them all: Haircloth is a fabric knotted from horsehairs. The souls resemble Biblical mourners, who wear haircloth and ashes, e.g., Lam. 2.10: "The ancients of the daughter of Sion sit upon the ground, they have held their peace: they have sprinkled their heads with dust, they are girded with haircloth, the virgins of Jerusalem hang down their heads to the ground" (cf. Gen. 37.34; 4 Kings 6.30; Judith 4.8; Ps. 68.12; Mt. 11.21).

59-60. each suffered . . . suffered them all: Thus while practicing compassion they practice the bodily attitudes that express it (see Additional Note 6).

61-66. Thus the blind . . . no lesser spur: "Pardons" were occasions for the granting and selling of indulgences (cf. *Decameron* 4.7.11), and beggars stationed themselves near church entrances to be visible (thus the passage evokes the door of a church). Compare the humbling of Provenzano Salvani (11. 109-11, 121-26, with notes) indirectly recalled in this canto (lines 116-17).

64-66. so that pity . . . no lesser spur: A comment on the compassionate use of the faculty of sight, as opposed to their misuse of it in life.

67-72. And as the sun . . . will not be still: The initial phases of training falcons involved "seeling" their eyes with gut thread as an aid in accustoming them to accepting food and handling from the falconer (the technique is described, with illustrations, in Frederick II, *De arte venandi cum avibus*, 2.53). The falconry images (cf. line 103, 14.147-51) coordinate the imagery of light, blindness, and nourishment and closely parallel the metaphors of whip, spur, and bridle (see the note to lines 37-42) in the two cantos of the envious; but the concepts are found not only at 14.147-51 (lure [*richiamo*]) but also at 19.61-66; indeed, the imagery is intrinsic to the themes of moral and political discipline (especially as administered by the emperor) that dominate the center of the poem; see *Inter cantica* to Canto 14.

83. the horrible sutures: For another sewing metaphor, see line 107, with note; for echoes of the weeping in Hell, see the *Inter cantica* to Canto 14.

85-90. I turned to them . . . descending through it: The pilgrim's elaborate address of the envious (with the *captatio* expressing confidence in their future sight) is often thought to anticipate the cleansing of the mind (see *Inf.* 2.8) in the river Lethe (28.127-28). The language transforms the just-described forcing of tears through closed eyelids, perhaps suggesting filtering (cf. 2.122-23, with note).

94-96. O my brother . . . as a pilgrim: Sapia's correction of the pilgrim marks her (only partial) distancing from her involvement in Sienese political life, and perhaps reflects her having (with her husband) endowed a pilgrim hostel near

Siena. For living on earth as a pilgrim—a condition that sharply affected the exiled Dante—see 2 Cor. 5-6; Eph. 2:17-22; Heb. 11:13-16; 1 Peter 2.11.

103-105. Spirit . . . by place or by name: "Mastering yourself" reiterates the idea of self-discipline for the sake of freedom to climb (as in *Ep.* 6.23, only one obedient to the law is free). For the formula interrogating identity, see 14.10-13 and note.

106-29. I was Sienese . . . in his charity: Born circa 1210, Sapia belonged to the important Sienese family of the Salvani (she was the aunt of Provenzano Salvani; see 11.109-11 and notes). It was probably as the widow of Ghinibaldo di Saracino (he died in 1269), when at the family castle of Castiglioncello, near Montereggioni (see map on p. xii) about five miles from the plain of Colle on which the battle was fought (lines 115-20), that Sapia rejoiced at the rout of her fellow-citizens. Sapia's ill feelings toward her fellow-citizens are not otherwise attested; Buti suggests that she was in exile at the castle at the time of the battle, hence her resentment. She died between 1274 and 1289. Dante's portrait of the haughty aristocrat is at once sharp and subtle, and should be read with his other harsh accounts of the Sienese (see 13.118-23, *Inf.* 29.121-39).

107-108: I repair my wicked life, weeping: "Repair" translates *rimendo* [literally, mend, darn] preferred by Petrocchi over *rimondo* [cleanse]. The sewing image, perhaps attributing to Sapia typically female work with the needle, should be seen in relation to the sewing up of the eyes.

109-11. I was not wise . . . my own good luck: Sapia implies that her name is derived from Lat. *sapio* [to know, to be wise]; such etymologizing was not unusual, for "names are the consequences of things" (cf. *VN* 1; 24; *Par.* 12.79-80), and many names were in fact chosen for their meaning. Lines 110-11 specify the mode of her folly and are an exact definition of envy as distinguished from pride (cf. 17.118-20). In this canto Dante draws extensively on the books of Proverbs and Wisdom, in which personified Wisdom (usually interpreted by the exegetes as the Logos) speaks at great length; see lines 9, 25, 27, 114-15, 122-23.

113-14. hear if I was mad . . . descending: The force of Sapia's statement is that she was mature (nearly sixty) and should have known better (cf. Prov. 1.20; attributed to Solomon, this book was thought to be for educating children). Dante discusses the "arc of life" in *Conv.* 4.23, the behavior appropriate to old age in *Conv.* 4.28; cf. *Inf.* 26.106-107, 27.79-81.

115. Colle: A town 14 miles northwest of Siena, near San Gimignano in the Val d'Elsa. Here on June 17, 1269, the Sienese Ghibellines, led by Sapia's nephew Provenzano Salvani and Count Guido Novello, were routed by the Florentine Guelphs aided by the French; Salvani was killed.

121. I turned my bold face upwards: The same gesture as at 13.101-102, but with opposite significance: it is a kind of parody of the traditional mark of the human being: "[the god] gave man a head uplifted and bade him see the sky and draw his upward gaze to the stars" (*Met.* 1.85-86; cf. also 12.25-63, 14.143-52, with notes). Sapia first *saw* (and rejoiced at) the rout, then *turned* her face insolently to God.

122-23. Now I fear you . . . a little sunshine: "When fair weather returns, [the blackbird] comes forth and seems to make fun of every other bird. In the fable about this bird, it is made to say: 'I do not fear you, Lord, for winter's over!'" (Buti). The commentators infer that the fable, recorded by Sacchetti in the late Trecento (*Novella* 149), was proverbial by Dante's time. Note the implicit reference to Prov. 1.7: "The beginning of wisdom is the fear of the Lord. Fools despise wisdom and instruction" (cf. Ps. 110.10; *Conv.* 4.21.12; *Ep.* 6.11).

124-29. I wished peace . . . in his charity: Though reconciled to God late in life, Sapia would still be waiting outside the gate, if not for the prayers of a saintly man, which diminished the period of delay (equal to the lifetime spent deferring repentance of mortal sin, according to Belacqua, 4.130-32).

127. Piero the comb-seller remembered me: Dubbed "a man full of God, Peter the comb-seller of Siena" by the radical Franciscan Ubertino da Casale (see *Par.* 12.124, with note), Piero was a hermit and tertiary of the Franciscan order who made and sold carding combs used in weaving; he died in 1289. The Sienese revered him for his piety and built him a tomb in the church of San Francesco; in 1328 the Sienese senate instituted an annual feast in his honor.

130-32. But who are you . . . as you speak: With her acute hearing, Sapia has noted the pilgrim's breathing; her tone is abrupt. This is the first direct challenge that the pilgrim identify himself; here, as at 14.16-21, he is evasive (cf. also 14.10-13 and note).

135. by being turned with envy: The use of "turned" here refers to the indirect eyes of Ovid's Envy (see the note to lines 48-72).

138. already the burden down there weighs on me: Dante was reputed to be proud, as Villani notes: "This Dante, because of his learning, was somewhat presumptuous, haughty, and disdainful, and being rude, as philosophers are, knew not how to speak with the unlearned."

139-41. Who then has led you . . . does not speak: Both here and in line 130, Sapia's interrogation is peremptory, without courtesy formulas; see 14.1-6 and note.

145-47. Oh, this is such . . . from time to time: "Strange new thing" translates "cosa nuova": Sapia is identifying the miracle of the pilgrim's journey (for "segno," cf. the note to line 7): here at least she rejoices at the grace shown to another, and begs for his prayers (note the parallel with the blind at Pardons, lines 61-62).

150. restore my good fame among my relatives: In order to reassure them of her salvation, so that they will pray for her (cf. 3.115-117).

151-54. that vain people . . . will lose even more: Sapia refers to two expensive Sienese fiascoes: the purchase of the port city of Talamone from the Counts of Santafiora, to gain an opening on the sea in order to compete with Genoese and Venetian shipping; and the attempts to locate water in an underground stream, the Diana. The term *admirals* could refer both to contractors and to ship captains. Sapia's final barb (note the close parallel with *Inf.* 29.121-23) is meant to distinguish her relatives from the rest of the citizens.

Inter cantica. The cantos 13 in *Inferno* and *Purgatorio* show many parallels, including similar beginnings ("a wood that no path marked," *Inf.* 13.2-3, "the bank and the road appear bare," *Purg.* 13.8) and conclusions, Sapia's review of Sienese folly (13.151-53), and the anonymous suicide's account of Florentine internecine violence (13.148-50). The spendthrifts hunted by dogs in 13.111-14 ("one who hears . . . the hunt approaching")—which includes the Sienese Lano, who died at the Toppo (120-21)—echoes the rout of the Sienese ("turned in the bitter steps of flight . . . hunted down," 13.118-19) that so pleased Sapia, a reversal of fortune like Pier delle Vigne's ("my bright honors turned to sad mourning"). Both Pier delle Vigne (but *Purg.* 13.128 also has a Piero, Pier Pettinaio) and Sapia—etymologically rich names both—wish to restore reputations impeached by envy (*Inf.* 13. 78, 13. 150). Pier delle Vigne holds envy, the "vice of courts" (*Inf.* 13.66) responsible for his doom; the radical status of this sin (Wisdom 2.24) and its "sluttish eyes" (*Inf.* 13.65) is punished with the loss of eyesight in *Purgatorio* (13.133-34). The vice of the imperial court in Piero's tragedy becomes that of a city-republic in Sapia (*Purg.* 13.115). The link is manifest in the verbal similarity of *Purg.* 13.37-38: "this circle whips the guilt of envy" and Piero's reference to his memory at *Inf.* 13.77-78: ". . . beneath the blow that envy dealt it." At a deeper level, the reference to seeling the eyes of the envious (*Purg.* 13.62-72) points to Pier delle Vigne's blinding by his lord and master Frederick II, who produced the principal medieval treatise on falconry, which in turn brings to mind the absence of imperial authority in Italy and the metaphors of moral discipline in 13.37-42 and 14.143-44 (see *Mon.* 3.15.9, Ps. 31.9).

With respect to line 121 ("turned upward my bold face"), readers also recall Capaneus' scornful upward gaze, *Inf.* 14.46-72; he "seems still to have God in disdain" (14.69-70).

CANTO 14

"Chi è costui che 'l nostro monte cerchia   1
prima che morte li abbia dato il volo,
e apre li occhi a sua voglia e coverchia?"

"Non so chi sia, ma so che non è solo;   4
domandal tu che più li t'avvicini,
e dolcemente, sì che parli, acco'lo."

Così due spirti, l'uno a l'altro chini,   7
ragionavan di me ivi a man dritta;
poi fer li visi, per dirmi, supini,

e disse l'uno: "O anima che fitta   10
nel corpo ancora inver' lo ciel ten vai,
per carità ne consola e ne ditta

onde vieni e chi se'; ché tu ne fai   13
tanto maravigliar de la tua grazia
quanto vuol cosa che non fu più mai."

E io: "Per mezza Toscana si spazia   16
un fiumicel che nasce in Falterona,
e cento miglia di corso nol sazia.

Di sovr' esso rech' io questa persona;   19
dirvi chi sia saria parlare indarno,
ché 'l nome mio ancor molto non suona."

"Se ben lo 'ntendimento tuo accarno   22
con lo 'ntelletto," allora mi rispuose
quei che diceva pria, "tu parli d'Arno."

E l'altro disse lui: "Perché nascose   25
questi il vocabol di quella riviera,
pur com' om fa de l'orribili cose?"

E l'ombra che di ciò domandata era   28
si sdebitò così: "Non so, ma degno
ben è che 'l nome di tal valle pèra:

CANTO 14

Second terrace, continued: Guido del Duca and Rinieri da Calboli—
denunciation of the Arno valley—prophecy—the decline of Romagna—
examples of envy

1   "Who is that, who circles our mountain before
death has given him flight, and opens and covers
his eyes at will?"

4   "I do not know who he is, but I know that he is
not alone; you ask him, since you are closer, and
greet him kindly, so that he will speak."

7   Thus two spirits, bending toward each other,
were discussing me off to my right; then to speak
to me they made their faces supine,

10   and one said: "O soul who still fixed in your
body are going up toward Heaven, in charity
console us and tell us

13   whence you come and who you are; for you
make us marvel at the grace you receive, as much
as befits a thing that has never been."

16   And I: "Through the midst of Tuscany there
flows a little stream that is born in Falterona, and a
hundred miles of flowing do not sate it.

19   From along its banks I bring this body of mine;
to tell you who I am would be to speak in vain, for
my name does not yet much resound."

22   "If I flesh out your meaning well with my
understanding," replied then the one who had
spoken earlier, "you are speaking of Arno."

25   And the other said to him: "Why did he conceal
the word for that river, just as one does of horrible
things?"

28   And the shade who was asked that question paid
his debt thus: "I do not know, but it is surely
fitting that the name of that valley perish:

ché dal principio suo, ov' è sì pregno   31
l'alpestro monte ond' è tronco Peloro
che 'n pochi luoghi passa oltra quel segno,
    infin là 've si rende per ristoro   34
di quel che 'l ciel de la marina asciuga,
ond' hanno i fiumi ciò che va con loro,
    vertù così per nimica si fuga   37
da tutti come biscia, o per sventura
del luogo o per mal uso che li fruga;
    ond' hanno sì mutata lor natura   40
li abitator de la misera valle,
che par che Circe li avesse in pastura.
    Tra brutti porci, più degni di galle   43
che d'altro cibo fatto in uman uso,
dirizza prima il suo povero calle.
    Botoli trova poi, venendo giuso,   46
ringhiosi più che non chiede lor possa,
e da lor disdegnosa torce il muso.
    Vassi caggendo, e quant' ella più 'ngrossa,   49
tanto più trova di can farsi lupi
la maladetta e sventurata fossa.
    Discesa poi per più pelaghi cupi,   52
trova le volpi, sì piene di froda
che non temono ingegno che le occùpi.
    Né lascerò di dir perch' altri m'oda;   55
e buon sarà costui, s'ancor s'ammenta
di ciò che vero spirto mi disnoda.
    Io veggio tuo nepote che diventa   58
cacciator di quei lupi in su la riva
del fiero fiume, e tutti li sgomenta.
    Vende la carne loro essendo viva;   61
poscia li ancide come antica belva;
molti di vita e sé di pregio priva.
    Sanguinoso esce de la trista selva;   64
lasciala tal che di qui a mille anni
ne lo stato primaio non si rinselva."
    Com' a l'annunzio di dogliosi danni   67
si turba il viso di colui ch'ascolta,
da qual che parte il periglio l'assanni:

31   for from its beginning where the high
mountain, from which Pelorus was broken off, is
so pregnant with water that few places exceed it,

34   down to the place where it restores what the sky
dries from the sea, whereby rivers gain what flows
in them,

37   virtue is avoided as an enemy by everyone as if it
were a snake, whether through bad influences on
the place or because of ill custom that goads them;

40   and the inhabitants of the wretched valley have
so changed their natures that it seems Circe has
been pasturing them.

43   Among ugly swine, more fit for acorns than for
any food made to human use, it first directs its
poor course.

46   Then, coming down, it finds curs who snarl
more than their power justifies, and from them,
disdainful, it twists away its snout.

49   It keeps falling, and the more it swells, the more
that cursed and baleful furrow finds the dogs
becoming wolves.

52   Descending then through many deep lagoons, it
finds foxes, so full of fraud that they do not fear
capture by any ruse.

55   I will not leave off speaking just because a
certain person may hear me, and it will be well for
this man if he keeps in mind what a true spirit is
unfolding to me.

58   I see your nephew become the hunter of those
wolves along the bank of the fierce river, and he
terrifies them all.

61   He sells their flesh while it is still living; then he
kills them like old cattle; he deprives many of life
and himself of praise.

64   All bloodied he comes forth from the wicked
wood; he leaves it such that a thousand years from
now it will not be reforested to its original state."

67   As at the announcement of grievous injuries the
face of one listening becomes clouded, from
whatever side danger may sink its teeth in him:

così vid' io l'altr' anima, che volta   70
stava a udir, turbarsi e farsi trista
poi ch'ebbe la parola a sé raccolta.

   Lo dir de l'una e de l'altra la vista   73
mi fer voglioso di saper lor nomi,
e dimanda ne fei con prieghi mista;

   per che lo spirto che di pria parlòmi   76
ricominciò: "Tu vuo' ch'io mi deduca
nel fare a te ciò che tu far non vuo'mi.

   Ma da che Dio in te vuol che traluca   79
tanto sua grazia, non ti sarò scarso:
però sappi ch'io fui Guido del Duca.

   Fu il sangue mio d'invidia sì rïarso   82
che, se veduto avesse uom farsi lieto,
visto m'avresti di livore sparso:

   di mia semente cotal paglia mieto.   85
O gente umana, perché poni 'l core
là 'v' è mestier di consorte divieto?

   Questi è Rinier, questi è 'l pregio e l'onore   88
de la casa da Calboli, ove nullo
fatto s'è reda poi del suo valore.

   E non pur lo suo sangue è fatto brullo,   91
tra 'l Po e 'l monte e la marina e 'l Reno,
del ben richesto al vero e al trastullo:

   ché dentro a questi termini è ripieno   94
di venenosi sterpi, sì che tardi
per coltivare omai verrebber meno.

   Ov' è 'l buon Lizio e Arrigo Mainardi?   97
Pier Traversaro e Guido di Carpigna?
Oh Romagnuoli tornati in bastardi!

   Quando in Bologna un Fabbro si ralligna? 100
quando in Faenza un Bernardin di Fosco,
verga gentil di picciola gramigna?

   Non ti maravigliar s'io piango, Tosco,   103
quando rimembro, con Guido da Prata,
Ugolin d'Azzo che vivette nosco,

   Federigo Tignoso e sua brigata,   106
la casa Traversara e li Anastagi
(e l'una gente e l'altra è diretata),

70   so I saw the other soul, who was turned to
listen, become troubled and sad, when it had
gathered his word to itself.

73   The speech of the one and the appearance of the
other made me wish to know their names, and my
request was mixed with prayers;

76   therefore the spirit who had spoken to me
earlier began again: "You wish me to condescend
to do for you what you will not do for me.

79   But since God wills that his grace shine through
you so much, I will not be stingy with you;
therefore know that I was Guido del Duca.

82   My blood was so afire with envy that, if I saw a
man becoming glad, you would have seen me turn
livid:

85   such is the straw I reap from my sowing. O
human race, why do you set your heart where
sharing must be forbidden?

88   This is Rinieri, this is the praise and the honor
of the house of Calboli, where no one since has
become heir to his nobility.

91   And not only his blood has gone barren,
between the Po and the mountain and the sea and
the Reno, of the good needed for truth and for
pleasure:

94   for within those bounds it is so full of poisonous
thickets that it is too late now for cultivation to
root them out.

97   Where is the good Lizio, and Arrigo Mainardi?
Piero Traversaro and Guido di Carpegna? Oh men
of Romagna, turned into bastards!

100   When in Bologna will a Fabbro take root again?
when in Faenza a Bernardino di Fosco, noble
shoot born of humble grass?

103   Do not marvel if I weep, Tuscan, when I
remember, with Guido da Prata, Ugolino d'Azzo
who lived in our midst,

106   Federigo Tignoso and his friends, the house of
the Traversari and the Anastagi (and both families
are without heirs),

le donne e ' cavalier, li affanni e li agi 109
che ne 'nvogliava amore e cortesia
là dove i cuor son fatti sì malvagi.

O Bretinoro, ché non fuggi via, 112
poi che gita se n'è la tua famiglia
e molta gente per non esser ria?

Ben fa Bagnacaval, che non rifiglia; 115
e mal fa Castrocaro, e peggio Conio,
che di figliar tai conti più s'impiglia.

Ben faranno i Pagan da che 'l demonio 118
lor sen girà, ma non però che puro
già mai rimagna d'essi testimonio.

O Ugolin de' Fantolin, sicuro 121
è 'l nome tuo, da che più non s'aspetta
chi far lo possa, tralignando, scuro.

Ma va via, Tosco, omai, ch'or mi diletta 124
troppo di pianger più che di parlare,
sì m'ha nostra ragion la mente stretta."

Noi sapavam che quell' anime care 127
ci sentivano andar; però, tacendo,
facëan noi del cammin confidare.

Poi fummo fatti soli procedendo, 130
folgore parve, quando l'aere fende,
voce che giunse di contra, dicendo:

"Anciderammi qualunque m'apprende!" 133
e fuggì come tuon che si dilegua,
se sùbito la nuvola scoscende.

Come da lei l'udir nostro ebbe triegua, 136
ed ecco l'altra con sì gran fracasso
che somigliò tonar che tosto segua:

"Io sono Aglauro, che divenni sasso!" 139
e allor, per ristrignermi al poeta,
in destro feci, e non innanzi, il passo.

Già era l'aura d'ogne parte queta; 142
ed el mi disse: "Quel fu 'l duro camo
che dovria l'uom tener dentro a sua meta.

109   the ladies and the knights, the labors and the leisures that love and courtesy made us desire, there where hearts have become so wicked.

112   O Bertinoro, why do you not disappear, now that your family has departed, and many more, so as not to become base?

115   Bagnacavallo does well to beget no sons; Castrocaro does ill, and Conio worse, that undertake to beget such counts.

118   The Pagani will do well, once their demon has departed, but not so that pure testimony will ever be left about them.

121   O Ugolino de' Fantolini, your name is safe, now that no one can be expected who could darken it by his degeneration.

124   But go away, Tuscan, for now weeping delights me much more than speech, our talk has so anguished my mind."

127   We knew that those dear souls could hear us walking; therefore by their silence they made us confident of our path.

130   When we had walked so far as to be alone, a voice that came against us seemed like a flash of lightning that cleaves the air, saying:

133   "Whoever finds me will kill me!" and it fled as a thunderclap fades, when suddenly a cloud has burst.

136   When our hearing had a truce from the first voice, behold the second, with so great a noise that it seemed like thunder that immediately follows:

139   "I am Aglauros who turned to stone!" and then, to draw closer to my poet, I made a step to the right, not forward.

142   Now the air was quiet on every side; and he said to me: "That was the hard bit that should keep one within his track.

Ma voi prendete l'esca, sì che l'amo   145
de l'antico avversaro a sé vi tira,
e però poco val freno o richiamo.
    Chiamavi 'l cielo e 'ntorno vi si gira,   148
mostrandovi le sue bellezze etterne,
e l'occhio vostro pur a terra mira:
    onde vi batte chi tutto discerne."   151

145   But you take the bait, so that the old adversary's
hook draws you to him, and therefore rein and
lure do little good.

148   The heavens call and wheel about you, showing
you their eternal beauties, and your eye still gazes
on the earth:

151   therefore he beats you who discerns all things."

1-9. Who is that . . . their faces supine: Uniquely in the poem, a canto begins with dialogue between unidentified spirits (not named until lines 81 and 87) who do not address the wayfarers. Farinata's address of the pilgrim (*Inf.* 10.22; also *Purg.* 8.88-114) is comparable, but does not begin the canto. Line 9 restates 13.102.

1-3. Who is that . . . opens and covers his eyes: The soul's surprised response to the pilgrim's ability to see elicits a counsel of courtesy from his companion (line 6). Cf. Is. 63.1, "Quis es iste, qui venit" [Who is this that cometh], which Christian exegesis and liturgy took as prophetic of Christ.

2. before death has given him flight: The soul's escape from the prison of the flesh, both Christian anagogy and Neoplatonic return of the soul to its source, are implied here; see *Commentarii* 1.11.3: "who have flown from the bonds of their bodies as from a prison" (see also Cicero *De amicitia* 4.14, *Consolation* 2.7, and *Purg.* 25.80, with note). For the taking flight of souls who complete their purgation, see 10.124-25 and note.

9. made their faces supine: See 13.121, with note.

10-12. O soul . . . in charity console us: These souls have presumably overheard Sapia's inference that the pilgrim is still alive (13.130-32). The request for consolation (cf. 2.109, to Casella) draws the pilgrim into the penitential action of the circle; note his *faux pas* at line 78.

12-15. tell us whence you come . . . has never been: See 13.130-32, with note. Pietro di Dante cites the interrogation of Tydeus and Polynices by Adrastus, king of Argos, in *Theb.* 1.443-46, 669-72 (see also *Purg.* 3.112-13 and note); although Tydeus at once proclaims his origins (1.451-65), Polynices, the son of accursed Oedipus, only identifies himself after further questioning (1.680-82): "But if you must learn the cares of the wretched, Cadmus gave rise to my fathers, my land is the Thebes of Mars, my mother is Jocasta."

16-21. Through the midst . . . does not yet much resound: The pilgrim's modesty implies the topic of fame, aired in the circle of pride (see 11.100-103, 109-11); see also 8.124-26 (the fame of the Malaspina family) and Sapia's concern for her reputation (13.150); the question of the reputations of poets will recur (26.124-26). The pilgrim's obscurity is juxtaposed with the infamy of the valley of the Arno.

22-27. If I flesh out . . . as one does of horrible things: Dante uses "horrible" rarely: see 13.83 ("horrible sutures"), and 3.121 for Manfred's sins; the last use in *Inferno* is 33.47, for Ugolino's tower.

28-66. And the shade . . . to its original state: The account of the Arno valley, beginning in the Casentino and eventually reaching the sea, is a kind of retrospective of Dante's Hell (see *Inter cantica* below). Dante begins by suggesting a personification of the river ("do not sate it") that is soon confirmed ("it twists away its snout"), except that it has become a beast.

29. paid his debt thus: A typical economic metaphor—at once feudal and purgatorial—for the "courtesy" between these souls.

29-30. it is surely fitting . . . that valley perish: Cf. Job 18.17: "Let the memory of him perish from the earth, and let not his name be renowned in the streets"; see also Ps. 108.13. After the harsh survey of European royalty in 7.94-136, these lines anticipate the second part of this canto (lines 88-123).

31-36. from its beginning . . . what flows in them: The course of the Arno, from its source on the Falterona massif (see 5.109-20 and notes), to its mouth (the "place where [the Arno] restores what the sky dries"), given in terms of the cycle of rain and evaporation, which, as Aristotle explains in his *Meteorology* 1, follows the seasons and creates a circular river traversing air and water. Aquinas (*In Meteorologiam Aristotelis commentarius* 1 lect. 13) summarizes: "When the sun comes closer, this rain of vapors goes upward; when the sun is more distant, it goes downward . . . Thus it can be concluded that when the ancients said the ocean to be a kind of river circling the earth, they were perhaps speaking obscurely about this river, which flows in a circle around the earth." See 5.109-11, with note.

32-33. the high mountain . . . was broken off: These lines refer to the entire chain of the Apennines, which extend the length of Italy, even into Sicily, where Mount Pelorus, across the straits of Messina, was thought to be originally its continuation, broken off from the mainland by an earthquake; cf. *Aen.* 3.410-19, and especially 414-17:

> Haec loca vi quondam et vasta convulsa ruina
> (tantum aevi longinqua valet mutare vetustas)
> dissiluisse ferunt, cum protinus utraque tellus
> una foret . . .
> [They say that these places once leapt apart forcibly,
> convulsed with huge ruin (so strong to change things is the vast
> antiquity of the ages), when previously the two lands
> had been one.]

Dante's lines are confusing in translation, since English word-order does not permit the inverted syntax "ov'è sì pregno l'alpestro monte" [where the high mountain is so pregnant] (Falterona), so the mention of Pelorus must interrupt it.

37-39. virtue is avoided. . . ill custom that goads them: The reverse of the valley in Canto 8, whence the serpent is expelled; compare also *Met.* 1.149-50

(Justice leaving the fallen world) and *Aen.* 3.44. The complaint over declining mores and civic life recurs at 16.115-26.

40-42. have so changed ... pasturing them: Circe, the witch of the *Odyssey*, is recalled in the *Aeneid* and in Ovid's *Metamorphoses*: In Homer she changes Odysseus's crew into animals (mostly pigs) by drugging their drink. Given an antidote (moly) by Hermes, Odysseus eludes her trap; she takes him to her bed and releases his crew. Medieval commentators read the tale as one of seduction by lust or avarice (Circe signified wordly goods, since she was a daughter of the sun, which creates abundance). See Boethius's moralizing (*Consolation* 4.3, 4. m.3, and 4. 4):

> Does the violent one who seizes another's goods burn with avarice? You might say he is like a wolf. He who, fierce and restless, employs his tongue in quarrels you will compare to a dog. Does the hidden intruder enjoy having stolen fraudulently? Let him be equaled with a fox . . . Does he wallow in rank and unclean lechery? He is held by the pleasures of a filthy sow. Thus it comes about that whoever, having abandoned right conduct, ceases to be a man, since he cannot pass into the divine condition, is transformed into a beast.

(Dante cites this passage in *Conv.* 2.7.3-4.) Dante's word for feeding (*pastura*) here prepares satirical uses of related terms in 16.98 and 110. For Circe in the pilgrim's second dream, see 19.22, with note.

43. Among ugly swine, more fit for acorns: Dante's word here, *galle*, literally means oak-galls, excrescences formed on oaks when infested by wasps; most critics take it as a synonym for *ghiande*, acorns, the food of swine (but also of the Golden Age: see *Met.* 1.106; *Consolation* 2. m. 5.4-5).

46-48. it finds curs ... it twists away its snout: The Arno passes near Arezzo, whose coat of arms shows a small dog baring its teeth at a boar, with the inscription: "A cane non magno saepe tenetur aper" [a small dog often holds a boar at bay]. The river is fully animated as it twists away its snout (cf. *Inf.* 31.126, Virgil to Antaeus: "non torcer lo grifo" [do not twist your snout away]), referring to the sharp bend that makes it flow north.

49-51. It keeps falling . . . the dogs becoming wolves: The rivalry of dogs and wolves refers to the traditional enmity of Guelph Florence and Ghibelline Arezzo. For hounds chasing wolves, see *Inf.* 33.28-33 and *Inter cantica* below; as in Boethius, the wolf is an emblem of avarice and cupidity throughout the *Comedy* (e.g., *Inf.* 1.49-51; *Purg.* 20.10-12).

52-54. finds foxes, so full of fraud: After passing Florence, the Arno enters the sea near Pisa. Known for stratagems and guile, the Pisans are compared to crafty foxes (see *Inf.* 33.30, 78).

55-57. I will not leave off . . . unfolding to me: Prophecy is furnished by the Holy Spirit, as in John 16.13: "But when the spirit of truth is come, he will teach you all truth. For he shall not speak of himself; but what things soever he shall hear, he shall speak; and the things that are to come, he shall shew you." For "unravelling," see *Conv.* 3.8.3: "intending . . . to disentangle some of such a great knot."

58-66. I see your nephew . . . its original state: The speaker predicts the future (relative to 1300), in which Fulcieri da Calboli, the nephew of his inter- locutor (see line 81), imposes a tyrannical regime on Florence (1303; he was also *podestà* of Milan, Parma, and Modena between 1297 and 1309). Dino Compagni (2.30) and Villani (8.59) report Fulcieri's roundups of prominent Whites, whom he tortured and killed at the behest of Blacks (such as Musciatto Franzesi; cf. Boccaccio, *Decameron* 1.1); they renewed Fulcieri's contract because of his effi- ciency. See *Inferno* Additional Note 9.

61-62. kills them like old cattle: Some critics take the phrase ending line 62 [literally, ancient beasts] to describe Fulcieri himself as an "ancient monster."

63. and himself of praise: Inverting what is said of Currado Malaspina, whose family maintains honor and worth at 8.128-29; compare also line 88 ("the praise and the honor") (Muresu 1985).

64. All bloodied . . . its original state: The antecedent of "he" in line 64 is ambiguous: given the personification of the "fierce river," the Arno and Fulcieri tend to coalesce, both leaving Tuscany (especially Florence; see *Inf.* 13.144-50 and note) deforested of citizens; for rivers running red with blood, see *Aen.* 6.87 (seen in a prophecy, as here) and *Inf.* 10.86. The construction in line 66 echoes the pessimism of 7.96 ("it will be long before any other revives her [Italy]").

67-72. As the announcement . . . his word to itself: The soul expresses regret at his nephew's future behavior (cf. 7.107-108 and note), but also sorrow at the misfortunes of others, an expression of charity. As when Guido decoded Dante's reference to the Arno (lines 22-24), exchanges of speech between the envious are slow and methodical—a refusal of their hasty, askance scrutiny of others when alive? (For danger's "teeth," see *Inter cantica* below.)

73-81. The speech . . . I was Guido del Duca: Naming himself, Guido notes the asymmetry of the exchange, for the pilgrim does not reciprocate. Out of charity and his perception of the pilgrim's election (note the metaphor of light in *traluca* [shines through]), he unfolds who he is (the term *deduca* in Italian means both "condescend" and "draw out"; cf. *Met.* 1.1-3, where *deducere* means "draw out [thread]" as in spinning and weaving. Since It. *guido* and *duca* mean respec- tively "I lead" and "leader," the name heralds the discussion of discipline at lines 143-47).

81. Guido del Duca: Only a few anecdotes recall this Ghibelline from Romagna, who died about 1250. Perhaps the son of Giovanni degli Onesti of the house of the Duchi (a family that included Saint Romuald and Pietro Peccatore), he was a judge in Faenza (1195) and Rimini (1199), and lived both in Bertinoro (1202-1218, of which he was lord) and Ravenna. He is one of several courtiers from previous generations that Dante invokes to condemn the present.

82-84. My blood was so afire . . . seen me turn livid: The commentators refer to the physiological effects of envy, which heats the blood, producing dark blotches on the skin. For burning as an expression of envy, cf. *Met.* 2.809-11: "uritur [Aglauros]" [Aglauros burns]).

85. such is the straw I reap: See Prov. 22.8, Hos. 8.7, and Gal. 6.8: "for what things a man shall sow, those also shall he reap." The metaphor is developed in lines 91-123.

87. why do you set . . . must be forbidden?: Del Lungo points out that "divieto di consorzio" is Florentine legal terminology: holding office required the exclusion (*divieto*) from that office of all family and clan members (*consorti*). For the implications of the phrase, and its roots in Augustine's discussion of the Earthly City (*De civ. Dei* 15.4-5) see 15.50, with note.

88. This is Rinieri: The Guelph Rinieri from Calboli (a town in the valley of the Montone, center of a small feudal holding corresponding to the modern Rocca San Casciano) participated in partisan struggles in Romagna in the mid-thirteenth century. *Podestà* of various cities between 1247 and 1292, during the Romagnole war of 1276 he rebelled against Forlì with the help of Florentine and Bolognese Guelphs, but had to yield the city to Guido da Montefeltro. Repacified with the Church, in 1291 he witnessed the accord with the papal rector, along with Malatesta da Verrucchio (27.46); he died in 1296 defending Forlì against Scarpetta Ordelaffi and the Ghibellines (27.43-44). Of the pair who speak here, one was Guelph, the other Ghibelline; one lived in the first half of the thirteenth century, the other in the second: distinctions like the division of the subject matter between Tuscany and Romagna.

89-90. no one since has become heir to his nobility: Explicit mention of the failure of heirs here and in line 108 hints at the theme of Guido del Duca's lament, the retreat of secular, imperial authority before the advance of papal ambition; cf. 6.76-151, 7.91-102, 16.103-20 and 20.67-96. The loss of inheritance has biblical resonance; cf. Lam. 5.2, on the loss of Jerusalem: "Our inheritance is turned to aliens"; the topic is also found in civic laments, such as Guittone d'Arezzo's for Arezzo, Florence, and Pisa; see 6.76-78, with note.

91-123. And not only . . . by his degeneration: Balancing his invective against Tuscany, Guido del Duca laments the decline of Romagna. Like Sordello's account of the failed rulers of Europe, it both mourns great men gone (using the

ubi sunt topos of biblical and epic resonance) and condemns the current genera-
tion, who cannot equal them. Guido's syntax is complex (see the multiple
chiasmus, lines 106-11); he uses difficult figures, such as the apostrophe of fami-
lies and personified cities, and tropes such as sarcasm, irony, antiphrasis, and
paranomasia (puns, as with the Conio family, who breed *conti*). Woven throughout
is the vegetation metaphor of family trees, of Romagna as a garden where weeds
choke nobler plants (cf. *Hamlet,* Act 1, 2.135-37: "Fie on 't, ah, fie, 'tis an unweeded
garden / That grows to seed. Things rank and gross in nature / Possess it merely").

92-93. between the Po and the mountain and the sea and the Reno: The
natural boundaries of medieval Romagna; see map, p. xii.

95-96. poisonous thickets . . . to root them out: For the old commentators,
these are, allegorically, the tyrants that flourished in contemporary Romagna (see
Inf. 27.36-39); see also *Inf.* 13.6-7, and *Inter cantica* below. Note again the phrasing
of 6.96, there in reference to emperors.

97-121: Lizio, and Arrigo Mainardi . . . O Ugolino de' Fantolini: In nine
terzinas, Guido deploys seventeen names (of families and places), arranged in
groups of two to four tercets. The first group (six names) denounces corrupt
families; the second (five names) laments the loss of noble manners; the third
(six again) praises the lack of new offspring as a blessing.

97-102. Where is the good Lizio . . . humble grass: Lizio was a Guelph of
Valbona, on the upper reaches of a tributary of the Savio (flowing into the Adriatic;
see the map on p. xii); he served Guido Novello da Polenta, *podestà* of Florence
in 1260, and assisted Rinieri da Calboli against the Ghibellines of Forlì. Arrigo
Mainardi of Bertinoro, held prisoner (along with Pier Traversaro) by the citizens
of Faenza in 1170 and who lived until 1228, was a friend of Guido del Duca, and
present at the nomination of Paolo Traversaro to be city procurator. Pier Traversaro
(1145-1225), of the Ravennate Traversari (of Byzantine origin), was a Ghibelline
lord in Ravenna; an ally of Frederick II, he was several times *podestà*. Guido da
Carpegna (d. 1283), of the counts of Miratoio of Carpegna in the Montefeltro,
was a Guelph adversary of Frederick II; he was *podestà* of Ravenna in 1251 and
claimed descent from the Odoacer who destroyed the Western empire in 476.
Fabbro (sometimes taken as a common noun [*smith*]) is probably Fabbro de'
Lambertazzi, head of the Ghibellines in Romagna and in Bologna; he was *podestà*
of Viterbo, Pistoia, Faenza, and Pisa and fought against Modena and Ravenna;
his death in 1259 presaged the decline of the Ghibellines and the ascent of the
Guelph Geremei in Bologna. Bernardin di Fosco, a humble farmer, later be-
came one of the first citizens of Faenza, which he defended against Frederick II
(he is remembered in a *sirventese* by Uc de Saint Circ) in 1240. He was *podestà*
in 1248 of Pisa, in 1249 of Siena.

99. Oh men of Romagna, turned into bastards: Sordello (6.74-75) writes in
his didactic *Ensenhamen d'onor*: "Alas, how can a nobleman be so shameless as to
bastardize his lineage for gold and silver?"

104-11. Guido da Prata ... become so wicked: Guido da Prata (near Faenza), is remembered in documents of 1184 and 1228 as present in Ravenna. Ugolino d'Azzo, whom Guido del Duca mentions as having lived among the Romagnoli, was a Tuscan. He married Beatrice Lancia, daughter of Provenzano Salvani of Siena (see 11.133-42 and note), and died in 1293; he was probably a member of the Ubaldini family, which included his uncle the cardinal Ottaviano (a heretic, see *Inf.* 10.120), his brother Ubaldino dalla Pila (a glutton, 23.28), and Ubaldino's son Archbishop Ruggieri (a traitor, *Inf.* 33.14). Federigo Tignoso (the surname means "mangy": a joke, given his copious hair) was associated with the Traversari. This family was linked and allied with the Anastagi, another Byzantine family of Ravenna; they reached the peak of their power in the early thirteenth century, but came to grief in an uprising against the Polentani in 1249, which deposed the *podestà,* a Church nominee. The Guelph exiles soon returned, and expelled the Ghibellines, though under threat of excommunication from Cardinal Ubaldino. Nine years later they made peace with the Church and returned, but never regained their former splendor; they had disappeared by Dante's time. All these families had reputations for generosity and courtesy; about many of them, tales and stories celebrating these virtues circulated that appear in the *Novellino* (97: Guido del Duca, Arrigo Mainardi) and in Boccaccio's *Decameron* (Lizio da Valbona, 5.4; the Traversari and Anastagi, 5.8). Lines 108-109 were adapted by Ariosto in the famous opening lines of the *Orlando furioso.*

112-21. O Bertinoro ... Ugolino de' Fantolini: Guido del Duca addresses four towns before returning to family names: Bertinoro, his own fief, between Forlì and Cesena, once known for the hospitality of its nobles to guests (Guido da Carpegna and Arrigo Mainardo had lived in its palace). The Anonimo Fiorentino identifies it as a place where the nobles vied with each other's acts of courtesy and largesse; now it is so neglected it may as well disappear. Bagnacavallo (115), was a town between Lugo and Ravenna, of which the counts Malvicini (Ghibellines) were lords. The family was extinct in the male line by 1300, thus "does well to beget no sons." Castrocaro and Conio were castles in the valley of the Montone, near Imola; the counts of Castrocaro were Ghibellines but submitted to the Church. In 1300 the castle passed into hands of the Ordelaffi of Forlì, and became the Guelph stronghold in Romagna. The counts of Conio, or Cunio, were Guelphs; in producing more offspring, they only do ill. The Pagani, Ghibelline lords of Imola and Faenza at the end of the thirteenth century, produced in Maghinardo Pagano da Susinana (cf. *Inf.* 27.50-51 and note), known as the "demon," their most notorious offspring; he died in 1302.

Guido del Duca concludes by addressing one man: Ugolino de' Fantolini, a Guelph nobleman of Cerfugano, lord of castles near Faenza. He died about 1278, and his two sons died without issue: Ottaviano at Forlì in 1282, when the Guelphs were repulsed by Guido da Montefeltro and Fantolino, about 1291. Without issue, the family is secure from further disgrace.

115. Bagnacavallo ... to beget no sons: Compare "Beatae steriles, et ventres qui non genuerunt" [Blessed the barren, and the wombs that have not borne] (Luke 23.29, a version of the "Little Apocalypse").

124-26. go away, Tuscan . . . anguished my mind: The choice of tears over speech is a topic of formal laments; see Sordello, "Planher vuelh Blacaz" [I wish to lament Blacaz] and the anonymous Latin lament for Troy, "Flere volo Pergama."

127-29. We knew . . . confident of our path: The commentators note that the wayfarers' trust in the mute good will of the two souls seals the exchange of courtesies in the canto. The silence prepares the subsequent clamor.

130-38. a voice . . . immediately follows: The speakers of the examples of envy are invisible, like the spirits in 13.25-36. They sound like lightning. Lightning and thunder signify God's wrath, or indeed that of Jove; compare the fall of Lucifer, "like lightning from heaven" (Luke 10.18), the model for the punishment of pride (cf. 12.26-27); see also 32.109-11 and note.

133. Whoever finds me will kill me: Cain's rejoinder to God when told he will be exiled for the murder of Abel (Gen. 4.14). God answers by marking Cain, shielding him from avengers. Cain was identified by Augustine as a principal founder of the Earthly City, based on envy, rivalry, and strife (*City of God* 15.5): "The first founder of the Earthly City was, as we have seen a fratricide, for, overcome by envy, he slew his own brother, a citizen of the Eternal City on pilgrimage in this world." He goes on: "Anyone whose aim was to glory in the exercise of power would obviously enjoy less power if his sovreignty was diminished by a living partner. Therefore, in order that the sole power should be wielded by one person, the partner was eliminated"(cf. 17.118-23 and notes).

139. I am Aglauros . . . to stone: Aglauros (*Met.* 2.708-832) was a sister of Herse, with whom the god Mercury fell in love. He enlisted the help of Aglauros, but Minerva, angry because of an earlier slight, commanded the goddess Envy to infect Aglauros, who then barred Mercury from entering. Taking up her challenge ("I'll never stir from here!") the god turned her to stone. Ovid underlines the lividity of the resulting statue: "Nec lapis albus erat, sua mens infecerat illam" [nor was the stone white, for her mind had stained it]. The transformation into the livid stone (see the note to 13.9) logically concludes the cantos of envy.

141. to the right, not forward: In anticipation of the reference to correct direction in the lines noted below.

143-51. That was the hard bit . . . discerns all things: Three metaphors of discipline: the bit and rein that steer the horse as it races between the goals or turning-posts, the *metae*; the bait and hook with which Satan, the adversary, would trick the "fish" (human souls, who must avoid it); and, set against that temptation, the lure that recalls the falcon, the soul, to its master, God. One term from each set is in rhyme in the Italian (for an earlier series of nautical, terrestrial, and aerial forms of guidance, see *Inf.* 17.100-129 and notes). The animal imagery recalls the bestial Arno valley, but the movement is—by way of Virgil's sharp reproof—heavenward. Implicit is the Platonic topic of humankind created to gaze upward at the heavens, unlike beasts whose heads hang down: see 13.102 and line 9 above, with notes, and see also *Consolation* 3.8.5: "Look back up at the breadth of heaven, its stability, its swiftness, and cease for a while to gaze on base things." Compare *Conv.* 3.5.22; cf. 19.62-63, with note.

151. who discerns all things: God; the phrase translates "Qui universa conspicit, Dominus Deus Israel," 2 Macc. 9.5 (cf. 6.120).

Inter cantica. Guido del Duca's moral geography of the Arno valley parallels the savage wood of *Inferno* 13 (cf. *sterpi*, "thickets" and "plants," *Inf.* 13.7, 37; *Purg.* 14.95, "poisonous thickets"), and especially the rivers of tears that flow from the Old Man of Crete into Hell (*Inf.* 14.112-20). Guido presents the Arno valley as, like Crete, a ruined land (66, "it will not be reforested to its original state"); the two accounts coordinate descending rivers and deteriorating moral conditions (see *Inf.* 14. 115, 117, 121-22; 126; and *Purg.* 14.45, 46, 51, 52); both use the words *valle* [valley] and *fossa* [ditch, furrow]; *Inf.* 14.115, 136; *Purg.* 14.10, 41, 51), with the clear implication that the Arno valley is a surface version of the river-valleys of Hell, beginning with the swinish (for early commentators, rustic and lecherous) inhabitants of the Casentino (parallel with Dante's gluttons, the "hog," and the wrathful "pigs in swill" of *Inf.* 8.50), continuing with the quarrelsome Aretines—"dogs," parallel with the aggressive Filippo Argenti in the Styx (8.42); then on to the Florentine wolves recalling the violent in Phlegethon (cantos 12-13); concluding with the foxlike Pisans, fraudulent and treacherous in their dealings with Ugolino (*Inf.* 33.79). Guido's bestiary also echoes the animal imagery Brunetto Latini heaps upon the Fiesolan stock in the Florentine population (see *Inf.* 15.67-75 and notes).

In Cocytus, the last and deepest of the rivers deriving from the Old Man of Crete, is Count Ugolino, whose death and revenge are elaborately recalled among the envious: he is indirectly named in Ugolino d'Azzo and Ugolino de' Fantolin (14.103); indeed the "twisted eyes" with which Ugolino seizes Ruggieri's skull (33.76) invoke the oblique gaze ("nusquam recta acies" [eyes never direct]) of Ovid's personified Envy herself, while the livid surface of the terrace (13.9, 48) echoes the stony lividity of the traitors (32.70, 33.49). Ugolino's dream of being hunted down like a wolf (33.29) is alluded to in Guido del Duca's vision of Rinieri da Calboli hunting his enemies (14.58-59).

The posture of the envious, their blind eyes turned upwards as they listen and speak (13.63, 14.9), resting against each other in mutual dependence (13.62), recalls the pairs of traitors frozen in the proximity of mutual hatred (32.45, 126); as the envious are denied the sun (13.66, 68, 86) Ugolino's prison is a "blind prison" (33. 57). That the envious are blinded like falcons seeled for training (13.70-72, 83) resonates with the situation of Ugolino shut up in a mews (*muda*, 33.22) for falcons.

To these parallel situations can be added the rhetorical attack of Sapia's address of the pilgrim ("But who are you" 13.130), which echoes the aggressiveness of Bocca degli Abati (*Inf.* 32.87); while the acknowledgment by the poet of the irresistibility of compassion before the torment of the envious (13.54, 14.103) echoes Ugolino's challenge to the pilgrim to weep (33.40-42): this is rooted in the charge to "love your enemies" (13.36, Matt. 5.44) and the invitation to the love-feast (13.26), which hark back to the eucharistic offer of Ugolino's sons in *Inf.* 33.59-63 and the allusions there to the Sermon on the Mount (see *Inferno* Additional Note 15).

CANTO 15

Quanto tra l'ultimar de l'ora terza   1
e 'l principio del dì par de la spera
che sempre a guisa di fanciullo scherza,

    tanto pareva già inver' la sera   4
essere al sol del suo corso rimaso:
vespero là, e qui mezza notte era.

    E i raggi ne ferien per mezzo 'l naso,   7
perché per noi girato era sì 'l monte
che già dritti andavamo inver' l'occaso,

    quand' io senti' a me gravar la fronte   10
a lo splendore assai più che di prima,
e stupor m'eran le cose non conte;

    ond' io levai le mani inver' la cima   13
de le mie ciglia e fecimi 'l solecchio,
che del soverchio visibile lima.

    Come quando da l'acqua o da lo specchio   16
salta lo raggio a l'opposita parte,
salendo su per lo modo parecchio

    a quel che scende, e tanto si diparte   19
dal cader de la pietra in igual tratta,
sì come mostra esperïenza e arte:

    così mi parve da luce rifratta   22
quivi dinanzi a me esser percosso,
per che a fuggir la mia vista fu ratta.

    "Che è quel, dolce padre, a che non posso   25
schermar lo viso tanto che mi vaglia,"
diss' io, "e pare inver' noi esser mosso?"

    "Non ti maravigliar s'ancor t'abbaglia   28
la famiglia del cielo," a me rispuose;
"messo è che viene ad invitar ch'om saglia.

CANTO 15

Late afternoon—the angel, erasure of a P, a Beatitude—climb—the pilgrim's question about sharing—Virgil's explanation: heavenly versus earthly goods—Third terrace, of anger—examples of forbearance—the cloud of smoke

1   As much as there appears, between the end of the third hour and the beginning of the day, of the circle that always plays like a little child,

4   so much the sun seemed still to have before it of its course toward evening: it was vespers there, and midnight here.

7   And the sun's rays were striking us from straight ahead, since we had circled so much of the mountain that already we were walking directly west,

10   when I felt my brow weighed down by the brightness much more than at first, and the things unknown amazed me;

13   so I raised my hands above the ridge of my brows and made myself a sunshade, that pares away at the excessive light.

16   As when from water or a mirror the ray jumps toward the opposite direction, rising in the same manner

19   as its descent, departing from the fall of a stone by an equal angle, as experience and science show:

22   so it seemed that I was being struck by light refracted there ahead of me, so that my sight was quick to flee it.

25   "What is that, sweet father, from which I cannot shield my sight sufficiently," I said, "and it seems to be moving toward us?"

28   "Do not marvel, if the family of Heaven still dazzle you," he replied; "it is a messenger who comes to invite us to ascend.

Tosto sarà ch'a veder queste cose   31
non ti fia grave, ma fieti diletto
quanto natura a sentir ti dispuose."

   Poi giunti fummo a l'angel benedetto,   34
con lieta voce disse: "Intrate quinci
ad un scaleo vie men che li altri eretto."

   Noi montavam, già partiti di linci,   37
e *"Beati misericordes!"* fue
cantato retro, e "Godi, tu che vinci!"

   Lo mio maestro e io soli amendue   40
suso andavamo; e io pensai, andando,
prode acquistar ne le parole sue;

   e drizza'mi a lui, sì dimandando: 43
"Che volse dir lo spirto di Romagna,
e 'divieto' e 'consorte' menzionando?"

   Per ch'elli a me: "Di sua maggior magagna   46
conosce il danno, e però non s'ammiri
se ne riprende perché men sì piagna.

   Perché s'appuntano i vostri disiri   49
dove per compagnia parte si scema,
invidia move il mantaco a' sospiri.

   Ma se l'amor de la spera supprema   52
torcesse in suso il disiderio vostro,
non vi sarebbe al petto quella tema:

   ché, per quanti si dice più lì 'nostro,'   55
tanto possiede più di ben ciascuno,
e più di caritate arde in quel chiostro."

   "Io son d'esser contento più digiuno,"   58
diss' io, "che se mi fosse pria taciuto,
e più di dubbio ne la mente aduno.

   Com' esser puote ch'un ben, distributo   61
in più posseditor, faccia più ricchi
di sé che se da pochi è posseduto?"

   Ed elli a me: "Però che tu rificchi   64
la mente pur a le cose terrene,
di vera luce tenebre dispicchi.

   Quello infinito e ineffabil Bene   67
che là sù è, così corre ad amore
com' a lucido corpo raggio vène.

31   Soon seeing these things will not be heavy for you but will give you pleasure as great as nature has disposed you to feel."

34   When we reached the blessed angel, with joyful voice he said: "Enter here on a stairway much less steep than the others."

37   We were climbing, already having left him, when *"Beati misericordes!"* was sung behind us, and "Rejoice, you who overcome!"

40   My master and I were going upward, alone; and I thought to gain profit from his words while climbing;

43   and I turned to him, asking: "What did the spirit from Romagna mean, mentioning both 'forbidden' and 'sharing'?"

46   Wherefore he to me: "He knows the harm done by his greatest fault, and therefore do not wonder if he reproaches us so that it may cause less weeping.

49   Because your desires point to where sharing lessens each one's portion, envy moves the bellows to sighing.

52   But if the love of the highest sphere bent your desire upward, you would not have that fear in your breasts:

55   for the more say 'our' up there, the more good each one possesses, and the more charity burns in that cloister."

58   "I am hungrier to be contented," I said, "than if you had been silent earlier, and I am gathering more doubt in my mind.

61   How can it be that one good, distributed among many possessors, can make them richer than if only few possess it?"

64   And he to me: "Because you are still thrusting your mind back into earthly things, you are plucking darkness from the true light.

67   That infinite and ineffable Good which is up there, runs to love just as a ray comes to a shining body.

Tanto si dà quanto trova d'ardore,   70
sì che quantunque carità si stende,
cresce sovr' essa l'etterno Valore.

E quanta gente più là sù s'intende,   73
più v'è da bene amare, e più vi s'ama,
e come specchio l'uno a l'altro rende.

E se la mia ragion non ti disfama,   76
vedrai Beatrice, ed ella pienamente
ti torrà questa e ciascun' altra brama.

Procaccia pur che tosto sieno spente,   79
come son già le due, le cinque piaghe
che si richiudon per esser dolente."

Com' io voleva dicer: "Tu m'appaghe,"   82
vidimi giunto in su l'altro girone,
sì che tacer mi fer le luci vaghe.

Ivi mi parve in una visïone   85
estatica di sùbito esser tratto
e vedere in un tempio più persone,

e una donna, in su l'entrar, con atto   88
dolce di madre, dicer: "Figliuol mio,
perché hai tu così verso noi fatto?

Ecco, dolenti, lo tuo padre e io   91
ti cercavamo." E come qui si tacque,
ciò che pareva prima, dispario.

Indi m'apparve un'altra, con quell'acque   94
giù per le gote che 'l dolor distilla
quando di gran dispetto in altrui nacque,

e dir: "Se tu se' sire de la villa   97
del cui nome ne' dèi fu tanta lite
e onde ogne scïenza disfavilla,

vendica te di quelle braccia ardite   100
ch'abbracciar nostra figlia, o Pisistràto."
E 'l segnor mi parea benigno e mite

risponder lei con viso temperato: 103
"Che farem noi a chi mal ne disira,
se quei che ci ama è per noi condannato?"

Poi vidi genti accese in foco d'ira   106
con pietre un giovinetto ancider, forte
gridando a sé pur: "Martira, martira!"

70 It gives itself according to the measure of the love it finds, so that however great is the charity that reaches out, by so much the eternal Worth grows upon it.

73 And the more people bend toward each other up there, the more there is to love well and the more love there is, and, like a mirror, each reflects it to the other.

76 And if my explanation does not satisfy your hunger, you will see Beatrice, and she will fully remove this and every other yearning.

79 Exert yourself that the five wounds, like the first two, may be quickly erased; they heal by hurting."

82 As I was about to say: "You satisfy me," I saw that I had arrived on the next ledge, so that my curious eyes made me silent.

85 There I seemed to be drawn suddenly into an ecstatic vision and to see many persons in a temple,

88 and a woman, on the threshold, with the sweet bearing of a mother, saying: "My son, why have you acted toward us in this way?

91 Behold, your father and I, grieving, have been searching for you." And as she fell silent here, what first appeared disappeared.

94 Then there appeared to me another woman with those tears running down her cheeks that grief distills when born in someone from great outrage,

97 and she was saying: "If you are lord of the city whose naming caused such strife among the gods and whence every knowledge sparkles forth,

100 take vengeance on those bold arms that embraced our daughter, O Peisistratus." And the lord seemed to me to be kind and mild

103 in replying to her, with a temperate look: "What shall we do to those who wish us ill, if one who loves us is condemned by us?"

106 Then I saw people on fire with wrath, killing a young man with stones, loudly crying to each other still: "Kill, kill!"

E lui vedea chinarsi, per la morte   109
che l'aggravava già, inver' la terra,
ma de li occhi facea sempre al ciel porte,

  orando a l'alto Sire, in tanta guerra,   112
che perdonasse a' suoi persecutori,
con quello aspetto che pietà diserra.

  Quando l'anima mia tornò di fòri   115
a le cose che son fuor di lei vere,
io riconobbi i miei non falsi errori.

  Lo duca mio, che mi potea vedere   118
far sì com' om che dal sonno si slega,
disse: "Che hai, che non ti puoi tenere,

  ma se' venuto più che mezza lega   121
velando li occhi e con le gambe avvolte,
a guisa di chi vino o sonno piega?"

  "O dolce padre mio, se tu m'ascolte,   124
io ti dirò," diss' io, "ciò che m'apparve
quando le gambe mi furon sì tolte."

  Ed ei: "Se tu avessi cento larve   127
sovra la faccia, non mi sarian chiuse
le tue cogitazion, quantunque parve.

  Ciò che vedesti fu perché non scuse   130
d'aprir lo core a l'acque de la pace
che da l'etterno fonte son diffuse.

  Non dimandai: 'Che hai?' per quel che face   133
chi guarda pur con l'occhio che non vede,
quando disanimato il corpo giace,

  ma dimandai per darti forza al piede: 136
così frugar conviensi i pigri, lenti
ad usar lor vigilia quando riede."

  Noi andavam per lo vespero, attenti   139
oltre quanto potean li occhi allungarsi
contra i raggi seròtini e lucenti.

  Ed ecco a poco a poco un fummo farsi   142
verso di noi come la notte oscuro;
né da quello era loco da cansarsi.

  Questo ne tolse li occhi e l'aere puro.   145

109   And him I saw falling to the ground with death already weighing him down, but his eyes he was still making into gates to Heaven,

112   praying the highest Lord, amid such strife, to forgive his persecutors, with the expression that unlocks pity.

115   When my soul returned outside, to the true things that are external to it, I recognized my not false errors.

118   My leader, who could see me behaving like one loosed from sleep, said: "What is the matter, that you cannot hold yourself,

121   but have walked more than half a league with your eyes veiled and your legs stumbling, like one whom wine or sleep bends over?"

124   "O my sweet father, if you listen, I will tell you," I said, "what appeared to me when my legs were taken from me so."

127   And he: "If you had a hundred masks over your face, your thoughts would not be closed to me, however slight.

130   What you have seen was so that you will not refuse to open your heart to the waters of peace, flowing from the eternal fountain.

133   I did not ask: 'What is the matter?' like one who looks only with an eye that does not see, when someone's body lies unconscious,

136   but I asked in order to give strength to your feet: so one must prod the lazy, slow to use their wakefulness when it returns."

139   We were walking toward the sunset, attentive ahead as far as our eyes could reach through the bright, setting rays.

142   And behold, little by little, a cloud of smoke coming toward us, dark as night; nor was there any place to turn aside from it.

145   This took away our eyes and the pure air.

NOTES

1-39. As much as . . . you who overcome: The encounter with the angel, the erasure of a *P*, and the singing of a Beatitude correspond to 12.73-114, another passage that begins with a periphrastic indication of the hour.

1-6. As much . . . midnight here: This elaborate periphrasis identifies the hour as three hours before sunset, the beginning of the division of the day called vespers, after the canonical hour that took place at its beginning (see Additional Note 5). The sun had as much of its daily course still to run (lines 4-5) as appears above the horizon in the first three hours of the day (lines 1-3); its angle above the horizon is the same in both cases (see lines 16-21, with notes). If it is three hours before sunset in Purgatory, it is three hours before sunrise in Jerusalem and consequently midnight in Florence, for Dante roughly 45° west of Jerusalem (line 6; see fig. 1). The repeated emphasis on light, reflected or refracted, in this canto will contrast strongly with the darkness in Canto 16.

1-3. As much . . . a little child: Dante's use of *spera* [sphere] here has occasioned some confusion, though the general sense is clear (see previous note). Both *spera* (line 2) and *corso* [course] (line 5) refer to the path of the sun across the sky, of which two segments are being compared (line 1: "as much"; line 5: "so much"). The reader is to visualize the position of the sun above the horizon in mid-morning and mid-afternoon (lines 7-9). The term *spera*, then, is being troped to mean "circle" (as in *Inf.* 7.96; *Par.* 24.1, 30, 114; 25.14). This circle is said to "play like a little child" because at any given latitude the apparent path of the sun changes from day to day.

1. the end of the third hour: Roughly 9 A.M. soon after the equinox.

7-33. And the sun's rays . . . disposed you to feel: The travelers are facing the sun; the intensification of light is due, Virgil explains, to the approach of the angel, so much brighter than the previous one (12.88-90) that the pilgrim cannot look at it. The brightness corresponds to the blindness imposed on the envious. According to Virgil, the pilgrim's sight will gradually become able to endure it; it thus represents a further step toward the strength of vision necessary for the direct vision of God (*Paradiso* 33). The dawning of new light is contrasted with the visible sun's declining path toward evening.

10-24. when I felt . . . quick to flee it: This is a passage of remarkably rich suggestiveness, drawing on Neoplatonic light metaphysics. It hinges on the pilgrim's inability to grasp intuitively what now confronts him. He is no longer "weighed down" by pride but by a heavenly light, and at first it seems that the increase of light is due to the reflection of the sunlight from a polished surface.

13-15. so I raised ... excessive light: The pilgrim shields his eyes with his hands in order to remain in relative darkness, because the light (*il visibile* [the visible]) is beyond his capacity. *Solecchio* [sunshade] is explained by Buti as a diminutive of *sole* [sun], from Lat. *soliculus* [little sun]: he must diminish the sun.

16-24. As when ... quick to flee it: The simile draws on the familiar theorem that the angle of reflection (of a ray of light falling [cf. Dante's *scende*] on a reflecting surface) is equal to the angle of incidence, established as early as Euclid's *Optics.* The notion that the equality of angles is to be applied to the light emanating from the angel (reflected, for instance, from the floor of the terrace), is similar to the error the pilgrim commits here. Like the sun, the angels are "mirrors" of God, but not in a mechanical sense.

19-20. from the fall of a stone: I.e., from the vertical.

22-23. that I was being struck by light refracted: The commentators explain that *luce rifratta* (line 22) means "reflected light," and that is indeed the pilgrim's supposition about his experience. But the terminology of reflection and refraction overlapped in the period; the distinction between them, a major subject of discussion and experimentation (see Grant 1986, "Optics"), was not entirely clear. The ambiguity is essential: the pilgrim supposes that mechanical laws of reflection apply; but in fact what he sees is metaphysical refraction: the angel is God's light *penetrating* the universe (see *Par.* 1.1-3, with note). The possible confusion of things *reflected* on a transparent surface with things *refracted* through it, is the subject of *Par.* 3.10-18.

29. the family of Heaven: The *family* of a lord are his household servants (see *Inf.* 30.88, with note).

30. a messenger: Literally translating Greek *ággelos* (see *Inf.* 9.85, with note).

30. to invite us to ascend: The implication is that the angel moves joyously (see line 35) toward every soul that mounts the stairway.

32-33. will give you pleasure ... disposed you to feel: Many commentators take the line to mean simply "as far as your nature can do so"; but the idea that human beings are disposed by nature to see angels, and that the sight of them will give the highest pleasure they can naturally feel refers to human nature as it was *before the Fall*, which in the ascent of the mountain is gradually being restored (Singleton 1955); Albert the Great, however, held that the human mind was by nature able to understand "separated substances" (see Additional Note 11).

35-36. Enter here ... than the others: Cf. 12.92-93, on the growing ease of the ascent. Some editors assign line 36 to the narrating poet, but the parallel seems to require it to be spoken by the angel.

37-39. We were climbing . . . who overcome: As in 12.109-11, a Beatitude is sung; here the source is not specified. See the note to 12.110-11.

38. *Beati misericordes*: The fifth Beatitude: "Beati misericordes, quia ipsi miseri-cordiam consequentur" [Blessed are the merciful, for they shall obtain mercy] (Matt. 5.7). The pairing of compassion and envy is traditional (Cicero, *Tusculan Disputations* 3.10. 21, *ST* 2.2 q. 36 a. 3); see the notes to 13.22-42 and 27.8.

39. Rejoice, you who overcome: No exact scriptural parallel to this phrase has been found; probably it alludes to the conclusion of the Beatitudes in Matt. 5.12: "Gaudete et exsultate, quoniam merces vestra copiosa est in coelis" [Be glad and rejoice, for your reward is very great in heaven].

40-84. My master and I . . . made me silent: The second part of the transition to the terrace of anger is the first of the great expositions of doctrine at the center of the *Purgatorio* (Cantos 15-18, the central cantos of the entire *Comedy*), setting forth its central themes: 15.40-81 (the nature of heavenly goods); 16.52-114 (the relation of free will to astrological forces; the causes of earthly disorder); 17.88-139 (love as the source of all merit; the structure of Purgatory); 18.13-75 (the psychology of love and free will).

44-45: What did the spirit . . . sharing: The reference is to 14.85-87, spoken by Guido del Duca. For *consorte* [sharer] see the note to lines 52-57.

46-81. Wherefore he . . . heal by hurting: Virgil's reply, in two parts, the first contrasting earthly and heavenly goods, the second stating more fully the nature of the sharing in Heaven.

46-48. He knows . . . less weeping: Virgil begins by paraphrasing Guido del Duca's admission that envy was his greatest fault (14.85), and attributes the rest of Guido's speech to Guido's desire to benefit others—his charity; cf. the note to 14.81-87. By implication, these lines identify the root motive of the writing of the poem itself.

49-57. Because your desires . . . in that cloister: According to the principle Virgil sets forth, temporal goods are not capable of being shared without being lessened for each sharer. There is no conception here of social goods enhanced by the pooling of resources (such as libraries, museums, hospitals, electricity). In this view, the spread of Christianity or the building of great churches are instances of the spiritual sharing characteristic of Heaven. This particular reductive view derives more from Gregory the Great than from Augustine (see the note to lines 52-57).

49. your desires point: The Italian *s'appuntano* [come to a point] is richly ambiguous: in addition to the sense adopted in the translation, it can refer to the focussing of light (*Par.* 21.83), to radiation or to dependence from a point (*Par.* 29.12). The light imagery of lines 64-75 is already implicit here.

51. envy moves the bellows to sighing: The bellows is of course the human breast with its diaphragm. According to Aristotelian physiology, the function of breathing (as of the brain) is to moderate the vital heat in the heart; in the case of envy or anger, however, intensified breathing may fan the fire. Here the fire imagery is restricted to the trope on *bellows*; it becomes explicit in line 57, for the fire of charity: cf. lines 106, 142-45, on the fire of anger.

52-57. But if the love . . . in that cloister: In his *Moralia in Job* 6.46.86, Gregory the Great cites the love of Heaven as the best antidote to envy, which he sees as resulting from the desire for temporal goods:

> Whoever wishes to be free of the plague of envy, let him love that heritage that is not diminished by the number of co-heirs, that belongs entire to all and each. . . . For when the mind draws back from desiring what must be divided among those who receive it, one loves one's neighbor all the more the less one fears [*pertimescit*] loss at his being provided for. And if one is rapt with love of the heavenly fatherland, one is confirmed solidly in love of one's neighbor without any envy.

Dante's emphasis on fear (line 54) is close to Gregory's *pertimescit*. That Dante also has in mind Augustine's identification of fratricide as the basis of the Earthly City is guaranteed by his emphasis on the term *consorte* (line 45; cf. 14.87).

57. in that cloister: This image of enclosure prepares for the mirror imagery of line 75; the Empyrean is supposed, of course, to be outside of space and time; see *Par.* 30.38-42, 100-123.

64-81. Because you are still . . . heal by hurting: Virgil develops the theory of beatitude in terms of light.

64-66. Because you are . . . from the true light: Because your thinking is dominated by the model of material things (cf. Augustine's analysis of this as a chief obstacle to his conversion, *Confessions* 7), the light seems darkness to you: cf. lines 10-24. Cf. also *SS* 4.1: "How long will your mind be fixed on the ground? Do you not see what temple you have entered?"

67-75. That infinite . . . reflects it to the other: Just as the sun gives its light to such objects as gold and precious stones in the measure of the "diaphanous" [transparent] that they contain, so God gives his grace in the measure of the love he finds in each soul. Dante had developed the analogy between God ("that infinite and ineffable Good") and the visible sun in *Conv.* 3.7.2-7, especially:

Truly each thing receives from that pouring out [of the divine goodness] according to the mode of its power and of its being, and of that we can have a visible example in the sun. We see that the light of the sun, which is one and derived from a single source, is differently received by different bodies; as Albert says, in his book On the Intellect, certain bodies, "because of the clarity of the diaphanous mixed in them, as soon as the sun sees them become so luminous that, because of multiplication of light in it and in their appearance, they give off a great brightness from themselves to other bodies, as do gold and certain stones."

(Cf. *Conv.* 3.14.) See the prolonged discussion of the analogy in the *De div. nom.* 4.113-29. Lines 67-75 are an important foretaste of the concepts and imagery of the *Paradiso*.

73. And the more people . . . up there: Most commentators take lines 73-74 as referring to the blessedness of Heaven, as we do; some, however, including Sapegno, take it to mean "the more people direct their love up there." For the "circulation of love," see Aquinas 1950 on the *De div. nom.*, lemma 330.

75. like a mirror . . . to the other: The mirror imagery of lines 16-24 recurs, now explicitly referring to the nature of Heaven; it derives ultimately from the Pseudo-Dionysius. For Dante's use of mirror imagery, see Pasquini 1976b.

85-138. There I seemed . . . when it returns: The second principal division of the canto: the pilgrim's ecstatic visions of the virtue contrary to anger and the discussion following them. They are to be correlated with the visions of the vice in 17.13-45, also identified as events within the pilgrim's imagination. "Ecstatic visions" were a recognized category of divine inspiration. Chiavacci Leonardi cites *ST* 1a q. 12 a. 3; cf. Alain of Lille's *Distinctiones* (*P.L.* 210, 1007). As lines 115-17 will point out, they involve the pilgrim's soul withdrawing itself from the outside world; see the note on 17.13-18. As products of inspiration; these visions are further instances of refraction of the divine light (cf. the note on lines 22-24).

85-114. There I seemed . . . unlocks pity: Three examples of the virtue contrary to anger, usually identified in Italian as "mansuetudine" [gentleness], derived from the seventh Beatitude, which will be heard in 17.69-70 (see note there); as always, the first example is drawn from the life of the Virgin Mary, the second, as in all but the first, from a classical source. There is a progression from the peacefulness of the first to the presence of a single angry person in the second (Peisistratus' wife, whose anger is readily disarmed), to the mob that stones Stephen. The progression sharpens the antithesis between the vice and its opposite. Few of the positive examples on the terraces of Purgatory include the vice to be corrected (Michal in 10.67-69; Helice in 25.131-32; perhaps Trajan's initial response to the widow in 10.85-90).

87-92. to see many persons . . . she fell silent: The episode is related in Luke 2. 42-51; see especially verses 42-49:

And when he was twelve years old, they going up into Jerusalem accord-
ing to the custom of the feast [Passover], and. . . when they returned, the
child Jesus remained in Jerusalem; and his parents knew it not. . . . And
not finding him, they returned into Jerusalem, seeking him. . . . after three
days they found him in the temple, sitting in the midst of the doctors,
hearing them and asking them questions. And all that heard him were
astonished at his wisdom and his answers. . . And his mother said to him:
Son, why hast thou done so to us? Behold, thy father and I have sought
thee sorrowing. And he said to them: How is it that you sought me? Did
you not know that I must be about my Father's business?

Dante's change from "in the midst of the learned men" [*in medium doctorum*],
verse 46) to "many persons" [*più persone*] helps prepare the mob scene of lines
106-114.

88-89. a woman . . . of a mother: The Virgin's identity must be inferred (like
the speaker of 13.29), and the presence of saint Joseph is not made explicit. That
the Virgin speaks from the threshold, a touch added by Dante, efficiently creates
a spatial frame. The Virgin's sweetness of *atto* [bearing, gesture] recalls the "atto
soave" [gentle bearing] of Gabriel (10.38) and the speaking *atto* of the Virgin's
humility (10.43).

94-105. another woman . . . condemned by us: The story is derived from
Valerius Maximus' *Facta et dicta memorabilia*, 5.1:

A memorable act of humanity on the part of Peisistratus, the tyrant of
Athens, shall be related. A certain young man, burning with love of
Peisistratus' young daughter, meeting her in the market-place, kissed her.
When his wife urged that he should punish the young man with death, he
replied: "If we are to kill those who love us, what shall we do to those who
hate us?"

As is evident, the description of the wife and the words attributed to her are
Dante's addition, as is the description of Peisistratus; his are closely translated
(except for "is condemned by us," somewhat softening "we are to kill"). Again,
the descriptions emphasize the bodily symptoms/expression of inner states, ab-
sent in the source.

94-101. another woman . . . O Peisistratus: A portrait of anger resulting from
an injury (cf. 17.121-23), strongly suggested to be injured pride (but see the note
to lines 104-106). Cf. the weeping widow in 10.73-93 (especially 10.78 and 87).

97-99. the city . . . sparkles forth: Dante read of Athens in many ancient au-
thors, including Cicero and Augustine (cf. the ironic comparison with Florence
in 6.139-41) The story of the contest for the naming of Athens between Poseidon
(who offered the horse) and Athena (who offered the olive tree) is told in *Met.*

6.70-82 (part of the tapestry woven by Athena in her competition with Arachne). There is considerable irony in the wife's appealing to the traditional symbol of peace to support her urgings to violence.

100-101. take vengeance . . . O Peisistratus: In Valerius Maximus the young man is said to have kissed the girl; Dante changes the emphasis.

104-106. What shall we do . . . condemned by us: By ending the first two examples with the defining speeches of the protagonists, Dante achieves notable concision. In both cases important elements are omitted (here, Valerius Maximus' admission that the girl had in fact been injured by the young man's impetuosity).

106-14. people on fire . . . that unlocks pity: The third example, less condensed than the others and considerably altered by Dante, is from Acts 7. After being accused of heresy and haled before the Council (presumably the Sanhedrin—cf. *Inf.* 23.109-123), Stephen preached a long sermon (Acts 7.2-53) denouncing Israel's pride. Dante has in mind especially verses 54-59:

> Now hearing these things they were cut to the heart, and they gnashed their teeth at him. But he being full of the Holy Ghost, looking up steadfastly [*intendens*] to Heaven, saw the glory of God, and Jesus standing at the right hand of God. And he said: Behold, I see the heavens opened, and the son of man standing on the right hand of God. And they crying out with a loud voice, stopped their ears, and with one accord ran violently upon him. And casting him forth without the city, they stoned him: and the witnesses laid down their garments at the feet of a young man whose name was Saul. And they stoned Stephen as he prayed, saying: Lord Jesus, receive my spirit. And falling on his knees, he cried with a loud voice, saying: Lord, lay not this sin to their charge. And when he had said this, he fell asleep in the Lord. And Saul was consenting to his death.

108. Kill, kill: The biblical account places the shouting in the Council scene, before Stephen is taken out of the city. The words attributed to the mob (added by Dante) are modeled on the shouts of "Crucify, crucify!" at the trial of Jesus (John 19.6; cf. Luke 23.2). Stephen was venerated as the first Christian martyr.

109-11. And him . . . gates to Heaven: Stephen falls to his knees in Acts 7.59; his eyes being gates to Heaven probably indicates that the vision of 7.55 is still present, also that anyone who looked into his eyes in the right spirit could pass through them into Heaven (refraction)—or see Heaven reflected in them.

112-14. praying . . . unlocks pity: Of the two last speeches attributed to the dying Stephen in Acts 7, both given in direct discourse, one (verse 58) is omitted and the other (verse 59) is given by Dante in indirect discourse, in contrast to the direct discourse of lines 89-92, 97-101, and 104-105. Stephen's last speech echoes Christ's "Father, forgive them, for they know not what they do" (Luke 23.34).

114. with the expression that unlocks pity: Probably to be taken, like line 111, in both possible senses: that his expression so expresses his love and forgiveness (Matt. 5.44) that it opens Heaven to him; and that it should unlock pity in anyone witnessing it.

115-17. When my soul . . . not false errors: See the note to lines 85-138. The "true things" [*cose . . . vere*] outside are of course the "real world," the world of sense-perception. The "not false errors," the visions, are "errors" because imagined in the absence of sense experience; they are "not false" because (like the carvings of Cantos 10 and 12) they are true representations of the events (12.68).

118-23. My leader . . . sleep bends over: Note the association of visions with sleep (lines 119 and 123) and death. Lines 122, "your eyes veiled," and 123, "sleep bends over," recall the famous phrase used of Stephen's death in Acts 7.59: "he fell asleep"); cf. also lines 135, 138, and the figure of saint John in 29.143-44.

127-29. If you had . . . however slight: This assertion of Virgil's ability to read the pilgrim's thoughts recalls *Inf.* 23.25-30. Both passages are close to personification allegory: here Dante is calling attention to the relation between imaginative ecstasy and the use to be made of it by waking consciousness (*vigilia* [waking], line 138)—themes all connected with dream-vision (see *Inf.* 1. 2 and 11 and *Inf.* 2.8, and notes).

130-32. What you have seen . . . eternal fountain: According to what Virgil says here, the remedy to anger is less the acquisition of a moral virtue than openness to God's calming grace, the "eternal fountain." The commentators note the allusion to John 4.13-14: "He that shall drink of the water that I will give him, shall not thirst forever; But the water that I will give him shall become in him a fountain of water springing up into life everlasting." The water imagery goes with the fire imagery (see the note to line 51): the waters of peace will quench the fires. Note the connection with 13.85-90.

134-35. one who . . . lies unconscious: The "eye that does not see" is the eye of the body, which cannot see the events taking place within someone who is outwardly unconscious, as the eye of the mind can do. Again the antithesis between the physical and the spiritual modes of vision (see the notes to lines 10-24, 16-24, 22-24, 64-66).

139-45. We were walking . . . the pure air: These lines establish both the parallel with the opening of the canto (especially with lines 7-9) and the antithesis between the new darkness and the sudden brightness of the angel (lines 10-30).

142-45. And behold . . . the pure air: Note the parallel with the motion toward them of the angel (lines 27 and 30). For smoke as metaphor for anger, see the notes to 16.1-7 and 15.51.

CANTO 16

Buio d'inferno e di notte privata   1
d'ogne pianeto, sotto pover cielo,
quant' esser può di nuvol tenebrata,

    non fece al viso mio sì grosso velo   4
come quel fummo ch'ivi ci coperse,
né a sentir di così aspro pelo

    che l'occhio stare aperto non sofferse;   7
onde la scorta mia saputa e fida
mi s'accostò e l'omero m'offerse.

    Sì come cieco va dietro a sua guida   10
per non smarrirsi e per non dar di cozzo
in cosa che 'l molesti o forse ancida:

    m'andava io per l'aere amaro e sozzo,   13
ascoltando il mio duca, che diceva
pur: "Guarda che da me tu non sia mozzo."

    Io sentia voci, e ciascuna pareva   16
pregar per pace e per misericordia
l'Agnel di Dio che le peccata leva.

    Pur "*Agnus Dei*" eran le loro essordia;   19
una parola in tutte era e un modo,
sì che parea tra esse ogne concordia.

    "Quei sono spirti, maestro, ch'i' odo?"   22
diss' io. Ed elli a me: "Tu vero apprendi,
e d'iracundia van solvendo il nodo.

    "Or tu chi se' che 'l nostro fummo fendi,   25
e di noi parli pur come se tue
partissi ancor lo tempo per calendi?"

    Così per una voce detto fue;   28
onde 'l maestro mio disse: "Rispondi,
e domanda se quinci si va sùe."

CANTO 16

Third terrace, continued: voices—Marco Lombardo—the pilgrim's question: do the stars cause our troubles?—Marco's explanation: the function of civil government, of the papacy—the good Gherardo

1   The darkness of Hell, or of a night deprived of every planet, under an empty sky, shadowed as much as possible by clouds,

4   never made so thick a veil to my sight as did the smoke that covered us there, nor a pelt so harsh to feel

7   that my eye could not bear to stay open; so my wise and faithful escort drew near and offered me his shoulder.

10   As a blind man goes after his guide so as not to be lost or collide with what might harm or even kill him:

13   so did I walk through the bitter, filthy air, listening to my leader, who kept saying: "Take care not to be cut off from me."

16   I heard voices, and each one was clearly praying for peace and for mercy to the Lamb of God who takes away sins.

19   "*Agnus Dei*" was ever their exordium; the same words came from all, and the same melody, so that all harmony appeared among them.

22   "Are these spirits, master, that I hear?" I said. And he to me: "You hear true, and they go untying the knot of wrathfulness."

25   "Now who are you who cut through our smoke, and speak about us just as if you still divided time by calends?"

28   Thus did one voice speak; and my master said: "Answer, and ask if one goes up on this side."

E io: "O creatura che ti mondi   31
per tornar bella a colui che ti fece,
maraviglia udirai, se mi secondi."

"Io ti seguiterò quanto mi lece,"   34
rispuose, "e, se veder fummo non lascia,
l'udir ci terrà giunti in quella vece."

Allora incominciai: "Con quella fascia   37
che la morte dissolve men vo suso,
e venni qui per l'infernale ambascia.

E se Dio m'ha in sua grazia rinchiuso   40
tanto che vuol ch'i' veggia la sua corte
per modo tutto fuor del moderno uso,

non mi celar chi fosti anzi la morte,   43
ma dilmi, e dimmi s'i' vo bene al varco,
e tue parole fier le nostre scorte."

"Lombardo fui, e fu' chiamato Marco,   46
del mondo seppi, e quel valore amai
al quale ha or ciascun disteso l'arco.

Per montar sù dirittamente vai."   49
Così rispuose, e soggiunse: "I' ti prego
che per me prieghi quando sù sarai."

E io a lui: "Per fede mi ti lego   52
di far ciò che mi chiedi; ma io scoppio
dentro ad un dubbio, s'io non me ne spiego.

Prima era scempio, e ora è fatto doppio   55
ne la sentenza tua, che mi fa certo,
qui e altrove, quello ov' io l'accoppio.

Lo mondo è ben così tutto diserto   58
d'ogne virtute come tu mi sone,
e di malizia gravido e coverto;

ma priego che m'addite la cagione,   61
sì ch'i' la veggia e ch'i' la mostri altrui;
ché nel cielo uno, e un qua giù la pone."

Alto sospir, che duolo strinse in "uhi!"   64
mise fuor prima; e poi cominciò: "Frate,
lo mondo è cieco, e tu vien ben da lui.

Voi che vivete ogne cagion recate   67
pur suso al cielo, pur come se tutto
movesse seco di necessitate.

31   And I: "O creature who are cleansing yourself so as to return beautiful to him who made you, you will hear a marvel, if you follow me."

34   "I will come after you as much as I am permitted," it replied, "and, if the smoke does not let us see, hearing will keep us together in its stead."

37   Then I began: "Still in the wrapping that death unties am I going up, and I have come here through the anguish of Hell.

40   And if God has enclosed me in his grace so much that he wills that I see his court in a manner entirely beyond modern usage,

43   do not hide from me who you were before your death, but tell me, and say if I am going toward the crossing, and your words will be our guides."

46   "I was a Lombard, and I was called Marco; I knew the world, and I loved that worth toward which everyone now has unstrung his bow.

49   To mount up, go straight ahead." Thus he replied, and added: "I pray you to pray for me once you are above."

52   And I to him: "In faith I bind myself to you to do what you ask; but I am bursting within a doubt, if I cannot free myself from it.

55   First it was simple, now it has been doubled by your pronouncement, which persuades me of what I combine with it here and elsewhere.

58   The world is surely as barren of every virtue as you say, pregnant with malice and covered with it;

61   but I beg you to point out the cause, so that I may see and show it to others; for some place it in the heavens and others down here."

64   A deep sigh, which sorrow dragged out into "uhi!" he uttered first, and then began: "Brother, the world is blind, and you surely come from there.

67   You who are alive still refer every cause up to the heavens, just as if they moved everything with them by necessity.

Se così fosse, in voi fora distrutto 70
libero arbitrio, e non fora giustizia
per ben letizia, e per male aver lutto.

Lo cielo i vostri movimenti inizia; 73
non dico tutti, ma, posto ch'i' 'l dica,
lume v'è dato a bene e a malizia,

e libero voler, che, se fatica 76
ne le prime battaglie col ciel dura,
poi vince tutto, se ben si notrica.

A maggior forza e a miglior natura 79
liberi soggiacete, e quella cria
la mente in voi, che 'l ciel non ha in sua cura.

Però se 'l mondo presente disvia 82
in voi è la cagione, in voi si cheggia,
e io te ne sarò or vera spia.

Esce di mano a lui che la vagheggia 85
prima che sia, a guisa di fanciulla
che piangendo e ridendo pargoleggia,

l'anima semplicetta, che sa nulla, 88
salvo che, mossa da lieto fattore,
volontier torna a ciò che la trastulla.

Di picciol bene in pria sente sapore; 91
quivi s'inganna, e dietro ad esso corre
se guida o fren non torce suo amore.

Onde convenne legge per fren porre; 94
convenne rege aver che discernesse
de la vera cittade almen la torre.

Le leggi son, ma chi pon mano ad esse? 97
Nullo, però che 'l pastor che procede
rugumar può, ma non ha l'unghie fesse;

per che la gente, che sua guida vede 100
pur a quel ben fedire ond' ella è ghiotta,
di quel si pasce e più oltre non chiede.

Ben puoi veder che la mala condotta 103
è la cagion che 'l mondo ha fatto reo,
e non natura che 'n voi sia corrotta.

Soleva Roma, che 'l buon mondo feo, 106
due soli aver, che l'una e l'altra strada
facean vedere, e del mondo e di Deo.

70   If that were so, free choice would be destroyed in you, and it would not be justice to have joy for good and mourning for evil.

73   The heavens begin your motions; I do not say all of them, but, supposing I say it, a light is given you to know good and evil,

76   and free will, which, if it lasts out the labor of its first battles with the heavens, afterwards overcomes all things, if nourished well.

79   To a greater Power and a better Nature you lie subject and therefore free, and that creates the mind in you, which the heavens do not govern.

82   Thus, if the present world has gone astray, in you is the cause, in you let it be sought, and now I will be a true spy of it for you.

85   From the hand of him who desires it before it exists, like a little girl who weeps and laughs childishly,

88   the simple little soul comes forth, knowing nothing except that, set in motion by a happy Maker, it gladly turns to what amuses it.

91   Of some lesser good it first tastes the flavor; there it is deceived and runs after it, if a guide or rein does not turn away its love.

94   Therefore it was necessary to set the law as a curb; it was necessary to have a king who would discern the tower at least of the true city.

97   The laws are there, but who lays hand to them? No one, because the shepherd that leads can chew the cud but does not have cloven hooves;

100   therefore the people, who see their guide striking at the thing that they themselves are greedy for, feed there and seek no further.

103   You can clearly see that bad government is the cause that has made the world wicked, and not nature corrupt in you.

106   Rome, which made the good world, used to have two suns that made visible the two paths, of the world and of God.

L'un l'altro ha spento, ed è giunta la spada   109
col pasturale, e l'un con l'altro insieme
per viva forza mal convien che vada,

  però che, giunti, l'un l'altro non teme: 112
se non mi credi, pon mente a la spiga,
ch'ogn' erba si conosce per lo seme.

  In sul paese ch'Adice e Po riga   115
solea valore e cortesia trovarsi
prima che Federigo avesse briga;

  or può sicuramente indi passarsi   118
per qualunque lasciasse per vergogna
di ragionar coi buoni o d'appressarsi.

  Ben v'èn tre vecchi ancora in cui rampogna   121
l'antica età la nova, e par lor tardo
che Dio a miglior vita li ripogna:

  Currado da Palazzo e 'l buon Gherardo   124
e Guido da Castel, che mei si noma,
francescamente, il semplice Lombardo.

  Dì oggimai che la Chiesa di Roma,   127
per confondere in sé due reggimenti,
cade nel fango, e sé brutta e la soma."

  "O Marco mio," diss' io, "bene argomenti,   130
e or discerno perché dal retaggio
li figli di Levì furono essenti.

  Ma qual Gherardo è quel che tu per saggio   133
di' ch'è rimaso de la gente spenta
in rimprovèro del secol selvaggio?"

  "O tuo parlar m'inganna, o el mi tenta,"   136
rispuose a me, "ché, parlandomi tosco,
par che del buon Gherardo nulla senta.

  Per altro sopranome io nol conosco,   139
s'io nol togliessi da sua figlia Gaia.
Dio sia con voi, ché più non vegno vosco.

  Vedi l'albór che per lo fummo raia   142
già biancheggiare, e me convien partirmi—
l'angelo è ivi—prima ch'io li paia."

  Così tornò, e più non volle udirmi.   145

109   One sun has extinguished the other, and the
sword is joined to the shepherd's staff, and it is ill
for those two to be violently forced together,

112   for, joined, neither fears the other: if you do not
believe me, consider the harvest, for every grass is
known by its seed.

115   In the land watered by Adige and Po valor and
courtesy used to be found, before Frederick found
opposition;

118   now anyone can pass through confidently who
is ashamed to speak with the good or to draw near
them.

121   It is true that three old men are still alive in
whom the former age reproaches the new, and
they find God slow to call them to a better life:

124   Currado da Palazzo and the good Gherardo, and
Guido da Castello, who is better known, in the
French way, as the faithful Lombard.

127   Say then that the Church of Rome, because it
has fused together in itself the two authorities, falls
in the mud and soils both itself and its burden."

130   "O my Marco, well do you argue, and now I
discern why the sons of Levi were excluded from
the inheritance.

133   But which Gherardo is the one you say remains
as an example of the departed people, to rebuke
this uncivil age?"

136   "Either your speech deceives me or it is testing
me," he replied, "for, speaking Tuscan to me, you
seem to know nothing of the good Gherardo.

139   I know him by no other surname, unless I were
to take it from his daughter Gaia. God be with
you, for I come no further with you.

142   You see the brightness that already shines
whitening through the smoke, and I must leave it
—the angel is there—before I appear to him."

145   Thus he turned back and would hear me no
longer.

NOTES

1-15. The darkness . . . cut off from me: The first fifteen lines of the canto present both the mode of suffering inherent in anger and a representation of its remedy, in so far as it lies in rational self-government (cf. the note to 15.130-32): anger blinds the soul, so that one must blindly obey the dictates of reason.

1-7. The darkness . . . to stay open: The idea of anger as fire and smoke goes back to the *Iliad* (18.107-10) and the Bible: "the smoke of his anger rose up, and its fire burned forth from his face," Ps. 17.9; Job 17.7: "my eye grew dark with indignation." Seneca's *De ira* 2.19, like many medical treatises, saw irascibility as due to the predominance of the hot humors (choler and black bile). Seneca adds: "Some say that anger derives from the boiling of the blood around the heart; the reason why this place should be assigned to anger is that the breast is the hottest part of the body." See 15.51, *Inf.* 11.70-75, and *Inter cantica* below.

1. The darkness of Hell: As in *Inf.* 3.22-30; see Apoc. 9.2: "And [the angel] opened the pit of the abyss, and the smoke of the pit rose up like the smoke of a great furnace, and the sun and the air were darkened by the smoke of the pit."

1-4. night deprived . . . so thick a veil: The early commentators took "sotto pover cielo" [lit., under a poor sky] to mean "deprived of stars, which are the riches of the heavens" (Benvenuto); some have (implausibly) taken "a poor sky" to refer to a view blocked by obstacles. Three elements, in any case, with increasing darkness: absence of planets, absence of stars, thick clouds.

6-7. a pelt . . . to stay open: The irritation of the smoke is compared to the touch of stiff hairs. There is no mention of any difficulty of breathing.

16-21. I heard voices . . . among them: The prayer is translated from the Ordinary of the Mass:

> Agnus Dei, qui tollis peccata mundi, miserere nobis [sung or recited twice],
> Agnus Dei, qui tollis peccata mundi, dona nobis pacem.
> [Lamb of God that takest away the sins of the world, have mercy on us [twice]
> Lamb of God that takest away the sins of the world, give us peace.]

That the voices are singing is conveyed by *modo* [melody], line 20: the harmony is musical as well as emotional. Line 19 implies continuous repetition.

24. untying the knot of wrathfulness: For the image of the knot, see Benvenuto's comment: "[anger] is indeed a strong knot that binds a man, depriving him of the free command over himself" (cf. Laing 1970 and 24.14-15, with note). Virgil's emphasis is on distentangling and straightening the souls' impulses (cf. 10.3, with note), as distinct from the punitive aspect of Purgatory (see the notes to 10.106-11, 9.126, 23.14-15, and 23.125-26, with notes).

25-145. Now who are you . . . no longer: The encounter with Marco of Lombardy. Several touches in Dante's characterization of Marco indicate that there is good reason for his being on this terrace, although his purging is well under way.

25-27. Now who are you . . . . by calends: The abruptness of the unseen soul's accosting of the pilgrim has a certain asperity, distantly recalling that of the angry Filippo Argenti (*Inf.* 8.33; *Purg.* 13.130-32); note the sharp distinction between *you* and *us* and the violence of *fendi* [cut through] (usually taken to mean that the soul has sensed a disturbance in the air). The soul's inference that the pilgrim is alive is based on line 22.

26-27. as if you still . . . by calends: As if your life were still governed by the civil calendar. In the Roman calendar (still in use in Italy in Dante's day), days were numbered according as they preceded the Calends (the first day) of the next or the Ides (in most cases the fifteenth day) of the current month. Marco does not mean that he and the other spirits are in eternity (Purgatory takes place in time), but that they count time differently from the living.

31-33. O creature . . . if you follow me: The pilgrim's reply goes beyond Virgil's suggestion (lines 29-30), so as to disarm the irritability in Marco's words, but also reminds us that Marco is undergoing purgation, as he will acknowledge.

34. I will come . . . permitted: Later in the canto a correlation is suggested between the thickness of the smoke and the stage of purgation, and Marco must return to the darkest part (lines 142-44).

37-45. Still in the wrapping . . . our guides: The pilgrim partly answers Marco's question (the pilgrim says that he is alive, but not who he is; cf. 14.20-21). Note the repetition of terms for the enclosure of the soul: *fascia* [wrapping, binding— always fabric], said of the body (line 37), and *rinchiuso* [enclosed] (line 40), of the soul (cf. Ps. 90.4, cited on 8.22-108). Both are clearly related to the veil of smoke (line 4); see the note to line 60.

42. in a manner . . . modern usage: Usually taken to mean (in conjunction with *Inf.* 2.36 and *Purg.* 14.15) that since saint Paul's vision (2 Cor. 12.1-7) no one has undertaken the journey. The invocation of a *moderno uso* [modern usage or custom] clearly implies an *antico uso* [ancient or former usage or custom] (as we have noted, the entire canto rests on such oppositions); Dante usually uses such expressions for *linguistic usage* and *linguistic change* (e.g., 26.113 and *Par.* 16.33; cf. Horace, *Ars poetica* lines 70-72—the principal source of the view of language change taken in *Par.* 26. 124-38). In addition to associating worldly corruption and religious change with the instability of language, the passage calls attention to the strictly linguistic aspect of the poem. Benvenuto's note on the line is acute:

"that is, by poetic speculation; indeed none of the ancients nor even any of the moderns ever ascended the heavens in the manner of this singular poet."

45. your words . . . our guides: Virgil does not speak for the rest of the canto.

46-51. I was a Lombard . . . you are above: Tersely, the soul names himself, characterizes his loyalties and disenchantment, and gives directions. After a pause, as if as an afterthought, he asks for the pilgrim's prayers (for "above" meaning "in the presence of God," see 26.127-32, with notes).

46-47. I was a Lombard . . . the world: According to the early commentators, this is the Marco Lombardo whom the *Novellino* (1280s) calls "a courtier and a man of great wisdom" and mordant wit. The *Novellino* uses *Lombardo* as a sur-name, which some commentators have seen as an impediment to the identifica-tion; but Dante expected his readers to know the *Novellino* and could easily have dissociated his personage from it. Rather, Marco's "I knew the world" and his princely acquaintances (lines 121-26) support the identification. Not much is known about him; according to Lana, Benvenuto, and Giovanni Villani, he was counselor and diplomat for several northern Italian princes, including Gherardo da Camino (line 124), and confronted Count Ugolino with a denunciation of his betrayal of the Guelphs. The parallels between his career and Dante's make him a kind of *alter ego* of Dante's.

46. I was a Lombard: The term *Lombard* may mean no more than that Marco was born in northern Italy, "the land watered by Adige and Po" (line 115); but cf. *Inf.* 27. 20-21, with note.

47-48. that worth . . . unstrung his bow: *Valore* [worth] here means *virtue* in general, including valor, courtesy, and concern for the common good (see lines 55-57, with note).

48. everyone now has unstrung his bow: "Has unstrung his bow" translates *ha disteso l'arco* [literally, has loosened his bow]; not only are people not aiming at the target, they have relaxed moral effort altogether (for the archery metaphor, see the note to *Par.* 1.126).

52-145. And I to him . . . hear me no longer: Marco's condemnation of the current state of the world leads the pilgrim to ask its cause: are human affairs in such disorder because of astrological influences ("the heavens," line 63) or be-cause of earthly causes ("down here," line 63)? Marco's reply and its corollaries form the second major doctrinal passage at the center of the poem (see the note to 15.40-84).

53-54. I am bursting . . . free myself from it: A particularly intense image: germination is about to burst open the seed casing; it can stand for the historic significance of the *Comedy* itself. For doubt as enclosure, see *Inf.* 10.95-96, 32.83; as sprouting, *Par.* 4.130-32.

55-57. First it was simple . . . combine with it here: The pilgrim is referring to what he heard from Guido del Duca in 14.88-126, which he now "combines" with what Marco has said. Guido del Duca's mention of the impossibility of sharing earthly goods has already led to the first of the central doctrinal passages (see the note to 15.40-84). More imagery of growth.

60. pregnant . . . covered with it: The metaphors of swelling and enclosure (the latter includes the cloud of smoke) now refer to the world as a whole (cf. lines 1-7 and 64-66).

61-63. I beg you . . . down here: The phrasing implies a sharp antithesis between the two possible answers, but Dante's position is much more nuanced, as Marco's reply will show.

62. so that I . . . to others: A reference to the writing of the present canto.

64-129. A deep sigh . . . and its burden: After his sigh and lament, Marco's reply follows a well-established scholastic pattern: *refutation* of the erroneous position (lines 67-81), and *confirmation* (proof) of the correct one (lines 82-129); for this pattern, see *Par.* 2.61-148. Marco's speech includes a digression (lines 121-26), as classical rhetorical theory provided.

   Here the great theme of the moral perfectibility of the individual is seen in the total context within which human beings must contend for autonomy: the forces of Nature acting on their bodies and thus on their inclinations, and the powerful influence of society, deeply affected by the failures of its civil and religious leaders. Dante does not deny astrological influences; he regards them as a major factor in human life. The souls in Purgatory must correct the temperamental bias due to heredity and the stars, as well as their habits. It is essential to Dante's position both that the stars are in some ways determining influences and that the faculty of rational choice can resist them.

64-66. A deep sigh . . . come from there: If the tendency to blame the stars for the state of the world was one of Marco's irascible tendencies, his mastering of the correct view would be an important part of his purgation.

67-83. You who are alive . . . let it be sought: The refutation has two parts: a. refutation of astrological determinism (lines 67-72); b. definition of the limits of astrological influences (lines 73-81).

67-69. You who are alive . . . by necessity: Marco identifies the erroneous doctrine accurately, but his attribution of it to all the living is an angry exaggeration, for according to the pilgrim they are debating it (lines 61-63).

70-72. If that were so . . . mourning for evil: The stars do not move everything by necessity; if they did, human beings would not have freedom of choice, and would not deserve reward or punishment in the next life. Technically this is a *reductio ad absurdum*; its validity depends on assumptions not always thought to be demonstrable, but assumed in the *Comedy* as facts: the freedom of the will, the immortality of the soul, the carrying out in the afterlife of God's justice.

73-81. The heavens begin . . . do not govern: Even on the most extreme hypothesis, that the stars "begin" all their impulses, human beings can achieve autonomy, but it is important to see how narrow a sphere Dante grants to their freedom. As 25. 37-78 will show, the bodies and temperaments of human beings are subject to Nature in both genesis and operation.

73. The heavens begin your motions: The "motions" (see 18.31-33, with notes) are the stirrings of impulse or desire: the "concupiscence" inherited from Adam (see the notes to lines 85-90) involves the partial independence of appetite from reason: desires contrary to reason cannot be entirely prevented. At what point the stirrings and fantasies of illicit desire become blameworthy was a matter of urgent discussion in the twelfth and thirteenth centuries; cf. 18.70-72, with notes.

76-78. free will . . . nourished well: The "first battles with the heavens" obviously take place in childhood, when the rational control of impulse must be learned. Only lifelong discipline enables one to achieve complete autonomy (see the note to lines 85-96).

79-81. To a greater Power . . . do not govern: Human beings are not ultimately subject to Nature as governed by the stars, but to God, who directly creates the intellect. God is the "greater Power" and "better Nature" (here in the sense of *natura naturans*; the phrase echoes *Met.* 1.21). The intellect is exempt from direct astrological influences both because directly created by God and because it does not, as Aristotle observed, have a bodily organ (see lines 73-81, Additional Note 11).

82-84. Thus, if the present . . . spy of it for you: The formal conclusion of the refutation and the transition to the confirmation.

85-129. From the hand . . . and its burden: The confirmation of the correct view: the disorder of the world is due to bad government, in two parts: a. the reason civil and religious authorities are needed (85-96), and b. its application to the state of the world (97-105); followed by c. historical analysis of the relations between empire and papacy. Dante's conviction that emperor and pope derived their authority from God independently and that the chief cause of the wretched state of the world was the popes' involvement in politics, is developed also in *Convivio* 4 and the *Monarchia*.

85-96. From the hand . . . of the true city: In defining the function of civil authority to be the moral education of the population, Dante voices his agreement with the central European tradition of political thought, going back to Plato and Aristotle and represented in medieval Europe by John of Salisbury, Aquinas, and many others.

85-90. From the hand . . . what amuses it: Dante's striking picture of the newly created soul, like a changeable little girl drawn instinctively to pleasure, has no direct literary antecedent, though it has an affinity with the opening of the emperor Hadrian's famous lyric, preserved in the *Historia Augusta*: "Animula vagula blandula" [little soul, wandering desirous, caressing, easily pleased]; it is doubtful, however, that Dante knew it. The image springs from the feminine gender of *anima,* from the iconography of the Last Judgment, often showing souls as infants, and from the observation of children. Dante emphasizes the origin of the soul in God's joyous love; the soul's capacity for delight derives from its "happy Maker," is part of its likeness to him. As Benvenuto observes, the newborn soul is a *tabula rasa*: it has no innate knowledge and is entirely innocent (see line 105, with note).

91-93. Of some lesser good . . . its love: What attracts the soul is a good, though a lesser one; all lesser goods are analogues of the highest good (*Par.* 13.52-66). There is no trace here of the idea that the human will inherently loves evil (see Gen. 8.21). The soul is deceived (line 92) about the magnitude of the lesser good, not in thinking it a good. This formulation agrees very closely with the view of original sin in Aquinas' early *Commentary on the Sentences* (liber 2, dist. 28, arts. 1 and 2), from which he retreated in the two *Summas.*

Augustine's view has been attributed to Dante recently by Chiavacci Leonardi; here is her summary: "human nature [is] vicious and inclined toward evil. That from his birth man has, because of Adam's sin, this inclination toward evil and ignorance of good, because of which, if he were permitted to act as he desires, he would fall into every sort of crime." This is simply not Dante's position. For him man is not inclined toward evil but weakened by Original Sin (see next note); he explicitly states that human nature as such is not corrupt (line 100).

94. to set the law as a curb: See *Mon.* 3.14-15: "These two authorities [empire and papacy] exist to direct man toward certain ends . . . if he had remained in the state of innocence where he was placed by God he would not have need of such direction: thus authorities of this kind are a remedy against the weakness of sin [*infirmitatem peccati*]."

96. the true city: Heaven, the City of God, "quella Roma onde Cristo è romano" [that Rome of which Christ is a Roman] (32.102). The authority of the king (the emperor), independent of the pope's, requires a kind of wisdom exemplified by Solomon (*Par.* 13.34-111) and not granted to the popes (see lines 106-14).

97-105. The laws are . . . corrupt in you: The second part of the confirmation, applying these principles to the current state of the world: the laws are not being enforced, mainly because the corrupt papacy has undermined the empire.

99. can chew . . . cloven hooves: The expression is derived from Lev. 11.2-4: "Whatsoever hath the hoof divided and cheweth the cud among the beasts, you shall eat. But whatsoever cheweth indeed the cud, and hath a hoof but divideth it not, as the camel, and others, that you shall not eat, but shall reckon it among the unclean." No longer bound by the Jewish dietary restrictions, Christians read the passage allegorically, and a long tradition applied it to the Christian clergy (they must be clean rather than unclean beasts). Chewing the cud was almost always taken to mean meditating on the Scriptures; there were several interpretations of the cloven hooves, such as: distinguishing between good and evil; accepting both OT and NT; understanding both literal and allegorical meanings.

Pietro di Dante explains: "The present clergy, though they are learned and thus chew the cud, still do not have cloven hooves in distinguishing and separating temporal matters from spiritual ones; instead they usurp temporal jurisdiction, from which they should be excluded" (see Maccarrone 1950). Dante's interpretation of the cloven hooves seems to have been unprecedented.

100-102. therefore the people . . . seek no further: The popes pursue temporal power and material wealth, and the people follow their example. The food imagery continues. *Fedir* [to strike] (line 101) seems to imply the image of a falcon diving at its prey.

103-105: You can clearly . . . corrupt in you: The formal conclusion of the confirmation.

105. not nature corrupt in you: An emphatic rejection of the pessimistic Augustinian view of the effects of Original Sin; see the note to lines 91-93, and cf. Agrimi 1966.

106-29. Rome . . . and its burden: The historical reasons for the present situation: the papacy has usurped the functions of the empire, with disastrous results exemplified by conditions in northern Italy.

106-108. Rome . . . and of God: Dante viewed the Romans as a second Chosen People, whose function was to bring the world under the rule of law and universal monarchy (to "make the good world," essential preparation for the coming of Christ). The two suns (line 107) are of course emperor and pope, who pointed the way to the happiness of this life and to that of the next life ("the two paths, of the world and of God"). Dante's fullest statement of this view is in *Mon.* 3.11.7-10:

> Thus God's ineffable Providence set before man two goals to pursue: the beatitude of this life, which consists in the operation of human virtue and is figured by the Earthly Paradise; and the beatitude of eternal life, which consists in the enjoyment of the vision of God, to which we cannot ascend by virtue of our powers unless aided by God's light, and which is signified by the Heavenly Paradise. To these beatitudes, as if to different conclu-

sions, we must come by different paths. For we come to the first by the teachings of philosophy, following them by operating according to the moral and intellectual virtues; but to the second we come by spiritual teachings that transcend human reason, following them by operating according to the theological virtues, namely faith, hope, and love. . . . For this reason man needed double guidance, according to his double goal: namely the pope, who should lead humankind to eternal life, according to the things revealed, and the emperor, who should direct human kind to temporal happiness according to the teachings of philosophy.

In the controversies of the thirteenth and fourteenth centuries both sides drew analogies between the pope and emperor and the two luminaries of Gen. 1.14-18 (sun and moon). The analogy between king/emperor and sun was common (as in Dante's *Ep.* 5.1.3), but the papal propagandists insisted that the emperor corresponded to the moon, subordinate to the sun (the pope); Dante's daring image of two suns, virtually unprecedented, is a response to the papal propaganda (see Kantorowicz 1957, Scott 1995 and 1996).

This is a passage of first importance, of course, and in terms of orthodox Church doctrine it is erroneous and smacks of Averroism, as was pointed out (after Dante's death) in the bitter attack on the *Monarchia* by the Dominican Guido Vernani; the *Monarchia* was on the Catholic Church's *Index of Forbidden Books* until the twentieth century.

109-14. One sun . . . by its seed: The popes have usurped the function of the emperors. The "sword" signifies civil authority (the power of life and death); the "shepherd's staff" (the bishop's crook) stands for spiritual authority. In Dante's view the two can only be joined together by violence.

113-14. consider the harvest . . . by its seed: These lines adapt Jesus' words in the Sermon on the Mount (Matt. 7.16-17; cf. Luke 6.44): "By their fruits you shall know them. Do men gather grapes of thorns, or figs of thistles? Even so every good tree bringeth forth good fruit, and the evil tree bringeth forth evil fruit." Dante has changed the figure of trees to grain; *spiga,* translated "harvest," is properly a spike of grain, the fruit or seed. These lines lead to the topic of the "harvest" in Italy.

115-17. In the land . . . found opposition: The turning point between the former age and the present is identified here as the development of opposition to Frederick II (reigned 1210-1250, from 1220 on as emperor; see the note to *Inf.* 10.119). Favored at first by the popes, Frederick was increasingly opposed by them, often in war, from the late 1220s on.

115. the land watered by Adige and Po: For Adige and Po, see the map on page xi. The geographical indication includes most of northern Italy (see the notes to 46-47 and 46), especially Lombardy-Emilia and the March of Treviso.

118-20. now anyone . . . draw near them: There are so few noble or virtuous people that the wicked need not fear being shamed by encountering them.

121-26. It is true . . . the faithful Lombard: The dark picture is somewhat relieved by this tribute (technically a digression) to "three old men"; they are reproaches to the new age because their virtues make its decadence evident. The "better life" they yearn for is of course Heaven. All three were prominent Guelphs (Marco was a Ghibelline).

124. Currado da Palazzo: Member of a noble family of Brescia, Currado had a distinguished political career, serving, among other posts, as Charles of Anjou's vicar in the north (1276), as head of the Guelph party (1277), and as *podestà* of Florence (1277) and Piacenza (1283).

124. the good Gherardo: Gherardo da Camino of Treviso (ca. 1240-1306), lord of Treviso from 1283 until his death, was famous for his hospitality to poets (Benvenuto says that Dante was a guest of Gherardo's early in his exile). Dante mentions Gherardo in *Conv.* 4.14.12 as one universally recognized to be truly noble.

125-26. Guido da Castello . . . the faithful Lombard: A member of the noble Roberti family of Reggio Emilia (ca. 1235–after 1315), Guido da Castello is similarly praised in *Conv.* 4.16.6. According to the Ottimo, the French called him the "simple [i.e., not duplicitous] Lombard" because of his generosity to French noblemen traveling through Reggio and to distinguish him from the Italian merchants in France, whom they despised.

127-29. Say then . . . and its burden: The formal conclusion to Marco's entire analysis, reiterating its central point. The "mud" is both failure and infamy; the "burden" of the Church is the responsibility laid upon it by Christ—spiritual guidance of society—not the powers it has usurped.

128. the two authorities: Dante's term *reggimento*, which occurs fourteen times in the *Convivio*, has rich connotations. Etymologically, it denotes an act of straightening, or directing. Thus it means "government" or "authority" actively asserted. Dante also uses it in the sense of one's "bearing" or "posture," clearly deriving from the governing oneself or holding oneself erect.

131-32. why the sons . . . the inheritance: The reference is to Num. 18.20-24, in which the tribe of Levi is appointed to be the priests of the temple and to receive tithes from the other tribes, but, unlike them, is not to possess a region of the Promised Land (the "inheritance"; cf. Jos. 13.33).

134. the departed people: Those of the previous age, most of whom are dead.

136-40. Either your speech . . . daughter Gaia: Marco's surprise at the pilgrim's question emphasizes the greatness of Gherardo's fame. That Gherardo was well known in Tuscany would be due to his connections with the Donati, especially Corso (see *Purg.* 24.82-90). About Gherardo da Camino's daughter Gaia little is known except that she married Tolberto da Camino and died in 1311; she is said by Lana and Benvenuto to have led a notoriously loose life; other early sources say she was famous for virtue. Sapegno comments: "The first interpretation seems more probable and more effective poetically: it discloses Marco's secret anger and prepares for the brusque tone of his farewell."

141-45. God be with you . . . hear me no longer: The ending of the canto effectively recalls its beginning and concludes the canto devoted to anger with Marco's need for purgation (see the notes to lines 25-145, 25-27, 34).

145. would hear me no longer: Implying that the pilgrim wished to continue the discussion.

Inter cantica. The themes of this fiftieth canto of the Comedy—the power of the stars, the causes of earthly disorder, the corruption of the papacy, the decadence of Dante's time, the value of earlier examples of civic virtue—recur throughout the *Comedy* and are given special prominence here at the center of the poem. See *Inferno* 6 (where the pilgrim asks Ciacco the reasons for the political upheavals in Florence), 7 (where Virgil explains the power of Fortune as related to the stars), 19 (where the pilgrim denounces the harm done by the corrupt papacy). *Purgatorio* 16, with its digression on the three noble survivors of the older generation, has a particularly close relation with *Inferno* 16, where the pilgrim encounters three Florentines representative of earlier civic virtues; they question him concerning the recent decadence of the Florentines in language closely parallel to that used in *Purgatorio* 16:

> "cortesia e valor dì se dimora
> ne la nostra città sì come suole,
> o se del tutto se n'è gita fora."
> (*Inf.* 16.67-69)
> [tell if courtesy and valor dwell in our city as they
> used to do, or if they have utterly forsaken it.]

Compare *Purg.* 16.116: "solea valore e cortesia trovarsi" [valor and courtesy used to be found]; *solere, cortesia,* and *valore* appear in both passages. In *Inferno* 16 the pilgrim attributes the decadence of Florence to "pride and excess" brought by prosperity; in *Purgatorio* 16 the analysis is placed in a cosmic context and derived from fundamental principles. All six are leading Guelphs: the corruption of the papacy casts an ironic light on their mistaken allegiance.

Marco Lombardo's observation that the pilgrim has been "speaking Tuscan" to him raises the important recurring theme of the regional nature of speech. See *Inf.* 10.22-29; 22.97-99; 23.76 , 91; 33.10-12; *Purg.* 6.72-75; 7.16-17; with notes.

CANTO 17

Ricorditi, lettor, se mai ne l'alpe   1
ti colse nebbia per la qual vedessi
non altrimenti che per pelle talpe,

come, quando i vapori umidi e spessi   4
a diradar cominciansi, la spera
del sol debilemente entra per essi,

e fia la tua imagine leggera   7
in giugnere a veder com' io rividi
lo sole in pria, che già nel corcar era.

Sì, pareggiando i miei co' passi fidi   10
del mio maestro, usci' fuor di tal nube
ai raggi morti già ne' bassi lidi.

O imaginativa, che ne rube   13
talvolta sì di fuor ch'om non s'accorge
perché dintorno suonin mille tube,

chi move te, se 'l senso non ti porge?   16
Moveti lume che nel ciel s'informa,
per sé o per voler che giù lo scorge.

De l'empiezza di lei che mutò forma   19
ne l'uccel ch'a cantar più si diletta
ne l'imagine mia apparve l'orma,

e qui fu la mia mente sì ristretta   22
dentro da sé che di fuor non venìa
cosa che fosse allor da lei ricetta.

Poi piovve dentro a l'alta fantasia   25
un crucifisso, dispettoso e fero
ne la sua vista, e cotal si moria;

intorno ad esso era il grande Assüero,   28
Estèr sua sposa e 'l giusto Mardoceo,
che fu al dire e al far così intero.

CANTO 17

Third terrace, continued: emergence from the smoke—examples of anger
—the angel, erasure, a Beatitude—climb—Fourth terrace, of sloth:
sunset and immobility—the structure of Purgatory: love distorted,
defective, excessive

1   Remember, reader, if ever in the mountains a
     fog caught you through which you saw no
     otherwise than a mole does through its skin,

4   how, when the moist, thick vapors begin to thin
     out, the sphere of the sun shines weakly through
     them,

7   and your imagination will easily come to see
     how I first saw the sun again, which was already
     setting.

10   Thus, making mine equal with my master's
     trusted steps, I came forth from that cloud into its
     rays, already extinguished on the lowest shore.

13   O imagination, that sometimes so steals us from
     the world outside that we do not hear though a
     thousand trumpets sound around us,

16   who moves you, if sense offers you nothing? A
     light moves you that is formed in the heavens, by
     itself or by a will that guides it downward.

19   The wickedness of her who changed her form
     into the bird that most delights to sing, appeared as
     a trace in my imagination,

22   and here my mind was so bound up within itself
     that it would receive nothing then that came from
     outside.

25   Next there rained into my deep fantasy one
     crucified, his gaze scornful and fierce, and such he
     died;

28   around him were the great Ahasuerus, Esther his
     wife, and the just Mordecai, who had such
     integrity in word and deed.

E come questa imagine rompeo   31
sé per sé stessa, a guisa d'una bulla
cui manca l'acqua sotto qual si feo,

    surse in mia visïone una fanciulla   34
piangendo forte, e dicea: "O regina,
perché per ira hai voluto esser nulla?

    Ancisa t'hai per non perder Lavina: 37
or m'hai perduta! Io son essa che lutto,
madre, a la tua pria ch'a l'altrui ruina."

    Come si frange il sonno ove di butto   40
nova luce percuote il viso chiuso,
che fratto guizza pria che muoia tutto:

    così l'imaginar mio cadde giuso   43
tosto che lume il volto mi percosse,
maggior assai che quel ch'è in nostro uso.

    I' mi volgea per veder ov' io fosse,   46
quando una voce disse: "Qui si monta,"
che da ogne altro intento mi rimosse,

    e fece la mia voglia tanto pronta   49
di riguardar chi era che parlava
che mai non posa, se non si raffronta.

    Ma come al sol, che nostra vista grava   52
e per soverchio sua figura vela,
così la mia virtù quivi mancava.

    "Questo è divino spirito, che ne la   55
via da ir sù ne drizza sanza prego,
e col suo lume sé medesmo cela.

    Sì fa con noi come l'uom si fa sego,   58
ché quale aspetta prego e l'uopo vede,
malignamente già si mette al nego.

    Or accordiamo a tanto invito il piede;   61
procacciam di salir pria che s'abbui,
ché poi non si poria, se 'l dì non riede."

    Così disse il mio duca, e io con lui   64
volgemmo i nostri passi ad una scala;
e tosto ch'io al primo grado fui,

    senti'mi presso quasi un muover d'ala   67
e ventarmi nel viso e dir: "*Beati
pacifici*, che son sanz' ira mala!"

31   And as this image burst by itself, like a bubble
losing the water beneath which it formed,

34   there arose in my vision a young girl, weeping
loudly, and she was saying: "O queen, why for
anger have you wished to be nothing?

37   You have killed yourself so as not to lose
Lavinia: now you have lost me! I am the one who
grieve, mother, for your ruin more than any
other's."

40   As sleep is shattered when suddenly new light
strikes our closed eyes, but wriggles as it breaks,
before it dies completely:

43   so my imagining fell down as soon as the light
struck my face, much greater than we are
accustomed to.

46   I was turning to see where I was, when a voice
said: "Here is the place to climb," and removed me
from any other thought,

49   and it made my desire so eager to see who was
speaking that it will never rest until face to face.

52   But as if at the sun, which weighs down our
gaze and veils its shape with excess, so my power
failed before him.

55   "This is a divine spirit, who directs us to the way
upward without being begged, and he hides
himself within his own light.

58   He treats us as one treats oneself, for whoever
waits to be asked when he sees a need, already
maliciously prepares to refuse.

61   Now let us make our feet accord with his
invitation; let us strive to climb before dark comes,
for then we could not, until day returns."

64   So said my leader, and with him I turned my
feet toward a stairway; and as soon as I was on the
first step,

67   I felt something like the motion of a wing near
me, and a wind in my face, and one saying: "*Beati
pacifici*, who are without sinful anger!"

Già eran sovra noi tanto levati   70
li ultimi raggi, che la notte segue,
che le stelle apparivan da più lati.

    "O virtù mia, perché sì ti dilegue?"   73
fra me stesso dicea, ché mi sentiva
la possa de le gambe posta in triegue.

    Noi eravam dove più non saliva   76
la scala sù, ed eravamo affissi
pur come nave ch'a la piaggia arriva.

    E io attesi un poco, s'io udissi   79
alcuna cosa nel novo girone;
poi mi volsi al maestro mio e dissi:

    "Dolce mio padre, dì, quale offensione   82
si purga qui nel giro dove semo?
Se i piè si stanno, non stea tuo sermone."

    Ed elli a me: "L'amor del bene, scemo   85
del suo dover, quiritta si ristora;
qui si ribatte il mal tardato remo.

    Ma perché più aperto intendi ancora,   88
volgi la mente a me, e prenderai
alcun buon frutto di nostra dimora.

    Né creator né creatura mai,"   91
cominciò el, "figliuol, fu sanza amore,
o naturale o d'animo, e tu 'l sai.

    Lo naturale è sempre sanza errore,   94
ma l'altro puote errar per male obietto
o per troppo o per poco di vigore.

    Mentre ch'elli è nel primo ben diretto   97
e ne' secondi sé stesso misura,
esser non può cagion di mal diletto,

    ma quando al mal si torce, o con più cura,   100
o con men che non dee corre nel bene,
contra 'l fattore adovra sua fattura.

    Quinci comprender puoi ch'esser convene   103
amor sementa in voi d'ogne virtute
e d'ogne operazion che merta pene.

    Or, perché mai non può da la salute   106
amor del suo subietto volger viso,
da l'odio proprio son le cose tute;

70 Already above us the last rays, those that night follows, had risen so far that the stars were appearing on many sides.

73 "O my strength, why do you disappear so?" I was saying to myself, for I felt a truce imposed on all the power of my legs.

76 We were where the stairway rose no further, and we were fixed like a ship that is beached.

79 And I waited a little, to see if I heard anything in the new circle; then I turned to my master and said:

82 "My sweet father, say, what offence is purged in the circle where we are? Though our feet stand still, let not your speech do so."

85 And he to me: "The love of the good, falling short of what is right, is here restored; here they ply and ply again the oar they did ill to slow.

88 But that you may yet more clearly understand, turn your mind to me, and you will take some good fruit from our delay.

91 Neither Creator nor creature ever," he began, "son, has been without love, whether natural or of the mind, and this you know.

94 Natural love is always unerring, but the other can err with an evil object or with too much or too little vigor.

97 As long as it is directed to the first Good and moderates its love of lesser goods, it cannot be a cause of evil pleasure,

100 but when it turns aside to evil, or when with more eagerness or less than is right it runs after some good, it employs his creature against the Creator.

103 Hence you can comprehend that love must be the seed in you of every virtue and of every action that deserves punishment.

106 Now because love can never turn its face away from the well-being of its subject, all things are safe from self-hatred;

e perché intender non si può diviso,   109
e per sé stante, alcuno esser dal primo,
da quello odiare ogne effetto è deciso.

  Resta, se dividendo bene stimo,   112
che 'l mal che s'ama è del prossimo, ed esso
amor nasce in tre modi in vostro limo.

  È chi, per esser suo vicin soppresso,   115
spera eccellenza, e sol per questo brama
ch'el sia di sua grandezza in basso messo;

  è chi podere, grazia, onore e fama   118
teme di perder perch'altri sormonti,
onde s'attrista sì che 'l contrario ama;

  ed è chi per ingiuria par ch'aonti   121
sì che si fa de la vendetta ghiotto,
e tal convien che 'l male altrui impronti:

  questo triforme amor qua giù di sotto   124
si piange. Or vo' che tu de l'altro intende,
che corre al ben con ordine corrotto.

  Ciascun confusamente un bene apprende   127
nel qual si queti l'animo, e disira,
per che di giugner lui ciascun contende.

  Se lento amore a lui veder vi tira   130
o a lui acquistar, questa cornice,
dopo giusto penter, ve ne martira.

  Altro ben è che non fa l'uom felice;   133
non è felicità, non è la buona
essenza, d'ogne ben frutto e radice.

  L'amor ch'ad esso troppo s'abbandona   136
di sovr' a noi si piange per tre cerchi;
ma come tripartito si ragiona,

  tacciolo, acciò che tu per te ne cerchi."   139

109   and because nothing can be conceived as self-existent or divided from the First, every creature is cut off from hating him.

112   There remains, if I judge well in my division, that the evil that is loved is that done to one's neighbor, and this love is born in your slime in three ways.

115   There are those who hope for supremacy through their neighbor's being kept down, and only on this account desire that his greatness be brought low;

118   there are those who fear to lose power, favor, honor, or fame because another mounts higher, and thus are so aggrieved that they love the contrary;

121   and there are those who seem so outraged by injury that they become greedy for revenge, and thus they must ready harm for others:

124   this triple love is wept for here beneath us. Now I would have you consider the other, which runs after the good with corrupted order.

127   Each confusedly apprehends a Good in which his spirit may be quieted, and desires it, and therefore each strives to reach it.

130   If slack love draws you to see it or to acquire it, this ledge, after just repentance, punishes you for that.

133   Other goods there are that do not make one happy; they are not happiness, they are not the good Essence, fruit and root of all goodness.

136   The love that abandons itself excessively to these is bewailed above us in three circles; but how one must speak of it as tripartite,

139   I do not say, that you may seek it out for yourself."

NOTES

1-12. Remember, reader . . . the lowest shore: This fourth and central address to the reader in the *Purgatorio* (see the note to 8.19-26) is the only one to begin a canto. Dante evokes memory of the sun emerging from mist: since it is nearly sunset, the sight joins a kind of "dawn" to the approaching dusk. The mole (line 3), the sun through mist, the approach of night: all emphasize the horizon of night and day, and the importance of memory and imagination to vigorous action: a nexus in the central cantos of the poem.

3. than a mole does through its skin: Brunetto Latini writes (*Trésor* 1.197): "the mole sees nothing, for nature does not wish to open the skin over his eyes, and so they are of no worth": cf. the envious (and see 14.3; "rough hair" recalls 13.58), the example also points to internal vision working when sight is impeded.

13-39. O imagination . . . than any other's: Introduced by the discussion of inspiration through the imagination are three examples of the punishment of anger, from Ovidian myth, the OT, and the *Aeneid*.

13-18. O imagination . . . guides it downward: Nardi 1966 paraphrases: "whether through the action of the light of the celestial body itself; by the action of the intelligences [the angels] that impress on the heavenly bodies light derived from the profound mind [of God]; or through divine action through the intelligences and the celestial bodies." Like those of 15.83-138, these are waking visions, whose causes were much discussed in the thirteenth century, along with dreams and prophetic visions; many maintained that such visions were instilled by the heavenly bodies. So Albertus Magnus: "The celestial forms directed at us, when touching our bodies, move them with great strength and impress their powers, though they are not perceived because of the tumult of outward distractions; when the soul is separated from the senses, in whatever way, then the motions are perceived . . . The imaginative soul, which the movements of these forms reach in this way, receives them according to the mode of its own possible movement, that is, the forms of the imagination" (*De somno et vigilia* 3.1, 8-9; in Gregory 1992; cf. *Conv.* 2.4.4-7).

Verbs of rising and falling used for the visions (*piovve, surse, cadde*: lines 25, 34, 43) are connected with the theme of lofty ambition brought low, twice in the ironic form of hanging. Consistent with Virgil's analysis of the vices at 17.112-23, the terms contrast also with the pilgrim's rising motion (line 47). For *imaginativa* [imaging faculty], cf. *apprensiva* [perceiving faculty], 18.22.

19-39. The wickedness . . . than any other's: The visions adapt and condense the events Dante found in his sources. The first is the most radically condensed; all that "appears" is the *empietà* [cruelty, wickedness] referring to infanticide and cannibalism, its author identified ambiguously: the reader must supply the tale of Procne and Philomela (*Met.* 6.412-676). Amata's suicide is seen through her daughter Lavinia's words of grief (invented by Dante). The second example presents a scene not in the source (see Silverstein 1953). The examples suggest how anger results from pride and envy; two examples involve fraud (Procne, Haman); in two of them virtuous figures appear (Mordecai, Lavinia). All suggest the ultimate transcending of suffering: birdsong is sweet to hear; Mordecai is vindicated; Lavinia marries Aeneas.

20. the bird that most delights to sing: This probably refers to Philomela; see the note to 9.16-18. But the swallow's (Procne's) infanticide is even more impious than Philomela's, she stabs her own child; Philomela slits his throat, and both sisters feed him to his father: the matter is left open. The desire to avenge outrage is shared: cf. lines 121-23.

22-23. my mind . . . within itself: Anticipating line 89; cf. the pilgrim's use of his mind's eye at 4.67-68; in each case a shift to the internal senses.

26-29. one crucified . . . the just Mordecai: According to the book of Esther, when the Jew Mordecai will not bow to Haman, minister of the Persian King Ahasuerus, Haman persuades the king to decree the death of all the Jews in the realm. Esther, Mordecai's niece and the King's favorite consort, invites Haman and the King to a feast: she confronts Haman, and as he entreats her mercy he is found lying on her couch by the king and is hanged on the scaffold prepared for the just Mordecai. The biblical text stresses Haman's pride in his high station and his envy of Mordecai; see lines 116-23.

26. one crucified. . . scornful and fierce: The Vulgate uses, along with *trabes* [beam] and *patibulo* [scaffold], the expression *affigi cruci* [to crucify] for Haman's execution. Dante clearly regards it as parodic of the crucifixion of Christ (see *Inferno* Additional Note 16). The description of Haman as "scornful and fierce" is not biblical; it contrasts with the suffering Christ of thirteenth-century iconography.

34-39. a young girl . . . more than any other's: Enflamed by the Fury Allecto (*Aen*. 7.341-53), Amata, wife of Latinus of Latium, vows not to see her daughter Lavinia married to Aeneas rather than to Turnus (*Aen*. 12.63-64: "at once I shall quit the hated light, nor will I ever, a captive, see Aeneas as my son-in-law"). Even before Turnus is killed Amata gives him up for dead and hangs herself from a beam (*trabes*; cf. previous note) in the palace. Dante draws on:

> When the wretched Latin women learned of this death,
> her daughter Lavinia first, tearing with her hands her lovely
> hair and rosy cheeks . . . rages (*Aen*. 12.604-606).

Lavinia's bitter grief reasserts the link of wrath and sorrow, *tristitia*. In *Ep*. 7.24 Dante predicts that the future despair of rebellious Florence will resemble Amata's.

38. now you have lost me: An ironic reflection on Amata's vow: Amata has lost Lavinia completely instead of only partly. "M'hai perduta" can also mean "you have destroyed me."

39. for your ruin more than any other's: Lavinia's grief for her mother is greater than her grief for Turnus.

40-45. As sleep is shattered . . . accustomed to: The visions are closely related to dreams, and Dante concludes with a simile of sleep shattered by strong light. The inner light (*lume*, line 17) that fashions the images is overcome by the light of the angel (*lume*, line 44).

46-60. I was turning . . . prepares to refuse: As the sun appears out of the smoke, the angel hidden in light suggests the virtue (love of peace) that counters wrath.

51. that it will never rest until face to face: This anticipates Virgil's account of perception leading to desire in 18.22-33.

53. veils its shape with excess: See Ps. 103. 2: "clothed with light as with a garment"; cf. line 57. For the angels as heralds of the *Paradiso*, see 15.10-33. Milton drew on this passage in *Paradise Lost* 3.372-82.

58-60. He treats us . . . prepares to refuse: See Mark 12.31, "Thou shalt love thy neighbor as thyself," the second of the two precepts of the New Law, here placed next to a saying of Seneca's: "To be slow to wish to give is not to wish it . . . he who delays is unwilling" (*De beneficiis* 2.5, another part of which Dante quotes in *Conv.* 1. 8.10; Gmelin).

61-84. Now let us . . . your speech do so: Near the center of the *cantica* and the poem, Dante articulates the interplay of physical ascent and mental contemplation fundamental to the *cantica*. The wayfarers replace diurnal walking with nocturnal talk (line 84), with an implicit allegory of the "*pes affectus*" ("foot of desire"; cf. *Inf.* 1.30; with note), whose lameness theologians often associated with the inertia of sloth (Wenzel 1967); cf. 18.44, 121, and 19.8.

62. let us strive to climb before dark: Cf. John 12.35-36: "Yet a little while, the light [i.e., Christ] is among you. Walk whilst you have the light, that the darkness overtake you not." See 7.43-57, with notes.

68-69. *Beati pacifici*, who are without sinful anger: The beginning of the seventh Beatitude (traditionally the last in the series): "Blessed are the peacemakers, for they shall be called the children of God"), rounded out with an application to the terrace of anger; for righteous anger, see John 2.13-17 (Christ driving the money-changers from the Temple), Eph. 4.26; cf. *Inf.* 8.43-45; *Ep.* 11.6.

70-75. Already above us . . . power of my legs: Sunlight and the strength to climb are correlated as both fail; cf. the note to lines 61-84.

77-78. fixed like a ship that is beached: Both here and in lines 87-88, the pilgrimage is metaphorically a sea-voyage. The figure was common for the return of the soul to God "as to that port from which she departed when she came to enter into the sea of this life" (*Conv.* 4.28.2), but is emphasized on the terrace of the slothful, in connection with the example of Aeneas' companions (18.133-38). Ulysses, the anti-type of the pilgrim's journey, is close by; see 19.19-24, with notes, and *Inferno* Additional Note 11.

82-87. My sweet father . . . did ill to slow: The pilgrim inquires about the vice purged on this terrace and receives a direct answer (lines 85-87); Virgil's definition of sloth as a deficiency of love has introduced the key term; this leads naturally into Virgil's long exposition. *ST* 1a q. 63 a. 2 ad 2 defines sloth [*acedia*] as "a kind of sadness [*tristitia*] whereby one becomes sluggish [*tardus*] in spiritual exercises because they weary the body."

91-139. Neither Creator . . . for yourself: At the center of the poem Dante places the central principle of all things, as well as the central problem of human life. Love is the motive of every action and is thus the key to understanding wrong as well as right actions, as well as the key to their correction. Therefore it provides the rationale of the ordering of Purgatory. Virgil proceeds by division: love is divided into natural and elective, and the distortions of elective love are divided into those of misdirection and faulty degree.

91-92. Neither Creator . . . without love: That God's love motivates his creation of the universe and his governing of it, and that love is the force that moves every created thing, from stones to angels, are basic tenets of Christian Neoplatonism (1 John 4.16; *Consolation* 3 m. 8, 4 m. 6; *City of God* 14.7; *De div. nom.* 4.113-22 with Aquinas 1950, par. 317-19; *ST* 1a q. 20 a. 1 ad 2, 1a 2ae q. 28 a. 6 resp), set forth in detail by Dante in *Conv.* 3.3.2-5.

93. whether natural or of the mind: It is not clear how this distinction applies to God, though it is clear enough with regard to created things.

94. Natural love is always unerring: *ST* 1a q. 60 a. 5 ad 4: "God, as he is the universal good, from which all natural goods depend, is naturally loved by all"; 1a q. 60 a. 1 ad 3: "As natural cognition is always true, so natural love is always right, as natural love is nothing else but the natural inclination grafted in us by the author of nature." This applies, then, to all creatures, though only angels and human beings have both natural and elective love. (According to the traditional view, derived from Augustine [*Confessions* 13, *De civ. Dei* 12.1-9], the angels' moment of choice was in the instant after their creation; some turned away from God and fell; the majority turned in love toward God who since then maintains them in grace; for the neutral angels, see *Inf.* 3.37-42.) Human beings are the principal focus, then, creatures capable of rational choice: the difficulty of maintaining freedom of choice is Marco's emphasis; rational choice as the basis of merit will be the subject of the next canto.

94-96. the other . . . too little vigor: Natural love aims at the ultimate end (discussed further in lines 127-29 and 18.55-63); elective love elects means to an end. Cf. *ST* 1a q. 82, a. 1 ad 3, quoting Aristotle (*Nichomachean Ethics* 3. 2 1111b): "We are lords of our own actions, insofar as we can choose this or that. Choice however is not of the end, but of those things that lead to the end . . . whence the desire of the ultimate end is not among those things of which we are lords." Natural love "tends to good existing in a thing," elective love "to a good which is apprehended"; for this reason, misjudgment of the good is possible. *ST* 1a 2ae q. 8, a.1 resp. cites Aristotle (*Physics* 2. 3, 195a) "As natural appetite tends to the good existing in the thing, the animal or voluntary appetite tends to the good that is apprehended or perceived. Thus when the will tends toward a given thing, it is not necessary that it be something truly good, but only that it be perceived to be good; and because of this the Philosopher says in 2 Physics that the end is the good, or what appears to be so."

Long thought of Dante's own devising, Virgil's analysis was shown to go back ultimately to the Dominican William Peraldus' *Summa de vitiis et virtutibus*, a penitential handbook based on Augustine, Gregory, and others, very widely read in the thirteenth and fourteenth centuries (Wenzel 1977); Pietro di Dante reports Peraldus' scheme without attribution.

95-105. the other can err . . . deserves punishment: The list of the errors of elective love is meant as an exhaustive classification: error in choice of object, error in degree of love. Elective love does not err when it is fixed on the highest good (it is not possible to love God too much: see Mark 12.30, *ST* 1a 2ae q. 64 a. 4 resp.) and moderate in its pursuit of lesser goods.

101. it runs after some good: The metaphor of "running" recalls the childish soul in 16.91-92, the running moon (18.79), and the running souls (18.97); see the note to lines 61-84.

102. it employs his creature against the Creator: Cf. Alain of Lille, *Anticlaudianus* 6.304: "Factorique suo movet factura querelam" [the thing made picks a quarrel with its maker] (Mazzoni 1972).

103-105. love must be . . . deserves punishment: See *ST* 1a 2ae q. 41 a.2 ad 4: "All passions of the soul derive from one principle, that is to say from love," and q. 46, a.1 resp: "Love then is the first root of all the passions." Implicit is a "tree" of distinctions, of loves (tree diagrams were common in the discussions of vices and virtues); cf. line 135.

106-11. Now because love . . . cut off from hating him: The suicides and Capaneus seem to contradict this. But Augustine and Aquinas, with nods to scripture (Eph. 5.29), observe that the suicide is persuaded he is seeking a good (*ST* 1a 2ae q. 29 a. 4 ad 2); while some souls, although they cannot hate the author of their own existence (cf. *Conv.* 3.2.7-8), hate his commandments or his authority (like Capaneus; see *ST* 2a 2ae q. 34, a. 1). See 18.15. and notes.

112. if I judge well in my division: Virgil calls attention to his Scholastic method: "there remains" is the scholastic "reliquitur in dividendo" [after dividing, there is left]. Terms like "divided from the First" or "cut off from hating him" echo the meaning of division in a divinely created and ordered cosmos, where no creature can be wholly cut off from the source of Being (cf. Durling/Martinez 1990).

113. the evil that is loved . . . to one's neighbor: For the role of malice in the ordering of sins, see *Inf.* 11.22-66, with notes. The emphasis there on the social effects of sin is consistent with the emphasis in the *Purgatorio* on restoring civic virtue through imperial authority, made explicit in the previous canto by Marco Lombardo (16.103-17; see 6.94-96, 7.94-96, 14.106-11, with notes).

114. in your slime: Compare Gen. 2.7: "And the Lord God formed man of the slime [*limo*] of the earth." The term recalls the discussions of human nobility among the lyric poets of the Duecento (see Guinizelli's "Al cor gentil rempaira sempre amore," lines 31-40; and cf. *Conv.* 3.7.3-4, 4.20.3-9). Cf.11.97-99, 26.91-114, with notes).

115-25. There are those who . . . here beneath us: Dante follows Peraldus and Aquinas in showing how envy and wrath form a sequence resulting from pride.

115-23. There are those who . . . ready harm for others: In addition to exemplifying the interrelation of the first triad of vices, Dante echoes how they generate the narrative of the Theban brothers Eteocles and Polynices in Statius, *Theb.* 1.316-19:

115-17. There are those . . . be brought low: See *ST* 2a 2ae q. 162 a. 4 ad 3: Pride is "love of one's own excellence, in that it is caused by the love of an inordinate presumption of exceeding others"; cf. *Purg.* 11.86-87.

118-20. there are those . . . love the contrary: See *ST* 2a 2ae q. 36 a. 1: "There is another way in which the good of another is judged to be one's own harm, in that it diminishes one's own glory or excellence; and in this manner envy sorrows at the good of others."

121-23. and there are those . . . harm for others: *ST* 2a 2ae q. 158 a. 4 resp: "He who is wrathful seeks the harm of another under the pretext of just revenge."

> . . . day and night, over and over he is gripped by
> but one wish: that he might see his brother humbled
> and quit the throne and he seize for himself the wealth
> of Thebes . . .

See also *Theb.* 1.123-30. Compare Benvenuto's gloss on 115-17, describing the proud man wishing "that his neighbor be cast down [*deiiciatur*] from his position, that he himself might be made great," echoing Aquinas and Statius.

126. runs . . . with corrupted order: Picks up Virgil's terminology from line 101.

127-29. Each confusedly apprehends . . . strives to reach it: Cf. *CG* 3.38: "There is a certain common, confused knowledge of God which is found among almost all men; whether this is because God's being is self-evident . . . or whether because man can through his natural reason immediately arrive at some knowledge of God." See also *ST* 1a q.2 a. 1 ad 1.

128. his spirit may be quieted: Cf. *Confessions* 1.1: "You have made us for yourself, and our hearts are restless until they rest in you."

130. to see it: The Good desired by the soul is the intellectual Vision of God; *ST* 2a 2ae q. 3 a. 4 resp.: "The essence of beatitude consists in the act of the intellect. But to the will pertains the enjoyment that follows on beatitude."

134-35. they are not . . . root of all goodness: God is beginning and end, Alpha and Omega (Apoc. 1.8, cf. Additional Note 15), both the root and ultimate fruit of good. See *ST* 1a q. 6 a. 4: "Thus each good is said to be good from the divine good, as the exemplary first, efficient, and final end of all goodness" (a good example of Aquinas' Pseudo-Dionysian Neoplatonism; see *De div. nom.* 4.173-78, Aquinas 1950, par. 442-50).

139. I do not say . . . for yourself: Left incomplete, the analysis stimulates the pilgrim and the reader to follow out its implications; cf. *VN* 19.33 and *Conv.* 3.5.20: "whoever has a noble wit can understand; it is well to leave them with some work yet to be done"; see Durling/Martinez 1990, Ch. 1.

Inter cantica. The parallels with *Inferno* 16-17 concern the central cantos of the respective canticas, and entail images central to the poem. The parallel cantos are linked by addresses to the reader, at *Inf.* 16.127-28 and *Purg.* 17.1-9; both appeal to personal experience, that of the *Inferno* to the pilgrim's, that of *Purgatorio* to the reader's, and both focus on the imagination or phantasy, the image-making power of the mind. In Canto 17 the appeal to the reader's imagination prepares the images of wrath that descend into the mind of the wayfarer; in the *Inferno* it is Geryon, the hybrid monster, who rises from the abyss, like the pilgrim's nightmare (*Inf.* 16.122), to represent the image of fraud (for the flight on Geryon as a microcosm of the poem itself, see *Inferno* Additional Note 6), and to assist the wayfarers to descend into the Malebolge. The rising and descending is programmatic: Geryon rises like a swimmer who has first descended into the ocean (16.133-36, *suso* 131, *giuso* 133), and begins his descent like a boat, bird, or arrow (17.98, 116, 130); the images in Purgatory descend ("rained" *Purg.* 17.25) but also vanish as if bubbles rising to the surface of consciousness (17.31-32) or a dream that dissipates (17.42), "wriggling" before it dies (*guizza*; and see *Inf.* 17.25), and the wayfarer's upward motion is arrested like a boat beaching itself in the sand (*Purg.* 17.72). The inertia of the wayfarers when the sun departs distantly recalls the seated usurers (*Inf.* 17.45), whose wealth was achieved without work.

In *Inferno*, the journey on Geryon, to which the wayfarers "bend" their steps (*si torca*, 17.28) risks becoming a flight like those of Phaëthon and Icarus, who left the right road (*strada*, *Inf.* 16.107) and followed a "bad course" (*mala via*, 17.111); once Phaëthon "abandoned the reins" (*abbandonò i freni*, 17.107), his doom was sealed. In *Purgatorio* Virgil discourses on how the will can err: it "turns [*si torce*] aside to evil" (17.100), or it "runs [*corre*] after the good with corrupted order" (17.126; see 16.92) and disregards both the bridle (*freno*, *Inf.* 17.107 / 16.94) and the right path (*strada*, *Purg.* 18.78-81), so that it goes off course (*disvia /sviare*, *Purg.* 16.82; see 29.82) and "must go astray" (*mal convien che vada*, *Purg.* 16.111). Thus "love that abandons itself [*s'abbandona*]" to lesser goods (*Purg.* 17.136) is the moral equivalent of Phaëthon's mad career, which as a model for the path of error (but also for the refusal of sloth; cf. Additional Note 3) is implicit here, though his name goes unmentioned.

Virgil's account implies a tree-diagram by which the genus in question is subdivided into species: Virgil first asserts the love of Creator and creatures alike; he then divides the love of creatures into natural and elective loves; error is possible only among the latter, as instinctual loves are not liable to praise and blame, and thus only among creatures capable of rational choice, which means humans (the domain of free will is the focus of Marco Lombardo's speech, 16.67-78, and again of Virgil's, 18.67-75; angels fix their wills immutably on God). Elective love is unerring when it aims at the final end (God) or when it gauges desire for secondary goods (like food, a necessity). It may err in two ways: when it turns to evil or approaches the good in a disordered way, either defectively or excessively. Virgil then further sifts the turn to evil: hate for the creator or the self being discounted, he concludes that the evil the soul chooses is that done to others , which the pilgrim has seen divided into pride, envy, and wrath. Finally, Virgil takes up the distinction between defective and excessive love, the first being insufficient desire for the supreme good, and the second. . . but Virgil stops, indicating only that the remaining vices distract one from the primary good that alone fully satisfies human desire.

CANTO 18

Posto avea fine al suo ragionamento   1
l'alto dottore, e attento guardava
ne la mia vista s'io parea contento;
    e io, cui nova sete ancor frugava,   4
di fuor tacea e dentro dicea: "Forse
lo troppo dimandar ch'io fo li grava."
    Ma quel padre verace, che s'accorse   7
del timido voler che non s'apriva,
parlando di parlare ardir mi porse.
    Ond' io: "Maestro, il mio veder s'avviva   10
sì nel tuo lume ch'io discerno chiaro
quanto la tua ragion parta o descriva.
    Però ti prego, dolce padre caro,   13
che mi dimostri amore, a cui reduci
ogne buono operare e 'l suo contraro."
    "Drizza," disse, "ver' me l'agute luci   16
de lo 'ntelletto, e fieti manifesto
l'error de' ciechi che si fanno duci.
    L'animo, ch'è creato ad amar presto,   19
ad ogne cosa è mobile che piace,
tosto che dal piacere in atto è desto.
    Vostra apprensiva da esser verace   22
tragge intenzione, e dentro a voi la spiega,
sì che l'animo ad essa volger face;
    e se rivolto inver' di lei si piega,   25
quel piegare è amor, quell' è natura
che per piacer di novo in voi si lega.
    Poi, come 'l foco movesi in altura   28
per la sua forma, ch'è nata a salire
là dove più in sua matera dura,

CANTO 18

*Fourth terrace, continued: Virgil expounds the nature of love: the
psychology of desire, love defined by its object, freedom of will—
moonrise—the souls of the slothful—examples of zeal—the Abbot of
San Zeno—examples of sloth—sleep*

1   My noble teacher had put an end to his
exposition, and he was gazing attentively into my
eyes to see if I was satisfied;

4   and I, prodded by yet another thirst, remained
silent without and within said: "Perhaps my
excessive questioning is burdensome to him."

7   But that truthful father, who perceived the timid
wish that I was not opening to him, by speaking
made me bold to speak.

10   Therefore I: "Master, my sight becomes so keen
in your light that I discern clearly whatever your
account divides or defines.

13   Therefore I beg you, dear sweet father, that you
expound love for me, to which you refer every
good action and its contrary."

16   "Direct," he said, "toward me the sharp eyes of
your intellect, and I will make manifest to you the
error of the blind who claim to lead.

19   The mind, created quick to love, can move
toward everything that is pleasing, as soon as it is
wakened into act by pleasure.

22   Your power of apprehension takes from some
real thing an intention and unfolds it within you,
so that it causes the mind to turn toward it;

25   and if, having turned, the mind bends toward it,
that bending is love, that is nature which by
pleasure is first bound in you.

28   Then, as fire moves upward because of its form,
which is born to rise to where it may last longer in
its matter,

così l'animo preso entra in disire,   31
ch'è moto spiritale, e mai non posa
fin che la cosa amata il fa gioire.

  Or ti puote apparer quant' è nascosa   34
la veritate a la gente ch'avvera
ciascun amore in sé laudabil cosa;

  però che forse appar la sua matera   37
sempre esser buona, ma non ciascun segno
è buono, ancor che buona sia la cera."

  "Le tue parole e 'l mio seguace ingegno,"   40
rispuos' io lui, "m'hanno amor discoverto,
ma ciò m'ha fatto di dubbiar più pregno;

  ché, s'amore è di fuori a noi offerto,   43
e l'anima non va con altro piede,
se dritta o torta va non è suo merto."

  Ed elli a me: "Quanto ragion qui vede,   46
dir ti poss' io; da indi in là t'aspetta
pur a Beatrice, ch'è opra di fede.

  Ogne forma sustanzïal, che setta   49
è da matera ed è con lei unita,
specifica vertute ha in sé colletta,

  la qual sanza operar non è sentita   52
né si dimostra mai che per effetto,
come per verdi fronde in pianta vita.

  Però, là onde vegna lo 'ntelletto   55
de le prime notizie, omo non sape,
e de' primi appetibili l'affetto,

  che sono in voi sì come studio in ape   58
di far lo mele; e questa prima voglia
merto di lode o di biasmo non cape.

  Or perché a questa ogn' altra si raccoglia,   61
innata v'è la virtù che consiglia
e de l'assenso de' tener la soglia.

  Quest' è 'l principio là onde si piglia   64
ragion di meritare in voi, secondo
che buoni e rei amori accoglie e viglia.

  Color che ragionando andaro al fondo   67
s'accorser d'esta innata libertate;
però moralità lasciaro al mondo.

31   so the captured mind enters into desire, which is a spiritual motion, and it never rests until the beloved thing causes it to rejoice.

34   Now can appear to you how hidden the truth is from the people who assert every love to be in itself a praiseworthy thing,

37   because perhaps its matter seems always to be good, but not every seal is good, although the wax be good."

40   "Your words and my wit, following them," I replied to him, "have shown love to me, but that has made me more pregnant with doubt;

43   for, if love is offered to us from without and the soul walks only with this foot, if it walks straight or crooked is no merit of its own."

46   And he to me: "As much as reason sees here, I can tell you; beyond that, you must wait for Beatrice, for it is a matter of faith.

49   Every substantial form, distinguishable from matter though joined to it, holds collected within it a specific power,

52   which, unless it operate, cannot be perceived, nor can be demonstrated, except by its effects, as green leaves reveal the life in a plant.

55   Therefore, whence may come our understanding of first notions no one knows, nor our desire for first desirables,

58   which are in you as in a bee the inclination to make honey; and this first desire deserves neither praise nor blame.

61   Now in order that to this first desire every other may be gathered, innate in you is the power that gives counsel and must guard the threshold of assent.

64   This is the principle that accounts for the cause of merit in you, according as it accepts or winnows good or evil loves.

67   Those who reasoned things out to their foundations recognized this innate liberty; thus they left morality to the world.

Onde, poniam che di necessitate   70
surga ogne amor che dentro a voi s'accende,
di ritenerlo è in voi la podestate.

La nobile virtù Beatrice intende   73
per lo libero arbitrio, e però guarda
che l'abbi a mente, s'a parlar ten prende."

La luna, quasi a mezza notte tarda,   76
facea le stelle a noi parer più rade,
fatta com' un secchion che tuttor arda;

e correa contra 'l ciel per quelle strade   79
che 'l sole infiamma allor che quel da Roma
tra ' Sardi e ' Corsi il vede quando cade.

E quell' ombra gentil, per cui si noma   82
Pietola più che villa mantoana,
del mio carcar diposta avea la soma;

per ch'io, che la ragione aperta e piana   85
sovra le mie quistioni avea ricolta,
stava com' om che sonnolento vana.

Ma questa sonnolenza mi fu tolta   88
subitamente da gente che dopo
le nostre spalle a noi era già volta.

E quale Ismeno già vide e Asopo   91
lungo di sé di notte furia e calca,
pur che i Teban di Bacco avesser uopo:

cotal per quel giron suo passo falca,   94
per quel ch'io vidi di color venendo,
cui buon volere e giusto amor cavalca.

Tosto fur sovr' a noi, perché correndo   97
si movea tutta quella turba magna,
e due dinanzi gridavan piangendo:

"Maria corse con fretta a la montagna!"   100
e: "Cesare, per soggiogare Ilerda,
punse Marsilia e poi corse in Ispagna!"

"Ratto, ratto, che 'l tempo non si perda   103
per poco amor," gridavan li altri appresso,
"che studio di ben far grazia rinverda!"

"O gente in cui fervore aguto adesso   106
ricompie forse negligenza e indugio
da voi per tepidezza in ben far messo,

70   Therefore, supposing that every love kindled in you arises by necessity, in you is the power to restrain it.

73   This noble power Beatrice understands as free choice, and therefore see that you remember it, if she speaks to you about it."

76   The moon, delayed almost until midnight, now made the stars seem fewer, shaped like a copper bucket still on fire,

79   and it was running against the heavens along those paths which the sun enflames when the Roman sees it set between the Sardinians and the Corsicans.

82   And that noble shade, because of whom Pietola is more famous than any other Mantuan village, had put off the burden I had laid upon him;

85   wherefore I, who had harvested an open and clear discussion of my questions, sat as one does whose mind wanders sleepily.

88   But this somnolence was taken from me suddenly by people who were coming round upon us from behind;

91   and, as Ismenus and Asopus once saw fury and trampling alongside them in the night, whenever the Thebans felt the need of Bacchus:

94   so around that circle—judging from the ones I saw coming—gallop those whose good will and righteous love ride them.

97   Suddenly they were upon us, for all that great crowd was running, and two in front cried, weeping:

100   "Mary ran with haste to the mountain!" and: "Caesar, to subdue Lerida, struck Marseilles and then hastened to Spain!"

103   "Quickly, quickly, that time not be lost through lack of love," cried the others following, "let eagerness to do well make grace grow green!"

106   "O people in whom keen fervor now perhaps makes up for negligence and delay that you, because lukewarm, brought your good works,

questi che vive, e certo i' non vi bugio,   109
vuole andar sù, pur che 'l sol ne riluca:
però ne dite ond' è presso il pertugio."

Parole furon queste del mio duca;   112
e un di quelli spirti disse: "Vieni
di retro a noi, e troverai la buca.

Noi siam di voglia a muoverci sì pieni,   115
che restar non potem; però perdona,
se villania nostra giustizia tieni.

Io fui abate in San Zeno a Verona   118
sotto lo 'mperio del buon Barbarossa,
di cui dolente ancor Milan ragiona.

E tale ha già l'un piè dentro la fossa   121
che tosto piangerà quel monastero
e tristo fia d'avere avuta possa:

perché suo figlio, mal del corpo intero   124
e de la mente peggio, e che mal nacque,
ha posto in loco di suo pastor vero."

Io non so se più disse o s'ei si tacque,   127
tant' era già di là da noi trascorso,
ma questo intesi, e ritener mi piacque.

E quei che m'era ad ogne uopo soccorso   130
disse: "Volgiti qua: vedine due
venir dando a l'accidïa di morso."

Di retro a tutti dicean: "Prima fue   133
morta la gente a cui il mar s'aperse,
che vedesse Iordan le rede sue!"

E: "Quella che l'affanno non sofferse   136
fino a la fine col figlio d'Anchise,
sé stessa a vita sanza gloria offerse!"

Poi quando fuor da noi tanto divise   139
quell' ombre che veder più non potiersi,
novo pensiero dentro a me si mise,

del qual più altri nacquero e diversi;   142
e tanto d'uno in altro vaneggiai
che li occhi per vaghezza ricopersi,

e 'l pensamento in sogno trasmutai.   145

109   this man, who is alive (and truly I do not lie to you), wishes to go upward as soon as the sun shines on us again: therefore tell us which way the opening is closer."

112   These were the words of my leader; and one of those spirits said: "Come after us, and you will find the hole.

115   We are so full of the desire to move that we cannot stop; therefore forgive us if our justice seems boorishness to you.

118   I was abbot in San Zeno in Verona under the reign of the good Barbarossa, of whom Milan still speaks with grief.

121   And he already has one foot in the grave who soon will weep for that monastery and will sorrow that he ever had power over it,

124   because he has put his son, diseased in his whole body, and worse in his mind, and a bastard, in the place of its true shepherd."

127   I do not know if he said more or was silent, he had already run so far beyond us, but this I heard and was pleased to retain.

130   And he who helped me in my every need said: "Look back here: see how two of them come scourging sloth."

133   Behind all the others they were saying: "First all the people died for whom the sea drew back, before Jordan saw their heirs!"

136   And: "Those women who did not endure hardship to the end with the son of Anchises, chose life without glory!"

139   Then when those shades had gone so far from us as to be seen no more, a new thought came into me,

142   from which a number of other, different ones were born; and from one to the other I so wandered on, that I closed my eyes in drowsiness

145   and transmuted thinking into dream.

NOTES

1-75. My noble teacher . . . speaks to you about it: Slightly more than half of this canto goes to further exposition of the theory of love. This section falls into two parts: a. Virgil's exposition of the psychology of love (lines 1-39); b. the pilgrim's doubt and Virgil's explanation of the power of free choice (lines 40-75). It culminates the series that began in Canto 15; see the note to 15.40-84.

1-9. My noble teacher . . . bold to speak: A needed pause following the intensity of the previous exposition of the ordering of Purgatory proper. Virgil's silence marks both the completeness he attributes to his explanation and his recognition of the pilgrim's need to digest it.

4-9. and I . . . bold to speak: For the pilgrim's fear of burdening Virgil, cf. *Inf.* 3.79-81.

7-9. that truthful father . . . bold to speak: In other words, noticing the pilgrim's hesitation, Virgil speaks in order to encourage him to speak. His actual words are omitted.

10-15. Master, my sight . . . and its contrary: The pilgrim pays tribute to the clarity of Virgil's exposition, which has defined and classified the function of Purgatory; he asks for a fuller discussion of the nature of love itself, the next logical step ("therefore") in his growth of understanding.

10-12. my sight . . . divides or defines: Like visual sight, intellectual sight takes place in a certain light, in this case the light of natural reason as represented by Virgil (for the light of revelation, see 29.16-57, with notes; for the thesis that the pilgrim's guides correspond to the "three lights" of Scholastic theory—those of nature, grace, and glory—see Singleton 1957).

14. expound love for me: The Italian *dimostri* [demonstrate] implies a philosophically rigorous discussion (including definition and division / classification: line 12); cf. line 41. There is an echo here of Cavalcanti's famous canzone "Donna me prega," lines 8-9: "Senza natural dimostramento / non ho talento di voler provare" [I have no desire to prove without natural (i.e., scientific) demonstration].

16-18. Direct, he said . . . claim to lead: The thinkers attacked here will be identified in lines 34-39.

19-39. The mind, created . . . wax be good: Virgil's account of the psychology of love is founded in Aristotelian psychology: it involves a close parallel between perception and desire. The major influence here is Aristotle's *De anima* [On the soul], intensively studied in the twelfth and thirteenth centuries; in addition to the highly controversial commentary by the great Averroës (see *Inf.* 4.142-44, with note), a number of prominent Scholastics, including Albertus Magnus and Aquinas, wrote commentaries on it, as well as treatises explicitly combatting Averroës' views (or, in some cases, defending them).

19-21. The mind, created . . . into act by pleasure: Virgil begins by recalling, in more technical language, Marco Lombardo's description of the innocent human soul being drawn by pleasure (16.85-90). The mind is created with the potentiality of loving: it is naturally ready to love ("quick to love"), but its love remains in potentiality until it is actualized ("wakened into act") by pleasure. This terminology of potentiality and act involves Aristotle's metaphysics: the bringing of any potentiality into actuality (act) always involves its taking on a form; only form is determinate. A particular love, then, is a case of the general potentiality for love becoming an actual love by taking on the form of a particular object of desire. (For the parallel with perception, see next note.)

22-27. Your power . . . bound in you: In Aristotle's theory of perception, the impressions taken from an external object are integrated by the so-called common sense into a single representation, and formed by the imagination into an image of the external thing, an "intention," so called because of the tension in focussed perception and also because it expresses intentionality (purpose). The "intention" is then presented to consciousness (this is the process Virgil sums up in lines 22-23). In this view the mind "mirrors" external things in an essentially passive way. The active power of the mind to transform perception will be Dante's focus in Canto 19.

Aristotle compares the receptivity of perception, which takes on the *form* of the external thing without its *matter*, to the capacity of wax to receive the form impressed by a seal without its matter, metal or terra cotta (*De anima* 2.12, 424a; cf. Aquinas 1959 pp. 138-39 and Albertus Magnus, *De anima* 2.4.1). This is the ultimate source of Dante's metaphor (explicit in lines 38-39); cf. Gmelin on 10.45.

There is an incipient personification allegory in these lines. The "mind" is like the occupant of a dwelling (perhaps a castle—see note to line 63), before whom the power of perception, like a servant, "unfolds" the image of the external world as if it were a painting or drawing (Aristotle in fact uses the analogy of paintings for images stored in the memory: *De memoria et reminiscentia* 450a). The "bending" of the mind toward the image implies that of an entire human figure: the passage combines both the subjective experience of desire (the impulse to move toward the object of desire) and an external view of the personified mind, which must, we are told in line 63, guard the "threshold of consent." This terminology is still alive: a desire is still an "inclination," a "leaning," a "bent."

22. real thing: The Italian is "esser verace" [literally, a truthful thing]. For the importance of this trope, see the note to 19.1-33.

27. that is nature . . . bound in you: "Nature" here is the inborn potentiality for love; by pleasure it is "bound," determined to an object.

28-32. Then, as fire . . . spiritual motion: In other words, when matter becomes fire (in itself pure potentiality, matter becomes fire by taking on the form of fire), the form determines its motion, which is naturally toward its "natural" place, the sphere of fire just below the moon (cf. *Conv.* 3.3.2, *Par.* 1.109-17), where no other form, such as that of water, will conflict with it. So the mind, "captured" by love (cf. "bound," line 27), takes on a motion whose direction is determined by its form. The association of love and fire is of course ancient; see *Inf.* 5.100-107.

32-33. it never rests . . . to rejoice: Like most commentators, we take "fin che" (line 33) to mean "until." The enjoyment of the object (*gioire*, Lat. *gaudere*, can have a sexual as well as a purely emotional meaning) is the goal of desire; when it is achieved, desire rests in the object, is satisfied (see *Conv.* 3.2.2).

34-36. Now can appear . . . a praiseworthy thing: Virgil's target is commonly identified as the Epicureans; Padoan 1965 cites Cicero's *De finibus* 2.10 ff., on the Epicurean arguments for pleasure being the highest good. But, as Bosco/Reggio observe, the attack is directed also at the ideology of courtly love. Dante probably also has in mind Ovid's permissiveness in the *Ars amatoria* and *Metamorphoses*. See *Inter cantica* below.

37-39. perhaps its matter . . . wax be good: The metaphor of wax and seal, implicit throughout Virgil's speech (see the note to lines 22-27), is now made explicit. Although the human potential for love (the matter, corresponding to the wax) is good in itself, not every determinate love is good, since its worth depends on its object (its form, corresponding to the seal).

40-75. Your words . . . speaks to you about it: The second part of the discussion of love, the pilgrim's doubt and Virgil's explanation of freedom of choice, on which all deserving rests.

40-45. Your words . . . merit of its own: The pupil has followed and accepted the teacher's definition of love, but his doubts are increased (for doubt as pregnancy and swelling, cf. 16.52-54). Virgil's account, especially lines 22-24, makes it seem that loves are necessarily imposed by the attractiveness of external objects; in that case, how can merit or demerit derive from them?

44. [If] the soul walks only with this foot: If love is the soul's only principle of motion. For the "two feet" of the soul, see the note to *Inf.* 1.30; the pilgrim has omitted one, as Virgil will now explain. The Platonic-Aristotelian notion of the soul as a principle of motion (*Phaedrus, De anima*) has of course been implicit all along (cf. 17.100-102).

45. straight or crooked: The mention of the straight versus the crooked path brings to the fore one of the basic images of the poem as a whole (*Inf.* 1.3; *Purg.* 17.100).

46-75. And he to me ... speaks to you about it: Virgil's reply introduces the question of the limits of the soul's knowledge of itself as considered by reason (see the note to lines 10-12). Although the soul cannot intuit the basis of its desire for the objects of its love, it is able to grasp that it is desire for *the desirable as such*, which in the last analysis is *the good as such*, and it can understand the need to order contingent goals according to that fundamental one.

46-48. As much as reason ... matter of faith: Virgil is excluded from the Christian revelation, and here he disclaims any knowledge deriving from faith. (How consistently Dante has treated this aspect of Virgil is a moot point: how does Virgil know what he says to Cato in 1.74-75?)

49-54. Every substantial form ... life in a plant: Every substance is such by virtue of its substantial form, its essence, which is distinct from its matter, though united with it. (Many commentators erroneously suppose that only the human soul is distinct from matter; but, as lines 28-32 point out, even the form of fire is distinct from its matter: all form is immaterial.) As distinguished from the visual form of a thing, the substantial form is not perceived directly but must be inferred from its effects, its operation. Each different substantial form possesses a "specific" power (a power proper to its species). The life in a plant, its substantial form, is revealed by its green leaves.

55-60. Therefore, whence ... praise nor blame: Virgil's *therefore* [però] introduces a shift in focus: just as the substantial form of a plant must be inferred, so also human beings must infer the nature of their own rational/appetitive souls. We do not know how it is that we understand "first notions" or love the "first desirables." The "first notions" are those on which all understanding rests, such as: truth, falsity, contradiction, existence, non-existence. The "first desirables" are those which constitute desirability: goodness, beauty, truth. Strictly speaking there is only one "first desirable": anything desired is desired as a good. Thus the object of desire, considered absolutely (without determination) is *the good*. From this formulation it is but a short step to seeing the fundamental object of human desire as *absolute good*: God. Even so, "this first desire deserves neither praise nor blame" because it is innate and not subject to control.

58-59. as in a bee the inclination to make honey: Chiavacci Leonardi observes that Virgil has drawn his instances of form, life, and desire from most levels of sub-lunar existence—fire (lines 28-30), plants (line 54), animals (lines 58-59)—as well as man.

61-66. Now in order ... good or evil loves: The "power that gives counsel" is of course reason (or, more generally, intellect); it must distinguish desires that are consistent with its most fundamental desire from those that are not. All deserving springs from this principle (cf. Marco Lombardo on objects of desire, 16.91-93).

63. guard the threshold of assent: This phrase makes explicit the house or castle image underlying lines 22-25: desires/loves that are allowed to cross this threshold, to enter the stronghold, in some sense gain the right to dwell there. Others are turned away from the door. Singleton cites a passage from Gregory the Great's *Moralia*, in which the metaphorical door in question is that of the soul's bedchamber, from which sensual desires especially are to be excluded. The notion of the castle or fortress of the soul is ancient and widespread (see the note to 5.74).

66. winnows: A striking image derived from the process of separating wheat or other grain from the chaff of its external husk, in Dante's time usually by a combination of beating (to loosen the chaff) and fanning (to blow it away).

67-69. Those who reasoned . . . to the world: These are the classical philosophers, especially Plato and Aristotle. The recovery of Aristotle's *Nichomachean Ethics* revolutionized ethical theory in Europe. Note the authority granted pagan thinkers: that of having, by natural reason, penetrated to the basic principles of moral conduct (see our Introduction, pp. 5-8).

70-75. Therefore, supposing . . . speaks to you about it: Even on the assumption that external objects unavoidably elicit desire, the counsel of reason makes it possible to control it. Virgil's *therefore* announces the formal conclusion of the proof. The last three lines recall the reference to Beatrice in lines 46-48 .

The issue of necessity versus freedom here is basically the same, if set forth in slightly different terms, as stated by Marco Lombardo in 16.67-78, and it is resolved similarly (there the compulsion mentioned was that of the stars; here it is the combined force of appetite in the temperament and the attraction of external objects; both are largely determined by the heavenly bodies).

76-145. The moon . . . thinking into dream: The second principal division of the canto, the pilgrim's sleepy meditation, interrupted by the souls purging sloth.

76-81. The moon . . . and the Corsicans: Another periphrastic indication of the time (compare 15.1-6): the moon, rising late, dims the light of surrounding stars, moving, in its monthly motion, from west to east and thus against the apparent daily east-west turning of the celestial sphere. The moon is in that part of the Ecliptic (most probably the sign Capricorn, since it was in Libra when full) where the sun sets, as seen from Rome, between Sardinia and Corsica (to the southwest, around azimuth 273°). According to *Inf.* 20.127, the moon was full on Thursday night: since this is Monday night, the moon is five days past full and has not yet reached its last quarter (cf. the note to 9.1-9); it is gibbous, with its illuminated side downward, thus resembling a bucket or kettle (it is red because near the horizon). At its last quarter, the moon rises at midnight; now it rises around 10 P.M., more than halfway from sunset to midnight. The exact hour, like the azimuth mentioned above, can only be approximately determined. The association of the moon and Capricorn (a house of Saturn, cf. 19.1-6, with notes) implies cold and slowness, associated with the pilgrim's sleepiness. The slothful may well have had saturnine temperaments, which they must now overcome.

82-87. And that noble shade . . . wanders sleepily: Virgil has fulfilled his obligation to answer the pilgrim's question (for "burden," cf. line 6), and the pilgrim has much to think about, though he is tired and sleepy.

82-83. because of whom . . . Mantuan village: Pietola, called Andes in Roman times, was Vergil's birthplace. Some commentators have taken the lines to mean that Pietola is more famous than the city (*villa*) Mantua, which is hardly the case. We follow the majority view, that Pietola is not a mere village, but something more.

88-140. But this somnolence . . . seen no more: The sudden appearance of the slothful, whose penance is continuous running. As Virgil has pointed out in 17.85-87, their love for the good was insufficient, and now they must ply their oar again and again. The relevance of this episode to the theory of love is clear enough; the contrast of the calm of the theoretical discussions with the penitents' noisy striving may be associated with the contemplative versus the active life. The scene is not without humor, particularly when connected with the picture of the indolent in 4.97-105: this is what Belacqua can look forward to!

88-90. But this somnolence . . . from behind: The penitents have been circling the mountain counterclockwise, as on other ledges. This would bring them up behind Virgil and the pilgrim, who are facing outward, from the right.

91-93. and, as Ismenus . . . need of Bacchus: Ismenus and Asopus are two rivers in Boeotia, a region in Greece; the Ismenus flows into the Asopus near Thebes, the center of the cult of Bacchus (Dionysus), worshipped in riotous nocturnal excursions, which Dante read about in Ovid's *Metamorphoses* (Books 3 and 4) and Statius' *Thebaid* (Books 7 and 9). The Bacchantes were proverbial for ecstatic dancing. Dante represents the rites as voluntary, his sources as involuntary possession.

94-96. so around that circle . . . love ride them: Already implicit in the mention of trampling (line 92), the horse metaphor becomes explicit here. The term *falcata* [being like a scythe], as Parodi observed, is used of the headlong gallop of a horse, when its legs (especially the forelegs) form a scythe-like curve. The souls' "good will and just love" are imagined as riders driving their horses as fast as they can go. The analogy with the training of horses and falcons is fundamental to the *Purgatorio* (see 13.37-40 and 67-72, with notes).

99-102. two in front . . . hastened to Spain: Like the examples of sloth recited later (lines 133-38), the two examples of zeal represent important moments in the history of church and empire respectively (cf. 16.106-29).

100. Mary . . . to the mountain: The reference is to Luke's account of the Visitation (1.39-56), which follows immediately upon the Annunciation and is motivated by the angel Gabriel's mention (1.36-37) of Elizabeth's pregnancy: "And Mary rising up in those days, went into the hill country [*in montana*] with haste [*cum festinatione*] into a city of Juda" (1.38-39).

101-102. Caesar . . . hastened to Spain: The turning point in the civil war between Julius Caesar and Pompey, in 48-49 BC, and a good example of Caesar's famous rapidity. Massilia (modern Marseilles) allied itself with Pompey just as he sent seven legions off to Spain. Caesar rapidly organized the siege of Massilia, delegated it to a lieutenant, marched his other legions to northern Spain, out-manoeuvered Pompey's generals, and within forty days secured the entire western portion of the Roman world. The main source for these events is Caesar's own account (*De bello civili* 1.34-87); it is doubtful that Dante knew it, but the sources usually alleged for Dante's lines (*Phars.* 3.453-55 and most of Book 4; Orosius, *Historia* 6.15) do not ascribe haste to Caesar in this case. See the note to 26.76-78.

106-108. O people . . . your good works: The lines do not imply that these souls failed to perform good works but rather that their performance of them was weakened by "negligence and delay."

111. the opening: The crack in the mountainside leading to the next level.

114. the hole: The soul uses the shortest—and crudest—word for the opening (see 19.35-36 and 64-69, with notes).

117. if our justice seems boorishness: Compare *Inf.* 33.150: "e cortesia fu lui esser villano" [and it was courtesy to treat him boorishly].

118-26. I was abbot . . . true shepherd: The abbey of San Zeno in Verona was particularly rich and powerful; its abbot under the emperor Frederick I Barbarossa was a certain Gerard, d. 1187, of whom nothing more is known. Dante spent years in Verona, under the patronage of the Scala family, and had access to local traditions. In any case, sloth—the "noontime demon"—was endemic in monasteries; this abbot was no doubt chosen in order to denounce the later one.

120. of whom Milan still speaks with grief: In 1167 Barbarossa destroyed Milan because of its rebelliousness. The "good" emperor's legitimate assertion of his power is praised, in contrast to the lord of Verona's abuse of his power.

121-26. And he already . . . true shepherd: Alberto della Scala (the father of Dante's patrons Bartolommeo and Cangrande: see *Par.* 17.70-93) died in 1301; thus in 1300 he was close to death. He will "soon" weep for his abuse of power, whether repentant before death or damned because unrepentant. Alberto forced the appointent of his crippled illegitimate son Giuseppe as abbot of San Zeno in direct violation of canon law and the prerogative of the Church.

127-29. I do not know . . . pleased to retain: A return of the humorous note that began the episode, perhaps with a note of defiance toward the powerful.

131-38. Look back here . . . without glory: The two runners are presumably shouting at the top of their lungs the denunciations of slothfulness, one a biblical example, one from the *Aeneid*; see the note to lines 99-102.

132. scourging sloth: Literally, "biting sloth"; this is a biting from behind and from their past: a kind of spatial figuration for *remorse* [from Lat. *remorsus*, biting again or from behind]; Ugolino bites Ruggieri from behind, *Inf.* 32.125-29.

133-35. First all the people . . . saw their heirs: The reference is to Num. 14.20-33, where, because of the Israelites' backsliding, entry into the Promised Land is to be delayed until all those who crossed the Red Sea (those responsible for the backsliding) have died off (forty years): Jordan, the boundary of the Promised Land, will see only their heirs.

136-38. Those women . . . life without glory: During the games in Sicily on the anniversary of Anchises' death, the Trojan women, urged on by Iris, set fire to Aeneas' ships so as to end the wanderings. Jupiter sends a rainstorm to put out the fires, and when Aeneas sets sail, the weary are left behind (*Aen.* 5.604-778).

139-45. Then when those shades . . . thinking into dream: The pilgrim's thoughts must be inferred from the dream of Canto 19. The drowsiness of lines 85-87 recurs and now prevails. As on the first night on the island, the pilgrim falls asleep because he "had with [him] something of Adam" (9.10), the flesh.

145. transmuted thinking into dream: An evocative phrase that can characterize an important dimension of the *Comedy* as a whole.

Inter cantica. These cantos are the theoretical keystone of the entire *Comedy* and have rich implications for all of it. There is perhaps a special intensity of reference to *Inferno* 5, where Francesca sets forth a mistaken theory of love that Dante attributes to the fashionable ideology of courtly love. Francesca's vision of herself as a passive victim of forces she was powerless to resist receives most explicit expression in *Inf.* 5.103: "Amor, che a nullo amato amar perdona" [Love, which pardons no one loved from loving in return], to which Virgil's exposition of the nature of free choice is a direct answer.

CANTO 19

Ne l'ora che non può 'l calor dïurno   1
intepidar più 'l freddo de la luna,
vinto da terra e talor da Saturno,
    quando i geomanti lor Maggior Fortuna   4
veggiono in orïente, innanzi a l'alba,
surger per via che poco le sta bruna,
    mi venne in sogno una femmina balba,   7
ne li occhi guercia e sovra i piè distorta,
con le man monche, e di colore scialba.
    Io la mirava; e come 'l sol conforta   10
le fredde membra che la notte aggrava,
così lo sguardo mio le facea scorta
    la lingua, e poscia tutta la drizzava   13
in poco d'ora, e lo smarrito volto,
com' amor vuol, così le colorava.
    Poi ch'ell' avea 'l parlar così disciolto,   16
cominciava a cantar sì che con pena
da lei avrei mio intento rivolto.
    "Io son," cantava, "io son dolce serena,   19
che ' marinari in mezzo mar dismago,
tanto son di piacere a sentir piena.
    Io volsi Ulisse del suo cammin, vago   22
al canto mio, e qual meco s'ausa
rado sen parte, sì tutto l'appago!"
    Ancor non era sua bocca richiusa   25
quand' una donna apparve santa e presta
lunghesso me per far colei confusa.
    "O Virgilio, Virgilio, chi è questa?"   28
fieramente dicea; ed el venìa
con li occhi fitti pur in quella onesta.

CANTO 19

Fourth terrace, continued: the dream of the Siren—the angel, erasure, a Beatitude—climb—comments on the dream—Fifth terrace, of avarice: the souls of the avaricous—Pope Adrian V

1   At the hour when the heat of the day can no
longer warm the cold of the moon, vanquished by
earth and sometimes by Saturn,

4   when the geomancers see their Greater Fortune
in the east, before the dawn, rising along a path
that stays dark for it but a short while,

7   there came to me in dream a female, stuttering,
cross-eyed, and crooked on her feet, with stunted
hands, and pallid in color.

10   I was gazing at her; and, as the sun strengthens
cold limbs that the night weighs down, so my gaze
loosed

13   her tongue, and then in a short while it
straightened her entirely and gave color to her wan
face, just as love desires.

16   Once her speech was loosened so, she began to
sing in such a way that I could hardly have turned
my attention from her.

19   "I am," she was singing, "I am a sweet siren,
who enchant the sailors on the deep sea, so full of
pleasure am I to hear!

22   I turned Ulysses from his course, desirous of my
song, and whoever becomes used to me rarely
leaves me, so wholly do I satisfy him!"

25   Her mouth had not yet closed when there
appeared a lady, holy and quick, alongside me, to
confound her.

28   "O Virgil, Virgil, who is this?" she was saying
fiercely; and he was approaching with his eyes
fixed only on that virtuous one.

L'altra prendea, e dinanzi l'apria,   31
fendendo i drappi, e mostravami 'l ventre;
quel mi svegliò col puzzo che n'uscia.

  Io mossi li occhi, e 'l buon maestro: "Almen tre   34
voci t'ho messe!" dicea, "Surgi e vieni:
troviam l'aperta per la qual tu entre."

  Sù mi levai, e tutti eran già pieni   37
de l'alto dì i giron del sacro monte,
e andavam col sol novo a le reni.

  Seguendo lui, portava la mia fronte   40
come colui che l'ha di pensier carca,
che fa di sé un mezzo arco di ponte,

    quand' io udi': "Venite: qui si varca,"   43
parlare in modo soave e benigno,
qual non si sente in questa mortal marca.

  Con l'ali aperte, che parean di cigno,   46
volseci in sù colui che sì parlonne,
tra due pareti del duro macigno.

  Mosse le penne poi e ventilonne,   49
"*qui lugent*" affermando esser "*beati,*
ch'avran di consolar l'anime donne."

  "Che hai che pur inver' la terra guati?"   52
la guida mia incominciò a dirmi,
poco amendue da l'angel sormontati.

  E io: "Con tanta sospeccion fa irmi   55
novella visïon ch'a sé mi piega
sì ch'io non posso dal pensar partirmi."

  "Vedesti," disse, "quell'antica strega   58
che sola sovr' a noi omai si piagne;
vedesti come l'uom da lei si slega.

  Bastiti, e batti a terra le calcagne;   61
li occhi rivolgi al logoro che gira
lo rege etterno con le rote magne."

  Quale 'l falcon, che prima a' piè si mira,   64
indi si volge al grido e si protende
per lo disio del pasto che là il tira,

    tal mi fec' io; e tal, quanto si fende   67
la roccia per dar via a chi va suso,
n'andai infin dove 'l cerchiar si prende.

31   The other he seized and opened in front, tearing
her clothes, and showed me her belly, which
awakened me with the stench that issued from it.

34   I turned my eyes, and my good master was
saying: "At least three times I have called you!
Arise and come: let us find the opening through
which you may enter."

37   Up I rose, and already all the circles of the
holy mountain were filled with broad daylight, and
we were walking with the new sun on our backs.

40   Following him, I was carrying my forehead
like one who has it laden with cares, who makes
of himself the half arch of a bridge,

43   when I heard, "Come: here is the crossing,"
spoken in a soft and kindly tone, such as one
does not hear in this mortal territory.

46   With open wings like those of a swan, the one
who had spoken thus directed us upward,
between the two walls of hard granite.

49   Then he moved his feathers and fanned us,
affirming "*Qui lugent*" to be "*beati*, whose souls
will be possessed of consolation."

52   "What is the matter, that you are staring at the
ground?" my guide began by saying to me, once
we had both climbed a little beyond the angel.

55   And I: "I walk so full of care because of a
strange vision that so bends me toward it that I
cannot leave the thought."

58   "You saw," he said, "that ancient witch who is
the only thing lamented here above us; you have
seen how one frees oneself from her.

61   Let it be enough for you, and strike the earth with
your heels; turn your eyes to the lure that the
eternal King keeps turning with the great wheels."

64   Like the falcon that first looks at its feet, then
turns toward the cry and stretches forward with
the desire for food that draws him there:

67   so I became; and thus through as much of the
rock as is split to provide the upward path, I went
to where circling begins again.

Com' io nel quinto giro fui dischiuso,   70
vidi gente per esso che piangea
giacendo a terra, tutta volta in giuso.

    "*Adhaesit pavimento anima mea!*"   73
sentia dir lor, con sì alti sospiri
che la parola a pena s'intendea.

    "O eletti di Dio, li cui soffriri   76
e giustizia e speranza fa men duri,
drizzate noi verso li alti saliri."

    "Se voi venite dal giacer sicuri,   79
e volete trovar la via più tosto,
le vostre destre sien sempre di fòri."

    Così pregò 'l poeta, e sì risposto   82
poco dinanzi a noi ne fu; per ch'io
nel parlare avvisai l'altro nascosto,

    e volsi li occhi a li occhi al segnor mio,   85
ond' elli m'assentì con lieto cenno
ciò che chiedea la vista del disio.

    Poi ch'io potei di me fare a mio senno,   88
trassimi sovra quella creatura
le cui parole pria notar mi fenno,

    dicendo, "Spirto in cui pianger matura   91
quel sanza 'l quale a Dio tornar non pòssi,
sosta un poco per me tua maggior cura.

    Chi fosti, e perché vòlti avete i dossi   94
al sù, mi dì, e se vuo' ch'io t'impetri
cosa di là, ond' io vivendo mossi."

    Ed elli a me: "Perché i nostri diretri   97
rivolga il cielo a sé, saprai; ma prima
scias quod ego fui successor Petri.

    Intra Sïestri e Chiaveri s'adima   100
una fiumana bella, e del suo nome
lo titol del mio sangue fa sua cima.

    Un mese e poco più prova' io come   103
pesa il gran manto a chi dal fango il guarda,
che piuma sembran tutte l'altre some.

    La mia conversïone, omè! fu tarda;   106
ma, come fatto fui roman pastore,
così scopersi la vita bugiarda.

70   When I was loosed onto the fifth circle, I saw
      people weeping there, lying on the earth, all
      facing downward.

73   *"Adhaesit pavimento anima mea!"* I heard them
      saying, with such deep sighs that what was
      spoken could hardly be understood.

76   "O chosen of God, whose sufferings both
      justice and hope make less harsh, direct us
      toward the high ascent."

79   "If you arrive here exempt from lying down,
      and wish to find the quickest way, let your right
      hands be ever on the outside."

82   So my poet begged, and so someone replied, a
      bit ahead of us; and by the speaking I knew
      where the rest was hidden,

85   and I turned my eyes to my lord's eyes, and he
      assented with glad sign to what my look of desire
      requested.

88   Since I could act according to my thought, I
      went to stand over that creature whose words
      had just now made me notice it,

91   saying: "Spirit in whom weeping ripens that
      without which one cannot return to God, for my
      sake suspend your greatest care a little while.

94   Who you were, and why you have your backs
      turned up, tell me, and whether you wish me to
      obtain anything for you back there, whence still
      living I have come."

97   And he to me: "Why Heaven turns our
      backsides toward itself, you will learn; but first
      scias quod ego fui successor Petri.

100   Between Sestri and Chiavari there descends a
      lovely river, and from its name my blood takes
      the pride of its title.

103   For one month and a little more, I felt how the
      great mantle weighs on one who keeps it from
      the mud, for all other burdens seem a feather.

106   My conversion, alas! was late; but, when I
      became the Roman shepherd, then I discovered
      life to be deceptive.

Vidi che lì non s'acquetava il core,   109
né più salir potiesi in quella vita:
per che di questa in me s'accese amore.

Fino a quel punto misera e partita   112
da Dio anima fui, del tutto avara;
or, come vedi, qui ne son punita.

Quel ch'avarizia fa, qui si dichiara   115
in purgazion de l'anime converse,
e nulla pena il monte ha più amara.

Sì come l'occhio nostro non s'aderse   118
in alto, fisso a le cose terrene,
così giustizia qui a terra il merse.

Come avarizia spense a ciascun bene   121
lo nostro amore, onde operar perdési,
così giustizia qui stretti ne tène,

ne' piedi e ne le man legati e presi;   124
e quanto fia piacer del giusto Sire,
tanto staremo immobili e distesi."

Io m'era inginocchiato e volea dire,   127
ma com' io cominciai ed el s'accorse,
solo ascoltando, del mio reverire:

"Qual cagion," disse, "in giù così ti torse?"   130
E io a lui: "Per vostra dignitate
mia coscïenza dritto mi rimorse."

"Drizza le gambe, lèvati sù, frate!"   133
rispuose; "non errar: conservo sono
teco e con li altri ad una Podestate.

Se mai quel santo evangelico suono   136
che dice '*neque nubent*' intendesti,
ben puoi veder perch' io così ragiono.

Vattene omai, non vo' che più t'arresti,   139
ché la tua stanza mio pianger disagia,
col qual maturo ciò che tu dicesti.

Nepote ho io di là c'ha nome Alagia,   142
buona da sé, pur che la nostra casa
non faccia lei per essempro malvagia;

e questa sola di là m'è rimasa."   145

109   I saw that my heart was not quieted there, nor could I rise any higher in that life: thus was kindled in me the love of this one.

112   Until that point I was a wretched soul separated from God, entirely greedy; now, as you see, I am punished for it here.

115   What avarice does is shown here in the penance of the inverted souls, and the mountain has no pain more bitter.

118   Since our eyes, fixed on earthly things, were not raised up, so here justice has sunk them to the earth.

121   Since avarice extinguished our love for every good, so that our power to act was lost, so justice keeps us fixed here,

124   bound and captive in feet and hands; and as long as it shall please our just Lord, so long will we stay immobile and stretched out."

127   I had knelt and wished to speak, but as I began, and he perceived, through hearing alone, my reverence,

130   "What cause," he said, "has bent you down so?" And I to him: "Because of your dignity my conscience reproached me when I stood erect."

133   "Straighten your legs, rise up, brother!" he replied; "do not err: I am a fellow-servant, with you and the others, of one Power.

136   If you have ever heard that holy sound in the Gospel that says '*neque nubent,*' you can see clearly why I speak thus.

139   Go away now; I do not wish you to stop here any longer; for your staying interrupts my weeping, with which I ripen the thing you mentioned.

142   I have a niece back there whose name is Alagia, good in herself, as long as our house does not corrupt her with its example;

145   and she alone is left to me back there."

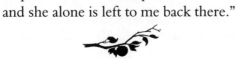

NOTES

1-69. At the hour . . . circling begins again: The pilgrim's second dream and the ensuing discussion form an essential supplement to the account of the psychology of love in Canto 18, incomplete because it takes for granted the accuracy of the "intention" presented to the mind by sense perception. The problem was signalled by the term *verace*: "La vostra apprensiva da esser verace / tragge intenzion" [Your power of apprehension takes from some real thing an intention] (18.22-23), which calls attention to itself: the primary meaning of *verace* is *truthful,* or *truth-speaking*; taken as meaning "objectively real," it is a trope, even a catachresis (Dante frequently tropes *verace*, always to mean "real" or "reliable"; see Niccoli in *ED, s.v. verace*). Perception is accurate on the whole, but there is a potentially weak link in the chain, the faculty known as *aestimatio* [judgment], which decides whether things are to be desired or feared. What if judgment is deceived (cf. 16.91-93)?

1-33. At the hour . . . issued from it: The indication of the time and the dream itself, as in Canto 9, occupy the first 33 lines of the canto. In both cases the circumstances involve the element earth (cf. 9.10-11, 19.3) and the moon (9.1-2, 19.2); in both cases the dream is terminated by a sensory event within the dream itself (sensations of burning in 9.32-33, of stench in 19.33).

1-6. At the hour . . . a short while: Like the first dream (9.13-33) and the third (27.94-108), the second takes place just before dawn, the hour thought since Antiquity the most propitious to prophetic dreams (cf. *Inf.* 26.7, *Purg.* 9.16-18). The insistence on cold (the element earth and the moon and Saturn were regarded as cold) is connected with the urge toward lesser goods (metals, including gold and silver, are forms of the element earth), and especially lust, traditionally due to the influence of Saturn and associated with freezing, flooding, and winter (see Panofsky 1946, Durling 1985, Durling/Martinez 1990). For the power of the heavenly bodies over the imagination, see 17.13-18.

4-6. when the geomancers . . . a short while: Geomancy [divining from earth signs] has been practiced in many cultures; the form envisaged by Dante, derived from the Arabs, associated random patterns of points (on the ground in sandy places, or on paper, often cast just before dawn) with zodiacal asterisms. "Greater Fortune" was six points in the shape of a quadrilateral with a tail (the letters indicate the order of rising in the figure discussed below):

$$
\begin{array}{cc}
A & B \\
C & D \\
 & E \\
 & F
\end{array}
$$

The passage has been intensively discussed by Chaucer scholars, for Chaucer echoes it in *Troilus and Criseyde* 3.1415-21; the best identification of the stars of

Greater Fortune (it seems to have been ignored by Dante scholars) is probably that proposed by Skeat in 1894, cited in Root 1945: θ Pegasus, α π γ Aquarius (AB CD), and ζ η Aquarius (EF). (See the very readable star charts in Ridpath 1993.) At the latitude of Florence on April 12 these stars would rise between 1:45 and 2:45 in the morning (sunrise would be at about 6:00 A.M.).

Greater Fortune was the most favorable of the sixteen geomantic figures and no doubt has an important but unrecoverable relevance to the dream (for the figures, see Charmasson 1980). All the commentators are agreed that Aquarius is involved, an important link with the first dream, for Aquarius (the Waterbearer) was thought to represent Ganymede (see 9.22-24). The mention of *Maggior Fortuna* also recalls Marco Lombardo's denial of astrological determinism, especially the phrase "a maggior forza e miglior natura / liberi soggiacete" [to a greater Power and a better Nature you lie subject and thus free] (16.79-80).

7-33. there came to me . . . issued from it: The dream represents the gradual seduction of the unwary soul by the Siren and its freeing by Virgil at the behest of a lady "holy and quick"; tearing open the Siren's clothing, Virgil reveals her essential ugliness. Virgil will later explain that this "ancient witch" is "the only thing lamented here above" (lines 58-59), "the love that excessively abandons itself" to lesser goods (17.133-36). The Siren, then, does not correspond to any external object of desire (cf. 18.22-25) but rather to a particular attitude toward external goods.

7-9. there came to me . . . pallid in color: This "female" is inherently deformed. The early commentators correlated her defects with the specific vices purged on the three upper terraces, but it seems rather that the defects are to be ascribed to fleshly vice in general: she stutters: vice loses the capacity for effective speech; she is cross-eyed: vice does not see the good accurately; she is lame: vice cannot move toward true goals; she has stunted hands: vice cannot accomplish good works (cf. lines 122-24); she is pallid: red is the color of love. In line 11 her defects are associated with cold and night.

Virgil will call the Siren "ancient" in line 58, giving her mythic status: her power is as old as humanity itself. That she is a withered crone is strongly implied, and the early commentators identify her with Circe (see the note on lines 22-23); that Virgil calls her a "strega" [witch] supports the association. She is the prototype of Ariosto's Alcina and other Renaissance enchantresses. As Toffanin 1921 showed, Dante draws on Christian legends, as in the *Vitae patrum* 5.5.23: a young monk sees "a certain work of the devil in the form of an ugly Ethiopian woman, so base that he could not bear her stench. He cast her from him, and she said: 'I appear sweet to the hearts of men, but because of your obedience and the labor of penitence you endure God does not permit me to seduce you, but has made known to you my stench.'" (For the *foetor peccati* [stench of sin] see *Inf.* 11.4.)

Compare *Queste del saint Graal* (Pauphilet, pp. 109-10): Perceval almost succumbs to a beautiful damsel (the devil in disguise); at the critical moment he sees the Cross inscribed on the hilt of his sword and blesses himself: "suddenly the tent was overturned, and he was surrounded by smoke and cloud so thick that he could not see, and he smelled so great a stench that he thought he must be in Hell." He prays, and the enchantments disappear.

10-15. I was gazing . . . as love desires: The dreamer's gaze transforms the Siren into an alluring young woman: that the attraction of lesser goods should be represented especially by that of sex is traditional (see the note to 17.136-39). The seduction of *aestimatio* (see the note to lines 1-69) is of course taking place on a secondary level, since it is not primarily external objects themselves that are misperceived, but the temptation to become engrossed by them (there is overlap with the theme of erotic illusion, however).

10-15. I was gazing . . . wan face: The pilgrim's "gaze" is the grammatical subject of all three verbs in the second clause: "loosed," "straightened," and "gave." It is the intensity of the gaze that makes it like the sun; in modern terms the process would be called projection: what the dreamer desires is what he sees.

16-24. Once her speech . . . I satisfy him: Dante knew of the myth of the sirens (*Odyssey* 12.39-54, 158-64, 181-200) indirectly, from Servius, Cicero's *De finibus*, Isidore of Seville, and others. He nowhere mentions the episode, which he could have known from Fulgentius and the Vatican mythographers, in which, so as not to be lured to shipwreck by the sirens, Odysseus filled his men's ears with wax and had himself bound to the mast. What Homer's sirens claim to offer is knowledge rather than pleasure, but the identification with pleasure is very early and dominates the mythographic tradition. A common allegory of the Medusa, in Fulgentius and others, saw her as sexual temptation (relating petri-faction to tumescence); see Dahlberg 1983, Freccero 1972.

19. I am . . . I am: The repetition, echoed and challenged by the lady in line 28, is similar to that in *Inf.* 19.62 (see *Inter cantica* below) and is possibly intended to parody "Ego sum qui sum" [I am who am], God's naming of himself (Ex. 3.14; see 24.52, with notes, and, especially, 30.73); the point would seem to be that what the Siren "is" is illusion, non-being, an anti-Beatrice (see 30.73, with note).

22-23. I turned Ulysses . . . of my song: These lines have also been read with commas setting off "del suo cammin vago," meaning "I turned Ulysses to my song, though he was eager to follow his path." Both readings are possible; their meanings differ only slightly. The commentators who identify the Siren as Circe take the "turning" here to refer to Ulysses' year-long stay with her; see lines 58-60, with notes, and *Inter cantica* below.

25-33. Her mouth . . . that issued from it: The most widely accepted identifica-tion of the lady seems to be Buti's; he saw her as Lady Philosophy. But her iden-tity is deliberately left vague; as Chiavacci Leonardi observes, if the lady were Philosophy, Reason (Virgil) would not have to be called. We agree with her that the lady represents some form of divine intervention that wakens the sleeping

Virgil: "One may think of St. Lucy (as Pietrobono proposes) or . . . of the grace that illuminates reason and gives it the power to penetrate the deceptive veils of seduction."

28. O Virgil, Virgil, who is this: The lady, calling on Virgil to identify the Siren, implicitly rejects her claim of line 19.

29-33. and he . . . issued from it: Virgil clearly corresponds to "the power" that "accepts or winnows good and evil loves" (18.62-64). That he keeps his eyes fixed on the lady indicates the refusal to become entangled in the mere appearance. There is a parallel with Perseus' killing of the Medusa: he avoids petrifaction by not looking at the Medusa directly but in the mirror-like shield loaned by Athena; see *Met.* 4.772ff., Fulgentius 1.21.

32-33. showed me her belly . . . issued from it: Chiavacci Leonardi writes: "the belly: that part of the human body that collects impurities, waste." The reference is clearly sexual, however, and is perhaps the only instance in Dante's works of expressed sexual disgust; see the note to lines 7-9.

33-36. awakened me . . . I have called you: Note the relation between the events of the dream and those in the world outside (cf. the notes to 9.52-63). In the dream the lady calls Virgil twice: outside the dream, Virgil calls the pilgrim three times; his third call would seem to be simultaneous with the perception of stench within it. The pilgrim's sleep itself, resulting from the heavy mortal body (see the note to 18.139-45) needs correction: the awakening takes place on several levels.

35-36. Arise . . . you may enter: As the commentators point out, the first phrase echoes several passages in the Gospels: e.g., "Surge et ambula . . . Surge, tolle lectum et vade in domum tuam" [Arise and walk . . . Arise, take up your bed and go to your home] (Matt. 9.5-6, said to the paralytic). In conjunction with the reference to the female organs in lines 32-33, these lines are an instance of Dante's theme of the transfer of sexual to religious eros; see lines 64-69.

37-39. already all the circles . . . sun on our backs: If it is broad daylight, an hour or more must have elapsed since dawn; the sun is still fairly low in the east, and the two are facing west.

40-69. Following him . . . circling begins again: The pilgrim's meditation on his dream, with Virgil's comment on it, dominates the transition to the next terrace; the encounter with the angel seems almost parenthetical.

40-42: I was carrying . . . arch of a bridge: The pilgrim is weighed down by his thoughts about the dream, so that the upper part of his body is bent over; continuing the motif of the weight of the cold elements (see lines 1-12, with notes).

45. this mortal territory: Literally, "this mortal march," a march being a border territory that requires special military vigilance (a metaphor of life as warfare).

50-51. affirming *Qui lugent . . . beati*: The angel quotes and adapts the third Beatitude (Matt. 3.5): "Beati qui lugent, quoniam ipsi consolabuntur" [Blessed are those that mourn, for they shall be consoled]. The appropriateness of this Beatitude to the absolution from sloth has been questioned; neither Augustine nor Richard of St. Victor makes the correlation. Dante was probably thinking along the lines of the *Glossa ordinaria*: "By 'mourning,' two types of compunction are to be understood: that is, [mourning] on account of the miseries of this life, and [mourning] on account of the desire for heavenly things." The latter has just been evidenced by the slothful; cf. 14.88.-126.

52-63. What is the matter . . . the great wheels: For Virgil's comment on the pilgrim's posture and the motivation of his question, see 15.120-38, with notes.

58-60. You saw . . . frees oneself from her: Virgil identifies the Siren as coterminous with excessive love of lesser goods, following the explanation of 17.133-39. His phraseology, "one frees oneself," disregards the strong suggestion in the dream of the need for the intervention of grace when reason has fallen asleep (see the note to lines 25-33).

61-63. Let it be enough . . . the great wheels: In other words, do not dwell on what must be transcended: direct your thoughts to the goal (replace the first mode of compunction above with the second, cf. the note to lines 50-51). Compare the urging to make progress in 15.136-38, here intensified into the violent "strike the earth with your heels" (as if to launch oneself into flight). The association with Matt. 10.14: "shake the dust from your feet," often cited, seems tenuous.

62-63. the lure . . . the great wheels: The turning heavens, with the sun and other stars and planets, are compared to a type of lure made of bright pieces of metal or glass on a cord, which the falconer whirls above his head to call a distant falcon (cf. another instance in 14.148-51). Note the characteristic reversal of higher and lower, and of container and thing contained: the falcon above the falconer, who whirls the lure above his head, versus the soul beneath and within the heavens, which are turned from above and beyond by God. Such patterns of reversal will become increasingly important (see 27.109-11, with note).

64-69. Like the falcon . . . circling begins again: With lines 35-36, the phallic reference in these lines is unmistakeable (cf. *protendere* [to stretch forward] in *Inf.* 15.114). Such instances are deliberate on Dante's part: his entire theory of human desire regards sexual desire as a specialization or determination of the desire for the good as such (see 17.127-34). Therefore the attachment to sexual objects can be broken, and desire can be redirected, metamorphosed (the modern, Freudian idea of sublimation involves no fundamental metamorphosis of libido, which remains irreducibly biological).

70-75. When I was loosed . . . hardly be understood: The first view of the repentant avaricious partly declares the nature of the penance, though it will be spelled out more fully in lines 118-26; it is based on the antithesis between earthward and heavenward impulses that has dominated the preceding cantos: the desires of the avaricious had in fact been directed toward the element earth (see the note to lines 1-6).

70. I was loosed: The phrase is probably not a falconry metaphor; the Italian "dischiuso" means "released from enclosure."

73. *Adhaesit pavimento anima mea* [My soul hath cleaved to the pavement]: The souls quote the first half of line 25 of the long acrostic Psalm 118 (a more literal translation of the Hebrew gives "dust" instead of "pavement"); the second half is: "vivifica me secundum verbum tuum" [quicken thou me according to thy word]. Nothing in the psalm applies specifically to avarice, but Augustine's influential commentary interpreted it as a prayer against attachment to earthly things; on verse 25 he writes: "What then is the pavement? If we take the entire universe as like a great house, its roof being the heavens, the earth will be its pavement. [The speaker] wishes to be freed from earthly things . . . For to adhere to earthly things is the death of the soul; against which he prays for its contrary, life, when he says *vivifica me*." *Adhaesit pavimento* was the very name of the posture of prayer in which the supplicant lay prone, associated with the reciting of the verse (see the note to 8.10).

81. let your right hands be ever on the outside: Toward the edge of the terrace: they are being told to turn to the right. By using plural pronouns and verbs the speaker shows that he has identified them as being more than one.

84-90. by the speaking . . . made me notice it: Locating the source of the spoken words by hearing alone, the pilgrim can identify the speaker (since he is face down on the terrace, the movement of his lips cannot be seen; "the rest" is his body). The pilgrim's curiosity is aroused, and Virgil consents to his desire, expressed by a glance, to interview this soul.

88-145. Since I could act . . . left to me back there: Almost half the canto is devoted to the interview with the soul the pilgrim has singled out. It turns out to be a nephew of pope Innocent IV, Ottobono dei Fieschi (ca. 1215-1276), who became pope as Adrian V.

91-96. Spirit in whom . . . I have come: The pilgrim addresses the soul ceremoniously (cf. Virgil in lines 76-77); perhaps this is to be explained by the humiliating nature of the penance.

91-92. weeping ripens . . . return to God: Exactly what this spirit, like all the others, is ripening by his weeping is unstated; presumably it is the full predominance of the desire for heavenly things.

93. suspend your greatest care: Interrupt your main concern in order to speak with me.

97-99. Why Heaven . . . *scias quod ego fui successor Petri* [know that I was a successor of Peter]: That Ottobono postpones answering the pilgrim's question about the penance until after his account of his conversion expresses perhaps not so much a feeling that his having been pope (a successor of saint Peter) is still of paramount importance to him, as his eagerness to confess his delusion and conversion (he does answer the pilgrim's questions in order). But he is still accustomed to hieratic modes of expression.

100-102. Between Sestri . . . pride of its title: Between Sestri Levante and Chiàvari, cities of the Ligurian riviera east of Genova, flows the river Lavagna, also called the Entella. The Fieschi family were the counts of Lavagna.

102. takes the pride of its title: *Cima* [summit], here translated "pride," may refer to the fact that the upper part of the Fieschi family's coat of arms carried the word *Entella* (Pedevilla in Bosco/Reggio).

103-105. For one month . . . seem a feather: Adrian V died after 38 days in office. The lines imply that his reputation for sanctity and probity was partly hypocritical (see *Inf.* 23.67: "Oh eternally laborious mantle"), but also that on election Ottobono strove to live up to his responsibilities. Cf. Marco Lombardo's metaphors for the corrupt papacy (16.127-29), and see *Inter cantica* below.

106-114. My conversion . . . punished for it here: Ottobono's realization of the falsity of his earlier goals, like his comment on the weight of papal responsibility (lines 103-105), is a close paraphrase of words attributed by John of Salisbury to an earlier pope, Adrian IV (1154-1159) in *Policraticus* 8.23 (Bosco/Reggio). Whether Dante confused the two popes (which seems unlikely, given his frequent use of the *Policraticus*), or knowingly adapted the passage is disputed.

109. I saw that my heart was not quieted there: Another allusion to Augustine's famous "You have made us for yourself, and our heart is unquiet until it rests in you" (*Confessions* 1.1). See the note to *Inf.* 4.42.

110. nor could I rise any higher: The papacy was the most exalted position a living person could attain. When commentators maintain that what Ottobono desired was power as opposed to wealth, they overlook line 113 and the fact that he is purging avarice.

114. I am punished for it here: Again the punitive view of Purgatory, characteristic of those in the early phases of purgation. Ottobono here speaks of himself in

the feminine gender: "punita" [punished] is feminine agreeing with the femi-
nine "anima" [soul], like "misera" [wretched], "partita" [separated], and "avara"
[greedy], but it is much less directly dependent on the noun.

115-26. What avarice does . . . and stretched out: Ottobono's second topic is
the nature of the penance: the nature of their vice ("what avarice does") is repre-
sented ("shown") in their bodily attitude.

117. the mountain has no pain more bitter: This line has occasioned discus-
sion; it is probably better to understand it as an expression of Ottobono's stage of
purgation and perception, rather than as an objectively valid statement: the bit-
terness of any penance would be a function of the soul's need for it.

118-20. Since our eyes . . . to the earth: Not only were their eyes not raised
up, they were fixed on things constituted by the element earth; this tercet is itself
a tropology of Ps. 118.25 (see the note to line 73). For the verb *ergere* [to lift up]
(here combined with the prefix *ad*), see *Inf.* 10.35-36, with the note.

121-24. Since avarice . . . feet and hands: Again the immobility of hands and
feet signifying inactivity or powerlessness (see the note to lines 7-9; for other
cases see *Inf.* 24.94-96 and 28.103).

125-26. as long as . . . stretched out: This soul does not seem to know how
long his purgation will take; he has progressed rapidly so far, having died only 24
years earlier, but we will soon learn that the process of purgation on this terrace
can take a very long time indeed.

127-32. I had knelt . . . I stood erect: Just as the pilgrim identified Ottobono as
the speaker of lines 79-81 by hearing alone, Ottobono knows that the pilgrim
has knelt beside him (see *Inter cantica* below).

130-45. What cause . . . left to me back there: Ottobono's third speech re-
bukes the pilgrim for his reverent posture and dismisses him in favor of return-
ing to penitential weeping; the brief mention of his niece Alagia is prompted by
the pilgrim's offer in lines 95-96, presumably with the unstated hope that she
will pray for him when she learns of his plight.

134-38. I am a fellow-servant . . . why I speak thus: Ottobono is echoing the
traditional formula: "servi servorum Dei" [servants of the servants of God], used
by the popes. Cf. Marco Lombardo's phraseology in 16.79-81.

136-38. If you have . . . speak thus: Ottobono is quoting Jesus' words to the
Sadducees (who denied the resurrection), when they asked him whose wife the
widow of seven men would be after the resurrection: "In the resurrection they
shall neither marry [*neque nubent*] nor be given in marriage: but they shall be like
the angels of God" (Matt. 22.30). Like other bishops, the pope (bishop of Rome)

is symbolically married to his diocese (as a figure of Christ the bridegroom); all such consecrations cease at death: the pilgrim owes Ottobono no more reverence than to anyone else.

141. the thing you mentioned: See lines 91-96, with notes.

142-45. I have a niece . . . left to me back there: Alagia dei Fieschi was the daughter of Ottobono's brother Niccolò; she married Moroello Malaspina, whose guest Dante had been in 1307 or 1308 (see 8.109-39, with notes); Dante presumably met her on that occasion. For the reliance of the repentant souls on female relatives, see 23.85-96, with notes.

Inter cantica. Since in *Inferno* 26 Ulysses's stay with Circe immediately precedes his prolonged exploration of the Mediterranean (lines 90-105), there is some basis for seeing the Siren of the present canto as representing one of the temptations that led to his last voyage, the fascination with the sensual surface of things (see the note to *Inf.* 26.112-20).

The connections of this canto with other parts of the *Inferno*, especially those concerning avarice and avaricious popes are very rich (for the connection between avarice and prodigality, see *Purg.* 22.22-54, with notes and *Inter cantica*). In all cases there is a strong association of the object of avaricious desire with the lowest of the elements, earth. In *Inferno* 7 the avaricious must push enormous stones around the circle until they collide (like the waves over Charybdis, a further connection with Ulysses) with the prodigal (*Inf.* 7.22-33). Virgil's scornful comment derives their sin from mental blindness (*Inf.* 7.40-42; cf. lines 118-20 here), and *Inf.* 7.46-51 identify it as prevalent among the clergy. The antithesis between the darkness of the element earth and the light of the heavens governs both cantos (cf. *Inf.*. 7.73-96—even there the theme of Fortune leads the eye upward—and lines 61-69 here).

Like *Purgatorio* 19, *Inferno* 19 is devoted to avaricious popes, and their simony (punished in the seventh Malebolgia) is attributed to avarice in one of the most indignant condemnations in the poem (*Inf.* 19.88-117). The connection with the element earth, again as stone, is developed in a savage way: the simoniacs are stuffed into the cracks in the stony floor of Hell, parodying the building of the Church on the foundation of the "rock" of saint Peter (Matt. 16.18). Damnation as entrapment within the stones of Hell (and within the full rigor of the Old Law) is a recurrent motif in the *Inferno* (see *Inf.* 32.1-12, with notes), and the punishment of simony is a particularly severe version of it. There is a clear continuity from the pushing of stones in *Inferno* 7 to being pushed into the rock in *Inferno* 19, to the closing in of the walls of stone in *Inferno* 32 and 33, which is then, in the *Purgatorio*, gradually reversed: the repentant proud have escaped enclosure by the rocks but must bear their weight as they learn humility (see *Inter cantica* for Canto 10); the avaricious are immobilized above the stone that was the object of their desire.

There are several other important parallels between these nineteenth cantos. Both former popes, Nicholas and Adrian, use the metonymy of "the great mantle" to refer to their former office (*Inf.* 19.69, *Purg.* 19.103-104). Both identify themselves as popes with the words "Know that . . .": Nicholas in Italian ("sappi che," *Inf.* 19. 69), Adrian in Latin ("scias quod," *Purg.* 19.99). Both allude to the Apostolic Succession: Nicholas by alluding to his predecessors (*Inf.* 19.73-74: "li altri . . . che precedetter me simoneggiando" [the others who preceded me in simony], Adrian explicitly (*Purg.* 19.99: "*ego fui successor Petri*" [I was a successor of Peter], where the parallel brings to the fore the names of Simon Magus and Simon Peter (see *Inferno*, Additional Note 7).

Another important parallel/contrast with *Inferno* 19 involves the bodily attitude of the pilgrim. In *Inferno* 19 he was "like the friar that confesses the treacherous assassin" (*Inf.* 19.49-50; it is clear from lines 52-53 that he is not kneeling). In *Purgatorio* 19 the layman kneels to show his respect for the office of pope (lines 127-29): no respect for the popes damned to Hell!

Note the parallels of phrasing: *Inf.* 19.46, "che 'l di sù tien di sotto" [who hold your up side down]; *Purg.* 19.94-95, "vòlti avete i dossi / al sù" [you have your backs turned up], and 97-98, "i nostri diretri / rivolga il cielo a sé" [Heaven turns our backsides toward itself]. There is a pattern of insistent repetition in the two cantos: *Inf.* 19.52-53, "Se' tu già costì ritto, se' tu già costì ritto" [Are you already standing there, are you already standing there] (like Adriano, Nicholas has derived the pilgrim's posture from hearing him speak), and 62: "Non son colui, non son colui" [I am not he, I am not he]; *Purg.* 19.19, "'Io son,' cantava, 'io son'" ["I am," she was singing, "I am"], and 28, "O Virgilio, Virgilio" [O Virgil, Virgil].

Finally, the lady's awakening of Virgil to rescue the dreamer from the Siren has a parallel in the chain of ladies who send Virgil to the pilgrim (*Inferno* 2). This parallel gives a strong indication that the Siren is to be connected with the she-wolf, before which the pilgrim is powerless (*Inf.* 1.52-60; see also *Purg.* 20.10-15). For her connection with the Medusa (*Inf.* 9.61-63), see the notes to lines 16-24 and 29-33.

CANTO 20

Contra miglior voler voler mal pugna: 1
onde contra 'l piacer mio, per piacerli,
trassi de l'acqua non sazia la spugna.

Mossimi, e 'l duca mio si mosse per li   4
luoghi spediti pur lungo la roccia,
come si va per muro stretto a' merli,

ché la gente che fonde a goccia a goccia   7
per li occhi il mal che tutto 'l mondo occupa,
da l'altra parte in fuor troppo s'approccia.

Maladetta sie tu, antica lupa,   10
che più che tutte l'altre bestie hai preda
per la tua fame sanza fine cupa!

O ciel, nel cui girar par che si creda   13
le condizion di qua giù trasmutarsi,
quando verrà per cui questa disceda?

Noi andavam con passi lenti e scarsi,   16
e io attento a l'ombre, ch'i' sentia
pietosamente piangere e lagnarsi;

e per ventura udi': "Dolce Maria!"   19
dinanzi a noi chiamar così nel pianto
come fa donna che in parturir sia,

e seguitar: "Povera fosti tanto   22
quanto veder si può per quello ospizio
dove sponesti il tuo portato santo."

Seguentemente intesi: "O buon Fabrizio,   25
con povertà volesti anzi virtute
che gran ricchezza posseder con vizio."

Queste parole m'eran sì piaciute   28
ch'io mi trassi oltre per aver contezza
di quello spirto onde parean venute.

CANTO 20

Fifth terrace, continued: denunciation of avarice—examples of liberality
—Hugh Capet—the crimes of the Capetians—examples of avarice—
earthquake and Gloria

1   Against a better will one's will fights but poorly:
therefore against my pleasure, to please him, I
drew my sponge unsated from the water.

4   I moved on, and my leader walked in the empty
spaces along the cliff, as one walks along a fortress
wall close under the battlements,

7   for the people, melting out through their eyes,
drop by drop, the evil that fills the whole world,
were too close to the edge on the outer side.

10   A curse be on you, ancient she-wolf, that more
than any other beast find prey for your endlessly
hollow hunger!

13   O heavens, whose turning, we believe, changes
conditions down here, when will he come who
will drive her away?

16   We went with careful, slow steps, and I walked
intent on the shades, whom I heard piteously
weeping and lamenting;

19   and I happened to hear one ahead of us calling
out, weeping: "Sweet Mary!" as a woman giving
birth will do,

22   and the voice continued: "How very poor you
were we can see by the shelter where you laid
down your holy burden."

25   Next I heard: "O good Fabricius, you wished to
possess poverty with virtue rather than great riches
with vice."

28   These words so pleased me that I walked
further, so as to make acquaintance with the spirit
whence they seemed to have come.

Esso parlava ancor de la larghezza   31
che fece Niccolò a le pulcelle
per condurre ad onor lor giovinezza.

"O anima che tanto ben favelle,   34
dimmi chi fosti," dissi, "e perché sola
tu queste degne lode rinovelle.

Non fia sanza mercé la tua parola,   37
s'io ritorno a compiér lo cammin corto
di quella vita ch'al termine vola."

Ed elli: "Io ti dirò, non per conforto   40
ch'io attenda di là, ma perché tanta
grazia in te luce prima che sie morto.

Io fui radice de la mala pianta   43
che la terra cristiana tutta aduggia,
sì che buon frutto rado se ne schianta.

Ma se Doagio, Lilla, Guanto e Bruggia   46
potesser, tosto ne saria vendetta,
e io la cheggio a lui che tutto giuggia.

Chiamato fui di là Ugo Ciappetta;   49
di me son nati i Filippi e i Luigi
per cui novellamente è Francia retta.

Figliuol fu' io d'un beccaio di Parigi;   52
quando li regi antichi venner meno
tutti, fuor ch'un renduto in panni bigi,

trova'mi stretto ne le mani il freno   55
del governo del regno, e tanta possa
di nuovo acquisto, e sì d'amici pieno,

ch'a la corona vedova promossa   58
la testa di mio figlio fu, del quale
cominciar di costor le sacrate ossa.

Mentre che la gran dota provenzale   61
al sangue mio non tolse la vergogna,
poco valea ma pur non facea male.

Lì cominciò con forza e con menzogna   64
la sua rapina; e poscia, per ammenda,
Pontì e Normandia prese e Guascogna.

Carlo venne in Italia, e, per ammenda,   67
vittima fé di Curradino; e poi
ripinse al ciel Tommaso, per ammenda.

31   He was speaking still of the generosity of
Nicholas to the maidens, done to lead their youth
to honor.

34   "O soul who speak of so much good, tell me
who you were," I said, "and why you alone repeat
these worthy praises.

37   Your words will not be without reward, if I
return to complete the brief path of the life that
flies to its end."

40   And he: "I will tell you, not for help that I
expect from there, but because so much grace
shines in you before you have died.

43   I was the root of the evil plant that overshadows
all the Christian lands, so that one rarely breaks
good fruit from it.

46   But if Douay, Lille, Ghent, and Bruges were
able, soon they would take vengeance, and I pray
for it to him who judges all.

49   I was called Hugh Capet back there; from me
are born the Philips and the Louis by whom
France in recent times is ruled.

52   I was the son of a Parisian butcher; when the old
kings had died out, save one gone to wear monkish
robes,

55   I found grasped in my hands the reins of the
government of the kingdom, and so much power
newly acquired, and so rich in friends,

58   that my son's head was promoted to the
widowed crown; from him the consecrated bones
of the others began.

61   As long as the great dowry of Provence had not
deprived my blood of shame, it was not worth
much, but still it did no harm.

64   There with force and fraud it began its
plundering, and then, to make amends, it took
Ponthieu and Normandy and Gascony.

67   Charles came into Italy, and, to make amends,
made a victim of Conradino; and then he drove
Thomas back to Heaven, to make amends.

Tempo vegg' io, non molto dopo ancoi,   70
che tragge un altro Carlo fuor di Francia
per far conoscer meglio e sé e ' suoi.

Sanz' arme n'esce e solo con la lancia   73
con la qual giostrò Giuda, e quella ponta
sì ch'a Fiorenza fa scoppiar la pancia.

Quindi non terra, ma peccato e onta   76
guadagnerà, per sé tanto più grave
quanto più lieve simil danno conta.

L'altro, che già uscì preso di nave,   79
veggio vender sua figlia e patteggiarne
come fanno i corsar de l'altre schiave.

O avarizia, che puoi tu più farne,   82
poscia c'ha' il mio sangue a te sì tratto
che non si cura de la propria carne?

Perché men paia il mal futuro e 'l fatto,   85
veggio in Alagna intrar lo fiordaliso
e nel vicario suo Cristo esser catto.

Veggiolo un'altra volta esser deriso,   88
veggio rinovellar l'aceto e 'l fiele,
e tra vivi ladroni esser anciso.

Veggio il novo Pilato sì crudele   91
che ciò nol sazia, ma sanza decreto
portar nel Tempio le cupide vele.

O Segnor mio, quando sarò io lieto   94
a veder la vendetta che, nascosa,
fa dolce l'ira tua nel tuo secreto?

Ciò ch'io dicea di quell' unica sposa   97
de lo Spirito Santo e che ti fece
verso me volger per alcuna chiosa,

tanto è risposto a tutte nostre prece   100
quanto 'l dì dura; ma com' el s'annotta,
contrario suon prendemo in quella vece.

Noi repetiam Pigmaliòn allotta,   103
cui traditore e ladro e paricida
fece la voglia sua de l'oro ghiotta,

e la miseria de l'avaro Mida   106
che seguì a la sua dimanda gorda,
per la qual sempre convien che si rida.

70   I see a time, not far in the future, that will bring another Charles out of France to make himself and his family better known.

73   Unarmed he comes forth, carrying only the lance that Judas jousted with, but this he will aim so that it will burst Florence's belly.

76   From this he will gain, not land, but sin and shame, all the heavier for him the more lightly he counts such harm.

79   The other, who once was captured aboard ship, I see selling his daughter and bargaining over her, as pirates do over their other female slaves.

82   O avarice, what more can you do to us, now that you have so drawn all my blood to you that it has no care for its own flesh?

85   So that its future crimes and those already done may seem less, I see the fleur-de-lys enter Anagni, and in his vicar Christ taken prisoner.

88   I see him mocked again, I see the vinegar and the wormwood renewed, I see him killed between living thieves.

91   I see the new Pilate so cruel that he is not sated, but without just decree moving with greedy sails against the Temple.

94   O my Lord, when will I be gladdened seeing the vengeance, now hidden, that makes your anger sweet in your secret counsel?

97   What I was saying of that only bride of the Holy Spirit, that made you turn to me for a gloss,

100   so much is the reply to all our prayers as long as the day lasts; but when night falls we take instead a contrary sound.

103   We recall Pygmalion then, whose gluttonous desire for gold made him traitor, thief, and parricide,

106   and the misery of grasping Midas that resulted from his greedy wish, for which he will always be ridiculed.

Del folle Acàn ciascun poi si ricorda,   109
come furò le spoglie, sì che l'ira
di Iosüè qui par ch'ancor lo morda.

Indi accusiam col marito Saffira;   112
lodiamo i calci ch'ebbe Elïodoro;
e in infamia tutto 'l monte gira

Polinestòr ch'ancise Polidoro;   115
ultimamente ci si grida: 'Crasso,
dilci, che 'l sai: di che sapore è l'oro?'

Talor parla l'uno alto e l'altro basso,   118
secondo l'affezion ch'ad ir ci sprona
ora a maggiore e ora a minor passo:

però al ben che 'l dì ci si ragiona   121
dianzi non era io sol, ma qui da presso
non alzava la voce altra persona."

Noi eravam partiti già da esso   124
e brigavam di soverchiar la strada
tanto quanto al poder n'era permesso,

quand' io senti', come cosa che cada,   127
tremar lo monte, onde mi prese un gelo
qual prender suol colui ch'a morte vada.

Certo non si scoteo sì forte Delo,   130
pria che Latona in lei facesse 'l nido
a parturir li due occhi del cielo.

Poi cominciò da tutte parti un grido   133
tal, che 'l maestro inverso me si feo,
dicendo: "Non dubbiar, mentr' io ti guido."

"*Glorïa in excelsis*" tutti "*Deo!*"   136
dicean, per quel ch'io da' vicin compresi,
onde intender lo grido si poteo.

No' istavamo immobili e sospesi,   139
come i pastor che prima udir quel canto,
fin che 'l tremar cessò ed el compiési.

Poi ripigliammo nostro cammin santo,   142
guardando l'ombre che giacean per terra,
tornate già in su l'usato pianto.

109   Then each remembers foolish Achan, how he stole the spoils, so that the wrath of Joshua seems still to bite him here.

112   Then we accuse Sapphira and her husband; we praise the hooves that kicked Heliodorus; and in infamy Polymnestor circles

115   all the mountain, he who killed Polydorus; finally we cry: 'Crassus, tell us, for you know: what flavor does gold have?'

118   Sometimes one speaks loud, another soft, according to the affection that spurs us now to greater, now to smaller steps:

121   thus, earlier, praising the good as we do during the day, I was not alone, but no other person was raising his voice nearby."

124   We had already left him and were struggling to leave behind as much of the way as was permitted to our power,

127   when I felt the mountain shake like a falling thing, and a chill seized me such as takes him who goes to death.

130   Surely Delos did not shake so violently, before Latona made her nest there to give birth to the two eyes of heaven.

133   Then on all sides began a shout so loud that my master drew closer, saying: "Fear not, while I am guiding you."

136   "*Gloria in excelsis Deo!*" they were all saying, as I grasped from those close by, from whom the shouting could be understood.

139   We were standing immobile and in suspense, like the shepherds who first heard that song, until the shaking ceased and the song was completed.

142   Then we took our holy way again, gazing at the souls who were lying on the earth and had already returned to their accustomed weeping.

Nulla ignoranza mai con tanta guerra 145
mi fé desideroso di sapere,
se la memoria mia in ciò non erra,

quanta pareami allor, pensando, avere; 148
né per la fretta dimandare er' oso,
né per me lì potea cosa vedere:

così m'andava timido e pensoso. 151

145   No ignorance ever assailed me with so much
desire to know, if here my memory does not err,

148   as it seemed to me I had then, pondering; nor in
my haste had I dared to ask, nor could I see
anything there:

151   so I walked on, timid and thoughtful.

NOTES

1-3. Against a better will . . . unsated from the water: The pilgrim's curiosity yields to Adrian's wish for purgation. The struggle echoes the rescue from the Siren (19.28-33) and the war of curiosity ending the canto (see lines145-148); it anticipates Statius's perfection of his will in 21.64-69 (see notes). That the pilgrim's desire for information is a sponge anticipates his "thirst" at 21.1-4, 39, and evokes the vinegar-filled sponge offered to Christ (Matt. 27.48); Fergusson 1953 speaks of the "magnetic effect of Christ's crucifixion" over this part of the poem (see also Carroll, Scott 1996). Physical hunger and or thirst express the vices of the upper ledges (22.149-50; 23.66; 24.28; 26.18, 20), finally of all human desire (27.117).

7-9. melting . . . the whole world: The image is of fusing metal, drawn from foundries, coining, or alchemy (cf. *Inf.* 7.18, 19.72, 30.88-90, with notes). The task is huge because avarice is universal.

10-14. A curse be on you . . . drive her away: As Dante's apostrophe of the she-wolf (echoing 1 Tim. 6.9) suggests, avarice is a chief target of the poet as prophet and moralist; the passage refers to the prophecy of the Greyhound in *Inf.* 1.91-112. Though associated with greed and violence (*Purg.* 14.49-51, *Inf.* 33.28-29), for the first time since *Inf.* 1.91 the she-wolf is labeled as avarice; the term "ancient" links her with the "old adversary" of 11.20. Saint Paul's naming of the vice became proverbial (1 Tim. 6.10): "Radix enim omnium malorum est cupiditas" [For cupidity is the root of all evils]; *avaritia* [avarice] was often substituted for the generic *cupiditas*.

After the terrace of pride, Dante devotes the most space to that of avarice (19.70-21.136), first of the last three vices (17.136-39), just as pride is the first of the first three. The two terraces are linked by their wealth of examples, and they alone earn reproach in the poet's voice (cf. 10.121). The Beatitude for those who defeat pride, "Beati pauperes spiritu" [Blessed are the poor in spirit] is a figurative form of the poverty that heals avarice.

10-12. A curse be on you . . . hollow hunger: Note the close echo of *Inf.* 1.97-99; cf. lines 82-84, 114-15 below.

16-18. We went . . . weeping and lamenting: The souls lament their sins, but also the corruption of the world, the loss of justice that makes all of Purgatory, as Singleton 1957 noted, a "lament for Eden." In this sense the beatitude *qui lugent* (19.50) of the central ledge applies to all Purgatory (see Martinez 1997).

19-33. one ahead of us . . . youth to honor: Three examples against avarice are called out, the first two as apostrophes, as if the souls were maintaining the poet's rhetorical tone. In last two examples Dante replaces the word for gold in his source with abstractions "riches" and "largesse"; for this elision of gold, see below.

20-24. Sweet Mary . . . your holy burden: The first example is the poverty of Mary, shown by the stable where she gave birth to Christ (Luke 2.7: "And she brought forth her firstborn son, and wrapped him in swaddling clothes, and laid him in a manger" [a manger is a bin from which cattle eat]). But Dante's emphasis is not on the manger scene, nor on Mary's labor (thought free of pain), but on the use of Mary's name against birth pangs, as women in antiquity had invoked the goddess Juno as Lucina. In a figure especially prominent on the terrace of avarice, the penitent souls are pregnant with their new being (see 10.124-26 and note); the analogy between childbirth and conversion/baptism, was traditional (see *Ep.* 11.15; *Confessions* 7.7, 9.9); cf. lines 75, 97.

25-27. O good Fabricius . . . riches with vice: C. Fabricius Luscius, Roman consul in 282 B.C., refused to be corrupted by bribes from Pyrrhus, mercenary general of the Samnites, designed to buy his betrayal of Rome. He was a pauper at his death; his funeral and the endowment of his daughters were paid by the state. He is one of several Roman Republican heroes Dante cited as proof the destiny of Rome had been providential (*Conv.* 4.5.13). See *Mon.* 2.5.11: "Did not Fabricius give us a lofty example of resisting avarice when, poor as he was, out of loyalty to the Republic he scorned the great sum of gold which was offered him— scorned and spurned it with disdain, uttering words in keeping with his character? The memory of this incident too is confirmed by our poet in his sixth book when he said: 'Fabricius, a great man in his poverty.'"

31-33. the generosity of Nicholas . . . their youth to honor: Saint Nicholas, bishop of Myra in Asia Minor (third-fourth century), is the third example. The legend relates that he dropped purses of gold through a window into the house of three impoverished sisters; the dowries made them marriageable, and they escaped prostitution. Highly popular (26 churches in Rome alone), Nicholas is the patron of children, sailors, unmarried girls, merchants, pawnbrokers (the three golden balls over pawnshops are symbols of his gifts), and apothecaries.

31. generosity: Also called largesse or liberality, this virtue is described by Aristotle (*Nichomachean Ethics* 4.1 [1119b-1122b]) as the mean, with respect to wealth, between avarice and its opposite, prodigality (see *Purg.* 22.49-54, with notes). For Dante, it was a crucial virtue: see *Inf.* 7.42, and the canzoni "Tre donne intorno al cor mi son venuto," 63 and "Doglia mi reca ne lo core ardire," 85-86, 121-22; see also *Conv.* 1.8, 4.17, 4.27.12-13.

34-36. O soul . . . worthy praises: The positive examples stand out against the general lament.

39. life that flies to its end: For this Augustinian formula see 33.54 and note. A traditional argument against greed: you can't take it with you (see *Inf.* 7. 61-66).

40-123. I will tell you . . . his voice nearby: Of the shade's answers to the pilgrim's questions (lines 34-36), that concerning his identity occupies 25 terzinas, the answer to the other only two terzinas.

43. I was the root . . . Christian lands: Hugh is the root of the genealogical tree of the Capetians, elaborately depicted in the official French royal chronicles (Hedemann 1991). Hugh's evil tree recalls the trees of *Inferno* (cf. 3.112-17, 33.118-20, with notes; see line 64, with note) and parodies the tree of Jesse, Christ's genealogy in Matt. 1.1-17 (see lines 87-93); it also suggests the tree of sins deriving from avarice, the "root of all evil" (see the note to lines 103-20); for the "trees" of love and desire, see 17.91-139, 27.115-16, with notes. The tree overshadows Christendom, for Capetian ambitions extended from Flanders to the Holy Land; see lines 91-93.

46-48. But if Douay, Lille, Ghent . . . who judges all:. After promising the Count of Flanders liberty in exchange for the surrender of Ghent, Philip IV violated the pact and imprisoned him; the free cities of Flanders reacted by crushing the king at Courtrai in 1302 (see *Inf.* 15.4-6, with note). The speaker alludes to the event as future (line 46; cf. 6.100-102, 121-23).

49. I was called Hugh Capet: Both Hugh Capet (d. 996) and his father, Hugh the Great, were *cappati*, or "mantled" because they were lay abbots. The royal house of France also possessed the mantle of Martin, the popular saint (often associated in devotions with St. Nicholas), who as a young officer in the Roman army divided his cape in half for a beggar (Dante's house in Florence was in the parish of San Martino al Vescovo). See Jacobus a Voragine, *Legenda aurea* (c. 1265): "the king of France had the habit of taking his mantle [*cappa*] into battle."

50. the Philips and the Louis: With the exception of Hugh's son Robert the Pious (see below) and Henry I, all the Capetians bore the names Philip (four) and Louis (five). Louis IX, St. Louis, is perhaps the "good fruit" that "rarely is plucked" in lines 44-45; in addition to figuring in this canto, Philip III the Bold and Philip IV the Fair are both mentioned elsewhere in the *Comedy*, the former at 7.109 ("father of the evil of France"), the second in *Inf.* 19.85-87, *Purg.* 7.109-11 and 32.152-60, and *Par.* 19.118-20.

52. the son of a Parisian butcher: Hugh Capet and his father Hugh the Great were dukes of France and counts of Paris and Orléans, not butchers' sons. But the legend of Hugh's humble origins was widespread in Dante's time; Villani reports it (5.4.3-9), along with more accurate information. In French dynastic history, the link of the Capetians to the Carolingians was contested; for some, the return to the lineage of Charlemagne occurred with Hugh; for others, it ended with Hugh and returned with Philip Augustus (d. 1223) or his son Louis IX.

54. one gone to wear monkish robes: The Carolingians became extinct with the death of Louis V the Slothful, who died without heirs; Charles of Lorraine, Louis's uncle, survived to claim the throne but was imprisoned at Orleans until his death. The story that Hugh forced Charles into a convent derives from Godfrey of Viterbo; there may be confusion with the fate of Childeric III, the last of the Merovingians, who became a monk in 752. Mattalia suggests that Hugh, conscious of having forced Charles, uses *renduto* (for becoming a monk; cf. *Purg* 3.119) ironically.

55-57. I found . . . so rich in friends: Anti-Carolingian factions concentrated power in the hands of Hugh: he was elected king at Senlis, and consecrated at Rheims by his ally the bishop on Christmas Day, 988. This combination of "the reins in hand" (cf. *Purg*. 6.88-92-7; 16.94; 18.96 and notes) and fortunate circumstances agrees with the French royal chronicle (*Grandes Chroniques*) on Hugh's success: "because Hugh saw that all the heirs and the line of Charlemagne were destroyed . . . and since there was no one to contradict him, he had himself crowned in Reims" (Hedemann 1991).

58-60. my son's head . . . the others began: Hugh's son was Robert I, the Pious, associated closely with his father's rule soon after his election. Emphasis on the anointing is richly ironic in view of what follows.

59. to the widowed crown: That is, vacant; but for the force of "widowed," see 1.76, 6.113, 32.50. As Italian *ciappetta* might suggest a chaplet or garland (see *Decameron* 1.1.9), a series of puns on "head" [It. *capo*, Lat. caput]), "hood" [cappa]) and "crown" [*ciappello*] is at work here.

61. the great dowry of Provence: The vast County of Provence, which Beatrice, last daughter of Raymond Berenguer (see the notes to 6.258-75, *Par*. 6.133-35) brought as her dowry to Charles of Anjou. According to one account, Charles wished to conquer the kingdom of Naples so that Beatrice could be a queen like her sisters. Commentators have seen a parallel between this dowry and the Donation of Constantine (called a dowry in *Inf*. 19.116, cf. lines 31-33 above), the great spur to the greed of the popes.

64. with force and fraud: Violence and fraud account for all of lower Hell; cf. *Inf*. 11.22-24, also *Purg*. 14.49-54: Hugh's account of his family is a kind of précis of Hell.

66. it took Ponthieu and Normandy and Gascony: Three great fiefs, formerly under English rule, absorbed by the Angevins in the thirteenth century.

67-69. Conradino . . . Thomas: After the defeat and death of Manfred in 1266 (see 3.118-29), Charles I of Anjou used treachery to defeat and capture the boy Conradino, grandson of Frederick II, early in 1268 at Tagliacozzo; he had him beheaded in the Piazza del Mercato at Naples, thus ending the Hohenstaufen dynasty. The chronicler Saba Malaspina saw Conradino as a Christ-like martyr: "Conradino . . . offered himself like a victim and patiently awaited the blow of the butcher" (see Acts 8.32-33, quoting Is. 53.7-8). The report that Charles had Thomas Aquinas poisoned at Fossanova in Campania, while en route to the Council of Lyons (1264), because he was going to "tell the truth" about Charles, is baseless; Aquinas seems to have died of a stroke.

65-69. to make amends: "Per ammenda" means both "so as to make amends" and "so as to better things," with obvious satirical import. These two terzinas offer the only case in the poem of Dante's using identical rhyme three times (except for the rhymes on "Cristo," *Par.* 12.71-75; 19.104-108; see Hardt 1973); they herald the explicit reference to Christ at line 91, and parody the "amends" that Christ's sacrifice made for Adam's sin. Each use of the rhyme, referring to violence and treachery in the service of greed, anticipates aspects of future Capetian misdeeds (related in lines 70-96), all of which Hugh relates to the Passion of Christ. Given that Hugh's *cappa* recalls that of Martin of Tours, a sartorial metaphor may be implicit: the gathering of feudal holdings by Hugh's descendants undoes Martin's generosity.

70-78. I see a time . . . such harm: Hugh foretells the entry into Italy in 1301 of Charles of Valois, the brother of Philip the Fair; he intended to recover Sicily for the Angevins (for the "Sicilian vespers," see 7.112, *Par.* 8.73-75). Charles conspired with Pope Boniface VIII to favor the Florentine Blacks (cf. *Inf.* 6.67-72); he is "unarmed" because at first he left his troops outside Florence. Judas' lance signifies treachery and avarice. Charles failed to recover Sicily, earning the shameful name "Lackland."

75. burst Florence's belly. The burst belly of Florence suggested to Benvenuto the expulsion of the Whites, confiscation of their goods and destruction of their houses. See Acts 1.18: "and being hanged, [Judas] burst asunder in the midst: and all his bowels gushed out"; like Judas's desperate act, Florence's reception of Charles was suicidal. For the city as a belly, see *Inf.* 6.49-50, 8.139-41, with notes, and *Inferno* Additional Notes 2 and 13. Thirteenth-century art saw in Judas' death a parody of childbirth (Derbes/Sandona in Ladis 1988); cf. lines 20-24, 97.

77-78. all the heavier . . . he counts such harm: The heedlessness of the unpunished malefactor is traditionally a consequence of his vicious behavior; cf. *Consolation* 4. pr. 4.

79-81. The other . . . other female slaves: Charles II of Anjou, the Lame (1248-1309), son of old Charles of Anjou (cf. 7.113, 124) and King of Naples and Sicily from 1285, was captured during the war of the Vespers by Ruggiero di Lauria, admiral of the Aragonese, then taking control of Sicily; held from 1284 to

1287, he was crowned king of Sicily in 1289 but never regained control of it. For Dante he is ineffectual and corrupt (*Conv.* 4.6.19-20; *DVE* 1.12.3-5; *Par.* 6.106-108, 19.127-29).

80-81. selling his daughter . . . as pirates do: In an act deplored by contemporaries, Charles II gave his daughter Beatrice in marriage to the unsavory Azzo VIII d'Este (*Inf.* 18.55-57), in return for an enormous sum. Dante draws a parallel with the money extorted by corsairs; the episode parodies Nicholas's generosity to the girls (and see 22.45 and note) and echoes Judas's betrayal of Christ (Luke 22.5: "pacti sunt pecuniam illi dare" [they covenanted to give him money]).

82-84. O avarice . . . no care for its own flesh: This apostrophe is the climax of Hugh's account of his family's misdeeds, echoing lines 8-9 cursing the she-wolf of avarice. The lines are a version of *Aen.* 3.56-57: "quid non mortalia pectora cogis, / auri sacra fames?" [To what do you not drive human breasts, O cursed hunger for gold]; see lines 114-115 below, and 21.40-42, with notes.

85-96. So that its future crimes . . . your secret counsel: Hugh continues to prophesy events future in relation to 1300 (cf. *Inf.* 19.52-54, 25.140-50). After Boniface VIII issued two bulls claiming papal authority over French royal prerogatives, Philip retaliated in 1303 by sending his agent Guillaume de Nogaret, along with Sciarra Colonna, chief of the pope's enemies, to arrest Boniface; they did so, and roughly, at the papal palace in Anagni, southwest of Rome. Though rescued by the townspeople, Boniface died of the shock within a month. Mention of the fleur-de-lys, the French royal device (cf. 6.105 and note), fixes responsibility for the outrage.

87-93. in his vicar . . . against the Temple: With the anaphora of lines 85, 88, and 91 (cf. also line 70), Hugh's discourse becomes exalted and allegorical; compare the pilgrim's denunciation of the simoniac popes in *Inf.* 19.88-117. The humiliation of the pope becomes a reenactment (introduced by the presentation of Charles of Valois as Judas) of Christ's arrest ("taken prisoner"), judgment (note Pilate, line 91), mocking, and crucifixion; the vinegar and wormwood (offered to Christ when he thirsted, John 19.28-30) are Boniface's humiliation; Colonna and Nogaret are "living thieves" corresponding to those crucified with Christ (Luke 23.33), of whom, however, one was saved. Although Dante attacked Boniface (*Inf.* 19.55-57, 90-117), he distinguished between the man and the office (cf. the note to 3.112-45): the person of the pope as Christ's vicar, however imperfect the man, was sacred.

91-93. the new Pilate . . . the Temple: Philip the Fair, who abandons Boniface to hired thugs as in the New Testament Pilate surrenders Christ to the Sanhedrin, is "the new Pilate." The passage summarizes events between 1307, when Philip the Fair ordered the arrest and torture of the leaders of the powerful Templars, Crusader knights (without authorization from the pope, their titular sovereign, hence line 92) and 1312, when, thanks to the king's pressure on Clement V, the order had been suppressed, and its leaders, including Jacques de Molay, the Grand Master, burned at the stake (most of the leaders had recanted the confessions obtained by torture). Thus the cash-poor King, who had owed a fortune to the Templars alone, though compelled to transfer some of the treasure to the Knights Hospitaller, acquired much of the vast Templar holdings (Barber 1994).

93. greedy sails: Charles II was portrayed as a corsair (lines 79-81); here Philip sails the metaphorical "ship of state" (see 6.79 and note) against the Templars. The metaphor suggests that Philip's attack is a parody of the crusade *passage* Philip attempted to organize in 1311: Philip destroyed the order devoted to defending not only the Holy Land, but the purity of the Temple itself (Bernard of Clairvaux 1983). For the association of sails and avarice, see *Inf.* 7.7-15.

94-96. O my Lord . . . secret counsel: With his last apostrophe, Hugh asks God to wreak vengeance on the Capetians; see the similar apostrophes of God in 6.100-102, 118-23, closely related in rhetorical intensity to this passage. Cf. Ps. 57.11: "The just shall rejoice when he shall see the revenge"; also Prov. 10.28. Philip and Clement V, who cooperated in the Templars' downfall, died within a few months of each other in 1314; see *Inf.* 19.85-86, with notes.

97. only bride of the Holy Spirit: The Virgin Mary (see *Purg.* 10.40-45, with notes, and cf. Matt. 1.20). The holy nuptials contrast with the debased marriages referred to in Hugh's speech: widowed crown, dowry, shame, prostituted daughter. Mentions of the Virgin surround Hugh's account of the Capetians (cf. *Inf.* 19.3-4).

100-102. so much . . . contrary sound: An explicit distinction between daytime and nighttime activities, the first that separates the examples of virtue and vice. The "contrary sound" recalls 13.40; see also 22.52-54, with notes, and *Inter cantica* below.

103-20. We recall . . . to smaller steps: Next to the examples of pride punished, this is the longest series of examples in the *Purgatorio.* Most commentators find Dante's list disappointing; but Scartazzini claimed that the seven examples correspond to the seven "daughters of avarice" listed by Aquinas (*ST* 2a 2ae q. 118. a. 8): treachery, fraud, lies, perjury, restlessness, violence, and obduracy. This is consistent with avarice as the root of all evil, since tree-diagrams and filiation schemes for sins were often superimposed in penitential treatises.

All but one of the sources of the examples include the Latin word for gold, *aurum.* Dante inserts a near-pun relating gold to avarice, It. *oro* to *avaro,* in lines 105-106, and threads the syllable *or* in the rhymes of 107-17, reserving *-oro* for the last set, and the full word itself for the last rhyme (line 117). Such emphasis on *oro* also points to the *oral* effects of avarice, seen in all but one example, and culminating in the last. For the curse of gold, see 22.40-41, with notes.

The order of the examples is important: the first and next to last are from the *Aeneid*, regarding Carthage and Troy respectively, Ovid furnishes the second. Within this Roman envelope are three moments from sacred history: first, the post-Exodus struggle for Jericho; last, the post-exilic Maccabean period; at the center, the post-Ascension scene from Acts, where avarice sins against the Holy Spirit.

103-105. We recall Pygmalion . . . parricide: *Aen.* 1.340-59 tells how Dido's wealthy husband Sichaeus, the richest of the Phoenicians, was murdered by her brother Pygmalion, "blinded by love of gold"; warned by her dead husband in a dream, Dido escaped with "ignotum argenti pondus et auri" [wealth uncounted of silver and gold] (line 359).

106. the misery of grasping Midas: Ovid (*Met.* 11.85-179) relates how Midas, king of Phrygia in Asia Minor, when offered a wish by Bacchus, asked that all he touched might turn to gold. He repented of his wish when his food turned to metal—the "misery" here recalled. Bacchus relented, ordering Midas to cleanse himself at the source of the Pactolus, thenceforth rich in gold nuggets from its contact with the king. In framing the oral frustration of Midas, and in calling his wish "gluttonous," Dante follows *Met.* 11.126-27: "If the gift of his patron [Bacchus' gift is wine] were mixed with water to drink, / flowing between his jaws you'd see the molten gold [*aurum*]."

109. foolish Achan: In Joshua 7.1-26, the soldier Achan is found to have stolen some of the booty of Jericho, including a "golden rule" [*regulam auream*]; accused by Joshua, he is stoned to death by the other soldiers.

112. we accuse Sapphira and her husband: Ananias and Sapphira, members of the Christian community of Acts 5.1-11, reserved to themselves a portion of the proceeds from the sale of a field; when denounced by Peter as defrauding the Holy Spirit, both die on the spot. The penitent souls ratify the accusation.

113. we praise the hooves that kicked Heliodorus: Heliodorus, treasurer of the Syrian king Seleucus IV, was ordered to plunder the treasury of the Temple in Jerusalem, but was prevented by a rider in "arma . . . aurea" [golden armor], whose horse "ran fiercely and struck Heliodorus with his forehooves" (2 Macc. 3.25). This example of vice is unique in including praise (cf. 2 Macc. 3.30, where the Jews bless the Lord for the miracle); medieval exegesis paired it with Christ's scourging of the moneylenders from the Temple (John 2.14-16; cf. *Ep.*11.6-7).

114-15. Polymnestor . . . Polydorus: Aeneas relates that the youngest of Priam's sons, Polydorus, was entrusted during the siege of Troy to Polymnestor, king of Thrace, along with a "great weight of gold" [*magnum auri pondus*] (cf. the note on lines 103-105). At Troy's fall, Polymnestor had the boy murdered for the money. Aeneas's condemnation is adapted in lines 82-84 above; see 22.40-42, with notes.

Dante's *infamia* [infamy] puns on Vergil's *fames* [hunger]. The episode is the basis of the wood of suicides in *Inferno* 13, especially lines 31-48.

116-17: Crassus . . . what flavor does gold have: Crassus, triumvir with Julius Caesar and Pompey, was one the richest men in Rome; defeated by the Parthians he was killed while attempting to surrender (59 B.C.). When the Parthian king Orodes received Crassus' head, he had molten gold poured into its mouth, saying: "aurum sitisti, aurum bibe" [you thirsted for gold, drink gold] (Florus, *Epitoma* 3.11; Cicero, *De officiis* 1.30).

118-20. Sometimes . . . smaller steps: A complicated metaphor: the loudness of each soul's calling out of the examples is an index of the intensity of its feeling at the moment, which "spurs" (the horse metaphor: cf. the story of Heliodorus) the progress (this word is also a metaphor of walking) of its purgation. The implications are rich: since they cannot walk, the souls migrate with their voices, and the examples move from mouth to mouth (the orality of avarice, again), girdling the mountain with edifying gossip. Note the many verbs for oral expression: "repeat," "deride," "recall," "accuse," "praise," "circles in infamy," "cries out"; all culminate in the apostrophe of Crassus, symmetrical with the apostrophes of the first two examples of virtue, and resonating with the other apostrophes in the canto (11 in all; see Martinez 1994).

127-29. I felt the mountain shake . . . who goes to death: Compare *Inf.* 5.142 and 12.31-45, with notes. The scriptural parallels are apocalyptic: cf. Luke 23.28-30, and Apoc. 6.16 (the opening of the sixth seal: "And they say to the mountains and the rocks: Fall upon us, and hide us from the face of him that sitteth upon the throne and from the wrath of the Lamb"); the source is Is. 2.19; see Additional Note 15.

130-32. Surely Delos . . . two eyes of heaven: The island of Delos was the birthplace of Apollo and Diana, the children of Latona, the sun and moon (cf. 18.80, 23. 120, 28.33, 29.78). According to *Aen.* 3.73-77, it was originally afloat and at the mercy of the winds, but after providing shelter for Latona (persecuted by the jealous Juno), it was secured by the grateful Apollo. The early commentators explain the myth as meaning that Delos had long been shaken by earthquakes.

133-41. Then on all sides . . . was completed: The abrupt and loud speaking of the Gloria, and the fright it instills, are explicitly associated with the angels at the Nativity (Luke 2.8-14), and Virgil's "Fear not" echoes theirs, as well as that of the angel at the tomb (Matt. 28.5). But as any medieval Christian would have known, the primary reference is to Easter midnight mass, when, for the first time since the beginning of Lent, the Gloria was sung, and every bell of every church rang loudly until it was completed (see Tucker 1960). Cf. 9. 46 and 21.78, with notes.

145-51. No ignorance . . . timid and thoughtful: The pilgrim's fear and suspense is modelled on that of the shepherds at the Nativity and that of the disciples at the Resurrection (see John 20.1-10; Luke 24.1-12; cf. 21.7-9, with notes).

Inter cantica. The avaricious in Purgatory are parallel with the simoniac popes in *Inf.* 19; simony was known to contemporaries of Dante as a "daughter of avarice" (*filia avaritiae*). Note how the hooves [literally, kicks] striking Heliodorus (113) echo the kicking popes at *Inf.* 19.105, 120; the reference to the book of Maccabees at *Inf.* 19.85-87 also prepares the example of Heliodorus and the reference to the Templars, known in the Middle Ages as "New Maccabees" (Bernard of Clairvaux 1983). In a more general sense, Hugh's account of the acts of Philip the Fair, especially the treatment of Boniface, echoes and complements the denunciation of the popes in *Inferno* 19, including the foreseen arrival of Boniface. Boniface's passion itself emerges from *Inf.* 19.82-87, for Dante thought of the relations of Philip the Fair and the Gascon Pope Clement V as analogous to the alliance of Pharisees and Pilate that compassed the condemnation of Christ (see Matth. 26-27).

The prostrate avaracious, as we saw in *Purg.* 19.94 and 97 ("your backs turned upward . . . Heaven turns our backs toward itself") and 130 ("turned you down so"), echo the twisted soothsayers in *Inferno* 20.11-12 (*travolto* [twisted]), 17 (*si travolse* [has contorted]) and 23 (*sì torta* [so twisted]). The distortions draw the pilgrim's tears in Hell (20.23), but the soothsayers themselves also weep, soaking the ground (20.6, "which was bathed with anguished weeping") as they proceed at the pace of a litany "silent and shedding tears" (20.8-9); so are the avaricious in Purgatory heard "piteously weeping and lamenting" (20.6-7, 20.18). *Inf.* 20.8-11 shares a set of rhymes (*basso, passo*) with *Purg.* 20.115-21, based on the idea of variably paced utterance; the wayfarers, too, move at a solemn pace (*Purg.* 20.16, "with careful, slow steps").

The "dead bones" of Manto on which the city of Mantua is built (*Inf.* 20.91) are recalled in the "consecrated bones" of the Capetians (*Purg.* 20.60); the expressions make clear the demystifying thrust of both discourses.

CANTO 21

La sete natural che mai non sazia,   1
se non con l'acqua onde la femminetta
samaritana domandò la grazia,

    mi travagliava, e pungeami la fretta   4
per la 'mpacciata via dietro al mio duca,
e condoleami a la giusta vendetta.

    Ed ecco, sì come ne scrive Luca   7
che Cristo apparve a' due ch'erano in via,
già surto fuor de la sepulcral buca,

    ci apparve un'ombra, e dietro a noi venìa   10
dal piè guardando la turba che giace,
né ci addemmo di lei, sì parlò pria,

    dicendo: "O frati miei, Dio vi dea pace."   13
Noi ci volgemmo sùbiti, e Virgilio
rendéli 'l cenno ch'a ciò si conface;

    poi cominciò: "Nel beato concilio   16
ti ponga in pace la verace corte,
che me rilega ne l'etterno essilio."

    "Come?" diss' elli, e parte andavam forte: 19
"Se voi siete ombre che Dio sù non degni,
chi v'ha per la sua scala tanto scorte?"

    E 'l dottor mio: "Se tu riguardi a' segni   22
che questi porta e che l'angel profila,
ben vedrai che coi buon convien ch'e' regni.

    Ma perché lei che dì e notte fila   25
non li avea tratta ancora la conocchia
che Cloto impone a ciascuno e compila,

    l'anima sua, ch'è tua e mia serocchia,   28
venendo sù non potea venir sola,
però ch'al nostro modo non adocchia.

CANTO 21

Fifth terrace, continued: Statius—explanation of the earthquake—
Statius identified—his love of Virgil—Virgil identified by the pilgrim

1   The natural thirst that is never sated, except by
the water of which the poor Samaritan woman
begged the gift,

4   travailed me, and haste spurred me along the
obstructed way behind my master, and I grieved in
sympathy for the just vengeance.

7   And behold, just as Luke writes for us that
Christ appeared to the two who were on the way,
when he was just risen from the hollow tomb,

10   a shade appeared to us, coming behind us, and
we were avoiding the crowd lying at our feet,
unaware of the shade until it spoke,

13   saying: "O my brothers, God give you peace."
We turned quickly, and Virgil answered him with
the appropriate sign;

16   then he began: "May the true court soon give
you peace in the blessed council, though it binds
me to eternal exile."

19   "What?" he said, while we were still hurrying
on: "If you are shades that God does not permit
above, who has guided you so far along his
stairway?"

22   And my teacher: "If you look at the signs this
man bears, outlined by the angel, you will see
clearly that he must reign with the good.

25   But because she who spins day and night had
not yet drawn off the skein that Clotho assigns and
gathers for each,

28   his soul, which is your sister and mine, in
coming up could not come alone, since it does not
see in our manner.

Ond' io fui tratto fuor de l'ampia gola   31
d'inferno per mostrarli, e mosterrolli
oltre, quanto 'l potrà menar mia scola.

Ma dimmi, se tu sai, perché tai crolli   34
diè dianzi 'l monte, e perché tutto ad una
parve gridare infino a' suoi piè molli."

Sì mi diè, dimandando, per la cruna   37
del mio disio, che pur con la speranza
si fece la mia sete men digiuna.

Quei cominciò: "Cosa non è che sanza   40
ordine senta la religïone
de la montagna, o che sia fuor d'usanza.

Libero è qui da ogne alterazione: 43
di quel che 'l ciel da sé in sé riceve
esser ci puote, e non d'altro, cagione.

Per che non pioggia, non grando, non neve,   46
non rugiada, non brina più sù cade
che la scaletta di tre gradi breve;

nuvole spesse non paion né rade,   49
né coruscar, né figlia di Taumante,
che di là cangia sovente contrade;

secco vapor non surge più avante   52
ch'al sommo d'i tre gradi ch'io parlai,
dov' ha 'l vicario di Pietro le piante.

Trema forse più giù poco o assai,   55
ma per vento che 'n terra si nasconda,
non so come, qua sù non tremò mai.

Tremaci quando alcuna anima monda   58
sentesi, sì che surga o che si mova
per salir sù, e tal grido seconda.

De la mondizia sol voler fa prova   61
che, tutto libero a mutar convento,
l'alma sorprende, e di voler le giova.

Prima vuol ben, ma non lascia il talento   64
che divina giustizia, contra voglia,
come fu al peccar, pone al tormento.

E io, che son giaciuto a questa doglia   67
cinquecent' anni e più, pur mo sentii
libera volontà di miglior soglia:

31   Therefore was I drawn forth from the wide throat of Hell to show him, and I will show him further, as far as my schooling can lead him.

34   But tell me, if you know, why the mountain shook so just now, and why all of it, down to its wet foot, seemed to shout all together."

37   With his question he so threaded the needle of my desire that the very hope made my thirst seem less acute.

40   He began: "Nothing that the rule of this mountain allows can be without order or beyond custom.

43   This place is free from any alteration: only what Heaven receives into itself by itself can be caused here, nothing else.

46   For this reason no rain, no hail, no snow, no dew, no frost falls any higher than the little stairway with but three steps;

49   clouds do not appear, whether dense or thin, nor lightning, nor the daughter of Thaumas, who often changes neighborhoods down there;

52   dry vapor does not rise above the highest of the three steps I mentioned, where Peter's vicar sets his feet.

55   Lower down, there may be tremors great or little, but up here wind hidden in the earth has never shaken it, I know not why.

58   Here the mountain trembles when some soul feels itself cleansed, so that it rises up or starts to climb, and that cry seconds it.

61   We know that we are cleansed when the will itself surprises the soul with the freedom to change convents, and the soul rejoices to will it.

64   Earlier it wishes to rise, certainly, but is not permitted by the yearning that God's justice puts to the torture, against the will, to the degree that it wished to sin.

67   And I, who have lain in this sorrow five hundred years and more, only now felt the free will of a better threshold:

però sentisti il tremoto e li pii   70
spiriti per lo monte render lode
a quel Segnor che tosto sù li ’nvii.”

  Così ne disse; e però ch’el si gode   73
tanto del ber quant’ è grande la sete,
non saprei dir quant’ el mi fece prode.

  E ’l savio duca: “Omai veggio la rete   76
che qui vi ’mpiglia e come si scalappia,
perché ci trema, e di che congaudete.

  Ora chi fosti piacciati ch’io sappia,   79
e perché tanti secoli giaciuto
qui se’, ne le parole tue mi cappia.”

  “Nel tempo che ’l buon Tito, con l’aiuto   82
del sommo Rege, vendicò le fóra
ond’ uscì ’l sangue per Giuda venduto,

  col nome che più dura e più onora   85
ero io di là,” rispuose quello spirto,
“famoso assai, ma non con fede ancora.

  Tanto fu dolce mio vocale spirto   88
che tolosano a sé mi trasse Roma,
dove mertai le tempie ornar di mirto.

  Stazio la gente ancor di là mi noma;   91
cantai di Tebe e poi del grande Achille,
ma caddi in via con la seconda soma.

  Al mio ardor fuor seme le faville,   94
che mi scaldar, de la divina fiamma
onde sono allumati più di mille:

  de l’Eneïda, dico, la qual mamma   97
fummi e fummi nutrice poetando:
sanz’ essa non fermai peso di dramma.

  E per esser vivuto di là quando   100
visse Virgilio, assentirei un sole
più che non deggio al mio uscir di bando.”

  Volser Virgilio a me queste parole   103
che viso che, tacendo, disse “Taci”;
ma non può tutto la virtù che vuole,

  ché riso e pianto son tanto seguaci   106
a la passion di che ciascun si spicca,
che men seguon voler ne’ più veraci.

70   therefore you felt the earthquake and heard the devoted spirits on the mountain returning praise to the Lord, may he soon send them upward."

73   So he spoke to us; and because one rejoices in drinking to the measure of one's thirst, I could not express how it profited me.

76   And my wise leader: "Now I see the net that entangles you here and how one gets free of it, why the mountain shakes, and in what you all rejoice together.

79   Now let it please you to tell me who you were, and let your words include why you have lain here so many centuries."

82   "At the time when the good Titus, with the help of the highest King, avenged the wounds whence the blood that Judas sold came forth,

85   with the name that lasts longest and gives most honor," replied that spirit, "I was very famous back there, but not yet with faith.

88   So sweet was my vocal spirit, that Rome drew me from Toulouse, and in Rome I became worthy to adorn my temples with myrtle.

91   Statius people back there call me still: I sang of Thebes and then of the great Achilles, but I fell along the way while carrying the second burden.

94   The seeds to my ardor were the sparks from which I took fire, of the divine flame that has kindled more than a thousand:

97   of the *Aeneid*, I mean, which was my mama and was my nurse in writing poetry: without it I did not make up a dram of weight.

100   And to have lived back there while Virgil was alive, I would agree to a sun more than I owe for my release from exile."

103   These words turned Virgil toward me with a look that silently said: "Be silent"; but the power of will cannot do everything,

106   for laughter and weeping follow so closely on the passion from which each springs, that they follow the will least in those who are most truthful.

Io pur sorrisi come l'uom ch'ammicca;   109
per che l'ombra si tacque e riguardommi
ne li occhi, ove 'l sembiante più si ficca,

   e: "Se tanto labore in bene assommi,"   112
disse, "perché la tua faccia testeso
un lampeggiar di riso dimostrommi?"

   Or son io d'una parte e d'altra preso: 115
l'una mi fa tacer, l'altra scongiura
ch'io dica; ond' io sospiro, e sono inteso

   dal mio maestro, e: "Non aver paura,"   118
mi dice, "di parlar, ma parla e digli
quel ch'e' dimanda con cotanta cura."

   Ond' io: "Forse che tu ti maravigli,   121
antico spirto, del rider ch'io fei;
ma più d'ammirazion vo' che ti pigli.

   Questi che guida in alto li occhi miei   124
è quel Virgilio dal qual tu togliesti
forte a cantar de li uomini e d'i dèi.

   Se cagion altra al mio rider credesti,   127
lasciala per non vera, ed esser credi
quelle parole che di lui dicesti."

   Già s'inchinava ad abbracciar li piedi   130
al mio dottor, ma el li disse: "Frate,
non far, ché tu se' ombra e ombra vedi."

   Ed ei, surgendo: "Or puoi la quantitate   133
comprender de l'amor ch'a te mi scalda,
quand' io dismento nostra vanitate,

   trattando l'ombre come cosa salda."   136

109   I but smiled, like one who gives a hint; therefore the shade fell silent and gazed into my eyes, where the expression is most visible.

112   and: "So may all your labor turn to good," he said, "why did your face just now show me a flash of laughter?"

115   Now am I caught on one side and the other: one makes me be still, the other conjures me to speak; hence I sigh, and I am understood

118   by my master, and: "Do not be afraid," he says, "to speak; but speak, and tell him what he asks with so much eagerness."

121   And I: "Perhaps you marvel, ancient spirit, at my having smiled; but I wish more wonderment to seize you.

124   This one who guides my steps to the heights is that Virgil from whom you took the strength to sing of men and gods.

127   If you believed that some other cause made me smile, dismiss it as untrue, and believe that it was those words you spoke about him."

130   Already he was bending to embrace my teacher's feet, but he told him: "Brother, do not, for you are a shade, and a shade is what you see."

133   And he, rising: "Now you can grasp the greatness of the love that burns in me toward you, when I forget our emptiness,

136   treating shades like solid things."

NOTES

1-75. The natural thirst . . . it profited me: The first half of the canto goes to resolve the suspense created by the earthquake and Gloria at the end of the previous canto, with the unexpected appearance of the Roman poet Statius, who explains them, to the pilgrim's great satisfaction, after the presence of the pilgrim has been explained.

1-6. The natural thirst . . . the just vengeance: The complex state of mind of the pilgrim, "travailed" by curiosity (he labors to grasp the meaning of the earthquake), spurred by haste to move forward, and grieving for the sufferings of the penitents. See the note to lines 73-75.

1-3. The natural thirst . . . begged the gift: "All men by nature desire to know" (Aristotle, *Metaphysics* 1.1), perhaps the philosopher's most famous dictum, is quoted by Dante as the opening of his *Convivio*. To what extent the philosophical enterprise of that work, which Dante identified as offering to laymen "the bread of the angels" (*Conv.* 1.1.7) overlaps the Christian idea of Wisdom as the second Person of the Trinity or is abandoned in the *Comedy*, has been hotly debated (see Additional Note 2, Nardi 1944, Scott 1990, 1995). In any event it is clear that in this passage Dante identifies the the natural desire to know as always including the desire for God; see 17.129-30, with notes. The metaphor of thirst is part of the gradual substitution of physical desire by spiritual desire in the upper reaches of Purgatory (see the notes on 18.58-59, 20.105, 117; 21.74; 22.6, 40, 67, 141-53; 23.27, 35, 86; 24.23-24, 28, 122-24; 25.39; 26.18).

2-3. the water . . . begged the gift: At a well in Samaria, Jesus asks a woman to give him to drink; she is surprised that a Judean should make the request of a despised Samaritan, and he replies contrasting her well-water with what he offers, which she then begs for: "the water I will give . . . shall become . . . a fountain of water, springing up into life everlasting" (John 4.5-15). In medieval exegesis, the incident is interpreted as the offering of salvation to the Gentiles in response to their desire for God (implications relevant to Statius, a Gentile convert).

7-15. And behold . . . the appropriate sign: This passage is the only instance in the *Purgatorio* of explicit comparison of a shade with the risen Christ (but see 1.31-39 and 88-90, with notes). Luke 24 relates that two disciples (by tradition, one was Luke) discuss the events of the Passion while walking to Emmaus: "And it came to pass, that while they talked and reasoned with themselves, Jesus himself also drawing near, went with them. But their eyes were held, that they should not know him" (verses 15-16). (See the notes to 8.43-60, which also draws on the passage.) Statius's greeting (line 13) draws on the events after the two return to Jerusalem (verses 35-36): "And they told what things were done in the way; and how they knew him in the breaking of bread. Now whilst they were speaking these things, Jesus stood in the midst of them, and saith to them: Peace be to you; it is I, fear not."

Pairing the consecutive scenes was common in medieval painting (e.g., Agostino di Duccio, on the reverse of the Siena *Maestà*).

Statius is said to appear before the travelers notice him; Luiselli in Zennaro 1981 pointed out that this departure from Dante's usual narrative point of view follows the wording of stage directions for miracle plays about the episode, in which Christ appears *behind* the disciples, dressed as a pilgrim (see Young 1933). Like the disciples, the travelers do not at first recognize Statius as *figura Christi*, but it now becomes apparent that although the earthquake was accompanied by explicit references to the Nativity (see the notes to 20.133-41 and lines 56-72), the governing parallel is with the Resurrection (as in Rom. 6.3-4).

14-15. Virgil answered him with the appropriate sign: Virgil's first response is a silent gesture (see next note), perhaps a bow or an inclination of the head.

16-18. then he began ... eternal exile: "He began" indicates that this is Virgil's first utterance to Statius, echoing his words by wishing him peace in Heaven ("the blessed council"), though he himself is barred from it (his striking last phrase echoes *Inf.* 23.126). This is the strongest expression of the pathos of Virgil's situation since 3.34-45 (though not the longest, cf. 7.7-33).

19-21. What? ... along his stairway: Statius' question echoes Cato's (1.40-48); Statius' rising from his penance (compared with the "hollow tomb," line 9) is a figural fulfillment of the wayfarers' emergence from the "eternal prison" (1.41); see our Introduction, pp. 14-16. For the stairway as a governing metaphor of the poem as a whole, see the Introduction to the *Inferno* volume, pp. 18-20.

22-24. look at the signs ... reign with the good: Virgil refers Statius to the three remaining *P*s on the pilgrim's brow (cf. the note to 3.110-12). For line 24, cf. 2 Tim. 2.11-12: "for if we be dead with him, we shall live also with him. If we suffer, we shall also reign with him."

25-27. she who spins ... assigns and gathers: A reference to the three Fates (Clotho allots the flax, Lachesis spins it, and Atropos, "the unbending," cuts it): the pilgrim is not yet dead. Paratore 1976 observes that this reference involves allusion to Statius, for in their epics neither Vergil, Ovid, nor Lucan names any of the Fates, whereas the *Thebaid* repeatedly names all three.

28-30. your sister and mine ... in our manner: The Italian for "soul" [*anima*] is feminine in gender; thus the souls of the three poets are three sisters (as are the Fates).

31-33. from the wide throat ... can lead him: Limbo is like the throat leading to the abyss of Hell (see *Inferno* Additional Note 2). Dante's *scola* [school] can also mean "little boat" (see 31.96, *Par.* 2.1-6, with notes), though the metaphor is unsupported by any other detail here.

34-78. But tell me . . . rejoice together: The principal focus of the canto is now reached (Statius himself), and the first of Virgil's questions, which propel the narrative through Canto 22, at last leads to the explanation of the earthquake. That Virgil's first question, asked before anything is known of this shade, concerns the earthquake expresses the strength of the impression it has made on the travelers.

40-72. He began: Nothing . . . send them upward: Statius's explanation first excludes any natural cause of the earthquake (lines 40-57) and assigns the true one, the freeing of a soul from penance (lines 58-60), commenting on the soul's coming to awareness of its freedom (lines 61-66); he then reveals that his freeing is the culmination of a very long process, at which all rejoiced (lines 67-72).

40-45. Nothing that the rule . . . nothing else: Statius begins with the general rule: Purgatory proper is governed by principles that exclude chance, irregularity, and "alteration" (the cycle of exchange of the elements), all operative only below. The meaning of lines 43-44 is disputed; some take "ciel" to refer to the physical heavens; this seems obviously wrong, for what is spontaneously (*da sé*) received from the mountain can only be liberated souls, not radiated light.

46-57. For this reason no rain . . . I know not why: The "alterations" from which the mountain is free above the gate of Purgatory (lines 48, 53-54) result from vapors drawn from the earth by sunlight: humid vapors produce winds, rain, hail, snow, dew, frost, cloud, and, when there are conflicting vapors within them, lightning (cf. *Inf.* 24.145-50, *Purg.* 5.109-14; the "daughter of Thaumas" is Iris, the rainbow); dry vapors, too, cause winds; subterranean winds were thought to be the cause of earthquakes (see *Inf.* 3.130-36).

58-72. Here the mountain . . . them upward: The general rule: the mountain trembles when a soul completes its purgation (cf. the earthquake at the Crucifixion, *Inf.* 12.27-45, with notes); for the idea of the universe in birthpangs, see Rom. 8.22: "omnis creatura ingemiscit et parturit usque adhuc" [all creation cries out and labors to give birth until now: our translation], an idea Dante connected with *Ecl.* 4.48-52 (see 22.76-78, with note). For the connection of Statius' explanation of the earthquake with *Inferno* 12, see *Inter cantica* to Canto 22.

61-66. We know . . . wished to sin: The soul is held to its penance as long as it retains the "yearning" ([*talento*], a weight: see the note to *Inf.* 5.39) that "wished to sin," the vice or inclination that divides the will against itself and must be purged (God's justice puts it to the torture according to its strength). There comes a moment, then, when the soul realizes that it is entirely free of its earlier yearning: the will is entirely whole, and by that very fact, in Dante's thinking, it has completed "satisfaction" (see our Introduction, pp. 9-10). For the problem of the two wills, see Rom. 7.15-25; Augustine's reliving of it is related in *Confessions* 8.8-12.

67-72. And I . . . send them upward: The application of the general observations to Statius himself, their latest instance. His purgation has taken a very long time indeed, since as we soon learn, he died ca. A.D. 96, some 1200 years earlier, of which "five hundred years and more" have been passed on the terrace of avarice/prodigality, four hundred on that of sloth (22.92-93); well may we think of 10.106-11!

70-72. heard the devoted . . . send them upward: All call out at Statius's rising because members of one body; see 1 Cor. 12.26: "And if one member suffer any thing, all the members suffer with it; or if one member glory, all the members rejoice together [*congaudent*] with it"; also Matt. 5.12, where the Beatitudes conclude with a call to exultation: "Be glad and rejoice, for your reward is very great in heaven." The Gloria (see the note to 20.123-41) is of course a long hymn of praise.

73-75. because one rejoices . . . it profited me: The pilgrim's thirst (21.1-3) is finally sated. Note the parallel phrasing for the pilgrim's feelings ("si gode" [one rejoices], line 73) and the penitent souls' ("congaudete" [you rejoice together], line 78), as well as for the correlation of intensity with desire (lines 66 and 74).

76-136. And my wise leader . . . like solid things: Virgil's second question (see the note to lines 34-75) is partly motivated by Statius's mention of his five hundred years of penance on this terrace (line 68). The second half of the canto, with Statius' identification of himself, including his status as a recognized poet during his lifetime, his works, his death, and his tribute to Virgil as the prime influence on his development, constitutes the first panel, so to speak, of his autobiography; his overcoming of his most serious vice and his conversion to Christianity (alluded to in line 82) will be the subject of Canto 22. This is the longest account of itself given by any shade in the entire *Comedy*.

The historical Statius (ca. 45-ca. 96) was from Naples, not Toulouse (Statius' *Silvae*, a collection of shorter poems, several of which mention his birthplace, was known to very few in the Middle Ages, but these did include Lovato dei Lovati and presumably others in Mussato's circle at Padua); the medieval life confuses him, following Jerome, with a Statius Ursulus (or Surculus) of Toulouse.

82-86. At the time . . . famous back there: Statius associates his entire poetic career with the rebellion of Judaea and the siege and destruction of Jerusalem by the Romans under Titus (A.D. 70), a major preoccupation of Dante's, soon to be an important focus (*Purg.* 23.28-30; see also *Inf.* 23.115-26, 27.87-90, with notes). Like most medieval Christians, in the wake of Jerome and Orosius, Dante regarded it as God's punishment of the Jews for the killing of Jesus, with the added complication that his theory of the Romans as a second chosen people led him to see it as one of the crowning glories of the Empire (*Par.* 6.82-93, 7.36-51).

82. the good Titus: The adjective refers specifically to Titus' function in carrying out God's will (*Par.* 6.89-90).

83-84. the wounds . . . that Judas sold: Judas betrayed Jesus for thirty pieces of silver (Matt. 27.5), a reminder that is appropriate to the terrace of avarice. For Judas, see the notes to *Inf.* 13.107, 33.124-33, 34.28-67, and *Purg.* 20.70-78, with notes. Christ's wounds save all humanity: for the phrasing "le fóra / ond' uscì 'l sangue" [the openings whence came forth the blood], compare *Inf.* 26.59: "la porta / ond' uscì de' Romani il gentil sangue" [the gate whence came forth the noble blood of the Romans], another passage involving Statius (see the notes on *Inf.* 26.58-60, 61-62). The parallel links Empire and Church (see the notes to 10.34-93).

85-90. with the name . . . temples with myrtle: The "name" is that of poet, of course; that it brings immortality and honor is the classical topos: Horace, *Odes* 3.30; *Geor.* 2.490-92; *Met.* 15.871-79; *Phars.* 9.983-86, the last of which Statius himself echoed in *Theb.* 12.810-19: "Will you *endure* [*durabisne*] and be read, surviving your author, O my Thebaid, my vigil of twice six years? . . . deserved *honors* will be paid after my death"; italics indicate the words quoted from Lucan, which Dante echoes in line 85 (he echoes the passage again in *Par.* 25.3).
    Statius was in fact quite successful (*Theb.* 12.812-15), as Juvenal also relates, in a passage that seems to have given Dante the idea that Statius was a prodigal (7.82-87):

> They run to hear his pleasant voice and their favorite poem
> the *Thebaid*, when Statius has cheered the whole town
> and set the day, he so captured their minds
> with sweetness [*tanta dulcdeine*], and the mob hears him
> with so much pleasure; yet though his verse brings down the house,
> he would have starved, except he sold his virgin *Agave* to a mime.

(*Agave* seems to have been a tragedy on the death of Pentheus, now lost.)

88. So sweet was my vocal spirit: This line seems to echo Juvenal's "tanta dulcedine" [so much sweetness], perhaps also his line 82. "Vocale spirto" [vocal spirit] should no doubt be taken in two senses: 1) Statius's speaking voice (his "sounding breath"); 2) his poetic inspiration. Dante calls Statius "dolce poeta" [sweet poet] in *Conv.* 4.25.6.

90. I became worthy . . . temples with myrtle: The *Silvae* mention a crowning with myrtle (usually associated with love poetry; the myrtle was sacred to Venus), but the sources Dante knew mention only the crowning with laurel. Aside from the pun on *meritai* [I merited], Dante is in all probability reserving the laurel crown for himself (*Par.* 1.22-33 and 25.1-12) and thinks of it as unassigned (but Mussato took it in 1315, followed by Petrarch in 1348).

91-93. Statius people . . . second burden: Statius's outline of his career peaks with his name and list of works (*Thebaid* and *Achilleid*). "Great Achilles" echoes *Achill.* 1.1-3: "Magananimum Aeaciden . . . diva, refer" [Tell, goddess, of the great-souled son of Aeacus], and in "second burden" Dante may be echoing Statius's claim of a second crown from Apollo (*Achill.* 1.9-10: "Phoebus . . weave a second garland [*fronde secunda*] for my locks"). Dante agrees with modern opinion in asserting that the *Achilleid* was left unfinished (a question debated in his time; 1167 verses survive). A poetic task as a burden, possibly too great a one, derives from Horace, *Ars poetica* 8-40; and for falling under the burden, *DVE* 2.4.4 (adapting Horace); cf. 16.127-29.

91. Statius people . . . call me still: Verrall 1906 identified the play on Statius's name as a descriptive adjective derived from Lat. *status* [a staying or delay]: *statius* [delayer]; thus his very name derives from his delays: see the notes to 22.90-93. According to the medieval life (following Jerome), Statius's other name was Surculus [twig for grafting], which Dante may have found significant in view of saint Paul's use of a grafting metaphor to refer to the Gentiles, who, he says, when the Jews rejected the Gospel, are "grafted" [*inserti*] on to the "root" of the olive tree (Romans 11); the passage is noteworthy in predicting the eventual salvation of Israel.

94-102. The seeds . . . release from exile: Statius's tribute to Virgil is based, again, on the conclusion of the *Thebaid* (12.810-19), addressing the poem, especially: "Live, I beg; nor strive with the divine *Aeneid*, but follow from afar and always adore its footprints" (lines 816-17, a passage imitated also by Chaucer, *Troilus and Criseyde* 5.1786-92). See Martinez 1995 and the note on lines 130-36. Note the parallels with the pilgrim's tribute to Virgil on first meeting him (*Inf.* 1.79-87).

94-97. The seeds . . . of the *Aeneid*: That sparks are the seeds of fire is Lucretian/Vergilian (*Aen.* 6.6), like the idea of the soul as essentially fire (*Aen.* 6.730-32) and the metaphor of spreading fire for the contagion of excitement (especially in war: *Aen.* 2.469-78); see Dante's use of it for the contagion of envy in *Inf.* 13.64-69. The *ardor* [burning] of Statius's love for Virgil will be recalled in *Par.* 1.34 ("poca favilla gran fiamma seconda" [a small spark is followed by a great flame]), expressing Dante's hopes for his own influence. These instances of the fire metaphor are versions *in bono* of the negative *ardor* (*Inf.* 26.97) of Ulysses, clearly associated by Dante with the metaphor of the tongue as a flame (James 3.5). See the note to *Inf.* 26.34-142 and to *Purg.* 22.10-12, 67-69.

96. more than a thousand: Note the close parallel with *Inf.* 5.67-68. "More than a thousand" in both cases indicates an indefinitely large number.

97-99. my mama . . . dram of weight: Statius attributes all his poetic achievements to Virgil's influence: cf. *Inf.* 1.85-87. From the elevated language of Statius's

speech so far, the change to the intimacy and colloquialism of these lines is strik-
ing, especially the term *mamma* (cf. 30.44-48, with the same rhyme-words), quite
foreign to the passage commonly cited, *De civ. Dei* 18.9 (of Athens): "mater et
nutrix liberalium artium" [mother and nurse of the liberal arts], a distant rela-
tive of our expression *alma mater*. As *mamma,* the *Aeneid* gave birth to Statius's
poetry; as nurse, it suckled it (cf. 22.102, of the Muses and Homer).

99. without it . . . dram of weight: The line refers, of course, to the worth of
Statius's poetry. Most commentators interpret *fermai* [I stopped, fixed] as mean-
ing "I wrote": Mattalia writes: "The metaphor is probably that of a balance, whose
arms 'stop' when the weights correspond. Statius did not write down a single
word or phrase that had not first been carefully weighed against the Vergilian
model." A dram was the eighth part of an ounce, the traditional minimum quan-
tity of apothecaries and gold merchants.

100-102. And to have lived . . . release from exile: "Sole" [sun] is ambiguous,
but it must mean "year" rather than "day" here, otherwise Statius' offer would
be rather paltry: considering how long he has been in Purgatory, one day would
not add much.

102. release from exile: "Exile" here translates *bando* [ban], a decree of exclu-
sion; earlier, Virgil used the term *esilio* [exile] (line 18).

103-36. These words . . . like solid things: One of the most delicious mo-
ments in the poem. It is worth considering why it is that Virgil wishes to prevent
the pilgrim from identifying him and why he then discourages Statius from
embracing him; he had no such hesitations when meeting and embracing
Sordello (7.4-15).

105-108. but the power . . . are most truthful: The most truthful are those
least practised in hiding their spontaneous reactions (good examples, in the bolgia
of the hypocrites: *Inf.* 23.85-90, 142, etc.). Laughter and weeping are singled out
also in 16.87 and 25.103-105.

107. each springs: "Si spicca" [usually, "stands out"] is difficult to interpret
here. Bosco/Reggio and Chiavacci Leonardi take it to mean "wells forth," thus
tacitly treating it as a catachresis, meaning *spiccia* [pours forth], as in 9.102. This
seems close to Dante's meaning.

109-20. I but smiled . . . so much eagerness: After silent words and laughter
and weeping (lines 103-104, 106), we have smiling, perhaps winking, and sigh-
ing; finally speech relieves the tension.

110-11. gazed into my eyes . . . most visible: See *Conv.* 3.8.9: "Which two
places [eyes and mouth] by a comely simile may be called the balconies of the

lady who lives in the edifice of the body, that is, the soul, because here, although somewhat veiled, she often reveals herself."

114. a flash of laughter: see *Conv.* 3.8.11: "And what is laughter but a flashing [*corruscazione*] of the soul, that is, a light appearing externally as it is within."

121-23. Perhaps you marvel . . . more wonderment: The episode has been a series of marvels and surprises, what the Middle Ages called *mirabilia*, after the marvels (associated especially with Rome and the Holy Land) described in medieval travel literature; see Marco Polo, *Milione*, Chapter 1 (cf. 25.106-108, with notes).

124-26. This one . . . men and gods: The pilgrim's careful phrasing connects his identification of Virgil with Virgil's explanation of his presence on the mountain (lines 22-33) and Statius's tribute (especially lines 92-97), thus providing a partial recapitulation of the canto.

125. is that Virgil from whom: Note the parallel of the phrasing with the pilgrim's expression of amazement in *Inf.* 1.79-80 ("Or se' tu quel Virgilio . . .").

127-29. If you believed . . . spoke about him: The mention of possible misunderstanding on Statius's part indicates that there are other possible meanings of the pilgrim's smile and that Dante wishes the reader to consider what they might be.

130-136. Already he was bending . . . shades like solid things: See 19.133-38, regarding Pope Adrian V, who refuses to allow the pilgrim to kneel. Possibly Virgil refuses homage from a Christian who exceeds him in the order of grace but who is in any case a mere shade, *ombra*, like himself. See the note to lines 103-36; there is a distant echo of *Aen.* 2.792-94 (quoted in the note to 2.79-81). In many respects, as Benvenuto noted, the whole exchange acts out Statius' *envoi* to his *Thebaid* (see the notes to lines 85-90, 94-102).

Inter cantica. See after Canto 22.

CANTO 22

Già era l'angel dietro a noi rimaso,   1
l'angel che n'avea vòlti al sesto giro,
avendomi dal viso un colpo raso,

e quei c'hanno a giustizia lor disiro   4
detto n'avea "*beati*," e le sue voci
con "*sitiunt*," sanz' altro, ciò forniro.

E io più lieve che per l'altre foci   7
m'andava, sì che sanz' alcun labore
seguiva in sù li spiriti veloci,

quando Virgilio incominciò: "Amore,   10
acceso di virtù, sempre altro accese,
pur che la fiamma sua paresse fòre;

onde da l'ora che tra noi discese   13
nel limbo de lo 'nferno Giovenale,
che la tua affezion mi fé palese,

mia benvoglienza inverso te fu quale   16
più strinse mai di non vista persona,
sì ch'or mi parran corte queste scale.

Ma dimmi, e come amico mi perdona   19
se troppa sicurtà m'allarga il freno,
e come amico omai meco ragiona:

come poté trovar dentro al tuo seno   22
loco avarizia, tra cotanto senno
di quanto per tua cura fosti pieno?"

Queste parole Stazio mover fenno   25
un poco a riso pria; poscia rispuose:
"Ogne tuo dir d'amor m'è caro cenno.

Veramente più volte appaion cose   28
che danno a dubitar falsa matera
per le vere ragion che son nascose.

CANTO 22

The angel, erasure, Beatitude—climb—Virgil's question: how could a poet be avaricious?—Statius' account of his conversion—Sixth terrace, of gluttony: the tree and stream—examples of abstinence

1   Already the angel had remained behind us, the
       angel who had turned us toward the sixth circle,
       having erased one wound from my brow,

4   and those who have their desire bent to justice
       he had called "*beati*," and his words had filled that
       out as far as "*sitiunt*," with nothing more.

7   And I walked lighter than after the other outlets,
       so that without difficulty I followed the swift
       spirits upward,

10   when Virgil began: "Love, kindled by virtue,
       always kindles other love, as long as its flame
       appears externally;

13   so from the hour when Juvenal came down into
       the Limbo of Hell among us and revealed to me
       your feelings,

16   my affection toward you has been greater than
       any ever felt for a person not seen, so that now
       these stairways will seem short to me.

19   But tell me, and as a friend forgive me if too
       much confidence loosens my rein, and as a friend
       speak with me now:

22   how could avarice find a place within your
       breast, among all the wisdom with which your
       studies had filled you?"

25   These words moved Statius to smile a little at
       first; then he replied: "Every word of yours is a
       dear sign of love to me.

28   Truly, often things appear that give false matter
       for doubt, because the true reasons are hidden.

La tua dimanda tuo creder m'avvera   31
esser ch'i' fossi avaro in l'altra vita,
forse per quella cerchia dov' io era.

Or sappi ch'avarizia fu partita   34
troppo da me, e questa dismisura
migliaia di lunari hanno punita.

E se non fosse ch'io drizzai mia cura   37
quand' io intesi là dove tu chiame,
crucciato quasi a l'umana natura:

'Perché non reggi tu, o sacra fame   40
de l'oro, l'appetito de' mortali?'
voltando sentirei le giostre grame.

Allor m'accorsi che troppo aprir l'ali   43
potean le mani a spendere, e pente'mi
così di quel come de li altri mali.

Quanti risurgeran coi crini scemi   46
per ignoranza, che di questa pecca
toglie 'l penter vivendo e ne li stremi!

E sappie che la colpa che rimbecca   49
per dritta opposizione alcun peccato,
con esso insieme qui suo verde secca:

però, s'io son tra quella gente stato   52
che piange l'avarizia, per purgarmi,
per lo contrario suo m'è incontrato."

"Or quando tu cantasti le crude armi   55
de la doppia trestizia di Giocasta,"
disse 'l cantor de' buccolici carmi,

"per quello che Cliò teco lì tasta,   58
non par che ti facesse ancor fedele
la fede, sanza qual ben far non basta.

Se così è, qual sole o quai candele   61
ti stenebraron sì che tu drizzasti
poscia di retro al pescator le vele?"

Ed elli a lui: "Tu prima m'invïasti   64
verso Parnaso a ber ne le sue grotte,
e prima appresso Dio m'alluminasti.

Facesti come quei che va di notte,   67
che porta il lume dietro e sé non giova,
ma dopo sé fa le persone dotte,

31   Your question shows me that you believe that I was avaricious in the other life, perhaps because of that circle where I was.

34   Know then that avarice was too distant from me, and thousands of months have punished this lack of measure.

37   And had it not been that I straightened out my desires, when I understood the place where you cry out, almost angry at human nature:

40   'Why do you, O holy hunger for gold, not govern the appetite of mortals?' I would be turning about, feeling the grim jousts.

43   Then I perceived that one's hands can open their wings too much in spending, and I repented of that as of my other vices.

46   How many will rise up again with shorn locks because of ignorance, which prevents them from repenting of this sin in life and at the end!

49   And know that the guilt which butts against any sin, by direct opposition, dries its greenness here together with it:

52   therefore, if I was purging myself among those people who bewail avarice, it happened to me because of the contrary."

55   "Now when you sang of the cruel war that caused the double sadness of Jocasta," said the singer of the bucolic songs,

58   "by what Clio touches on with you there, it seems that faith, without which good works are not enough, had not yet made you faithful.

61   If that is so, what sun or what candles dispelled your darkness so that then you set your sails to follow the fisherman?"

64   And he to him: "You first sent me to Parnassus to drink from its springs, and you first lit the way for me toward God.

67   You did as one who walks at night, who carries the light behind him and does not help himself, but instructs the persons coming after,

quando dicesti: 'Secol si rinova;   70
torna giustizia e primo tempo umano,
e progenïe scende da ciel nova.'
    Per te poeta fui, per te cristiano: 73
ma perché veggi mei ciò ch'io disegno,
a colorare stenderò la mano.
    Già era 'l mondo tutto quanto pregno   76
de la vera credenza, seminata
per li messaggi de l'etterno regno,
      e la parola tua sopra toccata   79
si consonava a' nuovi predicanti,
ond' io a visitarli presi usata.
    Vennermi mi poi parendo tanto santi   82
che, quando Domizian li perseguette,
sanza mio lagrimar non fur lor pianti,
      e mentre che di là per me si stette   85
io li sovvenni, e i lor dritti costumi
fer dispregiare a me tutte altre sette.
    E pria ch'io conducessi i Greci a' fiumi   88
di Tebe poetando, ebb' io battesmo;
ma per paura chiuso cristian fu' mi,
      lungamente mostrando paganesmo;   91
e questa tepidezza il quarto cerchio
cerchiar mi fé più che 'l quarto centesmo.
    Tu dunque, che levato hai il coperchio   94
che m'ascondeva quanto bene io dico,
mentre che del salire avem soverchio
      dimmi dov' è Terrenzio nostro antico,   97
Cecilio e Plauto e Varro, se lo sai;
dimmi se son dannati, e in qual vico."
    "Costoro e Persio e io e altri assai,"   100
rispuose il duca mio, "siam con quel Greco
che le Muse lattar più ch'altri mai
      nel primo cinghio del carcere cieco;   103
spesse fïate ragioniam del monte
che sempre ha le nutrice nostre seco.
    Euripide v'è nosco e Antifonte,   106
Simonide, Agatone e altri piùe
Greci che già di lauro ornar la fronte.

70   when you said: 'The age begins anew; justice returns and the first human time, and a new offspring comes down from Heaven.'

73   Through you I became a poet, through you a Christian: but so that you may better see what I have outlined, I will reach out my hand to color it.

76   Already the whole world was pregnant with the true belief, sown by the messengers of the eternal kingdom,

79   and your word, touched on above, agreed with the new preachers, and so I took up the custom of visiting them.

82   They grew to seem so holy to me that, when Domitian persecuted them, their weeping did not lack my tears,

85   and while I remained back there I helped them, and their righteous ways made me look down on all other sects.

88   And before I led the Greeks to the rivers of Thebes in my poetry, I was baptized; but out of fear I was a secret Christian,

91   for a long time feigning paganism; and this lukewarmness had me circling the fourth circle beyond a fourth century.

94   You therefore, who raised for me the cover hiding all the good I speak of, while we still have some distance to climb

97   tell me where our ancient Terence is, Caecilius and Plautus and Varro, if you know: tell me if they are damned, and to which district."

100   "They and Persius, and I, and many others," replied my leader, "are with that Greek to whom the Muses gave more milk than ever to any other,

103   in the first circle of the blind prison; often times we speak about the mountain that forever holds our nurses.

106   Euripides is with us and Antiphon, Simonides, Agathon, and many other Greeks who once adorned their brows with laurel.

Quivi si veggion de le genti tue   109
Antigone, Deïfile e Argia,
e Ismene sì trista come fue.

   Védeisi quella che mostrò Langia;   112
èvvi la figlia di Tiresia e Teti,
e con le suore sue Deïdamia."

   Tacevansi ambedue già li poeti,   115
di novo attenti a riguardar dintorno,
liberi dal salire e da' pareti,

    e già le quattro ancelle eran del giorno   118
rimase a dietro, e la quinta era al temo,
drizzando pur in sù l'ardente corno,

    quando il mio duca: "Io credo ch'a lo stremo   121
le destre spalle volger ne convegna,
girando il monte come far solemo."

   Così l'usanza fu lì nostra insegna,   124
e prendemmo la via con men sospetto
per l'assentir di quell'anima degna.

   Elli givan dinanzi, e io soletto   127
di retro, e ascoltava i lor sermoni,
ch'a poetar mi davano intelletto.

   Ma tosto ruppe le dolci ragioni   130
un alber che trovammo in mezza strada,
con pomi a odorar soavi e buoni;

   e come abete in alto si digrada   133
di ramo in ramo, così quello in giuso,
cred' io perché persona sù non vada.

   Dal lato onde 'l cammin nostro era chiuso,   136
cadea de l'alta roccia un liquor chiaro
e si spandeva per le foglie suso.

   Li due poeti a l'alber s'appressaro,   139
e una voce per entro le fronde
gridò: "Di questo cibo avrete caro."

   Poi disse: "Più pensava Maria onde   142
fosser le nozze orrevoli e intere
ch'a la sua bocca, ch'or per voi risponde.

109   There, of your people, can be seen Antigone,
Deiphile, and Argia, and Ismene as sad as ever.

112   There she can be seen who pointed out
Langia; Teresias' daughter is there, and Thetis,
and Deidamia with her sisters."

115   Both my poets fell silent now, intent again to
look about, freed from the climb and the walls,

118   and already four of the handmaids of the day
had remained behind, and the fifth was at the
pole, still pointing its burning horn upward,

121   when my leader: "I believe that we should turn
our right sides outward, circling the mountain as
is our custom."

124   Thus habit was our banner there, and we took
our way with less uneasiness because of that
worthy soul's assent.

127   They were walking ahead, and I all by myself
behind them, listening to their talk, which
instructed me in writing poetry.

130   But soon their sweet discourse was broken by
a tree that we found in the middle of the road,
with fruit sweet and good to smell;

133   and as a fir tree tapers upward from branch to
branch, so that one did downward, I believe so
that no one should climb it.

136   From the side where our path was closed, a
clear liquid was falling from the high cliff and
spreading over the leaves.

139   The two poets drew near the tree, and a voice
from within the foliage cried: "You shall not eat
this food."

142   Then it said: "Mary thought more about how
the wedding could be made honorable and
complete than about her mouth, which now
answers for you.

E le Romane antiche per lor bere   145
contente furon d'acqua; e Danïello
dispregiò cibo e acquistò savere.

Lo secol primo quant' oro fu bello: 148
fé savorose con fame le ghiande,
e nettare con sete ogne ruscello.

Mele e locuste furon le vivande   151
che nodriro il Batista nel diserto,
per ch'elli è glorïoso e tanto grande

  quanto per lo Vangelio v'è aperto."   154

145   And the ancient Roman women were content
        with water for their drink; and Daniel scorned
        food but acquired knowledge.

148   The first age was as lovely as gold: it made
        acorns tasty with hunger, and with thirst turned
        every stream to nectar.

151   Honey and locusts were the food that
        nourished the Baptist in the wilderness; therefore
        how glorious and great he is,

154   is set forth for you by the Gospel."

NOTES

1-6. Already the angel . . . with nothing more: The concluding rite of the terrace, given considerably less prominence than previous ones (12.79-99, 118-36; 15.34-39), especially by being narrated as already completed. For *raso* [erased], cf. 12.123; both cases refer to the result rather than to the action.

4-6. and those who . . . with nothing more: From the fourth Beatitude (Matt. 5.6): "Beati qui esuriunt et sitiunt iustitiam, quoniam ipsi saturabuntur" [Blessed are they that hunger and thirst after justice, for they shall have their fill], which Dante divides between two terraces. The implication of these lines seems to be that the angel said "Beati qui sitiunt iustitiam" [Blessed are those who thirst for justice], *esuriunt* [hunger] being reserved for the next terrace (see 24.151-54); this is the commonly accepted view. The choice of *sitiunt* [thirst] for the terrace of avarice is no doubt partly determined by the example of Crassus (see the note to 20.116-17 and 21.1-6), but the emphasis continues (see lines 39, 64-66, 88-90).

10-114. when Virgil . . . Deidamia with her sisters: As in 12.118-36, 15.42-81, and 25.10-108, the climb to the next terrace is occupied with talk, in this canto (as in the previous one) between Virgil and Statius.

10-18. when Virgil began . . . short to me: Virgil begins by replying to Statius' words of love (21.100-102, 133-36) with reciprocal affection.

10-12. Love, kindled . . . appears externally: This gnomic *sententia*, which continues the fire imagery of the previous canto (see the notes to 21.94-97), also stands as a direct refutation of Francesca's "Love which pardons no one beloved from loving in return" (*Inf.* 5.103; see the note to *Inf.* 5.100-107, another passage involving fire imagery, and *Purg.* 18 IC). Virgil's proviso, "kindled by virtue," marks the difference.

13-18. so from the hour . . . short to me: Dante's pleasant fantasy has Juvenal reporting Statius' veneration to Virgil, making it sound as if his knowledge was based on personal acquaintance. A friendship between Statius and Juvenal (ca. A.D. 60–ca. 130), though chronologically conceivable, is implausible: Juvenal had an inveterate animus against Domitian (whom Statius tirelessly flattered), and the tone of his famous lines about Statius is scornful (see Duff 1951 ad loc., *pace* Paratore 1971). Paratore does adduce grounds for believing that Dante knew at least several of Juvenal's *Satires* in their entirety (rather than mere anthologized excerpts).

16-17. my affection . . . person not seen: Dante read of such love as being characteristic of virtuous friendship in Cicero's *De amicitia* 8-9. Interestingly, Virgil's belief in Juvenal's report is a kind of faith in the unseen (cf. the note to 7.34-36 and Heb. 11.1-11).

19-93. But tell me . . . a fourth century: As in Canto 21, Virgil asks two questions, the first about Statius's supposed avarice (lines 19-24), the second about his conversion to Christianity (lines 55-63); Statius attributes the two great changes in his life to Virgil's influence. That Statius's moral awakening and achievement of self-control (line 37) precede and prepare his conversion is an instance of Dante's treatment of this theme on all levels, from Rome's establishment of law as the preparation for Christ's incarnation, to the pilgrim's preparation, under Virgil's authority, for the arrival of Beatrice.

22-54. how could avarice . . . because of the contrary: Virgil's question about Statius's supposed avarice leads to the explanation that he was a prodigal: avarice and prodigality are, in both *Inferno* and *Purgatorio*, the only sins/vices explicitly treated by Dante in terms of the Aristotelian conception of vice as the departure from the mean between two extremes (however, see 25.115-20 and 26.28-46, with notes). In *Inf.* 7.37-60 Virgil explains to the pilgrim the relation of avarice and prodigality; his failure to be alert to it now is part of the affectionate humor at his expense. On the relation between study and avarice, one may recall that the avaricious in Hell were all clerics (*Inf.* 7.46-48).

25-33. These words . . . circle where I was: In a brief introduction to his explanation, Statius is careful to reassure Virgil's anxiety about being presumptuous, as well as to cushion his correction of Virgil's surmise. His smile, like his words, is affectionate (see previous note). After the grimness of Hell, smiles and laughter return in the *Purgatorio* (see 2.83, 3.112, 4.122, 12.136, etc.) and become particularly associated with the poets (21.114, 25.103, 27.44, 28.146).

28-30. Truly, often . . . reasons are hidden: See *Inf.* 3.21, with note. Statius has replaced Virgil as the explainer of obscure and difficult matters, from the earthquake (21.40-72) to the shades' airy bodies and the development of the human foetus (25.31-108); Virgil is approaching the limit of his understanding (see the note to 27.127-30).

34-54. Know then . . . because of the contrary: This passage presents an important statement on several major themes of the cantica: techniques of reading, the relation of poetry and moral instruction, poetry as a vehicle of grace.

37-45. And had it not . . . my other vices: The central point here is the importance to Statius of the intellectual realization of the nature of prodigality as a vice/sin [*mali* is literally "evils"]. The realization enables him to identify not only his prodigality but his other vices as well (lines 43-45), and it leads to the achievement of self-control (line 37), but not, it is important to note, to the eradication of such inclinations, which have required long purging. Statius's other vices are not specified (cf. the note to 21.55-90).

38-44. I understood the place . . . too much in spending: There has been much discussion of these lines; many critics have supposed that they reflect a misunderstanding of Vergil's Latin on Dante's part (that is of course unlikely on the face of it: Dante was a brilliant Latinist). In *Aen.* 3.55-58 Aeneas condemns the cupidity that led Polymnestor to murder his guest, the boy Polydorus (see *Inf.* 13.31-51, with notes; Polymnestor has been denounced in *Purg.* 20.115): "fas omne abrumpit: Polydorum obtruncat et auro / vi potitur. quid non mortalia pectora cogis, / auri sacra fames?" [he violates every sacred obligation; he murders Polydorus, by force obtains the gold. To what do you not drive human breasts, O cursed hunger for gold?] Central to Dante's idea is that Lat. *sacer* has both a negative sense ("cursed"), foregrounded in Aeneas's speech, and a positive sense ("sacred"). We are to imagine Statius meditating on Vergil's choice of the word in this passage, focussing on its double meaning, and realizing that "quid non mortalia pectora cogis, auri sacra fames?" can correctly (i.e., in terms of Latin grammar) be taken as announcing the existence of a right rule in relation to riches. This is essential to Statius's realization of the sinfulness of his prodigality, just as deserving of eternal punishment as avarice, the opposite extreme (line 42): as Aristotle showed, the knowledge of the "right rule" is essential to virtue (see next note), and Statius is to be seen as achieving continence (see our Introduction, pp. 7-9, Shoaf 1978, Martinez 1989, also Picone in *LDV*).

The two meanings of *Aen.* 3.56-57 are readings *in malo* and *in bono*, basic to the techniques of allegorical reading (see *Inferno* Additional Note 16). Statius's derivation of the path to self-mastery from a text voicing condemnation and prohibition (the Old Law of retribution) leads ultimately to his understanding of the New Law of forgiveness and grace. As in the fourth *Eclogue,* Virgil revealed more than he himself understood.

46-51. How many will rise . . . together with it: Again stressing the necessity of rational understanding, these lines are particularly focused on *Inferno* 7 (especially *Inf.* 7.27 and 29: *voltando* [turning]; 30: *tornavano* [they returned]; 35: *giostra* [joust]; 45: *colpa contraria* [contrary guilt]; 55-56: "questi resurgeranno . . . coi crin mozzi" [these will rise up with shorn locks]; 55: *cozzi* [buttings]). Note, on moral blindness, *Inf.* 7.53: *sconoscente vita* [undiscerning life]. Like *Inferno* 7, the lines also target the Florentines (cf. *Inf.* 16.73-75, 26.1-6.)

55-93. Now when you sang . . . a fourth century: Virgil's second question now leads into Statius's account of his conversion.

55-63. Now when you sang . . . follow the fisherman: Virgil observes that he (unlike Dante, it would seem) sees no evidence in the *Thebaid* of Statius being a Christian (this implies that he knows the poem). In the *Inferno* Dante uses Statius's Thebes as the chief ancient embodiment of Augustine's Earthly City, Florence and Pisa as the modern ones (see the notes to *Inf.* 26.52-54, 33.88-90; Augustine's condemnation of Rome is of course rejected by Dante). Jocasta is the mother by her son Oedipus of the twins Eteocles and Polynices, who kill each other (hence her "double sorrow," which can also include the incest with Oedipus). Near the beginning of the poem, Jupiter announces his decision to destroy Thebes because of its wickedness (1.197-302). Dante seems to have regarded the compassionate intervention of Theseus and his establishing of the altar of Mercy (Book 12) as a veiled expression of Statius's Christianity (Padoan 1959). Dante probably knew the twelfth-century allegory of the *Thebaid* (attributed in his time to Lactantius), which viewed Thebes as sinful humanity within the body (the seven gates of the city representing the seven apertures of the body, the seven assailants the seven deadly sins), eventually saved by Theseus (figuring Christ).

57. the singer of the bucolic songs: Virgil as pastoral poet, preparing the importance of the fourth *Eclogue* (see the notes to lines 64-73 and 28.34-138).

58. Clio: Clio is the Muse of history, invoked in *Theb.* 1.41-42 and 10.628-31. Dante repeatedly expresses his belief that the ancient epic poems were based on historical fact (see especially *Conv.* 4.25-26).

59-60. faith, without which good works are not enough: A doctrine firmly held by Dante (see 7.34-36), central to saint Paul's teachings: "the just are saved by faith" (see especially Romans 4). For Statius's good works, see lines 79-87.

61-63. what sun . . . follow the fisherman: "Drizzasti" means literally "erected" (and cf. line 37). The fisherman is Saint Peter: "And Jesus walking by the sea of Galilee, saw two brethren, Simon who is called Peter, and Andrew his brother, casting a net into the sea (for they were fishers). And he saith to them: Come ye after me, and I will make you to be fishers of men. And they immediately leaving their nets, followed him" (Matt. 4.18-20). The light metaphors are of course fundamental to Christian tradition (John 1.1-14). For the ship imagery, see the notes to 1.1-12 and 130-32.

64-93. And he to him . . . a fourth century: Statius's account falls into two parts, an initial summary, termed by him an "outline," emphasizing the importance of Virgil's influence (lines 64-73), and a detailed, more literal explanation (lines 74-93). This is a major statement about Virgil and contains the nucleus of Dante's view of both the historical Vergil and his own fictional character.

64-73. You first sent me . . . through you a Christian: Statius's summary or outline begins and ends with the insistence on the close relation between poetic inspiration and illuminating grace. He identifies the fourth *Eclogue* (for text and translation, see pp. 584-87) as a prophecy of the birth of Christ to which Virgil himself was blind. Statius's openness to Virgil's influence is crucial to the awakening of his interest in the Christians (lines 79-81).

64-66. You first sent me . . . for me toward God: These lines correlate the metaphors of drinking (cf. *sitiunt*, line 6, lines 100-105; 21.1-3) and light. "Springs" translates "grotte" [cliffs or caves] (cf. 1.48); Castalia was the spring associated with Parnassus.

66. you first . . . toward God: We agree with Chiavacci Leonardi's arguments against the interpretation "you after God were the first to illuminate me," sometimes put forward: Statius is taking up the metaphor underlying Virgil's question (lines 62-63), and "appresso" [after] echoes "di retro a" [after] (i.e., "following").

67-72. You did as one . . . down from Heaven: By identifying the fourth *Eclogue* as the stimulus to Statius's conversion, Dante makes it the most important prophetic insight in Virgil's works; see the notes to lines 70-72 and *Inf.* 8.82-9.42, Additional Note 14.

67-69. You did as one . . . persons coming after: The metaphor is that of a lantern or candle (see the notes to 1.43, 8.112-14) held behind the back; it seems to be derived from Augustine's denunciation of the Jews in his third sermon *De symbolo ad catechumenos,* 4: "O Jews, carrying in your hands the lantern [*lucernam*] of the Law, that you might show the way to others, while you lead yourselves into the shadows." For turning away from the light, see *Confessions* 13.3-10, Martinez 1995.

70-72. when you said . . . down from Heaven: Although only three lines of the fourth *Eclogue* are cited here, the entire poem of 63 lines is invoked (see the note to lines 76-78); noteworthy is the omission of Vergil's insistent *iam* [now, already], the key term heralding the imminent birth of the child, which appears in the eclogue nine times (most conspicuously in lines 4, 6, 7, and 10, but also in lines 27, 37, 41, 43, 48). Statius's paraphrase echoes key terms (*saeclorum ordo* [cycle of the ages], *redit* [returns], *nova progenies* [new offspring], *caelo* [Heaven]), and it glosses allusions and metaphors: "giustizia" [justice] glosses "Virgo" [the Virgin], a reference to the goddess of justice, Astraea, traditionally the last of the immortals to abandon the earth with the Iron Age (*Met.* 1.149-50); "primo tempo umano" [the first human time] glosses "Saturnia regna" [the rule of Saturn], the Golden Age (*Met.* 1.107-15). Statius' translation is closest to the original in line 72, about the birth of the child. On the implications for Dante's conception of Virgil, see Additional Note 14.

73. Through you I . . . a Christian: An emphatic restatement, in more literal and compact form, of lines 64-66.

74-93. so that you may . . . a fourth century: The more detailed account of Statius's conversion, spoken of as a filling in and coloring of a visual sketch: Virgil's arousal of his interest in the Christians, his seeking them out, his growing admiration of them and his aid to them during the persecutions, finally his secret baptism and long concealment of his Christianity.

76-81. Already the whole . . . visiting them: Statius's narrative begins at a point subsequent to his study of the fourth *Eclogue;* we are to understand that (as with *Aen* 3.28-61) he was struck by it and began meditating on it.

76-78. Already the whole . . . eternal kingdom: "Already" [*già*] is Vergil's *iam*, associated with the motif of pregnancy (as in *Ecl* 4.48-52, which invoke the idea of labor and imminent birth; see the note to 21.58-72). Statius is echoing the parable of the sower (Matt. 14.3-9, 19-23: the seed is the word of God, the soil the hearer), and Christ's metaphor of himself as the vine (John 15.1-2), the metaphor of germination became traditional for the spread of Christianity, e.g., Orosius' *Against the Pagans* 7.9.5, on "the Church of God, already [*iam*] richly germinating throughout the world," explaining the futility of Domitian's persecution.

79-80. and your word . . . the new preachers: The agreement of the Cumaean Sybil's prophecy and Vergil's fourth *Eclogue* with Christian belief struck many; Lactantius, Augustine (*City of God* 10.27), Jerome all refer to it, and the question of whether Vergil was divinely inspired was debated by the Church fathers, most concluding that his prophecy was unwitting (see the chapter in Lubac 1964); the tradition was very much alive in the twelfth and thirteenth centuries: Abelard says that the *Eclogue* "openly prophesies" Christ's birth (*PL* 178, 1031-32); Vincent of Beauvais writes of conversions directly caused by the fourth *Eclogue* (Paratore 1976). Like the blessing of the baptismal water, the traditional beginning of the Easter Vigil Mass (after the baptism of catechumens) quotes the fourth *Eclogue*: "Deus . . . conserva in *nova* familiae tuae *progenie* adoptionis spiritum quem dedisti" [God, preserve in the *new progeny* of the family of your adoption the spirit you have given] (italics added).

82-87. They grew to seem . . . all other sects: The revelation of the New Law presupposes moral rectitude (see the note to lines 19-93). In having Statius clandestinely subvert Domitian's persecution of the Christians, Dante is also mitigating the historical Statius's flattery of that emperor (see *Theb.* 1.18-34, *Achill.* 1.14-19); see next note and that on lines 13-18. His sharing the grief of the Christians (see the note to 21.70-72) and his helping them are among the traditional "works of mercy" (Matt. 25.35-40).

88-89. And before I led . . . I was baptized: The story of Statius's conversion has no basis in historical fact (various legends seem to lie behind it; on the whole question see Padoan 1959, Paratore 1976, Picone in *LDV*). There has been much discussion of when his baptism is supposed to have taken place. *Theb.* 4.670-844 relate that the Argive army on the march toward Thebes is close to dying of thirst in a drought until led by Hypsipyle (see line 112) to the one stream still flowing, Langia. In our view, the importance of the theme of thirst in these cantos makes the arrival at the Langia the most probable reference of these lines, though it has also been argued that they refer to the arrival at Thebes (Book 7), and even that Statius was baptized before beginning the poem.

90-91. but out of fear . . . feigning paganism: This is an important motif in the NT (e.g., John 19.38 has Joseph of Arimathea request Jesus's body "secretly for fear of the Jews") and the Patristic period (*Confessions* 8.2 attributes Victorinus' delay in accepting baptism to fear of his pagan patrons).

92-93. this lukewarmness . . . a fourth century: With 500 years on the terrace of avarice/prodigality and 400 on that of sloth (four is the number of the element earth and may be alluded to here as the basis of sloth in the temperament; see the note to 19.1-3), 900 of the 1200 years since Statius's death are accounted for; the other 300 are left to the reader's imagination.

94-114. You therefore . . . with her sisters: Along with *Inf.* 4.79-144, this is the most extensive catalogue of classical figures in the *Comedy*; both lists include historical personages (in *Inferno* 4 mostly political figures and philosophers, here exclusively poets) and characters of myth (here figures from Statius's poems). They are a reminder of the richness of classical civilization, both Greek and Latin, culminating in Vergil, which prepared for the advent of Christianity.

94-95. raised for me . . . good I speak of: Note the motif of concealment: Statius's love for Virgil enabled him to see beyond the integument into the core of meaning, but he knowingly concealed it in his turn ("feigning paganism," line 91).

97-98. Terence . . . Caecilius . . . Plautus . . .Varro: Roman authors known to Dante only indirectly, through Cicero, Horace, Jerome, and others. The first three are dramatists; a variant "Vario" for "Varro" may refer to a dramatist mentioned by Horace (*Ars poetica* 55) or to Varus (*Ecl.* 9.27), a friend of Vergil's and one of the editors of the *Aeneid*. Terence (184-159 B.C.) wrote six comedies, all of which survive (for Dante's knowledge of them, see the note to *Inf.* 18.133-35); only fragments remain by Caecilius (d. 169 B.C., according to Jerome); of some 100 plays by Plautus (c. 250-184 B.C.), nineteen survive entire.

100-14. They and Persius . . . with her sisters: Virgil's reply has three parts: lines 100-105, introductory, includes the four just mentioned by Statius, Persius, Virgil, and Homer; lines 106-108 name Greek poets; lines 109-14 name mythical characters that appear in the *Thebaid* and *Achilleid*.

100-105. They and Persius . . . holds our nurses: Aulus Persius Flaccus (A.D. 34-62) left one book of satires. With this addition Dante completes his catalogue of Roman poets: Horace, Ovid, and Lucan are met in *Inf.* 4.85-90, along with Homer; Cicero appears in 4.141 with Seneca (it is not clear that Dante knew of the latter's plays); Juvenal is accounted for in this canto, lines 13-15; Pacuvius is referred to indirectly in 13.32. Of important Roman poets, Dante never mentions Catullus, Lucretius, or Martial.

101-105. with that Greek . . . holds our nurses: "That Greek" is of course Homer (who in *Inf.* 4.80-81 pays Virgil a similar compliment). For inspiration as suckling by the Muse, see 21.98.

106-108. Euripides . . . Antiphon . . . Simonides . . . Agathon: Except for Simonides, these are dramatists, about whom Dante learned from Cicero and Aristotle. By Euripides (484-406 B.C.) eighteen tragedies (and fragments of 60 more) survive. By Agathon (448-402 B.C.) a friend of Euripides and Plato, a speaker in the *Symposium*, nothing survives (see *Mon.* 3.6.7). Simonides (556-467 B.C.) was a lyric poet; various poems and fragments survive (cf. *Conv.* 4.13. 8). Only fragments survive by Antiphon, a poet at the court of Dionysius I of Sicily. With Homer, Virgil names five Greek and five Roman poets.

109-14. There, of your people . . . with her sisters: Of these all but the last two figure in the *Thebaid*: Antigone and Ismene are Oedipus's daughters, saved in Book 12 by Theseus; Deiphile and Argia are two daughters of Adrastus of Argos, wives respectively of Polynices and Tydeus: "she . . . who pointed out Langia" is Hypsipyle (see the note to lines 88-89); Teresias' daughter is Manto (discussed in the notes to *Inf.* 20.52-99 and *Inferno* Additional Note 8). Many figures from the *Thebaid* are seen in Hell (see the note to *Inf.* 26.52-54). In the *Achilleid*, Thetis is Achilles' mother, Deidamia his wife (see the note to *Inf.* 26.61-62).

115-54. Both my poets . . . by the Gospel: The group now arrives on the sixth terrace, purging gluttony; they turn to the right, as usual.

118-20. already four . . . burning horn upward: The image is that of the chariot of the sun, with the steering done by the successive Hours ("handmaids of the day"): the fifth hour is in progress (it is past 10 A.M.). The pole of the wagon points upward, as it will until noon.

121-23. I believe that . . . as is our custom: "Sides" translates "spalle" [shoulders], an obvious trope. For the turn to the right, see 13.13-21.

126. that worthy soul's assent: Statius tacitly approves the turn to the right (in 21.7-12 he was of course walking in the same direction as the travelers).

127-29. They were walking . . . writing poetry: The lines are clearly allegorical: studying the relation of Statius's poetry to Vergil's (their dialogue), Dante learns to conduct his own dialogue with them (also in *Inf.* 4.97-102, but less plainly).

130-54. But soon . . . by the Gospel: The rest of the canto is taken up with the description of the first of the two trees encountered on this terrace (the other appears in 24.101-54; see notes there). As yet no shades have appeared.

130-38. But soon . . . over the leaves: The tree itself is not upsidedown, as is sometimes claimed (that would be clearly indicated); it is rooted in the middle of the terrace, tapering toward the ground rather than upward as a fir tree does. The fruit intensifies the hunger of the shades (discussed in 23.64-75). Of all the trials of Purgatory, only this one represents the attractiveness of the object of appetite (cf. 19.19-24); this is the first reference to the sense of smell since 10.61-63. For *pomi* [fruit, plural] see 27.45, 115-17; *Inf.* 16.61, with notes. Cf. 24.106-11, with note.

136-38. From the side . . . over the leaves: The freshness of the water appeals to thirst as well as hunger. "Cadea da l'alta roccia" [was falling from the high cliff] excludes the idea, sometimes advanced, that the leaves are bathed from beneath. In a sense, Eden descends to meet the souls.

140-41. and a voice . . . eat this food: This is the only instance of any pronouncement preceding the examples of the corrective virtue (13.25-36 and 14.130-39 are the only other instances of disembodied voices). The quotation, like the attractiveness of the fruit, derives from Gen. 2.15-17: "And the Lord God took man, and put him into the paradise of pleasure, to dress it and to keep it. And he commanded him, saying: Of every tree of paradise thou shalt eat: But of the tree of knowledge thou shalt not eat [*ne comedas*]"; cf. 2.9: "And the Lord God brought forth of the ground all manner of trees, fair to behold, and pleasant to eat of"; and 3.6: "And the woman saw that the tree was good to eat, and fair to the eyes, and delightful to behold." We are perhaps to meditate on the connection with the Vergilian passage (lines 40-41), in which the right rule is derived from a prohibition; in any case; the reminder of Adam's and Eve's sin is part of the system discussed in the notes to 24.106-18.

142-54. Then it said: Mary . . . by the Gospel: The voice proclaims five examples (cf. the note to lines 106-108) of temperance/abstinence, the virtue corrective of gluttony, in the sequence:the Virgin Mary, Roman history, OT, classical myth, NT. The examples suggest a range of possibilities: the Virgin: solicitude for others amid abundance; the Roman women and the myth of the Golden Age: general austerity and simplicity of life; Daniel: refusal to break Jewish dietary laws for the sake of royal favor; John the Baptist: extreme asceticism.

142-44. Mary thought . . . answers for you: The example of the Virgin Mary at the wedding at Cana (John 2.1-11), the first example also on the terrace of envy (13.28; see Additional Note 12), emphasizes her ranking concern for others over pleasure. The proper use of the mouth will be a major focus of the next cantos.

145- 54. And the ancient . . . by the Gospel: These four examples in various ways evoke the Golden Age (cf. below, on lines 148-50); three of them involve prophecy. A pun, like that in 13.109, underlies the passage: Lat. *sapere*, the root of *sapientia* [wisdom], etc., means both "to know" and "to have flavor," "to be salty."

145-46. the ancient . . . for their drink: The temperance of the ancient Roman women was proverbial; for the prohibition of wine, see Valerius Maximus 2.1.5, *ST* 2a 2ae q. 149 a. 4 (Chiavacci Leonardi); cf. Juvenal 6.1-20, 286-319.

146-47. Daniel . . . acquired knowledge: Daniel leads the Jewish children at Nebuchadnezzar's court to live on lentils and water (cf. the note to lines 142-54): "And to these children God gave knowledge, and understanding in every book, and wisdom: but to Daniel the understanding also of all visions and dreams" (Daniel 1.17): on Daniel, Nebuchadnezzar's dream, the succession of empires, and the decline of humanity, see *Inf.* 14.106-14 and *Inferno* Additional Note 3.

148-50. The first age . . . nectar: The Golden Age itself (*Met.* 1.89-150; cf. above line 71, with note, and Shoaf 1978, Martinez 1989).

151-54. Honey and locusts . . . by the Gospel: In Matt. 3.4 John eats "locusts and wild honey"; Christ says of him, "No one has arisen greater than John the Baptist" (Luke 7.28; cf. Luke 1.15, Matth. 11.11, Mark 1.15). "Set forth for you" translates "v'è aperto" [literally, is opened to you]; cf. "Knock, and it shall be opened unto you" (Matt. 7.7):

Inter cantica. How seriously Dante believed that while writing the *Thebaid* (or even earlier) the historical Statius had become a Christian, we cannot be certain; however, with Cantos 21 and 22 he made it a significant feature of the entire *Comedy*, referring with special richness to the parts of the *Inferno* that draw upon Statius (most are enumerated in the note to *Inf.* 26.52-54 and 61-62), as well as to earlier sections of the *Purgatorio*, such as 9.34-45. See the notes to *Purg.* 21.82-86, 82, 83-84, 94-97; 22.46-51, 55-63, 67-69, 70-72, 88-89, 94-114, 109-14. An important focus is the "districts" of Hell (cf. 22.99) to which Statius might have been condemned. If he had not overcome his prodigality, he says, he would have gone to the "grim jousts" of *Inferno* 7 (see the note to 22.46-51); after mastering his vices (22.37-45), if he had not become a Christian, he might have been relegated, like the other classical poets, to Limbo, to which are many references in Canto 22 (see the notes to lines 53-63, 94-114, 127-29).

The implications of Statius's poems concealing Christian meaning are farreaching. Some of the possibilities (lost on Virgil—see next paragraph) are outlined in the note to 22.55-63. The implications of *Purgatorio* 21-22 for the entire design of the *Comedy*, for Dante's conception of the evolution of Roman poetry as a preparation for Christianity, and for his own function as "disciple" (Renucci 1965) of the classical world and fulfiller of the possibilities of Christian epic poetry (see *Par.* 1.22-36, with notes), are much in need of exploration.

These cantos shed light also on Virgil's damnation; they provide the probable key to Virgil's being blocked at the gate of Dis (see the note to 22.70-72); in another closely related episode (*Inf.* 12.31-45), Virgil is unable to explain the earthquake at Christ's death except in terms that he cannot believe. Virgil's failure in *Inferno* 12 and Statius's explanation in *Purgatorio* 21 are in the same relation as Virgil's not believing the fourth *Eclogue* and Statius's conversion through it (see Additional Note 14).

CANTO 23

Mentre che li occhi per la fronda verde   1
ficcava ïo, sì come far suole
chi dietro a li uccellin sua vita perde,

lo più che padre mi dicea: "Figliuole,   4
vienne oramai, ché 'l tempo che n'è imposto
più utilmente compartir si vuole."

Io volsi 'l viso, e 'l passo non men tosto,   7
appresso i savi, che parlavan sìe
che l'andar mi faccan di nullo costo.

Ed ecco piangere e cantar s'udìe   10
"*Labïa mëa, Domine,*" per modo
tal che diletto e doglia parturìe.

"O dolce padre, che è quel ch'i' odo?"   13
comincia' io; ed elli: "Ombre che vanno
forse di lor dover solvendo il nodo."

Sì come i peregrin pensosi fanno,   16
giugnendo per cammin gente non nota,
che si volgono ad essa e non restanno:

così di retro a noi, più tosto mota,   19
venendo e trapassando ci ammirava
d'anime turba tacita e devota.

Ne li occhi era ciascuna oscura e cava,   22
palida ne la faccia e tanto scema
che da l'ossa la pelle s'informava:

non credo che così a buccia strema   25
Erisittone fosse fatto secco
per digiunar, quando più n'ebbe tema.

Io dicea fra me stesso pensando: "Ecco   28
la gente che perdé Ierusalemme,
quando Maria nel figlio diè di becco."

CANTO 23

Sixth terrace, continued: the gluttonous—Forese Donati—explanation of the souls' appearance—how has Forese come up here so soon? his explanation—denunciation of the Florentine women—the pilgrim's account of himself

1   While I was probing with my eyes through the green foliage, as one does who wastes his life after the little birds,

4   my more-than-father was saying to me: "My son, come now, for our allotted time should be more usefully distributed."

7   I turned my face, and my steps no less quickly, following after the wise poets, whose talk was such that they made my going effortless.

10   And behold, we heard weeping and singing of "*Labia mea, Domine*," in a manner that gave birth to both delight and woe.

13   "Oh sweet father, what is that I hear?" I began; and he: "Shades who perhaps go untying the knot of their debt."

16   As care-filled pilgrims do, overtaking on the road people they do not know and turning toward them, but not stopping:

19   so from behind us, walking more quickly, a crowd of silent and devout souls, overtaking us and passing on, gazed wonderingly at us.

22   Each was dark and hollow about the eyes, with faces pallid and so wasted that the skin took its shape from the bones:

25   I do not think that Erysichthon was so dried up into his outer rind by fasting, when it made him most afraid.

28   I was saying in my thoughts: "Behold the people who lost Jerusalem, when Mary put her beak into her son."

Parean l'occhiaie anella sanza gemme: 31
chi nel viso de li uomini legge *omo*
ben avria quivi conosciuta l'emme.

   Chi crederebbe che l'odor d'un pomo   34
sì governasse, generando brama,
e quel d'un'acqua, non sappiendo como?

   Già era in ammirar che sì li affama,   37
per la cagione ancor non manifesta
di lor magrezza e di lor trista squama,

   ed ecco del profondo de la testa   40
volse a me li occhi un'ombra e guardò fiso;
poi gridò forte: "Qual grazia m'è questa!"

   Mai non l'avrei riconosciuto al viso,   43
ma ne la voce sua mi fu palese
ciò che l'aspetto in sé avea conquiso.

   Questa favilla tutta mi raccese   46
mia conoscenza a la cangiata labbia,
e ravvisai la faccia di Forese.

   "Deh, non contendere a l'asciutta scabbia   49
che mi scolora," pregava, "la pelle,
né a difetto di carne ch'io abbia,

   ma dimmi il ver di te, dì chi son quelle   52
due anime che là ti fanno scorta:
non rimaner che tu non mi favelle!"

   "La faccia tua, ch'io lagrimai già morta,   55
mi dà di pianger mo non minor doglia,"
rispuos' io lui, "veggendola sì torta.

   Però mi dì, per Dio, che sì vi sfoglia: 58
non mi far dir mentr' io mi maraviglio,
ché mal può dir chi è pien d'altra voglia."

   Ed elli a me: "De l'etterno Consiglio   61
cade vertù ne l'acqua e ne la pianta
rimasa dietro, ond' io sì m'assottiglio.

   Tutta esta gente che piangendo canta,   64
per seguitar la gola oltra misura,
in fame e 'n sete qui si rifà santa.

   Di bere e di mangiar n'accende cura   67
l'odor ch'esce del pomo e de lo sprazzo
che si distende su per sua verdura.

31   Their eye-sockets seemed rings without gems; those who read *omo* on the human face would have recognized the *M* there clearly.

34   Who would believe that the odor of a fruit and of water could have such an effect, generating hunger, unless he knew how?

37   Already I was wondering what makes them hunger so, for the cause of their leanness and sad scurf was not yet manifest,

40   and behold, one shade from the depths of his head turned his eyes toward me and stared fixedly; then he cried loudly: "What grace this is for me!"

43   Never would I have recognized him by his face, but in his voice was evident to me what his appearance had ravaged in itself.

46   This spark rekindled all my recognition for his changed features, and I made out the face of Forese.

49   "Ah, do not pay attention to the dry scales that discolor my skin," he begged, "nor to my lack of flesh,

52   but tell me the truth about yourself, tell who are those two souls that accompany you there: do not be silent, speak to me!"

55   "Your face, which I wept for at your death, gives me no less grief to weep for now," I replied to him, "seeing it so distorted.

58   Therefore tell me, for God's sake, what so strips you: do not make me speak while I am marveling, for he speaks ill who is full of some other desire."

61   And he to me: "From the eternal Mind there falls power into the water and the tree back there, and therefore I grow so thin.

64   All these singing and weeping people, because they followed their gullets beyond measure, in hunger and thirst here must make themselves holy again.

67   Desire to drink and eat is kindled in us by the fragrance that comes from the fruit and the spray that spreads over its foliage.

E non pur una volta, questo spazzo   70
girando, si rinfresca nostra pena:
io dico pena, e dovria dir sollazzo,

    ché quella voglia a li alberi ci mena   73
che menò Cristo lieto a dire 'Elì,'
quando ne liberò con la sua vena."

    E io a lui: "Forese, da quel dì   76
nel qual mutasti mondo a miglior vita,
cinqu' anni non son vòlti infino a qui.

    Se prima fu la possa in te finita   79
di peccar più che sovvenisse l'ora
del buon dolor ch'a Dio ne rimarita,

    come se' tu qua sù venuto ancora?   82
Io ti credea trovar là giù di sotto
dove tempo per tempo si ristora."

    Ond' elli a me: "Sì tosto m'ha condotto   85
a ber lo dolce assenzo d'i martìri
la Nella mia con suo pianger dirotto.

    Con suoi prieghi devoti e con sospiri   88
tratto m'ha de la costa ove s'aspetta,
e liberato m'ha de li altri giri.

    Tanto è a Dio più cara e più diletta   91
la vedovella mia, che molto amai,
quanto in bene operare è più soletta,

    ché la Barbagia di Sardigna assai   94
ne le femmine sue più è pudica
che la Barbagia dov' io la lasciai.

    O dolce frate, che vuo' tu ch'io dica?   97
Tempo futuro m'è già nel cospetto
cui non sarà quest' ora molto antica,

    nel qual sarà in pergamo interdetto   100
a le sfacciate donne fiorentine
l'andar mostrando con le poppe il petto.

    Quai barbare fuor mai, quai saracine,   103
cui bisognasse, per farle ir coperte,
o spiritali o altre discipline?

    Ma se le svergognate fosser certe   106
di quel che 'l ciel veloce loro ammanna,
già per urlare avrian le bocche aperte,

70   And not just once, as we circle this space, is our pain renewed: I say pain, and I should say solace,

73   for that desire leads us to the trees that led Christ to say '*Eli*' gladly, when he freed us with the blood of his veins."

76   And I to him: "Forese, from the day when you changed worlds for a better life, five years have not revolved until now.

79   If the power to continue sinning failed in you before the hour came of the good sorrow that marries us to God again,

82   how have you come up here already? I thought to find you down there below, where they repay time for time."

85   And he to me: "I have been so quickly brought to drink the sweet wormwood of our sufferings by my Nella and her broken weeping.

88   With her devoted prayers and sighs she has drawn me from the shore of waiting, and she has freed me from the other circles.

91   My little widow, whom I dearly loved, is the dearer to God and more beloved the more isolated she is in her good actions,

94   for the Sardinian Barbagia is much more modest in its women than that Barbagia where I left her.

97   O dear brother, what can I say? A future time is already in my sight when this hour will not seem very ancient,

100   when from the pulpit it will be forbidden to the brazen Florentine women to walk about showing their chests with their breasts.

103   What barbarian women, what Saracens ever needed either spiritual or other penalties to make them go covered up?

106   But if those shameless ones knew what the swift heavens are preparing for them, they would already have opened their mouths to howl,

ché, se l'antiveder qui non m'inganna,   109
prima fien triste che le guance impeli
colui che mo si consola con nanna.

   Deh, frate, or fa che più non mi ti celi!   112
Vedi che non pur io, ma questa gente
tutta rimira là dove 'l sol veli."

   Per ch'io a lui: "Se tu riduci a mente   115
qual fosti meco e qual io teco fui,
ancor fia grave il memorar presente.

   Di quella vita mi volse costui   118
che mi va innanzi l'altr' ier, quando tonda
vi si mostrò la suora di colui"—

   e 'l sol mostrai. "Costui per la profonda   121
notte menato m'ha d'i veri morti
con questa vera carne che 'l seconda.

   Indi m'han tratto sù li suoi conforti,   124
salendo e rigirando la montagna
che drizza voi che 'l mondo fece torti.

   Tanto dice di farmi sua compagna   127
che io sarò là dove fia Beatrice;
quivi convien che sanza lui rimagna.

   Virgilio è questi che così mi dice"—   130
e addita'lo—"e quest' altro è quell' ombra
per cuï si scosse dianzi ogne pendice

   lo vostro regno, che da sé lo sgombra."   133

109 for, if my foreseeing does not deceive me, they will grieve before hair grows on the cheeks of one who now can be consoled with a lullaby.

112 Ah, brother, now hide yourself no longer from me! See that not only I, but all these people are staring at where you veil the sun."

115 Therefore I to him: "If you call back to mind what you used to be with me, and I with you, the present memory will still be heavy.

118 From that life I was turned away by the one who goes ahead of me, the other day when the sister of that one was round"—

121 and I pointed to the sun. "He has led me through the deep night of those truly dead with this true flesh of mine that follows him.

124 From there his strengthenings have drawn me up, climbing and circling about the mountain that straightens you whom the world twisted.

127 He says he will keep me company until I am where Beatrice will be; there I must remain without him.

130 It is Virgil who tells me this"—and I pointed to him—"and this other is the shade for whom your kingdom just now

133 shook every slope, for it is freeing itself of him."

NOTES

1-3. While I was . . . the little birds: The pilgrim is trying in vain to see the speaker of 22.140-54. As in 24.115-29, the voice is left unidentified; the natural assumption is that it is an angel.

3. after the little birds: Usually taken to refer to fowling: hunting small birds with nets and birdlime was a popular sport in the Middle Ages and not, like falconry, restricted to the nobility; cf. the fowling imagery in *Inf.* 13.55-57, with notes.

7-9. I turned . . . going effortless: The first of a series of references to haste in this and the following canto. For the pilgrim's listening to Virgil and Statius, cf. 22.127-29, with notes.

9. effortless: The Italian is "di nullo costo" [of no cost]. Effort is not noticed or not begrudged, being amply repaid.

10-39. And behold . . . not yet manifest: The pilgrim will question Forese about the shades' emaciation (lines 55-75); these passages prepare Statius' explanation of their airy bodies in 25.19-111.

10-12. we heard . . . delight and woe: The group of shades first makes itself known through the sense of hearing; cf. lines 43-48, with note.

11. *Labia mea, Domine* [My lips, Lord]: The shades are singing one or more verses from Psalm 50 (see 5.24, with note), of which verse 17 is: "Domine, labia mea aperies, et os meum annuntiabit laudem tuam" [O Lord, thou wilt open my lips: and my mouth shall announce thy praise]. Ps. 50.16, "Deliver me from blood, O God, thou God of my health: and my tongue shall extol thy justice," is interpreted by Augustine (*Enarrationes in Psalmos*, 50) as referring to the need— due to Original Sin, in his view—for food and drink:

> For how can that be healthy which is declining, which is in need, which always has, as it were, the sickness of hunger and thirst? These things will no longer be [after the resurrection]: food for the belly and the belly for food will both be done away with by the Lord . . . and no failing will creep in, no change because of age, no fatigue from labor to need propping up or restoring by food. But we will not be without food and drink. God himself will be our food and our drink. That is the only food that truly restores and never fails.

The Eucharist is constantly in the background of this and the next canto. Mouths that sinned in gluttony now utter praise (see Abrams 1976, 24.50-55, with notes).

14-15. Shades who . . . knot of their debt: For knots, a central metaphor, see 16.24, 24.56, with notes; lines 125-26 are also closely related.

16-21. As care-filled pilgrims . . . wonderingly at us: Again the note of haste. These lines echo the sonnet of *VN* 40 (after the death of Beatrice): "Deh, peregrini che pensosi andate, / forse di cosa che non v'è presente, / venite voi da sì lontana gente / . . . / che non piangete quando voi passate / per lo suo mezzo la città dolente?" [Ah, pilgrims who go filled with care, perhaps for things that are not present to you, do you come from so distant a people . . . that you do not weep when you pass through the midst of the grieving city?]; cf. the note to lines 28-30. For "the grieving city" (an allusion to Lamentations), see the notes to *Inf.* 3.1 and *Purg.* 23.28-30, 29, 30. Compare the pilgrim similes that begin Canto 8: here the pilgrims are no longer nostalgic but firm in purpose and intent on their goal; compare the entire passage with 24.106-11, with note.

22-36. Each was dark . . . unless he knew how: A very elaborate passage on the appearance of the shades: three lines (22-24) on their faces; two comparisons involving divine punishment, each occupying three lines (25-27, 28-30): the first made by the poet, the other attributed to the pilgrim, the first from Ovidian myth, the other from Jewish history (though not from the OT); finally a return to direct description, with a startling graphic image (again three lines, 31-33); a general expression of wonder (three lines, 34-36).

22-24. Each was dark . . . from the bones: Dante derives a number of details from the portrait of the goddess Hunger in *Met.* 8.799-808, part of the story of Erysichthon (cf. lines 25-27; the italics mark verbal parallels): a dryad "saw her in a stony field, tearing up grass with her nails and teeth. Her hair was shaggy, *her eyes hollow* [*cava lumina*], *her face pallid* [*pallor in ore*] her lips pale with thirst, *her jaws rough with scabies* [*scabrae rubigine fauces*], *her skin leathery* [*dura cutis*], through which her viscera could be seen; *the dry bones stood out* [*ossa . . . exstabant arida*] below her shrunken pelvis . . ."

    Dante's description is limited to the shades' faces; the condition of the rest of the body, though implied, is not mentioned in this canto or the next; even the mention of the bones shaping the skin refers to the face (see next note), while in Ovid it refers to the pelvis and hips. Of the facial features only the eyes, nose, cheekbones, and brow are unmistakably referred to (the lips, of course, are mentioned in the psalm quoted in line 11; the mouth is a principal focus throughout (see 24.38-39, with note; for the scabies, see lines 39 and 49). Dante's "buccia strema" [outer rind] (line 25) was also suggested by this portrait.

23-24. with faces . . . from the bones: We take *scema* [wasted] as parallel with *pallor* [pallor] and thus as describing the face (both modify *ciascuna* [each]). It might be argued that *scema* refers to the general emaciation of the shades, but the governing focus on the face does not invite the eye to move downward; cf. lines 40-48, with notes. Marti 1984 calls attention to the biblical parallels: "Through the voice of my groaning, my bone hath cleaved to my flesh" (Ps. 101.6); "My flesh being consumed, my bone hath cleaved to my skin" (Job 19.20); "Their skin hath stuck to their bones, it is withered and is become like wood" (Lam. 4.8).

25-27. I do not . . . most afraid: The story of Erysichthon is told in *Met.* 8.739-878: he is punished with insatiable hunger after being cursed by the dryad of an oak sacred to Ceres, which he destroys; he consumes his wealth in order to feed, selling even his daughter (a shape-shifter who swindles her purchasers). The *Ovide moralisé* (8.3519-4398) interprets the tale as about the deceptive nature of worldly goods (cf. the Siren of Canto 19).

As Marti 1984 observed, contrary to Dante's lines (especially line 27: "per digiunare" [by fasting]), in Ovid's version Erysichthon does not fast, though his becoming emaciated is perhaps implied. There is no counterpart in Ovid of the moment of terror Dante attributes to Erysichthon (line 27).

28-30. Behold the people . . . into her son: The allusion is to Flavius Josephus' account (*De bello judaico*, Book 6) of Jerusalem during the siege by the Romans (70 A.D.), accepted as factual by Christian writers (see 21.82-86, with notes); large excerpts from it were included in their works by Vincent of Beauvais (*Specu lum historiale* 10.5) and others. In *Policraticus* 2 John of Salisbury uses Josephus' account of the Jews' blindness to the portents God sends in order to convert them (*De bello iudaico* 6.5.3) to explain their cruelty to each other during the siege. The *Ovide moralisé* gives a long interpretation of Erysichthon as representing the rejection of Christ by Jews, Muslims, and other unbelievers, attributing it to their greed for material goods.

29. the people who lost Jerusalem: The Christian commentators on Lamentations connected the siege of 70 A.D. with that of 586 B.C. (see next note). As Stephany (in Jacoff/Schnapp 1991) observes, these penitents have not lost Jerusalem: they are well on their way to the heavenly one.

30. when Mary put her beak into her son: Josephus (6.4.3) describes Mary's killing, roasting, and eating her nursing child as the result, at an advanced stage of starvation, of rage and desperation at being continually robbed of food by others. When she mockingly offers the thieves the uneaten half of her child, even the cruelest are speechless with horror. Josephus' highly rhetorical account is related both to Lam. 2.20 and 4.10 (on cannibalism during the siege of 586 B.C.) and to the Roman taste for the lurid, including cannibalism (see *Inter cantica* below). For Dante, Mary's cannibalism parodies Christ's self-sacrifice and the Eucharist and is set against the Virgin Mary's not thinking "about her mouth" (22.142-44; see the notes to 23.70-75). With the trope of *beak* for *teeth*, Mary becomes a metaphorical bird of prey—a far cry from the "little birds" of line 3. Note the parallel *when*-clauses (lines 27 and 30).

31. Their eye-sockets . . . rings without gems: The eyes are so sunken as to be almost invisible, and their sockets look like the mountings on rings from which the stones themselves have been lost. The comparison of the beloved's eyes to precious stones (especially crystals, sapphires, or topazes) is a topos of love-poetry; Dante exploits it in the *Rime petrose*. In. 31.116 Beatrice's eyes will be called emeralds.

32-33. those who read *omo* . . . the M there clearly: In inscriptions in Dante's time—in gothic characters—Os and other vowels were often inserted between the vertical strokes of *M* and other letters. The *M* in question is formed by the arching brows and the cheekbones, along with the line of the nose It is clear that Dante thinks of the conceit as well known. The Anonimo Fiorentino writes: "Some say that in everyone's face can be read *HOMO DEI* in this way: one of the ears is an *H* and the other, turned around, is a *D*: the eye is an *O*, the nose with the brows is an *M*, the mouth is an *I*." In Dante's treatment, the visibility of the *M* is at a first level a *memento mori* [reminder of death]; as such, it is closely related to the *VOM* of 12.25-68. The emaciation of the souls both expresses their desire for food and drink and is the sign of their progress toward Heaven (see the note to line 29); it will disappear when their vice has been completely purged.

34-36. Who would believe . . . unless he knew how: These lines foreground the exquisiteness of the torment on this level: the difficulty does not arise over the power of odors to arouse appetite (everyone knows it), but rather from the fact that the shades seem to need nourishment (cf. line 37). The pilgrim will only learn "how" (line 36) in Canto 25; cf. the note to 24.145-50. For nourishment by odor alone, see the Santagata 1996 note on Petrarch's *Rime sparse* 207.58.

37-133. Already . . . freeing itself of him: The rest of this canto and the first hundred lines (two thirds) of the next are devoted to the pilgrim's encounter with Forese Donati. This is one of the longest encounters in the *Comedy* (Sordello, for instance, is an interlocutor in 165 lines [Cantos 6-8], as opposed to 200 for Forese). It is a companion piece to Virgil's encounter with Statius, whose significance for Statius is parallel with the significance of this one for Forese. The encounter with Forese is notable for a series of marks of colloquial syntax and expressions (23.54, 56, 97, 112; 24.41, 46, 49, 52, 55, 75, 76, 77, 82, 91); repetition (23.49, 52, 54, 58, 59, 71-72, 87-88; 24.10-11, 19-20); deictic gestures (two each: 23.121, 131; 24.19, 89).

37-48. Already . . . face of Forese: The association of the appearance of the shades with that of decaying corpses underlies the entire canto; see the note to lines 55-60.

40-42. and behold . . . this is for me: For the parallels with the encounter with Brunetto Latini (*Inferno* 15), see Additional Note 10. Cf. also 7.19.

43-48. Never would I . . . the face of Forese: In contrast with the immediate legibility of the *M* on the souls' faces (lines 32-33), common to them all as human beings, Forese's individual appearance is at first undecipherable. The pilgrim's adjustment in perception, when his recognition of Forese's voice enables him to recognize his face as familiar, is remarkably imagined. Dante had evidently observed the resistance of the human voice to being changed by age or even by great changes in weight.

44-45. in his voice . . . ravaged in itself: The emaciation of Forese's features had destroyed their familiar outlines, but the sound of his voice was unchanged, his identity was evident in it.

48. Forese: Forese Donati (died 1296), member of a prominent Florentine family, was the brother of Corso Donati, the turbulent leader of the Black faction (Forese will predict Corso's demise in 24.82-87), and Piccarda (see 24.10-15 and *Par.* 3.37-120); he was a cousin of Dante's wife, Gemma Donati. This and the following canto, along with the famous "Tenzone" between them, are the only evidence about their friendship, which must have been very close. It is reasonable to suppose the two were near the same age, but there is no external evidence on that point. The charge of gluttony is one of the principal insults leveled at Forese in the "Tenzone." See Additional Note 10.

49-51. Ah, do not . . . lack of flesh: Forese's opening speech suggests a self-consciousness about his disfigurement appropriate to one used in life to presenting an elegant appearance and a no doubt handsome face. See *Inter cantica* below.

55-60. Your face . . . some other desire: Again the insistence on the face. Sharply evoked here is the memory of ceremonially mourning his dead body (see the note to lines 37-48). "La faccia tua . . . morta" means literally "the death of your face" (see the note to 31.47-48): obviously it was dear to Dante.

58. what so strips you: Italian *sfogliare* is derived from *foglia* [leaf] and means literally "to strip of leaves," here a plant or tree metaphor. Many commentators view it as referring to the scaling of skin, but it seems better to understand it as referring to the great loss of flesh.

61-75. From the eternal . . . of his veins: Forese gives a very full account of the penance of this level. Virgil's discussion of the upper terraces (17.133-39) had stated the general principle governing them, but it is only on each terrace that the vice to be purged is specified.

65. followed their gullets: Italian *gola* is Lat. *gula* [throat], a normal term for gluttony.

67-69. Desire to drink . . . over its foliage: At last the central point is stated: what the souls experience is indeed hunger and thirst. The purpose of the elaborate structure that surrounds this point is no doubt to emphasize the idea that hunger and thirst are of the soul, not of the body: it is the soul's inherent desire to form a body that is expressed in the sensations of hunger and thirst, seemingly so intrinsically "physical." The pilgrim's question in 25.20-21 is being prepared.

70-75. And not just once . . . of his veins: Forese is torn between suffering and joyful acceptance of suffering; he is a conspicuous instance of a soul exhibiting remnants of the vice even as he celebrates progress in overcoming it (cf. Oderisii in 11.73-117, Marco Lombardo in Canto 16).

72-75. I say pain . . . of his veins: These lines continue the theme set out in lines 10-12 (see also line 86, with note). Here we learn that it is the proximity of the trees that elicits the pangs of hunger and thirst the shades feel; the nearness of their approach to the trees seems to some degree a matter of choice.

73. the trees: Some commentators have inferred from this line the existence of a large number of such trees, but Dante has explicitly provided only two (22.130-54, 24.110-29); see the note to 24.100-154; we take "not just once" to refer to the intermittent nature of the shades' desire for food (see the note to 24.106-12).

73-75. that desire . . . of his veins: "*Elì*" quotes Christ on the Cross: "And about the ninth hour Jesus cried with a loud voice, saying: Eli, Eli, lamma sabacthani? that is, My God, my God, why hast thou forsaken me?" (Matt. 27.46, quoting Ps. 21.2; cf. Mark 15.34). For moderns, of course, it is particularly striking that the dying Christ of the Gospel should be said to be "joyful," but in medieval terms the idea is inevitable. In choosing the intensification of their suffering, the penitents are imitating Christ. See the note to 24.52-54.

76-111. Forese, from the day . . . with a lullaby: The pilgrim now raises a second question, the reason for Forese's rapid progress up the mountain. Forese's answer—that it is due to his devoted widow's prayers—leads into praise of her virtue and a denunciation of the shamelessness of the other Florentine women.

76-78. from the day . . . until now: Forese died in July, 1296; therefore in April, 1300 less than four years have elapsed.

79-84. If the power . . . time for time: Forese was a late repentant, then; his repentance ("the good sorrow . . .") took place only after he had lost the power to sin, i.e., when he was dying. The pilgrim expected to find him in the Ante-Purgatory, among the negligent (4.97-135, with parallels to the present canto: *martìri* [sufferings]: 4.128, 23.86; *buon sospiri* [good sighs]: 4.132, *buon dolor* [good sorrow], 23. 81; *orazione . . . di cuor* [prayer from the heart], 4.133-34, *prieghi devoti* [devoted prayers], 23.88).

85-90. I have been ... the other circles: The power of the prayers of the living to advance the souls in Purgatory has been a recurrent theme (see 3.142-45, 4.133-35, 6.28-42, 8.67-72, 11.31-36). Forese's progress is the single most striking example in the *Purgatorio*, given emphasis by being juxtaposed with the hundreds of years of Statius' penance. The tribute to Nella, then, has determined major elements of the structure of the cantica, including the numerous complaints of neglect uttered or implied by Manfred (3.142-45), Buonconte (5.88-89), and the entire group in 7.1-24. See Bosco in *LDS*, Additional Note 10.

87. my Nella: It is only from this passage that we know the name of Forese's wife; nothing else is known about her except what, if anything, can be inferred from the scornfully mocking portrait in the "Tenzone," according to which she was afflicted with perpetual colds and suffered greatly from Forese's neglect.

89-90. she has drawn me ... the other circles: Not only has Nella cut short the penalty for Forese's negligence, she has "freed" him from the penances for pride, envy, anger, sloth, and avarice—whether drastically shortening them or enabling him to skip them entirely.

91-96. My little widow ... I left her: As in the passages cited in the note to lines 85-90, only the prayers of those favored by God are efficacious; God's love for Nella is intensified, says Forese, by the contrast between her virtue and the general corruption of the women of Florence.

91. My little widow, whom I dearly loved: Although the first half of this line is warmly affectionate, the second is awkward: why does Forese feel it necessary now to tell his closest friend that he loved his wife? It is difficult to avoid the thought that the line is motivated by Dante's desire to repudiate the "Tenzone," which includes slurs at Nella from both participants.

94-96. the Sardinian Barbagia ... where I left her: *Barbagia* (derived from Lat. *barbaria* [barbarous region]) was the mountainous central region of Sardinia, said by the early commentators to be inhabited by a semi-barbarous people. Forese is saying that the Florentine women are more shameless than those of Barbagia.

97-111. O dear brother ... with a lullaby: The denunciation of the Florentine women leads into a prophecy that is almost in the manner of an Old Testament prophet; see the notes to lines 106-11.

98-102. A future time ... with their breasts: Cassell 1978 prints legislation promulgated by the bishop of Florence in 1310 (and no doubt read from the pulpits in the diocese) that prohibits women's dress from leaving uncovered any part of the torso, on pain of excommunication.

98-99. A future time . . . ancient: Similar assertions of the imminence of prophesied events occur in *Inf.* 26.7-12, *Purg.* 33.40-41; Forese will assert it again in 24.88-90.

103-105. What barbarian women . . . covered up: The medieval European ignorance of sub-Saharan Africa, where many tribes went entirely naked, is evident here. Muslim women were reputed to be particularly licentious in conduct (some of the stories from the *Thousand and One Nights* were already circulating). "Spiritual penalties" might range from penances to excommunication; "other penalties" or sanctions would be those imposed by the civil authorities. For NT injunctions to modest dress, see 1 Tim. 2.9. Abrams 1976 connects the the display of the breasts as sexual objects with the infantilism Dante sees as inherent in gluttony and lust (see 24.106-12, with note).

106-111. But if those . . . with a lullaby: The disaster is left vague but must affect the city as a whole; since the poem is set in 1300, it will occur before sixteen years have passed and one now a baby has begun a beard (lines 110-11); line 109 parallels a phrase ("Et si presaga mens mea non fallitur" [And if my prophetic mind is not deceived]) in Dante's ferocious *Epistle* 6 (March, 1311), to the city of Florence, denouncing its resistance to the emperor Henry VII and foretelling destruction and foreign domination (4.17). The destruction of Jerusalem is a subtext of the Epistle as well as of this and the following canto. Petrocchi 1969 suggests that the disaster is the defeat of Montecatini (1315).

107. the swift heavens: The heavens are swift both in their rotation and because disaster always seems to approach rapidly.

108. they would . . . to howl: Italian *urlare* is derived from Lat. *ululare* [to howl, especially with grief]; the word is characteristic of OT prophecies of destruction (see especially Is. 32.9-11, Jer. 9.20, 44.24, Ezek. 13.18, 23.48). Renewed emphasis on the mouth.

111. can be consoled with a lullaby: This child is presumably still at the breast; cf. the notes to lines 30 and 103-105.

112-14. Ah, brother . . . veil the sun: Forese has very fully answered the pilgrim's questions; now he can expect to have his own (lines 52-54) answered.

113-14. See that . . . veil the sun: For the shades' marveling at the pilgrim's shadow, see 3.88-99, 5.1-12, with notes.

115-33. If you call back . . . freeing itself of him: The pilgrim answers Forese more fully than he does other souls; only in this passage does he utter Beatrice's name. He does not name Statius. It is not true, however, that the pilgrim names Virgil only here: see 21.124-26. See *Inter cantica* to Canto 24.

115-19. If you call back . . . the other day: The pilgrim asserts that the life he and Forese led together was so deplorable as to cause grief even now that they have both left it behind. Furthermore, he states that the sinful patterns of his life with Forese were essentially the same as those represented in the Dark Wood of *Inferno* 1 (line 118: "that life"; line 119: "the other day"). These lines are often cited as evidence for dating the "Tenzone" in the early 1290's.

118-29. From that life . . . remain without him: A brief summary of the action of the *Comedy* until the end of the *Purgatorio*; compare Virgil's proleptic summary, *Inf.* 1.112-23; see *Inter cantica* for Canto 24.

120-21. the sister . . . the sun: The moon is mythologically Diana, twin sister of Apollo (cf. *Inf.* 10.79-81, *Purg.* 18.76-81, with notes). For the full moon in the Dark Wood, see *Inf.* 20.127-29, with notes.

121-23. through the deep . . . true flesh of mine: Summarizing the *Inferno*. The antithesis of "truly dead" and "true flesh" is striking, answering lines 113-14 and recapitulating the theme of the pilgrim's bodily presence in the other world.

124-29. his strengthenings . . . remain without him: Summarizing the *Purgatorio*. Lines 127-29 echo *Inf.* 1.121-23.

125-26. climbing . . . the world twisted: A striking formulation of some of the fundamental themes of the poem: the spiral (twisting) path of the pilgrim and the penitent shades, associated with the circling heavens and the spiral path of the sun; the "twisting" of the soul (the distortion of its nature by vice, resulting from its sins and from the influence of the world), which the mountain is "straightening" as if unwinding a skein. There may be a suggestion for this remarkable bundle of implications in Vergil's fourth *Eclogue*; see Additional Note 14.

131-33. this other . . . freeing itself of him: Statius. The reference is of course to the earthquake of 20.127-41, explained in 21.58-72. In the pilgrim's personification of the mountain, Statius is a weight being shaken from the shoulders.

Inter cantica. The reference to birding in lines 1-3 recalls *Inferno* 13, including the effort to see the hidden sources of voices (*Inf.* 13.22-27). The distortion of Forese's appearance and the grief it elicits recalls *Inf.* 20.10-26: cf. *torta* [distorted, twisted] (*Inf.* 20.23; *Purg.* 23.57); *Inferno* 20 focuses on the body below the neck, *Purgatorio* 23 on the face.

The deluge of rain in *Inferno* 6, signifying the indiscriminateness of gluttonous appetite, is contrasted with the "sprazzo" [sprinkling] of *Purg.* 22.136-38, discussed in 23.61-69 (examples of punishment that submerges—cf. *Inf.* 20.3—and penance that refines and purifies); and with the fact that the glutton Ciacco's suffering "perhaps" makes him unrecognizable (6.43-45). With 22.127-29, 23.7-9 recall the encounter with the poets in *Inf.* 4.85-103.

The prophecy of disaster to Florence recalls that in *Inf.* 26.7-12. The associated theme of the destruction of Jerusalem (lines 28-30) recalls the members of the Sanhedrin, who voted to put Jesus to death (*Inf.* 23.110-126) and are crucified in the way (cf. *Purg.* 23.73-75): ultimately they are the ones most responsible for the destruction of Jerusalem (*Inf.* 23.123; see *Purg.* 23.25-27). The lightness of the souls purging gluttony (see 24.69) enables them to hasten, unlike the hypocrites, who walk with painful slowness.

Finally, the references to starvation and cannibalism, parodying the Eucharist, recall the story of Count Ugolino (*Inferno* 32-33, see *Inferno* Additional Note 15) and in fact constitute strong evidence that *Inf.* 33.75 means that he fed on his children, since it involves a verbal echo of the act in Josephus (Martinez 1997).

CANTO 24

Né 'l dir l'andar, né l'andar lui più lento   1
facea, ma ragionando andavam forte,
sì come nave pinta da buon vento;

  e l'ombre, che parean cose rimorte,   4
per le fosse de li occhi ammirazione
traean di me, di mio vivere accorte.

  E io, continüando al mio sermone,   7
dissi: "Ella sen va sù forse più tarda
che non farebbe, per altrui cagione.

  Ma dimmi, se tu sai, dov' è Piccarda?   10
Dimmi s'io veggio da notar persona
tra questa gente che sì mi riguarda."

  "La mia sorella, che tra bella e buona   13
non so qual fosse più, trïunfa lieta
ne l'alto Olimpo già di sua corona."

  Sì disse prima, e poi: "Qui non si vieta   16
di nominar ciascun, da ch'è sì munta
nostra sembianza via per la dïeta.

  Questi"—e mostrò col dito—"è Bonagiunta,   19
Bonagiunta da Lucca; e quella faccia
di là da lui, più che l'altre trapunta,

  ebbe la santa Chiesa in le sue braccia: 22
dal Torso fu, e purga per digiuno
l'anguille di Bolsena e la vernaccia."

  Molti altri mi nomò ad uno ad uno,   25
e del nomar parean tutti contenti,
sì ch'io però non vidi un atto bruno.

  Vidi per fame a vòto usar li denti   28
Ubaldin da la Pila e Bonifazio,
che pasturò col rocco molte genti.

CANTO 24

Sixth terrace, continued: Forese, still—Bonagiunta da Lucca and others—Bonagiunta's prophecy—the Sweet New Style—the end of Corso—farewell to Forese—the second tree—examples of gluttony punished—the angel, erasure, a Beatitude

1   Speech did not slow our walking, nor walking
our speech, but we hastened on while speaking,
like a ship driven by a good wind;

4   and the shades, who seemed twice-dead
things, in through the pits of their eyes drew
amazement from me, perceiving that I was alive.

7   And I, continuing my speech, said: "His soul is
going on more slowly perhaps than it would, for
the sake of others.

10   But tell me, if you know, where is Piccarda?
Tell me if among these people who are looking at
me so, I see any person of note."

13   "My sister, of whose goodness and beauty I
know not which was the greater, already
triumphs joyous with her crown on high
Olympus."

16   So he said first, and then: "Here it is not
forbidden to name each one, since our
appearance has been so milked dry by fasting.

19   This"—and he pointed with his finger—"is
Bonagiunta, Bonagiunta of Lucca; and that face
beyond him, more pierced through than the others,

22   had Holy Church in his embrace: he was from
Tours, and by fasting he purges the eels of
Bolsena and the vernaccia."

25   Many others, one by one, he named for me,
and they seemed happy to be named, so that I did
not see one dark look because of it.

28   I saw Ubaldino da la Pila chewing the air for
hunger and Boniface, who pastured many people
with his rook.

Vidi messer Marchese, ch'ebbe spazio   31
già di bere a Forlì con men secchezza,
e sì fu tal che non si sentì sazio.

Ma come fa chi guarda e poi s'apprezza   34
più d'un che d'altro, fei a quel di Lucca,
che più parea di me voler contezza.

El mormorava, e non so che "Gentucca"   37
sentiv' io là ov' el sentia la piaga
de la giustizia che sì li pilucca.

"O anima," diss' io, "che par sì vaga   40
di parlar meco, fa sì ch'io t'intenda,
e te e me col tuo parlare appaga."

"Femmina è nata, e non porta ancor benda,"   43
cominciò el, "che ti farà piacere
la mia città, come ch'om la riprenda.

Tu te n'andrai con questo antivedere;   46
se nel mio mormorar prendesti errore,
dichiareranti ancor le cose vere.

Ma dì s'i' veggio qui colui che fòre   49
trasse le nove rime, cominciando:
'Donne ch'avete intelletto d'amore'?"

E io a lui: "I' mi son un che, quando   52
Amor mi spira, noto, e a quel modo
ch'e' ditta dentro vo significando."

"O frate, issa vegg' io," diss' elli, "il nodo   55
che 'l Notaro e Guittone e me ritenne
di qua dal dolce stil novo ch'i' odo.

Io veggio ben come le vostre penne   58
di retro al dittator sen vanno strette,
che de le nostre certo non avvenne;

e qual più a riguardar oltre si mette,   61
non vede più da l'uno a l'altro stilo."
E quasi contentato si tacette.

Come li augei che vernan lungo 'l Nilo   64
alcuna volta in aere fanno schiera,
poi volan più a fretta e vanno in filo:

così tutta la gente che lì era,   67
volgendo 'l viso, raffrettò suo passo,
e per magrezza e per voler leggera.

31 I saw messer Marchese, who formerly had
leisure to drink at Forlì with less thirst, and was
such that he never felt sated.

34 But as we do when we look and then prize one
more than another, so did I him from Lucca,
who most seemed to desire acquaintance with me.

37 He was murmuring, and I heard something
like "Gentucca" there where he felt the wound of
the Justice that so plucks them bare.

40 "O soul," I said, "who seem so eager to speak
with me, make me understand you, and with
your speech satisfy both you and me."

43 "A woman has been born, and she does not yet
wear the wimple," he began, "who will make my city
pleasing to you, however people may reproach it.

46 You will leave here with this foreseeing; if
from my murmuring you conceived an error, the
actual events will make it clear for you.

49 But tell me if I see here the one who drew
forth the new rhymes, beginning: 'Ladies who
have intellect of love'?"

52 And I to him: "I in myself am one who, when
Love breathes within me, take note, and to that
measure which he dictates within, I go signifying."

55 "O my brother, now I see," said he, "the knot
that held the Notary and Guittone and me back
on this side of the sweet new style I hear.

58 I see well how your pens follow close behind
him who dictates, which with ours certainly did
not happen;

61 and whoever most sets himself to looking
further will not see any other difference between
the one style and the other." And, as if satisfied,
he fell silent.

64 As the birds that winter along the Nile
sometimes flock in the air and then fly with
more haste, forming a line:

67 so all the people who were there, turning their
faces, hastened their pace, made light by both
leanness and desire.

E come l'uom che di trottare è lasso 70
lascia andar li compagni e si passeggia
fin che si sfoghi l'affollar del casso:

   sì lasciò trapassar la santa greggia 73
Forese, e dietro meco sen veniva,
dicendo: "Quando fia ch'io ti riveggia?"

   "Non so," rispuos' io lui, "quant' io mi viva, 76
ma già non fìa il tornar mio tantosto
ch'io non sia col voler prima a la riva,

   però che 'l loco u' fui a viver posto 79
di giorno in giorno più di ben si spolpa,
e a trista ruina par disposto."

   "Or va," diss' el: "ché quei che più n'ha colpa 82
vegg' ïo a coda d'una bestia tratto
inver' la valle ove mai non si scolpa.

   La bestia ad ogne passo va più ratto, 85
crescendo sempre, fin ch'ella il percuote,
e lascia il corpo vilmente disfatto.

   Non hanno molto a volger quelle ruote"— 88
e drizzò li occhi al ciel—"che ti fia chiaro
ciò che 'l mio dir più dichiarar non puote.

   Tu ti rimani omai, ché 'l tempo è caro 91
in questo regno, sì ch'io perdo troppo
venendo teco sì a paro a paro."

   Qual esce alcuna volta di gualoppo 94
lo cavalier di schiera che cavalchi,
e va per farsi onor del primo intoppo:

   tal si partì da noi con maggior valchi, 97
e io rimasi in via con esso i due
che fuor del mondo sì gran marescalchi.

   E quando innanzi a noi intrato fue 100
che li occhi miei si fero a lui seguaci
come la mente a le parole sue,

   parvermi i rami gravidi e vivaci 103
d'un altro pomo, e non molto lontani,
per esser pur allora vòlto in laci.

   Vidi gente sott' esso alzar le mani 106
e gridar non so che verso le fronde:
quasi bramosi fantolini e vani

70   And as one who is weary of trotting lets his companions pass on and so goes at a walk until the heaving of his chest has spent its fire:

73   so Forese let the holy flock go by and walked along behind with me, saying: "When will it be that I see you again?"

76   "I don't know," I answered him, "how long I am to live, but my return will not be so soon that in my desire I shall not have reached shore sooner,

79   for the city where I was placed to live strips itself of goodness day by day and seems bent on sad ruin."

82   "Believe it," said he: "for the one most to blame in this I see dragged at the tail of a beast toward the valley where guilt is never forgiven.

85   The beast goes faster with each step, ever growing, until it strikes him and leaves his corpse basely disfigured.

88   Those wheels have not far to turn"—and he raised his eyes to the sky—"before what my speech cannot further declare will become clear to you.

91   You stay behind now, for time is precious in this realm, and I lose too much coming along side by side with you in this way."

94   As sometimes a knight canters out from a company of horse and goes to gain the honor of the first encounter:

97   so he left us with greater strides, and I remained on the way with those two who were such great marshals of the world.

100   And when he had gone so far ahead of us that my eyes followed him as my mind did his words,

103   there appeared to me the laden, lively branches of another fruit tree, not far distant, since I had only then turned toward it.

106   I saw people beneath it raising their hands and shouting I know not what toward the foliage: like eager, silly little children

che pregano, e 'l pregato non risponde,　　109
ma, per fare esser ben la voglia acuta,
tien alto lor disio e nol nasconde.

　Poi si partì sì come ricreduta,　　112
e noi venimmo al grande arbore adesso,
che tanti prieghi e lagrime rifiuta.

　"Trapassate oltre sanza farvi presso:　　115
legno è più sù che fu morso da Eva,
e questa pianta sì levò da esso."

　Sì tra le frasche non so chi diceva,　　118
per che Virgilio e Stazio e io, ristretti,
oltre andavam dal lato che si leva.

　"Ricordivi," dicea, "d'i maladetti　　121
nei nuvoli formati, che, satolli,
Tesëo combatter co' doppi petti,

　e de li Ebrei ch'al ber si mostrar molli,　　124
per che no i volle Gedeon compagni
quando inver' Madïan discese i colli."

　Sì, accostati a l'un d'i due vivagni,　　127
passammo, udendo colpe de la gola
seguite già da miseri guadagni.

　Poi, rallargati per la strada sola,　　130
ben mille passi e più ci portar oltre,
contemplando ciascun sanza parola.

　"Che andate pensando sì voi sol tre?"　　133
sùbita voce disse, ond' io mi scossi
come fan bestie spaventate e poltre.

　Drizzai la testa per veder chi fossi,　　136
e già mai non si videro in fornace
vetri o metalli sì lucenti e rossi

　com' io vidi un che dicea: "S'a voi piace　　139
montare in sù, qui si convien dar volta:
quinci si va chi vuole andar per pace."

　L'aspetto suo m'avea la vista tolta,　　142
per ch'io mi volsi dietro a' miei dottori
com' om che va secondo ch'elli ascolta.

109   begging, and the one begged does not reply,
but, to sharpen their wish, holds high what they
desire and does not hide it.

112   Then they left as if changing their minds, and
now we came to the great tree, which refuses so
many prayers and tears.

115   "Pass further on without drawing near: there is
a tree further up that was bitten by Eve, and this
plant derives from it."

118   So spoke I know not who among the branches,
and therefore Virgil and Statius and I, drawing
together, walked past, on the side that rises.

121   "Remember," it was saying, "the cursed ones
formed in the clouds, who, gorged, fought
against Theseus with their double breasts,

124   and the Hebrews who were so indulgent in
drinking that Gideon would not take them as
comrades, when he went down the hills toward
Midian."

127   So, close against one of the two borders, we
passed on, hearing sins of gluttony followed of
yore by wretched earnings.

130   Then, freed into the empty road, a good
thousand paces and more carried us further, each
of us meditating without a word.

133   "What are you pondering as you walk by
yourselves, you three?" said a sudden voice, and I
started as frightened young animals do.

136   I raised my head to see who it might be, and
never has glass or metal in a furnace been seen so
shining and red

139   as one I saw, who was saying: "If you wish to
mount up, here you must turn: on this path go
those who wish to go toward peace."

142   His appearance had taken away my sight, so I
turned and followed my teachers like one who
goes by what he hears.

E quale, annunziatrice de li albóri,   145
l'aura di maggio movesi e olezza,
tutta impregnata da l'erba e da' fiori:
     tal mi senti' un vento dar per mezza   148
la fronte, e ben senti' mover la piuma,
che fé sentir d'ambrosïa l'orezza,
     e senti' dir: "Beati cui alluma   151
tanto di grazia che l'amor del gusto
nel petto lor troppo disir non fuma,
     esurïendo sempre quanto è giusto."   154

145   And as the breeze in May announcing the
dawn moves fragrant, all impregnated with the
grass and the flowers:

148   such a wind did I feel against my forehead, and
I heard the feathers moving, scenting the air with
ambrosia,

151   and I heard: "Blessed are those whom so much
grace illuminates that love of the palate does not
smoke with too much desire in their breasts,

154   hungering always for what is just!"

NOTES

1-3. Speech . . . good wind: The motif of haste (23.21) will become more insistent later in the canto.

3. like a ship driven by a good wind: Compare 12.5-6. The encounter is beneficial to both.

4-6. the shades . . . I was alive: These must be the shades of 23.16-21; Forese will let them move on (lines 64-74), and we catch up with them in lines 106-12. Apparently they have been listening to the pilgrim and Forese.

7. continuing my speech: Note the parallel with *Inf.* 10.74.

8-9. His soul . . . of others: Statius is slowing his upward progress in order to be with Virgil (see 21.100-102). Forese, too, is slowing his progress (cf. lines 91-93).

10. But tell me . . . Piccarda: The pilgrim's inquiry about Forese's sister is parallel to Statius's inquiry about the other ancient poets (22.97-99), also couched as "tell me . . . if you know." Cf. the note to 23.48.

13-15. My sister . . . high Olympus: Piccarda is in Heaven, with the Church Triumphant (her crown is not that of a martyr; Saint Paul uses the metaphor for salvation in general, 1 Cor. 9.25, quoted in the note to lines 94-97); she will appear in *Paradiso* 3.

16-18. Here it is not . . . dry by fasting: Nowhere in the *Purgatorio* has there been any such prohibition; attention is recalled to the emaciation that makes the souls unrecognizable (cf. the note to lines 52-54).

19-20. This . . . Bonagiunta of Lucca: Bonagiunta Orbicciani of Lucca was a prominent poet of the mid-thirteenth century, in all probability responsible for importing into northern Italy the style of Troubador-derived love poetry developed in Sicily (Contini 1960). He is known from documents dated between 1242 and 1257 to have been a notary; his dates are unknown (to qualify as a notary by 1242, he must have been born by 1215). He had poetic correspondences with other poets, including Guinizelli, whose new manner of using technical terms in love poetry he attacked; Guinizelli wrote an urbane sonnet ("Omo ch'è saggio non corre leggero" [A man who is wise does not lightly run]) in reply; see the note to 26.43-48. Several early commentators say that Dante and Bonagiunta were acquainted; this is not impossible, but there is no evidence except this canto (the *DVE* offers none; see the note to line 36).

19-20. Bonagiunta, Bonagiunta of Lucca: Forese repeats Bonagiunta's name and adds his natal city, as if the pilgrim knew him by reputation only. Nothing suggests that the pilgrim recognizes him; in lines 40-42 he does not even address him by name (cf. the note to lines 52-54).

20-24. that face . . . and the vernaccia: Martin IV was pope from 1281 to 1285. Lana relates that he personally supervised the drowning in wine of eels; at his death a satirical epitaph voiced the joy of the surviving eels.

21. more pierced through: The translation gives the literal meaning of *trapunto*; early commentators take it to refer to a greater prominence of this celebrity's bones. The term also refers to embroidery, needlepoint, or appliqué work, and some modern commentators take it as a reference to the shades' scabies (Vandelli, Pézard).

24. the eels of Bolsena and the vernaccia: Lake Bolsena is some fifty miles northwest of Rome (see the map on page xi); vernaccia is a Tuscan white wine.

25. Many others, one by one: Cf. *Inf.* 5.67-68, and see the note to line 48.

26-27. they seemed . . . dark look: Unlike the souls in lower Hell, who are reluctant to be identified (see *Inf.* 32.94-102, with notes); cf. also 23.22.

28. I saw . . . chewing the air for hunger: Cf. *Met.* 8.825-28:

> petit ille dapes sub imagine somni
> oraque vana movet dentemque in dente fatigat,
> exercetque cibo delusum guttur inani
> proque epulis tenues nequiquam devorat aures.
> [(Erysichthon) reaches for the food as he dreams its image,
> moves his lips in vain and grinds tooth against tooth;
> his deceived throat tries to swallow the nonexistent food,
> and instead of a banquet he devours thin air.]

29. Ubaldino da la Pila: Member of a prominent Tuscan Ghibelline family, the Ubaldini, father of archbishop Ruggieri (*Inf.* 33.13-18) and brother of Ottaviano, also a Ghibelline (see the note to *Inf.* 10.119); after Montaperti (1260) Ubaldino urged the destruction of Florence, as did Provenzano Salvani (see the note to *Inf.* 10.32, *Inter cantica* to Canto 11); he seems to have died in the 1290s; Pila was a castle in the Mugello region near Florence.

29-30. Boniface . . . with his rook: Bonifazio dei Fieschi, archbishop of Ravenna from 1272 to 1295. Lana explains: the archbishops of Ravenna "do not carry a bishop's staff in the form of a crook, but one surmounted by a shape like the rook used in chess."

31-33. messer Marchese . . . felt sated: Marchese degli Argugliosi (of a noble family of Forlì) died after 1296. Benvenuto relates: "Once [Marchese] prevailed upon his steward to tell what was said of him [in Forlì], and when the man fearfully replied: 'Lord, they say that you never do anything but drink,' he said, laughing: 'And why do they never say that I am always thirsty?'" Some version of this story must lie behind line 33.

36. seemed to desire acquaintance with me: For the text here, see "Textual Variants," p. 628.

37-48. He was murmuring . . . clear for you: Bonagiunta's first speeches concern a young woman (line 43) whose kindness will cause Dante to revise his negative opinion of Lucca (see *Inter cantica* below).

37. He was murmuring . . . Gentucca: No explanation is given for Bonagiunta's confused murmuring; he seems to be having a prophetic seizure whose import he has not yet grasped.

38-39. there where . . . plucks them bare: "There" is of course the mouth, problem area for the gluttons.

39. plucks them bare: Italian *piluccare* probably derives from a VL diminutive of Lat. *pilare* [to shear or tear out hair], **piluccare*. The modern meaning "to eat grapes one by one from a cluster" is a late troping of the original meaning.

40-42. O soul . . . both you and me: Bonagiunta's initial inarticulateness may be a sly dig at his poetry (cf. the note to lines 61-63).

43-48. A woman . . . clear for you: Modern commentators tentatively identify this lady as a Gentucca Morla, about the right age to have been known to Dante in 1306-1308, when it is most likely that he visited Lucca (see 8.109-39 and 121-39); by then she was the wife of a Bonaccorso di Fondara. A Giovanni Alighieri, thought to be Dante's oldest son, was living in Lucca at this time. For "femina" [female], see the note to lines 50-51. Whether there was a love relation between Dante and this lady is not known; the context would seem to suggest it.

43. she does not yet wear the wimple: She is not yet married (cf. 8.73-75, with notes).

45. however people may reproach it: Dante is thinking of his own denunciation of the corruption in Lucca (*Inf.* 21.37-49), and of the animosities among the Tuscan cities, forever scornful of their neighbors.

46-48. You will leave . . . clear for you: Like 8.133-39, this means that future experience will clarify his prediction; cf. also lines 89-90.

49-63. But tell me . . . he fell silent: This passage falls into two distinct parts: 1. lines 49-54, which concern Dante specifically; 2. lines 55-63, on the relation of the Sicilian and early Tuscan schools to later developments. This programmatic autocommentary is much more explicit than 2.106-33 or *Par.* 8.33-39.

49-51. But tell me . . . intellect of love: "Donne ch'avete intelletto d'amore" is the first of three canzoni forming the centerpiece of the *Vita nova*, where Dante represents it as the major turning point in his early poetry, from self-regarding poetry to the poetry of praise. His view of the importance in his development of "Donne ch'avete" was fully justified. Not only is the richness and grace of the stylistic garb of the poem unprecedented; Durling/Martinez 1990 have shown that the structure of "Donne ch' avete" involves a complex working out—the first in Dante's career—of the Christian Neoplatonic theme of the procession from God and return to him of all things, a structure that governs the *Vita nova* as a whole, as well as the *Comedy* (see also Martinez 1998, Durling 2001a).

49-50. drew forth the new rhymes, beginning: Bonagiunta echoes the prose narrative of *VN* 17-19 with "nove" [new] (cf. *VN* 18: "matera nova" [a new subject matter]) and "cominciando" [beginning]; *VN* 19 uses *cominciare* and its derivatives no fewer than eight times; see especially:

> Therefore I determined to take as the subject of my speech from then on what would be praise [*loda*] of this most noble lady; and thinking much about this, it seemed to me that I had embarked on an undertaking much too high for me, so that I did not dare to begin [*cominciare*], and thus I remained a number of days with the desire to compose and fear of beginning [*cominciare*].
>
> It happened then that as I was passing along a road beside which there ran a very clear stream, there came upon me so great a desire to compose that I began [*cominciai*] to consider the manner I might follow; and I considered that I should not write of her except speaking to ladies in the second person, and not every woman but only such as are noble and not mere females [*femine*]. Then, I say, my tongue spoke as if moved by itself, and said: "Ladies who have intellect of love."
>
> These words I stored in my memory with great joy, thinking to make them my beginning [*cominciamento*]; and later, having returned to the city mentioned above, meditating for several days, I began [*cominciai*] a canzone with this beginning [*cominciamento*], structured as will be seen below in its division.

The tongue speaking as if moved by itself is a version of Ps. 50.17: "Lord, thou shalt open my lips, and my mouth shall *announce* thy praise" (23.11); "Donne ch'avete" *announces* the new poetry of praise and the Neoplatonic return. For the "theory of the *incipit*" in Dante, see Gorni 1981.

52-54. I in myself . . . go signifying: These much-discussed lines are a manifesto. The early commentators took them as referring exclusively to love poetry (Benvenuto actually refers to the themes as "base"), and some modern commentators suppose that immediacy and sincerity of emotion are being identified as the hallmarks of "Donne ch'avete." But the nature of the Love that inspires is crucial here; in the context of the *Comedy*, *spirare* [to breathe] must be connected with *Par.* 10.1-2, "the Love that breathes [*spira*] equally between the Father and the Son," and with *Purg.* 25.71, where it is used of God's infusion of the rational soul. Dante is claiming that the spirit of love that inpires his poetry, beginning with "Donne ch'avete," is the Holy Spirit (see Hollander 1999, Durling 2001a).

The lines distinguish between an interior phase ("dentro" [within]) of listening and taking note of inspiration, and an external one of "signifying," best taken in its root meaning of "making signs": this would give due place to the constructive side of writing poetry, discussed at some length in *DVE* 2 and of great importance in "Donne ch'avete," as its "division" makes clear.

As Martinez 1983 showed, these lines are a naming of Dante's most characteristic activity (the poetry of praise), analogous with God's own self-naming in Ex. 3.14: "I' mi son un che" echoes "Ego sum qui sum" [I am who am]; the interiority of the reflexive *mi* mirrors in little the the tautology expressing the divine nature.

53. to that measure: Italian *modo* [measure] also takes on the extended senses of "proportion," "manner," "modality," "mode" (in music), "melody."

54. he dictates ... signifying: For the metaphor, cf. *Mon.* 3.4.11, on the writers of the Bible, and *Par.* 10.17. The image of the scribe copying from the Book of Memory governs the *Vita nova* from its first chapter

55-62. O my brother ... and the other: Bonagiunta's reply concerns, not Dante's achievement, but his own failure to develop: he is preoccupied with the "knot" that held him and others back. The early commentators were surely correct in taking line 57 as referring to the pilgrim's style in lines 52-54. On the other hand, Bonagiunta indicates that this "new style" represented a break with "the Notary and Guittone and me" (line 56), which can only reasonably be taken as a reference to the new style of Guinizelli and Cavalcanti, the first of whom Bonagiunta had attacked; Bonagiunta sees the pilgrim as carrying on their influence. Thus Dante is both acknowledging an important debt to his predecessors and claiming a major innovation for himself. The modern use of Dante's phrase *Dolce Stil Novo* to refer to Guinizelli and Cavalcanti and their followers, including Cino da Pistoia, Dante, and others, is both historically just and true to Dante's intention (as the encounter with Guinizelli in Canto 26 also shows).

55. now I see ... the knot: Gorni 1981 relates Bonagiunta's "knot" with the *vinculum linguae* [binding of the tongue] of the deafmute, loosed when he is cured (Mark 7.35); cf. the note to lines 50-51. "Now" most probably refers to Bonagiunta's being in Purgatory, rather than to illumination by the pilgrim's reply to him; as Abrams 1976 argues, the "knot" was probably his gluttony—or, more generally, his attachment to worldly pleasure (cf. 23.14-15; and see Mazzotta 1979). Pertile 1994 has shown that the passage also involves an extended metaphor from falconry; the "knot" is like the leash of a falcon that prevents it from leaving the pole or hand; it prevented the earlier poets' flight. See next note.

58-59. your pens follow close: Dante's "penne" can mean both "pens" and "feathers" (i.e., wings). The lines maintain both the metaphor of a scribe writing to dictation and that of a falcon flying to the falconer (Musa 1966, Pertile 1994).

61-63. whoever most sets . . . fell silent: In *DVE* 1.13.1 Dante dismissed Bonagiunta's style as merely "municipal"; the present passage, accounting for the new style exclusively in terms of fidelity to the inspiration of Love, takes a radically different view.

64-66. As the birds . . . forming a line: These are the cranes, drawn upon for similes in *Inf.* 5.46-47, with military connotations (a *schiera* is a battle line), and in connection with love poetry, and in *Purg.* 26.42-45. Forese's departure will be more vividly described (lines 70-72).

69. leanness and desire: Compare "leanness and sad scurf" (23.39).

70-72. And as one . . . spent its fire: This simile is correlated with lines 94-96.

76-78. I don't know . . . sooner: This reply to Forese is closely related to lines 52-54 (see next note): it describes the pilgrim's yearning [*voler*] to return [*tornar*, line 77, central in the canto], characteristic of Christian Neoplatonic eros, like his *contemptus mundi* [scorn of the world].

74, 76. walked along, am to live: Note the idiomatic reflexive pronoun in "sen veniva" [came along] and "mi viva" [am to live], to be connected with those in lines 8, 46, 52, 91 (cf. the note on lines 52-54 and 27.101); all indicate intimacy, inner life, inner awareness; see also 22.90.

79-90. for the city . . . clear to you: As in 23.91-111, the denunciation of Florence is followed by a prophecy, this time concerning an individual.

80. strips itself: The Italian *spolparsi* [to lose flesh] is apparently a coinage of Dante's; it is obviously related to the theme and terminology of emaciation (cf. *sfogliare* [to unleave], 23.58; *assottigliarsi* [to grow thin], 23.63; cf. the notes to 23.28-33).

82-87. Believe it . . . basely disfigured: The prophecy (for "I see," cf. the note to line 37) concerns Forese's brother, Corso Donati, leader of the Black Guelphs in Florence (see the notes to *Inferno* 6 and 15 and *Inferno* Additional Note 9). His corruption, arrogance, and Ghibelline family relations made him suspect to his party. In 1308 he was condemned to death for treason; escaping, he was captured near the city. According to Villani, after failing to bribe his captors he threw himself from his horse and was thrust through the throat by one of the soldiers; Compagni agrees as to the killing but does not mention the attempt to escape (see Singleton for passages from the chroniclers). Opinions differ as to whether Dante had heard some other version of events; in any case he drew on the folk motif of the demonic horse (he had probably already seen the sculpture of the one carrying off Theodoric at San Zeno in Verona [Singleton]).

82. Believe it: Both here and in 8.133 (where it introduces a favorable prophecy), *or va* implies corroboration: here the prophecy confirms the negative evolution of Florence and gives an instance of "sad ruin" (line 81) as divine retribution.

84. the valley: Hell.

86. ever growing: The reference seems to be to the speed of the beast rather than to its size.

87. basely disfigured: Or mutilated. According to Villani, Corso's body was left in the road and was buried by the monks of the nearby monastery.

88-90. Those wheels . . . clear to you: Compare 23.98-99, with note. For the deictic gesture—now limited to the eyes—see the note to 23.27-133.

91-99. You stay behind . . . marshals of the world: Forese's farewell and departure (he disappears in lines 100-102) have been prepared by lines 64-69. Forese's haste derives from his sense of the passage of time (lines 88-89); his circling the mountain is itself an analogue of the wheeling heavens (see the notes to 23.107 and 125-26). Note the contrast with Statius (lines 8-9); but Statius (the delayer) has completed his purgation.

93. side by side: As the pilgrim had done with Oderisi in 11.73-12.8; note the parallel 12.1, "di pari" [side by side], and see *Inter cantica* below.

94-97. As sometimes . . . greater strides: This evocation of chivalric gallantry inverts the image of Corso dragged at the beast's tail, as the "honor" (line 96) inverts "vilmente" [basely]: Forese's eagerness to joust with his penitential hunger makes his disfigurement a sign of honor (cf. Manfred in 3.106-11, with notes; for Dante's jousting metaphors, see Durling/Martinez 1990, Appendix 1).

Lana identifies the "gualoppo" as a collected canter. Forese has gathered strength and purpose from the encounter with the pilgrim (cf. "grace," 23.42); the control of the horse, the reverse of Corso's loss of control, is an instance of the governing metaphor of the *Purgatorio*, the training of the lower soul as like that of horses and falcons (see 13.37-40 and 14.143-44, with notes; *Conv.* 4.26.5-9).

Also important in the simile are the ideas of combat and emulation: the knight seeks to distinguish himself among his company, as well as to strike a blow against the enemy. There is an allusion to 1 Cor. 9. 24-27:

> Know ye not that they that run in the race, all run indeed, but one receiveth the prize? So run that you may obtain. And every one that striveth for the mastery, refraineth himself from all things: and they indeed that they may receive a corruptible crown; but we an incorruptible one. I therefore so run, not as at an uncertainty: I so fight, not as one beating the air: But I chastise my body, and bring it into subjection: lest perhaps, when I have preached to others, I myself should become a castaway.

98-99. on the way . . . marshals of the world: There is a strong suggestion that Forese is almost "a riva" [in port] (line 78); *in via* [on the way] implies the contrast with *in patria* [in the fatherland].

99. such great marshals of the world: It. *marescalco* (from Germanic *mahrskalk* [servant in charge of horses]) became the title of the head of the royal stables, eventually the chief officer under the emperor (Buti). The Ottimo takes it to refer to Vergil and Statius marshalling armies in their epic poems; they are educators of mankind for the warfare of life.

100-154. And when he . . . what is just: The symmetry of the second tree, associated with the examples of vice, and the first (23.130-54), associated with the examples of virtue, makes it unlikely that there are more (see the note on 23.73).

100-105. And when he . . . turned toward it: Forese does not join the shades beneath the tree, or he would presumably be mentioned in lines 106-11.

101-102. my eyes followed . . . did his words: Forese's prophecy was obscure and will require clarification by the event (lines 89-90); the pilgrim's mind follows it only so far, just as his eyes follow Forese himself only so far.

103-104. the laden, lively . . . fruit tree: The first tree also has "fruit sweet and good to smell" (22.132); there is no mention of the second tree having the unusual branches of the first (22.133-35) or of the liquid spraying over them (22.136-38).

106-12. I saw people. . . changing their minds: See the note to lines 4-6. In 23. 10-12 the shades were heard "weeping and singing" before they are seen: here formalized liturgical weeping and psalmody are replaced by unstructured—perhaps inarticulate—cries of desire, and the souls are compared to small children tantalized by an adult. The implications are complex: on the one hand the stripping away of adult habits and the reduction of feeling to pure desire is a step toward desiring the *good as such* (cf. 17.132-33, 18.61-62); on the other, recognizing the infantile component of gluttonous desire would seem essential to conquering it (see the notes to 23.103-105 and 27.43-46, Additional Note 6). For desire for an apple as typically infantile, see *Conv.* 4.12.16.

115-18. Pass further . . . among the branches: In 22.141 the prohibition of Gen. 3.3 is repeated; here it is revealed that the two trees are derived from the Tree of the Knowledge of Good and Evil. Eve's disobedience is mentioned here as the first example of the vice (others are recited in lines 121-26); the biblical, as usual, precedes the classical. The traditional view of Adam and Eve's sin was that it included every possible subversion of rationality, including gluttony and lust as well as pride.

118. So spoke . . . among the branches: As in 22.140 and 23.1-3, the speaker is invisible, but this time the pilgrim passes on without curiosity.

119-20. and therefore . . . the side that rises: The "side that rises" is the mountainside. The mention of "two borders" (line 127) makes it clear that this tree, too, occupies the center of the terrace.

121-29. Remember . . . wretched earnings: Further examples of the vice of gluttony and its punishment; both involve thirst (see the note to 151-54).

121-23. Remember . . . their double breasts: Theseus' comrade Pirithous was the son of Ixion, who had also begotten the centaurs by copulating with a cloud in the form of Juno. At Pirithous' wedding the centaurs became drunk ("satolli" [filled]) and attempted to carry off the women; Theseus led the Lapiths, Pirithous' people, defeating the centaurs (*Met.* 12.210-535; cf. *Od.* 21.295-304). The myth was a major example for the Greeks of the victory of reason over brute fury and violence; it was represented in the pediment of the temple of Zeus at Olympia and elsewhere; see *Inter cantica* below.

123. their double breasts: Dante saw the two natures of the centaurs (human and equine) as united at the breast (see *Inf.* 12.55-99 and especially 83-84, with notes, and *Inferno* Additional Note 2): a figure of the union in man of animal and rational, joined in the heart, according to Aristotelian theory. This is a version of the horsemanship metaphor (see the note to lines 94-97).

124-26. and the Hebrews . . . hills toward Midian: In a passage regularly cited as a warning against gluttony, God commands Gideon to lead only a few against Midian, so that the Israelites will not attribute the victory to themselves (Jud. 7.1-4). For the test, see verses 5-7:

> And when the people were come down to the waters, the Lord said to Gedeon: They that shall lap the water with their tongues, as dogs are wont to do, thou shalt set apart by themselves: but they that shall drink bowing down their knees, shall be on the other side. And the number of them that

had lapped water, casting it with the hand to their mouth, was three hundred men: and all the rest of the multitude had drunk kneeling. And the Lord said to Gedeon: By the three hundred men that lapped water I shall deliver you, and deliver Madian into thy hand: but let all the rest of the people return to their place.

132-33. each of . . . you three: Presumably the three are meditating on the nature of gluttony; the lines serve to remind us of the presence of Statius.

137-38: never has glass . . . shining and red: Superheated glass and metal are white (even blue); red color indicates a cooler temperature. Like his contemporaries, however, Dante thinks of the color red as that of the element fire.

141. to go toward peace: The expression can also mean "to go in peace."

145-50. And as the breeze . . . air with ambrosia: The breeze, dawn, May, grass, flowers, and fragrance all anticipate the Earthly Paradise (cf. 27.133-35).

150. ambrosia: The food of the gods in mythology. For the fragrance, see *Aen.* 1.402-405: "the hairs on [Venus's] head breathed divine ambrosial fragrance."

151-54. Blessed are those . . . what is just: Based on Matt. 5.6 (the fourth Beatitude; see the note to 22.4-6). "Esuriunt" [they hunger] is no doubt inevitable for gluttony, but note the references to drunkenness in Cantos 23-24. The association of gluttony with smoke rising in the breast derives from physiological theories attributing gluttony and lust to vapors rising from the belly; as well as the association of drunkenness and anger (cf. the smoke of Canto 16).

154. hungering always for what is just: The line is ambiguous: one view takes it to mean "always hungering for what is just," a second, to mean "always hungering (for food) to the right degree." The second meaning cannot be excluded: "quanto" [as much] is the correlative of "tanto" [so much] in line 152. Note the parallel with the two senses of Vergil's *sacer* in Statius' reading (22.38-44).

Inter cantica. Many passing references to the *Inferno* in Canto 24 are important in keeping alive our sense of the constant self-referentiality of the poem: see the notes to lines 7 (*Inferno* 20), 22 (*Inferno* 19), 25 (*Inferno* 5), 29 (*Inferno* 10 and 33), 46 (*Inferno* 21), 64-66 (*Inferno* 5), 82-87 (*Inferno* 6), 123 (*Inferno* 12). The echoes of *Inferno* 5 and 12 have a particular function in keeping before us the connections between gluttony (especially drunkenness) and lust and violence. By far the most elaborate system of parallels, spanning both Cantos 23 and 24, is with the episode of Brunetto Latini in *Inferno* 15, discussed in Additional Note 10.

CANTO 25

Ora era onde 'l salir non volea storpio,   1
ché 'l sole avëa il cerchio di merigge
lasciato al Tauro e la notte a lo Scorpio,

   per che, come fa l'uom che non s'affigge   4
ma vassi a la via sua che che li appaia,
se di bisogno stimolo il trafigge:

   così intrammo noi per la callaia,   7
uno innanzi altro prendendo la scala
che per artezza i salitor dispaia.

   E quale il cicognin che leva l'ala   10
per voglia di volare, e non s'attenta
d'abbandonar lo nido, e giù la cala:

   tal era io con voglia accesa e spenta   13
di dimandar, venendo infino a l'atto
che fa colui ch'a dicer s'argomenta.

   Non lasciò, per l'andar che fosse ratto,   16
lo dolce padre mio, ma disse: "Scocca
l'arco del dir, che 'nfino al ferro hai tratto."

   Allor sicuramente apri' la bocca   19
e cominciai: "Come si può far magro
là dove l'uopo di nodrir non tocca?"

   "Se t'ammentassi come Meleagro   22
si consumò al consumar d'un stizzo,
non fora," disse, "a te questo sì agro,

   e se pensassi come al vostro guizzo   25
guizza dentro a lo specchio vostra image,
ciò che par duro ti parrebbe vizzo.

   Ma perché dentro a tuo voler t'adage,   28
ecco qui Stazio, e io lui chiamo e prego
che sia or sanator de le tue piage."

CANTO 25

Climb—how can the shades become emaciated?—the
development of the human soul and foetus, the airy body—Seventh terrace,
of lust: the wall of fire—the souls in the fire—examples of chastity

1   It was an hour when our climbing brooked
no lameness, for the sun had left the meridian
circle to the Bull and night to the Scorpion;

4   therefore, as a man does not linger but goes
on his way no matter what he sees, if the
stimulus of need pierces him:

7   so we entered the passageway, taking the
stairs one before the other, for their narrowness
unpairs those who climb.

10   And like a little stork that lifts its wing out of
desire to fly, but does not attempt to leave the
nest and lowers it again:

13   so I, with my desire to ask first kindled and
then dampened, came as far as the gesture of
one who prepares to speak.

16   Though our climbing was rapid, my sweet
father did not hold back, but said: "Loose the
bow of speech, which you have drawn to the
very iron."

19   Then confidently I opened my mouth and
began: "How can thinness occur where there is
no need for nourishment?"

22   "If you brought to mind how Meleager was
consumed at the consuming of a log, this
would not," he said, "be so sour for you,

25   and if you thought how, when you wriggle,
your image in the mirror wriggles, what seems
hard to you would seem easy.

28   But so that you may be at ease within your
desire, here is Statius, and I call on him and beg
him now to be the healer of your wounds."

"Se la veduta etterna li dislego,"   31
rispuose Stazio, "là dove tu sie,
discolpi me non potert' io far nego."

 Poi cominciò: "Se le parole mie,   34
figlio, la mente tua guarda e riceve,
lume ti fiero al come che tu die.

 Sangue perfetto, che poi non si beve   37
da l'assetate vene e si rimane
quasi alimento che di mensa leve,

 prende nel core a tutte membra umane 40
virtute informativa, come quello
ch'a farsi quelle per le vene vane.

 Ancor digesto, scende ov' è più bello 43
tacer che dire; e quindi poscia geme
sovr' altrui sangue in natural vasello.

 Ivi s'accoglie l'uno e l'altro insieme, 46
l'un disposto a patire e l'altro a fare,
per lo perfetto loco onde si preme;

 e, giunto lui, comincia ad operare   49
coagulando prima, e poi avviva
ciò che per sua matera fé constare.

 Anima fatta la virtute attiva   52
qual d'una pianta, in tanto differente
che questa è in via e quella è già a riva,

 tanto ovra poi che già si move e sente 55
come spungo marino, e indi imprende
ad organar le posse ond' è semente:

 or si spiega, figliuolo, or si distende 58
la virtù ch'è dal cor del generante,
dove natura a tutte membra intende.

 Ma come d'animal divegna fante   61
non vedi tu ancor: quest' è tal punto
che più savio di te fé già errante,

 sì che per sua dottrina fé disgiunto 64
da l'anima il possibile intelletto,
perché da lui non vide organo assunto.

 Apri a la verità che viene il petto,   67
e sappi che, sì tosto come al feto
l'articular del cerebro è perfetto,

31   "If I unfold before him the eternal view,"
replied Statius, "in your presence, let my excuse
be that I am unable to refuse you."

34   Then he began: "If your mind, son, keeps
and receives my words, they will cast light for
you on the *how* that you ask.

37   Perfected blood, never drunk by the thirsty
veins, but left, like food one carries back from
the table,

40   takes on within the heart the power to shape
all human members, as does that which goes
out through the veins to become members.

43   Digested further, it descends to the place of
which it is better to be silent than to speak, and
then from there it flows onto another's blood
in a natural vessel.

46   There the two join together, the one disposed
to undergo and the other to shape, thanks to the
perfect place from which it is pressed,

49   and, once arrived, it begins to operate by
coagulating first, and then it quickens what it
has made firm to be its matter.

52   This active power, having become a soul like
that of a plant, but different in so far as it is still
under way, while the other is already in port,

55   next works until it moves and has feeling like
a sea sponge, and then it undertakes to shape
organs for the faculties of which it is the seed:

58   now it unfolds, my son, now the power
spreads out that comes from the heart of the parent,
where nature provides for all the members.

61   But how from an animal it becomes capable
of speech, you do not yet see: this is a point
that led one wiser than you into error,

64   so that in his teaching he separated the
possible intellect from the soul, not seeing any
organ occupied by it.

67   Open your breast to the truth that comes,
and know that as soon as in the foetus the
articulation of the brain has been completed,

lo Motor primo a lui si volge, lieto   70
sovra tant' arte di natura, e spira
spirito novo, di vertù repleto,

    che ciò che trova attivo quivi tira   73
in sua sustanzia, e fassi un'alma sola,
che vive e sente e sé in sé rigira.

    E perché meno ammiri la parola,   76
guarda il calor del sol che si fa vino,
giunto a l'omor che de la vite cola.

    Quando Làchesis non ha più del lino,   79
solvesi da la carne, e in virtute
ne porta seco e l'umano e 'l divino:

    l'altre potenze tutte quante mute;   82
memoria, intelligenza e volontade
in atto molto più che prima agute.

    Sanza restarsi, per sé stessa cade   85
mirabilmente a l'una de le rive;
quivi conosce prima le sue strade.

    Tosto che loco lì la circunscrive,   88
la virtù formativa raggia intorno
così e quanto ne le membra vive.

    E come l'aere, quand' è ben pïorno,   91
per l'altrui raggio che 'n sé si reflette,
di diversi color diventa addorno:

    così l'aere vicin quivi si mette   94
in quella forma che in lui suggella
virtüalmente l'alma che ristette;

    e simigliante poi a la fiammella,   97
che segue il foco là 'vunque si muta,
segue lo spirto sua forma novella.

    Però che quindi ha poscia sua paruta,   100
è chiamata ombra; e quindi organa poi
ciascun sentire infino a la veduta.

    Quindi parliamo e quindi ridiam noi;   103
quindi facciam le lagrime e ' sospiri
che per lo monte aver sentiti puoi.

    Secondo che ci affliggono i disiri   106
e li altri affetti, l'ombra si figura,
e quest' è la cagion di che tu miri."

70   the first Mover turns to it, rejoicing over the
greatness of Nature's art, and breathes into it a
new spirit, replete with power,

73   that draws into its own substance what it
finds active there, and becomes one single soul,
that lives and feels and turns itself back to itself.

76   And that you may wonder less at my words,
look how the heat of the sun becomes wine,
joined with the liquid that flows from the
grape.

79   When Lachesis has no more thread, the soul
is released from the flesh, and it carries off in its
powers both the human and the divine:

82   the other powers, all of them, are mute;
memory, understanding, and will are much
sharper in action than before.

85   Without delay it falls of itself, wondrously, to
one of the two shores; there first it knows its paths.

88   As soon as place circumscribes it there, the
formative power radiates around in the same
way and as much as in its living members.

91   And just as the air, when it is very moist,
becomes adorned with various colors because it
reflects another's rays:

94   so the air near there takes on the form that
the soul seals into it with its power, once it has
come to rest;

97   and then, like the flame that follows fire
wherever it changes, so its new shape follows
the spirit.

100   Because the soul now gains visibility through
this body, this is called a shade; and from it the
soul fashions organs for every sense, even as far
as sight.

103   Through this body we speak and laugh;
through it we make the tears and the sighs that
you may have heard around the mountain.

106   According as desires and other feelings afflict
us, so our shade configures itself, and this is the
cause of what you wonder at."

E già venuto a l'ultima tortura   109
s'era per noi e vòlto a man destra,
ed eravamo attenti ad altra cura.

  Quivi la ripa fiamma in fuor balestra,   112
e la cornice spira fiato in suso
che la reflette e via da lei sequestra,

  ond' ir ne convenia dal lato schiuso   115
ad uno ad uno, e io temëa 'l foco
quinci, e quindi temeva cader giuso.

  Lo duca mio dicea: "Per questo loco   118
si vuol tenere a li occhi stretto il freno,
però ch'errar potrebbesi per poco."

  "*Summae Deus clementïae*," nel seno   121
al grande ardore allora udi' cantando,
che di volger mi fé caler non meno,

  e vidi spirti per la fiamma andando,   124
per ch'io guardava loro e a' miei passi,
compartendo la vista a quando a quando.

  Appresso il fine ch'a quell' inno fassi,   127
gridavano alto: "*Virum non cognosco!*"
indi ricominciavan l'inno, bassi.

  Finitolo, anco gridavano: "Al bosco   130
si tenne Diana ed Elice caccionne,
che di Venere avea sentito il tòsco."

  Indi al cantar tornavano; indi donne   133
gridavano e mariti che fuor casti,
come virtute e matrimonio imponne.

  E questo modo credo che lor basti   136
per tutto il tempo che 'l foco li abbruscia:
con tal cura conviene e con tai pasti

  che la piaga da sezzo si ricuscia.   139

109 And now we had come to the last torture, turning to the right, and we were intent on a new concern.

112 There the bank throws out flame, and a wind blows upward from the edge, deflecting the flame and isolating a path;

115 therefore we had to walk along the exposed side one by one, and I feared the fire on this side, and on that I was afraid of falling down.

118 My leader was saying: "Through this place we must keep a close rein on our eyes, for straying would be easy."

121 "*Summae Deus clementiae,*" I heard singing in the bosom of the great fire, and it made me wish to turn as well,

124 and I saw spirits walking within the flames, and so I looked at them and at my steps, alternating my gaze from time to time.

127 After singing the end of that hymn, they loudly cried: "*Virum non cognosco!*" then they began the hymn again, softly.

130 Finishing it, again they cried out: "Diana held to the woods and drove out Helice, who had felt the poison of Venus."

133 Then they went back to singing; then they called out wives and husbands who were chaste, as virtue and matrimony require of us.

136 And this manner I believe lasts through all the time that the fire burns at them: with such care and such foods

139 must the wound at last be sewn up.

NOTES

1-9. It was an hour ... those who climb: The hour (see next note) permits no "lameness" [delay]; the travelers hasten, obeying "the stimulus of need," climbing the narrow stairs (see the note to 10.16) in single file.

1-3. It was an hour ... to the Scorpion: It is shortly after noon, not, as some commentators suppose, 2 P.M. (the sun is not at the first point of Aries—the equinox was March 13; at this date the first point of Taurus reaches the meridian a few minutes after the sun has passed it). As in 2.4-6, Night is imagined as a point circling opposite the sun, thus near the cusp between Libra and Scorpio, the first point of which has now passed the *Imum caeli* (see fig. 2).

10-108. And like a little stork ... what you wonder at: All but 40 lines of the canto are devoted to the pilgrim's question and its answer (as in Cantos 15 and 22 occupying the entire climb to the next terrace); again it is Statius who answers (thus he is the focus of almost three entire cantos: 21, 22, 25). The amount of space this question occupies is also an index of its importance.

10-15. And like a little stork ... prepares to speak: The simile of the fledgling stork recalls the motif of flight (see the notes to 24.55-59, 10.124-26; the pilgrim's wings will grow in 27.121-23, and he will be ready for flight in 33.145).

14-15. the gesture ... prepares to speak: This gesture is no doubt a general muscular tension (see the note to lines 16-18), as well as a facial expression including drawn breath and opened mouth (perhaps also raised eyebrows; cf. *Inf.* 15.20-21). For "s'argomenta" [prepares] see 6.129, with note; for the closely related idea of *arming oneself* to speak, cf. *Par.* 24.46.

16-18. Though our climbing ... to the very iron: The pilgrim's eagerness to let loose his question (his "arrow") is compared to the tension of the bow, drawn to the full length of the arrow (to the iron point). Both comparisons (lines 10-15 and 17-18) involve flight and the idea of teleology. The analogy between speaking and shooting an arrow is traditional (see the discussion of "Così nel mio parlar" in Durling/Martinez 1990). Arrow and archery imagery will increase in importance in the rest of the poem (for an important example see 31.16-21).

20-108. How can thinness ... what you wonder at: The question, prompted by the emaciation of the shades purging gluttony (cf. 23.34-36), brings into focus one of the central concerns of the cantica: the primacy, at all levels of human experience, of the principle of soul. The immediate, instinctive impulse to see hunger and lust as expressing the body—the mode of experiencing them *as* bodily—is illusory (it could almost stand as a definition of fleshliness). In Dante's view there is nothing in the body except what is fashioned by the soul, though of course out of materials presented to it (such body-soul monism was gradually emerging in Scholasticism; see Dales 1995, Bynum 1995). For a more traditional emphasis, seeing the body as almost a separate entity only tenuously controlled by the soul, cf. *De spiritu et anima* 14 (*PL* 270: a twelfth-century Cistercian text, drawing mainly on Augustine): "Both have similar extremes, namely the highest part of the body and the lowest of the soul, by which, *without confusion of natures*, they can be joined in a personal union. Thus the soul, which is truly spirit, and the flesh, which is truly body, at their extremes are fittingly joined, that is, in the imaginative faculty of the soul, which is not body, but is like body, and in the capacity for sensation of the flesh, which is almost spirit, since it cannot take place without the soul" [italics added].

22-30. If you brought . . . of your wounds: Virgil proposes two analogies, one from myth, the other from common experience; neither is very clear.

22-24. If you brought . . . so sour for you: The story of Meleager is told in *Met.* 8.260-525: at his birth the Fates decreed that his life would end with the burning of a log then on the fire; his mother snatched out and preserved the log, but when Meleager killed her brothers she cast it on the fire, and he perished as it burned. The point of the parallel is that Meleager's body is governed by a principle apparently extraneous to it.

25-27. and if you thought . . . would seem easy: The analogy of the mirror is clearer: the body is a mere reflection, a mirror image, of the soul; but this is hardly an explanation.

28-30. But so that you . . . of your wounds: Statius alone is capable of giving the full explanation, which requires illumination by revelation and faith. Virgil is echoing Augustine in referring to ignorance as a wound (for Augustine it is part of the *vulneratio naturae*; see Introduction, pp. 6-7). The imagery of wounds is important in Dante's treatment of the themes of food and sex, the most important focuses of concupiscence (see 24.37-39, 25.138-39): correct understanding of the relation of body and soul is necessary for the healing of the soul (see the note to 22.38-44).

31-109. If I unfold . . . what you wonder at: Briefly introduced and concluded (lines 34-36 and 106: note the rounding out of "the *how* that you ask" with "the cause of what you wonder at"), Statius's speech explains the nature of the shades' bodies as typical of the functioning of the soul, the formal principle of the body; it has two main parts: lines 37-78, on the development of the foetus; and 79-106, on the shade or airy body produced by the soul after death. Dante's position is a version of the new monism (see the note to lines 21-106), but he follows out its implications more consequentially than any of the theologians, who are still to some extent caught in the old dualism in their treatment of the soul as a "form" that cannot change; Dante carefully avoids this trap. But it must be remembered that his account is compressed and schematic, leaving untouched many difficult distinctions, and that it serves a poetic purpose as well as a "scientific" one.

37-78. Perfected blood . . . from the grape: In certain important respects
Dante follows the views of Albert the Great (Albertus Magnus), as set forth in
his *De natura et origine animae* and *De animalibus* (see Nardi 1960, 1967). Accord-
ing to Nardi, these are: 1. that the sensitive (i.e., animal) soul developed in the
foetus was *combined* with the rational soul, a view shared by Peckham and others
(attacked by Aquinas, who does not name its proponents, in *CG* 2.89.6-22, *ST*
1a q. 118, and elsewhere: Aquinas maintained that the rational soul infused by
God included the vegetative and sensitive principles and entirely replaced the
soul already in the foetus); 2. that the soul of the foetus governed the forming of
the body (Aquinas partly shared this view, but others, e.g. Alexander of Hales,
did not). For Dante's differences from Albert, see the critique of Nardi by Cogan
1999, Additional Note 11, and the notes to lines 46-51, 53-54, and 58-60.

37-45. Perfected blood . . . natural vessel: In Aristotelian physiology (see
especially *De part. anim.* 3.4-7), the heart was the seat of the soul (see 5.73-75,
with note, and see the note to lines 76-78 below) and communicated to the
blood the formative power to develop the organs, formed like alluvial deposits
from the bloodstream (although Aristotle uses the analogy of a river, there was of
course no conception of the circulation of the blood until its discovery in the late
sixteenth century; the heart was thought to be like a well or cistern). Lines 37-39
identify the blood that will eventually become semen, which is never shared out
to the veins (the "table" corresponds to the heart, not the veins); lines 40-42
describe the so-called "third digestion" of food (the first two take place in the
stomach and liver respectively; see the notes to *Inf.* 30.52-57, 73-74, and 117, and
Durling 1981a), undergone in the heart by all the blood; the "fourth digestion"
is the subject of lines 43-45: a portion of the unused blood is transformed into
semen (in the heart) and descends into the genitals to be deposited in the mother's
womb, the "natural vessel." For *geme* [literally, oozes], cf. *Inf.* 13.41.

46-51. There the two . . . to be its matter: In the first stage of the development
of the foetus, the father's semen, as the active formative power ("disposed . . . to
shape"), coagulates and solidifies the matter furnished by the mother's blood,
which is passive ("disposed to undergo"). The "perfect place" of line 48 is the
father's heart (mentioned again in line 59). Dante adopts the reactionary Aristo-
telian theory, common to most thinkers of the period, according to which the
father contributes the active principle, the mother only passive matter (see Addi-
tional Note 11).

48. from which it is pressed: Note the implicit image of a wine- or oil-press.

50-51. it quickens . . . to be its matter: The formative power gives life ("avviva"
[quickens]) to the matter it is shaping; most other accounts, including Albert's,
also stress the shaping influence of the stars.

52-60. This active power . . . all the members: These lines unambiguously
encapsulate the most important difference from Aquinas; for Dante the active

power of the semen *becomes* the soul of the foetus, passing in a natural evolution from an initial stage of plant life, through an intermediate stage like the life of a sponge (see the note to liines 55-56); to a final phase (lines 56-60) in which the characteristic animal structures of specialized organs are fashioned: this phase receives particular emphasis; as line 61 implies, the result is that the foetus has a human body, but not yet a human soul.

53-54. different in so far . . . already in port: "The other" (the soul of a plant) has reached its completion, its *télos* or "port," while the soul of the foetus will develop further. Aquinas would not have accepted this point; for him "form" could not evolve; Albert's position is possibly inconsistent (Additional Note 11).

55-56. until it moves . . . sea sponge: Aristotle classed sponges as defective animals (*Historia animalium,* 5.16). One notes that this ascent on the scale of being is carried out by every animal and human foetus: the distant ancestor of modern theories, in which ontogeny repeats phylogeny. The powers of locomotion and sensation mark the transition to animal.

56-57. it undertakes . . . of which it is the seed: Until the soul has fashioned the organs for perception and locomotion, as well as nutrition, it possesses these faculties [*posse*] virtually, as their seed. The correlation of the faculties of the soul with bodily organs was central to Aristotle's conception. The metaphor of the formative power in the semen as a craftsman's tool or sculptor's chisel is prominent in Albert's discussions of generation; cf. *De animalibus* 16. tr. 1, c. 6; see notes to 76-78 and 94-96 and *Inter cantica* below.

58-60. now it unfolds . . . all the members: The subject of the verbs "si spiega" [unfolds itself] and "si distende" [spreads out] is "virtù" [power]. In Albert's *De natura et origine animae* 1.6, the "spreading out" and the "continuitas motus continue exeuntis de potentia ad actum" [the continuity of the motion continuously going out from potency to act], which Nardi argued was the source of Dante's idea here, refer to the *potentiality* of the foetus, not to the formative principle itself (again, see Additional Note 11).

61-78. But how from an animal . . . flows from the grape: The climactic account of the infusion of the rational soul is introduced by a warning about the delicacy of the problem and concludes with the analogy of the metamorphosis of grape juice into wine. Following Gregory of Nyssa, the Greek church placed the infusion of the rational soul at conception (this is the present position of the Church), but in the medieval West the creation of Adam in Genesis 2, in which the fashioning of the body precedes the "breathing in" of the soul, provided the dominant model.

61-66. But how from an . . . occupied by it: The error targeted here is that of Averroës. According to Aristotle no organ can be found for the possible intellect; Averroës therefore attributed to him the view that both the possible and the active intellect were external to the human soul, being angelic intelligences operating through the heavenly bodies (the possible intellect was the capacity to form abstractions that could be the focus of the act of intellection). His claim that Aristotle denied individual immortality was probably correct, but most of the Scholastics, including Albert and Thomas, rejected the idea that Aristotle did so; Siger of Brabant and other "Averroists," very possibly including Guido Cavalcanti (see *Inf.* 10. 61-69, with notes), accepted his having done so.

67. Open your breast . . . that comes: This truth is only accessible through faith in divine revelation.

68-69. as soon as . . . has been completed: In Dante's time the body was thought to be completely structured by the fortieth day; his mention of the articulation of the brain is unusual.

70-72. the first Mover . . . replete with power: Based on Gen. 2.7: "And the Lord God formed [*formavit*] man of the slime of the earth, and breathed into his face the breath of life; and man became a living soul."

71. the greatness of Nature's art: The formation of the foetus has been overseen by Nature in the larger sense, i.e., the formative power of the heavenly bodies (explicitly acknowledged in virtually all medieval discussions of embryology, and strongly featured in Albert's).

71-75. a new spirit . . . back to itself: Dante's account of the union of the "new spirit" with the sensitive soul in the foetus is a version of Albert's theory (see the note to lines 37-78), but we know of no other medieval text that states that the infused rational soul draws the soul of the foetus "into its own substance" (discussed in Additional Note 11).

75. that lives . . . back to itself: The line enumerates the three principal powers of the unified soul: it *lives* (vegetative powers), *feels* (sensitive/animal powers), and *knows* (intellectual powers); knowing necessarily involves self-awareness, or *reflection* ("turns itself back to itself"); cf. the related passage in *Conv.* 4.2.18.

76-78. And that you . . . from the grape: The analogy operates on several levels. At the embryological level, it was thought that the seed (see the notes to lines 46-51) formed the foetus by means of its vital heat. At a more general metaphysical level, it is a form of the Neoplatonic analogy between the sun (the "heart" of the cosmos—see Durling 1981b) and God (see the note to *Inf.* 10.97-108), from whom all things radiate like light (cf. lines 88-96). Finally, there is an important connection with the miracle at Cana, when Christ (the "Sun of Justice") turned the water into wine. Underlying all these levels—and the entire account of embryology—is Dante's fundamental category of *metamorphosis* (see 10.121-29, with note, and *Inter cantica*, below).

79-108. When Lachesis . . . what you wonder at: Statius now turns to the question of the "shade" [*ombra*], the visible body of the soul after death, whose fashioning is explained on the same principles as the development of the living body. The account presupposes two phases: 1. immediately after death, in which we are to understand that the soul does not occupy space (lines 80-84); 2. circumscription by place, beginning when the soul arrives on one of the two shores of embarkation (Acheron: *Inferno* 3; Tiber: *Purgatorio* 2). Naturally enough, there is nothing in earlier literature, theological or otherwise, like this passage, but it is integral to Dante's conception of the unified human person.

79. When Lachesis has no more thread: That is, when death comes; see the notes to lines 103-108 and to 21.27.

80-84. the soul is released . . . action than before: Some early Fathers believed in a subtle body of the soul, but the Scholastics agreed that the soul was entirely immaterial; they held that the intellectual powers of the soul were strengthened after death; there were differences on the survival of the vegetative and sensitive powers (the "human," though the term might be taken to exclude the vegetative powers), though all agreed that they were inactive ("mute," line 82). This phase of Statius's account corresponds to the traditional conception (cf. *De spiritu et anima* 15 on the disembodied soul after death: "moving only in time . . . not in space, since it is not spread out [*non distenditur*] in any place"; and cf. lines 58, 21-22).

83-84. memory . . . than before: These are all aspects of the rational soul (for *will* as rational, see the notes on 18.63 and 66), more intense because no longer hampered by the mortal body. A tradition going back to Augustine (*De trinitate* 10.11.18) conceived of these three intellectual powers as the seal of the Trinity in the human mind.

85-102. Without delay . . . as far as sight: The production of the airy body follows the same principles as that of the foetus and achieves the same degree of perfection as in the living members (line 90), including fashioning internal organs at least for sense perception (lines 101-102), though probably not for the functions of the vegetative soul (see note to lines 80-84). Barański in *LDT* calls attention to *ST* Ia, q. 51, a. 2, ad 3, on angels' assuming airy appearances of body (cf. our note on 5.112-14), and to the *Visio Baronti,* in which the visionary assumes a body of air and light.

87. there first it knows its paths: The souls of both damned and blest must move through space to their proximate and their ultimate destinations (see *Inf.* 3.1-12, 4.52-63, and 5.4-15; *Purg.* 25.105; *Par.* 9.112-26).

88-102. As soon as place . . . as far as sight: "Radiates" [*raggia*] again involves the analogy with the cosmic heart, the sun (see the notes on lines 37-78 and 76-78). There is also a submerged analogy with the action of sound waves, supporting the basic analogy between the body of the text and the human body, discussed in Durling 1981a, Freccero 1983 (for Virgil's works as his *voice*, see *Inf.* 1.62-63).

88. As soon as place . . . there: This "falling" to the embarkation points sets the production of the airy body (in orthodox terms probably a heretical idea) within Dante's fiction or myth, insulating it from awkward questions. Nevertheless the immediate working of the soul to construct a body out of the materials available underlies Dante's entire conception of the other world, is so central to his poetics and his view of the relation of soul and body, and is given such prominence here, that it demands to be taken seriously. Note the difference from the traditional position (note to lines 80-84; the locomotion of the soul is mentioned again in lines 97-99). There is of course a considerable background in folklore (ghosts, etc.; cf. the note to lines 85-102) and the classical notion of the shade (as in *Aeneid* 6): for all of it Dante furnishes a Christian philosophical foundation!

91-96. And just as the air . . . come to rest: "Another" is once more the sun; the analogy with the rainbow will be used to describe the pilgrim's final vision of the Trinity (*Par.* 33.115-20).

94-96. so the air . . . with its power: Note that the soul *imposes* the form on the air. For the metaphor of seal and wax, see the note to 18.22-27. For the traditional notion of begetting as like coining or stamping a seal on wax, see *Ep. mor.* 84.8 and Durling 1981a.

97-99. like the flame . . . follows the spirit: Properly speaking the element fire was thought to be invisible; flame was understood to be heated air. This analogy is closely related to Virgil's example of the mirror image (lines 25-26).

100-101. Because the soul . . . called a shade: Virgil's shades seem made of air, into which they dissolve; see the passages quoted in the notes to 2.79-84.

103-108. Through this body . . . you wonder at: These lines make it clear that the soul, not the body, is the source of affects and their expression. Dante is providing a countertext to the famous passage (*Aen.* 6.730-47—a principal source of the idea of Purgatory, quoted in our Introduction, pp. 3-4; cf. *Inf.* 10.58, with note) attributing the perturbations of the soul and the need for purgation to the infection of the body. In "quindi . . . quindi" [literally, hence . . . hence], Dante is echoing Vergil's line 733: "hinc metuunt cupiuntque, dolent gaudentque" [hence—i.e., because of the body—they fear and desire, grieve and rejoice], but with opposite meaning. It is possible, too, that Dante's *quanto* [as much] (line 90, of the formative power exercized by the soul after death) echoes Vergil's *quantum* [in so far as] (line 731, of the body as burden).

108. what you wonder at: The emaciation of the shades of the gluttonous is thus attributed to the souls' desire to indulge in gluttony, which is shown to be independent of any bodily need (as, indeed, it was in this life).

109-39. And now we had . . . be sewn up: The last section of the canto, the arrival on the seventh and last terrace of Purgatory proper, devoted to the purgation of lust.

115-20. therefore we had . . . would be easy: Another case in which virtue is suggested to be a middle path between extremes, although the contrary of lustful burning (line 117) is not specified.

121-39. *Summae Deus* . . . at last be sewn up: The last twenty lines of the canto introduce the souls that are purging lust. The pilgrim apparently does not see them at first; then his attention is drawn by their singing, and the report of their utterances ends the canto.

121. *Summae Deus clementiae*: A very old hymn, though not by St. Ambrose, it is attested as early as the tenth century (*Analecta hymnica,* 1), associated liturgically with Saturday night. Omitting the final invocation of the Trinity, it reads:

Summae Deus clementiae,	God of highest clemency,
mundi factor machinae,	maker of the fabric of the world,
unus potentialiter,	one in power
trinusque personaliter,	and triple in Persons,
nostros pios cum canticis	accept our pious weepings
fletus benigne suscipe,	with our songs graciously,
quo corde puro sordibus	by which may we more fully
te perfruamur largius.	enjoy you, pure heart cleansed of stains.
Lumbos iecurque morbidum	Our loins and liver, diseased,
adure igne congruo,	burn out with suited fire,
accincti ut sint perpeti,	so may they ever be girt up,
luxu remoto pessimo.	all sinful lust put away.
Ut quique horas noctium	As all of us interrupt
nunc concinendo rumpimus,	the hours of night with singing,
donis beatae patriae	so with the riches of our blest homeland
ditemur omnes affatim.	may we all be enriched beyond desire.

See the note to 27.8, and note the parallel with "Te lucis ante" (8.13): the first and last hymns of the *Purgatorio* beg for help against sexual urges.

121-26. I heard singing . . . from time to time: The sight, from outside the fire, of spirits walking within it echoes Daniel 3.24 and 91-92, on Shadrak, Mishak, and Abednago, cast into the fiery furnace for refusing to worship Nebuchadnezar's statue (the episode is echoed again in 27.25-30): "And they walked in the midst of the flame, praising God and blessing the Lord . . . Then the king was astonished and rose up in haste and said to his nobles . . . Behold, I see four men loosed and walking in the midst of the fire. And there is no hurt in them."

127-35. After singing the end . . . require of us: The singing of "Summae Deus clementiae" (like a liturgical antiphon preceding each verse of a chanted psalm) precedes the recitation of each example of chastity, first that of the Virgin, then a classical example, then an indeterminate number of examples of chaste husbands and wives, who are all unnamed, uniquely among the examples in the cantica. It is particularly striking that no instance of monastic or celibate virtue is mentioned.

128. *Virum non cognosco* [I know not man]: This is the Virgin's reply to Gabriel at the Annunciation (Luke 1.34); see the note to 10.34-45 (on the references to the virtues of the Virgin see Additional Note 12).

130-32. Diana held . . . poison of Venus: Helice is Callisto, whose story is told in *Met.* 2.401-507: a nymph of Diana, she is raped and made pregnant by Jupiter. When her nakedness reveals her advanced state, she is banished from the woods by Diana. After Callisto gives birth, she and her son are turned into bears by the jealous Juno, but Jupiter makes them constellations (the Big and Little Bear).

136-39. And this manner . . .at last be sewn up: There is again a pun on *modus* [manner, measure] and *modus* [melody, musical mode]; see *Inf.* 3.34-36, 19.88.

Inter cantica. As our notes to *Inferno* 18-30 and *Inferno* Additional Note 13 point out, the Malebolge are the belly of the Body of Satan (the parallel rests on the idea that truth is the food of the soul, fraud its poison); they involve countless references to the nutritive and reproductive functions of the human belly, of which the sins of fraud represent symbolic distortions. The nutritive functions of the belly are especially prominent in *Inferno* 18 (the flatterers: excretion) and 30 (the falsifiers: disorders of digestion; parallel with coining: see below). The reproductive functions are featured in *Inferno* 18, where the panders are said to turn women into coin, parodying the imposition of form on the foetus, and especially in *Inferno* 24-25, where the thieves undergo three types of infernal metamorphosis (see *Inferno* Additional Note 10): 1. combustion and immediate reconstitution (24.97-120; compared to the Phoenix, and parodying resurrection); 2. agglutination (25.49-78; parodying nutritional agglutination and the sexual act); 3. exchange of human and reptile forms, mediated by smoke issuing from mouth and navel (parodying the gradual transformation of the fetus in the womb through vegetative and animal stages, and no doubt referring to theories of the operation of the "spirit" in the father's seed). Some of the key terms of Statius's exposition occur in *Inferno* 24-25: "nature" (25.100; cf. *Purg.* 25.60, 71), "form" and "matter" (24. 125, 25.101-102, 125; cf. *Purg.* 25.41, 51, 89, 95), forms of the verbs *to generate* (25.119; cf. *Purg.* 25.59) and *to join* (24.104; cf. *Purg.* 25.46), "limbs" and "members" (25.60, 75, 106, 116; cf. *Purg.* 25.60), as well as related ideas, such as concealment of the genitals (25.116; cf. *Purg.* 25.44-45), the importance of heat (24.85-90, 25.61-66; implicit in *Purg.* 25), the chain of being, with descent from human to reptile (25, with comparison to the snail in line 132) or ascent from plant to human (emphasized especially in *Purg.* 25. 51-57—with comparison to the sponge—and 61), speech as distinctive of man (24.64, 25.136-41; cf. *Purg.* 25.61-63), disordered sexuality as part of the *vulneratio naturae* (there is the wound at the nape, *Inf.* 24.98; the wound [*piaga*] at the navel, *Inf.* 25.85-86, 92; the wounds [*piage*] of ignorance, *Purg.* 25.30; and the wound [*piaga*] of concupiscence, *Purg.* 25.139).

Not surprisingly, these cantos present an unusual density of references to Ovid (named, along with Lucan, in *Inf.* 25.99) and Ovidian myths: Arethusa (*Inf.* 25.97-99), Cadmus (*Inf.* 25.97), Callisto (*Purg.* 25.130-32), Io (*Inf.* 24.100), Meleager (*Purg.* 25.20-24), Pasiphaë (*Purg.* 26.41-42, 82, 86-87), the Phoenix, Salmacis, and Hermaphroditus (*Inf.* 25.57-59; *Purg.* 26.82). (As can be seen, because of the close connection between sexuality and poetic creation, the system of parallels involves also *Purgatorio* 26; see also *Inter cantica* there.) *Inf.* 25.94-102, the poet's boast at surpassing the classical descriptions of metamorphosis, finds its counterpart in the humility with which Statius sets forth (see lines 31-33) the miracle of divine creativity which the infernal transformations parody, and this is an even greater triumph of Dante's art. The climax, in Hell, of the loss of speech of the emerging serpent and the spitting misuse of speech by the emerging human (fraud being possible precisely because of the gift of speech), is overgone in the crowning moment of human generation, when "it becomes capable of speech"— and, as Dante intends us to remember, of poetry.

CANTO 26

Mentre che sì per l'orlo, uno innanzi altro,   1
ce n'andavamo, e spesso il buon maestro
diceami: "Guarda: giovi ch'io ti scaltro,"

feriami il sole in su l'omero destro,   4
che già raggiando tutto l'occidente
mutava in bianco aspetto di cilestro,

e io facea con l'ombra più rovente   7
parer la fiamma; e pur a tanto indizio
vidi molt' ombre, andando, poner mente.

Questa fu la cagion che diede inizio   10
loro a parlar di me, e cominciarsi
a dir: "Colui non par corpo fittizio."

Poi verso me quanto potëan farsi   13
certi si fero, sempre con riguardo
di non uscir dove non fosser arsi.

"O tu che vai, non per esser più tardo   16
ma forse reverente, a li altri dopo,
rispondi a me, che 'n sete e 'n foco ardo.

Né solo a me la tua risposta è uopo,   19
ché tutti questi n'hanno maggior sete
che d'acqua fredda Indo o Etïopo.

Dinne com' è che fai di te parete   22
al sol, pur come tu non fossi ancora
di morte intrato dentro da la rete."

Sì mi parlava un d'essi, e io mi fóra   25
già manifesto, s'io non fossi atteso
ad altra novità ch'apparve allora:

ché per lo mezzo del cammino acceso   28
venne gente col viso incontro a questa,
la qual mi fece a rimirar sospeso.

CANTO 26

Seventh terrace, continued: Guido Guinizelli—homosexuals and heterosexuals—examples of lust—Guinizelli identified—the pilgrim's debt to him—Arnaut Daniel

1   While thus, one before the other, we walked
       along the edge, and often my good master said to
       me: "Look out; profit from my alerting you,"

4   the sun was striking me on the right shoulder,
       for already its rays were changing all the west from
       blue to white,

7   and with my shadow I was making the flame
       seem ruddier; and even to so small an indication I
       saw many shades pay heed as they walked.

10   This was the cause that led to their speaking of
       me, and they began by saying to each other: "That
       one does not look like a factitious body."

13   Then some approached me as closely as they
       could, always taking care not to come out where
       they would not be burned.

16   "O you who are walking behind the others, not
       because you are slower, but perhaps reverent,
       answer me, who am burning in thirst and fire.

19   Nor do I alone need your reply, for all these
       have greater thirst for it than ever Indian or Ethiop
       for cold water.

22   Tell us how it is that you make a wall of yourself
       to the sun, as if you had not yet entered the net of
       death."

25   So one of them was saying to me, and I would
       already have made myself known, if I had not
       attended to another novelty that appeared then:

28   for down the center of the burning path came
       people facing toward these, and they made me
       suspend my reply so as to gaze.

Lì veggio d'ogne parte farsi presta   31
ciascun' ombra e basciarsi una con una
sanza restar, contente a brieve festa:

    così per entro loro schiera bruna   34
s'ammusa l'una con l'altra formica,
forse a spïar lor via e lor fortuna.

    Tosto che parton l'accoglienza amica,   37
prima che 'l primo passo lì trascorra,
sopragridar ciascuna s'affatica,

    la nova gente: "Soddoma e Gomorra!"   40
e l'altra: "Ne la vacca entra Pasife
perché 'l torello a sua lussuria corra!"

    Poi, come grue ch'a le montagne Rife   43
volasser parte, e parte inver' l'arene,
queste del gel, quelle del sole schife:

    l'una gente sen va, l'altra sen vène;   46
e tornan lagrimando a' primi canti
e al gridar che più lor si convene;

    e raccostansi a me, come davanti,   49
essi medesmi che m'avean pregato,
attenti ad ascoltar ne' lor sembianti.

    Io, che due volte avea visto lor grato,   52
incominciai: "O anime sicure
d'aver, quando che sia, di pace stato,

    non son rimase acerbe né mature   55
le membra mie di là, ma son qui meco
col sangue suo e con le sue giunture.

    Quinci sù vo per non esser più cieco;   58
donna è di sopra che m'acquista grazia,
per che 'l mortal per vostro mondo reco.

    Ma se la vostra maggior voglia sazia   61
tosto divegna, sì che 'l ciel v'alberghi
ch'è pien d'amore e più ampio si spazia,

    ditemi, acciò ch'ancor carta ne verghi: 64
chi siete voi, e chi è quella turba
che se ne va di retro a' vostri terghi?"

    Non altrimenti stupido si turba   67
lo montanaro e rimirando ammuta,
quando rozzo e salvatico s'inurba,

31 There on both sides I see each soul make haste,
and each one kiss another, without stopping,
contented with brief welcomes:

34 so in their dark ranks the ants nuzzle each other,
perhaps to spy out their path and their luck.

37 As soon as they break off their friendly greetings,
before they take the first step to depart, each labors
to outshout the other,

40 the newcomers: "Sodom and Gomorrha!" and
the others: "Into the cow goes Pasiphaë, so that the
young bull will run to her lust."

43 Then, like cranes, who might fly, some toward
the Riphaean mountains, some toward the sands,
these avoiding frost, those the sun:

46 so one group goes off, the other comes along;
and they return, weeping, to their first songs and
the cry that most befits them;

49 and the same ones who had begged me came
back to me as before, eager to listen, by their looks.

52 I, who twice had seen what would please them,
began: "O souls sure to enjoy, whenever it may be,
the state of peace,

55 my limbs have not remained back there either
green or ripe, but are here with me with their
blood and with their joints.

58 I am going up through here so as to be blind no
longer; there is a lady above who gains me grace,
and so I bring my mortal part through your world.

61 But so may your greatest desire soon be
satisfied, so that the heaven may shelter you that is
full of love and encloses the most ample space,

64 tell me, that I may rule paper for it still: who are
you and who are that throng going off behind your
backs?"

67 Not otherwise is the mountain peasant struck
with awe and troubled, falling silent as he gazes,
when, crude and rustic, he enters the city:

     che ciascun' ombra fece in sua paruta;   70
ma poi che furon di stupore scarche,
lo qual ne li alti cuor tosto s'attuta:

     "Beato te, che de le nostre marche,"   73
ricominciò colei che pria m'inchiese,
"per morir meglio, esperïenza imbarche!

     La gente che non vien con noi offese   76
di ciò per che già Cesar trïunfando
'Regina' contra sé chiamar s'intese;

     però si parton 'Soddoma' gridando,   79
rimproverando a sé com' hai udito,
e aiutan l'arsura vergognando.

     Nostro peccato fu ermafrodito,   82
ma perché non servammo umana legge,
seguendo come bestie l'appetito,

     in obbrobrio di noi per noi si legge,   85
quando partinci, il nome di colei
che s'imbestiò ne le 'mbestiate schegge.

     Or sai nostri atti e di che fummo rei;   88
se forse a nome vuo' saper chi semo,
tempo non è di dire, e non saprei.

     Farotti ben di me volere scemo: 91
son Guido Guinizelli, e già mi purgo
per ben dolermi prima ch'a lo stremo."

     Quali ne la tristizia di Ligurgo   94
si fer due figli a riveder la madre,
tal mi fec' io—ma non a tanto insurgo—

     quand' io odo nomar sé stesso il padre   97
mio e de li altri, miei miglior, che mai
rime d'amor usar dolci e leggiadre,

     e sanza udire e dir pensoso andai   100
lunga fïata rimirando lui,
né, per lo foco, in là più m'appressai.

     Poi che di riguardar pasciuto fui,   103
tutto m'offersi pronto al suo servigio
con l'affermar che fa credere altrui.

     Ed elli a me: "Tu lasci tal vestigio   106
per quel ch'i' odo in me, e tanto chiaro,
che Leté nol può tòrre né far bigio.

70   than each soul then appeared; but when their
amazement had been laid aside, for it is quickly
blunted in high hearts:

73   "Blessed are you, who from these border lands
of ours," began the shade who had inquired of me
previously, "are taking on a cargo of experience, so
as to die better!

76   Those who are not coming with us committed
the offense for which Caesar, in his triumph, once
heard himself reproached as 'Queen':

79   therefore they depart crying, 'Sodom,' blaming
themselves as you have heard, and they help the
burning by feeling shame.

82   Our sin was hermaphrodite; but because we did
not keep human law, following our appetite like
beasts,

85   in our own reproach we read out, when we part,
the name of her who made herself a beast within
the beast-shaped planks.

88   Now you know our deeds and what our sin was:
if perhaps you wish to know who we are by name,
there is not time to tell, and I could not.

91   I will rid you of your ignorance of me: I am
Guido Guinizelli, and now I purge myself here
because I repented well, before the last."

94   Such as in Lycurgus' grief the two sons became,
seeing their mother again: so did I become—
though I do not rise so high—

97   when I hear our father name himself, the father
of me and of the others, my betters, who ever used
sweet and graceful rhymes of love,

100   and without hearing or speaking I walked full of
thought, gazing at him a long time, but because of
the fire I approached no closer.

103   When I had fed myself with gazing, I offered
myself all eager to serve him, with the kind of
affirmation that gains belief.

106   And he to me: "You are leaving such a trace in
me because of what I hear, and so clear a one, that
Lethe cannot take it away or make it fade.

Ma se le tue parole or ver giuraro,   109
dimmi che è cagion per che dimostri
nel dire e nel guardar d'avermi caro."

   E io a lui: "Li dolci detti vostri,   112
che, quanto durerà l'uso moderno,
faranno cari ancora i loro incostri."

   "O frate," disse, "questi ch'io ti cerno   115
col dito," e additò un spirto innanzi,
"fu miglior fabbro del parlar materno.

   Versi d'amore e prose di romanzi   118
soverchiò tutti, e lascia dir li stolti
che quel di Lemosì credon ch'avanzi.

   A voce più ch'al ver drizzan li volti,   121
e così ferman sua oppinïone
prima ch'arte o ragion per lor s'ascolti.

   Così fer molti antichi di Guittone,   124
di grido in grido pur lui dando pregio,
fin che l'ha vinto il ver con più persone.

   Or se tu hai sì ampio privilegio   127
che licito ti sia l'andare al chiostro
nel quale è Cristo abate del collegio,

   falli per me un dir d'un paternostro,   130
quanto bisogna a noi di questo mondo,
dove poter peccar non è più nostro."

   Poi, forse per dar luogo altrui secondo   133
che presso avea, disparve per lo foco
come per l'acqua il pesce andando al fondo.

   Io mi fei al mostrato innanzi un poco,   136
e dissi ch'al suo nome il mio disire
apparecchiava grazïoso loco.

   El cominciò liberamente a dire: 139
"Tan m'abellis vostre cortes deman,
qu'ieu no me puesc ni voill a vos cobrire.

   Ieu sui Arnaut, que plor e vau cantan;   142
consiros vei la passada folor,
e vei jausen lo joi qu'esper denan.

   Ara vos prec, per aquella valor   145
que vos guida al som de l'escalina,
sovenha vos a temps de ma dolor."

   Poi s'ascose nel foco che li affina.   148

109 But if your words swore truly just now, tell me the reason why you show by your speech and your gaze that you hold me dear."

112 And I to him: "Your sweet poems, which, as long as modern usage lasts, will make precious their very ink."

115 "O my brother," he said, "he I point out to you with my finger," and he indicated a spirit further on, "was a better fashioner of his mother tongue.

118 All verses of love and romances in prose he surpassed, no matter what the fools say who think that the one from near Limoges is better.

121 They turn their faces more to reputation than to the truth, and thus they fix their opinion before listening to art or reason.

124 Thus of old many did with Guittone, still praising him in cry after cry, until the truth overcame him in the judgments of more people.

127 Now if you have such ample privilege that you are permitted to go to the cloister where Christ is abbot of the college,

130 say a Paternoster to him for me, as much of one as we in this world need, where the power to sin is no longer ours."

133 Then, perhaps to make room for another who was near him, he disappeared into the fire like a fish into the water when it goes to the bottom.

136 I went forward a little to the one he had pointed out, and said that my desire was preparing a gracious place for his name.

139 He began freely to say: "*So pleasing to me is your courteous request, that I cannot nor will not hide myself from you.*

142 *I am Arnaut, who weep and go singing; with chagrin I view my past folly, and rejoicing I see ahead the joy I hope for.*

145 *Now I beg you, by the Power that guides you to the summit of the stairway, remember my suffering at the appropriate time!*"

148 Then he hid himself in the fire that refines them.

NOTES

1-15. While thus, one . . . would not be burned: The narrative continues without transition, combining vivid imagining of the scene with an indication of the hour; the naturally motivated reintroduction of the theme of the pilgrim's body, casting its shadow on the wall of flame (which we know he will have to traverse) leads to the opening of the dialogue that will occupy almost the entire canto.

1-3. While thus, one . . . my alerting you: A reminder of the obvious symbolism of the narrow path, set forth more fully in 25.115-20.

4-6. the sun was . . . from blue to white: The sun has moved perhaps halfway from noon to its setting, since the west is now white rather than blue, as earlier: it is around 3 P.M. In 4.56-57 the sun struck the pilgrim from the left as he faced east at mid-morning; here the sun strikes him from the right as he faces southwest in mid-afternoon.

7-9. and with my shadow . . . as they walked: The pilgrim's shadow has not been mentioned since 23.114, where it prompted Forese's question on behalf of the group of shades; that the shadow cast on the flames makes them seem hotter (to the pilgrim), while indicating to the shades that his body is real, is a brilliant touch; as in other cases, the shades are struck with amazement.

10-12. This was the cause . . . factitious body: The observations connects the events with Statius's exposition (especially 25.88-108); the somewhat denigrating term *factitious* is a reminder of the insubstantiality of the airy body and its temporary status, as well as its being a literary fiction (Dante uses the term *fittizio* of the fictitious literal sense of the canzoni of the *Convivio*, e.g. 2.12.10, 15.2). See Additional Note 11. *Fittizio/factitious* is the first of many words in the canto derived from Lat. *facere* [to make] and its synonyms.

13-15. Then some approached . . . would not be burned: For the care taken by souls to observe their penance, cf. 16.142-44, 18.115-16, 19.140-41, and Statius's explanation, 21.61-66; cf. Foster 1984, *Purg.* 11.73, 16.142 and 18.115, 19.139, and 24.91. The fire is also a container, a "womb" (see 27.25-27 and the notes to *Inf.* 30.102-20).

16-135. O you who . . . goes to the bottom: All but some 20 lines of the canto are devoted to the meeting with Guido Guinizelli (identified in line 92), though interrupted, in lines 27-48, by the arrival and departure of the repentant homosexuals.

18. burning in thirst and fire: This speaker is Guido Guinizelli; in his sonnet, "Lo vostro bel saluto," the speaker burns in love ("in gran pene e 'n foco ardo" [in great pain and in fire I burn], Folena 1977). Guinizelli's words recall those of

Dives in Hell, who thirsts for water "to cool my tongue: for I am tormented in this flame" (Luke 16.24).

19-21. Nor do I alone . . . for cold water: The metaphor of thirst for sexual desire is replaced by thirst as the desire for knowledge; see 21.1-6, with notes (cf. Wisdom 6.23; *Conv.* 4.6.18).

21. Indian or Ethiop: They are mentioned as inhabiting proverbially hot climates; cf. *Inf.* 24.89-93 (where *Etiopia* [Ethiopia] rhymes with *elitropia* [heliotrope]). The line may reflect speculation about the location of Eden in the parts of the earth most remote from Europe (see Introduction, pp. 10-12).

22-24. Tell us how . . . the net of death: This is the last instance of the shades' amazed curiosity about the pilgrim's shadow, first introduced in Canto 3 (see our notes to 3.22-45, 88-90, 118-19). The underlying system of references to Ovid's Pyramus and Thisbe will soon become explicit: see 27.37-39, with notes, and Additional Note 13.

24. the net of death: That sin and death (but also Love) net or hook the living as if they were fish or birds is traditional (see Koonce 1959); see also 22.77-78. The net is a container, it is "entered" (see line 41).

25-26. would have made myself known: The pilgrim's distraction by the new group of souls (see line 40) defers the interview with this soul until line 73.

28-46. for down the center . . . the other comes along: A second file of souls now meets the first, moving in the opposite direction from the first; they provide the only instance of souls' moving clockwise around the mountain during their purgation (see the note to 10.100), obviously to be correlated with the sin's being "against nature." After embracing, the two groups shout phrases that identify the corresponding vices of homosexual lust (the newcomers) and heterosexual lust, each group reproaching itself (the shouting is no doubt an allusion to the scandal caused by these vices when revealed; for the relevance of the shouts, see lines 76-87). There is some suggestion (cf. the note to 25.115-20) that the two vices are departures from a just middle course (cf. "down the center," line 28). The raising of cries at meeting connects the passage with *Inf.* 7.25-36, where the the avaricious and prodigal reproach each other, not themselves (cf. *Inf.* 5.34-36).

31-33. There on both sides . . . brief welcomes: The two groups exchange the "holy kiss" that saint Paul counseled as a sign of peace (2 Cor. 13.12).

34-36. so in their dark ranks . . . path and their luck: The commentators recall *Aen.* 4.404 ("nigrum agmen" [dark column]) and Pliny, *Natural History* 11.6. One may think of *Aen.* 1.430-36, Vergil's portrait of the harmonious society of the bees, also praised in *Georgics* 4.

40. Sodom and Gomorrha: See the note to *Inf.* 14. 8-39 and *Inferno* Additional Notes 4 and 5; cf. Foster 1984. For the eagerness of souls to purge themselves, see *Purg.* 11.73, 16.142 and 18.115, 19.139, and 24.91.

43-48. Then, like cranes . . . that most befits them: Cranes in Egypt appear in similes in *Phars.* 5.711-16, 7.831-34 and *Theb.* 5.11-16, 12.515-18; see *Inf.* 5.46-48 and *Purg.* 24.54-56, with notes. Their noisiness (especially in Statius's similes) may have contributed to the invention of the incident. For the relevance of cranes to love poetry, see 24.64-66 and *Inf.* 5.46-48, with notes. Dante may also wish to allude to Guinizelli's sonnet to Bonagiunta (see 24.19-20), "Omo ch'è saggio" lines 9-14, where different styles of love poetry are compared with different species of birds (Martinez 1983).

43. Riphaean mountains: Traditionally Europe's northern border, as in *Geor.* 1. 240; cf. Orosius 1.2.4: "Europe begins . . . under northern skies, where the Riphaean mountains . . . pour forth the Tanais river."

47. they return, weeping, to their first songs: As elsewhere, the souls lament their inclination toward the sin. For the mournful tone cf. line 142 and 25.121, with notes.

55-57. my limbs have not . . . with their joints: The most detailed reference so far to the pilgrim's body, the "mortal part" he "bring[s] through your world" (line 60), contrasting with the "factitious bodies" of line 12. Neither "green" nor "ripe" mean "neither child nor old man" (cf. *Inf.* 1.1, with note).

58. so as to be blind no longer: The pilgrim speaks generically (cf. 16.66), but the ledges of pride, envy, wrath, avarice, and lust (see 25.118-20) all restrict or impede sight for their inmates.

62-63. the heaven . . . the most ample space: The Empyrean, the heaven of pure light and love (see *Par.* 30.39-40), "in which the whole world is included and outside of which there is nothing" (*Conv.* 2.3.10-11). *Empyrean* is derived from Gr. *en* [in] + *pyr* [fire]; the purgatorial fire in some sense anticipates it; see 9.30, with note, and Additional Note 15.

64. tell me, that I may rule paper for it still: The wayfarer refers to the preparation of the blank page with ruled lines to guide the pen (thus establishing limits, ultimately in imitation of God's setting the boundaries to the universe; see Prov. 8.23-29; Durling/Martinez 1990). For other references to the labor of writing the poem, see *Inf.* 17.127-128; *Purg.* 24.52-54, 29.97-98, 33.139-41, *Par.* 25.1-3, with notes; and *Inter cantica* below.

67-69. Not otherwise . . . he enters the city: The rustic amazed by the city (cf. *Ecl.* 1.19-25) prepares for Eden as an anticipation of the Heavenly City (an important subtext for the *Purgatorio*: see *Purg.* 32.100-102, *Par.* 31.31-36 , with notes). Another reference to enclosed space, and in a border area (line 73)—just above is Eden.

71-72. amazement . . . in high hearts: Inured to Purgatory, the souls are not long stupefied; compare 3.79-93 and note, and see *Conv.* 4.25.6 for Dante's analysis of this passion (Adrastus); see also *Ep.* 5.20 and 6.12.

73-75. Blessed are you . . . so as to die better: The knowledge of Purgatory, the border land (a "march": see the note to 19.45), will give the pilgrim wisdom for the ordering of his life. The passage is a tissue of citations of Arnaut and Guinizzelli, whose shades both appear in this canto; both wrote poems using the difficult rhyme "embark" (Prov. *embarc*, Ital. *imbarco*; see Wilkins 1917, Martinez 1991). Rhymes, of course, provide the *borders* of verses.

76-87. Those who are not . . . beast-shaped planks: The explanation of the self-reproachful shouts of the two groups.

76-78. the offense . . . Queen: Suetonius writes that Julius Caesar became the passive sexual partner of the King of Bithynia; his own troops taunted him with the title *regina* [queen] (Dante seems to have got the story from Uguccione da Pisa: Toynbee 1897). Caesar is the only individual to be cited in the poem both as an example of virtue (18.10-102) and as an example of vice (for which, however, he is not damned: see *Inf.* 4.123). This ambiguous status may be connected, like a number of popular legends about him, with Caesar's famous Caesarean birth: preternaturally, he was "not born of woman." This is one of the passages, incidentally, that make it quite certain that the sin of violence against Nature in *Inferno* 15-16 is homosexuality; see *Inter cantica* below.

79-81. therefore they depart . . . by feeling shame: Their shame strengthens the desire to purge themselves (cf. the shadow making the flame redder, lines 4-6): repentance itself was sometimes thought to be the "fire" of Purgatory (Le Goff 1991; see Introduction pp. 7-10). Self-reproach will be emphasized again in lines 85-87.

82. Our sin was hermaphrodite: Heterosexual lust is "hermaphrodite," as in *Met.* 4.285-388. Overcome by desire for the boy Hermaphroditus (so named because son of Hermes and Aphrodite), the nymph Salmacis embraces him when he swims in her pool and, as he resists, is granted her wish to be fused with him. Ovid's character emerges a *semivir* (half-male), expressing the traditional idea that copulation diminishes manhood, as Guinizelli's use of the term implies (see *Inter cantica* below).

83-87. because we did not keep . . . beast-shaped planks: Pasiphaë, the wife of Minos (himself progeny of Zeus, who had taken the form of a white bull to rape Europa), lusted for a young bull (also white) from Minos' herd; she had Daedalus fashion a wooden cow, within which she received the bull, conceiving the Minotaur (see *Ecl.* 6.45-55; *Met.* 9.738-740; Ovid's *Art of Love* 1.290-326, 2.21-24; and Martinez 1991; for the Minotaur, *Inf.* 12.11-25, with notes). The monstrosity of the hermaphrodite is here surpassed by lust compounded with fraud (the bull is deceived by the artifice), as well as by bestiality. The troping of *hermaphrodite* as a modifier (line 82) leads to the virtuosity of Guinizelli's elaborate paranomasia *bestie* [beasts], line 84; *s'imbestiò* [imbeasted herself] and *imbestiate schegge* [imbeasted planks], line 87, cf. Ovid's "vacca . . . acerna" [maple cow], line 326: the insistent trope acts out the negative imposition of form in Daedalus's abuse of his craft and Pasiphaë's acceptance of pseudo-bestial form: multiple subversions of the order of Nature (human to beast, plant to beast, etc.).

89-90. if perhaps you wish . . . not time to tell: Virgil pointed out "more than a thousand" of the carnal sinners in *Inf.* 5.52-69; Brunetto chose to be silent regarding the many sodomites; cf. also 24.16-39.

92-148. I am Guido Guinizelli. . . fire that refines them: The encounters with Guinizelli (lines 16-135) and Arnaut Daniel (lines 136-48), which dominate the canto, are the last of the series in this cantica of encounters between poets (Virgil, the pilgrim, Sordello, Statius, Forese, Bonagiunta—others are mentioned: the Roman poets, Giraut de Bornelh, the Notary, Guittone d'Arezzo, Guido Cavalcanti) and craftsmen (Casella, Belacqua, Oderisi—others are mentioned: Daedalus the archetype, Policlitus, Franco Bolognese, Cimabue, Giotto).

92. I am Guido Guinizelli: A Bolognese jurist and partisan of the Guelf Lambertazzi (see *Purg.* 11.97-98), "noble Guido Guinizelli" (as Dante calls him in *Conv.* 4.20.7) was in exile from 1274 on and dead by 1276. Dante refers to him as "Maximus Guido" in *DVE* 1.15.6, holding up his poems as models (2.5.4; 6.6). Guido's great canzone "Al cor gentil rempaira sempre amore" [Love always repairs to the noble heart] is alluded to in a sonnet in *Vita nova* 20, where Guido is called "il saggio" [the wise man].

92-93. now I purge myself. . . before the last: Guinizelli's emphasis on timely repentance perhaps involves an implicit contrast with Statius, the "dallier" (see 22.89-92, with note). "The last" [*lo stremo*] (i.e., the end of life) refers to a *temporal* border.

94-96. Such as in Lycurgus' grief . . . not rise so high: In *Theb.* 5.534-753, Opheltes, the infant son of Lycurgus, king of Nemea (between Argos and Thebes), is killed by a giant snake while left untended by his nurse, Hypsipyle (22.88-89 and 112, with notes). Lycurgus demands her death, the Argives prepare to defend her, but she is joyfully recognized by two of Lycurgus' men, her sons (by Jason the Argonaut), whom she had abandoned twenty years before, fleeing Lemnos (see the note to *Inf.* 18.88-94; *Conv.* 3.11.16 recalls Hypsipyle's devotion to Opheltes), and so the romance plot ends with the reunion of mother and sons.

The simile is compressed and arduous; Dante assumes that the reader knows the *Thebaid* as well as he does! The parallels are oblique: the pilgrim's offer to serve Guinizelli echoes the offers made by the sons to Hypsipyle (as well as by the Argives); the joy of Hypsipyle's sons at finding their mother expresses the pilgrim's joy (tempered by the context of Lycurgus's grief) at finding his and others' poetic father. Hypsipyle's sons embrace her, but the pilgrim "approached no closer" (line 102; see *Inter cantica* below, and 2.76-85, 21.130-36, with notes). For the relation of this scene to the motif of lament, see Martinez 1997. That Guinizelli, a lyric poet, evokes a simile from a digressive romance episode from Statius is striking; one might suppose Latin epic has become ancillary to the Tuscan lyric, except that the compendious *Comedy* "takes up into its substance" both traditional epic and lyric.

97-99. our father name himself . . . and graceful rhymes: Although he is not mentioned in 24.49-63, the central passage on the "sweet new style," these lines make it clear that Dante considered Guinizelli to be its originator or "father" (see especially our note on 24.55-63). The metaphor of paternity for literary influence is traditional (see Seneca *Ep. mor.* 84), but it acquires a special resonance after Statius's discourse on embryology, with its applicability to literary creation (see 25.88-102, 94-96, and Additional Note 11).

103. fed myself with gazing: Fixation through the eyes, displaced from the gaze at or of the lady in love poetry, most fully developed by Dante in the *Rime petrose* (see Durling/Martinez 1990). We are required to consider the relation of this moment with the theme of homosexuality and sexual desire in general.

106-108. You are leaving . . . make it fade: Guido speaks of memory and immortality, but it is the pilgrim's affection that emerges. Ital. *vestigio* [footprint] implies reciprocity here with the language of Guido as a father (whose texts leave traces in his imitators), as well as a metaphor of writing, which deposits the traces of thought (Augustine); see line 64. The pilgrim passes from audition to writing, without mediation.

109-11. you show by your speech . . . you hold me dear: Again, as if the pilgrim were a love-poet writing for his lady; this also recalls Virgil of Statius; see 22.10-18 and notes. See *Inter cantica* below.

112-14. Your sweet poems . . . precious their very ink: Poems are here named metonymically by their ink, another reference to the material aspect of writing (see lines 64, 106-108 and notes). Expressing esteem by collecting an author's poems (cf. Cavalcanti, "I' vegno il giorno," line 8: "tutte le tue rime avea ricolte" [I had collected all your poems]) and the veneration of written documents were established practices in the Due- and Trecento, but a hint of literary fetishism is implied by speaking of Guinizelli's poems as if religious relics. Guinizelli's surviving corpus is small: some twenty poems.

Note the respectful *voi*, used elsewhere in the poem only to Brunetto, Farinata, Cacciaguida (in *Paradiso* 16, whereas in Cantos 15 and 17 the pilgrim addresses him with *tu*), and Beatrice (in lines 140-46, Arnaut addresses respectful pronoun forms to the pilgrim no fewer than five times).

113. as long as modern usage lasts: Compare 11.97-99 and notes. Dante means the vernacular principally, but "modern" also suggests "new," recalling the "sweet new" of lines 112-14 (for "modern usage," see 16.42, with note): the fashion that Guinizelli is credited with originating.. Dante wrote (*VN* 25.4) that poetry in Romance vernaculars dated back about 150 years, in Italian less.

114. ink: It. *inchiostro* is from Lat. *encaustum* [burned]: ink was often made from lampblack: love poems are traces of combustion, of ardor.

115-17. O my brother . . . fashioner of his mother tongue: Pointing to the poet (cf. line 8), Guinizelli's use of *fabbro* [artisan] voices Dante's conception of the craft of poetry: *fabbro* denotes any artisan working in "hard" materials such as iron, stone, and wood (cf. Dante's use of the Latin terms in *DVE* 1.5.1 [of God], 1.6.7). Arnaut characterized himself as an artisan (Provençal *obrador*), and his writing as shaping and filing words ("obr' e lim / motz"). The lines invoke the rich analogies by which human art imitates Nature's (her "hammers" are the planetary spheres) and ultimately God's. The imagery of craft is also evoked in 1 Cor. 3.12-15, one of the founding texts of the idea of Purgatory: the fire will test each man's "work," which may be of gold, silver, jewels, straw, or hay; see Introduction, pp. 4-6.

115-48. O my brother . . . the fire that refines them: Guinizelli modestly applies the pilgrim's praise to the Provençal troubadour Arnaut Daniel (1140–ca. 1190; named in line 142). Born in Ribérac in the Dordogne, Arnaut was active at the court of Richard the Lion-hearted in Poitiers; he exchanged poems with Bertran de Born (see *Inf.* 28.134, with notes). He was a chief master of the *trobar clus* [closed or difficult style] and an important influence on Dante (see Perugi 1978; cf. *DVE* 2.2.8; 2.6.6; 2.10.2, 2.13.2).

118-26. All verses of love . . . the judgments of more people: Guinizelli presents Arnaut as the best vernacular poet, including Provençal lyric and Old French narrative romances, dismissing as shallow the popularity of Giraut de Bornelh (compare lines 121-22 to 11.100-102 regarding earthly fame). The same proportion disadvantages Guittone (see 24.55-57), who wrote both amorous and moralizing canzoni.

119-20. no matter what . . . the one from near Limoges: Again the theme of competing literary reputations (see 11.91-102, with notes). "The one from near Limoges" is Giraut de Bornelh, ca. 1160-1210, whom Dante had praised for his moralizing verses (see *DVE* 1.9.3; 2.2.8; 2.5.4; 2.6.6; *Conv.* 4.11.10). In Guinizelli's reference to "fools" Dante is echoing Guinizelli's sonnet answering Bonagiunta's criticisms, "Omo ch'è saggio," line 5: "Foll'è chi crede sol veder lo vero" [Foolish is he who thinks he alone sees the truth].

122. and thus they fix their opinion: The verse echoes, although it alters the intention of, "Omo ch'e saggio," line 3, "quand'ha pensato riten lo suo pensero" [when he has thought, he holds to his thought]; cf. *Par.* 13.115-20.

124-26. Thus of old many . . . judgments of more people: Another condemnation of Guittone d'Arezzo, as in 24.55-57 and *DVE* 2.6.8 ("Let the sectaries of ignorance therefore cease to extol Guittone d'Arezzo and certain others, who never lost the habit of plebeian constructions and diction"; see also 1.13.1). Dante's spokesman Guinizelli, speaking from beyond the grave, is asserting an absolute standard of artistic excellence ("the truth," lines 121 and 126), which he sees as eventually winning out over the poor judgment of the mob (the "many," "fools"); cf. *Par.* 17.106-20. Cf. also "Omo ch'è saggio," line 4: "infin a tanto che 'l ver l'asegura" [until the truth makes him secure].

125. cry after cry: The "cries" of reputation (cf. the shouted reproaches of lines 39-42); in 11.100-103 fame is "nothing but a breath of wind that comes now from here and now from there."

127-32. Now if you have such ample . . . no longer ours: Guinizelli requests a Paternoster with omission of the last petition ("Lead us not into temptation but deliver us from the evil one"; cf. 11.19-24). The "cloister where Christ is abbot" is of course the Empyrean. "Abbot" is derived from *abba*, Hebrew for father; cf. Gal. 4.6.

133-35. Then, perhaps to make room . . . goes to the bottom: The "other" for whom Guinizelli perhaps makes room is not Arnaut, who since line 115 has been visible "a little ahead" (line 136), but probably another of the shades curious to see the living man (as in lines 19-21). For the fish image, see *Par.* 5.100-105. Folena 1977 recalls the image of the love-poet as salamander, a cold animal ("freddo animale," like a fish) that thrives in flames (see Guinizelli, "Lo fin pregio avanzato," line 38); and cf. *DVE* 1.6.3.

136-48. I went forward . . . fire that refines them: There is some suggestion that Arnaut is ahead of Guinizelli as a penitent as well as a poet. This encounter is unique in the poem in including a speech in a modern language (as opposed to Latin) other than Italian. Dante's tribute shows how deeply he has studied Arnaut and other Provençal poets.

137-38. said that my desire . . . place for his name: The pilgrim prepares a place for Arnaut in his memory and thus in his poem, in the text of the *Comedy*: an ultimate container, tomb or monument, for Arnaut. The trope is appropriate to Arnaut, whose famous sestina "Lo ferm voler" [My steadfast desire] explores the erotic obsession with the beloved's chamber, which he wishes to enter (with erotic pun) and is based on repeated rhyme-words that shift their places according to a fixed rule (see Durling/Martinez 1990, Martinez 1991).

140-47. So pleasing to me . . . the appropriate time: Arnaut's conciliatory words are untypical of his difficult style: he speaks openly and "will not hide." The commentators have identified echoes of Arnaut ("vei jauzens lo joi" recalls the sestina; see note to lines 133-38); and of other Provençal poems: "Tan m'abellis" [so pleasing to me] is an incipit used by Sordello and Folquet of Marseilles (the latter is cited in *DVE* 2.6.6); many Provençal poems end with "Ara vos prec" [now I beg you]. The passage summarizes a whole tradition; see *Inter cantica* below.

142-44. I am Arnaut . . . the joy I hope for: Like the other penitents, Arnaut bewails the past, rejoices in the future, suffers in the present.

142. I am Arnaut, who: An echo of Arnaut's "signature" at the end of his poem "En cest sonet," characterizing his erotic pursuit: "I am Arnaut, who gather the wind and hunt the hare with an ox" (cf. Ecclus. 34.1-2: "like to him that catcheth at a shadow, and followeth after the wind"; see Perugi 1978).

145-47. Now I beg . . . the appropriate time: The last request made of the pilgrim in Purgatory: after the opening salutation, Arnaut begins and ends on a note of pain, but he is on the cusp of regret and anticipation; cf. Paul, Phil. 3.13: "But one thing I do: forgetting the things that are behind, and stretching forth myself to those that are before, I press toward the mark, to the prize."

148. hid himself . . . fire that refines them: *Affina*, meaning "finishes" as well as "refines," announces the canto's—and Purgatory proper's—final border.

Inter cantica. *Purgatorio* 26 has rich parallels to *Inferno* 26-27, as well as to earlier treatments of lust. Guinizelli's burning (*ardo*, 26.18) echoes Guido da Monte-feltro's (*ardo*, *Inf.* 27.24), while the ship image of 26.73 (*embark*) resonates with the ship of Ulysses (*Inf.* 26.100-101; see also 26.124) and with the ship of human life reaching port (*Inf.* 27.79-81). Guido's reference to his real mother (*Inf.* 27. 74), and his spiritual father, the wily pope (*padre*, 27.108), return in the pilgrim's hailing of Guinizelli as poetic mother and father (*Purg.* 26.95, 97) and in Guinizelli's account of poetry as the shaping of the "mother" tongue (*Purg.* 26.117). These parallels point to the focus in the cantos 26 on speech and writing; language as a container of meaning; poetic reputation; rivalry; and filiation.

To the "cry" of reputation (26.125) we can juxtapose, from the *Inferno*, the bad reputation of the Florentines (26.1) and of Guido da Montefeltro (27.28); to the "sweet words" (26.112) of Guinizelli's poems in the "mother" tongue and to Arnaut's actual Provençal can be matched the idiom used by Virgil to Ulysses (*Inf.* 27.21: "istra ten va" [*istra* you may go]; 27.20: "parlavi mo lombardo" [just now you spoke Lombard]; 27.34: ("parla tu: questo è latino" [You speak: this one is Italian]) and with Ulysses (26.75-76: "perhaps they would shun, because they were Greek, your words." That translation is fundamental emerges from the focus on the speech production of the flaming tongues (*Inf.* 26.31, 38; 27.7-9) that envelop Ulysses and Guido (see James 3.3-6, cited in the note to *Inf.* 26.85-90).

More than nuances of speech is at stake. The several references in 26 to the labor of writing (26.64, "rule paper"; 114, "precious their inks") recall the letters, paper, and pen of *Inf.* 24.100-101, 25.64-66, and 25. 143-45. Dante's analysis includes the verbal sign as a container of meaning: in *Purg.* 26 the Daedalian cow of Pasiphaë, but also the refining fire ("he hid himself," 26.142); at 25.121 ("the bosom of the great fire") and at 27.25-26 ("the womb of this flame") are containers, one a fraudulent disguise abetting lust, the other a matrix of regeneration. These echo the flames enclosing Ulysses and Diomedes (26.48-49, 55, 61, 79) and ultimately the "deceit of the [Trojan] horse" (26.58-60) and the bull of Phalaris (27.7-9), which figure the fraudulent transformation of signs (see *Inf.* 30.73-74 and notes and *Inferno* Additional Note 13). The relation of container to thing contained describes the structure of the signifier, externally audible or visible and containing an immaterial rational meaning (see *DVE* 1.3); but is also based on the form-matter relation: matter may seem to house form, but in fact form encloses matter.

The image of the fire as a womb, site of both regenerated conscience and of the intentions behind speech, also grounds the references to progenitors, biological and spiritual: *Inf.* 15. 82-85, on Brunetto's remembered paternal image, is echoed in Guido's status as literary progenitor (26.97-99); both men are forerunners (26.112-114; *Inf.* 15.86-87); both stimulate writing (26.64: "that I may rule paper for it still"; *Inf.* 15.89: "I am writing down and keeping to be glossed"). Both episodes appeal to the "treasury" of memory, where the pilgrim places Arnaut (26.138), as Brunetto survives in his *Treasure* (*Inf.* 15.119-20). Memory is the matrix of literature.

The swarm of parallels with *Inferno* 5 emphasizes literature as serving love and lust. One set of parallels concerns courtly behavior, including greetings (26.37, *Inf.* 5.88); conversation (26.100; *Inf.* 5.95); requests and petitions (26.145; *Inf.* 5.92); expressed desire (26.137; *Inf.* 5.82); the longing for peace (26.53-54; *Inf.* 5.99); and, finally, kissing (26.32: "each one kiss another"; *Inf.* 5.136: "kissed my mouth all trembling"). The close link of love-thoughts and lyric poetry is also at issue: (26.99 and 112, "sweet words"; *Inf.* 5.113: "how many sweet thoughts"); also 26.100 and *Inf.* 5.111; as are love's sorrows (26.142: "I am Arnaut, who weep and go singing"; *Inf.* 5.139: "While one spirit said this, the other was weeping"). Doleful lovers are changed by simile into cranes (26.43; *Inf.* 5.46), whose complaints are of similar tenor, "cries" and wails (26.47-48: *Inf.* 5.48).

The most important nexus involves Pasiphaë and Semiramis, both taxed by the tradition with sexual sins. Minos, Hell's warden (*Inf.* 5.1-3), had been Pasiphaë's consort as king of Crete. A rhyme links Pasiphaë's legend (26. 85-86, "we read [*si legge*] out . . . the name of her who made herself a beast") and Semiramis' law (*Inf.* 5.56, "in her laws [*legge*] she made licit whatever pleased"), and each is tagged with the word for lust (*lussuria*: 26.40-41, *Inf.* 5.55): the cantos name lust in a similar way (26. 82-84, "we did not keep human law, following our appetite like beasts"; *Inf.* 5.39, "the carnal sinners, who subject their reason to their lust").

CANTO 27

Sì come quando i primi raggi vibra   1
là dove il suo Fattor lo sangue sparse,
cadendo Ibero sotto l'alta Libra

e l'onde in Gange da nona rïarse: 4
sì stava il sole, onde 'l giorno sen giva,
come l'angel di Dio lieto ci apparse.

Fuor de la fiamma stava in su la riva   7
e cantava *"Beati mundo corde!"*
in voce assai più che la nostra viva.

Poscia: "Più non si va, se pria non morde,   10
anime sante, il foco: intrate in esso,
e al cantar di là non siate sorde,"

ci disse come noi li fummo presso;   13
per ch'io divenni tal, quando lo 'ntesi,
qual è colui che ne la fossa è messo.

In su le man commesse mi protesi,   16
guardando il foco e imaginando forte
umani corpi già veduti accesi.

Volsersi verso me le buone scorte,   19
e Virgilio mi disse: "Figliuol mio,
qui può esser tormento, ma non morte.

Ricorditi, ricorditi! E se io   22
sovresso Gerïon ti guidai salvo,
che farò presso più a Dio?

Credi per certo che se dentro a l'alvo   25
di questa fiamma stessi ben mille anni,
non ti potrebbe far d'un capel calvo.

E se tu forse credi ch'io t'inganni,   28
fatti ver' lei, e fatti far credenza
con le tue mani al lembo d'i tuoi panni.

CANTO 27

*Seventh terrace, continued: the angel, Beatitude—the pilgrim's fear
overcome—through the fire—an angel, erasure—climb—night on the stairway—
the dream of Leah—dawn—climb—the pilgrim crowned and mitred*

1   As when he shoots the first rays to where his
Maker bled, when Ebro falls beneath high Libra

4   and the waves of Ganges are scorched by noon:
so stood the sun, and thus day was fading, when
the glad angel of God appeared to us.

7   He was standing outside the flame, on the bank,
and he was singing, "*Beati mundo corde!*" with a
voice much more alive than ours.

10   Then: "You go no further, holy souls, unless the
fire bites first; enter into it, and be not deaf to the
singing over there,"

13   he said to us as we came near; and when I heard
him, I became like one placed in the grave.

16   Over my clasped hands I stretched forward, staring
at the fire, and vividly imagining human bodies I
had in the past seen burning.

19   My good guides turned toward me, and Virgil
said to me: "My son, here there can be torment,
but not death.

22   Remember, remember! And if I guided you
safely upon Geryon, what will I do here, closer to
God?

25   Believe it certain that if you stayed within the
womb of this flame for a good thousand years, it
could not make you bald by one hair.

28   And if you perhaps believe I am deceiving you,
approach it and reassure yourself with your own
hands and the edge of your robe.

Pon giù omai, pon giù ogne temenza,   31
volgiti in qua e vieni: entra sicuro!"
E io pur fermo e contra coscïenza.

    Quando mi vide star pur fermo e duro,   34
turbato un poco disse: "Or vedi, figlio:
tra Bëatrice e te è questo muro."

    Come al nome di Tisbe aperse il ciglio   37
Piramo in su la morte e riguardolla,
allor che 'l gelso diventò vermiglio:

    così, la mia durezza fatta solla,   40
mi volsi al savio duca, udendo il nome
che ne la mente sempre mi rampolla.

    Ond' ei crollò la fronte e disse: "Come,   43
volenci star di qua?" Indi sorrise
come al fanciul si fa ch'è vinto al pome.

    Poi dentro al foco innanzi mi si mise,   46
pregando Stazio che venisse retro,
che pria per lunga strada ci divise.

    Sì com' fui dentro, in un bogliente vetro   49
gittato mi sarei per rinfrescarmi,
tant' era ivi lo 'ncendio sanza metro.

    Lo dolce padre mio per confortarmi   52
pur di Beatrice ragionando andava,
dicendo: "Li occhi suoi già veder parmi."

    Guidavaci una voce che cantava   55
di là; e noi, attenti pur a lei,
venimmo fuor là ove si montava.

    "Venite, benedicti Patris mei!"   58
sonò dentro a un lume che lì era,
tal che mi vinse e guardar nol potei.

    "Lo sol sen va," soggiunse, "e vien la sera: 61
non v'arrestate, ma studiate il passo
mentre che l'occidente non si annera."

    Dritta salia la via per entro 'l sasso   64
verso tal parte ch'io tagliava i raggi
dinanzi a me del sol, ch'era già basso.

    E di pochi scaglion levammo i saggi,   67
che 'l sol corcar, per l'ombra che si spense,
sentimmo dietro e io e li miei saggi.

31   Lay aside now, lay aside every fear; turn this way and come: enter confidently!" And I being still fixed and against conscience.

34   When he saw me still standing fixed and rigid, a little perturbed he said: "Now see, son: between Beatrice and you is this wall."

37   As at the name of Thisbe Pyramus opened his eyelids on the point of death and gazed at her, then when the mulberry turned crimson:

40   so, my rigor softening, I turned to my wise leader, hearing the name that burgeons always in my memory.

43   And he shook his head and said: "Well? do we want to stay on this side?" Then he smiled as one does at a little boy who is won over by an apple.

46   Then ahead of me he put himself in the fire, begging Statius to come after, who for a long way had divided us.

49   As soon as I was within, I would have thrown myself into boiling glass to be cooled, so without measure was the burning there.

52   My sweet father, to strengthen me, walked ever speaking of Beatrice, saying: "Already I seem to see her eyes."

55   A voice was guiding us that was singing on the other side; and, ever intent upon it, we came forth where we could ascend.

58   "*Venite, benedicti Patris mei!*" sounded within a light that was there, so bright that it vanquished me and I could not look at it.

61   "The sun departs," it added, "and evening comes; do not stop, but hasten your step, while the west has not gone dark."

64   The path mounted straight ahead within the rock, so that I cut the rays of the sun in front of me, for it was already setting.

67   And we sampled but few steps before my sages and I perceived, by my shadow's disappearing, that the sun had set behind us.

E pria che 'n tutte le sue parti immense   70
fosse orizzonte fatto d'un aspetto,
e notte avesse tutte sue dispense,

   ciascun di noi d'un grado fece letto;   73
ché la natura del monte ci affranse
la possa del salir più e 'l diletto.

   Quali si stanno ruminando manse   76
le capre, state rapide e proterve
sovra le cime avante che sien pranse,

   tacite a l'ombra, mentre che 'l sol ferve,   79
guardate dal pastor, che 'n su la verga
poggiato s'è e lor di posa serve:

   e quale il mandrïan che fòri alberga   82
lungo il peculio suo queto pernotta,
guardando perché fiera non lo sperga:

   tali eravamo tutti e tre allotta,   85
io come capra ed ei come pastori,
fasciati quinci e quindi d'alta grotta.

   Poco parer potea lì del di fòri,   88
ma per quel poco vedea io le stelle
di lor solere e più chiare e maggiori.

   Sì ruminando e sì mirando in quelle,   91
mi prese il sonno, il sonno che sovente,
anzi che 'l fatto sia, sa le novelle.

   Ne l'ora, credo, che de l'orïente   94
prima raggiò nel monte Citerea,
che di foco d'amor par sempre ardente,

   giovane e bella in sogno mi parea   97
donna vedere andar per una landa
cogliendo fiori, e cantando dicea:

   "Sappia qualunque il mio nome dimanda   100
ch'i' mi son Lia, e vo movendo intorno
le belle mani a farmi una ghirlanda.

   Per piacermi a lo specchio qui m'addorno,   103
ma mia suora Rachel mai non si smaga
dal suo miraglio, e siede tutto giorno.

   Ell' è d'i suoi belli occhi veder vaga   106
com' io de l'addornarmi con le mani:
lei lo vedere e me l'ovrare appaga."

70 And before the horizon in all its immense
regions had become of one appearance, and night
had assumed all its dispensation,

73 each of us made his bed on a step; for the nature
of the mountain had broken our power to climb
further and our delight in it.

76 As the she-goats are still and tame as they
ruminate, though they were swift and wild on the
hilltops before having fed,

79 silent in the shade while the sun burns, guarded
by the goatherd, who leans on his staff and
provides them with rest:

82 and as the shepherd who dwells outdoors spends
the night resting alongside his flock, taking care
that no wild beast disperse them:

85 so were all three of us then, I like a she-goat,
they like shepherds, enclosed on this side and that
by the high rock.

88 Little could be seen there of outside things, but,
by that little, I saw the stars brighter and larger
than their custom.

91 Thus ruminating and gazing at them, sleep took
me, sleep that often, before the event comes,
knows the news.

94 At the hour, I believe, when from the east
Cytherea first shone on the mountain, she who
seems always aflame with the fire of love,

97 in dream I seemed to see a lady, young and
beautiful, walking in a meadow gathering flowers,
and singing she said:

100 "Whoever asks my name, let him know that I
myself am Leah, and I go moving my lovely hands
about in order to make myself a garland.

103 To please myself at the mirror I here adorn
myself, but my sister Rachel is never distracted
from her looking-glass, and sits there all day long.

106 She is as desirous to see her lovely eyes as I am
to adorn myself with my hands: seeing satisfies
her, doing satisfies me."

E già per li splendori antelucani,   109
che tanto a' pellegrin surgon più grati
quanto, tornando, albergan men lontani,

    le tenebre fuggian da tutti lati,   112
e 'l sonno mio con esse: ond' io leva'mi,
veggendo i gran maestri già levati.

    "Quel dolce pome che per tanti rami   115
cercando va la cura de' mortali
oggi porrà in pace le tue fami."

    Virgilio inverso me queste cotali   118
parole usò, e mai non furo strenne
che fosser di piacere a queste iguali.

    Tanto voler sopra voler mi venne   121
de l'esser sù ch'ad ogne passo poi
al volo mi sentia crescer le penne.

    Come la scala tutta sotto noi   124
fu corsa, e fummo in su 'l grado superno,
in me ficcò Virgilio li occhi suoi

    e disse: "Il temporal foco e l'etterno   127
veduto hai, figlio, e se' venuto in parte
dov' io per me più oltre non discerno.

    Tratto t'ho qui con ingegno e con arte;   130
lo tuo piacere omai prendi per duce:
fuor se' de l'erte vie, fuor se' de l'arte.

    Vedi lo sol che 'n fronte ti riluce,   133
vedi l'erbette, i fiori e li arbuscelli
che qui la terra sol da sé produce.

    Mentre che vegnan lieti li occhi belli   136
che lagrimando a te venir mi fenno,
seder ti puoi e puoi andar tra elli.

    Non aspettar mio dir più né mio cenno: 139
libero, dritto e sano è tuo arbitrio,
e fallo fora non fare a suo senno.

    Per ch'io te sovra te corono e mitrio."   142

109   And already, because of the splendors preceding
dawn, which rise the more welcome to pilgrims as,
returning, they sleep less far from home,

112   the shadows were fleeing on every side, and my
sleep with them: therefore I rose up, seeing my
great masters already risen.

115   "That sweet apple which the zeal of mortals goes
seeking along so many branches, today will bring
peace to your hungers."

118   Virgil used toward me these very words, and
never were there gifts that were equal in pleasure
to them.

121   So much did desire upon desire grow in me to
be above that at every step I felt my wings grow for
flight.

124   When the stairway was all below us, quickly
climbed, and we were on the uppermost step,
Virgil fixed his eyes on me

127   and said: "The temporal fire and the eternal
have you seen, my son, and you have come to a
place where I by myself discern no further.

130   I have drawn you here with wit and with art;
your own pleasure now take as leader: you are
beyond the steep ways, beyond the narrow.

133   See the sun that shines on your brow, see the
grasses, the flowers, and the bushes that here the
earth brings forth of itself alone.

136   Until the lovely eyes arrive in their gladness
which weeping made me come to you, you can sit
and you can walk among them.

139   No longer await any word or sign from me: free,
upright, and whole is your will, and it would be a
fault not to act according to its intent.

142   Therefore you over yourself I crown and mitre."

NOTES

1-60. As when he shoots . . . look at it: The previous purgations have been vicarious: the pilgrim has observed but has been exempt from direct experience of them. Now he must enter the fire himself, if briefly.

1-6. As when he shoots . . . appeared to us: A complicated periphrasis indicating the time as close to sunset, parallel with 2.1-9 (of which it is the inversion) and 15.1-12, both of which also require elaborate visualization. It is dawn in Jerusalem, the antipodes of Purgatory (lines 1-3); thus in Purgatory the sun is setting (see fig. 1). Libra, opposite Aries, is above the Ebro, in Spain (line 3), where it is midnight, and it is noon on the Ganges (line 4).

The four terrestrial locations are momentarily aligned with the four cardinal points of the zodiac: those of the two equinoxes (Ganges with Aries, Ebro with Libra) and the two solstices (Purgatory with Cancer, Jerusalem with Capricorn); we are probably to think of the sun as having almost reached the boundary between Aries and Taurus: see the note to 25.1-3 and the diagram on p. xiii. As usual, Dante simplifies and schematizes.

As Frattini (*LDS*) observes, the mention of the four cardinal points evokes the image of the Cross, already referred to in line 2; the aligning of Capricorn, the sign of the lustful goat, with Jerusalem is germane to the passage through the fire.

6-13. the glad angel . . . came near: See the notes to 12.110-11. Until now, the angel of the terrace has been met on leaving the terrace, has in most cases been the source of the Beatitude, has erased one of the pilgrim's *P*s with his wing (implied in 15.16-36), and invited the travelers to climb. Here the three functions are divided: a first angel sings the Beatitude, a second (lines 55-63) urges the climb (neither angel's wings are mentioned, nor the *P*s). The division intensifies the drama of the pilgrim's refusal to enter the flames, and the second angel proclaims the completion of the entire purgation, not simply of one of its stages, as previously (cf. the notes to lines 55-63). Both angels stand outside the fire (lines 7 and 57-59), marking its boundaries.

8. *Beati mundo corde*: The sixth Beatitude, Matt. 5.8: "Beati mundo corde, quoniam ipsi Deum videbunt" [Blessed are those of pure heart, for they shall see God], appropriate both to the purging of lust and to the completion of the entire process. Looking back over Dante's use of the Beatitudes, one notes that his use of the fourth (Matt. 5.6) for two terraces (avarice and gluttony; see the notes to 20.116-17 and 24.151-54) requires him to omit one (the second, "Blessed are the meek, for they shall inherit the earth," Matt. 5.4, to which, as the corrective to envy, he preferred the fifth; see 15.38-39, with notes). The traditional exegesis, going back at least to Augustine, saw the order of the Beatitudes as correlated with the seven petitions of the Lord's Prayer (see the notes to 11.1-24) and the seven Gifts of the Spirit (Is. 11.1-3), and as tracing an ascent, beginning in humility (Beatitude 1) and ending in the peace of Heaven (Beatitude 7; see the note to line 117). Disregarding this traditional exegesis allows Dante to sharpen the applicability of each Beatitude to the correlative vice. His freedom is characteristic—and portentous.

11. enter into it: Nardi 1967 (1922, on Eden) quotes saint Ambrose on Psalm 118 (cap. 3): "The great Baptist . . . will brandish the flaming sword saying . . .: 'Enter you who dare, who do not fear the fire' . . . since we have been purged here it will be necessary to be purged again there, and he will purify us there, for the Lord will say: 'Enter into my rest'; that each of us, burned, but not consumed, by the flaming sword, entering that delightful paradise, may give thanks to the Lord."

12. be not deaf to the singing over there: The first reference to the second angel.

14-15. when I heard . . . placed in the grave: These lines are usually taken to refer to the pilgrim's pallor. Opinions differ on whether the "one placed" is a corpse or a living person being buried alive (a punishment for certain crimes, mentioned in *Inf.* 19.49-51). Since the focus is on the pilgrim's inner state, including his memories of barbarous punishments (line 18; cf. 20.128-29), the second is more relevant.

16-18. Over my clasped hands . . . seen burning: Both horror and revulsion (clasped hands close to the chest) and fascination (leaning forward and staring) are expressed here.

17-18. vividly imagining . . . seen burning: Public execution by burning was not uncommon in Tuscany in Dante's time, for crimes such as heresy, counterfeiting (*Inf.* 30.61), sorcery (*Inf.* 29.109-17), homosexuality; a sentence of death by fire was passed in absentia on Dante (1302; see *Inferno* Additional Note 9).

20-32. My son, here . . . enter confidently: Virgil's brief oration is constructed according to established principles. It defines the issue (*status,* line 21), appeals to past experience and inference (*narration* and *enthymeme* [implied syllogism]), urges an empirical test, appeals to established trust (ethical proof) and to authority, and rises in peroration to intensified urgings (lines 31-32).

27-30. it could not make . . . edge of your robe: Dante again draws on the story of the three Israelites in the fiery furnace (see 25.121-26, with note). The reference to the hair and the urging to test the effect of the fire on garments draw on Dan. 3.94: All the witnesses "considered these men, that the fire had no power on their bodies and that not a hair of their head had been singed, nor their garments altered, nor the smell of the fire had passed on them" (cf. Luke 21.18).

33-34. fixed . . . fixed and rigid: The immediate repetition of "fixed" [*fermo*] intensifies the sense of the duration of the refusal and its reassertion.

33. against conscience: In spite of his awareness that what Virgil has said is true.

34-36. When he saw . . . is this wall: Virgil's slight annoyance occurs after his careful speech has failed: apparently he had expected it to succeed. The appeal to the pilgrim's love is represented as an afterthought, although the theorist of love of Cantos 17 and 18 might have been expected to think of it earlier.

37-42. As at the name . . . in my memory: Not rational persuasion, but the power of love conquers the pilgrim's fear (cf. Cant. 8.6: "love is strong as death"). For the power of Beatrice's name, see 6.43-51, with notes (and, of course, *Inferno* 2).

In *Met.* 4.51-166, Pyramus, supposing Thisbe to have been killed by a lioness, stabs himself, staining the white berries of the mulberry with his blood; although Thisbe repeatedly calls his name, he responds only to her naming of herself: "ad nomen Thisbes oculos iam morte gravatos / Pyramus erexit visaque recondidit illa" (4.145-46) [At Thisbe's name his eyes already weighed down by death / Pyramus opened, and, having seen her, closed them again in death].

For the exegetical tradition, Pyramus' death in proximity to the bloodstained tree represented Christ's death on the Cross for love of mankind, represented by Thisbe (see Ortiz 1925, Fergusson 1953, Freccero 1965). The simile continues the christological opening of the canto (see lines 1-4; cf. the notes to 23.30 and 73-75). For the relevance of the myth to the *Comedy* as a whole, see Additional Note 13.

41-42. the name that burgeons always in my memory: Note the plant imagery, introduced in line 39 (for *rampollare* [to sprout] cf. *Purg.* 5.16 , *Par.* 4.130).

43-45. And he shook . . . by an apple: Virgil's affectionate amusement at the pilgrim's childlike response to Beatrice's name and the simile of the little boy continue the motif of 24.111, as will lines 115-17. The rationale is derived from Matt. 18.2-4: "Amen I say to you, unless you . . . become as little children, you shall not enter the kingdom of Heaven"; cf. Matt. 19.14. Contini 1959 notes the frequency of this topos in lyric poetry.

46-48. Then ahead of me . . . divided us: Statius has been walking with Virgil, ahead of the pilgrim, at least since 22.125; from 28.1 on, the pilgrim will lead. For the enclosing of the pilgrim, cf. lines 85-87, with note.

54. Already I seem to see her eyes: For Virgil on Beatrice's eyes, see *Inf.* 2.55 and 116-17, and below, lines 100-108 and 136-37, with notes.

55-63. A voice . . . not gone dark: The encounter with the second angel of the terrace. The separation of the angel's urgings (lines 61-63) from his singing and eventual appearance allow lines 55-60 to round out the first section of the canto.

55-57. A voice . . . we could ascend: What the angel is singing is not specified (see the note to line 58). Note the correlation of sight and hearing here and in line 54. Once within the fire they can see nothing else, it would seem.

58-60. *Venite* . . . look at it: Presumably the purification just undergone makes the pilgrim unable to bear the angel's brightness. At the successive levels of the ascent the angels have increased in brightness (see 9.79-132; 12.88-99; 15.16-36;

17.46-67; 19.43-51; 22.1-6; 24.133-54; 27.6-13 and 58-63; also 30.16-30, 82-96; and 31.76-78). The brightest so far has been in 24.137-44.

58. *Venite, benedicti Patris mei* [Come, ye blessed of my Father]: Quoted from Matt. 25.34, which gives the words that at the Last Judgment Christ will say to welcome the just into Heaven: "Come, ye blessed of my Father, possess you the kingdom prepared for you from the foundation of the world." (The Baptistery in Florence includes in its mosaic of the Last Judgment an angel speaking these words from behind an opening door.) Here the phrase signals the end of the entire purgation, and it carries the apocalyptic associations of its source. Puzzlement has been occasioned about its applicability to Virgil (as of line 11, "anime sante" [holy souls]), and some have argued from it that Virgil will eventually be saved (see Iliescu in Franco/Morgan 1995).

61-63. The sun departs . . . not gone dark: The commentators note the parallel with John 12.35: "Yet a little while, the light is among you. Walk whilst you have the light, that the darkness overtake you not" (see the note to 33.10-12).

64. The path mounted straight ahead: The last stairway, then, mounts toward the east (cf. 26.4-6), and the setting sun is at their backs; since in 3.15-18 the morning sun was directly behind them, they have now circled 180° of the mountain; this is probably to be associated with the 180° turn in *Inf.* 34.76-81.

65-69. I cut the rays . . . set behind us: This passage is the last reference to the pilgrim's shadow in the *Purgatorio* and thus in the entire *Comedy,* and it is carefully planned so that the disappearance of this sign of the pilgrim's fleshliness coincides with the completion of his purgation.

70-75. before the horizon . . . delight in it: Between sunset and total darkness the three adopt their positions for the night, each on a different degree of the stairway. The clear implication of "made his bed" is that all three recline; Virgil and Statius, of course, do not sleep.

70-72. before the horizon . . . dispensation: In these impressive lines an omniscient point of view is adopted, not that of the pilgrim (to whom only a small part of the sky is visible: line 88).

72. dispensation: That night has *dispense* [literally, allotments] is partly a reminder that night is the shadow of the earth, of which half is always in daylight. See the note to lines 109-14.

74-75. the nature of the mountain . . . delight in it: For the souls' inability to climb after sunset, cf. 7.43-45 and 53-60, 17.62-63 and 75, as well as lines 121-23 below. Line 75 refers to the climb now being pleasurable; cf. Virgil's predictions in 4.88-95, 12.126.

76-87. As the she-goats . . . by the high rock: A double simile, the first part focussed mainly on the flock of goats and invoking noontime, the second on the shepherd and invoking nighttime. Although there is no explicit statement, there is a clear implication that the arrangement of lines 47-48 still obtains: Virgil is on the highest of the three steps and Statius on the lowest. Note the parallel with the enclosing positions of the two angels in 8.31-33, and see the note on line 87.

76-81. As the she-goats . . . provides them with rest: This first part of the double simile contrasts the stillness of the early afternoon with the lively activity of the morning (mirroring the transition from hurried ascent to rest). There is a strong suggestion of youth and capriciousness in the she-goats (see the note on 16.85), but their choice, as opposed to he-goats, is no doubt partly motivated by considerations of euphony (in all nine lines there are only three words ending in *-i* in lines 76 and 82, but if *capri* had been used instead of *capre*, eight more would have been required, a total of eleven; note also the verbs and adverbs ending in *-e* and *-a*). She-goats are frequent in bucolic poetry (e.g., *Ecl.* 2.64, 10.77, etc.; see Dante's *Ecloga* 1.3).

82-83. as the shepherd . . . his flock: Although in modern Italian *mandria* [herd] refers properly to larger animals and *mandriano* would probably be translated "herdsman," the early commentators unanimously take the lines to refer to sheep and a shepherd. Mattalia notes the parallel with *Geor.* 4.433-36: "He [Proteus], like a guardian of the fold in the mountains, when Evening leads the calves from pasture home and the lambs with their loud bleating arouse the listening wolves, sits on a rock in the midst and reviews their number."

84. wild beast: Dante's imagined beast [*fiera*] is most probably the wolf, too.

85-86. so were all three . . . like shepherds: The rounding out of the simile, emphasizing especially the watchfulness of Virgil and Statius on either side of the pilgrim, who of course is the only one who has had to use a body to climb.

87. enclosed on this side and that: Benvenuto observes that there is no danger of falling here, as there had been along the edge of the last terrace (25.112-20), also described with the terms *quinci* [on this side] and *quindi* [on that side]. Italian *fasciare* (from *fascia* [wrapping]) means *to wrap* or *to bundle*; it is used by Dante of the various enclosures of the souls, e.g., *Inf.* 26.48, *Par.* 26.135; in *Purg.* 16.37 *fascia* is used of the body itself, the soul's primary "wrapping," from which the others are derived (see *ED*, s.v. *fascia*). In the *DVE* (e.g., 2.5.8) Dante uses the metaphor of a bundle [*fascis*] of sticks for the canzone stanza (rhymes are the binding).

88-108. Little could be seen . . . doing satisfies me: The pilgrim's sleep and his third dream.

88-96. Little could be seen . . . the fire of love: The earlier passages introducing the pilgrim's dreams (9.1-12, 18.139-42) do not mention the pilgrim's contemplating the heavens, although both indicate the hour astronomically. In the first he sleeps because he is weighed down by the flesh, in the second when thinking back on Virgil's expositions. Here his gazing at the stars, like their greater brightness and size, suggests a new openness to the celestial and foreshadows the *Paradiso*.

89-90. the stars . . . than their custom: Dante may have attributed the greater brightness of the stars to the purity of the air near the summit of the mountain (cf. 21.40-54, with notes), but the idea of their greater size probably derives from *SS* 3.7: "From there all the stars seemed extremely bright and wondrous—and there were stars that from here we have never seen—and the magnitudes of all were such as we have never supposed to exist."

91. ruminating: A reprise of the she-goats' chewing of the cud (line 76), with the same term, closely related to the coming of sleep in 18.139-45.

92-93. sleep that often . . . knows the news: These lines are more explicit than 9.16-18, on the same theme.

94-108. At the hour . . . doing satisfies me: The third of the pilgrim's three dreams, a prefiguration of the events of the coming day and a partial key to their interpretation (see the notes on 28.40-42, 31.115-26). It is the most explicit of the pilgrim's three dreams, its meaning the least disguised; see the notes to 9.16-18 and 19.1-6.

94-96. At the hour . . . fire of love: Like the first two dreams, this one begins with an indication of the hour (just before dawn): "Ne l'ora . . . che" [At the hour when]. In the two earlier cases, the indications were negative, associated with violent impulse (9.13-15) or cold (19.1-6). Here the hour is warmed by Venus ("Cytherea," from Cythera, her birthplace).

97-108. in dream . . . doing satisfies me: Only twelve lines long, this is the shortest of the dreams.

97-99. in dream . . . singing she said: Although Leah and Rachel are OT figures (see the note on lines 100-108), the scene draws on a variety of sources, including Ovid and Claudian, to be discussed in the notes to Canto 28.

97-98. in dream . . . gathering flowers: The inverted syntax of these lines cannot be reproduced idiomatically in English. Their elements, literally translated, in the original order, are: "Young and beautiful in dream it seemed to me a lady to see to walk in a meadow gathering flowers." Until "donna vedere" [to see a lady] "giovane e bella" [young and beautiful] could refer to Venus, and the grammatical construction is undefined; the occurrence of "donna vedere" thus creates the impression of a sudden apparition. Furthermore, although the construction could stand alone after "vedere" [to see], the complementary infinitive "andare" [to walk] follows without more than the slightest pause (though technically there is a caesura). It is one of the most remarkable sentences in the *Comedy* (see the even more spectacular one in 30.22-33, with notes, and cf. the note on 28.37-42).

100-108. Whoever asks . . . satisfies me: The lady identifies herself as Leah, daughter of Laban: in Genesis 29-30, Jacob visits his uncle Laban and falls in love with his younger daughter, Rachel; he agrees to serve Laban for seven years in order to gain her hand. At the end of the seven years, Laban substitutes Leah on the marriage night; reproached by Jacob the next morning, Laban justifies his action by the custom of giving the oldest in marriage first, but he offers to let Jacob marry Rachel at once if he agrees to serve him for seven more years; Jacob accepts. The exegetes identified the two daughters as representing the active and contemplative life; Augustine's discussion was influential (*Contra Faustum* 22.52):

> I believe that Jacob's two wives who were free [not slaves, like his concu-
> bines] refer to the New Law, under which we are called to freedom, and
> that it is significant that they are two. For two lives are preached to us in the
> Church: one temporal, in which we labor; one eternal, in which we will
> delight in the contemplation of God. The former is declared by the Lord's
> Passion, the latter by his Resurrection . . . Thus the living of this mortal
> human life, in which we live by faith, doing many laborious works though
> uncertain whether they will be beneficial to those we wish to help, that is
> Leah, Jacob's first wife, and that is why she is said to have weak eyes, for the
> cogitations of mortals are timid and our previsions are uncertain. But the
> hope of the eternal contemplation of God, with the certain and delectable
> knowledge of Truth, that is Rachel, and that is why she is said to be beautiful
> and of goodly features. . . . For in the just training of a man the performing of
> what is just comes before the pleasure of understanding what is true.

(See also Augustine's *De consensu Evangelistarum* 1.5.8; Gregory the Great, *Homiliae in Ezechielem* 2.2.10.) The pairing of Leah and Rachel is similar to that of Martha and Mary, also sisters, in Luke 10.38-42, discussed in *Conv.* 4.17 as figures of the active and contemplative life. This traditional distinction is close to Dante's distinction between the two goals of human life in *Mon.* 3.6-8; see the note to 16.106-108.

101-103. I go moving . . . adorn myself: Leah's gathering flowers signifies the operation of moral virtues (the works of her hands); the garlands that will adorn her signify the merits she gains through her works (see the note to 19.121-24).

104-106. my sister Rachel . . . her lovely eyes: The mirror is a virtually universal symbol of contemplation in the Middle Ages; what Rachel sees—her eyes— is at one level her own capacity for reflection and contemplative vision (see 25.73-75, with notes), at another the vision of God (cf. the notes on line 54 and 31.115-26); see also lines 136-37.

109-142. And already . . . crown and mitre: The last phase of the ascent to the summit of the mountain, culminating in the crowning of the pilgrim.

109-114. And already . . . already risen: Before dawn on the last day on the mountain. The pilgrim's two previous awakenings had occurred later in the day: in 9.43-45 the sun is two hours high; in 19.33-39 it is broad daylight. In the latter passage the pilgrim's heavy sleep is a figure of the content of the preceding dream, the attachment to lesser pleasures; here the lightness of his sleep and his early rising—not due to any painful happening in the dream (cf. 9.31-32, 19.33)— express his new state. The *Comedy* begins on the night of Holy Thursday; the sun rises in *Inferno* 1 on Good Friday (see the notes to *Inf.* 21.112-14, 29.10-11, 34.68). The *Purgatorio* begins just before dawn on Easter Sunday (see the notes to 1.88-90, 109); the three nights spent on the mountain are those of Sunday, Monday, and Tuesday; thus this last day is a Wednesday—*Mercurii dies*. Night will not come again in the *Comedy*, since the *Paradiso* quickly moves beyond the shadow of the earth (it is not true, however, as some commentators assert, that the *Paradiso* takes places entirely beyond time: that is true only beginning with *Paradiso* 28).

110-11. which rise . . . far from home: This mention balances the first mention of pilgrims in the cantica, 8.1-6, and is placed in a roughly symmetrical position (separated from the end by six cantos, versus seven from the beginning). In 8.1-6 the travelers have just begun their journey; here they are drawing nearer home, Heaven being the *patria*. The change from the sense of earth as home, dominant in the early cantos, to Heaven as home is a major shift in the gravitation of the poem. It will be intensified through the *Paradiso*, and the axial symmetry of the *Comedy* around *Purgatorio* 17 will become more and more evident. See also 26.67-69, with notes.

114. seeing my great masters already risen: See the note to lines 76-87.

115-20. That sweet apple . . . in pleasure to them: The "sweet apple" is of course earthly happiness; the commentators cite *Consolation* 3.2.2: "Every striving of mortals, exerted in a multitude of pursuits, proceeds along different paths but strives to attain only the one goal of happiness. That is the good beyond which, once one attains it, nothing further can be desired." Many such passages could be cited (e.g., Augustine, *De Trinitate* 13.4.7). Dante's image of the apple or fruit brings with it also that of the tree ("branches," line 115), while the image of paths is more common in such contexts. See 24.103-12, with notes.

117. peace: The imminence of peace has been a recurrent theme; see 25.54, 27.8.

119. gifts: Italian *strenna* [Lat. *strena*] refers to a gift given for good luck, traditionally on January 1; the practice survived in Dante's time and was denounced as pagan by Cavalca. The new day marks an epoch for the pilgrim.

121-23. So much did . . . grow for flight: The first mention of the growth of wings since the introduction of the analogy with insect metamorphosis in 10.124-29 (see the notes there, and the note on the textual variant in 12.5) and *Par.* 1.67-75 (where flight will begin). We are meant to recall the failure to climb the "delightful mountain" in *Inferno* 1 (the beasts, especially the she-wolf, were recalled in line 84).

124-42. When the stairway . . . crown and mitre: At the summit, but still outside the Earthly Paradise (mentioned but not yet seen directly), Virgil announces the pilgrim's justification to be complete—Original Justice has been restored (see Singleton 1957)—and renounces his authority over him.

124-25. When the stairway . . . uppermost step: The last phase of the climb is here seen only in retrospect. Not only the stairway from the level of lust is now behind them; as Virgil will indicate in line 132, the entire mountain (and the descending stairway of Hell—cf. *Inf.* 17.82, with note) is included in "la scala tutta" [all the stairway].

126. Virgil fixed his eyes on me: The solemnity of the moment is emphasized by the direct gaze. Compare the earlier references to Virgil's facial expressions (lines 35, 43-44; cf. *Inf.* 10.34).

127-42. The temporal fire . . . crown and mitre: Virgil's graduation address, as it were, conferring the degree on the candidate, and recapitulating the entire journey so far.

127-30. The temporal fire . . . with wit and with art: These lines echo those in which Virgil assumed authority over the pilgrim, especially *Inf.* 1.112-20. The "temporal fire" (cf. *Inf.* 1.119-20) is that of Purgatory, where the souls are "contenti nel foco" [content in the fire] (*Inf.* 1.118-19) since they know it is temporary; the "eternal fire" is of course Hell, the "loco etterno" [eternal place] of *Inf.* 1.114. Now Virgil "can judge no further" (line 129), whereas in *Inf.* 1.112-13 he assumed authority with the words "penso e discerno / che tu mi segui" [I think and judge that you shall follow me]. "Tratto t'ho qui" [I have led you here] echoes *Inf.* 1. 114 "trarrotti di qui" [I shall lead you from here]. *Inferno* 1 and 2 do not specify *where* Virgil will leave the pilgrim, only that it will be with a worthier soul, obviously Beatrice (cf. 23.127-29, and see the note on lines 133-35 below).

130. with wit and with art: Wit [*ingegno*] as native talent, art as acquired knowledge and skill, are two ingredients of all fashioning. They are fully applicable to the *Aeneid,* produced by Vergil's wit and art, the reading of which is an ultimate allegorical reference of the figure of Virgil's guidance on the journey.

133-35. See the sun . . . of itself alone: This is the very first description in the *Comedy* of the Earthly Paradise, heretofore only vaguely referred to; 1.24 mentions "the first people" (Adam and Eve) as having seen the four bright stars, implying that Eden is on the mountain; 6.46 mentions the summit as a place of happiness; 8.114 mentions its flowers; 24.116 identifies the gluttons' trees as derived from the Tree of the Knowledge of Good and Evil "above"; 25.112 introduces the fire of the ledge of lust, which an informed reader would associate with the traditional wall of fire surrounding Eden (Nardi 1967). Although as readers of the *Purgatorio* we are continually aware that Eden is at the summit of the mountain, that is partly the product of the commentary tradition within which we read. Only in the next canto will we see Eden through the pilgrim's eyes.

136-37. Until the lovely eyes . . . come to you: See *Inf.* 2.116-17: "li occhi lucenti lagrimando volse, / per che mi fece dal venir più presto" [she turned her shining eyes, shedding tears, which made me quicker to come here], and cf. *Inf.* 2.55: "Lucevan li occhi suoi più che la stella" [Her eyes shone brighter than the morning star], and, in this canto, lines 54 and 106-108. For the gladness of Beatrice's eyes, which will contrast with their earlier weeping, 6.46-48.

139-42. No longer await . . . crown and mitre: The earlier assertions of the pilgrim's autonomy (lines 131-32, 138) and of Virgil's withdrawal of supervision (line 129) are now completed and made fully explicit in the impressive climax of the speech, concluding the canto and the entire process of purgation.

139. await . . . from me: As the pilgrim does, for example, in 1.49-51, 1.112, 3.10-13, 21.115-20, 25.10-19, to mention only instances from the *Purgatorio*. This is in fact Virgil's last speech before his disappearance.

140. free, upright, and whole is your will: The Italian term *arbitrio* (Lat. *arbitrium* [decision]) refers properly to the power of choice (see 16.71, 18.74, with notes). The pilgrim's power to choose is now free, no longer enslaved by habit or limited by unruly impulse; it is upright in that it will spontaneously choose the good; it is whole (healthy) because it has been cured of its diseases or wounds and made whole in the restoration of the natural harmony and interrelation of the faculties of the soul, formerly overturned and fragmented by sin and vice. The goal announced in 1.71-72 has been attained.

141. it would be . . . its intent: Contini 1959 calls attention to the frequency of alliterative effects ("*fallo fora non fare a suo senno*") in the canto (cf. lines 19, 27, 88, 106, 128-29), as well as other preciosities, especially rare words and neologisms (*pernotta, antelucano, immenso, dispensa, manse, pranse*).

142. you over yourself I crown and mitre: The pilgrim is crowned king over himself by Virgil, representing both reason and the entire cultural tradition stemming from antiquity: he is fully qualified to govern himself (for the kingdom, cf. the note to line 58). Note "te sovra te" [you over you], expressing this ideal integration and autonomy, correlated with the civil war in the soul of Pier delle Vigne, expressed in his "me contra me" [me against me] (see *Inf.* 13.72, with note).

Both kings and bishops wore mitres, and there has been dispute whether Virgil's "crown and mitre" refers to both king and pope (meaning that the pilgrim is now beyond the authority of the corrupt papacy, as well as of the empire), or exclusively to the crowning of kings and emperors (Contini 1959). Although the pilgrim's ascent in the *Paradiso* is beyond the authority of kings, emperors, and corrupt popes, it is explicitly placed under the authority of the Church Triumphant (see especially *Paradiso* 24-26).

Inter cantica. As the culmination of the process of purgation—which has extended not merely through Purgatory proper but can be seen to include the penitential descent into Hell as well—this canto represents a major turning point. For this reason, its many important connections with the *Inferno* have been discussed in the notes; see also *Inter cantica* for Canto 28.

CANTO 28

Vago già di cercar dentro e dintorno   1
la divina foresta spessa e viva,
ch'a li occhi temperava il novo giorno,

    sanza più aspettar lasciai la riva,   4
prendendo la campagna lento lento
su per lo suol che d'ogne parte auliva.

    Un'aura dolce, sanza mutamento   7
avere in sé, mi feria per la fronte
non di più colpo che soave vento,

    per cui le fronde tremolando pronte   10
tutte quante piegavano a la parte
u' la prim' ombra gitta il santo monte,

    non però dal loro esser dritto sparte   13
tanto, che li augelletti per le cime
lasciasser d'operare ogne lor arte;

    ma con piena letizia l'ore prime   16
cantando ricevieno intra le foglie,
che tenevan bordone a le sue rime:

    tal qual di ramo in ramo si raccoglie   19
per la pineta in su 'l lito di Chiassi,
quand' Ëolo scilocco fuor discioglie.

    Già m'avean trasportato i lenti passi   22
dentro a la selva antica tanto ch'io
non potea rivedere ond' io mi 'ntrassi,

    ed ecco più andar mi tolse un rio   25
che 'nver' sinistra con sue picciole onde
piegava l'erba che 'n sua ripa uscìo.

    Tutte l'acque che son di qua più monde   28
parrieno avere in sé mistura alcuna
verso di quella, che nulla nasconde,

CANTO 28

The Earthly Paradise—the breeze—the stream—Matelda
—the pilgrim's desire—his puzzlement—Matelda's explanation—the
Golden Age

1   Eager already to search within and about the
divine forest, thick and alive, which tempered the
new day to my eyes,

4   without further waiting I left the bank, taking
the plain slowly, slowly, over ground that breathed
fragrance from every side.

7   A sweet breeze, unchanging in itself, struck my
brow with no greater force than a gentle wind,

10   by which the pliant branches, trembling, were
bent, all of them, toward where the holy mountain
casts its earliest shadow,

13   but not parted so much from their straightness
that the little birds in the treetops left off exerting
their every art,

16   but with full gladness they welcomed the first
hours, singing among the leaves, which kept the
bass note to their rhymes:

19   like the note that gathers from branch to branch
in the pine-forest on the shore of Classe, when
Aeolus looses the scirocco.

22   Already my slow steps had transported me into
the ancient wood so far that I could not see back to
the place whence I had entered,

25   and behold, walking further was denied me by a
stream flowing toward the left with its little waves
and bending the grass that grew along its bank.

28   All the waters that back here are purest, would
seem to have some impurity in them next to that
one, for it hides nothing,

avvegna che si mova bruna bruna 31
sotto l'ombra perpetüa, che mai
raggiar non lascia sole ivi né luna.

 Coi piè ristetti e con li occhi passai 34
di là dal fiumicello, per mirare
la gran varïazion d'i freschi mai;

 e là m'apparve—sì com' elli appare 37
subitamente cosa che disvia
per maraviglia tutto altro pensare—

 una donna soletta che si gia 40
e cantando e scegliendo fior da fiore
ond' era pinta tutta la sua via.

 "Deh, bella donna che a' raggi d'amore 43
ti scaldi, s'i' vo' credere a' sembianti,
che soglion esser testimon del core,

 vegnati in voglia di trarreti avanti," 46
diss' io a lei, "verso questa rivera
tanto ch'io possa intender che tu canti.

 Tu mi fai rimembrar dove e qual era 49
Proserpina nel tempo che perdette
la madre lei, ed ella primavera."

 Come si volge, con le piante strette 52
a terra e intra sé, donna che balli,
e piede innanzi piede a pena mette:

 volsesi in su i vermigli e in su i gialli 55
fioretti verso me, non altrimenti
che vergine che li occhi onesti avvalli,

 e fece i prieghi miei esser contenti, 58
sì appressando sé che 'l dolce suono
veniva a me co' suoi intendimenti.

 Tosto che fu là dove l'erbe sono 61
bagnate già da l'onde del bel fiume,
di levar li occhi suoi mi fece dono.

 Non credo che splendesse tanto lume 64
sotto le ciglia a Venere, trafitta
dal figlio fuor di tutto suo costume.

 Ella ridea da l'altra riva, dritta, 67
trattando più color con le sue mani,
che l'alta terra sanza seme gitta.

31   although it moves dark, dark under the
     perpetual shade, which never lets sun or moon
     shine through.

34   With my feet I stood still, and with my eyes I
     passed beyond the stream, to gaze at the great
     variety of the fresh May branches,

37   and over there appeared to me—as sometimes a
     thing will suddenly appear that for wonder scatters
     every other thought—

40   a solitary lady, who was walking along both
     singing and choosing flower from flower among
     those that colored all her way.

43   "Ah, beautiful lady who warm yourself in the
     rays of love, if I am to believe your expression,
     which usually bears witness to the heart,

46   let it be your desire to move forward," I said to
     her, "toward this stream so far that I may
     understand what you are singing.

49   You put me in mind of where and what
     Proserpina was, in the time when her mother lost
     her and she the spring."

52   As a lady turns who is dancing, with her feet
     pressed to the ground and together, scarcely
     placing one foot before the other:

55   so she turned on the crimson and yellow flowers
     toward me, not otherwise than a virgin who lowers
     her modest eyes,

58   and she contented my prayers, drawing so near
     that the sweet sound reached me with its
     meanings.

61   As soon as she was where the grass is already
     bathed by the lovely river, she made me the gift of
     raising her eyes.

64   I do not believe so much light shone under
     Venus' brow when she was transfixed by her son,
     beyond all his custom.

67   She was laughing from the other bank, standing
     upright, arranging in her hands many colors,
     thrown forth by the noble earth without any seed.

Tre passi ci facea il fiume lontani,   70
ma Elesponto—là 've passò Serse,
ancora freno a tutti orgogli umani—
    più odio da Leandro non sofferse   73
per mareggiare intra Sesto e Abido,
che quel da me perch' allor non s'aperse.
    "Voi siete nuovi, e forse perch' io rido,"   76
cominciò ella, "in questo luogo eletto
a l'umana natura per suo nido,
    maravigliando tienvi alcun sospetto;   79
ma luce rende il salmo *Delectasti*,
che puote disnebbiar vostro intelletto.
    E tu che se' dinanzi e mi pregasti,   82
dì s'altro vuoli udir, ch'i' venni presta
ad ogne tua question tanto che basti."
    "L'acqua," diss' io, "e 'l suon de la foresta   85
impugnan dentro a me novella fede
di cosa ch'io udi' contraria a questa."
    Ond' ella: "Io dicerò come procede   88
per sua cagion ciò ch'ammirar ti face,
e purgherò la nebbia che ti fiede.
    Lo sommo Ben, che solo esso a sé piace,   91
fé l'uom buono e a bene, e questo loco
diede per arr' a lui d'etterna pace.
    Per sua difalta qui dimorò poco;   94
per sua difalta in pianto e in affanno
cambiò onesto riso e dolce gioco.
    Perché 'l turbar che sotto da sé fanno   97
l'essalazion de l'acqua e de la terra,
che quanto posson dietro al calor vanno,
    a l'uomo non facesse alcuna guerra,   100
questo monte salìo verso 'l ciel tanto,
e libero n'è d'indi ove si serra.
    Or perché in circuito tutto quanto   103
l'aere si volge con la prima volta,
se non li è rotto il cerchio d'alcun canto,
    in questa altezza ch'è tutta disciolta   106
ne l'aere vivo, tal moto percuote,
e fa sonar la selva perch' è folta;

70   The river kept us three paces apart, but Helles-
pont, where Xerxes passed—a bridle still on all
human pride—

73   suffered no more hatred from Leander when the
sea was high between Sestos and Abydos, than that
river from me for not opening then.

76   "You people are new, and perhaps because I
laugh," she began, "in this place chosen to be the
nest for human nature,

79   some doubt keeps you marveling; but light is
shed by the psalm *Delectasti*, which can uncloud
your intellects.

82   And you who stand in front and begged me,
say if you wish to hear more, for I have come ready
for your every question, as much as will suffice."

85   "The water," I said, "and the sound of the forest
conflict with a new belief in me, in what I heard
contrary to this."

88   Then she: "I will explain how what you marvel
at proceeds from its cause, and I will purge the fog
that strikes you.

91   The highest Good, who alone pleases himself,
made man good and for the good, and this place he
gave as a token to him of eternal peace.

94   Because of his own fault he dwelt here but little;
by his own fault he changed into weeping and
labor his virtuous laughter and sweet play.

97   That the disturbances made below by the
exhalations of water and earth, which follow heat
as much as they can,

100   should not offer any harm to man, this
mountain rose thus far toward Heaven and is free
of them above the gate that is locked.

103   Now because the sphere of air turns in a circle
all together, following the first turning, if its circle
is not broken in some place,

106   this height, rising altogether free into the living
air, is struck by that motion, which makes the
forest resound because it is so dense;

e la percossa pianta tanto puote 109
che de la sua virtute l'aura impregna
e quella poi, girando, intorno scuote;

e l'altra terra, secondo ch'è degna 112
per sé e per suo ciel, concepe e figlia
di diverse virtù diverse legna.

Non parrebbe di là poi maraviglia, 115
udito questo, quando alcuna pianta
sanza seme palese vi s'appiglia.

E saper dei che la campagna santa 118
dove tu se' d'ogne semenza è piena,
e frutto ha in sé che di là non si schianta.

L'acqua che vedi non surge di vena 121
che ristori vapor che gel converta,
come fiume ch'acquista e perde lena,

ma esce di fontana salda e certa 124
che tanto dal voler di Dio riprende
quant' ella versa da due parti aperta.

Da questa parte con virtù discende 127
che toglie altrui memoria del peccato;
da l'altra d'ogne ben fatto la rende.

Quinci Letè, così da l'altro lato 130
Eünoè si chiama, e non adopra
se quinci e quindi pria non è gustato:

a tutti altri sapori esto è di sopra. 133
E avvegna ch'assai possa esser sazia
la sete tua perch' io più non ti scuopra,

darotti un corollario ancor per grazia, 136
né credo che 'l mio dir ti sia men caro
se oltre promession teco si spazia.

Quelli ch'anticamente poetaro 139
l'età de l'oro e suo stato felice,
forse in Parnaso esto loco sognaro.

Qui fu innocente l'umana radice; 142
qui primavera sempre e ogne frutto;
nettare è questo di che ciascun dice."

Io mi rivolsi 'n dietro allora tutto 145
a' miei poeti, e vidi che con riso
udito avëan l'ultimo costrutto;

poi a la bella donna torna' il viso. 148

109   and the plant that is struck is so vigorous that it impregnates the air with its formative power, and the air then, in its circling, scatters it abroad;

112   and the rest of the earth, as it is worthy in itself and because of its sky, conceives and bears divers trees from the divers powers.

115   Hearing this, it would not seem a marvel back there when a plant takes root without visible seed.

118   And you must know that the holy field where you are is full of every sowing, and has fruit in itself that is not gathered back there.

121   The water that you see does not rise from a vein that vapor condensed by cold restores, like a river that gains and loses fullness,

124   but issues from a firm, sure fountain that takes from the will of God as much as it pours forth, opened in two directions.

127   On this side it descends with the power to take away all memory of sin; on the other it gives back the memory of every good deed.

130   Here it is called Lethe, as on the other side Eunoè, and it is not effective before it is tasted both on this side and on that:

133   this is a savor above all others. And while your thirst might be well satisfied though I should discover nothing more to you,

136   I will give you still a corollary, as a grace, nor do I think my speech will be less precious to you if it ranges with you beyond my promise.

139   Those who in ancient times wrote in their poetry of the Age of Gold and its happy state, perhaps on Parnassus dreamed this place.

142   Here the human root was innocent; here there is always spring and every fruit; this is the nectar of which each one tells."

145   I turned entirely around, back to my poets, then, and I saw that they had smiled hearing her last construction;

148   then to the beautiful lady I returned my gaze.

NOTES

1-36. Eager . . . May branches: These lines set the scene for the last portion of the cantica and are the only passage of direct description of the Earthly Paradise through the eyes of the pilgrim, except for scattered details (as in lines 61-62, 67-70, and 29.31-33); direct description is quickly replaced by the figure of Matelda with her scientific explanations.

Dante draws heavily on the classical myth of the Golden Age (see lines 139-41) and the classical, biblical, and medieval tradition of the *locus amoenus* [delightful place], or *plaisance,* which regularly featured springlike weather with gentle breezes, trees, singing birds, varied flowers, and a pleasant river or stream; examples abound in Vergil's *Eclogues* and the later pastoral tradition, and a noteworthy biblical example is Psalm 22. In Christian writers the *locus amoenus* (cf. 8.100) was associated with Eden (Nardi 1967, Graf 1925, Curtius 1949).

Dante dwells particularly on the dawning, springlike newness and temperateness of conditions in the Earthly Paradise (see lines 3, 7-9, 13-15, 26, 33, with notes); it is a figure of the body in its original harmony and innocence, into which the pilgrim is now newly born. This dimension of the symbolism derives from the exegetical tradition that saw the Garden as a figure for the natural justice—the harmonious integration of spirit and body—in unfallen humanity. See the notes to lines 22-33.

1-6. Eager . . . from every side: Only now do we learn that the Earthly Paradise is a deep forest (see 27.133-35, where there is no mention of trees) of infinite fertility. The pilgrim's eagerness to explore Eden has of course been whetted by long preparation; the profound sense of erotic curiosity and exploration (see especially *dentro e dintorno* [within and around] and *prendendo* [taking]) draws on deep childhood and adolescent memories.

3. tempered . . . to my eyes: As lines 31-33 will reveal, the entire Earthly Paradise is entirely shaded by the leaves of the forest: the light filters in, subdued to the capacity of the inhabitants (see the note to lines 32-33), an important instance of accomodation, as well as of the motif of the veil, which will recur.

5. the plain slowly, slowly: The term *campagna* here refers less to the landscape being open to the view (as a thick forest it cannot be) than to its being level. Dante frequently uses the idiomatic repetition of modifiers, often single words, for emphasis, e.g., *Inf.* 17.101 ("indietro indietro"), 17.115 ("lenta lenta"), 21.89 ("quatto quatto"), 29.70 ("passo passo"); *Purg.* 18.103 ("ratto ratto"), 28.31 ("bruna bruna"); *Par.* 5.138 ("chiusa chiusa"). See Cavalcanti's ballata (pp. 588-89), line 12 and the note to lines 37-42 below.

7-12. A sweet breeze . . . earliest shadow: The pilgrim is facing east (see 27.64-69); the breeze comes from there and bends the branches toward the west (line 12) and toward the pilgrim.

16-18. with full gladness . . . to their rhymes: The birds are the only fauna encountered in the Garden (cf. Gen. 2.19-20). The joyous singing with which they greet the dawn is an instance of the happiness of the Creator reflected in the creatures (cf. 16.89-90 and Ps. 148.7-10); the musical references remind us that their singing is an analogue of the prayer service of Lauds (see Additional Note 5 and *Inter cantica,* below).

18. kept the bass note: Dante's word is *bordone* [drone, from Fr. bourdon], a frequent feature of medieval music, surviving today especially in musette and bagpipe.

19-21. like the note . . . looses the scirocco: The bass note of line 18 is like the note the ear gathers in the famous pine forest just north of Classe (the Roman and medieval port of Ravenna); Aeolus is the classical god of the winds (see *Aen.* 1.50-91); the scirocco is the southeast wind (Eurus). See the note on lines 103-20.

22-24. Already . . . had entered: The narrative returns to the motion of the pilgrim, echoing lines 1 ("already") and 5 ("slow"). The motif of the backward glance refers back to *Inf.* 15.13-15 and *Purg.* 9.131-32 and 10.5-6, but without echoing the biblical warnings (Lot's wife, Gen. 19.26; and Luke 9.62); the indicative in "non potea" [I could not] perhaps implies that he has looked back (cf. lines 145-48).

Eden is "ancient" because created before man (Gen. 2.8: "And the Lord God had planted a paradise of pleasure, from the beginning"); the term *selva* [wood] strengthens the association with the Dark Wood of *Inferno* 1 (see *Inter cantica,* below) as well as the Platonic use of the term to refer to the world of matter (see the note to *Inf.*1.2): the pilgrim's entry into the forest is a figure of the soul's entry into the material world, strongly suggested by his inability to see whence he entered, an allusion to the new-born soul's forgetfulness of its heavenly origin (for the reflexive *mi* here, see the notes to *Inf.* 1.2, *Purg.* 24.74,76; and cf. 16.88)—but here in non-fallen mode (and in contrast to the sleep of *Inf.* 1.10-12).

25-33. and behold . . . shine through: This river (we soon learn that it is Lethe) is the culmination in this cantica of an important strand of imagery and symbolism extending over the entire poem. A major clue to its significance is provided by 13. 87-90, in which the goal of purgation is called the cleansing of the "river of the mind." This association is but one of many indications that the landscape of Eden is to be taken both as the literal Garden of Genesis 2-3 and as an inner one, figuring the new relation between soul and body (in this Dante is quite traditional; the biblical commentators recognized both the literal/historical and the allegorical meanings of the Garden). Events in the Earthly Paradise are primarily inner ones. (For the relation of the rivers of Eden to those of Hell, see *Inter cantica,* below.)

That the pilgrim's steps are halted by the river (flowing toward the left—north, since the pilgrim is facing east) recalls the romance motif of a river as the boundary between this world and the next (as in Marie de France's *Lanval*, or the *Lai of Graelent*). Separating the pilgrim from a section of the Earthly Paradise currently reserved, Lethe here recalls the Jordan, last boundary, after the Red Sea, separating Moses and the Israelites from the Promised Land (Deut. 34, Jos. 1): like Moses, Virgil will not cross this last barrier.

30. it hides nothing: Associated with the theme of self-knowledge and confession in Cantos 30-31. The *Ovide moralisé* allegorizes the stream Arethusa (whose nymph reveals Proserpina's whereabouts to Ceres) as oral confession (see the note to lines 49-61).

31. dark, dark: See the second note to line 5.

32-33. the perpetual shade . . . shine through: See line 3. These lines are the principal statement about the light in the Garden; not until *Par.* 1.46-48 will any heavenly body be seen directly; until the end of this cantica all events take place within the shade of the forest.

34-148. With my feet . . . I returned my gaze: The remainder of the canto is devoted to the encounter with Matelda. There has been much discussion of her identity and significance. On the assumption that, like Beatrice, Virgil, and Statius, Matelda must have had a real historical existence, commentators have identified her with Countess Matilda of Canossa (1046-1115), the powerful supporter of Pope Gregory IX (in her courtyard the emperor Henry IV stood barefoot in the snow as penance); as one of the German mystics, Mechthilde of Hageborn or Mechthilde of Reichenau; or as an otherwise unknown Florentine lady who died young. However, that Matelda is named only in 33.119 is an indication that her symbolic significance, which the reader must grasp for himself, is more important than her relation to any historical figure.

Embodying the innocent happiness of Eden, Matelda is a kind of nymph of the wood or protective spirit of the place; Singleton 1957 urged her identification with Astraea, the virgin goddess of justice of classical myth, last of the immortals to leave the earth (cf. *Ecl.* 4.6). That Matelda is singing and gathering flowers connects her with Leah, the figure of the active life in the pilgrim's last dream; with her Beatrice will be correlated as a figure of the contemplative life (like Rachel in the dream; see the notes to 27.100-108). Matelda will soon explain that her singing expresses her delight in God's creative power, which is of course also a branch of the contemplative life (see the notes to lines 76-84).

Although Virgil and Statius are present in this scene, they are spectators rather than participants (see lines 145-48); the pilgrim is in the lead, and the pairing of pilgrim and Matelda (cf. line 37: "là m'apparve" [over there appeared *to me*]) is an important aspect of Matelda's significance, as a wealth of imagery and mythological allusion will emphasize: The effects of sin have been purged, Original

Justice has been restored; the pilgrim is a new Adam to Matelda's blameless Eve, he is Leander to her Hero (lines 70-75). Matelda represents innocent joy in desire; at one level she is an aspect of the pilgrim's psyche—in Jungian terms his "anima." The paired male and female figures strongly recall the idea of the celestial Twins, Gemini, which in calendars of the period are frequently represented as male and female (not coincidentally, Dante considered himself a Gemini; see *Par.* 22.112-33, with notes, and Durling/Martinez 1990).

36. May branches: Italian *maio* (a variant of *maggio* [May], usually used in the plural), referred to the flowering branches carried in May festival processions.

37-42. and over there . . . all her way: Matelda's sudden appearance is more directly narrated than Leah's (27.97-99), to which it is closely parallel though slightly more particularized ("choosing flower from flower," as opposed to the generic "gathering" of 27.99). While Leah's song is quoted at some length, we are never told what Matelda is singing, though line 80 gives an important hint. For the significance of the flowers, see the note to 27.101-102. Both Leah and Matelda draw heavily on the *pastourelle* tradition, in which the narrator meets a beautiful shepherdess in a *locus amoenus* and usually gains her favors: the most famous Italian example is Cavalcanti's "In un boschetto" (pp. 588-89), to which Dante here makes several allusions, all in the direction of eliminating the profane sexual theme while retaining the springlike freshness and lyric charm (see Barolini 1984, De Robertis 1985). The daring of his approach is noteworthy in lines 43-44, 64-66, 73-74.

43-51. Ah, beautiful lady . . . she the spring: The pilgrim's first address to Matelda derives in tone and vocabulary (at least until line 45) from the tradition of lyric love poetry, including the *pastourelle*; his explicit request to hear her song helps control the sexual overtones of the passage.

44-45. your expression . . . to the heart: See 21.102-108.

49-51. You put me . . . she the spring: Dante's main source of knowledge of the myth of the rape of Proserpina was *Met.* 5.341-571: the only child of Ceres (goddess of grain), carried off by Dis (for the name, see *Inf.* 8.68 and the note to *Inf.* 6.115) to become queen of Hades, while she was gathering flowers in Enna in Sicily, near a lake shaded by thick trees (a passage Dante is remembering in lines 1-3, 31-33): "silva coronat aquas cingens latus omne suisque / frondibus ut velo Phoebeos submovet ictus. / frigora dant rami, Tyrios humus umida flores: / perpetuum ver est" [The wood is a crown to the waters, girding every side, and with its leaves, like a veil, bars every ray of the sun. The boughs give cool shade, the damp ground gives flowers of Tyrian purple, spring is perpetual there.]
  Like Milton (*Paradise Lost* 4.268-272), Dante connected the eternal spring of Enna with that of Eden; Proserpina is an obvious figure of Eve (an important instance of classical myth treated as a version of biblical truth; see lines 139-44,

with notes). The "spring" Proserpina loses is Enna (in figure, Eden) as well as her youth and virginity; "what [she] was" refers to her beauty and innocence (cf. line 57). Kirkham in *LDV* points out that here and in lines 73-75 (on Leander) the references are to moments just before loss, supporting the theme of the recuperation of Paradise. Some details of Dante's description of Eden and references to Proserpina may derive from Claudian: while Ovid has her gathering flowers in a basket, Claudian has her weaving garlands (*Raptus* 2.127-50; cf. *Raptus* 2.101-106, 114-18).

The *Ovide moralisé* allegorizes the story in Christian terms: Ceres, who searches everywhere to reclaim her daughter, represents the Church; Proserpina is the erring human soul; Dis is the devil (cf. the note on line 30). Dante's earlier references to Proserpina as queen of Hell (*Inf.* 9.43-44, 10.79-80) associate her with Hecate and the moon and omit mention of her name.

52-60. As a lady . . . with its meanings: As Singleton observes, this passage is an important document of styles of dancing and attitudes toward them; there is a further reference to Cavalcanti's ballata here; see fig. 10.

61-66. As soon . . . all his custom: The encounter with Matelda, like the encounter with Beatrice in Cantos 30-31, reaches a preliminary climax in the close and direct gaze into the lady's eyes (cf. *Inf.* 10.34, with note).

64-66. I do not believe . . . all his custom: The intensity of Venus' gaze is not an Ovidian theme but a Lucretian one (see *De rerum natura* 1.28-40, which it is just possible Dante knew). The accidental wounding of Venus referred to here (*Met.* 10.525-28) leads to her falling in love with Adonis (*Met.* 10.529-739). Interestingly, both Ovid (*Met.* 10.729-31) and Claudian (*Raptus* 2.122-23) associate Proserpina with Adonis. The lovers' gaze is a major theme of Italian love lyric, not least in Dante's own (cf. the note to 26.103, Durling/Martinez 1990).

69. without any seed: See the note to lines 103-20.

71-75. Hellespont . . . not opening then: Two famous episodes connected with the Hellespont (the modern Dardanelles) occupy the principal clause ("Hellespont . . . suffered," etc.) and a subordinate clause ("where Xerxes," etc., lines 71-72; see next note). The principal clause refers to the lovers Hero and Leander, living in cities facing each other across the narrowest part of the Hellespont, Sestos and Abydos respectively. To keep their love secret, Leander swam across the water at night, except when the winter brought storms; eventually he could not bear to wait and was drowned; Hero leapt to her death from her tower. The earliest surviving literary reference to the story (*Geor.* 3.258-63) cites it as an example of love as ungovernable impulse and makes clear the tragic outcome, though without mentioning the lovers' names; Ovid's *Heroides* includes a letter from each of the lovers, written during a winter storm; Hero voices her fears, but neither lover expresses hatred of the Hellespont itself, protesting instead against the weather.

71-72. where Xerxes . . . human pride: Dante knew from Orosius of Xerxes' invasion of Greece, crossing the Hellespont on bridges resting on specially constructed boats; they collapsed under his panicked, retreating army, drowning thousands. Greek and Latin tradition treated Xerxes as a prime instance of overweening pride punished with humiliating defeat. According to Herodotus, when a storm destroyed his bridge at an early stage of construction, Xerxes had the water whipped for its presumption.

75. for not opening then: In the Italian this is an additional subordinate clause ("perché . . ." [because]); it is an obvious reference to the opening of the Red Sea in Ex. 14.21 and implicitly a reminder that Lethe is figurally related to Jordan (see the note to lines 25-33).

76-84. You people . . . as will suffice: Matelda now reveals herself as a kind of receptionist and guide, capable of explaining every aspect of the Garden. Exactly what the doubt or fear is that Matelda attributes to the group is not clear; the suggestion of some commentators that since Eden was the scene of Adam's fall it might be puzzling to find Matelda happy, seems beside the point.

80. light is shed by the psalm *Delectasti* [You have delighted]: The reference is to Ps. 91.5-6: "For thou has given me, O Lord, delight in thy doings: and in the works of thy hands I shall rejoice. O Lord, how great are thy works!" Psalm 91 would not seem to be what Matelda has been singing, but it was a staple of the prayer service of Lauds, sung at sunrise, and its mention, like lines 16-18, identifies such acts of praise as natural and instinctive (cf. 23.11 and 24.50-59, with notes).

85-148. The water . . . I returned my gaze: The rest of the canto is devoted to the pilgrim's question and Matelda's "scientific" reply and its "corollary."

85-87. The water . . . contrary to this: The flowing of the river seems to imply a source fed by rain, the wind to imply variable weather, both contradicting Statius' account of the meteorological unchangeability of the mountain (21.40-57).

88-133. Then she . . . above all others: Matelda's explanation amounts to a complete theory of the nature and function of the Garden. The statement of general principles (lines 91-96) is followed by their application to 1) the height of the mountain (lines 97-102); 2) the two items mentioned by the pilgrim: a. the breeze (lines 103-20); b. the rivers (lines 121-33).

91-96. The highest Good . . . sweet play: The general principles underlying the nature of the Garden, based on Genesis 1-3 as interpreted by the exegetical tradition: God created man to be deathless and to share his own happiness (cf. *Par.* 13. 57-60), "good and for the good"; because they disobeyed the commandment not to eat of the Tree of the Knowledge of Good and Evil, Adam and Eve were expelled from the Garden into hardship and mortality.

94-96. Because of his own fault . . . sweet play: "Virtuous laughter and sweet play" are not mentioned in Genesis 1-3, but Dante saw them as implied in "paradise of pleasure." "Weeping and labor" recall Gen. 3.16: "I will multiply thy sorrows . . . in sorrow shalt thou bring forth children" and 17: "with labour and toil shalt thou eat . . . all the days of thy life."

97-102. That the disturbances . . . that is locked: The first consequence of the fundamental principles, the height of the mountain: the Garden was placed on the summit of the highest mountain, extending far higher than meteorological disturbances (Statius's account is corroborated), both as a pledge and foretaste of Heaven (lines 93-94) and to protect man.

103-120. Now because the sphere . . . gathered back there: The second consequence, deriving directly from the first: the great height of the mountain brings it up into the portion of the sphere of air that, since it is meteorologically undisturbed, prolongs the motion imparted to it by the daily revolution from east to west of the heavens (lines 103-108); this motion serves to disseminate from the Garden the plants found in other parts of the world (lines 109-120); it also indirectly connects the music of the plants with the music of the spheres (cf. the note to 31.144-45). The idea that all plants had their origin in Eden was widely accepted by the biblical exegetes; it is based on Gen. 2.5-9; see especially 2.5: "And every plant of the earth before it sprung up in the earth, and every herb of the ground before it grew: for the Lord God had not rained upon the earth"; and 2.9: "And the Lord God brought forth of the ground [in the Garden] all manner of trees."

112-13. as it is worthy . . . its sky: That is, the other regions of the earth are more and less fertile and fit for different crops in themselves, and they are exposed to different portions of the sky and consequently to different astrological influences.

121-33. The water . . . above all others: The third consequence of the fundamental principle. First the source of the rivers, then their functions (both functions are internal to the mind; see the note to lines 25-33). Like the "formative power" in the plants, the rivers are not fed naturally but directly by God's creative will. Gen. 2.10: "And a river went out of the place of pleasure to water paradise, which from thence is divided into four heads"; verses 11-14 enumerate Phison, Gehon, Tigris, and Euphrates: there was debate as to whether these rivers existed within Eden or gained their names only after leaving it.

126. two directions: Nardi 1960 pointed out the connection of these two streams with streams in Boeotia said by Pliny and Isidore alternately to restore and obliterate memory; crossed with Cupid's golden and leaden arrows, they will have a large fortune in Renaissance epic.

127-32. On this side . . . and on that: The meaning of these lines has been disputed. The most natural and idiomatic reference of the singular verb "si chiama" [is called] is "acqua" [water] in line 121: by this reading, strongly supported by the series of singular verbs beginning in line 124, neither Lethe nor Eunoè take effect until both have been tasted. The difficulty is that in 33.91-99 the pilgrim has forgotten earlier sins after having drunk from Lethe but before drinking from Eunoè (see 33.124-45). Barbi and others resolve the problem by taking lines 131-33 to refer only to Eunoè, which is logical but lacks the support of any syntactical marking.

131. Eunoè: The name is a coinage of Dante's, from Greek *eu* [well] and *noêsis* [knowledge], meaning "knowledge of good"; In *Conv.* 2.3.11 he made a similar coinage, *Protonoè* [first Mind], from *prótos* [first] and *noêsis*.

136-48. I will give . . . I returned my gaze: Matelda's "corollary" shows that not only all plants and human beings have their origins in the Garden, but also a major classical myth, that of the Golden Age. Dante did not know Hesiod's *Works and Days*, but he had studied with great care the references to the Golden Age in Vergil, especially in *Eclogue* 4 (pp. 584-87; cf also *Aen.* 8.314-27) and Ovid's influential description in *Met.* 1.89-112, which lists five main characteristics: 1. men did right without laws or fear of punishment; 2. no ships sailed the sea; 3. there were no fortifications, no weapons, no fighting; 4. men did not till the earth, all food was provided by the earth spontaneously, and the rivers ran milk and nectar; 5. there was perpetual spring. That mining began in the Iron Age was a commonplace.

136-38. I will give . . . beyond my promise: Note the metaphor of walking in "si spazia" [ranges]; her discourse walks further with him, but this is not a digression (from Lat. *digradior* [to walk aside]). The term *corollary* (from Lat. *corollarium* [crown, wreath, garland], originally used of a prize or reward, was adapted by Boethius to logic, to mean a supplementary conclusion already implicit in a proof. Matelda's corollary is a garland the classical poets may wear (cf. 27.102, with note).

139-41. Those who . . . dreamed this place: Rather than attributing the distortion of the truth to the agency of demons (see the notes to *Inf.* 1.72, 3.82-111), Matelda emphasizes the depth of insight reached by poets through dream: outside the fiction of the poem, the lines are equally applicable to the poem itself as dream-vision: Dante is dreaming on Parnassus of this place (see the notes to *Inf.* 1.2, 2.8).

142-44. Here the human root . . . each one tells: These lines enumerate the respects in which the classical myth of the Golden Age coincides with the biblical truth: the first human beings were innocent; Eden had and has perpetual spring; food was gathered without labor; the rivers ran nectar.

142. the human root: Adam and Eve, the root of the human family tree; cf. *Inf.* 3.115, with note.

145-46. I turned . . . to my poets: The pilgrim turns back to his ancient poets, especially to Virgil, on whose account he has become a poet (*Inf.* 1.85-87): they represent his point of entry into poetry as well as into the Garden (see lines 22 -24).

146-47. I saw . . . last construction: Both classical poets, even Virgil, who will presumably soon have to return to Limbo, are pleased by Matelda's accreditation of classical myth.

Inter cantica. This canto has important links with the forests of *Inferno* 1 and 13, the "dark wood" and the wood of the suicides, places of bewilderment, danger, and horror. The dark wood of the beginning of the poem is set at the foot of the "delightful mountain" the pilgrim wishes to climb and above the deeper dangers, related by the imagery to the abyss and to damnation, and it is lit by the actual sun; it is a figure of the situation of humanity between the heights and the depths; our notes to *Inferno* 1 call attention to this schematic symbolism, which dominates the entire *Purgatorio* as well: the mountainside as the scene of moral struggle and progress, the divine forest at the summit as the figure of the harmonious and innocent integration of body and soul.

The wood of the suicides is more diametrically opposite to Eden, it is suicide as the sterile and distorted refusal of the divine plenitude and the joy shared by all creation. With *Inferno* 13 the parallels are very pointed: no green leaves, no fruit, but thorns and poison; no birds or birdsong, but the laments of the filthy Harpies and trees that bleed, sputter, and speak. Like Satan himself at the bottom of Hell, the suicides have no alternative but to mirror in their shadowy and distorted fashion the wonders of Eden.

The two rivers of Eden recall the rivers of Hell. Vergil had followed tradition in assigning both the Elysian Fields and Lethe to the underworld (*Aen.* 6.679-720), and in the discussion in *Inf.* 14.85-138, Dante's Virgil notes that Lethe will be found above. Like Lethe and Eunoè, the rivers of Hell are spiritual states (see *Inferno* Additional Note 2), and all derive from the Old Man of Crete (see *Inferno* Additional Note 3).

Except for his head, which is of gold, each part of the Old Man's body is cracked, and from the cracks come tears that flow together into the four rivers of Hell. The Old Man of Crete, who stands erect within Mount Ida on Crete, under whose king the world saw the Age of Gold: *Inf.* 14.94-96, is both a figure of fallen humanity (and thus of Hell, whose summit contains Limbo and its hemisphere of light) and of the mountain of Purgatory, which corrects the *vulneratio naturae* (the wound in human nature caused by the Fall and represented by the cracks), and whose summit is crowned by Eden (the Golden Age), parallel to the Old Man's golden head. Other important points of comparison include the parallel between the fissure in the Old Man's body and the cracks in the rock of the mountain through which the travelers climb (on which cf. Additional Note 13), the theme of mourning (cf. Martinez 1997), and the contrast beween the fertility of Eden/early Crete and the wasteland of present-day Crete and Purgatory proper (*Inf.* 14.97-99, *Purg.* 10.20-21). As we shall see, the *Paradiso*, in its ascent into the spherical heavens, draws on the macro-microcosmic relation between them and the human head (see Durling/Martinez 1990, Chapters 2 and 4). There is thus a certain continuity among the various versions of the body analogy in the three cantiche of the poem.

CANTO 29

Cantando come donna innamorata,   1
continüò col fin di sue parole:
"Beati quorum tecta sunt peccata."

E come ninfe che si givan sole   4
per le salvatiche ombre, disïando
qual di veder, qual di fuggir lo sole,

allor si mosse contra 'l fiume, andando   7
su per la riva, e io pari di lei,
picciol passo con picciol seguitando.

Non eran cento tra ' suoi passi e ' miei,   10
quando le ripe igualmente dier volta,
per modo ch'a levante mi rendei.

Né ancor fu così nostra via molta,   13
quando la donna tutta a me si torse,
dicendo: "Frate mio, guarda e ascolta."

Ed ecco un lustro sùbito trascorse   16
da tutte parti per la gran foresta,
tal che di balenar mi mise in forse.

Ma perché 'l balenar, come vien, resta,   19
e quel, durando, più e più splendeva,
nel mio pensier dicea: "Che cosa è questa?"

E una melodia dolce correva   22
per l'aere luminoso, onde buon zelo
mi fé riprender l'ardimento d'Eva,

che là dove ubidia la terra e 'l cielo,   25
femmina, sola e pur testé formata,
non sofferse di star sotto alcun velo,

sotto 'l qual se divota fosse stata   28
avrei quelle ineffabili delizie
sentite prima e più lunga fïata.

CANTO 29

The Earthly Paradise, continued: walking upstream—the strange
light and melody—invocation—candelabra—the procession:
twentyfour elders, four animals, gryphon and chariot, seven
nymphs, seven elders—halt

1   Singing like a lady in love, she continued, at
the end of her words: "*Beati quorum tecta sunt
peccata!*"

4   And like nymphs that used to walk alone
through the forest shadows, some desiring to
see, others to flee, the sun,

7   she then moved against the stream, walking
along the bank, and I even with her, matching
little steps with little steps.

10   There had not been a hundred, between her
steps and mine, when the banks made equal
turns, so that I faced east.

13   Nor had we walked much further, when the
lady turned to face me, saying: "My brother,
look and listen."

16   And behold, a shining suddenly ran through
the great forest on all sides, such that it made
me wonder if it were lightning.

19   But since lightning, as soon as it comes,
ceases, and this, lasting, shone brighter and
brighter, in my thought I said: "What thing is
this?"

22   And a sweet melody ran through the
luminous air, at which good zeal made me
reproach the boldness of Eve,

25   who there, where earth and sky obeyed, a
female, alone, and just then fashioned, could
not bear to stay beneath any veil,

28   under which if she had humbly remained, I
would have felt those ineffable delights sooner
and for a longer time.

Mentr' io m'andava tra tante primizie   31
de l'etterno piacer tutto sospeso,
e disïoso ancora a più letizie,
    dinanzi a noi tal quale un foco acceso   34
ci si fé l'aere sotto i verdi rami,
e 'l dolce suon per canti era già inteso.
    O sacrosante Vergini, se fami,   37
freddi o vigilie mai per voi soffersi,
cagion mi sprona ch'io mercé vi chiami:
    or convien che Elicona per me versi,   40
e Uranìe m'aiuti col suo coro
forti cose a pensar mettere in versi.
    Poco più oltre, sette alberi d'oro   43
falsava nel parere il lungo tratto
del mezzo ch'era ancor tra noi e loro;
    ma quand' i' fui sì presso di lor fatto   46
che l'obietto comun, che 'l senso inganna,
non perdea per distanza alcun suo atto,
    la virtù ch'a ragion discorso ammanna   49
sì com' elli eran candelabri apprese,
e ne le voci del cantare *"Osanna."*
    Di sopra fiammeggiava il bello arnese,   52
più chiaro assai che luna per sereno
di mezza notte nel suo mezzo mese.
    Io mi rivolsi d'ammirazion pieno   55
al buon Virgilio, ed esso mi rispuose
con vista carca di stupor non meno.
    Indi rendei l'aspetto a l'alte cose   58
che si movieno incontr' a noi sì tardi
che foran vinte da novelle spose.
    La donna mi sgridò: "Perché pur ardi   61
sì ne l'affetto de le vive luci,
e ciò che vien di retro a lor non guardi?"
    Genti vid' io allor, come a lor duci   64
venire appresso, vestite di bianco,
e tal candor di qua già mai non fuci.
    L'acqua imprendëa dal sinistro fianco,   67
e rendea me la mia sinistra costa,
s'io riguardava in lei, come specchio anco.

31 While I walked along among so many first
fruits of the eternal pleasure, all in suspense
and desirous of still greater gladness,

34 ahead of us the air beneath the green
branches became like a blazing fire, and the
sweet sound could now be heard as singing.

37 O sacrosanct Virgins, if ever I have suffered
hunger, cold, or vigils for you, I am spurred by
need to call to you for help:

40 now must Helicon pour forth for me, and
Urania with her chorus help me to put into
verse things difficult to conceive.

43 A little further on, a false appearance of
seven golden trees was caused by the long tract
of air that was still between us and them;

46 but when I had come so close to them that
the ambiguous object that deceives the sense no
longer lost through distance any of its features,

49 the power that gives reason the manna for its
discourse perceived that they were candelabra
and, in the singing voices, "*Hosanna.*"

52 Overhead the beautiful array flamed much
brighter than the moon in a clear sky at
midnight, in the middle of its month.

55 I turned full of amazement to the good
Virgil, and he replied with a look laden with no
less awe.

58 Thence I turned my eyes back to the high
things that moved toward us so slowly that new
brides would have overtaken them.

61 The lady scolded me: "Why do you burn so
with feeling for the living lights and do not
look at what comes after them?"

64 Then I saw people coming after as if
following their leaders, dressed in white, and
back here such whiteness never was.

67 On my left the water was ablaze and
reflected my left side, if I looked down at it, just
as a mirror would.

Quand' io da la mia riva ebbi tal posta   70
che solo il fiume mi facea distante,
per veder meglio ai passi diedi sosta,

  e vidi le fiammelle andar davante,   73
lasciando dietro a sé l'aere dipinto,
e di tratti pennelli avean sembiante,

  sì che lì sopra rimanea distinto   76
di sette liste, tutte in quei colori
onde fa l'arco il Sole e Delia il cinto.

  Questi ostendali in dietro eran maggiori   79
che la mia vista, e, quanto a mio avviso,
diece passi distavan quei di fori.

  Sotto così bel ciel com' io diviso,   82
ventiquattro segnori, a due a due,
coronati venien di fiordaliso.

  Tutti cantavan: "*Benedicta* tue   85
ne le figlie d'Adamo, e benedette
sieno in etterno le bellezze tue!"

  Poscia che i fiori e l'altre fresche erbette   88
a rimpetto di me da l'altra sponda
libere fuor da quelle genti elette,

  sì come luce luce in ciel seconda,   91
vennero appresso lor quattro animali,
coronati ciascun di verde fronda.

  Ognuno era pennuto di sei ali;   94
le penne piene d'occhi, e li occhi d'Argo,
se fosser vivi, sarebber cotali.

  A descriver lor forme più non spargo   97
rime, lettor, ch'altra spesa mi strigne
tanto ch'a questa non posso esser largo;

  ma leggi Ezechïel, che li dipigne   100
come li vide da la fredda parte
venir con vento e con nube e con igne,

  e quali i troverai ne le sue carte   103
tali eran quivi, salvo ch'a le penne
Giovanni è meco e da lui si diparte.

  Lo spazio dentro a lor quattro contenne   106
un carro, in su due rote, trïunfale,
ch'al collo d'un grifon tirato venne.

70 When I was so placed on my bank that only the river separated me from them, I halted my steps in order to see better,

73 and I saw the flames move on, leaving the air behind them painted, and they seemed like brushes drawn along,

76 so that the air overhead was marked with seven stripes, all in those colors with which the Sun makes his bow and Delia her belt.

79 These banners extended backward further than my sight; and, in my estimate, the outer ones were ten paces apart.

82 Under the beautiful sky that I describe, twenty-four elders, two by two, were coming, crowned with lilies.

85 All were singing: "*Benedicta* are you among the daughters of Adam, and blessed in eternity be your beauties!"

88 After the flowers and the other fresh grasses opposite me on the other bank were free of that chosen people,

91 as light follows light in the sky, after them came four animals, each crowned with green leaves.

94 Each was feathered with six wings; the feathers were full of eyes, and the eyes of Argus, were they alive, would be such.

97 To describe their shapes I scatter no more rhymes, reader, for another outlay constrains me so that I cannot be liberal with this one;

100 but read Ezekiel, who depicts them as he saw them coming from the cold region with wind and cloud and fire,

103 and as you find them in his pages, such were they there, except that as to the feathers John is with me, and departs from him.

106 The space amid the four of them contained a triumphal chariot with two wheels, which was drawn harnessed to the neck of a gryphon.

Esso tendeva in sù l'una e l'altra ale 109
tra la mezzana e le tre e tre liste
sì ch'a nulla, fendendo, facea male;
 tanto salivan che non eran viste. 112
Le membra d'oro avea quant' era uccello,
e bianche l'altre, di vermiglio miste.

 Non che Roma di carro così bello 115
rallegrasse Affricano o vero Augusto,
ma quel del Sol saria pover con ello:
 quel del Sol, che svïando fu combusto 118
per l'orazion de la Terra devota,
quando fu Giove arcanamente giusto.

 Tre donne in giro da la destra rota 121
venian danzando, l'una tanto rossa
ch'a pena fora dentro al foco nota;
 l'altr' era come se le carni e l'ossa 124
fossero state di smeraldo fatte;
la terza parea neve testé mossa;
 e or parëan da la bianca tratte, 127
or da la rossa, e dal canto di questa
l'altre toglien l'andare e tarde e ratte.

 Da la sinistra quattro facean festa, 130
in porpore vestite, dietro al modo
d'una di lor ch'avea tre occhi in testa.

 Appresso tutto il pertrattato nodo 133
vidi due vecchi in abito dispari,
ma pari in atto e onesto e sodo.

 L'un si mostrava alcun de' famigliari 136
di quel sommo Ipocràte che Natura
a li animali fé ch'ell' ha più cari;
 mostrava l'altro la contraria cura 139
con una spada lucida e aguta,
tal che di qua dal rio mi fé paura.

 Poi vidi quattro in umile paruta, 142
e di retro da tutti un vecchio solo
venir dormendo, con la faccia arguta.

109   He extended upward his two wings, between
the center stripe and the three and three, so that
he harmed none of them by splitting it;

112   his wings rose higher than could be seen.
His members were gold as far as he was a bird,
the others white mixed with crimson.

115   Not only did Rome never gladden Africanus
or Augustus with so glorious a chariot, but that
of the Sun would be poor beside it:

118   that of the Sun, which when it strayed was
burned up at the prayer of the humble Earth,
when Jove was mysteriously just.

121   Three ladies came dancing in a circle at the
right wheel, one so red that she would hardly
be noticed within fire;

124   the next was as if her flesh and bones had
been fashioned of emerald; the third appeared
like newly fallen snow;

127   and now they seemed drawn by the white
one, now by the red one; and from the latter's
song the other two took their slow or rapid
pace.

130   On the left side four others rejoiced, clothed
in purple, following the melody of one of them
who had three eyes in her head.

133   After the whole cluster here described, I saw
two old men, differently clothed, but equal in
bearing, both virtuous and strong.

136   One seemed to be a familiar of that highest
Hippocrates whom Nature made for the
animals she loves most;

139   the other showed the opposite intent, with a
sword so shining and sharp that even on this
side of the stream it frightened me.

142   Then I saw four of humble bearing, and
behind them all a solitary old man walking
asleep, with his face alert.

E questi sette col primaio stuolo   145
erano abitüati, ma di gigli
dintorno al capo non facëan brolo,

    anzi di rose e d'altri fior vermigli;   148
giurato avria poco lontano aspetto
che tutti ardesser di sopra da' cigli.

    E quando il carro a me fu a rimpetto,   151
un tuon s'udì, e quelle genti degne
parvero aver l'andar più interdetto,

    fermandosi ivi con le prime insegne.   154

145   And these seven were dressed like the first
regiment, though they had no lilies garlanding
their heads,

148   but roses instead, and other crimson flowers;
a gaze somewhat removed would have sworn
that all were burning above the brow.

151   And when the chariot was opposite me, a
peal of thunder was heard, and those worthy
folk seemed forbidden to go further,

154   for they halted there with the first standards.

NOTES

1-9. Singing like a lady . . . steps with little steps: Matelda begins singing again, as when the pilgrim first saw her (see 28.8), and begins walking upstream (thus toward the pilgrim's right), and he moves with her.

1. Singing like a lady in love: The line echoes "cantava come fosse' nnamorata" [she was singing as if she were in love], line 7 of "In un boschetto" (pp. 588-89; see the note to 28.37-42), just after Matelda's identification of Eden with the Golden Age, fusing pagan myth with an Italian vernacular *ballata*.

3. *Beati quorum tecta sunt peccata* [Blessed those whose sins are covered]: The first verse of Psalm 31, a penitential psalm sung at Matins, with which Dante provides a kind of summarizing allusion to the Beatitudes sung on the terraces of Purgatory.

4-6. And like nymphs . . . the sun: For nymphs that are stars, see 31.106, with note [1.23, four stars; 8.89, three]. For the contrasting groups (line 6), compare the cranes in 26.44-45, and see *Geor.* 4.382-383 (dryads keep to the woods, oreads to the mountains, cf. also 33.49, with note).

11-12. the banks made equal turns, so that I faced east: At the bend in the river, to continue walking upstream, the group must turn to the left. In 27.133 and 28.25 the river flowed from south to north; now its course is from east to west, and all four personages are facing toward the rising sun (cf. 4.52-54, 27.133). Moving upstream toward the source is of course one of the many figures of return to origins.

14-15. the lady turned . . . look and listen: Matelda's call to attention has been compared to that of the angel who announces Italian miracle plays (*sacre rappresentazioni*); cf. also Lam. 1.1 and Apoc. 6.1. For her mode of addressing the pilgrim, cf. 26.115, 33.23.

16-30. And behold . . . for a longer time: The sudden lightning brings light to the dark forest (cf. 28.31-33), evidently supernatural in not fading but gradually increasing in brightness; thunder will occur in lines 151-52. This is the first of many references in these final cantos to the Apocalypse; see Apoc. 4.5: "And from the throne proceeded lightnings, and voices, and thunders; and there were seven lamps burning before the throne, which are the seven spirits of God."

21. What thing is this: Cf. Zach. 1.19, Mark 1.27: "What thing is this?"; also Acts 2.12 (at Pentecost): "What meaneth this?"

22-30. And a sweet melody . . . for a longer time: Had Eve not sinned, humankind would have inherited Eden (see 33.1 and note). Medieval opinion emphasized Eve's responsibility for Adam's fall; see *ST* 2a 2ae q. 163, a. 4, resp.: "the woman not only sinned herself, but also suggested the sin to the man. Thus she sinned both against God and neighbor" (see *DVE* 1.4.2). The guilt of Adam will be mentioned at 32.37. Note the implicit analogy between the covering foliage and the covering veil, and the continuation of cosmological ideas in these cantos, the "music of the spheres" (cf. 28.16-21, 31.143-45, and *Par.* 14.121-23, with notes). For Eve "alone" [*sola*] compare *soletta* [all alone], of Matelda (28.40). Note the reminder of the brevity of the pilgrim's stay in Eden in line 30.

31-36. While I walked . . . heard as singing: The mention of "first fruits" and the gradual intensification of the light and the sound create ever greater suspense. The early commentators took the fire as representing the Holy Spirit; cf. Milton in the proem to *Paradise Lost*, Book 3: "living fount, fire, charity, unction," quoting the Pentecost hymn "Veni creator spiritus" [Come creator Spirit], lines 5-6. On the entire procession see Additional Note 15.

37-42. O sacrosanct Virgins . . . difficult to conceive: This is only the second request for poetic inspiration in the *Purgatorio* since1.7-12 (also implicitly referred to at 22.65). Cf. *Aen.* 10.163: "Throw open Helicon now, goddesses, move your songs."

37-38. hunger, cold, or vigils: See 2 Cor. 11.27, referring to the vicissitudes of Paul's ministry: "In labor and painfulness, in much watchings, in hunger and thirst, in fastings often, in cold and nakedness"; see also Horace, *Ars poetica* 412-13. Cf. *Conv.* 3.1; *Par.* 25.1-3, with notes.

40-41. Helicon . . . Urania: Helicon, in Boeotia, was one of the mountains sacred to Apollo and the nine Muses; its fountains were Aganippe and Hippocrene (*Met.* 5.312; see 22.65-66 and 31.140-41, with notes). Urania is the muse of astronomy (her name means "heavenly"); her mention indicates that what follows will have cosmological significance. Cf. *Commentarii* 2.3.1-2: "cosmogonists consider the nine Muses to be the tuneful song of the eight spheres and the one predominant harmony that comes from all of them . . . In the *Theogony*, Hesiod calls the eighth Muse Urania because the eighth sphere, the star-bearer, situated above the seven planetary spheres, is correctly referred to as the sky [*ouranós*]" (see line 82, with note).

43-50. A little further . . . that they were: Compare *Inf.* 31.19-45, with note, and *Inter cantica* to Canto 33. Dante refers to the Scholastic concept of "common sensibles" (number, size, and shape): these are perceptible by several senses, in contrast to specific sensibles such as color. Because sight and hearing do not perceive number and size without correlation, it is possible for them to err in respect to them, whereas sight does not err with respect to color unless it is diseased. When the procession comes nearer, the pilgrim's powers of sensation furnish to his reason the necessary data (*manna*) to make the correct judgment ("discourse"). See Aristotle *De anima* 418a; Aquinas 1959 2.13 [385]; and *Conv.* 3.9.6.

50-52. they were candelabra . . . the beautiful array flamed: The trees prove to be candelabra; later they are said to be held severally by the seven nymphs (32.97-99). Dante's use of the term invokes the text of the Apocalypse, see the note to line 76.

51. *Hosanna*: The Hebrew word originally meant "we beseech, save," but became a joyous acclamation, as in Matt. 21.9: "Hosanna to the son of David: Blessed is he that cometh in the name of the Lord [quoting Ps. 117. 26]. Hosanna in the highest," greeting Christ as he enters Jerusalem (as prophesied by Zach. 9.9: "Behold thy king cometh to thee, meek, and sitting upon an ass") to celebrate the Passover and accomplish his Passion; it is chanted on Palm Sunday. Dante uses it in *VN* 23.7 and 25 for his vision of Beatrice entering Heaven. The cry implies that the procession is an advent of Christ (Singleton 1954); cf. 30.19.

52-54. Overhead the beautiful array . . . middle of its month: See 28.33, with note; the forest, where the sun and moon never penetrate, is now the scene of supernatural illumination; cued by Urania, we have an astronomical reference to the chief luminaries, which God made "to be for seasons and times" (Gen. 1.14).

55-57. I turned full . . . with no less awe: This is our last glimpse of Virgil; his awe and amazement are a reaction to this invasion of time from eternity (for the importance of this moment, see Additional Note 14).

60. new brides: Evoking thirteenth-century Florentine marriage rituals, the simile suggests that the procession has nuptial meanings; see lines 85-89.

61-63. Why do you burn so . . . what comes after them: Matelda takes over Virgil's function (cf. *Purg.* 10.46-48) of directing the pilgrim's gaze (in 33, this role is assumed by Beatrice). Note terms for light and fire (61, cf. 16, 35, 52, 67, 73).

64-66. people coming . . . such whiteness never was: Cf. Matt. 21.9, "and the multitudes that went before and that followed, cried Hosanna" (see the note to line 51); for the white garments, lines 82-84.

67-72. On my left . . . to see better: The pageant is moving along the river, toward the pilgrim's left; he is reflected in the stream. The commentators note an echo here of the myth of Narcissus (*Met.* 3.339-510; cf. *Par.* 3.17-18, with note); the motif also recalls 9.94-96; cf. 30.76-77: the pilgrim is not yet disturbed by his reflection, but later there will be a further, more intense reenactment of the sacrament of penance.

73-78. I saw the flames . . . and Delia her belt: Dante's description of the air as painted by the lights borne on the candelabra continues the references to the visual arts in the cantica (cf. 10-12, 21-22; 23-25); *pennelli* has been taken to mean "pennons" (cf. next lines) as well as "brushes". The position of these streaks of light, like the comparison with the rainbow (cf. Gen. 9.12-17) and the lunar halo, make this canopy a "heaven" (line 82): Dante is drawing on *Confessions* 13.18.

77. seven stripes: For seven candelabra, see Apocalypse 1.12: "And I turned to see the voice that spoke with me; And being turned, I saw seven golden candlesticks; And in the midst of the seven golden candlesticks, one like the Son of Man"; and 1.19: "Write therefore the things which thou hast seen, and which are, and which must be done hereafter. The mystery of the seven stars, which thou sawest in my right hand, and the seven golden candlesticks. The seven stars are the angels of the seven churches. And the seven candlesticks are the seven churches."

Most commentators take the lights to represent the sevenfold spirit of God and/or the stripes of color the seven gifts of the Spirit (see *Conv.* 4.21.11-12), often shown in iconography crowning the tree of Christ's genealogy (from Jesse and David through Mary). See Apoc. 4.5: "And there were seven lamps burning before the throne, which are the seven spirits of God." The candelabra may also represent the seven-pillared ideal Church; cf. Additional Note 15.

78. the Sun makes his bow and Delia her belt: In Apoc. 4.4, the figures here shown processionally surround the Lamb; cf. the note to 82.

79-81. These banners . . . ten paces apart: The stripes of color "painted" by the seven lights extend over the whole procession; cf. Augustine on Gen 1.2 in *Confessions* 13.7. Benvenuto identifies Dante's banners [*ostendali*] with imperial insignia: "the standards of an emperor are termed banners . . . these are the standards of the highest emperor, who was coming with his army." See line 154 and 10.79-81, with notes.

82-154. Under the beautiful sky . . . with the first standards: The description of the procession, in 73 lines (24 terzinas plus one line), divided into three sections: 1) figures representing the books of the OT; 2) the Chariot, drawn by the gryphon; and 3) figures representing the books of the NT. Like the Bible, from Genesis to Apocalypse, so the procession contains all of time, with Christ at the center (for Dante he was crucified at the center of history and in the center of the earth). Three epochs are differentiated by the garlands on the figures (repectively white, green, and red, see note to lines 121-29 below). As a whole the procession is cruciform, with the OT figures representing the support, the gryphon and Chariot the center and crossbeam, and the NT figures the headpiece; the Cross is represented also by the intersection of the two paths of procession and pilgrim (Singleton 1954).

82. Under the beautiful sky that I describe: After references to the luminaries, Dante explicitly compares the seven stripes of light to the sky: at 30.1 the seven candlesticks serve as the "Septentrion of the first heaven," that is, the Little Dipper of the Empyrean, but also of the procession, and of the Chariot of the Church, which are guided by it as sailors by the constellation; the present procession is literally a "descent of Heaven" into Eden.

83-84. twenty-four elders . . . crowned with lilies: The twenty-four white-clad elders derive from Apoc. 4.1-8: John, in exile on the island of Patmos, is rapt "in the spirit" to Heaven, where he sees the throne of the Lamb of God: "And round about the throne were four and twenty seats; and upon the seats four and twenty ancients sitting, clothed in white garments, and on their heads were crowns of gold." The white lilies signify faith (in the Redeemer to come), purity, and justice (and the Virgin as bride of the Song of Songs, "lilium convallium" [lily of the valley]). In the *Prologus Galeatus* to his translation of the Bible, St. Jerome notes: that "they took the old law to be twenty-four books, which John's Apocalypse introduces as twenty-four elders adoring the lamb" (see *Par.* 5.76).

85-86. *Benedicta* [blessed] . . . daughters of Adam: Part of Gabriel's greeting to the Virgin at the Annunciation (see 10. 34-45, with note), reiterated by Elizabeth in Luke 1.42 (the episode mentioned in *Purg.* 18.100). Mary does not figure in the procession (although Beatrice will do so). Since the twenty-four elders represent the books of the OT, the utterance alludes to Christ's birth from the house of David, from which Mary traced her descent. Judith (see 12.58-60 and note) was also blessed in this way (Judith 13.3, 15.11); the supposed "harmony" of the two Testaments is on view here.

90. that chosen people: Chosen, in that among the elect; but the phrase recalls the election of the people of Israel, which these figures also represent.

91. as light follows light in the sky: As stars pass successively over the sky.

92-105. after them . . . departs from him: The four evangelists, in the symbolic forms in which they surround the throne in Apoc. 4.6-8 (based on Ezek. 1.10-11, with the difference noted in lines 100-105, that Ezekiel mentions four wings, John six): "And round about the throne, were four living creatures, full of eyes before and behind. And the first living creature was like a lion: and the second living creature like a calf: and the third living creature, having the face, as it were, of a man: and the fourth living creature was like an eagle flying. And the four living creatures had each of them six wings" (see fig. 9). Unique to Dante, the green crowns signify the hope of the gospel (1 Tim. 1.1: "Christ, our hope"; for the colors, see 30.31-33).

95-96. the eyes of Argus, were they alive: *Met.* 1.622-723 relates how Argus was set by Juno to guard Io (see the note to *Inf.* 24.100 and *Inferno* Additional Note 10), whom the jealous Juno had changed into a cow; but Jove sent Mercury, who charmed Argus to sleep (with the tale of the nymph Syrinx, changed into the panpipes when fleeing rape; see 32.64-66) and then cut off his head. Juno took Argus' many eyes to adorn her peacock's tail, itself compared to the starry night sky. In *Met.* 1.664 Argus is "star-eyed" (*stellatus*); see also lines 625-27: "Argus of the hundred eyes, all watching and on duty round his head; whichever way he stood he looked at Io, Io before his eyes behind his back."

97-105. To describe their shapes . . . and departs from him: It is not surprising that the NT Apocalypse should be more accurate than the OT prophet, but it is a surprise that the poet claims to be able to corroborate and criticize their accounts! The biblical writer agrees with Dante! With this bold move, Dante inserts himself into the visionary company of Ezekiel and John and claims the roles of prophet and scribe (cf. Apoc. 4.9-11). For the rhymes in lines 97-99, evoking a poem by Arnaut Daniel, see Martinez 1991.

100-102. but read Ezekiel . . . cloud and fire: See Ezek. 1.4: "And I saw, and behold, a whirlwind came out of the North, and a great cloud, and a fire infolding it, and brightness was about it: and out of the midst thereof . . . as it were the resemblance of amber."

106-32. The space amid . . . three eyes in her head: Dante gives nine tercets to the central group of the procession: three to the gryphon drawing it, two to the chariot, four to the virtues at its two wheels (three to the theological virtues, one to the cardinal virtues).

107-108. a triumphal chariot . . . the neck of a gryphon: The two-wheeled chariot is explicitly compared with the *biga* of Roman triumphs; but contemporary readers would think also of the four-wheeled *carrocci*, war-wagons of the Italian communes. For terms used of the chariot, see 32. 95 and note.

108-14. harnessed to the neck . . . white mixed with crimson: The gryphon drawing the chariot has the head, breast, and wings of an eagle (perhaps front legs like an eagle's legs), the body and hindquarters of a lion (see the logo on p. 1). Most commentators take it to be a representation of Christ, his divine nature represented by the golden eagle, his human nature by the royal lion. The colors echo descriptions of the bridegroom of the Song of Songs, interpreted in medieval texts as Christ, spouse of the Church: "his head is pure gold," 5.11; "my beloved is white and ruddy," 5.10. Gold is the noblest metal; white and red signify Christ's purity in the flesh and his blood shed for mankind.

115-16. Not only did Rome . . . so glorious a chariot: A comparison of the chariot of the Church with the triumphal chariots of Scipio (see *Inf.* 31.115-17, with note) and Augustus (for Augustus' triple triumph, see *Aen.* 8.715: "Caesar, borne into the walls of Rome with threefold triumph"; also *Phars.* 8.553-54).

117. that of the Sun would be poor beside it: Dante draws from *Met.* 2.107-109 for the chariot of the sun: "Golden was its axle, golden its pole, golden its wheelrims and silver the array of their spokes; along the yoke chrysolites and gems in orderly design returned with bright light the reflection of the sun." See *Conv.* 4. 23.14; *Ecl.* 2.1-4.

117-20. that of the Sun . . . mysteriously just: Dante refers to Phaëthon, who loses control of the horses of the sun; at the plea of the Earth, scorched by the fire, Jove strikes Phaëthon with a thunderbolt—"mysteriously" just, because for Dante Phaëthon's death signifies the correction owed the Church, led astray by pope and Curia: see *Ep.* 11.5, where Dante compares the Cardinals with the "false charioteer" Phaëthon. The *Ovide Moralisé* reads him as Lucifer (see *Inf.* 34.121-26).

121-29. Three ladies . . . slow or rapid pace: The three theological virtues, love the greatest (fire-red), hope (green as emerald), and faith (white as new snow), are led alternately by faith and love, but love always gives the measure of the dance; they are next to the right, the preferred, wheel of the chariot.

130-32. On the left side . . . three eyes in her head: One terzina is given to the four cardinal virtues. Prudence gives the measure, as she is both an intellectual and a moral (or active) virtue; she sees past, present, and future; see *Conv.* 4.27.5; and *ST* 1a 2ae q. 57 a. 5. The other virtues are justice, temperance, and fortitude; all are purple because regal but also because tinged, since the coming of Christ, with the red of charity.

133-50. After the whole cluster . . . burning above the brow: After the central group come seven figures representing the other books of the NT, brows girt with red roses to signify the Passion and the triumph of love.

136-40. One seemed to be . . . a sword so shining and sharp: The book of Acts, signified by a physician because its author, Luke, was a "most dear physician" (Colossians 4.14). Acts is juxtaposed to the epistles of saint Paul (all 14 counting as one book), signified by a sword, Paul's traditional attribute (derived from Eph. 6.17, which calls the Word "the sword of the Spirit"; cf. Heb. 4.12, Apoc. 1.16; also, Paul was beheaded).

142-44. Then I saw four . . . with his face alert: After Paul's letters come the epistles of saints James, Peter (2 letters), John (3 letters), and Jude, each represented by one figure/author—humble because the letters are brief and familiar in tone. The procession ends with the figure of the author of the Apocalypse, traditionally represented as sleeping (as in the Paris Apocalypse manuscript—see Apoc. 1.10—or the visionary Ezekiel in the relief on Amiens cathedral, c. 1235, Mâle 1958, fig. 87); more than any other author, John inspires the canto, and Dante identifies strongly with him.

151-54. And when the chariot . . . the first standards: The procession of the
Church halts with the chariot opposite the pilgrim. The peal of thunder answers
the flash of lightning that opened the procession (lines 16-17), as if it had filed
past in the pause between them.

Figure 9. The four Evangelists.

CANTO 30

Quando il Settentrïon del primo cielo,　　　　　1
che né occaso mai seppe né orto
né d'altra nebbia che di colpa velo,

e che faceva lì ciascuno accorto　　　　　4
di suo dover, come 'l più basso face
qual temon gira per venire a porto,

fermo s'affisse, la gente verace　　　　　7
venuta prima tra 'l grifone ed esso,
al carro volse sé come a sua pace,

e un di loro, quasi da ciel messo,　　　　　10
"*Veni, sponsa, de Libano!*" cantando
gridò tre volte, e tutti li altri appresso.

Quali i beati al novissimo bando　　　　　13
surgeran presti ognun di sua caverna,
la revestita voce alleluiando:

cotali in su la divina basterna　　　　　16
si levar cento, *ad vocem tanti senis*,
ministri e messaggier di vita etterna.

Tutti dicean: "*Benedictus qui venis!*"　　　　　19
e, fior gittando e di sopra e dintorno,
"*Manibus, oh, date lilïa plenis!*"

Io vidi già nel cominciar del giorno　　　　　22
la parte orïental tutta rosata
e l'altro ciel di bel sereno addorno,

e la faccia del sol nascere ombrata,　　　　　25
sì che per temperanza di vapori
l'occhio la sostenea lunga fïata:

così, dentro una nuvola di fiori　　　　　28
che da le mani angeliche saliva
e ricadeva in giù dentro e di fòri,

CANTO 30

The Earthly Paradise, continued: Expectation—Angels—Beatrice—
disappearance of Virgil—Beatrice's severity—the angels' compassion—
the pilgrim weeps—Beatrice's accusations

1   When the Septentrion of the first Heaven,
       which has never known setting or rising, nor the
       veil of any other fog than that of sin,

4   and which made each one there aware of his
       duty—as the lower Septentrion does him who
       turns the helm so as to arrive in port—,

7   when it came to a halt, the truthful people who
       had come between the gryphon and it, turned
       toward the chariot as if to their peace,

10   and one of them, like a messenger from Heaven,
       singing cried: "*Veni, sponsa, de Libano!*" three times,
       and all the others after him.

13   As at the last trumpet the blessed will swiftly
       arise, each from his cavern, singing hallelujah for
       the reclothing of the voice,

16   so on the divine wagon arose a hundred, *ad
       vocem tanti senis*, ministers and messengers of eternal
       life.

19   All were saying: "*Benedictus qui venis!*" and,
       casting flowers up and around, "*Manibus, oh, date
       lilia plenis!*"

22   I have sometimes seen, at the beginning of the
       day, the eastern sky all rosy, and the rest adorned
       with cloudless blue,

25   and the face of the sun rising shadowed, so that
       by the tempering of vapors the eye endured it for a
       long while:

28   so, within a cloud of flowers that from the
       hands of the angels was rising and falling back
       within and without,

sovra candido vel cinta d'uliva   31
donna m'apparve, sotto verde manto
vestita di color di fiamma viva.

    E lo spirito mio, che già cotanto   34
tempo era stato ch'a la sua presenza
non era di stupor tremando affranto,

    sanza de li occhi aver più conoscenza,   37
per occulta virtù che da lei mosse
d'antico amor sentì la gran potenza.

    Tosto che ne la vista mi percosse   40
l'alta virtù che già m'avea trafitto
prima ch'io fuor di püerizia fosse,

    volsimi a la sinistra col respitto   43
col quale il fantolin corre a la mamma
quando ha paura o quando elli è afflitto,

    per dicere a Virgilio: "Men che dramma   46
di sangue m'è rimaso che non tremi:
conosco i segni de l'antica fiamma!"

    Ma Virgilio n'avea lasciati scemi   49
di sé—Virgilio, dolcissimo patre,
Virgilio, a cui per mia salute die'mi—,

    né quantunque perdeo l'antica matre   52
valse a le guance nette di rugiada
che, lagrimando, non tornasser atre.

    "Dante, perché Virgilio se ne vada,   55
non pianger anco, non piangere ancora,
ché pianger ti conven per altra spada."

    Quasi ammiraglio che in poppa e in prora   58
viene a veder la gente che ministra
per li altri legni, e a ben far l'incora:

    in su la sponda del carro sinistra,   61
quando mi volsi al suon del nome mio,
che di necessità qui si registra,

    vidi la donna che pria m'appario   64
velata sotto l'angelica festa
drizzar li occhi ver' me di qua dal rio,

    tutto che 'l vel che le scendea di testa,   67
cerchiato de le fronde di Minerva,
non la lasciasse parer manifesta.

31   her white veil girt with olive, a lady appeared to me, clothed, beneath a green mantle, in the color of living flame.

34   And my spirit, which already for so long a time had not known in her presence the awe that overcame it with trembling,

37   without having more knowledge through the eyes, because of hidden power that moved from her, felt the great force of ancient love.

40   As soon as my sight was struck by that high power that had transfixed me before I was out of boyhood,

43   I turned to the left with the appeal with which a little boy runs to his mama when he is afraid or when he is hurt,

46   to say to Virgil: "Less than a dram of blood is left me that is not trembling: I recognize the signs of the ancient flame!"

49   But Virgil had left us deprived of himself— Virgil, most sweet father, Virgil, to whom I gave myself for my salvation—,

52   nor did everything our ancient mother lost suffice to prevent my cheeks, though cleansed with dew, from turning dark again with tears.

55   "Dante, though Virgil depart, do not weep yet, do not weep yet, for you must weep to another sword."

58   Like an admiral who comes to stern and prow to see the people who serve on the other ships, and heartens them to do well:

61   on the left side of the chariot, when I turned at the sound of my name, which of necessity is here set down,

64   I saw the lady who had just appeared to me veiled beneath the angelic welcome, directing her eyes toward me across the stream,

67   although the veil that came down from her head, circled with Minerva's foliage, did not permit her to appear openly.

Regalmente ne l'atto ancor proterva,   70
continüò come colui che dice
e 'l più caldo parlar dietro reserva:

   "Guardaci ben! Ben son, ben son Beatrice.   73
Come degnasti d'accedere al monte?
non sapei tu che qui è l'uom felice?"

   Li occhi mi cadder giù nel chiaro fonte,   76
ma, veggendomi in esso, i trassi a l'erba,
tanta vergogna mi gravò la fronte:

   così la madre al figlio par superba   79
com' ella parve a me, perché d'amaro
sente il sapor de la pietade acerba.

   Ella si tacque, e li angeli cantaro   82
di sùbito: *"In te, Domine, speravi,"*
ma oltre *"pedes meos"* non passaro.

   Sì come neve tra le vive travi   85
per lo dosso d'Italia si congela,
soffiata e stretta da li venti schiavi,

   poi, liquefatta, in sé stessa trapela   88
pur che la terra che perde ombra spiri,
sì che par foco fonder la candela:

   così fui sanza lagrime e sospiri   91
anzi 'l cantar di quei che notan sempre
dietro a le note de li etterni giri;

   ma poi che 'ntesi ne le dolci tempre   94
lor compatire a me—par che se detto
avesser: "Donna, perché sì lo stempre?"—

   lo gel che m'era intorno al cor ristretto   97
spirito e acqua fessi, e con angoscia
de la bocca e de li occhi uscì del petto.

   Ella, pur ferma in su la detta coscia   100
del carro stando, a le sustanze pie
volse le sue parole così poscia:

   "Voi vigilate ne l'etterno die,   103
sì che notte né sonno a voi non fura
passo che faccia il secol per sue vie;

   onde la mia risposta è con più cura   106
che m'intenda colui che di là piagne,
perché sia colpa e duol d'una misura.

70   Still regal and haughty in bearing, she continued
like one who speaks but holds in reserve the hotter
speech:

73   "Look at us well! Truly I am, truly I am
Beatrice. How have you deigned to approach the
mountain? Did you not know that here mankind is
happy?"

76   My eyes fell down to the clear spring, but,
seeing myself there, I turned them to the grass,
such shame weighed down my brow:

79   so a mother seems severe to her son as she
seemed to me, for bitter is the flavor of
compassion still unripe.

82   She fell silent, and the angels sang suddenly: "*In
te, Domine, speravi*," but beyond "*pedes meos*" they
did not pass.

85   As snow on the living beams along the back of
Italy turns to ice, driven and compressed by the
Slavic winds,

88   and then, liquefied, trickles into itself as soon as
the land that loses shadow breathes, so that it
seems fire is melting the candle:

91   so I was without tears or sighs prior to the
singing of those whose notes ever follow the notes
of the eternal spheres;

94   but when I perceived in their sweet harmonies
their compassion for me—as much as if they had
said, "Lady, why do you so untune him?"—

97   the ice that had tightened around my heart
became spirit and water, and with anguish of my
mouth and eyes came forth from my breast.

100   She, still motionless on the aforesaid flank of the
chariot, to those merciful substances then turned
her words:

103   "You keep watch in the eternal day, so that
neither night nor sleep steals from you any step the
world may take along its ways;

106   wherefore I reply with more concern that he
understand me who is weeping over there, so that
guilt and grief may have the same measure.

Non pur per ovra de le rote magne   109
che drizzan ciascun seme ad alcun fine,
secondo che le stelle son compagne,

  ma per larghezza di grazie divine,   112
che sì alti vapori hanno a lor piova
che nostre viste là non van vicine,

  questi fu tal ne la sua vita nova,   115
virtüalmente, ch'ogne abito destro
fatto averebbe in lui mirabil prova.

  Ma tanto più maligno e più silvestro   118
si fa 'l terren col mal seme e non cólto,
quant' elli ha più di buon vigor terrestro.

  Alcun tempo il sostenni col mio volto: 121
mostrando li occhi giovanetti a lui,
meco il menava in dritta parte vòlto.

  Sì tosto come in su la soglia fui   124
di mia seconda etade e mutai vita,
questi si tolse a me e diessi altrui:

  quando di carne a spirto era salita,   127
e bellezza e virtù cresciuta m'era,
fu' io a lui men cara e men gradita,

  e volse i passi suoi per via non vera,   130
imagini di ben seguendo false,
che nulla promession rendono intera.

  Né l'impetrare ispirazion mi valse,   133
con le quali e in sogno e altrimenti
lo rivocai, sì poco a lui ne calse!

  Tanto giù cadde che tutti argomenti   136
a la salute sua eran già corti,
fuor che mostrarli le perdute genti.

  Per questo visitai l'uscio d'i morti,   139
e a colui che l'ha qua sù condotto
li preghi miei, piangendo, furon porti.

  Alto fato di Dio sarebbe rotto   142
se Letè si passasse e tal vivanda
fosse gustata sanza alcuno scotto

  di pentimento che lagrime spanda."   145

109   Not only through the workings of the great
wheels that direct every seed to some end,
according as the stars are companions,

112   but through abundance of divine graces, which
rain from such high vapors that our sight cannot
approach them,

115   he was such in his new life, potentially, that
every good habit would have produced a
marvelous result in him.

118   But all the more malignant and wild becomes
the soil with bad seed and without cultivation, the
more it has in it of good earthly vigor.

121   For a time I sustained him with my
countenance: showing him my youthful eyes, I led
him with me, turned in the right direction.

124   When I was on the threshold of my second age
and changed lives, he took himself from me and
gave himself to another:

127   when I had risen from flesh to spirit, and beauty
and power had increased in me, I was to him less
dear and less pleasing,

130   and he turned his steps along a way not true,
following false images of good, which keep no
promise fully.

133   Nor did it avail me to obtain inspirations, with
which in dreams and in other ways I called him
back, so little they mattered to him!

136   He fell so low that all means for his salvation
had already fallen short, except to show him the
lost people.

139   For this I visited the threshold of the dead, and
to the one who has guided him up here, my
prayers, weeping, were carried.

142   The high decree of God would be broken, if
Lethe were passed and such nourishment were
tasted without any fee

145   of such repentance as pours forth tears."

NOTES

1-33. When the Septentrion . . . color of living flame: The elaborately pre-pared appearance of Beatrice, with the sense of expectation already high because of the strange, hieratic procession. The contrast with the abrupt appearance of Matelda (28.34-42), whose analogy with Leah (27.97-108) includes the forecast of a figure that will correspond to Rachel (27.104-105), is an important element.

1-7. When the Septentrion . . . came to a halt: The halt of the procession (cf. 29.151-54), described again, this time in terms of an elaborate analogy between the candelabra (the "sevenfold Spirit of God," see the note to 29.76), leading and directing it, and the polar constellation Ursa Minor. The term *Septentrion* (from Lat. *septem triones* [seven plow-oxen]) was used of both polar constellations, Ursa Major (the Big Dipper) and Ursa Minor (the Little Dipper), each of which has seven conspicuous stars; that Dante is referring to Ursa Minor is guaranteed by the reference to navigation (line 6), involving the fixed polestar, Polaris (α UrsMin). All seven stars of Ursa Minor can be seen as far south as 22° N.

3. nor the veil . . . that of sin: The application of the analogy with the visible constellation implicitly reminds us that Purgatory proper and the Earthly Para-dise are above the clouds, and that the souls' final purgation does away entirely with the blindness of sin (but cf. Beatrice's veil, only lifted at the end of Canto 31).

7-9. the truthful people . . . to their peace: The figures in the first part of the procession (between the candelabra—29.43-54—and the gryphon), represent-ing the books of the OT, turn back to face the chariot as if to the fulfillment of their desires ("their peace," line 9). Already identified as the central item in the procession, and directly opposite the pilgrim, the chariot now becomes the cen-ter of converging lines of sight, two being those of the books of OT and NT (cf. *Par.* 32.22-27, of the heavenly rose: "On this side . . . are seated those who be-lieved in Christ to come; on the other side . . . are those who had their faces toward Christ already come," and *Par.* 20.104-105), the third being that of the pilgrim and the others with him. See the note to lines 13-18.

10-12. one of them . . . after him: Presumably the singing is led by the figure representing the source of the quotation, the Song of Songs; see next note.

11. *Veni, sponsa, de Libano* [Come, bride, from Lebanon]: A slightly altered quo-tation of Cant. 4.8; the Song of Songs, a collection of wedding songs, was inter-preted in Jewish tradition as expressing the love between God and Israel, in Christian tradition on several levels: as the love between Christ and the Church, between God and the Virgin Mary, between Christ and the individual soul: in each case the Bridegroom is God or Christ, the Bride is the Church, the Virgin, or the soul. For the application to Beatrice, see Additional Note 15. After an extended, lush description of the Bride's physical beauty (Cant. 4.1-7), verse 8 reads: "Veni de Libano, sponsa mea, veni de Libano, veni, coronaberis" [Come from Lebanon, my bride, come from Lebanon, come, you will be crowned]; the following verses associate the crowning with the summits of a series of mountains.

The triple summons (actually six-fold in Dante, according to line 12) is already in the biblical verse; in having the phrase repeated, Dante assimilates it to liturgical patterns (e.g., "Sanctus, sanctus, sanctus" [Holy, holy, holy] (Is. 6.3) in the Mass, or the "Agnus Dei"—see the note to 16.16-21). Cant. 4.8 was adapted to prayers in honor of virgin saints ("Veni, sponsa Christi, accipies coronam quam praeparavit tibi Dominus" [Come, bride of Christ, to receive the crown the Lord has prepared for you]), but otherwise does not seem to have been used liturgically.

13-18. As at the last . . . eternal life: While the analogy of lines 1-7 began with the tenor of the comparison, this elaborate simile begins with the vehicle, like that in lines 22-33, both delays serving to prolong and intensify expectation. The Resurrection of the Dead, invoked here, will take place at the Second Coming of Christ (see Matt. 24-25), of which, as Singleton 1954 showed, the coming of Beatrice here is an analogue(as her life on earth was an analogue of his Incarnation). Compare the association of Statius's freeing with Christ's Resurrection (21. 7-9), which of course prefigures the general Resurrection. The cross formed by the pilgrim's path and the procession, which in a sense are at right angles, figures both the intersection of time and eternity that takes place in each operation of God's grace in the individual soul, and the Last Judgment itself, when, at the end of time, and with all humankind, Dante will stand before Christ "come to judge."

13. the last trumpet: The Italian "novissimo bando," means literally "last proclamation," drawing on the ancient practice of announcing public proclamations with trumpet fanfares (still current in Dante's time), as well as echoing Matt. 24.31 and 1 Cor. 15.52: "in novissima tuba, canet enim tuba, et mortui resurgent incorrupti . . . oportet enim corruptibile hoc induere incorruptionem: et mortale hoc induere immortalitatem" [at the last trumpet, for the trumpet shall sound, and the dead shall arise incorruptible . . . for this corruptible must put on incorruption: and this mortal must put on immortality]. For the clothes metaphor in *induere* [to don], see the note to line 15.

14. cavern: An unusual word for the grave. Buti writes: "A cavern is a hollow place, and thus the pit, the grave, and the tomb can all be called caverns."

15. singing hallelujah for the reclothing of the voice: The resurrected body as a garment that will absorb the mortal body is a favorite metaphor of saint Paul's; see 1 Cor. 15.53 (quoted above) and 2 Cor. 5.4: "Nam et qui sumus in hoc tabernaculo, ingemiscimus gravati: eo quod nolumus expoliari sed supervestiri, ut absorbeatur quod mortale est a vita" [For we also, who are in this tabernacle (i.e., the mortal body), do groan, being burdened: because we would not be stripped of clothing, but clothed over, that what is mortal may be absorbed by life]. "Revestita" [clothed again, or clothed over], then, has a rich ambiguity of meaning; cf. the emphasis on Beatrice's clothing in lines 31-33.

Dante's daring trope is best understood as a metonymy for the body, to be connected with the theme of the use of the mouth in Cantos 23-24 (see the notes to 23.11 and 30, 24.50-51).

16-18. so . . . eternal life: The reference in "cotali" [such] is both to the joyous singing and to the suddenness of the apparition, which will occur "in the winking of an eye" (1 Cor. 15.52).

17-18. a hundred . . . eternal life: A throng of angels ("a hundred" is no doubt to be taken as indicating an indefinitely large number).

17. *ad vocem tanti senis* [at the voice of so great an elder]: The phrase seems to be Dante's own, not a quotation, though it certainly contributes to the hieratic atmosphere, as well as providing the required (though approximate) Latin rhyme for *venis* and *plenis*. The "elder" (cf. 29.83) is not explicitly identified but must be the one representing the Song of Songs (cf. the note to line 11).

19. *Benedictus qui venis* [Blessed are you who come]: This phrase is adapted from Ps. 117.26, "Benedictus qui venit in nomine Domini" [Blessed is he who comes in the name of the Lord]. Note that *benedictus* is masculine; while "Veni sponsa" is feminine and can refer to Beatrice, this verse is addressed to Christ (note the second person of the verb). See the note on "hosanna," 29.51. Liturgically, the verse is prominent in the Mass, quoted in the *Sanctus* (from the song of the angels before God), just before the Preface and Canon (the prayers of consecration of the bread and wine), thus at a moment of heightened expectation of the coming of Christ in the miracle of transubstantiation.

20. *Manibus, oh, date lilia plenis* [Oh, give lilies with full hands]: Quoted from *Aen.* 6.883, where it is part of Anchises' long lament for the death in 23 B.C. of Augustus' sister's son Marcellus at the age of nineteen (*Aen.* 6.868-70, 882-86):

> O gnate, ingentem luctum ne quaere tuorum;
> ostendent terris hunc tantum fata nec ultra
> esse sinent . . .
> heu miserande puer, si qua fata aspera rumpas,
> tu Marcellus eris. manibus date lilia plenis,
> purpureos spargam flores animamque nepotis
> his saltem accumulem donis et fungar inani
> munere.
> [O son, do not seek to know the great grief of your people;
> the Fates will merely show him on earth, no further
> permit him to be . . .
> Alas, pitied boy, if ever you break your harsh fate,
> you will be Marcellus. Give lilies with full hands,
> let me scatter purple flowers, and the soul of my descendant
> with these gifts at least let me honor, and carry out
> an empty duty.]

Dante was evidently struck by the fact that Vergil's catalog of the glorious heroes of Rome (*Aen.* 6.756-892) ends on this note of profound sadness; he no doubt saw it as integral to the *Aeneid*'s being a tragedy (see *Inf.* 20.113–21.3, with notes). That the angels should quote Vergil's line is a striking and powerful tribute to the Roman poet, but it is important to note the violent wrenching of Vergil's expression of pagan mourning to Christian rejoicing (cf. 22.40-41, with notes). While one may see an analogy between the early death of Marcellus and that of Beatrice, the context asserts the Christian victory over death; in Christian terms, lilies are associated with the Bride (see especially Cant. 2.1-2, 16; 4.5) and with the Resurrection. On the entire episode, see Bologna 1998.

22-33. I have sometimes . . . living flame: One of the most elaborate similes in the *Comedy,* a single sentence of twelve lines (cf. the note to 27.97-99), evenly divided into six lines (22-27) for the vehicle, six (28-33) for the tenor. The groups are parallel: in each pair of terzine the first depicts the surroundings, the second the main focus, with the additional refinement that in each case the principal subject is placed spatially *within* several layers of what is said to surround it (rosy clouds + sun + vapors; flowers, veil + lady + garments); in the final terzina (31-33), the eye first moves up from Beatrice's head ("sovra" [above]) to her olive wreath and then descends beneath [sotto] her mantle to her dress, closer and closer to her body (the sequence of layers is explicit in the description of Beatrice; the rosy clouds of line 23 are possibly to be taken as identical with the "vapori" [vapors] of line 26). Vividly contrasting colors—rose, blue, white, two greens—climax in fiery red.

31-33. her white veil . . . living flame: Beatrice's garments bring together the three colors dominating the procession (white, 29.84; green, 29.83; red, 29.148) and correspond to the three theological virtues (29.122-29; faith, hope, and love respectively). They also recall the colors of Beatrice's clothing on the first occasions she appears in the *Vita nova* (at the beginning of her ninth year: "sanguigno," *VN* 2; at the beginning of her eighteenth year: white, *VN* 3—these occasions are datable 1274 and 1283; Beatrice's death occurred in 1290. The present epiphany is taking place, then, in the twenty-seventh year since the first (on the "friendship" of the number nine for Beatrice, see *VN* 28-29).

34-39. And my spirit . . . ancient love: The focus shifts to the pilgrim's reaction, in another sentence that builds slowly to its climax: although he cannot see her face, he is able to recognize her by the strange power that emanates from her; these lines are the motivation for the elaborate establishment (lines 22-33) of the obstacles to sight. The long interval since the pilgrim's last sight of Beatrice corresponds to the clouds; line 37 alludes to her veil, behind which is located the hidden power that strikes him in line 39.

34-36. And my spirit . . . trembling: The "trembling" of line 36 finds its most drastic instance in *VN*14, in which, just before unexpectedly seeing Beatrice at a social gathering, he is seized by a "mirabile tremore" [wondrous tremor] that he feels "incominciare nel mio petto da la sinistra parte e distendersi di subito per tutto il mio corpo" [beginning in my breast, on the left side, and quickly extending itself to my entire body], and that brings him close to death.

40-54. As soon as . . . dark again with tears: Virgil has not been mentioned since 29.55-57, when he returned the pilgrim's gaze. This now turns out to have been our last sight of him, for at some moment, left unspecified, Virgil has departed, presumably to return to Limbo (but perhaps not as a pedestrian; cf. *Inf.* 12.56; but also *Inf.* 9.22-30 and 21.79-89).

41-42. transfixed me . . . boyhood: According to *VN* 2, when he had just turned nine.

43-48. I turned . . . ancient flame: The intensity of the pilgrim's emotions reduces him to a childlike state of vulnerability and spontaneity (already suggested in the allusion to boyhood) at the moment when Virgil's paternal authority (see line 50; for the parallel with that of the Roman Empire, see the note to 22.19-93) is replaced by Beatrice's maternal authority (corresponding to that of the Church; cf. lines 79-81).

43. to the left: In 29.10-12, when the group turned to mount the course of the stream, the pilgrim was ahead of his companions, the stream to his left. Here the pilgrim evidently expects Virgil to be still behind him (cf. 28.145-46, and see next note; had Virgil been beside him, his departure could hardly have gone unnoticed). The pilgrim is pivoting on his left side (cf. *Inf.* 15.97-98), associated with the heart and the emotions (cf. the notes to 13.14-15, *Inf.* 1.30, and see Additional Note 14).

43. appeal: It. *respitto* (from Lat. *respectus* [a looking back]) has many shades of meaning, including "trust," "regard" (perhaps "facial expression"), "respect." We take it as expressing the idea that the child "looks back to" its mother, "appeals from" what confronts it. In terms of the powerful forward motion of the poem, reliance on Virgil is being identified as retrograde, as Beatrice will point out.

46-48. to say to Virgil . . . ancient flame: The pilgrim expects to find sympathy and indulgence in Virgil; his impulse is to confide his feelings to the poet of pathos and tender feeling. So far Beatrice has given no sign of having seen the pilgrim: he is focused on himself, absorbed by the effect the meeting is having on him.

46-47. less than a dram . . . not trembling: For the heart as the source of trembling, which is then communicated to all the blood, see the note to lines 34-36.

48. I recognize the signs of the ancient flame: The line echoes the words of Dido to her sister Anna (*Aen.*4.23), confessing that for the first time since the death of her husband she feels a reawakening of love (now for Aeneas: cf. *Inf.* 5.61-62, with note): "agnosco veteris vestigia flammae" [I recognize the embers of former love]. Like the adaptation of *Aen.* 6.882 to rejoicing, this echo of Vergil, again placed as a tribute to him at a supreme moment of the poem, inverts the original context: in Dante's view, Dido "broke faith" with her dead husband, and this weakness caused her death, but here the context is that of reestablishing love beyond the grave, directed to its original object. Dante's substituting "segni" [signs] for Vergil's "vestigia" [remnants] introduces an important ambiguity (see Hawkins 1999).

49-54. But Virgil . . . dark again with tears: One remarkable moment after another in this extraordinary canto! Virgil has of course already abdicated his authority (27.127-42, which includes line 139: "No longer await any word or sign from me," is in fact his very last utterance in the poem).

Note the parallel between Virgil's departure and the death of Moses, who because of his disobedience was not permitted to cross the Jordan into the Promised Land. For the relation of the moment of Virgil's departure to Dante's interpretation of the fourth *Eclogue*, see Additional Note 14.

As Moore 1887 observed, in these lines Dante draws once more on Vergil, this time on *Geor.* 4.525-27, according to which Orpheus' head, torn off by the raging Maenads and thrown into the river Hebrus, still called out the name of Eurydice (cf also *Geor.* 4.465-66) :

> "Eurydicen!" vox ipsa et frigida lingua,
> "a miseram Eurydicen!" anima fugiente vocabat,
> "Eurydicen!" toto referebant flumine ripae.
> ["Eurydice!" the voice itself and the tongue cold in death,
> "ah, wretched Eurydice!" they called, as the soul fled,
> "Eurydice!" the shores replied across the expanse of the river.]

52-54. nor did everything . . . with tears: All Eden (lost by Eve; cf. the similar theme, with verbal parallels, in 28.50-52) does not prevent the pilgrim from shedding tears at the loss of Virgil (note the reference to 1.121-29, where Virgil had cleansed the pilgrim's face of his tears and of the stains of Hell).

55-145. Dante . . . pours forth tears: Two thirds of the canto are now devoted to the first phase of Beatrice's confrontation of the pilgrim with her accusations, in two stages: 1. her hostile challenge and naming of herself, the angels' compassion for the pilgrim, which triggers his weeping (lines 55-99); 2. her speech to the angels, detailing her accusations (lines 100-145).

55-57. Dante . . . to another sword: Gmelin points out the parallelism of the triple use of the word *piangere* in these lines with the triple mention of Virgil's name (lines 49-51).

55. Dante: The only place in the entire poem where Dante's name appears, to great dramatic effect; it will be matched in line 73 with Beatrice's naming of herself.

57. weep to another sword: The sword of Beatrice's reproaches. See 29.139-41, with note; cf. Dido's sword in "Così nel mio parlar" line 36, Durling/Martinez 1990.

58-69. Like an admiral . . . to appear openly: These twelve lines have a complex transitional function: precisely registering the new spatial arrangements (Beatrice now directly facing the pilgrim, the pilgrim turning back toward his right to face her) and circumstances (the rain of flowers has ceased, but Beatrice is still veiled), and emphasizing the significance of the mention of the pilgrim's name.

58-60. Like an admiral . . . to do well: The simile not only emphasizes Beatrice's official standing and her authority; the naval reference reminds us that the Church is also a ship. In these terms the pilgrim is "in a little bark" (*Par.* 2.1).

60. heartens them to do well: This phrase somewhat softens the harshness of Beatrice's words: her ultimate purpose is positive.

61-69. on the left side . . . to appear openly: Note the elaborate structure of the sentence, in which the center is occupied by the pilgrim's turning and his new sight of Beatrice.

62. when I turned: Note the references to the pilgrim's turning to his left toward Virgil (line 43) and toward Farinata (*Inf.* 10.1-36, with notes); the latter involves a series of references to the Last Judgment, of which the encounter with Beatrice is an even more elaborate prefiguration. If in the *Inferno* the pilgrim corresponded to Christ the Judge (see *Inferno* Additional Note 16), now it is Beatrice who does so (for face-to-face confrontation, see 1 Cor. 13.12).

62-63. my name . . . here set down: Benvenuto writes: "The poet excuses himself lest he seem a vain boaster; for it does not seem appropriate for a philosopher to introduce his own name into his works, except rarely and for good reason." The Ottimo (cited by Sapegno) writes: "It was necessary for the lady to call him by name for two reasons: first, to make it clear who among so many persons was being addressed; second, because, just as human speech is sweeter when a person to whom affection is being shown is called by name, so reproaches are sharper when the one being reproached is named by the reproacher." Cf. also *Conv.* 1.2.2-3.

67-69. although the veil . . . to appear openly: We are reminded of the continuing presence of the veil and of the pilgrim's ability to perceive Beatrice in spite of it, as in lines 31-39. For the punctuation, see "Textual Variants," p. 629.

67-68. the veil . . . Minerva's foliage: Beatrice's white veil is girt with an olive wreath (line 31). The olive was Athena's gift to mankind, for which Athens bore her name (see the note to 15.77-79); it represents peace and reconciliation.

70-75. Still regal . . . mankind is happy: Beatrice's next speech both balances her naming of the pilgrim with her naming of herself and voices her anger sarcastically but not yet explicitly.

73. Look at us . . . I am Beatrice: For the interestingly garbled manuscript tradition of this line and the reasoning behind the adoption of this reading, see "Textual Variants," p. 629. Although "guardaci" can mean "look over here" (Sapegno), and can also mean "look at all of us," in our view it expresses a royal we, and there is no reason why Beatrice should not shift to the more direct and intimate first person singular in the rest of the line.

We regard the repetition ("ben son, ben son") as both characteristic of Beatrice's emphatic speech here (cf. line 56; 31.5, 25, and 28) and carefully prepared by *Inf.* 19.52-53 and 62-63, *Purg.*19.19 and 28, and 24.52-54 (see our notes on these passages). Note the transition from the naval and masculine (lines 58-60) to the increasingly feminine and personal in lines 70 and 73 (cf. also line 79). De Robertis 1997 calls attention to the echo of Is. 43.11 and 25: "Ego sum, ego sum Dominus" [I am, I am the Lord].

74-75. How have you deigned . . . mankind is happy: There has been disagreement about the meaning of "degnasti": Buti took it to mean "considered yourself worthy," Landino to mean "condescended," which seems more appropriate to Beatrice's scornful anger. The apparent slight logical inconsistency between the two lines is part of Beatrice's sarcasm: "Why did you bother to come here, since you had chosen the path of unhappiness?"

76-81. My eyes fell . . . compassion still unripe: As line 82 will make clear, these lines refer to the reactions of the pilgrim during Beatrice's speech. There has been no hint in the poem up to this point that the pilgrim's going astray involved a specific disloyalty to Beatrice or that she has any reason to be angry with him, other than the very general indications of the nature of the Dark Wood of *Inferno* 1 (cf. *Inf.* 2. 61-66 and 94-108). For the moment of sharp self-knowledge essential to true repentance, cf. 9.94-96. The locus classicus is *Confessions* 8.7.16. The natural gesture of shame is hanging the head, as that of defiance is holding the head erect (cf. *Inf.* 10.35-36). We connect these two terzine as a unit; the second qualifies what the pilgrim sees in line 64; see "Textual Variants," p. 629.

80-81. for bitter . . . still unripe: The mother's stern rebuke expresses compassion and love, which must correct the child before "ripening" into sweet expressions of affection. The fruit metaphor recalls the occasion of the first Fall.

82-99. She fell silent . . . from my breast: The first phase of the confrontation, which has led to the pilgrim's shamed and frightened silence, is now interrupted by the angels' song of compassion, at which the pilgrim's rigidity dissolves in tears.

83-84. *In te, Domine, speravi* [In you, Lord, have I hoped] ... *pedes meos* [my feet]: The angels sing Ps. 30.2-9 (verse 1 is a title):

> In thee, O Lord, have I hoped, let me never be confounded: deliver me in thy justice. Bow down thy ear to me: make haste to deliver me. Be thou unto me a God, a protector, and a house of refuge, to save me. For thou art my strength and my refuge; and for thy name's sake thou wilt lead me, and nourish me. Thou wilt bring me out of this snare, which they have hidden for me: for thou art my protector. Into thy hands I commend my spirit: thou hast redeemed me, O Lord, the God of truth. Thou hast hated them that regard vanities, to no purpose. But I have hoped in the Lord: I will be glad and rejoice in thy mercy. For thou hast regarded my humility, thou hast saved my soul out of distresses. And thou hast not shut me up in the hands of the enemy: thou hast set my feet in a spacious place.

(The remaining sixteen verses of the psalm treat themes of defeat and ultimate reward.)

85-99. As snow ... from my breast: An even longer simile than lines 22-33, also beginning with the vehicle. The "living rafters along the back of Italy" are the branches of trees on the slopes of the Apennines or, more probably once the mountains have been metaphorized as the spine of a body, the outbranchings of the mountain range itself: in either case they correspond to the ribs of a human body. The snow is turned to ice by the wind from Slavonia (to the northeast); the "land that loses shadow" is Africa (especially the Tropical Zone), where the sun is higher in the sky, thus casting shorter shadows. For the geography, the notion of cold as a kind of pressure, and the macro- microcosmic correlations, see Dante's canzone "Io son venuto al punto de la rota" [I have come to the point of the wheel], translated and discussed in Durling/Martinez 1990. For the association of ice and sin, cf. Cocytus in *Inferno* 32-34: the ice around the pilgrim's heart is the last remnant of sin.

The passage, like others in Dante, goes back to the emblematic description of the frozen giant Atlas, figuring Aeneas' paralysis in Carthage, in *Aen.* 4.246-51:

> [Mercury] now in his flight discerns the top and steep sides
> of Atlas, who supports the heavens on his strong neck,
> of Atlas, whose pinebearing head is always girt
> with dark clouds, beaten with wind and rain;
> the snow gathered hides his shoulders, and rivers rush
> down the old man's chin, and his beard is stiff with bristling ice.

As in lines 21-33, the weaving together of the macro- and microcosmic levels in Dante's simile does much to suggest the intensity of the pilgrim's emotions.

88. trickles into itself: The phrase is important in bridging the external description of the winter landscape and the internal experience of the pilgrim.

89. as soon as . . . breathes: As soon as a warm wind comes from the south (like "Io son venuto," the passage draws on *Phar.* 9.528-31). The cold wind was Beatrice's hostile speech (Chiavacci Leonardi).

90. it seems fire is melting the candle: Juxtaposition of the enormous landscape with the intimacy and speed of the melting of an ordinary candle.

92-93. the singing of those . . . the eternal spheres: The "notes of the eternal spheres" seem most naturally to refer to the harmony of the spheres, in the *SS* and *Commentarii* explained as the product of the mathematical ratios of the intervals between them. Here the singing of the angels is said to follow the spheres; Buti observes: "In singing, *notare* is to follow the notes, that is, the written signs in the book." In this interpretation the "notes" followed by the angels would be those fixed by God for their singing as they govern the spheres (Chiavacci Leonardi). This perhaps makes better sense, but it seems to force the Italian.

94-96. in their sweet harmonies . . . untune him: Complex play on the idea of *tempering*, whose root meaning refers to musical tuning. The term was extended to include psychological temperament, as well as transient moods; see Spitzer 1963. Beatrice is "untuning" the pilgrim by placing him under great stress (for the body as a musical instrument, see *Inf.* 30.49-51).

98-99. with anguish . . . from my breast: The melting of the ice of fear and guilt results in violent sobbing (spirit, breath) and tears (water); for the relation of ice and tears, see Dante's canzone "Amor, tu vedi ben che questa donna" [Love, you see well that this lady], the third of the *petrose* (see the note to lines 85-99).

100-145. She, still motionless . . . pours forth tears: The second phase of the confrontation, Beatrice's presentation of the case against the pilgrim, as if arguing before a court (cf. 31.40-42; this aspect of the episode is a particularly clear figure of the Last Judgment). This passage provides the essential narrative framework for the entire *Comedy*, and it is not duplicated anywhere else in the poem or in other works. The principal basis for this grand outline is the *Vita nova*, which narrates Dante's early love for Beatrice; a series of confusions leading to her denying him her greeting, which in turn leads him to the major turning point of the poetry of praise (see the notes to 24.50-52); Beatrice's death, followed by another period of confusion involving the temptation of a second love; several visions of Beatrice that lead him to the resolution "to write of her what was never written of any woman," with which the book ends. To what extent the present passage departs from, or even radically alters, the perspective of the *Vita nova* has been the subject of considerable controversy.

Beatrice's speech has an elaborate formal structure derived from rhetorical doctrine: proem, setting forth the purpose of the speech (lines 103-108); narration of events (lines 109-41), including logical definition of the offence (lines 127-32); conclusion (lines 142-45).

109-17. Not only through . . . result in him: Both natural causes and divine grace had provided the pilgrim in his youth with high potential. A similar pairing governs *Inf.* 26.23-24; cf. *Conv.* 4.21.7.

109-11. the great wheels . . . are companions: A succinct statement of the basic medieval conception of nature as consisting primarily in the astrological influence of the heavenly bodies, which direct the development of all natural potentiality ("every seed" is not exclusively biological in reference); the stars that accompany the development determine its course. Note the explicitly teleological conception of the functioning of the heavens (governed, of course, by divine Providence).

112. abundance: The Italian *larghezza* includes the idea of generous bestowal.

113-14. which rain . . . cannot approach them: Rain or dew is a common metaphor for divine grace or mercy ("it droppeth as the gentle rain from heaven," *Merchant of Venice* 4.1.182); as rain results from the condensation of water vapors high in the atmosphere, so God's grace results from his love, but his reasons are too high for any creature (Beatrice's "our" is addressed to the angels) to understand them.

116-17. every good habit . . . result in him: Here the term *habit* is to be taken in the extended sense including intellectual as well as other modes of activity.

121-23. For a time . . . right direction: According to the *Vita nova*, from the age of 9 to the age of 25, Beatrice being about eight months younger. For the pattern—leading in the right direction one who then turns away—see the note to *Inf.* 15.124.

124-35. When I was . . . mattered to him: "When I was entering maturity and when I died." The conflict between loyalty to Beatrice's memory and the attraction of a new love is the subject of the last quarter of the *Vita nova*; the *rime petrose* and several other poems also celebrate other loves. In the *Convivio* the love for the "noble lady" of the *Vita nova* is treated as an allegory of Dante's newly discovered love for philosophy. To what extent the *Convivio* is touched by Beatrice's condemnation here has been the subject of much debate; in our view Beatrice's anger and the terms of her condemnation of the pilgrim's other loves (in line 126 and in 31.55-60) identify them as attractions to the merely temporal, which would not seem to apply to the study of philosophy (cf. Additional Note 2).

124-25. When I was . . . second age: According to *VN* 29, Beatrice died on September 8, 1290, about four months before her twenty-fifth birthday. According to *Conv.* 4.24.2 (on the four ages of man), the first age ("adolescence") lasts "until the twenty-fifth year."

125. changed lives: That is, exchanged temporal existence for eternal: went to Heaven.

126. he took himself ... to another: This is the language of a jealous woman: never is Beatrice more alive than in this canto. The Italian *altrui* (from the Lat. dative singular of *alter* [other]) can have either a singular or a plural referent, thus "diessi altrui" can also mean "gave himself to others."

127-32. when I had risen ... no promise fully: This is the logical definition of the offense, which is to be seen as contrary to reason as well as disloyal. Things of the spirit are of course invisible, though their primacy over the merely visible is assumed. The episode of the "noble lady" in the *Vita nova* is the culminating example in the book of the recurrent theme of obstacles to sight/insight, both external and internal. For the visible world as barrier to true vision, see 2.119-23, with notes, and for the deceptiveness of transitory goods, see 16.85-96, 18.18-75, with notes. Chiavacci Leonardi cites parallel descriptions in *Consolation* 3.8.1, 3.9.30. See also Additional Note 13.

130. a way not true: Clear reference to *Inf.* 1.2: "the straight way was lost."

133-35. Nor did it avail ... mattered to him: *VN* 39-42 relate a series of visions and imaginations that recall the protagonist from the love of the "noble lady" to Beatrice. Within the *Vita nova* itself this change is narrated as definitive. Beatrice's temporal perspective is larger.

136-41. He fell so low ... were carried: The last lines of Beatrice's narrative recapitulate what Virgil had told the pilgrim in *Inferno* 2.

139. the threshold of the dead: The proper meaning of It. *uscio* is "exit." The reference is of course to Beatrice's descent to Limbo, narrated by Virgil.

141. weeping: A direct reference to *Inf.* 2.116: "lacrimando" [shedding tears].

142-45. The high decree ... pours forth tears: Beatrice's peroration invokes the ritual of contrition, as well as the idea that the sacrifice God prefers is that of the contrite heart (Ps. 50.17).

142. The high decree of God: Dante's *fato* is a Latinism; Lat. *fatum* is the past participle of the verb *for, fari* [to speak], thus "something said" or a decree.

143-44. if Lethe were passed ... nourishment were tasted: See 28.127-32.

144. fee: Italian *scotto* meant literally "payment for a meal" (in a public house).

CANTO 31

"O tu che se' di là dal fiume sacro,"   1
volgendo suo parlare a me per punta,
che pur per taglio m'era paruto acro,

    ricominciò, seguendo sanza cunta: 4
"Dì, dì se questo è vero: a tanta accusa
tua confession conviene esser congiunta."

    Era la mia virtù tanto confusa   7
che la voce si mosse e pria si spense
che da li organi suoi fosse dischiusa.

    Poco sofferse, poi disse: "Che pense?   10
Rispondi a me, ché le memorie triste
in te non sono ancor da l'acqua offense."

    Confusione e paura insieme miste   13
mi pinsero un tal "sì" fuor de la bocca
al quale intender fuor mestier le viste.

    Come balestro frange, quando scocca   16
da troppa tesa, la sua corda e l'arco,
e con men foga l'asta il segno tocca:

    sì scoppia' io sottesso grave carco,   19
fuori sgorgando lagrime e sospiri,
e la voce allentò per lo suo varco.

    Ond' ella a me: "Per entro i mie' disiri,   22
che ti menavano ad amar lo Bene
di là dal qual non è a che s'aspiri,

    quai fossi attraversati o quai catene   25
trovasti, per che del passare innanzi
dovessiti così spogliar la spene?

    E quali agevolezze o quali avanzi   28
ne la fronte de li altri si mostraro,
per che dovessi lor passeggiare anzi?"

CANTO 31

The Earthly Paradise, continued: the pilgrim's confession and explanation—Beatrice's further reproaches—his faint—the crossing of Lethe—taken to Beatrice—the gryphon's changes in her eyes—Beatrice unveiled

1   "O you who are beyond the sacred river," turning toward me the point of her speech, whose mere edge had seemed sharp to me,

4   she began again, continuing without delay: "say, say if this is true: to so great an accusation your confession must be joined."

7   My strength was so confounded that my voice began but gave out before it was released from its organs.

10   She endured this briefly; then she said: "What are you pondering? Answer me, for your memories of evil have not yet been erased by the waters."

13   Confusion and fear mixed together drove such a "Yes" out of my mouth that to hear it one needed eyes.

16   As a crossbow cracks, when it is loosed after cord and bow have been drawn too far, and the bolt strikes the target with less force:

19   so I broke under this heavy burden, gasping forth tears and sighs, and my voice was weakened along its passage.

22   Therefore she to me: "Within your desires for me, which were leading you to love the Good beyond which there is nothing one can aspire to,

25   what ditches across your way, or what chains did you find, that you should so strip yourself of the hope of passing beyond them?

28   And what comforts or what advantages did you see displayed on others' brows, that you should parade before them?"

Dopo la tratta d'un sospiro amaro,   31
a pena ebbi la voce che rispuose,
e le labbra a fatica la formaro;
 piangendo dissi: "Le presenti cose   34
col falso lor piacer volser miei passi
tosto che 'l vostro viso si nascose."
 Ed ella: "Se tacessi o se negassi   37
ciò che confessi, non fora men nota
la colpa tua: da tal giudice sassi!
 Ma quando scoppia de la propria gota   40
l'accusa del peccato, in nostra corte
rivolge sé contra 'l taglio la rota.
 Tuttavia, perché mo vergogna porte   43
del tuo errore, e perché altra volta,
udendo le serene, sie più forte,
 pon giù il seme del piangere, e ascolta: 46
sì udirai come in contraria parte
mover dovieti mia carne sepolta.
 Mai non t'appresentò natura o arte   49
piacer quanto le belle membra in ch'io
rinchiusa fui, e sono in terra sparte;
 e se 'l sommo piacer sì ti fallio   52
per la mia morte, qual cosa mortale
dovea poi trarre te nel suo disio?
 Ben ti dovevi, per lo primo strale   55
de le cose fallaci, levar suso
di retro a me, che non era più tale.
 Non ti dovea gravar le penne in giuso,   58
ad aspettar più colpo, o pargoletta
o altra novità con sì breve uso.
 Novo augelletto due o tre aspetta,   61
ma dinanzi da li occhi d'i pennuti
rete si spiega indarno o si saetta."
 Quali fanciulli, vergognando, muti   64
con li occhi a terra stannosi, ascoltando
e sé riconoscendo e ripentuti:
 tal mi stav' io; ed ella disse: "Quando   67
per udir se' dolente, alza la barba,
e prenderai più doglia riguardando."

31   After heaving a bitter sigh, I hardly had the voice to reply, and my lips formed it with difficulty;

34   weeping I said: "Present things with their false pleasure turned my steps as soon as your face was hidden."

37   And she: "If you were silent or denied what you confess, your guilt would be no less remarked: by such a judge is it known!

40   But when the accusation of the sin bursts forth from the sinner's own cheek, in our court the whetstone turns against the edge of the sword.

43   Still, so that you may now bear the shame of your error, and so that another time, hearing the sirens, you may be stronger,

46   lay aside the seed of weeping, and listen: you will hear how the burial of my flesh should have turned you in the contrary direction.

49   Never did nature or art present to you such beauty as did the lovely members in which I was enclosed, and now they are scattered in earth;

52   and if the highest beauty thus failed you with my death, what mortal thing should later have drawn you to desire it?

55   After the first arrow from deceptive things, you should have risen up after me, for I was no longer such.

58   Your wings should not have been weighted down, to await more blows, by either a young girl or some other new thing of such short duration.

61   A young bird waits for two or three, but before the eyes of one full-fledged, nets are spread and arrows shot in vain."

64   As boys stand ashamed, silent, with their eyes on the ground, listening, and recognizing themselves, and penitent:

67   so I stood; and she said: "If you are pained by listening, lift up your beard, and you will have more pain gazing."

Con men di resistenza si dibarba   70
robusto cerro, o vero al nostral vento
o vero a quel de la terra di Iarba,
   ch'io non levai al suo comando il mento;   73
e quando per la barba il viso chiese,
ben conobbi il velen de l'argomento.
   E come la mia faccia si distese,   76
posarsi quelle prime creature
da loro aspersïon l'occhio comprese;
   e le mie luci, ancor poco sicure,   79
vider Beatrice volta in su la fiera
ch'è sola una persona in due nature.
   Sotto 'l suo velo e oltre la rivera   82
vincer pariemi più sé stessa antica,
vincer che l'altre qui, quand' ella c'era.
   Di penter sì mi punse ivi l'ortica   85
che di tutte altre cose qual mi torse
più nel suo amor, più mi si fé nemica.
   Tanta riconoscenza il cor mi morse   88
ch'io caddi vinto, e quale allora femmi
salsi colei che la cagion mi porse.
   Poi, quando il cor virtù di fuor rendemmi,   91
la donna ch'io avea trovata sola
sopra me vidi, e dicea: "Tiemmi, tiemmi!"
   Tratto m'avea nel fiume infin la gola,   94
e tirandosi me dietro sen giva
sovresso l'acqua, lieve come scola.
   Quando fui presso a la beata riva,   97
"*Asperges me*" sì dolcemente udissi
che nol so rimembrar, non ch'io lo scriva.
   La bella donna ne le braccia aprissi,   100
abbracciommi la testa e mi sommerse,
ove convenne ch'io l'acqua inghiottissi.
   Indi mi tolse e bagnato m'offerse   103
dentro a la danza de le quattro belle,
e ciascuna del braccio mi coperse.
   "Noi siam qui ninfe e nel ciel siamo stelle;   106
pria che Beatrice discendesse al mondo,
fummo ordinate a lei per sue ancelle.

70   With less resistance is a massive oak uprooted, whether by a wind of ours or one from the land of Iarbas,

73   than was my chin raised at her command; and when she referred to my face by my beard, I knew well the venom in the point.

76   And when I lifted my face, my eye perceived that those first creatures had ceased their scattering of flowers,

79   and my eyes, still unsure, saw Beatrice turned toward the beast that is but one person in two natures.

82   Under her veil and beyond the river she seemed to me to surpass her former self more than she surpassed other women here, when she was here.

85   The nettle of repentance so pricked me then, that whatever other thing had most turned me toward its love, now became most hateful to me.

88   So much recognition bit my heart that I fell overcome, and what I then became, she knows who was the cause.

91   Then, when my heart gave me back my external powers, the lady whom I had found alone I saw above me, and she was saying: "Hold me, hold me!"

94   She had drawn me into the river up to my throat, and, pulling me after her, she was walking on the water as light as a little boat.

97   When I drew near the blessed shore, "*Asperges me*" was heard so sweetly that I cannot remember, let alone write it.

100   The beautiful lady opened her arms, embraced my head, and submerged me, so that I had to swallow some of the water.

103   Then she took me and, drenched as I was, inserted me into the dance of the four beauties, and each of them covered me with her arm.

106   "We are nymphs here, and in the sky we are stars; before Beatrice descended into the world, we were appointed to be her handmaidens.

    Merrenti a li occhi suoi, ma nel giocondo   109
lume ch'è dentro aguzzeranno i tuoi
le tre di là, che miran più profondo."

    Così cantando cominciaro, e poi   112
al petto del grifon seco menarmi,
ove Beatrice stava vòlta a noi.

    Disser: "Fa che le viste non risparmi: 115
posto t'avem dinanzi a li smeraldi
ond' Amor già ti trasse le sue armi."

    Mille disiri più che fiamma caldi   118
strinsermi li occhi a li occhi rilucenti,
che pur sopra 'l grifone stavan saldi.

    Come in lo specchio il sol, non altrimenti   121
la doppia fiera dentro vi raggiava
or con altri, or con altri reggimenti.

    Pensa, lettor, s'io mi maravigliava   124
quando vedea la cosa in sé star queta,
e ne l'idolo suo si trasmutava!

    Mentre che piena di stupore e lieta   127
l'anima mia gustava di quel cibo
che, saziando di sé, di sé asseta,

    sé dimostrando di più alto tribo   130
ne li atti, l'altre tre si fero avanti,
danzando al loro angelico caribo.

    "Volgi, Beatrice, volgi li occhi santi,"   133
era la sua canzone, "al tuo fedele,
che per vederti ha mossi passi tanti!

    Per grazia, fa noi grazia che disvele   136
a lui la bocca tua, sì che discerna
la seconda bellezza che tu cele."

    O isplendor di viva luce etterna: 139
chi palido si fece sotto l'ombra
sì di Parnaso, o bevve in sua cisterna,

    che non paresse aver la mente ingombra,   142
tentando a render te qual tu paresti
là dove armonizzando il ciel t'adombra,

    quando ne l'aere aperto ti solvesti?   145

109   We will lead you to her eyes, but to the joyous
light that is in them yours will be sharpened by the
three over there, who see more deeply."

112   Thus singing they began, and then they led me
with them to the breast of the gryphon, where
Beatrice stood, turned toward us.

115   They said: "Do not spare your eyes; we have
placed you before the emeralds whence Amor
formerly drew his bow at you."

118   A thousand desires hotter than flame drew my
eyes to her shining ones, which were still fixed
unmoving on the gryphon.

121   Like the sun in a mirror, not otherwise shone
there the double beast, now with one bearing, now
with another.

124   Think, reader, if I marveled when I saw that the
thing in itself remained unchanged, but in its
eidolon transmuted itself!

127   While, full of awe and joyful, my soul tasted that
food which, by satisfying, makes one thirst for it,

130   the other three, showing their more noble rank
in their bearing, came forward, dancing to their
angelic carol.

133   "Turn, Beatrice, turn your holy eyes," was their
song, "to your faithful one, who has come so far to
see you!

136   For grace, do us the grace of unveiling your
mouth to him, so that he may discern the second
beauty that you conceal."

139   O splendor of eternal, living light: who has
become so pale beneath the shadow of Parnassus,
or has drunk so deeply from its well,

142   that he would not seem to have a laboring mind,
attempting to portray you as you appeared there,
where, harmonizing, the sky is your only veil,

145   when you disclosed yourself in the open air?

NOTES

1-63. O you who . . . shot in vain: Almost half the canto is devoted to the continuation of Beatrice's reproaches, his confession and explanation, followed by a further lecture from her.

1-15. O you who . . . one needed eyes: At Beatrice's urging, the pilgrim confesses that her accusations are justified.

1. beyond the sacred river: Marking the rift still existing between them. The second half of the canto will take the pilgrim across the river to her side.

2-3. turning toward me . . . sharp to me: The metaphor of the sword again (cf. 30.57, with note, and the note to 30.62). Beatrice turned the "edge" of the sword toward the pilgrim when addressing the angels, referring to him in the third person; now, addressing him, she points it directly at him.

5. say, say: For Beatrice's emphatic repetitions, see 30.55-57 and 73, with notes.

5-6. to so great . . . must be joined: Beatrice's legalistic formulations continue the analogy with a criminal trial (cf. the note to 30.100-145) under Roman law.

10. What are you pondering: The question repeats verbatim Virgil's question in *Inf.* 5.111; see *Inter cantica* below.

13-15. Confusion and fear . . . one needed eyes: That is, the pilgrim says "Yes," but so faintly as to be inaudible; that it could be understood visually implies that he nodded his head or made some other affirmative gesture.

16-21. As a crossbow . . . along its passage: A further development of the analogy between the human body and a stringed instrument (cf. 30.94-96, with note), this time not a musical one, although the bolt of the crossbow is the analogue of the voice, whose projection in fact depends on muscular tension (the lines have also been taken to mean, "as a crossbow, when it is loosed after being drawn too far, breaks its cord and bow"; as Chiavacci Leonardi observes, the parallel with line 19 supports the interpretation followed here). The loosing of the crossbow causes additional strain because the trigger causes the stop to move slightly backward; *frange* should be understood as meaning "cracks," since if the bow were entirely broken the bolt would not be projected at all.

22-30. Therefore she . . . parade before them: Beatrice's question is double: a. What internal difficulties—"within your desire" (or within your desire for the good, which I inspired)—made you lose hope of reaching me? The ditches and chains are metaphors derived from military fortifications. b. What external advantages did you expect from others? The mention of "parading" before others (cf. the note to line 35) seems a direct reference to *VN* 35-37, where the protagonist becomes aware of the lady watching him from her window and later seeks her out, presumably by walking past her window (see Gorni's 1996 notes).

31-36. After heaving . . . face was hidden: The disappearance of the visible Beatrice was indeed an obstacle, but only an external one (see the previous note); she was replaced by the deceptive appearances of "present things." One notes how all the concreteness of actions now judged to have been wrong is converted into abstract terminology.

35. turned my steps: Cf. 30.130, with note. For walking as metaphor for the pursuit of desire, see *Inf.* 1.28-30 and *Purg.* 16.91-93 and 18.43-45, with notes.

37-63. If you were silent . . . arrows shot in vain: Another elaborately structured speech from Beatrice (cf. 30.100-145), beginning with acceptance of his confession as adequate (see the division of the body of the speech in the note to lines 43-63).

37-39. If you were silent . . . is it known: "Such a judge" is of course Christ, present as the gryphon, from whose knowledge and sentence there is no appeal; cf. *Inf.* 5.54-55, where the souls confess their sins to Minos (obviously without any possibility of prevarication).

40-42. But when the accusation . . . against the edge: Again the sword metaphor (cf. lines 2-3). The "whetstone" is explicitly a wheel in the Italian (*rota*, line 42): her speech will no longer be as sharp as until now.

43-63. Still, so that . . . shot in vain: The main body of the speech on the principle that should have guided the pilgrim: proem, lines 43-48; death of Beatrice as treachery of "present things," lines 49-54; summation of the lesson, with bird analogy, lines 55-63.

43-44. bear the shame of your error: That is, endure being publicly shamed, on the assumption that the memory will deter future lapses.

45. hearing the sirens: Encountering the allurements of "present things," with obvious reference to the Siren of the dream in 19.7-33.

46. lay aside the seed of weeping: A striking phrase that has been interpreted in several ways: "put aside your confusion and fear (causes—i.e., seeds—of weeping)" (Sapegno); "stop sowing tears," on the analogy with Ps. 125.5 ("Those who sow in tears shall reap in exultation"—Buti, Chiavacci Leonardi).

47-48. the burial . . . contrary direction: In the Italian "mia carne sepolta" [my flesh buried], the past participle is to be taken in the strong sense (*Gerusalemme liberata* means "The freeing of Jerusalem," as *Paradise Lost* means "The losing of Paradise"); cf. 23.55-60. The "contrary direction" is away from "present things."

49-57. Never did nature . . . no longer such: The focus is still on Beatrice's flesh (line 48): the beauty of her body is strongly asserted, its only imperfection being its mortality. The intensity of that first loss ("the first arrow") should have prevented any further attachment to merely mortal beauty and turned you to follow me, since "I was no longer such" (mortal and thus deceptive). For the term *piacere* [here, beauty], see *Inter cantica* below.

58-63: Your wings . . . shot in vain: The bird metaphor, implicit in lines 55-57 ("arrow," "risen"), is now made explicit; the attachment to transitory things ("a young girl or some other new thing") becomes a weight hampering the flight of the soul and making it an easy target for loss ("more blows" of the "arrows" of transient things). The metaphor derives from a widespread tradition of "Satan the fowler" (see Koonce 1959; for the biblical basis of the idea, see the note to line 63).

62. one full-fledged: The adult bird: a reminder that when Beatrice died Dante had already passed from "adolescence" to adulthood; see the note to 30.124-25.

63. nets: "Nets" correspond, obviously, to the beauties that snare the unwary; the lines adapt Prov. 1.17: "Frustra autem iacitur rete ante oculos pennatorum" [For a net is spread in vain before the eyes of the full-fledged], quoted by Dante also in *Ep.* 6.21 (Chiavacci Leonardi).

64-67. As boys . . . so I stood: Even without the explicit reference to scenes of parental rebuke, the entire section from 30.58 on (see especially 30.79-81) has exploited the paradox of the imposition of this model on adult confrontation. The difference between Dante's treatment of the pilgrim's relation to father figures (Virgil, and Cacciaguida in *Paradiso* 15-17) and the mother figure (Beatrice) will repay study.

67. so I stood: The pilgrim has had his eyes on the ground since 30.77, as lines 67-75 make clear.

67-75. If you are pained . . . venom in the point: Although Beatrice's tone is severe and she promises further pain, the invitation to raise his head to look at her directly motivates the transition to the second half of the canto powerfully (and is placed at the exact center).

70-72. With less resistance . . . land of Iarbas: The figure of the oak in the wind renews in part the terms of the simile of 30.85-99; there the Slavonian wind turned the snow to ice, the African wind melted it, here a violent African wind may uproot the oak (there is a distant allusion to the famous simile in *Aen.* 4.437-49). The violence of this wind does not correspond to anything external in the action.

70-71. a massive oak uprooted: Dante's term for "uprooted" here is "si dibarba," a trope based on the analogy between the roots of a plant and the hairs of a beard (cf. modern Italian *abbarbicarsi* [to take root] and *barbetta* [the barb of a fishhook]). Dante uses the term *barbare* [to take root] metaphorically for amorous attachment in "Al poco giorno e al gran cerchio d'ombra" [To the brief day and the great circle of shadow], the second of the *rime petrose*, lines 4-5.

73. the land of Iarbas: Iarbas was the king of Libya who wooed Dido; his outraged prayer to Jupiter protesting her shameless love affair with Aeneas (*Aen.* 4.198-218) leads directly to the sending of Mercury to speed Aeneas' departure (see the note to 30.85-99).

74-75. when she referred . . . venom in the point: The pilgrim identifies the trope used by Beatrice in line 68; Italian *viso* refers properly to the eyes or the power of sight; it is often used of the face (cf. French and English *visage*). The term *argomento* includes the idea of sharpness (cf. *arguto* [sharp, in the metaphorical sense, used of understanding, witticisms, eyes]); this is a continuation of the sword metaphor of lines 1-3. In Italian the phrase "velen dell'argomento" has become proverbial.

76-145. And when I lifted . . . in the open air: The second half of the canto: the pilgrim's direct gaze at Beatrice, whose beauty causes him to faint with remorse; his crossing of the river; his entering the dance of the virtues; Beatrice's unveiling. The whole is framed by the two protagonists offering their faces to direct view, first the pilgrim (line 76, prepared by lines 67-75), then Beatrice (lines 133-45); but the two moments are separated by an elaborate series of allegorical events that lessen the erotic charge of the moment of unveiling and confrontation; cf. the notes to lines 79-81, 103-17.

77-81. my eye perceived . . . in two natures: The pilgrim's first glance takes in further changes in the arrangements: the cessation of the rain of flowers and Beatrice's having turned toward the gryphon (see the note to 30.58-69).

77-78. my eye perceived . . . scattering of flowers: The rain of flowers was last mentioned in 30.65, and the exact moment of its cessation is left unspecified (30.65, in its immediate context, might be taken to mean that the rain had already ceased, but now we learn that that was not the case). The angels are the "first creatures" because in the traditional (Augustinian) interpretation of Gen. 1.1, "heaven" is taken to refer to the angels.

79-81. and my eyes . . . in two natures: Beatrice's last speech (lines 67-69) might naturally be taken to indicate that she will return the pilgrim's gaze, but that is postponed until the moment of full unveiling. Her turning away begins the series of allegorical, ritualistic events that both intensify the expectation of the direct gaze and desexualize it: the gryphon is more important to Beatrice than the pilgrim.

80-81. the beast . . . in two natures: The gryphon is here identified in language that is appropriate only to Christ, referring to the hypostatic union of his divine and human natures in one person (the second person of the Trinity); cf. the notes to lines 121-26.

82-84. Under her veil . . . when she was here: The sense of the obstacles between the two is reasserted. Note the emphatic anaphora of "vincere" [to vanquish] in lines 83 and 84, with the daring syntactical inversion in both (normal order would be: "pariemi vincer sé stessa antica più che [pariemi] vincere l'altre qui").

85-90. The nettle of repentance . . . was the cause: These lines are the final resolution of the penitential aspect of the encounter with Beatrice, which, with its exquisitely gradated and orchestrated stages has occupied 181 lines (30.54-145, 31.1-90), or 194, if one includes lines 91-103. New here is the addition to the yearning toward Beatrice of the hatred of the things that had led him astray.

88-90. So much recognition . . . was the cause: For the parallels with *Inferno* 5, see *Inter cantica* below. The great complexity of meaning of *riconoscenza* [recognition, acknowledgment, gratitude] (cf. line 66 and *Par.* 22.113) makes these lines particularly untranslatable.

91-145. Then, when my heart . . . in the open air: The final movement of the canto: symbolic baptism in Lethe, participation in the dance of the cardinal and theological virtues, contemplation of the two natures of Christ reflected in Beatrice's eyes, unveiling.

91. when my heart . . . external powers: Fainting takes place when the powers of the soul withdraw into the chamber of the heart (the seat of the soul, see the notes to 5.74 and 25.37-42); consciousness returns as the vital powers in the heart spread forth through the veins once again.

92-102. the lady . . . some of the water: Matelda assures the pilgrim's passage of Lethe, the taste of which will obliterate all memory of sin (28.127-28; cf.

31.11-12). Exactly what the significance of its being Matelda who performs this function is unclear, though it is consistent with her being a guardian appointed to various tasks (cf. 33.123-35, with notes).

98. *Asperges me* [you will sprinkle me]: Another quotation from Psalm 50 (verse 7; see the notes to 5.24 and 23.11): "Asperges me hysopo et mundabor, lavabis me et super nivem dealbabor" [You will sprinkle me with hyssop and I shall be clean, you will wash me I shall become whiter than snow]. Probably the angels sing the verse.

98-99. so sweetly . . . write it: The sweetness that transcends memory is a version of the "inexpressibility topos" (Curtius 1946) that will be a major aspect of the *Paradiso* (see *Par.* 1.4-9, with notes).

103-14. Then she took me . . . turned toward us: Matelda inserts the pilgrim into the circle of the four cardinal virtues (cf. 29.130-32); they in turn lead him to Beatrice and the gryphon. The lines imply that he becomes the center of the circle and that the dancers join their hands above his head, with obvious allegorical significance: the acquisition of the moral virtues precedes and prepares the reception of divine revelation, which in turn will lead to the infusion of the theological virtues: this allegorical sequence recapitulates the action of the entire *Purgatorio* to this point (as well as all human history previous to the Incarnation; cf. the notes to 22.19-93 and 29.82-154).

106-109. We are nymphs . . . to her eyes: In 29.120 the virtues were called *donne* [ladies]; Matelda is compared with a nymph in 29.4-6. Figures of myth, nymphs were most characteristically associated with woodlands, mountains, and streams (the literal meaning of the Greek word is "bride"). That the virtues are also "stars" recalls the constellations of 1.23-24 and 8.88-93, discussed in the notes; the point is partly that they reflect the providential ordering of history, governed, like all things sublunar, by the heavenly bodies (it is not clear whether Dante means the stars to be thought of as real or merely symbolic; see the note to 8.89-93).

108. we were appointed . . . handmaidens: The symbolism applies to Beatrice both as she is represented in the *Vita nova* and in her symbolic function in the *Comedy,* which will become increasingly predominant.

109-11. We will lead . . . see more deeply: The emphasis on contemplation that dominates the rest of the canto fulfills the parallel between Beatrice and Rachel, as Matelda does that with Leah (see 27.100-108). In *Conv.* 3.15, interpreting his canzone "Amor che ne la mente mi ragiona" [Love that discourses to me in my mind] as an allegory of the love of the personified Wisdom, Dante writes, "Here it is necessary to know that the eyes of Wisdom are her demonstrations, with which one sees the truth most certainly; and her smile is her persuasions, in which is shown the inner light of wisdom under some veil." Later in the same paragraph he cites Wisdom 7.26: "For [Wisdom] is the brightness of the eternal light and the spotless mirror of the majesty of God." See also *VN* 19 (on "Donne ch'avete intelletto d'amore"; see the notes on 24.50-54): "I speak of her eyes, which are the beginning of love . . . and of her mouth, which is the goal of love; and that every vicious thought may be removed hence, let it be remembered by the reader that it is written above that this lady's greeting, which was one of the operations of her mouth, was the goal of my desires while I was able to receive it."

113. they led me . . . of the gryphon: As we know from *Inf.* 12.83-84, the breast is "where the two natures are joined" (see Durling 1981a), in man the rational and the animal, in Christ the divine and the human. As in the centaurs man and horse meet at the breast, so in the gryphon the eagle and lion.

118-26. A thousand desires . . . transmuted itself: In Beatrice's eyes, as in a mirror, the pilgrim sees alternately the two natures of the gryphon, divine and human. The comparison with the sun, the dual natures, the inexhaustibility of the "food" (lines 128-29), these are only appropriate if the gryphon is Christ (the principal other candidate is the ideal Roman emperor: Armour 1989). The gryphon is not an allegory of Christ but must be understood as Christ himself, seen according to the present stage of the pilgrim's capacity: at first entirely opaque as an arbitrary joining of eagle and lion, the gryphon is understood analytically, separately, by theology in the light of revelation. The principle of the union of the two natures is beyond human understanding; but it is the ultimate goal of the pilgrim's entire journey, the culmination of the vision in which the pilgrim's eye penetrates further and further in the infinite transparency of God (see *Par.* 33.130-41, with notes); here there is an implicit reference to 1 Cor. 13.12: "Now we see as in a mirror into an enigma, but then face to face." Thus this vision of the gryphon prefigures the climax of the entire poem, and to see it as a mere political allegory is a drastic reduction of its significance.

121. Like the sun in a mirror: Since Beatrice will remove her veil only in lines 139-45, we are to understand the brightness of the images of the gryphon as imposing itself through the veil (that the veil covers Beatrice eyes is clearly indicated by its being girt with olive, 30.31, 67-69; see the note to lines 139-45).

124-26. Think, reader . . . transmuted itself: This is the sixth of the seven addresses to the reader in the *Purgatorio*; see the note to 8.19-21 and *Inter cantica* below.

126. eidolon: Dante uses the learned term (it is Greek; cf. Isidore, *Etym.* 8.9.13) for "image" or "reflection."

127-45. While, full . . . in the open air: The three theological virtues beg Beatrice to remove her veil, interrupting the pilgrim's vision of the gryphon.

128-29. that food . . . thirst for it: Only the vision of God has the quality of increasing desire rather than satiating it.

131-38. the other three . . . that you conceal: Presumably the theological virtues must make this request because of the miraculous nature of Beatrice's beauty.

133-38. Turn, Beatrice . . . that you conceal: Beatrice will now turn to face the pilgrim directly for the first time since the beginning of the canto (cf. 30.66); but the goal of the unveiling will be the mouth, not the eyes (see the note to lines 109-11 above). For "your faithful one" cf. *Inf.* 2.61, 98, 103.

133, 136. Turn . . . turn; grace . . . grace: Note the consecutive repetitions, and cf. line 5, and 30.73, with notes.

139-45. O splendor . . . in the open air: There is no direct description of Beatrice's face (neither eyes nor mouth), no evocation of the direct gaze as in "Così nel mio parlar voglio esser aspro" [So in my speech I would be harsh] (the last of the *rime petrose*), lines 74-78, but instead a particularly elaborate version of the inexpressibility topos: even the most learned and inspired poet would seem to be a struggling beginner if he tried to describe Beatrice unveiled.

139. O splendor . . . living light: A translation of Wisdom 7.26, quoted in the note to lines 109-11. Beatrice's beauty is a reflection (for *splendore* [brightness] as referring especially to reflected light, see *Conv.* 3.14.9) of the eternal light of the divinity.

140-41. who has become . . . from its well: What poet, no matter how pale from study of the poets and from self-denial for the sake of poetry (the "shadow of Parnassus"), and no matter how inspired (the spring Castalia is associated with Mt. Parnassus). Note how the suggestion of indoor enclosure in these lines intensifies the force of lines 144-45.

144-45. there, where . . . in the open air: These lines have been variously understood: "armonizzando" [harmonizing] has been taken to refer to the harmony of the spheres (cf. *Par.* 1.76-78); to the singing of the angels (cf. 30.94-96); to the beauty of Eden itself. "T'adombra" [literally, shades you] has been referred to the flowers thrown by the angels; to Eden itself as a shadowy reflection of the divine; to the stripes left in the air by the candelabra (29.73-82); and—as in our version—to the absence of a veil.

145. in the open air: This phrase, like the entire passage, seems to indicate that the event takes place in a clearing where the sky is visible. As described earlier, however (see 28.3, 31-33, 35), the scene is entirely enclosed by foliage. In 32.18 the presence of the seven candelabra is reasserted, but there has been no further mention of the stripes since 29.73-82; they would be particularly inappropriate to an unveiling "in the open air."

Inter cantica. There are a number of conspicuous parallels in this canto with *Inferno* 5, most importantly with the episode of Francesca da Rimini. The parallels serve to emphasize the thematic relation between the two episodes, both of them crucial to Dante's representation of the problematic of human desire and love, and to intensify the contrast between them. In one case we have the pair of adulterous lovers, whose yielding to desire led them to "one death" (*Inf.* 5.106), since which they have been together; in the other case we have virtuous lovers (though the pilgrim has been a backslider) who were separated by death and who now meet again. In one case the woman narrates the critical moment of temptation and fall, while the man weeps uncontrollably; in the other case the woman sternly reproaches the man with a general pattern of disloyalty, for which he weeps brokenly, acknowledging the justice of her reproaches. In both cases the complexity of the pilgrim's feelings (in the first case, vicarious) leads to his fainting: in Hell this provides the transition to the next circle; in the Earthly Paradise, to the baptismal crossing of the river Lethe that has separated him from Beatrice.

The verbal parallels between the two cantos are pointed. In *Inferno* 5, the sequence of the pilgrim's reactions indicate the degree to which he is vulnerable to the self-deception and death-oriented yielding of Francesca. In both cases he bows his head under the weight of unresolved sorrow (and guilt) and provokes the same question: "Che pense?" [What are you pondering?] (*Inf.* 5.111; *Purg.* 31. 10), drawing on the etymological connection of this word for thinking with *weight*, in the subjunctive to emphasize the dubiousness of his delay; the importance of the connection is reinforced by the use of the identical words in rhyme with *pense* in both cantos ("spense" [extinguished]: *Inf.* 5.107, *Purg.* 31.8; "offense" [harmed]: *Inf.* 5. 109, *Purg.* 31.12). In both cases his faint is announced with the term *caddi* [I fell] (*Inf.* 5.142, *Purg.* 31.136). The ambiguous complexity of the pilgrim's reactions in *Inferno* 5 focuses a problematic—the nature of sexual temptation and self-deception, the possibility of religious sublimation—that is continuous with *Purgatorio* 30 and 31. The amalgam of sublimated erotic feeling with religious devotion now governs the resolution of these issues, asserting (as the *Vita nova* had done) the possibility of direct continuity between the love of woman and love of God.

Both cantos make conspicuous use of the ambiguous term *piacere*, which contains ideas both of beauty and of pleasure (it is used by both Francesca and Beatrice with reference to the Provençal vocabulary of courtly love: *Inf.* 5.104, *Purg.* 31.50, 52). Both cantos involve wind imagery (*Inf.* 5.28-36, 75, 96; *Purg.* 31.70-72) and bird imagery (*Inf.* 5.40-48; *Purg.* 31.55-63), used to sharply differing purposes.

Finally, our notes on *Purgatorio* 30-31 have traced the extreme care with which Dante has modulated, both evoking and evading, the erotic charge of the direct gaze into the beloved's eyes, the moment of unveiling, and the revealing of the beloved's mouth/smile: compare the importance of eyes and mouth/smile in *Inf.* 5.127-36, especially lines 130, 133, 136.

Figure 10. Ladies dancing and singing a ballata.

CANTO 32

Tant' eran li occhi miei fissi e attenti 1
a disbramarsi la decenne sete,
che li altri sensi m'eran tutti spenti.

Ed essi quinci e quindi avien parete 4
di non caler—così lo santo riso
a sé traéli con l'antica rete!—

quando per forza mi fu vòlto il viso 7
ver' la sinistra mia da quelle dee,
perch' io udi' da loro un "Troppo fiso!"

e la disposizion ch'a veder èe 10
ne li occhi pur testé dal sol percossi,
sanza la vista alquanto esser mi fée.

Ma poi ch'al poco il viso riformossi— 13
e dico "al poco" per rispetto al molto
sensibile, onde a forza mi rimossi—

vidi 'n sul braccio destro esser rivolto 16
lo glorïoso essercito, e tornarsi
col sole e con le sette fiamme al volto.

Come sotto li scudi per salvarsi 19
volgesi schiera e sé gira col segno,
prima che possa tutta in sé mutarsi:

quella milizia del celeste regno 22
che procedeva, tutta trapassonne
pria che piegasse il carro il primo legno.

Indi a le rote si tornar le donne, 25
e 'l grifon mosse il benedetto carco,
sì che però nulla penna crollonne.

La bella donna che mi trasse al varco, 28
e Stazio e io seguitavam la rota
che fé l'orbita sua con minore arco.

CANTO 32

The Earthly Paradise, continued: the procession to the Tree—the pilgrim's sleep—the gryphon gone—emblematic events: the eagle's blow to the chariot, the dragon, the chariot covered with feathers, the seven heads, the whore and the giant

1   So fixed and attentive were my eyes to slake their ten-year thirst, that all my other senses were extinguished.

4   And my eyes on this side and that had walls of non-concern—her holy smile so drew them to itself with its ancient net!—

7   when those goddesses forcibly turned my face to the left, for I heard from them a "Too fixedly!"

10   and the disposition that affects eyes just now struck by the sun left me without sight for a time.

13   But when my sight adapted itself again to the lesser object—and I say "lesser" with respect to the excess of the visible, from which I had been forcibly removed—

16   I saw the glorious army had turned on its right side and was going back with the sun and the seven flames at its head.

19   As a battle-line turns about under its shields to save itself, and must wheel with its standards, before it can all change direction:

22   so those warriors of the heavenly kingdom who came in front of the others all passed by us before the chariot turned its pole.

25   Then the ladies returned to its wheels, and the gryphon drew the blessed burden, but in such a way that none of his feathers were shaken loose.

28   The beautiful lady who had drawn me through the crossing and Statius and I were following the wheel that made its orbit with a smaller arc.

Sì passeggiando l'alta selva vòta,   31
colpa di quella ch'al serpente crese,
temprava i passi un'angelica nota.

    Forse in tre voli tanto spazio prese   34
disfrenata saetta quanto eramo
rimossi, quando Bëatrice scese.

    Io senti' mormorare a tutti "Adamo";   37
poi cerchiaro una pianta dispogliata
di foglie e d'altra fronda in ciascun ramo.

    La coma sua, che tanto si dilata   40
più quanto più è sù, fora da l'Indi
ne' boschi lor per altezza ammirata.

    "Beato se', grifon, che non discindi   43
col becco d'esto legno dolce al gusto,
poscia che mal si torce il ventre quindi."

    Così dintorno a l'albero robusto   46
gridaron li altri; e l'animal binato:
"Sì si conserva il seme d'ogne giusto."

    E vòlto al temo ch'elli avea tirato,   49
trasselo al piè de la vedova frasca
e quel di lei a lei lasciò legato.

    Come le nostre piante, quando casca   52
giù la gran luce mischiata con quella
che raggia dietro a la celeste lasca,

     turgide fansi, e poi si rinovella   55
di suo color ciascuna, pria che 'l sole
giunga li suoi corsier sotto altra stella:

     men che di rose e più che di vïole   58
colore aprendo, s'innovò la pianta,
che prima avea le ramora sì sole.

    Io non lo 'ntesi, né qui non si canta   61
l'inno che quella gente allor cantaro,
né la nota soffersi tutta quanta.

    S'io potessi ritrar come assonnaro   64
li occhi spietati udendo di Siringa—
li occhi a cui pur vegghiar costò sì caro—

     come pintor che con essempro pinga   67
disegnerei com' io m'addormentai,
ma qual vuol sia che l'assonnar ben finga.

31   Thus, pacing through the lofty wood, empty
by the fault of her who trusted the serpent, our
steps were tempered by an angelic song.

34   Perhaps an arrow loosed three times would
cover the space through which we had moved,
when Beatrice descended.

37   I heard all murmur: "Adam"; then they
encircled a tree stripped of leaves and all else in
every branch.

40   Its head, which spreads out more the more it
goes up, would be admired by the Hindus in
their woods for its height.

43   "Blessed are you, gryphon, who tear not with
your beak this tree so sweet to taste, since the
belly is ill twisted by it."

46   Thus around the massive tree the others
shouted, and the double animal: "Thus is
conserved the seed of all righteousness."

49   And, turning to the pole he had drawn, he
drew it to the foot of the widowed stem and, as
belonging to the tree, left it tethered there.

52   As our plants, when the great light comes
down mixed with that which shines next after
the heavenly carp,

55   swell and then renew their color, before the
sun yokes his horses beneath another star:

58   so, opening out color less than roses and
more than violets, that plant renewed itself,
whose branches earlier had been so bare.

61   I did not understand, nor is it sung back
here, the hymn those people sang then, nor did
I endure all its melody.

64   If I could portray how the cruel eyes fell
asleep when they heard of Syrinx—those eyes
whose wakefulness cost so dear—

67   like a painter painting from a model, I would
depict how I fell asleep; but he must be one
who imitates sleepiness well.

Però trascorro a quando mi svegliai,   70
e dico ch'un splendor mi squarciò 'l velo
del sonno, e un chiamar: "Surgi: che fai?"

Quali a veder de' fioretti del melo   73
che del suo pome li angeli fa ghiotti
e perpetüe nozze fa nel cielo,

Pietro e Giovanni e Iacopo, condotti   76
e vinti, ritornaro a la parola
da la qual furon maggior sonni rotti,

e videro scemata loro scuola   79
così di Moïsè come d'Elia,
e al maestro suo cangiata stola:

tal torna' io, e vidi quella pia   82
sovra me starsi che conducitrice
fu de' miei passi lungo 'l fiume pria.

E tutto in dubbio dissi: "Ov' è Beatrice?"   85
Ond' ella: "Vedi lei sotto la fronda
nova sedere in su la sua radice.

Vedi la compagnia che la circonda;   88
li altri dopo 'l grifon sen vanno suso
con più dolce canzone e più profonda."

E se più fu lo suo parlar diffuso   91
non so, però che già ne li occhi m'era
quella ch'ad altro intender m'avea chiuso.

Sola sedeasi in su la terra vera,   94
come guardia lasciata lì del plaustro
che legar vidi a la biforme fera.

In cerchio le facevan di sé claustro   97
le sette ninfe, con quei lumi in mano
che son sicuri d'Aquilone e d'Austro.

"Qui sarai tu poco tempo silvano;   100
e sarai meco sanza fine cive
di quella Roma onde Cristo è romano.

Però, in pro del mondo che mal vive,   103
al carro tieni or li occhi, e quel che vedi,
ritornato di là, fa che tu scrive."

70   Therefore I pass on to when I awoke, and I say that a brightness rent the veil of sleep for me, and a call: "Arise: what are you doing?"

73   As, when brought to see the budding flowers of that apple tree which makes the angels greedy for its fruit, holding perpetual wedding-feasts in Heaven,

76   Peter and John and James were overcome by them, and awoke again to the voice that had broken deeper sleep than theirs

79   and saw that their school was deprived both of Moses and of Elijah, and that their master had changed his stole:

82   so I awoke, and I saw the compassionate lady standing over me who had guided my steps along the river earlier.

85   And all in doubt I said: "Where is Beatrice?" And she: "Behold her under the new leaves, sitting upon their root.

88   See the company that surrounds her: the others are going back up, following the gryphon, with a sweeter and a deeper song."

91   And if her speech extended further, I do not know, for already my eyes were on the one who had barred me from perceiving anything else.

94   She was sitting solitary upon that true earth, as if left as a guard there for the wagon that I saw tethered by the beast of double form.

97   In a circle, the seven nymphs enclosed her, with those lights in their hands which are safe against Aquilon and Auster.

100   "Here you will be but briefly a dweller in the wood; and with me, without end, you will be a citizen of that Rome of which Christ is a Roman.

103   Therefore, for the good of the world that lives ill, keep your eyes now on the chariot, and what you see, returning back there, be sure that you write."

Così Beatrice; e io, che tutto ai piedi   106
d'i suoi comandamenti era divoto,
la mente e li occhi ov' ella volle diedi.

Non scese mai con sì veloce moto   109
foco di spessa nube quando piove
da quel confine che più va remoto,

   com' io vidi calar l'uccel di Giove   112
per l'alber giù, rompendo de la scorza,
non che d'i fiori e de le foglie nove,

   e ferì 'l carro di tutta sua forza,   115
ond' el piegò come nave in fortuna,
vinta da l'onda or da poggia, or da orza.

   Poscia vidi avventarsi ne la cuna   118
del trïunfal veiculo una volpe
che d'ogne pasto buon parea digiuna;

   ma, riprendendo lei di laide colpe,   121
la donna mia la volse in tanta futa
quanto sofferser l'ossa sanza polpe.

   Poscia per indi ond' era pria venuta,   124
l'aguglia vidi scender giù ne l'arca
del carro e lasciar lei di sé pennuta;

   e qual esce di cuor che si rammarca,   127
tal voce uscì del cielo, e cotal disse:
"O navicella mia, com' mal se' carca!"

   Poi parve a me che la terra s'aprisse   130
tr'ambo le ruote, e vidi uscirne un drago
che per lo carro sù la coda fisse;

   e come vespa che ritragge l'ago,   133
a sé traendo la coda maligna,
trasse del fondo, e gissen vago vago.

   Quel che rimase, come da gramigna   136
vivace terra, da la piuma—offerta
forse con intenzion sana e benigna—

   si ricoperse, e funne ricoperta   139
e l'una e l'altra rota e 'l temo, in tanto
che più tiene un sospir la bocca aperta.

106   Thus Beatrice; and I, all devoted to the very foot of her commandments, turned my mind and eyes where she willed.

109   Never has fire from a dense cloud descended with such swift motion, raining from the boundary that moves most remote from us,

112   as I saw Jove's bird fall through the tree, tearing its bark, not to mention its blossoms and new leaves,

115   and it struck the chariot with all its force, making it lurch like a ship in a tempest, overcome by the wave now to leeward, now to windward.

118   Then I saw hurling itself into the cradle of the triumphal vehicle a vixen that seemed to lack all good nourishment;

121   but, reproaching it for ugly sins, my lady turned it in such flight as its fleshless bones could achieve.

124   Then I saw the eagle descend from where it had earlier come, into the ark of the chariot, leaving it feathered like itself,

127   and a voice, like one that comes from a grieving heart, came forth from Heaven and said: "O my little ship, what an evil burden you have!"

130   Then it seemed to me that the earth opened between the two wheels, and I saw a dragon come forth and drive its tail up into the chariot;

133   and, like a wasp withdrawing its sting, pulling toward itself its evil tail, it tore off some of the base and went off aimlessly.

136   What remained, like fertile earth covering itself with grass, with the eagle's plumage—offered perhaps with healthy, benign intention—

139   covered itself all over, and both wheels and the pole were covered with it, in the time a sigh holds the mouth open longest.

Trasformato così, 'l dificio santo   142
mise fuor teste per le parti sue,
tre sovra 'l temo e una in ciascun canto.

Le prime eran cornute come bue,   145
ma le quattro un sol corno avean per fronte:
simile mostro visto ancor non fue.

Sicura, quasi rocca in alto monte,   148
seder sovresso una puttana sciolta
m'apparve con le ciglia intorno pronte;

e come perché non li fosse tolta,   151
vidi di costa a lei dritto un gigante,
e basciavansi insieme alcuna volta.

Ma perché l'occhio cupido e vagante   154
a me rivolse, quel feroce drudo
la flagellò dal capo infin le piante;

poi, di sospetto pieno e d'ira crudo,   157
disciolse il mostro e trassel per la selva
tanto che sol di lei mi fece scudo

a la puttana e a la nova belva.   160

142   Thus transformed, the holy structure put forth heads along its parts, three along the pole and one on each corner.

145   The first were horned like oxen, but the four had each a single horn on its forehead; such a monster has never yet been seen.

148   Confident as a fortress on a high mountain, I saw an ungirt whore sitting upon it, with brow ready to look about;

151   and, as if to prevent her being taken from him, I saw a giant standing beside her, and they kissed together from time to time.

154   But because she turned her greedy, wandering eye toward me, that ferocious lover whipped her from head to soles;

157   then, full of suspicion and harsh anger, he untied the monster and drew it into the wood so far that he made the wood alone a shield against me

160   for the whore and the strange beast.

1-12. So fixed and attentive . . . sight for a time: The wayfarer's vision, in which all his attention is concentrated (cf. 4.1-12), is dazzled and isolated from all else when he looks at Beatrice. For some commentators line 9 means that the theological virtues reproach a premature attempt to see in Beatrice providential designs; a more recent view is that he is fixated on Beatrice's "physical" beauty.

2. to slake their ten-year thirst: As the ideal date of the journey is 1300 (see *Inf.* 21.12-14, with note), the interval is calculated from Beatrice's death on June 8, 1290 (*VN* 29); for other echoes, see 30.34-36 and 115, with notes.

5-6. her holy smile . . . its ancient net: Love's net (and cf. 26.24) is a metaphor from vernacular love-poetry (cf. Dante's "Io son venuto," lines 23-24). Antici-pated in 31.138 (the "second beauty"), Beatrice's smile is her first in the poem (Gmelin); more await in the *Paradiso*. As a term of blessedness, her smile harks back to *VN* 19.20; "ancient" evokes both 30.48, where the pilgrim claims an inveterate love for Beatrice, and the reference to Eden at 30.52: lost by "ancient Eve," Beatrice's advent has recovered Eden for the wayfarer, as it is regained by all purified souls who achieve the return there. Recalling how Beatrice's beauty brought him to the right path (cf. 30.121-23, 31.49-54), the passage evokes the trajectory of Dante's love, but allowing that the fixation on her physical beauty must be transcended (31.52-57).

7-8. my face to the left: To the right side of the car, which stands in front of him, thus to the theological virtues (cf. 29.121-22).

14-15. I say lesser . . . excess of the visible: Line 15 ends with a technical phrase (cf. *multum sensibile*) referring to an overcharging of the sense in question: the procession is only relatively less dazzling than Beatrice's sun-like smile. See the note to 31.109-11; the complexity of the passage reflects the fusion of Beatrice as historical person with her role as personified abstraction.

16-27. I saw the glorious army . . . shaken: Now those leading the procession wheel about to the right, reversing from a westerly to an easterly direction, until the chariot too turns back, still pulled by the gryphon, whose unshaken feathers mark the immutability of the divine nature, represented by the upper, aquiline half (lines 26-27). For the easterly direction, see Luke 1.78 ("visitavit nos oriens ex alto" [the Orient from on high hath visited us]); Zach. 6.12. See Additional Note 15.

19-20. As a battle-line . . . wheel with its standards: Already called an "army," (line 16; and see, below, "warriors," line 22), the procession, appearing as the Church Militant, is compared to a troop executing a well-disciplined retreat ("to save itself," line 19) under upraised shields. Uses of "army" suggesting a disci-plined multitude were found at 8.22 and *Inf.* 18.28; see 29.79-84, 154, with notes.

24. the chariot . . . its pole: For this crucial part of the chariot, see lines 49-51, with note.

25. the ladies returned to its wheels: They had left them at 31.131.

28-30. The beautiful lady . . . with a smaller arc: Matelda and Statius, unmentioned since 28.145-48, accompany the pilgrim behind the right wheel of the chariot (see line 8, with note). For the arc, see *Par.* 12.112-14, with note; in his letter to the Cardinals (*Ep.* 11.5), Dante speaks of the "clear wheel-track" that Phaëthon failed to follow (see 29.118, with note).

31-36. Thus, pacing . . . Beatrice descended: This resumption of the walk with Matelda heralds a new stage of the procession (now recession) of the Ark (compare 28.1-6 and 29.7-12), marked by Beatrice's descent from the chariot, a gesture variously interpreted: Scartazzini thought it the homage to empire of the Church, after Romans 13.1: "Let every soul be subject to the higher powers." Others see a reference to the poverty of the apostolic Church. For the singing, cf. 30.93, with note.

37-60. I heard all murmur: Adam . . . so bare: After noting how Eve emptied Eden by heeding the serpent (lines 31-32), the procession recalls the guilt of Adam, and circles the tree Adam's sin has despoiled. Most commentators take this to be the Tree of the Knowledge of Good and Evil (Gen. 2.17, 3.1-8; *Purg.* 33.64-72). The Atonement is heralded by the tree's reacquisition of foliage after the gryphon ties to it the pole of the chariot (whose stave-and-crossbeam shape suggests the Cross). For interpretations of the tree, see 33.64-72, with notes, and Additional Note 15.

38. a tree stripped of leaves: Other Biblical trees Dante probably had in mind: Judges 9.8; Ezek. 17.24; 31.4-18. Dan. 2.20-22, 4.10-12, and 4.17 ("the tree high and strong, whose height reached to the skies"; see lines 43-46).

40-42. Its head . . . for its height: The tree, like its offshoots (22. 130-38 and 24. 112-17), is conical in shape, the branches becoming longer the higher on the tree they grow, suggesting a prohibition. This was also acknowledged as the shape of palm trees, though Dante mentions a fir tree at 22.133; other trees supposed represented in the Cross were the mulberry (see 27.37-39, with note), the apple tree (73-75, with note), and the terebinth. The great height of trees in India was proverbial (*Geor.* 2.122-24), but the exotic reference also appeals to traditional speculation on the distant location of Eden.

43-47. Blessed are you . . . the others shouted: The fourth blessing spoken during the procession, after the general *Beati* of 29.3, *Benedicta* of 29.85 and *Benedictus* of 30.19, acknowledging how Christ, the second Adam, by eschewing Adam's plucking of the tree, reverses the ancient curse (see 10.34-45, with notes):

a good example of the gestural symbolism of the poem. For words sweet on the palate but bitter in the belly compare Apoc. 10.8-11 and *Par.* 17.130-132.

48-51. Thus is conserved . . . tethered there: Lines 48-49 contain the only words spoken by the gryphon, paraphrasing Christ's words asking for baptism by John the Baptist (Matt. 3.15: "For so it becometh us to fulfill all justice"; cf. *Ep.* 7. 14). By attaching the cross-pole of the chariot to the tree, Christ submits to the justice that required his sacrifice to atone for Adam's sin (see *Par.* 7.85-120, with notes, Philippians 2.5-11).

49-50. he had drawn, he drew it: Compare lines 6, 28, and 158; see *Mon.* 3.3.12, where Dante cites Song of Songs 1.3: "This is what the Church says to the Spouse: 'Draw me after you.'" For other citations of the Song of Songs, and the nuptial meaning of the procession, see lines 73-75, 118-123, with notes.

51. as belonging to the tree: Literally, "that which was from it left tied to it." Many commentators take this to mean that the wood of the pole (thus, the Cross) derives from the Tree of the Knowledge of Good and Evil; others suggest that one of the branches of the Tree was used to tether the chariot, and that it is unsuitable for the Cross to be degraded as in lines 142-47. The former view reflects medieval legends (the story of the finding of the true Cross in the *Legenda aurea* by Jacobus a Varagine [c. 1265], and the *Estoire del Graal* of the Lancelot cycle, about 1225), which identified the wood of the Cross as from a tree going back to a cutting from the Tree of Knowledge, taken by Adam and Eve when expelled from Eden.

52-60. As our plants . . . had been so bare: The renovation of the tree is like the natural renewal of foliage in the spring: when the "the great light," the sun, joins its light with the influence of Aries (March-April), which follows Pisces, "the heavenly carp," plants swell in growth and regain the color of their flowers (again, Dante does not clearly distinguish between the zodiacal signs and constellations). For the chariot and horses of the sun, see *Purg.* 29.117-120, with note, *Aen.* 1.568: "equos . . . Sol iungit" [the sun . . . yokes his horses], and Additional Note 15.

55. swell: The detail is drawn from Vergil's poems on the natural world; see *Ecl.* 7.48: "Already the grapes swell on the drooping vine," and *Geor.* 1.315.

58-59. color less than roses and more than violets: Duller than rose-red but brighter than violet (almost black), this is crimson, vermilion, or reddish-purple, hues associated with Christ's shed blood (see 27.37-39, 29.130-132, of the virtues, and 29.148 for crimson). The hymn "Vexilla regis prodeunt" by Venantius Fortunatus, sung on Passion Sunday (see the note to *Inf.* 34.1), includes: "O tree beautiful and shining, adorned with the king's purple" (Raby 76-78).

61-90. I did not understand . . . with a sweeter and deeper song: The hymn that accompanies the regeneration of the tree puts the pilgrim to sleep (cf. Apoc. 1.17, 4.1, 5.9, and 14.3); when he awakes, the procession and the gryphon have returned to Heaven, accompanied by transcendent music, leaving Beatrice sitting on the root of the tree. Gmelin refers the pilgrim's nap to *Ep.* 1.9: "sopor tranquillitatis et pacis" [a slumber of calm and peace].

64-69. If I could portray . . . sleepiness well: Another nod to Ovid's tale of Argus; see 29.95-96, with note. Dante suggests the difficulty of narrating his own loss of consciousness as he hears the angelic music; Ovid's tale, Dronke 1986 notes, furnishes the "model" [*essemplo*] Dante claims not to have.

71. rent the veil of sleep for me: Compare *Inf.* 33.26-27, Ugolino's "the evil dream that rent the veil of the future for me"; see *Inter cantica* after Canto 33.

73-81. As, when brought to see . . . changed his stole: The simile evokes Christ's Transfiguration, in the presence of Peter, John, and James (Matt. 17.1-13): he shines like the sun in a garment whiter than snow, flanked by Moses and Elijah. The evocation is cued by line 72 ("Arise, what are you doing"), which echoes Matt. 17.7, "Surgite, nolite timere" [Arise, fear not], Christ's words waking the disciples after they have been overwhelmed (they "fall on their faces"). When they arise, he has resumed his normal appearance and is alone.

73-75. when brought to see . . . wedding-feasts in Heaven: Medieval commentary treated the Transfiguration as a foretaste of Christ in glory. For the feasts, see Apoc. 19.9: "Blessed are they who are called to the marriage supper of the Lamb" (cf. Ps. 67.25 and Wisdom 16.20; see *Conv.* 1.1.7; *Par.* 2..10-12, 24.1-6, with notes). For the apple, see Cant. 2.3: "as the apple tree among the trees of the woods, so is my beloved among the sons," of the Bridegroom.

76. Peter and John and James: These Apostles, after whom Dante's sons were named (of the probable firstborn, Giovanni, little is known; see the note to 24.43-48), will examine the wayfarer in Heaven; see *Par.* 24-26.

77-78. the voice that had broken deeper sleep: The reference is to Christ's resurrection of Lazarus (John 11.43-44: "When he had said these things, he cried with a loud voice: Lazarus, come forth. And presently he that had been dead came forth"). The pageant has now assembled a suite of allusions to Christ's life, including his Incarnation (cf. *Benedicta*, 29.85), baptism (32.48), entry into Jerusalem (29. 51, 30.19), Transfiguration (lines 73-81), Crucifixion (mystically, line 38), and Ascension (lines 89-90); the next canto refers to Christ's farewell to his disciples and his crucifixion (33.10-12, 33.6). In commentary, the Transfiguration is said to summarize salvation history in a single vision of glory (Moses the lawgiver, who died in the flesh; Elijah the prophet assumed to Heaven, and Christ who died and was resurrected); for another compendium of Christ's life (also at a climax of the poem), see *Purg.* 20-21, with notes, and see Additional Note 15.

82-85. I saw the compassionate lady . . . Where is Beatrice: A new stage of the pageant, again marked by the intervention of Matelda and a shift in the position of Beatrice. In terms of the allegory of Church history Dante deploys here, this phase corresponds to the apostolic Church after the Ascension.

94-96. She was sitting . . . beast of double form: Beatrice, said earlier (lines 86-87) to be beneath the new shade of the tree and sitting on its root ("that true earth" remains enigmatic), represents for some readers the Church in its correct apostolic poverty, for others the created Wisdom that should guide the Church in the absence of Christ, the gryphon. Beatrice is solitary, as Christ was said to be after the Transfiguration (Matt. 17.8), but also as the city of Jerusalem, bereft of the Redeemer, in the words of Lam. 1.1 as sung during Holy Week ("Quomodo sedet sola civitas" [How doth the city sit solitary]).

95. for the wagon: Dante uses here the Italian form of Lat. *plaustrum*, used in the Vulgate (2 Kings 6.3) for the chariot that bore the Ark of the Covenant. In Cantos 29-32, eight or nine different terms name the chariot: 29.107, *carro*; 30.16, divina *basterna*; 32.95, *plaustro*; 32.118, *veiculo*; 32.129, *navicella*; 32.142. *diflelo*; 158, *mostro*; 160, *belva*, 33.34, *vaso*; 33.39, "*mostro . . . preda.*"

97-99. In a circle . . . Aquilon and Auster: The seven nymphs are plausibly identified as the seven Virtues in their role as handmaidens of Wisdom, a well-known iconographic program (cf. Ambrogio Lorenzetti, Sala della Pace, Siena 1338). Other explanations have been proposed (Beatrice is theology based on the moral law; the root is Rome, basis of the secular and sacred powers; or she is humility; and so on.). The seven lights are probably those originally carried on the candelabra leading the procession (29. 43-45, with note), as these could carry lamps as well as candles (Tatlock 1945).

99. Aquilon and Auster: Dante uses the Latin names Aquilo and Auster, with recall of Cant. 4.16: "Arise, O north wind, and come, O south wind."

100-102. Here you will be . . . Christ is a Roman: As the commentators note, this is an explicit guarantee of the pilgrim's salvation; his brief time in Eden (allegorically, his mortal life, under the rule of the Empire—but all mortal life is brief) will be followed by life with Beatrice in the Heavenly City, here conspicuously not called the New Jerusalem (see Apoc. 21.2, and Additional Note 15), but Rome. For Christ's submission to Roman authority, see lines 48-51, *Mon.* 2.11 and *Par.* 7.46-48, with note. At *Conv.* 3.14.15 Dante speaks of the Heavenly City as the "celestial Athens."

103-105. for the good of the world . . . that you write: An echo of the command to John to write his Apocalypse (a passage emphasized by frequent illustration in manuscripts): "What thou seest, write in a book" (Apoc. 1.11; seee also 1.19. 10.4, 14.2, 19.9). The metaphor of the book (see Curtius 1954) is implicit through the cantos of Eden, influenced by passages in the Apocalypse (e.g. the "book of life" at 3.5, 13.8, 20.12; and the book of the future written "within and without," that is a scroll written on both sides, also an image of allegory, at 5.1-2.). In Giotto's Scrovegni Chapel the rolling up of the heavens "as a book [scroll]" (Apoc. 6.14) is illustrated. Again, see Additional Note 15.

106-107. to the very foot of her commandments: Typical of medieval high rhetorical style, as commentators observe, this metaphor also mirrors Beatrice's position at the foot of the tree of the moral law (see 33.71-72, with notes).

109-60. Never has fire . . . the strange beast: The last section displays to the wayfarer, distributed over seventeen tercets, seven tribulations of the Church from its foundation until its corruption in Dante's day. With one exception, descents of the eagle alternate with insidious attacks from internal enemies; the final two scenes are prophecies after the fact. The tribulations recall the seven plagues of the Apocalypse loosed by the opening of the seven seals; for these correspondences, again, see Additional Note 15.

The commentators note that Dante's prophecies are often close in content, manner, and sometimes detail to the writings of the Spiritual or Radical Franciscans, who adopted the doctrine of the three great ages of sacred history in the prophetic texts of Joachim of Fiore and his visions of tribulations afflicting a Church corrupted by wealth. But Dante's adherence to world empire as a possible agent of restoration (see lines 100-102 above) sharply distinguishes him from Joachimism, if not always from the Franciscan radicals; from these however he takes his distance elsewhere (see *Par.* 12.124-26, with note).

109-17. Never has fire . . . now to windward: The first affliction is the eagle of empire (or of an emperor, or emperors), "Jove's bird" (*Aen.* 1.394, in the omen of Aeneas' ships as birds) damaging the tree of the moral law, stripping away bark, leaves, and blossoms, and putting in peril the ark of the Church, compared to a ship on the high seas (see note to 116-17). The Church recognized ten major persecutions from Nero to Diocletian; see 9.28-30, 12.26-27, with notes.

109-11. Never has fire . . . most remote from us: The eagle descends with the impetus of lightning, understood in Dante's milieu as vapors that ignite through friction and explode out of the clouds toward the earth (cf. *Purg.* 5.37-40, 21.49-54, 28.97, with notes); the remote boundary is the upper limit of the sphere of air, which touches the sphere of fire (itself near that of the moon, see *Par.* 1.115-26).

113. fall through the tree, tearing its bark: Commentators recall Ezek. 17.3-4: "A large eagle with great wings . . . came to Libanus, and took away the marrow of the cedar."

116-17. like a ship in a tempest . . . now to windward: The ship and the chariot or wagon are often paired in medieval accounts of the Church, whose guises include both the Ark of the Covenant and the "ship of Peter" (*navicula Petri*, see *Par.* 11.119-20); for line 16 ("in a tempest") compare 6.72-76, with notes.

118-23. Then I saw hurling . . . bones could achieve: On the basis of Ezek. 13.4, "thy prophets are like foxes in the desert" and Cant. 2.15: "the little foxes have spoiled the vines," the vixen of the second affliction is usually identified as the heresies that troubled the early Church (e.g., Gnostic, Montanist, Sabellian, Arian, Donatist, Nestorian, and others). See Augustine's *Enarrationes in Psalmos* 80.9-10: "insidious foxes principally signify heretics, deceitful and fraudulent." The vixen's invasion of the "cradle" suggests an attack on fundamental doctrine; she is repulsed by Beatrice in her role as Theology. The leanness of the vixen may indicate the supposed weakness of heretical doctrines; but cf. the she-wolf of *Inf.* 1.49-51.

124-29. Then I saw . . . an evil burden you have: The second descent of the eagle, leaving the chariot feathered, represents the Donation of Constantine (see the notes to *Inf.* 19.115-17 and *Purg.* 27.94-96; *Mon.* 3.10-15), the supposed grant by the emperor Constantine of power in the West to Pope Sylvester I. With it came the Church's corrupting temporal power and wealth. The legend of the voice from Heaven, perhaps that of Saint Peter, lamenting the "evil burden" [literally, how badly freighted] of the Church, appears in the apocryphal Acts of Peter.

130-35. Then it seemed . . . went off aimlessly: The fourth and central affliction, closely echoing Apoc. 12.4: "his tail drew the third part of the stars of heaven, and did cast them to the earth," and 13.1 and 11, the ascent of the beasts ("et vidi aliam bestiam ascendentem de terra" [and I saw another beast, coming up out of the earth]), usually identified as the removal of one third of the faithful of Christendom, due to the growth of Islam (founded A.D. 611). This affliction is related to the second affliction in that Mohammed was regarded by Christians as schismatic and heretical (see the notes to *Inf.* 28.22-33). Pietro di Dante thinks of a more generic demon of cupidity. The dragon, whose tail works like that of a wasp, recalls the infernal Geryon.

136-41. What remained . . . mouth open longest: The fifth affliction, balancing the third, has been identified with later grants of property and privileges to the Church by kings Pepin and Charlemagne (A.D. 755 and 775). Dante maintained that the original Donation, although illegal ("for whoever embodies imperial authority is not allowed to divide the empire," *Mon.* 3.10.9) had been well meant (see *Par.* 6.1-3, 20.55-57, with notes). Opponents of the thesis that the chariot-pole represents the Cross object that it could not be thus corrupted; but Dante distinguishes between the pageant that returns to Heaven with Christ (the gryphon) and the Church remaining in the world.

142-47. Thus transformed . . . has never yet been seen: The seven heads with ten horns, attributes of the first beast of the Apocalypse (13.1: "And I saw a beast coming up out of the sea, having seven heads and ten horns"). In *Inf.* 19. 109-10, Dante refers to these heads and horns as the sacraments and command- ments; here these offspring or excrescences of the corrupt Church (see *Ep.* 11.15) have usually been taken as the capital sins corrected on the cornices of Purga- tory; two horns each for the grave social sins of pride, envy, and avarice (see 17.112-14), one each for the rest. After having just referred to the chariot, even covered with plumage, as a "holy structure" [*dificio santo*], Dante now calls the chariot a "monster" (lines 146, 158), "beast" (line 160), and "prey" (33.39), as well as "vessel" (33.34): once the Church breeds vices it loses not only its exter- nal form, but its very essence (see 33.34-36, with note). Even under the "veil of allegory," these are radical views.

148-60. Confident as a fortress . . . the strange beast: The seventh and final affliction, four tercets rather than two (or three, like the first), reiterates the de- scription of the great whore of Babylon (Apoc. 17.1): for saint John, Rome; for Dante, the papacy, which committed fornication with the kings of the earth. This affliction probably refers to the vicissitudes of the Church after the fic- tional date of the pilgrim's journey: most commentators agree that the "ungirt whore" denotes the papacy, perhaps Boniface VIII (1294-1303; see *Inf.* 19.52-54, with notes) or Clement V, and the giant the French monarchy, notably Philip the Fair (1300-1314); their amorous passages (parodies of earlier nuptial imagery: see *Inf.* 19.4, with note; and *Par.* 9.142), represent the secret talks between the Pope and the French crown that led to the invasion of Italy by Charles of Valois (1301; see 20.70-78, with notes); while the beating inflicted on the whore re- flects the humiliation of Boniface by Philip's henchmen in 1303 (see 20.85-90, with notes). The detachment of the Ark itself from the Tree and its removal to the wood is usually taken to refer to the removal of the papacy and curia from Rome in 1305 (they settled in Avignon in 1309, thus initiating the "Babylonian captivity" of the Church, which lasted, with an interruption, until 1378). Dante considered it a cosmic catastrophe; see *Ep.* 11.5, 13.

155-59. her greedy, wandering eye . . . a shield against me: The attempted seduction recalls aspects of 19.16-18 (see notes). No persuasive explanation has been offered for these hints of the pilgrim's involvement in the foretold degra- dation of the Church; see 30.130-32, 31.55-63, with notes. He may stand for Florence as an object of papal designs.

CANTO 33

"*Deus, venerunt gentes,*" alternando   1
or tre or quattro dolce salmodia,
le donne incominciaro, e lagrimando,

    e Bëatrice sospirosa e pia   4
quelle ascoltava, sì fatta che poco
più a la croce si cambiò Maria.

    Ma poi che l'altre vergini dier loco   7
a lei di dir, levata dritta in pè
rispuose, colorata come foco:

    "*Modicum, et non videbitis me;*   10
et iterum, sorelle mie dilette,
modicum, et vos videbitis me."

    Poi le si mise innanzi tutte e sette,   13
e dopo sé, solo accennando, mosse
me e la donna e 'l savio che ristette.

    Così sen giva, e non credo che fosse   16
lo decimo suo passo in terra posto,
quando con li occhi li occhi mi percosse,

    e con tranquillo aspetto: "Vien più tosto,"   19
mi disse, "tanto che, s'io parlo teco,
ad ascoltarmi tu sie ben disposto."

    Sì com' io fui com' io dovëa seco,   22
dissemi: "Frate, perché non t'attenti
a domandarmi omai venendo meco?"

    Come a color che troppo reverenti   25
dinanzi a suo maggior parlando sono,
che non traggon la voce viva ai denti,

    avvenne a me, che sanza intero suono   28
incominciai: "Madonna, mia bisogna
voi conoscete, e ciò ch'ad essa è buono."

CANTO 33

*The Earthly Paradise, continued: Beatrice's grief—her obscure prophecy
—the pilgrim to write what he has seen—loss of memory of his
unfaithfulness—noon—Eunoè*

1   *"Deus, venerunt gentes,"* alternating their sweet psalmody, now by three, now by four, the ladies began, weeping,

4   and Beatrice, sighing and grieving, listened to them, becoming such that Mary at the Cross changed but little more.

7   But when the other virgins made room for her to speak, coming to her feet erect she replied, in color like flame:

10   *"Modicum, et non videbitis me; et iterum,* my beloved sisters, *modicum, et vos videbitis me."*

13   Then she put all seven before her, and behind her, by beckoning only, she placed me and the lady and the sage who remained.

16   So she walked along, and I do not believe she had taken her tenth step upon the earth, when with her eyes she dazzled mine,

19   and with tranquil expression: "Come more quickly," she said to me, "so that, if I speak to you, you will be well placed to listen."

22   As soon as I was positioned with her, as I was bidden, she said to me: "Brother, why do you not venture to question me now, walking with me?"

25   As happens to those who, too reverent when speaking before their elders, do not bring their voices alive as far as their teeth:

28   so it was with me, for without full voice I began: "My lady, you know my need and what is good for it."

Ed ella a me: "Da tema e da vergogna   31
voglio che tu omai ti disviluppe,
sì che non parli più com' om che sogna.

Sappi che 'l vaso che 'l serpente ruppe   34
fu e non è; ma chi n'ha colpa, creda
che vendetta di Dio non teme suppe.

Non sarà tutto tempo sanza reda   37
l'aguglia che lasciò le penne al carro,
per che divenne mostro e poscia preda,

ch'io veggio certamente, e però il narro,   40
a darne tempo già stelle propinque,
secure d'ogn' intoppo e d'ogne sbarro,

nel quale un cinquecento diece e cinque,   43
messo di Dio, anciderà la fuia
con quel gigante che con lei delinque.

E forse che la mia narrazion, buia   46
qual Temi e Sfinge, men ti persuade,
perch' a lor modo lo 'ntelletto attuia,

ma tosto fier li fatti le Naiade   49
che solveranno questo enigma forte
sanza danno di pecore o di biade.

Tu nota, e sì come da me son porte   52
così queste parole segna a' vivi
del viver ch'è un correre a la morte.

E aggi a mente, quando tu le scrivi,   55
di non celar qual hai vista la pianta
ch'è or due volte dirubata quivi.

Qualunque ruba quella o quella schianta   58
con bestemmia di fatto offende a Dio,
che solo a l'uso suo la creò santa.

Per morder quella, in pena e in disio   61
cinquemilia anni e più l'anima prima
bramò colui che 'l morso in sé punio.

Dorme lo 'ngegno tuo, se non estima   64
per singular cagione essere eccelsa
lei tanto e sì travolta ne la cima.

E se stati non fossero acqua d'Elsa   67
li pensier vani intorno a la tua mente,
e 'l piacer loro un Piramo a la gelsa,

31   And she to me: "From fear and shame I would have you disentangle yourself now, so that you speak no more like one who dreams.

34   Know that the vessel the serpent broke was and is no more; but let him who is to blame believe that God's vengeance fears no sop.

37   Not for all time without heir will the eagle be who left his feathers on the chariot, whereby it became a monster and then booty,

40   for I see clearly, and therefore I relate it, stars already near, secure from all obstacle and all barrier, that will give us a time

43   in which a five hundred ten and five, messenger of God, will slay the thieving woman and the giant that transgresses with her.

46   And perhaps my narrative, dark like Themis and the Sphinx, persuades you less, because in their manner it blunts the intellect,

49   but soon events will be the Naiads who will solve this hard enigma, without loss of sheep or grain.

52   Do you take note and just as they come from me write these words to those who live the life that is a race to death.

55   And remember, when you write, not to hide what you have seen of the tree that has now been robbed twice here.

58   Whoever steals from it or tears it, with an act of blasphemy offends God, who created it holy, for his own use alone.

61   For having bitten of it, in punishment and desire five thousand years and more the first soul yearned for him who punished in himself that bite.

64   Your wit is asleep if it does not judge that a singular cause made the tree so tall and so inverted at the top.

67   And if your vain thoughts had not been water of Elsa around your mind, and their delight a Pyramus at the mulberry,

per tante circostanze solamente   70
la giustizia di Dio ne l'interdetto
conosceresti a l'arbor moralmente.

  Ma perch' io veggio te ne lo 'ntelletto   73
fatto di pietra e, impetrato, tinto
sì che t'abbaglia il lume del mio detto,

  voglio anco—e se non scritto, almen dipinto—   76
che 'l te ne porti dentro a te per quello
che si reca il bordon di palma cinto."

  E io: "Sì come cera da suggello,   79
che la figura impressa non trasmuta,
segnato è or da voi lo mio cervello.

  Ma perché tanto sovra mia veduta   82
vostra parola disïata vola,
che più la perde quanto più s'aiuta?"

  "Perché conoschi," disse, "quella scuola   85
c'hai seguitata, e veggi sua dottrina
come può seguitar la mia parola,

  e veggi vostra via da la divina   88
distar cotanto quanto si discorda
da terra il ciel che più alto festina."

  Ond' io rispuosi lei: "Non mi ricorda   91
ch'i' stranïasse me già mai da voi,
né honne coscïenza che rimorda."

  "E se tu ricordar non te ne puoi,"   94
sorridendo rispuose, "or ti rammenta
come bevesti di Letè ancoi;

  e se dal fummo foco s'argomenta,   97
cotesta oblivïon chiaro conchiude
colpa ne la tua voglia altrove attenta.

  Veramente oramai saranno nude   100
le mie parole quanto converrassi
quelle scovrire a la tua vista rude."

  E più corusco e con più lenti passi   103
teneva il sole il cerchio di merigge,
che qua e là, come li aspetti, fassi,

  quando s'affisser, sì come s'affigge   106
chi va dinanzi a gente per iscorta,
se trova novitate o sue vestigge,

70   through so many circumstances alone you
would have recognized the tree to be, in the moral
sense, God's justice in his prohibition.

73   But because I see that your intellect has turned
to stone and, petrified, is so darkened that the light
of what I say dazzles you,

76   I wish, too, that you carry it back within you—
and if not written, at least depicted—for the reason
that pilgrims bring their staffs back wreathed with
palms."

79   And I: "As wax is marked by the seal so that it
does not change the figure stamped on it, so my
brain has now been signed by you.

82   But why does your speech, so much desired, fly
so far above my sight that the more my sight
strives, the more it loses it?"

85   "So that you may know," she said, "the school
you have followed and see how well its teaching
can follow my words,

88   and may see that your way is as distant from
God's as the heaven that most hastens on high
differs from earth."

91   Therefore I answered her: "I do not recall that I
ever estranged myself from you, nor does my
conscience gnaw at me for that."

94   "And if you cannot recall that," smiling she
replied, "remember now how you have drunk
from Lethe this very day;

97   and if fire is betokened by smoke, this forgetting
clearly shows the guilt of having turned your desire
elsewhere.

100   Truly now my words shall be naked, as far as
shall be fitting to uncover them to your untutored
sight."

103   Both blazing brighter and with slower steps, the
sun held the circle of midday, which moves from
side to side with him who gazes,

106   when the seven ladies stopped, as one halts who
precedes people as their guide, if he finds
something new or signs of it,

le sette donne al fin d'un'ombra smorta,   109
qual sotto foglie verdi e rami nigri
sovra suoi freddi rivi l'alpe porta.

Dinanzi ad esse Ëufratès e Tigri   112
veder mi parve uscir d'una fontana
e, quasi amici, dipartirsi pigri.

"O luce, o gloria de la gente umana,   115
che acqua è questa che qui si dispiega
da un principio e sé da sé lontana?"

Per cotal priego detto mi fu: "Priega   118
Matelda che 'l ti dica." E qui rispuose,
come fa chi da colpa si dislega,

la bella donna: "Questo e altre cose   121
dette li son per me, e son sicura
che l'acqua di Letè non gliel nascose."

E Bëatrice: "Forse maggior cura,   124
che spesse volte la memoria priva,
fatt' ha la mente sua ne li occhi oscura.

Ma vedi Eünoè che là diriva: 127
menalo ad esso e, come tu se' usa,
la tramortita sua virtù ravviva."

Come anima gentil, che non fa scusa   130
ma fa sua voglia de la voglia altrui
tosto che è per segno fuor dischiusa:

così, poi che da essa preso fui,   133
la bella donna mossesi, e a Stazio
donnescamente disse: "Vien con lui."

S'io avessi, lettor, più lungo spazio   136
da scrivere, i' pur cantere' in parte
lo dolce ber che mai non m'avria sazio,

ma perché piene son tutte le carte   139
ordite a questa cantica seconda,
non mi lascia più ir lo fren de l'arte.

Io ritornai da la santissima onda   142
rifatto sì come piante novelle
rinovellate di novella fronda,

puro e disposto a salire a le stelle.   145

109 at the edge of a pale shadow, like that cast in the mountains under green branches and black boughs over cold streams.

112 In front of them I seemed to see Euphrates and Tigris issuing from a single fountain and, as if friends, separating slowly.

115 "O light, O glory of the human race, what water is this that spreads forth from one beginning and distances itself from itself?"

118 To this request came the answer: "Beg Matelda to tell you." And here the beautiful lady, like one who frees herself from blame,

121 replied: "This and other things I have told him, and I am sure the waters of Lethe have not hidden them from him."

124 And Beatrice: "Perhaps a greater care, which often robs the memory, has darkened the eyes of his mind.

127 But see Eunoè that pours forth there: lead him to it and, as is your custom, revive his languishing powers."

130 As a noble soul makes no excuse but makes another's will its own as soon as any sign discloses it:

133 so, having taken my hand, the beautiful lady moved, and to Statius with gracious command she said: "Come with him."

136 If, reader, I had more space to write, I would continue to sing in part the sweet drink that could never satiate me,

139 but because all the pages are filled that have been laid out for this second canticle, the bridle of art permits me to go no further.

142 I returned from the most holy wave refreshed, as new plants are renewed with new leaves,

145 pure and made ready to rise to the stars.

NOTES

1-12. *Deus venerunt gentes . . . et vos videbitis me*: Beatrice and the Virtues lament the separation of the Church from the tree; Beatrice rises to announce that she will disappear and later return, intimating the restoration of the Church. What is prophesied here is in part explained in the balance of the canto.

1-3. *Deus venerunt gentes* [God, the heathens have come] **. . . weeping:** The Latin words are the first hemistich of Psalm 78, grieving over the destruction of the Temple by Nebuchadnezzar in 587 B.C. (the event that gave rise to Lamentations); the psalm was used after 1187 for the liturgy mourning the loss of Jerusalem to Saladin. Seventh and last of the psalms cited in *Purgatorio*, this is the only one in Dante's poem to begin a canto (*Inf.* 34.1, the only other canto-beginning in Latin, parodies the verse of a hymn, while *Par.* 7.1-3 adapts liturgical Hebrew to Latin). Canto 33 is one of two cantos in the *Purgatorio* with a first line addressing God directly (the other is Canto 11), one of only three such in the poem (see *Par.* 7.1; but also cf. *Inf.* 25.1-3): The psalm begins: "O God, the heathens are come into thy inheritance, they have defiled thy holy temple, they have made Jerusalem as a place to keep fruit . . . we are become a reproach to our neighbors: a scorn and derision to them that are round about us . . . How long, O Lord, wilt thou be angry forever?" (1, 4-5). The "inheritance" is Israel itself (Deut. 32.9). During the Crusades, the "inheritance" was thought to be the Holy Land; for Dante it is the Church, torn from Rome by the French monarchy and the Gascon pope, Clement V. The passage hardly shows serene faith, as has been claimed; the crisis is apocalyptic.

4-6. Beatrice . . . Mary: Hearing of the defilement of the Church, Beatrice adopts the mournful attitude of Mary at the foot of the Cross, echoing the *planctus Mariae*, a dramatic genre appearing at Monte Cassino about 1100 and popularized by the *Stabat Mater* by the Franciscan Jacopone da Todi (c. 1290; a version attributed to Boniface VIII also exists); versions of the lament were also featured in meditations on the Passion in both prose and verse.

9. in color like flame: Ardent in her wrath; alternation of lament and indignation is traditional, going back to Ciceronian rhetoric and the Provençal *planh-sirventes* (see 6.106-26, 7.91-36, 14.124-26, with notes; *Par.* 27.28-36).

10-12. *Modicum . . . videbitis me*: Beatrice is quoting John 16.16-19: "A little while, and now you shall not see me; and again a little while, and you shall see me: because I go to the Father" (the entire sentence appears three times in the Gospel; the pronoun *vos* [you] is Dante's addition). The quotation of an enigmatic utterance made to the disciples introduces the obscure portents of this final canto of the *Purgatorio*, which mourns future vicissitudes of the Church but ends in joy; see the balance of the passage (John 16.20), which also links the Gospel with Psalm 78: "Amen Amen I say to you, that you shall lament and weep, but the world shall rejoice; and you shall be made sorrowful, but your sorrow shall be turned into joy."

13-21. Then she put all seven . . . well placed to listen: The walk through Eden resumes, with the Virtues walking in front, Beatrice next (midmost), and the pilgrim, Matelda, and Stazio behind: this reiterates in miniature the pageant of the Church in Canto 29 (Pasquazi 1966 calls the group a "saving remnant" of the Church), even as it marks a new stage of the events in Eden. In having the pilgrim catch up with her, Beatrice advances him but also puts him on the spot again.

16-17. do not believe she had taken her tenth step: Beatrice's steps have been interpreted to suggest a lapse of time (nine or ten years) bringing the events alluded to down to 1309-10 or 1314; some claim a reference to Beatrice's association with the number nine in the *Vita nova*. For the emphasis on intervals of time, see Additional Note 15.

23-30. Brother . . . what is good for it: Beatrice addresses the pilgrim in the familiar manner of Purgatory (cf. 13.94 and 26.115); her insistence on active attention recalls Virgil's (cf. 10.46). See also *Aen.* 6.51-53: "'Are you slow to vow and beg,' she said, 'Trojan Aeneas? Are you slow? But until then the great [mouths] of the terrified house will not open.'"

31-33. From fear and shame . . . like one who dreams: The words recall Hellmouth (*Inf.* 3.1-14), where Virgil invokes the pilgrim's fortitude ("Every cowardice must die here"). That the pilgrim is like a dreaming sleepwalker recalls the opening of the poem (*Inf.* 1.11, "so full of sleep was I"). What ensues confirms that he is being asked to make a leap of understanding.

34-102. Know that the vessel . . . untutored sight: After attacking his moral deviation in Canto 31, Beatrice now emphasizes the pilgrim's limited understanding before she discloses the future and explains the meaning of Eden; this testifies to the restriction on human desire signified by the inverted tree.

34-51. the vessel . . . loss of sheep or grain: Beatrice sees in the stars that celestial causes will soon bring an heir of the eagle (cf. 20.13-15, with notes): that is, of the empire or emperor (Constantine) who first corrupted the Church: this heir will destroy the whore (the corrupt Church) and the Antichrist (see Apoc. 17.8-11): probably the Avignon papacy and French monarchy. Clement V and Philip the Fair both died in 1314 (April 20 and November 29, respectively), a year Dante thought might mark a turn in European politics; see *Epistle* 11.

34-35. the vessel . . . was and is no more: Dante paraphrases the Apocalypse on the beast thrown into the lake of fire: (17.11: "And the beast which was, and is not . . . and goeth into destruction") to describe the corruption of the Church (see *Par.* 27.22-24). The word here for the Church, the "vessel," focuses on the

Ark itself, which traditionally held the manna, Aaron's rod, and the tablets of the Law; use of "vessel" also invokes the idea of the Ark as foreshadowing Mary's womb and the eucharistic tabernacle; see Additional Note 15.

36. God's vengeance fears no sop: The early commentators claim that this refers to a feudal custom: if a murderer ate a sop of bread on the grave of his victim, he might escape the vendetta; but no measures can deflect God's vengeance. For the poet's desire for vindication, see lines 1-3 above and 6.118-20, 20.13-15.

37. Not for all time without heir: Between the death of Frederick II in 1250 and the coronation of Henry VII in Rome in 1312 (not by the Pope, however), no Holy Roman Emperor had been crowned in Rome; thus Dante considered the post to have been vacant for over fifty years; this is an argument for seeing Henry VII, or another emperor, as the "heir" to the eagle (see 7.96 , with notes).

39. a monster and then booty: First the corrupting transformation, then the detachment of the Church from the tree, Christ's cross, by the Antichrist-figure, the French monarch. Grandgent observed that "booty" (*preda*) echoes the rhymes in 20.11-15, in the passage on the depredations of the Capetians (see also *Inf.* 31.115-17).

41. will give us a time: The glorified Beatrice can read in the stars the future Providence prepares; for the phrasing, see *Inf.* 8.128-30 and 9.814-85, with notes.

43. a five hundred ten and five: With the enigma of the *Veltro* [greyhound] (see the note to *Inf.* 1.101-105), which it complements, this code for the name of the eagle's heir ranks as one of the most challenging riddles in the poem. Rendering the number in Roman numerals (DXV), and applying the same decoding (*gematria*) that produces, in Apoc. 13.18, the number of the Antichrist (or, in commentaries, the giant) as 666, "the number/name [*numerus*]" of the emperor Nero, 515 has yielded no plausible name, though the technique suggests it must be that of an emperor (perhaps Henry VII) or other leader (such as Can Grande, lord of Verona and Dante's protector after 1316). Other interpreters (Sarolli 1971, Kaske 1974) point out that the Roman numerals, reversed (VXD), correspond to a monogram found in liturgical books, an abbreviation of "Vere dignum et iustum est" [It is truly fitting and just], the beginning of the Canon of the Mass: the initials V and D are joined by an X, read as Christ's initial or as a Cross (often bearing an image of Christ). Thus the number would refer to the Second Coming.

For Dante, however, the emperor represented Christ quite as much as the pope did; when expecting his advent, Dante had clothed him in christological terminology (the "lamb of God," *Ep.* 7.10; the bridegroom, *Ep.* 5.5; also 6.25). Beatrice makes it explicit that the difficulty is material to the meaning here; compare *Par.* 17.31-33, with notes, and *Aen.* 6.98-100: "the Cumaean Sybil sings the fearsome windings, and she echoes in her cave, wrapping true things with dark ones."

44-45. will slay the thieving woman and the giant: In the Apocalypse, Babylon, the "great whore," is destroyed (18.2), the Antichrist (beast) is thrown into the pit of fire (19.20), and Satan, the dragon, is bound and placed in the abyss (20.2-3).

46-48. And perhaps my narrative . . . it blunts the intellect: The enigma itself darkens the intellect of its auditor and is thus a form of interdict, like the riddles of Themis and the Sphinx. Themis, a consort of Jove and lawgiver of archaic times, proposed to Deucalion and Pyrrha, pious survivors of the Deluge, that they should throw "the bones of their mother" (rocks, earth's bones) behind them to restore the human race (*Met.* 1.375-415); the Sphinx (*Theb.* 1.66-67) proposed the riddle of a creature who walks first with four, then two and finally three legs. Both riddles concern human origin and thus nature, appropriate to cantos that recall the sin of Adam and the shortcomings of the pilgrim.

49-51. but soon events . . . without loss of sheep or grain: Ghisalberti 1932 showed that Dante read, in his text of *Met.* 7.759-65, *Naiades*, instead of *Laiades* [son of Laius, i.e., Oedipus], for the solver of the riddle of the Sphinx. Thus Dante compares future events, which alone will disclose the heir to the eagle, to prophesying water-nymphs (Naiads), with which, as Ghisalberti showed, medieval glosses tried to make sense of the corrupted passage. The same glosses explain line 51, relating how Themis, enraged that the Naiads had solved a riddle she could not (in other versions, that her own riddle is solved), summons a beast (*belva*) to destroy livestock and crops. The riddle names a beast that cannot be caught and a hound (Laelaps) that cannot be outrun, but when the beast and the hound are turned to stone by the gods, the riddle is solved by the event itself. See *Inf.* 20.85-87, 23.97-99, 24.46-48, with notes.

Isidore observes that *enigma* is allegory so obscure it must be decoded for the reader; similarly, the contingent events of the future are so difficult to foresee that only their unfolding in time will permit the pilgrim to understand Beatrice's riddle—in short, no human mind unaided by revelation can understand it at all; see the note to 31.118-26, *Inf.* 10.100-102, with note).

52-102. Do you take note . . . your untutored sight: Beatrice now explains the meaning of the reverse cone-shaped tree (see 32.37-42, with notes), again chiding the pilgrim for an intelligence dulled by empty pleasures (67-69) and intellectual errors (85-87); though her words mark his memory, he does not understand them (79-84); he also forgets his truancy (91-93), which, Beatrice says, confirms his passage of the river that deletes memory of sin (94-99). Even while charging the wayfarer with the duty of recording his vision, Beatrice recalls his shortcomings of memory, apprehension, and understanding (see 25.75 and note).

52-54. Do you take note . . . a race to death: For the charge to write, cf. 24.52-54, 32.103-105 and *Par.* 17.127-32, with notes; with the charge in 32.103-105 (see notes), this is the explicit institution of the protagonist as God's scribe, and as a prophet. The "race to death" is Augustine's description of human life (*City of God*, 11.21), appropriate to a procession of the Church through time, unfolding sacred history. Some readers find the reference to mutability forced, but this canto, like the pageant of Eden as a whole, stages the disorienting encounter of the human with the eternal (see Additional Note 15).

56-58. the tree . . . or tears it: Exactly which "robberies" of the tree are meant has been much discussed; many readers leave the matter vague. Although Adam's original theft (32.37) is the remote cause of all harm to the tree, it is probably not referred to here (see 61-63). Leading candidates for the robbers are the dragon (who removes a portion of the chariot bottom) and the giant (who removes the chariot); for the tearing, the first descent of the eagle is likely, but the Donation of Constantine, which divided the Empire (see *Mon.* 3.10.5-6), has also been suggested as both a robbery and a laceration (Nardi 1944); in this sense "tears" would also describe the effect of the dragon, and might be Dante's prophetic intuition of the ultimate effect of the captivity of the Church in Avignon: the Great Schism of 1381-1409, when two (and sometimes three) popes reigned.

58-63. Whoever steals . . . punished in himself that bite: Adam's eating of the tree led to his exile in Hell (see *Inf.* 4.55; *Purg.* 1.40-41) until freed by Christ's sacrifice; Dante here uses the calculation of Eusebius of Caesarea, 5232 years, as the interval between the Fall and the Crucifixion.

59-60. with an act of blasphemy . . . his own use alone: Foster 1957 emphasizes that Adam's transgression was not only disobedience but injustice: wishing to become like a god, Adam exceeded the limit set for him by the tree, which represents "iustitiam propter se servatam" [justice observed for its own sake] (Anselm, in Kaske 1971). Seizing the fruit was "blasphemy" not in words but in act (see Augustine); "use" suggests full enjoyment of a wisdom reserved to God alone.

64-72. Your wit is asleep . . . God's justice in his prohibition: The height and shape of the tree visibly discourage climbing: its fruit cannot be plucked, nor its knowledge approached by man. Thus the "moral" sense of the tree, in the fourfold scheme of literary interpretation that Dante sets out in *Conv.* 2.1, is prohibition itself, the basis of God's law: "Thou shalt not." The literal sense is the actual tree of Genesis, the "allegorical" sense its provision of the wood for the Cross (and for the chariot-pole of the Church).

67-75. And if your vain thoughts . . . what I say dazzles you: The calcium-carbonate-rich waters of the Elsa river in Tuscany coat immersed objects with a mineral crust; Pyramus' blood stained dark red the white fruit of the mulberry tree (Ovid, *Met.* 4.162-66; see Additional Note 13, *Inf.* 34.39-45). Similarly, Beatrice's wisdom is lost on the pilgrim, whose mind is hard (will not take impressions) and darkened (will not receive light). The terms echo Aristotle's discussion of memory, best if neither too hard to accept impressions nor too soft to retain them; see lines 79-81. For petrifaction, cf. *Inf.* 9.52-57, 33.57, with notes.

76-78. I wish, too . . . wreathed with palms: If unable to relate what he has seen in words, the pilgrim is to return with a visible token (*dipinto* [painted]) proving that he has witnessed the pageant of Eden, like a pilgrim who returns from the Holy Land with his staff wreathed with palm fronds; other such devices were the vernicles (*veroniche*) of Romers and the scallop-shells of Compostela pilgrims. See *VN* 40; *Par.* 31.104, with notes.

79-84. As wax is marked . . . the more it loses it: The account of memory, both verbal and visual, as impressions on a wax tablet is ancient; see Plato, *Theaetetus* 191d-196a. Dante is claiming that Beatrice's words mark his mind, but that their meaning goes over his head.

85-90. So that you may know . . . differs from earth: The obtuseness of the pilgrim shows his inadequate preparation: God's ways are as distant from human as the Primum Mobile, the first movable and moving sphere, is from the immobile earth: see Is. 55.9: "For as the heavens are exalted above the earth, so are my ways exalted above your ways, and my thoughts above your thoughts." What "school" Dante refers to here is much debated (cf. *Inf.* 4.94, *Purg.* 24.58-60), just as the precise nature of his transgression with the *pargoletta* remains unclear (31.59; see Sturm-Maddox 1987, Durling/Martinez 1990, Scott 1991). Views arguing that a specific intellectual error is meant, such as that supposedly represented by Lady Philosophy in the *Convivio*, or Averroism (see 25.63 and note), seem too restrictive: as the pilgrim's limitations are associated with universal history and the Fall of Adam, Beatrice may be noting the pilgrim's share in Adamic arrogance—what the height and shape of the tree expressly forbid.

91-102. I do not recall . . . your untutored sight: The final blow to the pilgrim is his failure to remember betraying Beatrice's memory; he suffers no "remorse of conscience." Beatrice claims that the erasure of his memory by Lethean waters is proof that it recorded sinful acts, including his apostasy. Strictly speaking, to deduce from their present oblivion that past sins existed is fallacious: the lack of memory of sin might indicate the absence of sin, not the cancellation of one.

97. if fire is betokened by smoke: See Augustine, *On Christian Doctrine* 2.1 (and the note to lines 106-108): "For a sign is a thing which, over and above the impression it makes on the senses, causes something else to come into the mind as a consequence of itself . . . when we see smoke, we know there is a fire beneath . . ."

100-101. my words shall be naked: Cf. *VN* 12.3: " tempus est ut pretermictantur simulacra nostras" [it is time to set aside our deceptions]; see also John 16. 25, in a passage already used in this canto: "These things I have spoken to you in proverbs. The hour cometh, when I will no more speak to you in proverbs, but will shew you plainly of the Father"; and Num. 12.6-8, God speaking to Miriam and Aaron: "Hear my words: if there be among you a prophet of the Lord, I will appear to him in a vision, or I will speak to him in a dream. But it is not so with my servant Moses, who is most faithful in all my house: for I speak to him mouth to mouth: and plainly, and not by riddles and figures doth he see the Lord." See 32.71 and note.

103-45. Both blazing brighter . . . to rise to the stars: Beatrice, the Virtues, and Matelda, along with Statius and the pilgrim, all reach the source of the rivers of Purgatory; finally Statius and the pilgrim are bathed in the second river. As the sun reaches the meridian at noon, the action that began as the pilgrim entered Eden with the rising sun on his brow (27.133) is now complete (for the positions of the sun, cf. 32.18, with notes). The action of the poem began on the previous Thursday (it is now Wednesday, *Mercurii dies,* thus the seventh day, appropriate both to the regaining of Eden and the flight to Heaven); the six cantos spent in Eden correspond to the six hours spent there by Adam (*Par.* 26.139-42).

104-105. the sun held the circle . . . with him who gazes: The last temporal reference in Purgatory places the sun on the meridian, where it seems to move slowly because at the midpoint of its course (the meridian is said to move because it depends on the longitude of the observer). Once the pilgrim leaves the earth the relevance of the luminaries for telling time ceases; see *Par.* 1.37-48, with notes.

106-108. as one halts . . . or signs of it: See Augustine, *On Christian Doctrine,* 2.1: "as when we see a footprint [*vestigium*], we conclude that an animal whose footprint this is has passsed by."

109-11. at the edge . . . over cold streams: The landscape of Eden, wooded and shaded (see 28.31-33, 29.17), is characteristic of the mountainous and rural Casentino (where Dante was in 1311, probably working on the *Purgatorio*; Migliorini-Fissi 1989); the *Purgatorio* again echoes a natural mountainous landscape.

112. Euphrates and Tigris: Two of the traditional four rivers of Eden (in Gen. 2.11-14 the four are Gihon, Phison, Tigris and Euphrates; Augustine identified the former pair with the Nile and the Ganges: *De Genesi ad litteram* 1.160). For Augustine the single fountain from which they flow is the fount of Wisdom. The commentators recall *Consolation* 5 m. 1, 3-4: " The Tigris and Euphrates flow from the one fount but soon disjoin their forking streams." Cf. 28.121-32.

115-26. light, O glory . . . the eyes of his mind: The wayfarer's failings again underlined: he has forgotten Matelda's account of the rivers (28.121-33). The "greater care" that caused his forgetfulness is not the result of Lethe, which removes memory of sin, but the chastisement in Cantos 30-31, or the vicissitudes of the Church he has witnessed.

119. Matelda: Beatrice casually supplies the name of the lady first seen at 28.40; see the notes to 28.38-148, and 28.49-51.

127. But see Eunoè: The second river restores memory of good actions; for its name, see 28.130-31, and note.

134-35. to Statius . . . Come with him: Long ignored, Statius is once again mentioned (see line 15, "the sage who remained"), now by name. There may be a distant echo of Christ's words to the blest at the Last Judgment, quoted by the last angel (see 27.58, with note).

136-41. If, reader . . . to go no further: With the pilgrim's taste of Eunoè, his darkness of mind yields to ineffable joy (for Adam's bitter taste of the tree, see 32.45 and note). His limitations coincide with the boundaries of the poem, which impose a "bridle" parallel to the discipline imposed by the mountain on its tenants (see 13.39-40, 16.92-93, with notes): thus the poem's form channels the dynamism of its content—ultimately, desire (see 17.91-93, 18.19-21, with notes)— that might run astray and fail of its true object (see 16.85-96, 18.34-39, with notes). For Dante's ideas of poetic form, see Durling/Martinez 1990.

139-40. all the pages . . . this second canticle: The pre-established number of ruled pages (see 26.64 and note) has been filled; there is also a weaving metaphor, for ruled pages are like warp awaiting their weft (see 12.43-45 and note). Using for the first time the term *cantica* to designate each of the poem's three parts (cf. *Inf.* 20. 3, with note), Dante adopts the scribal convention of marking material limits to the poem: the *Inferno* is 4,720 lines long, the *Purgatorio* 4,755, and the *Paradiso* 4,758; no cantos are shorter than 115 lines, none longer than 160; the vast majority have between 139 and 154 lines (these lengths compare to those of the longer Italian canzoni of the period). The *terza rima* runs throughout (Freccero 1986). The poem's formal discipline expresses the physical, moral, and intellectual integrity of the poem; container is suited to thing contained. See 26.64-65, 115-17, with notes; cf. Apoc. 22.18-19.

138. sweet drink: Drinking from a fountain is a traditional image for salvation attained; cf. 21.1-3. Cf. Augustine's lamented Nebridius, *Confessions* 9.3: "his spiritual mouth [is] at your fountain and drinks of wisdom, as much as he can, in accord with his desire, endlessly happy." Nebridius is also said to be "on the mountain of God, a fat mountain" (Ps. 67.16) and "in Abraham's bosom" (Luke 16.23).

142-45. I returned . . . to rise to the stars: Concluding with the same word as the *Inferno* (discipline again, as above), the *Purgatorio*'s last lines renew the pilgrim as the tree was renewed (32.59), echoing the rebirth of the rush when plucked (1.134-36). In Purgatory, hope springs anew (cf. 3.135, 8.28-30, with notes). The insistence on the prefix *re-* and on the newness of the leaves is retained in translation, but English cannot render the richness of the double consonants in the Italian, six in four lines (*-ss, -tt, -ll, -ll, -ll*), or how *new* and *renew* weave a wreath of sound that closes the *cantica*.

Inter cantica (Cantos 29, 32-33). Dante's invocation of the "sacrosanct virgins" and appeal to the springs of Helicon (29.37-42) parallel his appeal to the Muses "who helped Amphion enclose Thebes" (*Inf.* 32.7-11). The Muses' fount, as later the two rivers of Purgatory (33.111-12), contrasts with the icecap of Cocytus compared to the icebound Danube and Don (32.25-26). The principal action of these cantos is the procession and return of the pageant, led by the seven candelabra (29. 43), evoking Roman triumphs (29.115) and Christ's entry into Jerusalem (29.50); similarly, the view of Satan in *Inferno* begins with the processional "Vexilla regis" (like *Inf.* 34.1, 33.1 is a Latin verse). The "procession" of cold from Satan's wings congeals the floor of Hell (34.36, 52) and contrasts with the dynamism of the pageant itself, which represents the Church, led by the fire of the Holy Spirit, proceeding through time (see Additional Note 15).

The conclusions both to *Inferno* and *Purgatorio* question the pilgrim's vision, both physical and intellectual: in Hell, after taking the giants for towers (31.20), he is instructed "how sense is deceived by distance" (31.26); later, darkness deceives him into taking Lucifer for a land-mill (34.4-9). In Purgatory distant candelabra appear to be trees (29.43-47) as the pilgrim is again deceived by distance (29.44-45, "the long tract of air"); finally his intellectual vision will prove obtuse before Beatrice's prophecies (33.102, "your untutored sight"), in part because his mind is "darkened" by preoccupation over his failings (33.126). The limitations of sight are juxtaposed with the disclosures in these cantos: both at *Inferno* 33.27 and at *Purg.* 32.71 the expression "rent the veil" (of the future, in Hell; of sleep, in Purgatory) alludes to the violence of the invasion of time by eternity, and, like Beatrice's words, the pilgrim's purgation requires "unwrapping" earthly cares so as to clarify perception (cf. "ti disviluppe," 33.32); by contrast, traitors in Hell are blinded by icy visors the pilgrim refuses to clear (33.98, 148-149); the "veil over their hearts" (2 Cor. 3.13-16) is material as well as spiritual.

Most striking is how the pageant revises the dark spectacle of Lucifer: his three faces on one head (34.38); six weeping eyes (34.53) and especially his colors off-white, vermilion, and black (34.39-45), are signs of his parodic representation of the Trinity (see note to *Inf.* 34.28-67), and of the Crucifixion of Christ (see notes to *Inf.* 34.39-45; 70-93 and *Inferno* Additional Note 16; thus the *Vexilla regis* that begins Canto 34). In *Purgatorio* these details are re-evoked in the three eyes of Prudence (29.132) and in the reference to Pyramus and the mulberry (33.65), its white fruit stained red and black by Pyramus' blood; most strikingly with the gold, white, and red of the gryphon (29.113-14), which, as Christ, opposes Satan (both are partly birds, cf. 34.47, 29.113). That the gryphon's head is gold, while one of Satan's is black, reiterates a scriptural image for the degradation of

Jerusalem ("How is the gold become dim [obscuratus], the finest color is changed" (Lam. 4.1) which medieval exegetes applied to the falling away of the Church from its head, Christ; while Satan's darkening heads parody Christ's beauty, devastated on the Cross, recalled in the devotional literature of popular Franciscan piety (Bestul 1996)—especially his ruddy and white complexion darkened by the lividity of bruises and bloody wounds (Ubertino da Casale 1961). A related set of parallels concerns Satan, first misperceived as a *dificio* or "edifice" (34.7), and the Ark itself, a *dificio santo* (32.142) that degenerates into a "monster" and "beast" (32.160).

How the fall of Satan established the island of Purgatory is spelled out at *Inferno* 34.112-26 (see note to 106-26), including mention of the Crucifixion (34.112-15), where the hemisphere of water is *contraposto* to that of land. In Eden this contraposition is evoked most obviously with the echo of Adam's fall and Christ's redemption (acted out at 32.37-51, explictly mentioned at 33.61-63) but also in subtler ways: in a consummation of the poem's bihemispheric vision, Eden becomes a virtual Jerusalem like the real one at its antipodes: Mount Zion in Jerusalem was the destination of the Ark of the Covenant (see 32.125, 10.56, with notes), and it is the Jerusalem temple that is defiled in Psalm 78 (33.1); Jerusalem is the site whence pilgrims return wreathed with palms (33.78), and Jerusalem is the city Christ enters to undergo the Passion (29.51, 30.19, with notes): it is of course the focus of the version of Christ's life deployed over the course of the pageant (see Additional Note 15), and the new Jerusalem, adorned as a bride, is the city John sees descending from Heaven in Apoc. 21.1-2. Yet once these associations are assessed, 33.102 tells us that Heaven is the Rome of which Christ is Roman, and it is not the Jerusalem temple that Beatrice laments in 33.1-7, but the "widowed" papal city (cf. 6.112-13 and note). The pageant and its sequel represent not the fate of Jerusalem, but of Rome; Rome will be the chief model for Dante's Empyrean (see *Par.* 31.31-42, 103-108, with notes).

Vergili Ecloga IV

Sicelides Musae, paulo maiora canamus;
non omnis arbusta iuvant humilesque myricae;
si canimus silvas, silvae sint consule dignae.
Ultima Cumaei venit iam carminis aetas
magnus ab integro saeclorum nascitur ordo.   5
iam redit et Virgo, redeunt Saturnia regna,
iam nova progenies caelo demittitur alto.
tu modo nascenti puero, quo ferrea primum
desinet ac toto surget gens aurea mundo,
casta fave, Lucina: tuus iam regnat Apollo.   10
teque adeo decus hoc aevi, te consule inibit,
Pollio, et incipient magni procedere menses;
te duce, si qua manent sceleris vestigia nostri,
inrita perpetua solvent formidine terras.
ille deum vitam accipiet divisque videbit   15
permixtos heroas et ipse videbitur illis,
pacatumque reget patriis virtutibus orbem.
At tibi prima, puer, nullo munuscula cultu
errantis hederas passim cum baccare tellus
mixtaque ridenti colocasia fundet acantho.   20
ipsae lacte domum referent distenta capellae
ubera, nec magnos metuent armenta leones;
ipsa tibi blandos fundent cunabula flores,
occidet et serpens, et fallax herba veneni
occidet; Assyrium vulgo nascetur amomum.   25
At simul heroum laudes et facta parentis
iam legere et quae sit poteris cognoscere virtus,
molli paulatim flavescet campus arista
incultisque rubens pendebit sentibus uva

Vergil, Eclogue IV

Sicilian Muses, let us sing for a while of greater things;
not all are pleased by shrubs and the humble tamarisk:
if we sing of woods, let them be woods worthy of a Consul.
    The last age of Cumaean song has now come;
the great cycle of the ages is born anew.   5
Now the Virgin returns, Saturn's reign returns,
now a new offspring is being sent down from high heaven.
The boy soon to be born, with whom at last the iron
shall cease and a golden people arise through all the world:
O chaste Lucina, favor him; your Apollo now reigns.   10
While you are Consul this glorious age shall begin—you,
Pollio—and the great months begin to march forth;
you leading, if any vestiges of our guilt remain,
dissolved they shall free earth from its perpetual fear.
He will accept the life of the gods and see the heroes   15
mingling with the gods, himself be seen by them;
and with his father's virtues he will rule the peaceful globe.
    But for you, little boy, its first gifts without tilling
the ground will pour forth: wandering ivy with scattered
berries and the lotus mixed with laughing acanthus.   20
By themselves the she-goats will bring home their milk-
swollen udders, and the flocks will not fear the great lions.
Your very cradle will pour forth soft flowers,
the serpent also shall die, and the deceitful poison-plant
shall die; everywhere Assyrian balm will breed.   25
    But as soon as you come to read the praises of heroes
and your father's deeds, and you learn what manhood is,
then the field, untilled, will grow blond with tender grain,
on untended vines the grape will hang reddening,

et durae quercus sudabunt roscida mella.   30
pauca tamen suberunt priscae vestigia fraudis,
quae temptare Thetim ratibus, quae cingere muros
oppida, quae iubeant telluri infindere sulcos.
alter erit tum Typhis et altera quae vehat Argo
delectos heroas; erunt etiam altera bella   35
atque iterum ad Troiam magnus mittetur Achilles.
    Hinc, ubi iam firmata virum te fecerit aetas,
cedet et ipse mari vector, nec nautica pinus
mutabit merces; omnis feret omnia tellus.
non rastros patietur humus, non vinea falcem;   40
robustus quoque iam tauris iuga solvet arator.
nec varios discet mentiri lana colores,
ipse sed in pratis aries iam suave rubenti
murice, iam croceo mutabit vellera luto;
sponte sua sandyx pascentis vestiet agnos.   45
    "Talia saecla" suis dixerunt "currite" fusis
concordes stabili fatorum numine Parcae.
adgredere o magnos (aderit iam tempus) honores,
cara deum suboles, magnum Iovis incrementum!
aspice convexo nutantem pondere mundum,   50
terrasque tractusque maris caelumque profundum:
aspice, venturo laetentur ut omnia saeclo!
o mihi tum longae maneat pars ultima vitae,
spiritus et quantum sat erit tua dicere facta!
non me carminibus vincet nec Thracius Orpheus   55
nec Linus, huic mater quamvis atque huic pater adsit,
Orphei Calliopa, Lino formosus Apollo.
Pan etiam, Arcadia mecum si iudice certet,
Pan etiam Arcadia dicat se iudice victum.
    Incipe, parve puer, risu cognoscere matrem   60
(matri longa decem tulerunt fastidia menses)
incipe, parve puer: qui non risere parenti,
nec deus hunc mensa, dea nec dignata cubili est.

and the rugged oaks will sweat with honey, like dew.   30
Still there will lurk some few vestiges of original fraud
that will drive men to probe Thetys with ships, to gird
fortresses with walls, to cut furrows in the earth.
There will be another Tiphys and another Argo, to
convey the chosen heroes; there will be other wars,   35
and once more great Achilles will be sent to Troy.

    Thereafter, when strong maturity has made you a man
at last, the sailor himself will quit the sea, the pine vessel no
longer exchange its wares; every land will bear every thing.
The soil will feel the plow no more, nor the vine the pruning
       hook,   40
the sturdy plowman now will release the bulls, too, from the yoke.
Nor will the wool any longer learn deceits of varied color,
instead the ram himself in the meadows now to soft ruddy
purple will change his fleece, now to saffron yellow;
of its own accord vermilion will clothe the pasturing lambs.   45

    "Run through such ages," the Sisters bade
their spindles, united in the fixed power of Fate.
O step forward to your great honors (the time is now at hand),
beloved offspring of the gods, great increment of Jove!
Behold the world trembling with its ponderous sphere,   50
the lands, the expanses of the sea, and the deep heaven:
behold how all things rejoice at the coming age!
Oh for me let there be a last portion of long life
and breath enough to relate your deeds:
not even Thracian Orpheus will conquer me in song,   55
not Linus, though the mother of the one, the father of the other,
though Calliope help Orpheus, though beauteous Apollo help
       Linus.
Even Pan, should he compete with me with Arcadia judging,
even Pan would declare himself surpassed, though Arcadia judge.

    Begin, little boy, to recognize your mother with a   60
laugh (to your mother the ten months brought long
weariness), begin, little boy: those who have not laughed
to their parent no god welcomes to his table, no goddess
       to her bed.

                    (Translated by R.M.D.)

Pastorella di Guido Cavalcanti

In un boschetto trova' pastorella   1
più che la stella—bella, al mi' parere.

Cavelli avea biondetti e ricciutelli   3
e gli occhi pien' d'amor, cera rostata;
  con sua verghetta pastorav' agnelli;
discalza, di rugiada era bagnata;
  cantava come fosse 'namorata:
er' adornata—di tutto piacere.

D'amor la saluta' imantenente   9
e domandai s'avesse compagnia;
  ed ella mi rispose dolzemente
che sola sola per lo bosco gia,
  e disse: "Sacci, quando l'augel pia,
allor disia—'l me' cor drudo avere."

Po' che mi disse di sua condizione   15
e per lo bosco augelli audio cantare,
  fra me stesso diss' i': "Or è stagione
di questa pastorella gio' pigliarc."
  Merzé le chiesi sol che di basciare
ed abracciar,—se le fosse 'n volere.

Per man mi prese d'amorosa voglia   21
e disse che donato m'avea 'l core;
  menòmmi sott' una freschetta foglia,
là dov' i' vidi fior' d'ogni colore,
  e tanto vi sentìo gioia e dolzore,
che 'l dio d'amore—mi parea vedere.

(Text from Contini 1960)

Guido Cavalcanti's Pastorella

1   In a little wood I found a shepherdess, more
beautiful than the morning star, it seemed to me.

3   Her hair was blond and curling, her eyes full
of love, her complexion rosy;
    with her staff she was pasturing lambs; her
bare feet were wet with dew;
    she was singing as if she were in love: she was
adorned with every beauty.

9   Amorously I greeted her at once and asked if
she had a companion;
    and she replied sweetly that she was walking
all alone through the wood,
    and she said: "You know, when the
nightingale sings its longing, then my heart
desires to have a sweetheart."

15   When she had told me of her desire and all
through the wood I heard the birds singing,
    I said within myself: "Now is the season to
take joy of this shepherdess."
    I begged her for the mercy of but kissing and
embracing, if she should desire it.

21   She took me by the hand with amorous
desire and said she had given me her heart;
    she led me beneath the fresh green boughs,
where I saw flowers of every color,
    and so much joy and sweetness did I experience
there that I seemed to see the very god of love.

(Translated by R.M.D.)

ADDITIONAL NOTES

1. Cato of Utica
(Canto 1)

The presence of Cato in Purgatory has long challenged readers, since as an apparent pagan, a suicide, and an enemy of Caesar, founder of the Empire, Cato would seem unfit for salvation by Dante. Most early commentators (Pietro di Dante and Bernardino Daniello are exceptions) evaded the difficulties by insisting Dante thought Cato a symbol of human virtue; only in modern times did the consensus emerge that the moral exemplum and historical character coincide. But Cato's presence in the *Purgatorio*, like that of the excommunicated Manfred a few cantos later, was probably intended to surprise. Although other pagans are extraordinarily saved (e.g., Ripheus and Trajan), none is so prominent in the poem, nor is his acquisition of the faith necessary to salvation left inexplicit; and though other prominent Romans of the Republican era are mentioned (e.g., Scipio Africanus), these had not opposed Caesar in war. Placing Cato on the threshold between Hell and Purgatory, Dante has him mark the historical and cultural horizon where the moral and civic values sacred to Rome touch those of Christian humility and sacrifice—a sufficiently remarkable feat. What is more, Roman history in Dante's day had made of Cato an exemplum for medieval defenses of the *bonum commune* [common good], or local communal government, against tyrannical overlords of all stripes, as in texts of Remigio de' Girolami, a Dominican preacher in Florence known to Dante. In this context, Cato's suicide, as Ernst Kantorowicz pointed out, exemplified the resurgent ideal of dying nobly for one's country (*pro patria mori*).

Cicero (*De officiis* 1.31) had reasoned that, given Cato's perfect probity, his suicide, unlike all other cases, lay beyond suspicion of cowardice or self-interest. Lucan for his part shows Cato wishing to shed his blood as an expiatory scapegoat that might spare Rome civil war (*Phars.* 2.306-13), a passage whose resemblance to the voluntary sacrifice of Christ did not escape medieval readers. Thus, in *Mon.* 2.5.15-16 (expanding on *Conv.* 4.5.10-20), Dante makes Cato not only the "stern guardian" of liberty, but praises his suicide as an *inenarrabile sacrificium* [ineffable sacrifice] for the common good, while pointedly grouping Cato with Romans like the Decii who gave their lives for their country. Cato's self-sacrifice reveals the hand of God shaping the history that endowed Rome with universal Empire; and with the clear implication that Cato's manner of death was sanctioned by God, Dante contradicts the skeptical account of its merit by Augustine (*City of God*, 1.23).

Though mollified by Virgil's mention of the divine assistance offered by Beatrice, Cato is unmoved by Virgil's ingratiating reference to Marcia, for the worldly bond to his wife was broken when he departed Limbo (*Purg.* 1.76-93):

Cato, liberated during Christ's descent into Hell, is thus clearly among the saved. Indeed, Virgil's reference to Cato's suicide as driven by love of liberty, because of which his body, shed at Utica, will one day be glorified (75: *che al gran dì sara sì chiara* [which on the great day will be so bright]), confirms that Cato is destined for Paradise; his devotion to freedom seems to anticipate St. Francis' devotion to Poverty (*Par.* 11.58-84). However, if the guardian of all or part of the island, Cato would probably remain in Purgatory until the Day of Judgment; to what extent this implies a penitential delay imposed on him remains controversial.

Virgil's mention of Utica, which identifies Cato, also indicates that his salvation was not in spite of, but because of his suicide: thus for Mazzotta 1979 Cato's suicide renders literally the ethical self-mortification by which the "new man" puts off the "old" (Eph. 4.22-24). Also dictated by Christian values is Cato's requirement that the pilgrim be girded with a rush and cleanse his face of the tears and soot left by the passage through Hell (93-99); following his instructions, the wayfarers descend to the shore and use the humble dew collected there to wash the pilgrim's face, possibly invoking Christian humility as the "custodian of all the virtues" (121-36).

After Cato returns to break up the rapt audition of Dante's "Amor che nella mente mi ragiona" (see 2.120-23, with notes), Cato neither reappears nor is mentioned again in the poem, though his monitory function might be seen echoed in the "whips" and "bridles" (*Purg.* 13.39-40; *Mon.* 3.16.9) of moral example that reeducate the souls on the seven terraces.

Constructing the relation of Cato's self-sacrificing love of political liberty to the moral freedom that is the goal of a Christian Purgatory is thus arguably central to Dante's conception of Cato. The view of Auerbach 1957, that Cato, as a figure who fulfills in the afterlife his historical existence on earth, transposes a love of political freedom into one signifying not "civic virtue and the law," but the "freedom of the immortal soul in the sight of God," has been influential. But Auerbach too hastily transcends Cato's secular political meaning. More balanced is Scott 1996, for whom Dante's Cato is the embodiment of the glorious tradition of Republican Rome: along with Ripheus and Trajan, Cato was devoted to the justice and law that steered Dante's idea of universal empire. For the souls that arrive in Purgatory to be purified, Cato's surprising example, no less than his admonitions, exhorts to the discipline of moral liberation that lies ahead; but for contemporary readers of the poem, and, given that for Dante political freedom consisted in uncoerced adherence to Roman law (*Ep.* 6.23), Dante's Cato, in his possession of justice, embodies the moral freedom that Roman law, administered by the empire, was divinely appointed to foster. Thus, although the opponent of Caesar (whom Dante erroneously considered the first Roman emperor), Cato represents the virtuous citizen Dante's Empire was designed to fashion: one that lived not for himself, but his fellow citizens and all the world (*Phars.* 2.380-83; *Conv.* 4.27.3). Cato's salvation is evidence of the sacred task of Roman law in promoting that happiness in *this* life that Dante saw figured in the Earthly Paradise at the summit of Purgatory (*Mon.* 3.16.7).

R.L.M

2. The Meeting with Casella

(Canto 2)

Casella is the first acquaintance of Dante's to appear in the *Purgatorio*, and the choice was undoubtedly carefully considered. That the very first soul encountered should be that of a friend contributes to the central theme of reconciliation and contrasts strongly with most of the encounters in Hell. Since the action of the poem is set in 1300 (and Casella's reference to the Jubilee unmistakably identifies the date), the question must naturally arise as to the status of the arriving souls in relation to the plenary indulgence offered to pilgrims (in Catholic doctrine, a plenary indulgence was one that freed the soul entirely from Purgatory). The figure of Casella, among its other functions, allows Dante to refer to the Jubilee but to evade the question of its effect on the souls in Purgatory. The text requires us to infer that Casella died well before the beginning of the Jubilee: lines 94-96 clearly mean that his desire to board the angelic boat had been repeatedly denied previously to Christmas, 1299, "three months" earlier, when Boniface VIII's proclamation took effect. Thus lines 97-99 make it clear that the Jubilee facilitates the progress of souls already dead, without the necessity of explaining how it has affected souls who have died within its chronological limits—particularly the others who have just arrived in the angelic boat, all of whom are clearly required to undergo the discipline of the mountain but, like Casella, may have died before the beginning of the Jubilee. In fact Dante never acknowledges the possibility of plenary indulgence, though he is repeatedly explicit on the efficacy of the prayers of the living in speeding souls through Purgatory (3.142-45, 8.71-72, 11.133-42, and especially 23.85-90; see Aurigemma 1965); no other soul in either *Purgatorio* or *Paradiso* is said to have been affected by the Jubilee. The design of the *Purgatorio*, especially those levels of meaning that refer to moral discipline in this life, requires a downplaying of the very idea of indulgences, especially plenary ones (but see 11.127-42, with notes), and in *Par.* 29.115-26 he condemns the foolish belief that they can be bought.

Although a number of passages in the *Inferno* echo or allude to earlier poems of Dante's (see the notes to *Inf.* 5.100, 6.14-16-18, 32.72), *Purgatorio* 2 gives an actual quotation from one of Dante's most ambitious earlier poems, "Amor che ne la mente mi ragiona" [Love that discourses with me in my mind], the second of three canzoni in what survives of the *Convivio*. Three such explicit autocitations occur in the *Comedy* (critics have naturally been tempted to see significance in their ordering—see Barolini 1984 and our notes on the passages involved): in addition to Canto 2, Canto 24 quotes the opening of the first canzone of the *Vita nova* in line 31, and *Paradiso* 8 the first canzone in the *Convivio* (Book 2), "Voi che intendendo il terzo ciel movete" [You who through intellection move the third heaven].

According to the *Convivio,* both "Voi che intendendo" and "Amor che ne la mente," though literally love poems concerning a "donna gentile" [noble lady], actually celebrate the poet's love for philosophy, interpreted as the love of the biblical figure of Wisdom (cf. Prov. 8, especially verses 22-36, and Ecclus. 1 and 24), often identified in exegesis as the second person of the Trinity. There has been debate whether or not these poems were originally written with allegorical intent (for texts, translation, and copious notes, see Foster/Boyde 1967, also *ED* on each poem).

That Casella's singing of this canzone is rebuked by Cato is interpreted by a number of critics as expressing a rejection of the view of philosophy taken in the *Convivio* (see Freccero 1973, Hollander 1975 and 1993; somewhat more moderately, Shoaf 1975, Barolini 1984). Exactly what that view is and in what respect it is rejected tends to be left unexplored, as well as its relation to the view of philosophy taken in the *Comedy*. Opponents of the view (see Scott 1990 and 1995, with bibliography) point out that the *Paradiso* sets forth a closely related conflation of philosophy and Wisdom in the figure of Beatrice, and insist that Dante never published and almost certainly did not expect his readers to know the *Convivio*. Nevertheless it is hard to avoid the conclusion that, at least for Dante himself and those of his intimates who knew of the unfinished treatise, some kind of comment on it is involved, though probably not so negative as outright rejection; the canto includes an unusually dense complex of allusions to it (Hollander 1995). On the whole question see Baldelli 1994.

The beauty of Casella's singing—and, implicitly, of Dante's poem—is identified as both genuine and good, but as a lesser good, especially when contrasted with the singing of psalms the newly arrived souls have just been engaged in. Cato's rebuke does not accuse the souls of focussing on an evil object but of neglecting the highest one. They are still to be purged, of course, but they have been reborn, and one of the keys to the episode is that their condition is very much akin to that of the soul when it is literally newborn, as described by Marco Lombardo in 16.85-93, especially 88-93: "it [knows] nothing except that . . . it gladly turns to what amuses it. Of some lesser good it first tastes the flavor; there it is deceived and runs after it, if a guide or rein does not turn away its love." Cato corresponds to the "guide or rein." (One notes the feeding image; cf. 2.124-26.). Their pleasure in the song is not condemned as sinful; otherwise, after the pilgrim's journey, it would not be sweetness that remained within him from it (line 114; cf. *Inf.* 1.6, 32.71-72, *Purg.* 19.31-33). The elusive charm of these cantos resides precisely in the fact that judgment has been lifted and full-scale discipline has not yet begun.

R.M.D.

3. Belacqua and the Horizons of Purgatory
(Canto 4)

Jacques Le Goff 1981 suggests that Purgatory is a "mountain of the virtues": the pilgrim climbs to achieve the prize of prelapsarian justification at the summit. The idea of representing virtue as a mountain climb is ancient, going back to the choice made by the hero, Hercules, when faced with a crossroads (Panofsky 1999): one fork sloping into idleness and oblivion, the other rising to the temple of glory. A previous choice was offered at *Inf.* 9.132, and an anticipation of the purgatorial climb is found at *Inf.* 24.46-57, where Virgil contrasts a life of repose to the climb necessary for renown; there too the obstacle was sloth, the faintness that besets the spirit wearied by the "heavy body."

In *Purgatorio* 4, Dante draws on this traditional idea (see the note to lines 88-96), and he juxtaposes it with the idea, also traditional, of the distinction between the active and contemplative lives (see the note to 27.100-108, cf. *Conv.* 1.5.11; *ST* 2 2ae q. 179 a. 2). Although the acquisition and practice of the moral virtues is strictly speaking internal to the soul, the active life has a partly external goal, since it always involves relations with other persons and with external goods (*ST* 2a 2ae q. 180 a. 1; q. 181 art. 1; and see *Conv.* 3.15.12, 4.17.8). But because the intellect is man's highest gift, the contemplative life is superior to the active (2 2ae q. 179 a. 1; q. 182 a. 1; *Conv.* 4.22.14-18). The contemplative life maintains external calm ("it consists mostly in repose," q. 179 a. 1) but it has *internal* action which may be described with similes from exterior action (q. 179 a. 1 ad 3). The final goal of the contemplative life is the vision of God, while its mediate end is the contemplation of truths deriving from and leading to God (q. 180 a. 4 ad 3; *Conv.* 3.11.14). Aquinas concedes that, in practice, human life combines both activities, it is "blended from both," "for means are fixed between extremes" (q. 179 a. 2 ad 2); thus Dante speaks in *Conv.* 4. 28.5 of the "good acts and contemplations" of the "noble soul" as it reaches the end of life. Even the angels (*Conv.* 2.4.13) have an active life, in that they govern human affairs (*Conv.* 2.4.10).

The action of Canto 4 can be understood as a systematic deployment of the two forms of life: the pilgrim's climb expresses the active life, which despite Virgil's stimulation (49) leads to physical fatigue (43); on the other hand, the wayfarer gazes back to contemplate the departure point (54) and upward (55) to view the heavenly motions created to inspire humans (*Purg.* 14.148-50 and notes; cf. *Conv.* 3.5.21-22, and *Consolation* 1 m. 2). The wayfarer's arduous journey is also juxtaposed with Belacqua's enforced leisure (126), which echoes and chastises his tardy repentance in life, and with the image of him as the allegorical "brother of sloth" (111). Belacqua is a caricature of the contemplative, who becomes "prudent and wise by sitting still" (see 4.99 and note). As the pilgrim stops to sit, the chief subject of contemplation (or, in other words, of *consideration*, looking at the stars, *sidera*) turns to an investigation of the motion of the sun (61-84). But this entails mention of the heroic, if failed, attempt of Phaëthon to master the horses of the solar chariot, so that the *vita activa* appears again, although we should recall that Dante's future poetic correspondent, the Bologna rhetoric professor Giovanni del Virgilio, interpreted Phaëthon's flight as an allegory of contemplation; allegory again rebalances and complicates the equation, so that Dante's text is "blended from both."

Just as important is the mental effort Virgil calls for in inviting the wayfarer to visualize the globe and the motions of the sun within his imagination (67-68), that is, within the inner forum of intellectual contemplation. Virgil's teaching might seem to focus on the active life: his astronomical lesson on the sun's course (61-66) recalls Apollo instructing Phaëthon on the hazards of steering the solar chariot (*Met.* 2.126-41). But in explaining solar motion Virgil is also contemplating the "truths" of astronomy and geography: this recalls how, in Aquinas' view, teaching can be oriented to serve both the active and contemplative lives (*ST* 2 2ae q. 181 a. 3). By the same token the reference to the Hebrews gazing at the ecliptic circle to the south by as much as the wayfarers see it to the north again links the wayfarer's journey to one of its archetypes, the passage of the desert by Moses: what is, in other terms, the *vita activa* of movement toward salvation, which found its goal on Mount Zion (mentioned at line 70), interpreted in the Middle Ages to mean "contemplation."

These juxtapositions of the two lives may also be construed in terms of the horizon-line, invoked by Virgil at line 70. For Dante's epoch, the horizon was both a subjective effect of perception, the "visual horizon" ("linea terminans visum"; see *Purg.* 1.15 , 7.60, 27.71 and notes) and an objective geoastronomical concept: for example, the Equator, the great circle that bisects the northern and southern terrestrial hemispheres, is a horizon, the boundary between two hemispheres. But the horizon is also a metaphor for the boundary on the scale of being suited to humans, who are both subject to time as mortal animals and free from time as immaterial souls. This concept, applied by Neoplatonism to the world-soul (cf. "Neoplatonism" in Lansing 2000), was adapted by the Scholastics to refer to the human soul (see 25.70-75 and notes). Dante too draws on the metaphorical horizon in *Mon.* 3.16.3-6 (see Nardi 1966) to account for the two distinct goals of human striving: since the embodied human soul is on the horizon of the eternal and the temporal, it is fitting that it have two goals, justice in this life and beatitude in the next, a *vita activa* and a *vita speculativa*. Dante's mention of the term explicitly recalls its astronomical meanings. Thus, in Dante's use, human life taken whole must, as in Aquinas's comment regarding the active and contemplative lives, "have some taste . . . of the extremes it unites" [*sapere utramque naturam*]. See Durling/Martinez 1990, and discussions of the various "souls" in *DVE* 2.2.6, and at *Conv.* 3.2.10 and 4.7.14-15. As we can see from mention of the horizon [*orizzòn*] in line 70 (cf 139), the text itself may be said to have a "boundary between two hemispheres" precisely where Virgil's explanation indentifies the threshold between a view of the external world (the division of the earth into two hemispheres, one with Jerusalem at its center, one with Purgatory at its center) and the inner life of the pilgrim, the microcosm ("turning inward" [*dentro raccolto*]). That is, Virgil invokes not only the hemispheric division of the earth, but also the boundary between exterior action and inner contemplation, between outer and inner man.

In fact the idea of the horizon is deeply implicated in the text. The canto ends with Virgil's telling time by putting the leading edge of the shadow of night over Morocco: this makes it noon in Purgatory and midnight in Jerusalem, "thus bringing in the idea of the two hemispheres" (Singleton), and also implying the great circle that is the horizon of day and night. At the other extreme of the canto, Dante's short excursus on the soul's attention (4.1-12) raises, again implicitly, the question of the threshold between "souls" in the person (see 4. 5-6: "if one soul is kindled over another in us"—the position Dante is concerned to refute).

Canto 4 itself is like a small globe traversed by the motion of the sun: noted as having risen high in the sky in lines 15-16, the sun is mentioned seven times (four times before line 70, three after it); it reaches the meridian (noon), the circle drawn through the highest point it reaches at this latitude, just as the canto ends (line 139). Thus the end of Canto 4 is precisely centered between the moment the pilgrim sees the sun break the horizon at dawn (2.1) and the moment of sunset in Purgatory (8. 1-6; cf. 7.60): this makes the canto the central one of the first day of Purgatory: it is itself a "horizon."

More than a frame for a humorous anecdote (although it is also that), the canto of Belacqua establishes a model for the Purgatorial mountain as a "horizon" of this life and the next, poised between time and eternity, where human personality is regenerated through a mixed regimen ("ex utroque composita") of active exercise, and quasi-liturgical devotions. The diurnal exercise of the moral virtues is signified (and instilled) by the four morning stars signifying the cardinal virtues (see 1.22-24 and notes); the nocturnal, spiritual exercise by the three theological virtues appearing at evening, the threshold of day and night (8.85-93 and notes). The horizon of body and soul, the threshold of the outer and inner person, of the external and internal senses, of perception and imagination, will be constantly at issue in the cantica (see 12.7-9, 17.84, 25.106-108 and notes).

R.L.M.

4. Vergil's Palinurus in *Purgatorio* and the Rudderless Ship of State

(Canto 6)

In *Purg.* 6.45 Dante refers to *Aen.* 6.373-76, where the Sybil, Aeneas' guide, reproaches Palinurus, Aeneas' helmsman, for requesting that Aeneas help him across Acheron, though his body still lies unburied on an Italian beach. The case of Palinurus is treated by Augustine in comparing pagan and Christian treatment of the dead, and may have stimulated Dante's focus on the character (*De cura pro mortuis gerenda* 10, *PL* 40, 601). Allusion to Palinurus allows Dante to recapitulate the predicament of souls delayed, as well as souls excluded from the *Ante-Purgatorio*.

Palinurus has a proleptic view of Italy (*Aen.* 6.357: "I made out [*prospexi*] the Italian shore when high on the summit of a wave"), though he perishes upon reaching shore. This recalls Dante's Ulysses, the first character in history to see Purgatory; and he too perishes, after catching sight of the mountain, "higher than any I had seen" (*Inf.* 26.134-35). Casella, held on a Tiber bank explicitly contrasted with infernal Acheron (2.105), and unable to cross the sea to Purgatory until received by the angel boatman, is like Palinurus, who is blocked from crossing Acheron (*Aen.* 6.329: "for a hundred years they wander and flutter around these shores"); and Casella also closely echoes, with his profession that "no outrage has been done me" (2.96-99), Palinurus' admission that "Neither Phoebus' prophetic cauldron deceived you . . . nor did a god drown me in the sea" (*Aen.* 6.347-348).

Next is Manfred, whose body is cast out from the *Regno* and tossed by wind and rain: he famously echoes (*Purg.* 3.130-31) Palinurus' account of his dead body (*Aen.* 6.362: "Now the flood has me, and the winds toss me along the shore"). Ditto for Buonconte, his body cast into the Arno and rolled by its waters (5.128-129). Chiavacci Leonardi notes that Dante's question to Buonconte (5.91-93: "What force or chance carried you away from Campaldino, so that your burial place was never known?") recalls Aeneas question to Palinurus (*Aen.* 6.341-42: "Which of the gods, Palinurus, snatched you from us and drowned you in the middle deep?"). And the storm that drives Buonconte's body shares details with the storm described by Palinurus (*Aen.* 5.8-18).

The identification of Palinurus and Manfred was made long ago (Moore 1896; d'Ovidio 1906), and has been recently reiterated (Gmelin, Brugnoli 1993). Additional cases parallel to Palinurus' have also emerged (Cioffi 1991): Jacopo del Cassero's recollection of what might have been (5.79-81: "But if I had fled toward Mira . . . I would still be back there where people breathe" [s'io fosse fuggito . . . ancor sarei di la dove si spira]) echoes Palinurus' account of how he was killed after supposing he was safe on shore (*Aen.* 6.358-361: "already I was out of danger . . . except that a savage tribe . . . attacked me with iron weapons" [iam tuta tenebam, ni gens crudelis . . . ferro invasisset]). Manfred too had ruminated this way at 3.124-29.

With so many refractions of an unmentioned Palinurus in play, it is no surprise that it is Virgil instead who in part embodies this character. Palinurus-Virgil reiterates several of the figures mentioned so far. In his regret—mentioned both at 3.40-45 and 7.28-36—over the virtuous pagans "suspended" [*sospesi*] in Limbo (3.40-42: "and you have seen those yearning fruitlessly whose desire would be stilled, which is given them eternally as their grief" [disiar vedeste sanza frutto / tai che sarebbe lor disio *quetato* / ch'etternalmente è dato lor per lutto]), Virgil mourns the lack of *quies*, of satisfied repose, afflicting those who cannot yet traverse Acheron (6.328-329: "before his bones are quiet [*quierunt*] in the tomb"; 6.371: "so that at least in death I may rest [*quiescam*] in a quiet place"). This group is typified by a sorrowful demeanor (6.333: "cast down [*maestos*] and deprived of the honors of death," as is Palinurus when Aeneas first sees him (6.340: "covered as he was with sadness [*maestum*] and deep shadow"); Virgil shares their melancholy: "and here he bent his brow . . . and remained perturbed" (3.44-45).

Virgil-Palinurus is especially recalled in Manfred and Buonconte. The honorable translation of Virgil's body from Brindisi for burial in Naples (3.25-27) contrasts by design with the casting out of Manfred's (3.131); and the contrast is reiterated if we set 3.127-28 ("the bones of my body would still be . . . under the protection of the heavy cairn") next to 7.5 ("my bones were buried by Octavian"). Indeed Manfred's cairn, the *grave mora*, recalls the "ingenti *mole*" [enormous heap] of Misenus' tomb (*Aen.* 6.212), one whose initial unburied status parallels that of Palinurus.

More significantly, Buonconte's eventual, natural burial in the Arno recalls the promise made by the Sybil that Palinurus would find a future tomb: "'warned by heaven-sent wonders, [the Lucanians] will consecrate your bones and build you a tomb and by it keep yearly rituals; and eternally the place will keep the name of Palinurus [*aeternumque locus* Palinuri nomen habebit].' By her words his cares were lightened, for a moment the grief is driven from his sad heart: he rejoices in name of the land" (*Aen.* 6.379-83).

Like Palinurus, Virgil is honored by Sordello's encomium of him as the "*eternal* honor of the *place* I was from" [pregio *etterno* del *luogo* ov'io fui], based on the Sybil's prophecy to Palinurus. The two phrases correlate eternal fame with a place; while the third element, the name, explicit in the Latin, remains implicit in the Italian, as Sordello's "place" is Mantua and Virgil is the "Mantuan" by antonomasia. In the present context this recalls Vergil's epitaph (see *Purg.* 6.72-

74 and note) and thus his tomb. And as Palinurus can rejoice in the association of his name with a place, Sordello's celebration of Virgil arises "merely for the *sweet sound* of his *city* to make much of his fellow-citizen there [sol per lo *dolce suon* de la sua *terra* / di fare al suo cittadin quivi *festa*]," 6.79-81, the very sound of Virgil's Mantuan accent. Name, place, fame, and tomb are correlated.

Sacrificed by the Fates to the larger purposes of Aeneas' imperial destiny, the unnamed Palinurus thus serves in Dante's poem to summarize the exclusions (*divieto*, 3.144; see 10.36) of Ante-Purgatory: temporary exclusion from passage to Purgatory (Casella) or from promotion once there; from physical burial, through either human or demonic agency (Manfred, Buonconte); from physical safety (Jacopo del Cassero; La Pia); from the sacraments of the Church (Manfred); finally, from divine grace absolutely (Ulysses in Hell; Virgil in Limbo). Brugnoli 1993 suggests that Cato's "blind river" [*cieco fiume*] (1.40-41) echoes Vergil's "stern river" [*amnem severum*] that blocks Palinurus: the exclusionary system of Ante-Purgatory is juxtaposed with the prohibition imposed by Acheron, which for Cato divides Purgatory from "the eternal prison" of Hell.

Yet the significance of Palinurus should not be limited to reasserting (as in 6.28-42) the differences between paganism, with its universal relegation of souls to Hades, and Christianity, with its promise of merits and grace accessible through prayer; or, even less, to providing one more confirmation of Virgil's failure as a pagan. In refracting Palinurus through many figures, Dante imitates Vergil's recurring insistence in the *Aeneid* that the providential imperial enterprise requires sacrificial victims, from Misenus drowned to Pallas killed in the war in Latium (see *Inf.* 1.106-108; also *Par.* 6.35-36 and notes). Blood sacrifice is not only pagan, of course: early medieval commentators on Vergil heard in the prophecy of Palinurus' death ("unum pro multis dabitur caput" [one's life shall be given for many], *Aen.* 8.515) an anticipation of the sacrifice of Christ (John 11.50; Courcelle 1984); while Palinurus' request to be ferried over the river ("eripe me his . . . malis" [rescue me from these evils], *Aen.* 6.365) resonates with the Catholic liturgy ("eripe me, Domine, de inimicis meis" [Deliver me, Lord, from my enemies], Ps. 58.1).

If the idea of a sacrificial economy touches both on Dante's representation of Virgil as a pagan excluded from grace and on the continuities of pagan and Christian sacrifice, it also exceeds the bounds of Purgatory and includes contemporary history, where winners and losers are less easy to distinguish. Thus the most complex allusion to Palinurus in the *Purgatorio*—perhaps echoing Palinurus' proleptic sight of Italy from a wave-crest—comes during the speech on "Slavish Italy" (6.76-151), where Dante refers to Italy as "a ship without a pilot" (6.77) nigh foundering in the tempest of history. In this case it is the absent Albert, or, as Perugi 1983 would have it, the recently deceased Henry VII (d. 1313), who stands for the missing helmsman. We are bound to recall Palinurus' claim that after falling into the sea his main worry was for Aeneas' ship, pilotless amid dangerous seas, (6.351-55: "the bristling seas, I swear, caused me no such great fear as I had that your ship, robbed of its tiller and master [*spoliata armis, excussa magistro*], would sink, so great were the waves that surged"). Dante recalls this passage when writing to the Florentines in 1311, when finishing the *Purgatorio*, to describe an Italy adrift without the emperor, "abandoned to private wills and bereft of all public guidance [*publico moderamine destituta*]," *Ep.* 6.3). Palinurus' anxiety for Aeneas' ship, which he places above concern for his own life, suggests the anxieties of Dante the author as he witnesses from exile the peril of the Italian ship of state lacking a helmsman or *gubernator* (cf. 6.96), Palinurus's title when introduced by Vergil at *Aen.* 6.337 (and see 5.858-59), and a traditional designation for the Roman Emperor. With no imperial hand guiding the state, Italy succumbs to the "fierce hands" of Ghino di Tacco (6.13-14).

The poet's anxiety is linked to the question of whether prayers are answered, which had triggered mention of the lost helmsman in the first place; and this same anxiety links the poet to Palinurus. One thing to proclaim the comforts of Christian prayer as represented in the poet's own text; something else to grasp the working of the divine plan on the historical scene of 1312-1314. Dante wants *his* prayers heard, but fears God has averted his face (see *Purg.* 6.120 and note); he wants Italy saved from chaos, but fears it may not be. The hands Federigo Novello extends in prayer (6.16) may reflect the poet's own, for it seems only prayer can call forth the steadying hand Italy needs. This anxiety over Providence—it hints at, but stops short of, a crisis of faith—is never far from the political texts of *Purgatorio*, and it is to the poet's fear of the historical failure of Italy, with no consolation but the cold comfort of literary fame, that the recurring specter of Palinurus may perhaps be assigned.

R.L.M.

5. The Canonical Hours; Compline

(Canto 8)

The "canonical hours," also known as the Office (Lat. *officium* [duty]), are prayer services fixed by canon (decree). In the Latin West, the pattern was essentially established in the sixth century by the *Rule of Saint Benedict*, the foundation of Benedictine monastic practice, which in turn was based on the Roman liturgy. Many local variations survived or grew up over time, and there were numerous efforts to reform and shorten the Office, which every cleric had the obligation of reciting daily, whether singing in the convent or cathedral choir, or privately, perhaps silently. In the thirteenth century a major effort of reform was carried out by the Franciscans.

The basic structure of the Office centered on the reading or chanting (usually antiphonal) of the entire Book of Psalms each week, along with appropriate prayers, hymns, canticles, ancillary chants (versicles, responses, antiphons), and, in some of the services (most notably Matins), extensive readings from the Bible, the Fathers, and the lives of the saints, all varied according to the Church seasons and feasts. Not counting Matins (which began several hours after midnight), there were seven diurnal services (see Ps. 118.164: "seven times a day let me praise thee"): Lauds (before dawn), Prime (at dawn, "at the first hour"), Terce ("at the third hour"), Sext ("at the sixth hour"), Nones ("at the ninth hour"), Vespers (named after the evening star), and Compline (soon after dark, at bedtime). The hours referred to are the so-called unequal hours: day and night were each divided into twelve "hours" whose length varied according to the proportion of daylight to darkness: in winter the night hours were longer, in summer the day hours. Terce, Sext, and None were called "minor hours" because very much shorter than the others (often only a few minutes long). In the course of time, the actual time of performance of a number of the diurnal hours shifted. Our use of the term *noon* for midday derives from the gradual shifting of the service of Nones to that time; likewise, Vespers came to be performed in the middle of the afternoon rather than at sunset.

Certain psalms had relatively fixed places in the cycle of services, for instance Psalms 144-150, the great psalms of praise, in Lauds; Psalms 4, 90, and 133 in Compline. In the high Middle Ages, especially in Benedictine monasteries, the Office (like all other forms of the liturgy and its music: the Mass and other sacramental ceremonies, the Burial Services, consecrations of churches or bishops, etc.) was extremely elaborate; in the most highly developed form, each verse of a psalm was preceded by an introductory antiphon, and especially elaborate forms of music were performed on Sundays and feast days. Alongside the Office properly speaking there arose in the course of the Middle Ages several other, shorter cycles, most importantly the Office of the Virgin and the Office of the Dead, whose prayers were often appended to the corresponding services of the regular Office.

The *Purgatorio* and *Paradiso* include countless references to the canonical hours, but the one to which the references are most fully developed is Compline (Lat. *Completorium* [that which completes]), in *Purgatorio* 7 and 8. Here is an outline of a typical monastic Easter Sunday Compline service of Dante's time; it would have taken about three quarters of an hour:

Versicle and response

Blessing

Short reading (1 Peter 5.8: "Brothers, be sober and awake, for your adversary the devil, roaring like a lion, goes about seeking whom he may devour: resist him, strong in faith. But you, Lord, have mercy on us"), followed by versicles and responses.

Confiteor and absolution

Versicles, Gloria

Psalms (with antiphon: Hallelujah): 4, 90, 133, followed by a longer Hallelujah antiphon

Hymn:

1. Te lucis ante terminum,	[1. Before the ending of the light,
rerum Creator, poscimus,	Creator of all things, we beg
ut pro tua clementia,	that in your mercy
sis praesul et custodia.	you be our help and guardian.
2. Procul recedant somnia,	2. Let dreams recede far off,
et noctis phantasmata:	and the phantasms of the night:
hostemque nostrum comprime,	And keep down our enemy,
ne polluantur corpora.	lest our bodies be polluted.
3. Praesta, Pater piissime,	3. Be present, most merciful Father,
Patrique compar Unice,	and Only-begotten of the Father,
cum Spiritu Paraclito,	with the Spirit, the Paraclete,

regnans per omne saeculum.	reigning through all ages.
Amen.	Amen.]

Chapter: Jeremiah 14.9

Responsorium ("Into thy hands I commend my spirit: Hallelujah")

Canticle of Simeon (Luke 2.29-32: "Now thou dost dismiss thy servant, O Lord, according to thy word in peace; Because mine eyes have seen thy salvation, Which thou hast prepared before the face of all peoples: A light to the revelation of the Gentiles, and the glory of thy people Israel"), with antiphon

Prayers: Kyrie; Credo (silently)

Versicles, Benediction

One of the four Marian antiphons: at Eastertide, "Regina caeli":

Regina caeli, laetare, alleluia:	[Queen of Heaven, rejoice, halleluiah:
quia quem meruisti portare,	for he whom you were worthy to carry,
alleluia:	hallelujah:
resurrexit, sicut dixit, alleluia:	has risen, as he foretold, hallelujah.
Ora pro nobis Deum, alleluia.	Pray God for us, hallelujah.]

Versicles and Responses, closing prayers.

Psalm 90 seems to have been the nucleus of the earliest form of the Compline service (Eisenhofer 1932); its relevance to Dante's text is striking (see the notes to Canto 8). The close of day is of course associated in medieval sensibilities with the close of life; the texts chosen (e.g., the Canticle of Simeon) reflect this preoccupation, explicit in medieval commentaries on the service, such as Durandus'.

The addition of a Marian antiphon to the Compline service seems to have taken place in the eleventh century; the melodies (several of them by the famous Hermannus Contractus) were among the most popularly beloved in the liturgy. The four were eventually assigned to different seasons (when these assignments were made is not entirely clear, and local practice varied): "Alma Redemptoris mater" (easily the most popular; see Chaucer's *Prioress' Tale*) from the the eve of the first Sunday in Advent until the Feast of the Purification; "Ave Regina caelorum" from February 2 through Holy Thursday; "Regina caeli" from Easter Sunday until the Friday before Trinity Sunday; and "Salve, Regina" from Trinity Sunday until the Saturday before Advent. One of the most striking aspects of Dante's allusions to Compline is the fact that the Marian antiphon he imagines the souls singing in the Valley of Princes is not "Regina caeli," which is later sung in *Par.* 23.128, but "Salve, Regina," the longest and most penitential of the four:

Salve, Regina, mater misericordiae,	[Hail, Queen, mother of compassion,
vita, dulcedo, et spes nostra, salve.	our life, our sweetness and our hope, hail.
Ad te clamamus, exsules, filii Hevae.	To you we cry out, exiles, sons of Eve.
Ad te suspiramus, gementes et flentes	Toward you we sigh, groaning and weeping
in hac lacrimarum valle.	in this vale of tears.

Eia ergo, advocata nostra,	Ah therefore, our advocate,
illos tuos misericordes oculos ad nos converte,	turn those compassionate eyes of yours to us,
et Jesum, benedictum fructum ventris tui,	and Jesus, the blessed fruit of your womb,
nobis post hoc exilium ostende.	show him to us after this exile.
O clemens: O pia:	O merciful, O compassionate,
O dulcis Virgo Maria.	O sweet Virgin Mary.]

The penitential spirit of the negligent rulers is particularly emphatic against the background of Easter rejoicing that would inform the Compline service on earth.

R.M.D.

6. The Terrace of Pride: i. Structure and Rationale

(Cantos 10-12)

The first terrace of Purgatory proper, that of pride, sets forth Dante's conception of the purgative process more fully than any of the later ones. This is partly because much is to be set forth that will be assumed later, partly because pride, as the source and fundamental motive of all sin (see the discussion in *Confessions* 2.9-14), is the most serious disposition to be corrected in Purgatory, and its correction must be particularly elaborate.

The target of the purgative process, on this as on the other terraces, is a disposition or tendency of the will: in the case of pride, the tendency to set oneself up above others, or, as Virgil explains in 17.115-17, the desire to see others lowered so that one can be superior. This tendency or inclination is not an action; the wrong actions—sins—to which it led have all been forgiven (see Introduction, pp. 8-9).

The medieval adaptation of the Aristotelian doctrines of virtuous and vicious habit, while retaining their general framework, operates a profound transformation on them (Dante's is a preeminent example): it insists that all actions spring from love, that all habits of the will are modes of love, and that the active expression of God's love—his grace—is always available to the repentant. This approach is so central for Dante that he devotes to it the central cantos (16-18) of the *Purgatorio* and thus of the entire *Comedy*.

The scene of the process of purgation is, with some variation, the same on each of the terraces of Purgatory proper: a narrow shelf circling the entire mountain, without any vegetation (there is one exception). The expanded paraphrase of the Lord's Prayer recited by the souls of the proud (11.1-24) calls it a "harsh desert" (11.14), and in the governing figural parallel with the Exodus, the terraces correspond to the Desert of Sinai, where, because of their stiff-necked disobedience, the children of Israel had to wander for forty years, until all those born in Egypt had died (commonly interpreted in the Middle Ages as referring to the penitential death of the "Old Man").

The process of purgation, as Dante represents it, is essentially that of redirecting love; it has two phases, destructive and constructive. In Aristotelian terminology, the old habit or form taken by the will must be broken down and the new habit or form imposed; destruction of the old form may accompany the imposition of the new form. On the terrace of pride, as well as on the others, this double process of discipline, of learning, involves a mode of suffering and a practice of meditation, including prayer and the contemplation of examples of the vice to be unlearned and the virtue to be learned. At the end of the process, one of the *P*s inscribed by the angel at the gate is erased by the wing of the angel guarding the ascent, and the victory over vice is celebrated by the singing of one of the Beatitudes (Matt. 6.1-11); this moment obviously corresponds to that of priestly absolution in the sacrament of penance (in the very last case the singing of the Beatitude precedes the pilgrim's purgation, and the erasure of the *P* is not mentioned). The process is a reshaping and redirection of the will, and at the same time it is accompanied and made effective at each step of the way by God's help. Dante draws no sharp distinction between nature and grace, one of the respects in which he is not Thomistic.

The terrace of pride gives special prominence to the Lord's Prayer, which Dante clearly considered a chief corrective to pride, since its sincere utterance requires an attitude of deep humility, which the penitent souls on the terrace practice and internalize as they recite it. As the notes to 11.1-24 suggest, Dante seems to have studied Augustine's discussions of the Lord's Prayer with great attention; he may even have derived from them the suggestion of the mode of suffering of the proud. Commenting on the words "deliver us from evil," Augustine observes that in this life we cannot be entirely freed from it: "but this cannot be hoped for in this life, as long as *we carry about that mortality* [*istam mortalitatem circumferimus*] into which we were drawn by the persuasion of the serpent" (*De serm. Dom.* 63; italics added).

This passage, written near the end of Augustine's life, involves a clear echo of one of the most striking passsages in his *Confessions* (1.1), written much earlier: "And man, a certain portion of your creation, wishes to praise you; even man, carrying about [*circumferens*] his mortality, carrying about the testimony of his sin and testimony that you, God, resist the proud." The three "weights" man is said here to "carry about," his mortality, the testimony to his sin, and the testimony that God resists the proud, are identical in reference, since, first, his mortality is the punishment for his sin (Gen. 2.17) and thus testifies to it; and, second, his sin resulted primarily from rebellious pride, and thus its punishment testifies to God's resisting the proud. It is but a small step from these correlations to seeing that the weight is also pride itself, since sin is always its own punishment.

In addition to its obvious connection with Augustine's metaphor, the logical structure of the circumambulatory penance done on the terrace of pride is also closely related to it: the penance is at the same time both punitive and expressive of the vice itself. Furthermore, the association between the weight of pride and that of mortality is obvious in Virgil's mention in Canto 11 of the pilgrim's being weighed down by mortality (11.43-45, especially "lo 'ncarco" [the burden]), which calls attention to the analogy. However, Dante represents the weight also as a mode of practising and thus acquiring the corrective virtue. When in *Purg.* 11.53 Omberto Aldobrandeschi speaks of the weight "that masters my proud neck," he is using the terminology of retributive justice: he was proud and stiff-necked in life (among the many biblical occurrences of the idea, see in particular Deut. 10.16, and cf. *Purg.* 12.70-72), now he is forced to bend. He thus reveals that he has not yet understood that the weight that bends him down is that of his pride itself. We know from Omberto (11.52-57) that the weight of his stone prevents him from turning his head sufficiently to see the pilgrim; souls at a later stage of purgation, like Oderisi da Gubbio, are able to turn their heads (11.73-78).

One implication of these passages is that those in the initial stages of the process are not able to see the examples of humility; they must gaze at the ground, able to contemplate only the examples of pride punished that are visible there (12.16-69): when the weight of their pride has lightened sufficiently, they can contemplate the examples of humility as they pass them, as well as see and identify others near them (as in 11.109-26). (Thus although on each terrace the examples of virtue are presented to the pilgrim before those of vice, that is not necessarily how the souls inhabiting the terraces experience them.) The practicing of the virtue of humility, then, involves practicing the bodily postures and gestures that express it even though at first these may be merely imposed and not understood. Although Dante exploits this idea with great originality, it is by no means original with him. The medieval practice of adopting specific bodily positions for different kinds of prayer rested on such a recognition; as the *Modi orandi Sancti Dominici* put it: in such a mode of prayer "the soul moves the members of the body that it may be the more swiftly lifted to God, that the soul that moves the body may be moved by the body . . . such a mode of prayer instills devotion alternately, from the soul into the body and from the body into the soul."

The examples of pride punished and humility exalted, clearly enough, present what is to be avoided and what imitated, respectively. They have an important rational function: it is critical to the acquisition of virtue that the nature of the "right rule" be grasped by the mind. The examples of pride cast down not only instill fear; more importantly they address the understanding, which must grasp the inherent absurdity of pride and identify the brevity and mortality of all human pretension. Hence the anagram *VOM* is built, sculpted, as it were—like the mark of a tool, or a genetic characteristic—into the very material of the text (see the notes to 12.25-63, and cf. *OMO* in 23.32-33): if he does not rise above his mere human state, man is dust and returns to dust, a worm (cf. 10.121-29). The association of these carvings with those on the covers of tombs on church floors of course emphasizes that aspect of the lesson; it also suggests that the ultimate feeling they are to instill is that of humbled grief, whose bodily expression is the bowed head. The lesson in the self-destructiveness of pride is essential preparation for learning from the examples of humility. The souls must be ready to see why, in order to see the examples, they must look up to them, spiritually as well as spatially. (It is made clear that the souls who appear at the end of Canto 10 are coming from the pilgrim's left as he faces the carvings; thus the examples of humility are to the penitent souls' left also—the side of the heart, as 10.48 reminds us; cf. 10.100).

One of the most interesting and subtle psychological insights set forth in Purgatory proper is that the mode of penance, especially on the three lowest levels, involves a separation of the self from its vice: the distinction between body and flesh we have traced involves the representation of pride, envy, and anger as distinct from the body and thus from the true self. On the terrace of pride, the stones that closed around the damned (cf. *Inferno* 10, 31; 32-33) have been escaped, and though they still weigh the souls down, they can ultimately be trodden under foot (as practiced in *Purgatorio* 12); the same principle separates the iron wires, the livid garments, and the livid rock from the souls/bodies of the envious and the smoke from the angry. This distinction between the tendency to be corrected and the essence of the body-soul complex is itself a theme of meditation for the penitents and is a hallmark of Purgatory proper: in the Ante-Purgatory the pro-grammatic separation has not taken place (Belacqua is the best example: his iden-tification with his sloth is quite unreflecting). In the Ante-Purgatory a generic striving upward draws on the traditional parallel between the acquisition of vir-tue and the difficult ascent of a mountain; in Purgatory proper, however, the actual process of discipline takes place on the terraces, which are level, and its result *facilitates* the climb, which is no longer itself the locus of moral effort but of theoretical discussion, a form of contemplation.

R.M.D.

7. The Terrace of Pride: ii. The Theme of Art
(Cantos 10-12)

The process of reeducation set forth by Dante on the terraces of Purgatory, and most fully on the terrace of pride, involves all the dimensions of the human being, intellectual, sensory, imaginative, emotional, physical. It expresses Dante's profound sense of the unity of the human body-soul complex, the central theme of the entire *Purgatorio*. In this process he gives art a major role. With their ex-tended descriptions of the marble sculptures and of the reaction to them of the pilgrim and certain of the pentitents, Cantos 10-12 are a major statement about the nature and function of the visual arts and, by implication, of poetry and of the *Comedy* itself.

As has often been observed, Dante attributes to the sculptures what had been recognized since Antiquity as a chief virtue of art: mimetic vividness, life-like representation, the holding of the mirror up to nature. The miraculous qualities he ascribes to the sculptures, such as the conveying of imagined dialogue, are intensifications of qualities he sees and values in the products of human art (see the note to 10.28-99). As on all the terraces, the virtue is first exemplified by the Virgin Mary (see Additional Note 12), and in Cantos 10, 13, 15, and 25—a ma-jority of the cases—the words spoken by Mary in the Gospels are quoted. The very first example, in Canto 10, is particularly interesting, since repeated empha-sis is placed on the sculptures' actual silence: they are so vivid that the viewer can imagine exactly what is said. "One would have sworn that he [the archangel Gabriel] was saying '*Ave!*'" In the case of the Virgin, Dante's words are particu-larly significant: "in her bearing was stamped this speech: '*Ecce ancilla Domini,*' exactly as a figure is sealed in wax" (10.43-45). In other words, the Virgin's hu-mility of soul so permeates her bodily gestures as to stamp them legibly with her utterance; her body is mere wax to the forming power of her soul. (We may note in passing that it is the Virgin's legibility that guarantees that of the archangel:

note the *perché* [because] of line 41.) Perfection of virtue requires—is—the perfection of the relation of soul to body, and in this, as in all things, the Virgin is the model the souls must strive to follow. This conception of the permeating of the body with the "word" of the soul is close to what is said of the angel in 2.44: "parea beato per iscritto" [he seemed to have blessedness inscribed on him]: every detail of his appearance and bearing expressed his beatitude.

Important light is cast by these passages on Dante's conception of personification allegory: he connects it with the representation of bodily appearance and gesture, as in the pilgrim's description of Belacqua, who "appears more negligent than if Laziness were his sister" (4.110-11): it is as if there were a blood relation between Belacqua and the personification: again, his laziness permeates his body. Dante's conception of personification and his treatment of the Virgin as the true exemplar of each virtue are closely allied.

The shining beauty attributed to the carvings in Canto 10—perceived, of course, through the sense of sight—is also an integral part of their function; it draws the soul to love both the representation and what is represented. The delight felt by the pilgrim and his gratitude toward the Maker (10.97-99; cf. 26.97-114 for the analogous principle in relation to poetry) are presumably shared by the penitent souls able to contemplate them. Although the point is not made explicit here, the Virgin, as the most virtuous and most beautiful human being (the two are virtually synonymous for Dante), is supremely lovable. The example of the Virgin's humility is not only to instruct the souls in the nature of the virtue, it is meant to arouse their love and through it their ability as well as their desire to imitate her (on the order of the examples, see Additional Note 12). Thus the first appeal made through the beautiful carving representing the Virgin's humility, is to the imagination and to the power of empathy: it is obviously Dante's conception that the images of virtue and vice remain in the penitents' imaginations and are to govern and inform their prayers and their meditations: they enable them to "think of what follows" (10.110). Important light is cast by these passages on Dante's hopes for the effect on the reader of the beauty of the *Comedy*.

That effect depends, of course, not only on the reader's admiration and love of the beauty of the poem but also on his vicarious participation in it. Here again, the pilgrim is the model: in order to see and speak with Oderisi, the pilgrim must bend equally low, and he preserves the posture throughout his dialogue with him. As he listens to Oderisi's account of the futility of artistic pride, his own pride is chastened, he says (11.118-19). This occurs when he is bent over and to that extent sharing the penance. But, throughout the *Comedy*, the pilgrim's relation to the souls he meets is primarily that of an observer who participates vicariously in what he witnesses. In this respect the figure of the pilgrim gazing intently upon the sculptures of the terrace of pride is an analogue of the relation of the reader to the poem itself, with its plethora of examples (Boccaccio may well have found a suggestion here for his metanovellas, such as *Decameron* 5.8). Just as the pilgrim's vicarious participation includes a strong empathic element (see 10.130-35, with note), so too does the reader's, and through it the poet obviously hopes to involve the reader's body as well. And, again, all this takes place through the bodily, empathic image-making faculty. See also Additional Notes 10 and 13.

R.M.D

8. San Miniato al Monte and
Dante's Pride of Workmanship
(Canto 12)

A reference to San Miniato, the Romanesque basilica (built 1078-1207) just outside Florence on a hill above the Rubaconte bridge (blown up in 1944 and replaced by the present Ponte alle Grazie; the abutments of the original bridgehead emerged during road repairs in the spring of 1999), marks the center of the wayfarer's first passage from a terrace of purgation (lines 73-136) and summarizes key ideas of the circle of pride and of Purgatory in general. Chiavacci Leonardi points out that in Landino's commentary (1481) the "right hand" to which the poet refers must refer to paths formerly ascending the Monte San Miniato (also known as Monte alle Croci): on the left hand, a path led to the crest where now stands Cronaca's church of San Francesco al Monte (built about 1470; previously the site of a small Franciscan chapel); on the right hand, a much steeper path, provided with steps, led directly to the basilica. The map drawn by Pietro del Massaio for a manuscript of Ptolemy's *Geography* as translated by Jacopo d'Angelo in 1470 (Cod. Vat. Urb. Lat. 299; see fig. 8) illustrates these paths, which Landino claimed corresponded to the layout of the slope in Dante's day. In this way Dante gives Florentine locality to the fundamental image of the "stairway" leading to the summit of Purgatory. In addition to the terms for "stairway" and "steps" (*scalee*, 12.104; *scaglion*, 12.115), note the rhyme on *ale, sale* ("wings," "climb") at lines 91, 93.

In the context of the ascent of the mountain, a "right-hand" path has moral significance (see Additional Note 3); indeed, everything about Dante's mention of San Miniato is closely related to actions performed by the pilgrim as he exits the first terrace, of pride. The church of San Miniato is said to "subjugate" or dominate the city (It. *soggioga*, 12. 101), as if burdening the "ben guidata" [well-guided city]—an ironic jab at a city that Dante saw as proud and out of control. The church thus stands to the city as the stones that subjugate the proud (see 11.53, with note). Overlooking the city from outside all three circles of walls, the church is sited like the poet himself, reproaching the city from the distance of exile, but from the proximity of his own acknowledged pride as well (see 12.1).

The steep, staired path the pilgrim ascends is called the *cruna* [needle's eye] or *tagliata* [cut], and this language links the path to the sculptured examples against pride. Dante says the narrow path "scrapes" (12.108, *rade*) on either side as he climbs, and this—in light of other uses such as *raso* and *scemo* (12.9, 12.123; respectively "diminished" and "erased")—suggests the abrasion of the scurf of sin (*scoglio*) that Cato informed the souls is the function of the mountain. One implication of the biological metaphor of 10.128-29 is that purgation entails self-sculpting (Michelangelo, ever attentive to Dante's artisanal metaphors, later conceived of both sculpture and moral progress as freeing the figure from the block, by "taking away" [*levando*] and carving [*l'intaglio*], thus purifying it of its scurf [*scorza, scoglio*]). Hence the wayfarer's gesture of feeling with his hand for the abraded (*scempie*) signs of sin (12.133-35); the pilgrim must manually verify his polishing.

The bridge Dante knew was named after the popular *podestà* from Milan, Rubaconte di Mandello, who ordered the paving of Florence within the first girdle of walls, a massive job of stone-dressing not irrelevant to a rocky terrace displaying sculpture. Villani (*Istorie* 6.26), tells how Rubaconte bore the first load of lime, clay and stone for the bridge that bore his name (Davidsohn 1957); Rubaconte was also legendary for commonsensical judgments that calmed private disputes (Sachetti, *Trecentonovelle* 196). With Rubaconte's good government Dante contrasts the scandal of the stave removed from the salt-measure by Donato Chiaramontesi, which entailed a distortion of measure, weight, and number (Prov. 11.10); also mentioned is the alteration and falsification of notarial records ordered by the *podestà* Monfortino Coderta: Compagni (*Chronicle*, 1.19) reports that the entry had been scraped away (*raso*; other witnesses speak of pages torn out). It is by deliberate antithesis to mismeasurement and falsification that Dante, a true son of mercantile Florence, exhibits on the terrace of pride careful measurement and ordered rankings (10.24: the terrace is three times as broad as the length of a human body; Canto 11 assesses the relative merits of poets and painters; cf. 11.84), and a just distribution of burdens (*pondo, incarco, sasso, soma, peso*; 11.26, 43; 52; 57, 70); also found are canonical statements of purgatorial suffering as payment (11.88, 125-126). The terrace is also a showcase for authorized graphic representation, from visible, sculpted "texts" (the "visible speech" of 10.95, authored by God) to acrostics (12.25-63, inscribed by the poet): and of course it narrates the incipient *erasure* of the "notes" or marks of sin (12.122-35). In short, the San Miniato terzine, narrating the pilgrim's exit from the terrace and the "staircase" of Purgatory, include references to sculpture, the judgment of merit and castigation of error, and writing—and, implicitly, the writing of the poem. As this is the first such passageway and exit (note the comparison at lines 112-114 with the passages of Hell), Dante may be said to establish the standard measures, so to speak, for the purgatorial edifice that rises from the ledge of Pride as its base; in short, for the moralized "architecture" of the seven-terraced mountain that remedies the effects of sin (see Additional Notes 6 and 7).

And well he might. Dante writes in *Conv.* 1.2.8-10 of the risks of self-evaluation precisely in terms of false measures and false testimony, given the difficulty of impartially weighing one's own faults (for this problematic, see Ascoli 1989). Pondering his own pride by foreseeing its painful expiation (13.136-38), already "measuring" himself in the attitudes of the proud (cf. 12.1), Dante implicitly sides with those artists (in the medieval sense of any skilled worker) who worked with due regard for honest weights and measures, as indeed the scruples expressed at the end of the *cantica* (see 33.136-41 and notes) bear out. In conceiving the terrace with its pavement reliefs, Dante may have found suggestive the signed and dated (1207) inlaid floor of San Miniato, where leonine hexameters ordered by "Josephus, metricus et iudex" [Joseph, metrician and judge] testify to the completion of the floor. As poet and judge this Joseph would have fitted words to measure and pondered just decisions: his skills are evident on the floor in the metrical apportionment of credit to God, "celesti numine *dante*" [the heavenly godhead granting]. That poetry, judgment, and piety might coincide surely resonated with the vernacular poet who expected his own handiwork to be "tried in the fire" (1 Cor. 3.12-14; see 26.117, 27.10-11 and note, and Introduction) as part of his purgation as man and artist.

R.L.M.

9. Number, Light, Motion, and Degree at the Center of the *Comedy*
(Canto 17)

Singleton (1965) pointed out that the seven cantos of the center of *Purgatorio* (thus of the whole poem) have a symmetrical disposition of line lengths: 151 145 145 139 145 145 151; these seven cantos are in turn "bounded" by sevens (151 = 7, by addition of digits) and include further symmetry based on the two mentions of free will in cantos 16 and 18 (lines 72, 73), each 25 tercets from the beginning and end, respectively, of those cantos (more sevens, as 25 = 7). Singleton viewed this pattern as a "signature" at the center of the poem of the poet as maker, marking the poem's completeness and perfection; such a mark recalls those left in creation by the Maker of all (see 25.70-72, 26.117, with notes; *Mon.* 2.7; and Shaw 1996 xix-xxiii). Although the meaningfulness of the pattern has been questioned, further work has confirmed it (Ferrante in Jacoff/Schnapp 1988 observes a seven-canto pattern in cantos 4-10); for the schemes in the *Paradiso* and *Inferno*, see *Par.* 17.70-79.

Of course, the importance of numerical patterns to the *Comedy* has never been in doubt. The poem's one hundred cantos, arranged in three cantiche (of 34, 33 and 33 cantos) are part of its rhetorical form, its *forma tractandi,* as Dante points out in the Letter to Can Grande (if he is its author), a form that also embraces the division of each individual canto into rhymed (i.e., "numbered") terzinas (Freccero 1991). In medieval culture, numerical schemes with multiple meanings (seven was particularly rich: virginity, planets, vices and virtues, sacraments, ecclesiastical orders, liberal arts, etc.) are widespread; Prov. 11.10, stating that all things are made in number, weight, and measure was taken with great seriousness and evidence sought high and low to confirm its truth (cf. Bonaventura's *Mind's Journey to God,* 1.5-6).

Order, as evidence of a divine plan expressed in numbers, is a dominant theme of the center of Purgatory, especially insofar as it is an expression of the love that rules the universe: writers that may have influenced Dante, such as Peraldus (see Wenzel 1984), followed Augustine in defining vice as disordered love, and virtue as the setting of love in order; it was precisely the task of the sage to "set in order" according to the pattern of Wisdom (*CG* 1.1, citing Aristotle). In Dante's poem such order is proclaimed in Marco Lombardo's and Virgil's expositions of human desire and its need for guidance, both external, through the laws administered by the Empire, and internal, through the innate counsel of reason: in short, the balanced co-operation of natural impulse and discipline both intrinsic and imposed. In particular, Virgil's exposition in Canto 17 itself, adopting logical schemes of definition and distinction, constructs a logical diagram of human loves (Fergusson 1953), divided into genera and species. As in Aristotle's biology, such a logic of classes involves a hierarchy of value: thus, animals include the species man and lion; hierarchically, man is the summit of animals, the lion the noblest beast, and so on down the scale including fish, snails, worms; animals are in turn subordinate to the class of angels, but superior to the class of plants (cf. *Conv.* 3.2.11-14, 4.7.14-15). The principle of order in Purgatory is most conspicuous in the seven terraces of purgation, marked by the seven beatitudes and seven examples of the virtues of the Virgin; see Additional Note 12 and the note to *Purg.* 11.1-24.

The dynamism, complexity, and detail of Dante's application of numerical schemes distinguish the *Comedy*. Take for example two important patterns of imagery that help Dante express the order embedded in his poem: that of light from the heavens and from angels (cf. 14.149-51; 15.10-24, 67-75; 16.142-45; 17.9-18, 40-45, 52-57, 70-72; 18.76-81; 19.61-63), and that of the journey by steps, degrees, distributed throughout Purgatory (indeed the whole poem), centered on Canto 17. Significantly, one of these patterns primarily expresses the downward, guiding effect of natural light (including planetary influence) or of the divine ray (15.67-75; for the importance of the "reflected" ray; see *Par.* 1.49-51 and note); the latter unifies and vivifies the creatures and provides the image of a community where increased participation increases joy and satisfaction (counteracting pride, envy, and wrath; the latter two entail darkening of sight and thus of light). The downward ray is also the echo of the original creation, which began with light ("*Fiat lux*"; see *Par.* 29.25-30). The other pattern is that of the motion of the creature's return by degrees to its creator, up the Jacob's ladder that Bonaventura compares to an Exodus (*Journey* 1.9). Perhaps the most detailed indication of this pattern is Dante's use of the rhymes based on *ala* [wing], *scala* [ladder], *mala* [evil] or *cala* [descend] as verbal links for adopting the "ladder of being" as an organizing pattern for the *Comedy* (see Morgan 1991 and our Introduction to the *Inferno*); *ala* or variants appears in rhyme 13 times in the *Purgatorio*; *scala* six times with it and *cala* five (for the "staircase" see especially 12.104 and note, and Additional Note 8). The rhymes also appear at key moments in the poem: *scala* was used in Hell of the wayfarer's use of Geryon and Satan as ladders (*Inf.* 17.82-86; "per sì fatte scale" [by such stairs]; *Inf.* 34.82; allegorically, the Cross, cf. *Inferno* Additional Note 16, Freccero 1991), and now, as the poem comes up to its exact center, *Purg.* 17.70 (65-69, "ad una scala" [toward a stairway]; *ala, mala*), the center of the *cantica* is line 72; and just there, between that terzina (70-72) and the one following (73-75, the twenty-fourth and twenty-fifth terzinas of the canto; of course 25 = 7), the pilgrim's motion is arrested by the division of day and night that governs upward progress in *Purgatorio*. Or, in other words, by a law manifested by the presence, and regular interruption, of light, one that echoes the Creator's dividing the light from the darkness (Gen. 1.2), and the day from the night (Gen. 1.14: "Let there be lights made . . . to *divide* the day and the night"). Thus the poet sets his journey in order.

As Manfred Hardt 1989 showed, however, the exact center of the *Commedia* is at *Purg.* 17.125, the verse that divides the poem into two equal parts, each 7, 117 verses long; this point also marks the midpoint of Virgil's exposition of Love. Thus the centers of the canto and the cantica (17.70, 72) respectively mark the cessation of motion at the division of light and dark, phenomena specific to Purgatory; while the center of the whole work (17.125) marks the center of Virgil's exposition of the hierarchy of loves according to a logic of classes: for the "great chain of being" runs through not only the seven terraces of Purgatory, but through the whole poem. Number, light, motion, and degree are all interrelated at these two junctures.

The numerical patterns are also wedded to the other structures through which the poem makes its meanings. Singleton's pattern, stretching from Cantos 14 to 20, has as its extreme terms cantos including political lament-invectives and images of ramifying structures (the Arno valley in Canto 14; the Capetian genealogical descent in 20), while the center of the pattern observed by Ferrante 1988 is at Canto 7, midmost of the three cantos spent in the valley of the Princes, where genealogical trees and political invective are thematized.

R.L.M.

10. Dante and Forese
(Cantos 23-24)

Interpretation of the encounter of the pilgrim with Forese Donati (Cantos 23-24) is closely bound up with that of the series of six sonnets traditionally known as the "Tenzone" between Dante and Forese (numbers 26-28a in *Rime* 1946, 72-74a in *Dante's Lyric Poetry* 1967; three are ascribed to Dante—26/72, etc.—each paired with one ascribed to Forese—26a/72a, etc.). Although apparently unknown to the early commentators (the earliest mention of them is by the Anonimo Fiorentino, dating from the late fourteenth century), and never together in a single manuscript earlier than the seventeenth century (27-27a appear in one late fourteenth-century ms., the rest in another), the six sonnets are closely related in theme and style. Their attribution has been debated since Guerri 1931 argued that their closeness in manner to early-fifteenth-century Florentine "poesia giocosa" [jocose poetry] made it unlikely that they were by Dante and his friend. More recently Lanza 1971, Cursietti 1995, and Stefanini 1996 have renewed the discussion; Cursietti arguing that the poems date from the last decade of the fourteeth century and were written by the burlesque poet Stefano Finiguerri, called "il Za," as deliberate parody attacking a prominent Dantista and his homosexual lover.

In any reading the six poems are scurrilous; Cursietti's edition juxtaposes the more literal interpretations, favored by Barbi 1941 and other proponents of the traditional attribution, with the obscene meanings—mainly punning references to sodomy—found by him and others, which he documents with parallels in Boccaccio, Finiguerra, and others. To an unprejudiced reader at the turn of our century, no longer burdened with the need to see Dante as "respectable," the existence in these poems of a whole range of obscene puns seems undeniable. How the puns affect the question of attribution, however, in the absence of unambiguous external evidence (see now Alfie 1998, who argues for an early dating of one of the mss.), is another matter. In fact, citing the *Decameron* (ca. 1350) as a witness to slangy and obscene punning like that in the "Tenzone" is both appropriate and indicative of a major problem: many of the slang sexual puns current in any age have centuries of life behind them. With the *Decameron* we are within a mere twenty-five years of Dante's death, and the possibility that such jargon dates from Dante's time (and that he contributed to it—there is nothing in Finiguerra's dismal writings that remotely resembles the metaphorical inventiveness of the "Tenzone")—cannot be excluded. No doubt the scurrility of the "Tenzone" is an embarrassment, if three (or perhaps even all) of the poems are by Dante, but Dante—unlike Finiguerra—obviously had the ingenuity for such punning. On the other hand, the fact that none of the earliest commentators mention the "Tenzone" and the lateness of the manuscript tradition, if it is not refuted, do weaken the attribution.

The traditional view, which assumes that the "Tenzone" is authentic on the basis of the manuscript attributions, sees the following points of contact with the *Purgatorio*: 1. Canto 23 has Forese praise his faithful and virtuous widow at some length, asserting that he loved her dearly (lines 85-96); this is seen as a palinodic correction of the "Tenzone," where he is said to neglect her sexually in favor of other activities. 2. In Canto 23 the pilgrim implies that he and Forese had led particularly sinful lives together, and he associates their activities with the wood of *Inferno* 1 (lines 115-120). 3. Forese is doing penance in Purgatory for gluttony, one of the literal charges against him in the "Tenzone." Critics of the traditional view argue that the author of the forgery simply used these aspects of the episode as his grafting points, which without the "Tenzone" would have raised no question. They point to the fact that in *Purgatorio* 23 there are no verbal echoes of it, as one would expect if it were authentic.

It seems to us that the position occupied by the encounter with Forese in the larger structures of the *Purgatorio*—especially his prominence as the most conspicuous and carefully prepared example in the entire poem of the efficacy of prayer to help souls in Purgatory (the case of Trajan is of quite a different kind; see our notes to 10.73-93 and *Par.* 20.43-48)—is strong evidence in favor of the traditional view. On balance it seems to us that the preponderance of the evidence indicates that the simplest hypothesis is the most satisfactory: that Dante is indeed the author of the "Tenzone," probably with the collaboration of Forese, and that *Purgatorio* 23 and 24 are an effort to make amends for it, in particular for its insults to Forese's wife.

These considerations are strengthened by the fact that Dante has associated the Forese episode with the theme of homosexuality in a very pointed way, by making it parallel with the encounter with Brunetto Latini in *Inferno* 15. With the exception of Beatrice, Brunetto and Forese are the most important Florentine figures the pilgrim meets on his journey, a father-figure and a brother-figure. The number and closeness of the parallels between the episodes is extraordinary, even in the *Comedy* (see Giovanuzzi 1998, Durling [forthcoming]).

As in other structures of parallels between *Inferno* and *Purgatorio,* the differences help dramatize the contrast between Hell and Purgatory, especially the self-involvement, hopelessness, and despair of Hell as the background to the sense of hope, progress, and reliance on grace of the souls in Purgatory. The emphatic parallel between Brunetto's "What a marvel!" and Forese's "What grace is this for me!" is typical: Brunetto interprets the encounter with the pilgrim in terms of Fortune or astral determinism, but Forese understands immediately that like everything else that touches him now, the encounter is an expression of

God's love, providing encouragement and strength for both Forese and the pilgrim, while the effect of meeting the pilgrim on Brunetto is left ambiguous, to say the least; if Brunetto meditates on the relevance to his case of 1 Cor. 9.24-27, it can only deepen his suffering.

But the significance of the parallels is far from exhausted in this pattern, which they share with others. As our notes to *Inferno* attempt to trace, a major part of the penitential lesson of Hell for the pilgrim is his experience of his kinship with the damned, his discovery in himself of the potentiality for each of the sins punished there. There is no escaping the central relevance to the episode of Forese—and to the *Comedy* as a whole—of the theme of homosexual desire and its relation to Dante's love for Beatrice and the poetics deriving from it. That Dante was no stranger to homosexual feelings is clear, and the evidence indicates that he did not radically distinguish them from "purer" forms of love. He regarded homosexual desire as extremely common, perhaps affecting as much as half of human kind (see 26.76-87, with notes), and in the *Comedy* he expresses what is, for his times, an unusually liberal—though by no means permissive—attitude toward it (see also *Inferno*, Additional Note 5).

R.M.D.

11. Embryology and Heredity
(*Canto 25*)

The effort to assimilate Aristotle's metaphysics and biology, with his complicated theories of the relation of form and matter, of potency and act, of the soul as the substantial form of living bodies, led to much debate among the Scholastics, particularly since they had to reconcile with Aristotle's theories their Christian belief in the immortality of the soul and of the direct creation of each human soul by God. The questions involved had direct relevance also to the fundamental idea of Original Sin: it was clear that all our imperfections went back to Adam and Eve, but how exactly were they transmitted, through the body, the soul, or both? Until the rediscovery of Aristotle, this question was not particularly critical, though there were several opinions. A number of Fathers of the Church took the view that human souls were derived from Adam's *ex traduce* [by transmission], that is, by the "passing along" of a "part" of the father's soul in his seed, a view vigorously opposed by the Scholastics; others saw the body as the vehicle of transmission, a separate entity only tenuously controlled by the soul (see our note to 25.21-106).

Our remarks on this complicated subject will necessarily brief and simplified. A key passage in Aristotle's very difficult *De generatione animalium* reads:

> Thus it is clear that [semens and fetations] possess nutritive soul . . . It is while they develop that they acquire sentient soul as well, in virtue of which an animal is an animal—I say "while they develop," for it is not the case that when an animal is generated, at that same moment a human being, or a horse, or any other particular sort of animal is formed, because the end or completion of each thing comes into being [*génetai*] last of all, and that which is the end [*télos*] of its process of generation. (2.3)

In keeping with his view of the importance of classes in the logical structure of things, Aristotle believes that the generic aspect of each generated thing must in some sense exist before additional determinations take place: a thing must exist before it has life, have life before being plant or animal, etc. Later he says: "It is clear that we must posit that semens and fetations that are not separated from the parent possess nutritive soul *potentially,* though not *in actuality*" (2.10).

Naturally enough, such passages created great difficulties for the Scholastics. For one thing, if soul is form and appears last, perhaps being actualized only at birth, it would seem that some other agency must govern the formation of the animal, especially since only something "in act" (fully realized) could bring any-thing from potentiality into act. Following Aristotle, most Scholastics adopted his theory that the active principle in the development of the foetus was the father's seed, the mother supplying only the matter, identified with the menstrual blood. Galen had recognized that what we now call the Fallopian tubes brought into the womb a substance that joined with the sperm, but he remained uncertain as to its exact function. Albert the Great considerably qualified the Aristotelian antithesis:

> The subjected matter in the humor of the female has much receptivity and preparation for form; nor is the semen of the male entirely without matter, nor the liquid released by the female entirely without form: but the former is closer to form and the latter is closer to matter. In generation both are united in one, and then the thing in which both have joined becomes one, having the powers both from the male and the female: for this reason nei-ther by itself, but only when joined to the other, has the potentiality for life and soul (*De animalibus* 16.1.3).

As he makes clear in *De natura et origine animae,* Albert attributes to matter in general what he calls *incohatio formae,* a version of Augustine's *rationes seminales* [seminal principles], predispositions to form, or incipient forms; he does not see matter as merely formless (Dante, on the other hand, does not refer to any for-mal principle in the mother's blood, and *Par.* 29.24-36 seems to exclude *rationes seminales* entirely).

Aquinas saw the foetus as exercizing the powers of nutrition and eventually of motion in the womb, but, because of his conviction that forms as such are un-changing, he held that the father's semen, acting on the mother's blood, fash-ioned the body and soul of the foetus as far as the animal stage and then evaporated; in this process a large number of intermediate forms (souls) succeeded each other in the foetus, each destroyed as the next came into being, until God in-fused the rational soul, entirely replacing the last animal soul fashioned by the semen (*CG* 2. 89.6-22, *ST* 1a q. 118). One of the difficulties such a view entails is that although it may account for the imperfections of the offspring as deriving from the mother's blood and the father's seed, still, if the earlier sensitive soul is *replaced* by the directly created rational soul, there is no reason to attribute the imperfections resultant from Original Sin to the soul. Albert's view, in which the infused rational soul was combined with the already existing sensitive soul in the foetus, kept the source of imperfection clearly in the soul.

Nardi was surely correct in asserting that Dante rejected the doctrine of the succession of forms. But Dante is very far from taking over Albert's theory in every respect. Here is the crucial passage (*De natura et origine animae,* 1.5), also quoted by Nardi:

> The human soul is partly from within [i.e., biologically produced] and partly comes from outside, for, although the vegetative and the sensitive [soul] are drawn forth from matter by the formative principle that is in the combined blood of mother and father, still this formative principle would not have brought them forth so as to be the powers of a rational and intellectual form and substance, unless the very formative principle were informed and moved by the Intellect that moves all things in the work of generation. And thus the last complement, the intellectual form, is not infused by the pure first Intellect, the First Cause, through an instrument or through matter, but through his own light. Thus God is not said to create the rational soul out of anything preexisting; the intellect enters the embryo from what is extraneous to matter, but not from what is extraneous to nature, for the Intellect, the Author of nature, is not external to nature, except in so far as he is pure and unmixed with matter . . . but is more intimately within natural things than all other natural principles, none of which can operate any effect unless it is moved and shaped by him.

The last statement is a version of the famous first proposition of the *Liber de causis,* according to which, when a higher cause operates through a secondary cause, the effect of the higher cause is always greater than that of the secondary one (no autonomy of nature in Albert). It is not at all clear, *pace* Nardi, that Albert disagreed with Aquinas on the supercession of forms; he is evasive and perhaps inconsistent on this point, since he insists that *formans* [shaper] and *formatum* [thing shaped] cannot be the same entity (as in *De nat. et orig.* 1.1), and repeatedly, as here, calls the rational soul "the last form." Dante's "anima fatta" [having become a soul] (line 52) is unambiguous.

Although Albert would no doubt have had to agree that the creation of every rational soul mirrored Genesis 2, there is nothing in his account corresponding to Dante's "the first Mover turns to it, rejoicing over the greatness of Nature's art," since in Albert's account God has been actively present all along. Notice also that Albert's view that God illuminates the rational soul "with his own light" involves the proposition that the human being can directly know "separated substances" (i.e. angels and perhaps God himself), a doctrine that Aquinas vigorously opposed, maintaining that human knowledge is naturally derived from sense experience exclusively (Dante seems to subscribe to his view in *Par.* 2.40-42).

One of the most interesting points in Canto 25 is the assertion that the "new spirit" (the infused rational soul) "draws into its own substance what it finds active" in the foetus. Busnelli 1934 (who argued that "what it finds active" refers to the body, an idea conclusively refuted by Nardi 1938) pointed out the similarity of Dante's phrase with Aquinas's description of the conception of Christ: "As in the usual process of generation, the seed of the man *draws into its own substance* the matter supplied by the mother; so that same matter [i.e., in the Virgin's womb], in the generation of Christ, the divine Word assumed to be unified with himself" (*CG*, 4.45), and: "he draws human nature into his own substance, that it may subsist there" [*naturam humanam . . . ad suam substantiam trahit, ut in ea subsistat*] (49). In reply Nardi (1938, now in 1990) scornfully pointed out that the terminology was traditional for the assimilation of food, although he had to acknowledge that the human embryology in the passage was inconsistent with Aquinas's usual Aristotelian embryology. Indeed, it has very different implications from Aquinas's theory of the evaporation of the formative power of the semen, which cannot apply to the Word. Nardi regarded Dante's phrase as merely metaphorical, but we believe the matter goes very deep, as the importance given to the miracle at Cana and the repeated analogy with the sun indicate (see the notes to 25.76-78 and 88-102, and *Par.* 33.127-32). Dante's poetics constantly models itself on the Incarnation, the "Word made flesh" (see Martinez 1983, Cogan 1999).

R.M.D.

12. The Virtues of the Virgin Mary
(After Canto 27)

On each of the terraces of Purgatory, the souls are instructed in their practice of virtue by examples of it, and in each case the first example is the Virgin Mary's conduct in an incident from the Gospels:

1. 10.34-45	Humility	Annunciation	Luke 1.26-38, esp. 38
2. 13.28	Compassion	Wedding at Cana	John 2.1-11, esp. 3
3. 15.85-93	Mildness	Jesus in the Temple	Luke 2.42-51, esp.48
4. 18.100	Zeal	Visitation	Luke 1.39-56, esp. 39
5. 20.1-24	Poverty	Nativity	Luke 2, esp. 7
6. 22.142-44	Abstinence	Wedding at Cana	John 2.1-11, esp. 3
7. 25.128	Chastity	Annunciation	Luke 1.26-38, esp. 34

Four out of five of these incidents are from the Gospel of Luke, indeed from the first two chapters of Luke; they are not related in any of the other Gospels. The fifth incident is the Virgin's intervention at the Wedding at Cana; it appears in the Gospel of John and in no other.

One is immediately struck by the symmetry and chiastic relation of examples 1-2 and 6-7. The importance of the Annunciation was enormous in theology, in the liturgy (the Ave Maria, based on the Visitation as well, is probably the most frequently uttered prayer in the Christian tradition, especially in the High Middle Ages), and in the visual arts, and it is no surprise to find the Virgin's role on that occasion given the place of honor—first and last, alpha and omega—among her virtues. The Annunciation is also, of course, the very earliest Gospel event involving the Virgin Mary, and it is immediately followed by the Visitation; the other events from Luke are among the earliest in which Jesus appears. The Wedding at Cana, the occasion of Jesus's first miracle (John 1.11), marks the beginning of his public ministry, in which the Virgin has little role (for further observations on these events, see Additional Notes 6 and 7). The five events, then, as a group, have a certain self-contained completeness.

The chronological order of these five events in the Gospels is as follows:

I. Annunciation
II. Visitation
III. Nativity
IV. Jesus in the Temple
V. Wedding at Cana

The order in which Dante makes use of the events is interestingly complex, and he must have considered it carefully, given its importance to the whole framework of the *Purgatorio*; we should not be deceived by the sense of inevitability that Dante's masterful arrangement creates. A table can perhaps best set forth the interrelationships (Arabic numerals refer to the order in the *Purgatorio*; Roman numerals to the chronological order according to the Gospels):

1	2	3	4	5	6	7
I	V	IV	II	III	V	I

|———> <——————||——————> <———|

As the arrows indicate:

1-2	The order is chronological (I-V).
2-3-4	The chronogical order is reversed (V-IV-II).
4-5-6	The order is chronological (II-III-V).
6-7	The chronological order is reversed (V-I).

It is striking how the entire system points at Cana; see the note to 25.76-78 and, on the importance of Cana for Dante's poetics, Additional Note 11.

R.M.D.

13. Dante and Ovid's Pyramus
(Canto 27)

The brief reference in 27.36-39 to Ovid's tale of Pyramus and Thisbe (*Met.* 4.51-166) has a much richer significance than the commentary tradition has recognized; it calls attention to fundamental metaphors in both *Inferno* and *Purgatorio*. Commentators have, accurately enough, related lines 37-39 to the crisis of Ovid's story, pointing out that the analogy is with the power of Thisbe's name: because of Pyramus' great love for Thisbe, hearing her name calls him back momentarily from death. But line 36, with its reference to the wall, refers to a fundamental strain of imagery both in Ovid's tale and in the *Purgatorio*.

The metaphorics of Ovid's famous story is extremely rich and can only be briefly discussed here (for further discussion, see Durling/Durling, in preparation). The tale is introduced as an explanation of the change in color (from white to dark red or black) of the berries of the mulberry tree (cf. 27.39). It is centered on the image of the body as the house of the soul: the human psyche is enclosed within its body as if in a house, communicating with the world and with other human beings through the apertures in the walls—eyes, ears, mouth, and so on. This theme is most clearly expressed in Pyramus and Thisbe's conversing through the chink in the wall that separates their two houses. Fire imagery is also fundamental to Ovid's text: the youthful passion of Pyramus and Thisbe burns the more intensely the more strictly their parents forbid it (line 64), and it finds its way through the chink in the wall (introduced in line 65). The two escape parental and societal restraint (the latter figured in the walls of Babylon, according to legend the first walled city in history, lines 57-58) into the realm of powerful impulses they are not equipped to control, especially not Pyramus, whose very name includes *fire* (Greek πῦρ). The tragic outcome of the tale is due primarily to the fact that Pyramus' agitation—the excitement of sexual desire and rebellious escape from authority—makes him hasty and precarious, ready to imagine disaster: he supposes Thisbe dead and in an agony of guilt and despair stabs himself, soon after followed in death by Thisbe.

Beginning in the emblematic scene of the chink in the wall, Ovid's story moves out of the symbolic and social containers into the forest, to the white mulberry looming in the darkness, another figure for the body, this time as erotic goal, and in doing so the story moves ever closer to the lovers' literal bodies, first in the metonymy of Thisbe's veil, then to their literal bodies, to the sudden and irrevocable destruction of those fragile containers, whose life blood escapes through the small cuts made in their walls by Pyramus' sword, whose most intense moment is the terrifying image of Pyramus' blood spurting over the mulberry tree, compared to the water spurting from a chink in a leaden water pipe (lines 122-24).

Thisbe's veil, whose finding by Pyramus precipitates the catastrophe, is another well-established symbol: the body as the veil of the soul. Fleeing the thirsty lioness that comes to the fountain where she is to meet Pyramus, she lets it fall, to be torn and stained with blood by the lioness (a figure for ungovernable impulse); Thisbe's panic, which causes her to lose her veil as she runs to hide, is as crucial to the story as Pyramus' misinterpretation of it. For him the veil is both metonymically and metaphorically Thisbe's body; though ambiguous, it is in reality the sign of Thisbe's escape, but in his panic Pyramus leaps to the conclusion that it signifies her death. The story is a classic treatment of the misreading of ambiguous signs, and for this reason, among others, it was of great interest to Dante.

Dante read Ovid's story as a study in fleshliness, especially in the power of fear and guilt to distort perception. Dante repeatedly uses the symbolism of the body as the house of the soul (see *Conv.* 3.8.9), and he rightly connected Ovid's house-metaphor with *Aen.* 6.724-34, on the body as the prison of the fiery soul, itself one of Ovid's sources. Cavalcante's "cieco carcere" [blind prison] (*Inf.* 10.58-59) echoes *Aen.* 6.734 in a context using the body/house metaphor and featuring the misreading of an ambiguous sign (*Inf.* 10.58-72). The story of Ugolino is Dante's darkest version of the flesh as the prison of the soul, lit only by a small opening [*pertugio*] (*Inf.* 33.22). Not only do the walls and "pertugio" of the Tower of Hunger allude to Pyramus and Thisbe; there is also a rending of the veil in Ugolino's prophetic dream (*Inf.* 33.27), an ambiguous sign to which Ugolino, like Pyramus and Cavalcante (misinterpreting the pilgrim's "ebbe"), gives the worst possible construction.

In Canto 3, where the motif of the pilgrim's shadow is introduced, the parallels are richly developed (see our notes to 3.17-18, 22-45, 88-99, 118-19): the central motif is that the fleshly body is a wall that blocks the sun lines 94-99): "Without your asking, I confess to you that this is a human body you see, by which the light of the sun is *split* upon the ground. Do not marvel, but believe that not without power that comes from Heaven does he seek to surmount this *wall*" (emphasis added; note the ambiguity of the term *wall* in line 99). In the next canto the pilgrim will be confronted with the chink in the wall of the mountain (4.19-21). The allusions to the famous scene in the myth of Pyramus and Thisbe could hardly be clearer; see *Met.* 4.65-66: "*fissus* erat tenui rima, quam duxerat olim, / cum fieret, *paries* domui communis utrique . . ." [*Split* by a narrow crack, which had opened long ago when it was made, was the *wall* common to both houses].

Note the inversion of the term *fesso* [Lat. *fissus,* split] of the sunlight (3.96; cf. 3.17 and 88), before the arrival at the split in the wall. It is an inversion of Ovid's symbolism that subtly but effectively establishes the correlation of the flesh as wall with the wall of the mountain. Dante's sytematic use of Ovid's myth allows the identification of another inverted parallel: in 3.87-91: the shades, in doubt and hesitant, draw back at the sight of the pilgrim's living body, as the hesitant Thisbe draws back when she sees the dying Pyramus: "dum dubitat, tremebunda videt pulsare cruentem / membra solum, retroque pedem tulit" [while she is in doubt, she sees the trembling members pounding the bloody ground, and she stepped back]. The sense of the fragility of the body in Ovid's account recurs in Manfred's body being "broken" by "two points," making chinks in the bodily walls (cf. also *Inter cantica* to Canto 3). Canto 5 continues these systems of imagery.

The entire *Comedy* thus involves a metaphorical reversal of the tale of Pyramus and Thisbe (as well as a complex reversal of the "tragedy" of the *Aeneid*): it moves from confrontation with a lion and other beasts in the Dark Wood to the safety of home (the *patria*; cf. *Inf.* 15.54). The simile of *Purg.* 27.37-42 makes at last explicit the relation to Ovid's story of this fundamental system of imagery also governing the *Purgatorio.* It was introduced by Cato's "the slough [*scoglio*] that keeps God from being manifest to you" (2.122-23), a version of the veil, related to the scales [*squamae*] that blind saint Paul (Acts 9.18); see Pertile 1995. But *scoglio* is both *slough* and *rock*. If the veil adheres to its wearer, the wall confronts him externally; it is the projection of his own condition. As Pyramus and Thisbe communicate through the chink in the wall, the travelers mount toward Beatrice through chinks in the rock, beginning in 4.19. The wall of rock is finally attenuated, becoming the wall of fire of Canto 27. Finally, Beatrice's veil (in place from 30.31 to 31.145) is an ultimate version of Thisbe's veil, but it is removed, as Thisbe's should have been, in a supreme moment of amorous reunion.

R.M.D.

14. Virgil and the Fourth *Eclogue*

(After Canto 30)

When in Canto 30 the pilgrim turns to Virgil to express his turmoil at the appearance of Beatrice, Virgil is no longer there: he has "left us deprived of himself" (lines 49-50), and his departure is a capital event in the poem. Dante avoids specifying when it takes place, but there are a number of clues that suggest both the moment of Virgil's departure and its significance. Central to the issues is Dante's conception of the fourth *Eclogue* (for text and translation, see pp. 584-87) as a clearly designated moment of prophetic inspiration—nothing less than the prophecy of the imminent birth of Christ. As Statius says, as the poet of the fourth *Eclogue* Virgil was "like one who walks at night, who carries the light behind him and does not help himself, but instructs the persons coming after, when [he] said: 'The age begins anew . . .'" (lines 67-69). The clear indication of these lines is that in some sense Virgil turned his back on the prophetic light of the eclogue, and the simplest explanation is that he simply did not believe in it.

In Canto 30 the moment at which Virgil chooses (or is required) to disappear occurs at a point after the seven moving lights become clearly identifiable as candelabra, for that is the moment of our last glimpse of him (lines 43-57). Immediately thereafter, Matelda urges the pilgrim to look further ahead to the procession itself, to "what comes after" (lines 61-63; cf. 10.110: "think what follows"). Since the procession represents both a) the entire history of the world and b) the process of the biblical revelation of the meaning of world history, at some point there must be a moment that corresponds to 40 B.C. (the date of the consulship of Pollio and thus of the composition of the fourth *Eclogue*); this moment must be before the arrival of the four Evangelists opposite the pilgrim and his companion, since their arrival corresponds to the Incarnation, and Vergil died in 19 B.C.

Matelda's urging of the pilgrim to direct his gaze further ahead is connected with an elaborate series of turnings in Canto 29. First, in lines 1-9, Matelda turns to her left and walks upstream; the pilgrim, followed by the other two poets, turns to the right and keeps pace with her, facing south. Then, in lines 10-12, the group follow the turn in the river and turn left, so that they are walking toward the east, and at this moment occurs the initial flash of lightning that announces the procession. The entire group continues to walk eastward as the procession approaches (lines 31-54), and we have our last view of Virgil (still behind the pilgrim, as in 28.145-46). As the elders representing the OT draw near, we have the first reference to another turn toward the left (lines 67-69, couched hypothetically); when the elders of the OT are opposite the pilgrim he stops walking (and so must anyone still behind him). In what remains of the canto the rest of the procession becomes visible, but in lines 151-54 it comes to a halt when the chariot is directly opposite the pilgrim. If he is still facing east, it is to his left, but at some unspecified moment, perhaps precisely at lines 151-54, the pilgrim turns to his left in order to face it directly, and in 30.43 the pilgrim again turns to the left in order to speak to Virgil.

The entire context, then, invites us to understand that whenever Virgil leaves, it involves his *turning*; in other words, he reenacts turning his back on the prophetic vision of the fourth *Eclogue* (and on the offer of salvation implicit in his being granted it). At some point Virgil turns toward his own left, away from the direction indicated by Matelda for the pigrim to look. Now in Dante's eyes the fourth *Eclogue* is one of the testimonies of the invasion of the world of history by the light of revelation; the moment of Matelda's injunction—

because it is an injunction to look (prophetically) forward—is probably the one that corresponds most closely to the historical moment of the composition of the eclogue as Dante conceived it, and is the one most likely to be that of Virgil's departure.

Virgil reenacts the moment of the fourth *Eclogue* in another important passage, when he and the pilgrim are blocked from entering the gate of Dis (*Inf.* 8.82–9.15). At the end of *Inferno* 8, Virgil has a moment of clear prophetic insight: he sees exactly the whereabouts of the angel descending to help them: "'already, on this side of [the main gate of Hell] there comes down the slope . . . such a one that by him the city will be opened to us'" (lines 128-30). But at the beginning of Canto 9 Virgil has lost that certainty and is close to despair. That "già" [already, now] of *Inf.* 8.128 is a clear allusion to the insistent *iam* of the eclogue (where it occurs in lines 4, 6, 7, 10, 27, 37, 43, 48); cf. Statius's use of it in *Purg.* 22.76 and its omission in 22.70-72. As our note to *Inf.* 8.82-117 shows, Dante also connected this episode with the fact that in the *Aeneid* the Sybil and Aeneas are not permitted to enter Dis. Although it is indirectly and subtly suggested, then, Dante's interpretation of the fourth *Eclogue* is integral to his entire treatment of the figure of Virgil.

The treatment of Virgil's departure is integral also to the meditation on poetry and on European poetic tradition so prominent in *Purgatorio* 23-26. Virgil, Statius, and Dante himself represent a spectrum of possible relations to divine inspiration and the fashioning of the external sign, and they form a historical sequence: 1) *Virgil.* Divine inspiration speaks, but it is not recognized as such nor accepted; the deeply yearning but skeptical poet produces a mystified pagan text, setting forth partial truths distorted by his misunderstanding and lack of belief. 2) *Statius.* Divine inspiration is accepted (Statius becomes a Christian), but the external signs he fashions—in both his practical conduct and his poetry—hide his belief. 3) *Dante.* Divine inspiration is recognized, accepted, and proclaimed as the primary source of poetry itself, as in fact it had been for the first two ("quando Amor mi spira, noto" [when Love breathes within me, I take note]), and the external sign is consciously and coherently fashioned as Christian allegory ("a quel modo / ch'e' ditta dentro vo significando" [to that measure which he dictates within, I go signifying]). The first words of the pilgrim's reply to Bonagiunta, "I' mi son un" [I in myself am one] (24.52) are parallel to Statius' "fu'mi" [I was in myself], where he is relating that "out of fear in myself I was a secret Christian for a long time, feigning paganism" (22.90-91). In both cases the reflexive pronoun intensifies the distinction between inner and outer. Statius is saved, but he has had to atone—for four hundred years, he says (22.92-93)—for not integrating his inner life and his outward expression. Dante asserts his commitment to integration of inner being and outer expression in his answer to Bonagiunta.

This great arc of relation among major poems (*Aeneid, Thebaid, Comedy*) is not explicitly the subject of the exchange between the pilgrim and Bonagiunta in Canto 24, but it provides the controlling context; what the pilgrim says to Bonagiunta there is true of the *Comedy* as well as of the *Vita nova*, and in the Earthly Paradise the pilgrim will begin to understand the task that is set before him.

R.M.D.

15. Rolling Out the Apocalypse
(*Cantos 29-33*)

At six cantos, the pilgrim's stay in the Earthly Paradise (28.1– 33.145) is the longest so far in the poem; its central event, the pilgrim's meeting with Beatrice (Cantos 30-31) is framed by the procession and recession of the Biblical books (Cantos 29, 32), and the sojourn is capped by the pilgrim's vision of both the history and immediate future of the Church (33; a tripartition of the episode in Eden is offered by Lansing 1994). That the pageant of the Church unfolds where it does may reflect Augustine's allegorical identification of Eden with the Church (*City of God* 13.21).

Charles S. Singleton (1949) observed that cantos 28-30 constitute the "advent of Beatrice" at the center of the part of the *Comedy* that unfolds in time (*Purg.* 1-33, *Par.* 1-28; only Hell and the Empyrean are beyond time). Beatrice's judgment of Dante imitates the coming of Christ at the fulcrum of history, dividing Old Law from New, and preparing, with his first advent in the flesh, his second advent at the Last Judgment, when time will be swallowed up in eternity. In this sense, as Singleton noted, the parade of biblical books, from Genesis to the Apocalypse, represents the sweep of created time in the form of a liturgical pageant. The thirteenth-century *Golden Legend* states that Christ comes to *free* humankind from time: a gesture well suited to Eden, which stands above Ante-Purgatory, where the obligation was to "restore time for time" (23.84) and above Purgatory itself, where time is spent purging sin (18.103, 24.91).

That a series of books should represent linear time recalls Augustine's comparison of created time to a verse of a hymn, only fully intelligible when it ends (*Conf.* 11.27-28; see Freccero 1991). The events in Eden rehearse the narrative of sin and redemption of sacred history, but recursively rather than consecutively: there is mention of the Fall (29.24, 32.32, 37), of King David the Psalmist, when Israel worshiped at the Ark of the Covenant (29.107, 33.2), of the Exile in Babylon (33.1), of the exilic prophet Ezekiel (29.100). These echoes from the Pentateuch, the historical books, and the Prophets are complemented with material from the Solomonic books of Wisdom, especially the Song of Songs (see 29.113-14, 30.11, 32.73, 149-60). The life of Christ, from his Incarnation to his Ascension, is sketched (see 32.77-78 and note). OT and NT naturally overlap here, since for Christians the history of the Church, the "true Israel," has always been single (Catholic teaching denied that Jews were any longer part of the "true" Israel, though Dante does not unduly emphasize this; but see *Par.* 7.46-48 and notes). The life of Christ is the "form" of the Church (see *Mon.* 3.15.3), as the soul is that of the body.

Like other medieval Neoplatonists, Dante imagined time as born out of eternity at the Creation and absorbed back into eternity at the Last Judgment; the procession is therefore described in cosmological terms. Suggesting how time was displayed by the moving heavens, Dante refers to the seven bands of color streaming from the candlesticks as "the beautiful heaven that I devise." The Ark of the Church is compared to the chariot of Helios or Apollo, the sun (29.117), echoing the tradition of the sun as "the chariot of time" (Gen. 1.14; see *Conv.* 4.23.12-14, Silverstein 1932, Ghisalberti 1934). Dante introduces similes using the stars, sun and moon (29.53, 78, 91). And he is explicit in referring to the seven candlesticks guiding the procession, as "the Septentrion of the first heaven" around which the procession rotates as it prepares its return to Heaven, just as the stars of the northern hemisphere rotate around the polestar. Thus the procession turns in a manner analogous to the stars that rise and set, it descends and returns (see below). As Tatlock 1934-35 pointed out, the shape of the procession represents this movement through time, for in the Apocalypse the twenty-four elders representing the books of the Bible are gathered around the Lamb in a circular figure of eternity, rather than in the linear distension of the cross-shaped pageant. This "circular" nature of eternal Godhead is reiterated by naming God as "who is, who was, and is to come" (Apoc. 1.8, 4.8, 11.17, 16.5), as well as "Alpha and Omega, the beginning and the end" (Apoc. 1.8, 21.5, 22.13); Beatrice-Wisdom surrounded by the virtues in 32.97-99 also appears to be a trace of John's vision of the "circular" eternal.

This astronomical panorama is closely related to the numerological patterns observed by commentators (Porcelli, *LDN* 1989), which bear out how Creation was according to "number, weight, and measure" (Prov. 11.10). Indeed the pageant is quite at sixes and sevens, associated in medieval Christian numerology with the six days of creation, the six ages of secular history, and with the Sabbath beyond time (the seventh day, God's day of rest and a figure of the next life). The pilgrim remains in Eden for six cantos, as Adam and Eve dwelt in Eden six hours (see *Par.* 26.141-42), while the Fall, which emptied it (29.24), took place on the sixth day, also destined to be the Good Friday of redemption through the Cross (32.51); and since the time of Augustine the Crucifixion was understood to inaugurate the beginning of a sixth age, under the New Law. The number seven clearly functions as well: led by a sevenfold beacon, the procession is parsed in seven groups (OT books; Gospels, gryphon and chariot; grouped virtues; Luke-Acts paired with Paul; the Catholic Epistles; John by himself; Luke through John form a group of seven— those wearing red flowers—and the virtues also make a distinct group of seven). Dante was surely struck by the sevens that organize John's Apocalypse (seven angels, churches, stars, seals, ages, trumpets, plagues, heads on the beast, etc.), and seven was also the number of the Wisdom books, which included the Song of Songs. Twenty-eight, numbering the canto where the pilgrim enters Eden, is perfect in being both the sum of its possible factors (1, 2, 4, 7, 14) and of numbers one through seven (see Kirkham 1998). As Kirkham points out, numbers also represent the ideal Church, which was seven-pillared (cf. the "seven pillars of wisdom" [Prov. 9.1]) in that it was sustained by the sevenfold Spirit. Bede's influential treatise also claimed that the Church displayed "perfect" Solomonic temple proportions in length, breadth, and height (6:4:2:3; 1, 2, and 3 are the factors of the perfect number six): the length signifies the faith of the Church "which in the pilgrimage of exile tolerates all adversities patiently"; breadth signifies charity, and height, hope. In Dante's procession, the pilgrim at first takes the seven candlesticks as "trees" (or pillars?), while the community of faith is represented in the biblical books; the width of the procession is determined by the breadth of the seven lights, which, as the manifestation of the Holy Spirit, suggest the spread of charity, as the soaring wings of the gryphon point to the hope of heaven. Numerology often informs prophecy, and in Dante's day apocalyptic expectations, stimulated by the prophetic works of Joachim of Flora (1135-1202) and his radical Franciscan followers, strove to discern the transition from the sixth to the seventh age (by Dante's death, various dates had been proposed, from 1260 to 1324), but another tradition, going back to Augustine, was more cautious in anticipating the end of time.

The procession has more to tell us, however. Commentators have called attention to the resemblance of Dante's pageant to mosaic images of processions in Ravenna, Rome, and Anagni; popular medieval visions like St. Patrick's Purgatory also culminated with processions (Morgan 1991). Tatlock suggested that Dante's model is the liturgical description (Honorius of Autun, *Gemma animae*, 5-6, PL 172.544-546) of episcopal processions signifying the advent of Christ. Preceded by deacons and subdeacons signifying the prophets and canons signifying the apostles, the bishop is brought, amidst choral singing, by a *comitatus* signifying the "chariot" ("quasi curru vectus"), as Christ was brought into the world by the chariot of Scripture; seven acolytes with candles signify the gifts of the spirit informing the sacraments of the Mass; the whole procession, Durandus observes, is "like an army set in array" (Cant. 6.3; see 29.19-23 and note). But if the Mass represents the sending of Christ to redeem mankind, the processions of the Church community from one church to another, as during Palm Sunday, when *Hosanna* is sung (29.51) are figurally the Exodus, the passage of Israel into the Promised Land, led by the column of fire (the candles, the Holy Spirit) and bearing the tablets of the Law (the Gospels), the Tabernacle (chests) with the Ark (reliquaries); when these are deposited in the sanctuary, as David and Solomon placed the ark under the wings of the cherubim, they represent Christ's ascent to heaven. Durandus, Dante's elder contemporary, puts it succinctly (*Rationale* 1859): "as the sending [*legatio*] of Christ into the world is figured in the Mass, so in our processions our return to our homeland [*reversio ad patriam*] is denoted, through whose solemnity the exodus of the people from Egypt [*egressum populo de Aegypto*] is imitated in nearly all aspects."

That the descent and return of Christ and the *reversio ad patriam* are models for liturgical movement goes back to the metaphysical underpinnings of Byzantine church architecture and liturgy: these ultimately rely on the Neoplatonic understanding of Creation as a descent and return (*exitus, reditus*) of God's creative love (see *Par.* 1.103-36, 29.13-36), the concept that determined the arrangement of works such as Aquinas' two *Summae* (Chenu 1964). In Dante's procession, the *reditus* is evident in that the procession approaches from the East, the direction of the rising Sun (Beatrice appears as the sun, 30.22-27), and then turns around and recedes towards the east, thus moving from its origin back to its origin; and just as the procession is about to turn back, Dante refers to this movement with the verb *procedere* (32.23), anticipating use of the same word in *Par.* 7.113 to describe the "humiliation" of God in the Incarnation (see also *Purg.* 22.70-72 and notes), and at *Par.* 29.20 (*procedette*, of the Creation), and recalling how sorrow *procede* from Satan in Hell (*Inf.* 34.36 and note; see also 28.88 and note) in a parody of God's creation through love. In a Christmas hymn using the figure of descent and return, Ambrose, the fourth-century bishop of Milan glossed Psalm 18, sung liturgically during the Advent and Nativity, as recounting how Christ, the bridegroom (*sponsus*) proceeds from the womb of the Virgin: "let him proceed [*procedat*] from his chamber, the royal hall of chastity, a giant of twin substance, that he may eagerly run his course, having stridden forth [*egressus*] from the Father, and returned [*regressus*] to the Father, run forth [*excursus*] even to hell and run back [*recursus*] to the throne of God" (Raby 1959).

Procession and return could of course be along a ladder or stairway, as in Jacob's dream and in medieval adaptations of the "scale of being," such as Bonaventura's *Mind's Journey to God*, which cites the "ascensions" of Psalm 83, and develops a meditative ladder (in 1.5 and 7.1 using both a sevenfold ladder of numbers and the "six steps to the throne of Solomon" (3 Kings 1.19) to "the high mountain," the seat of God. More relevant to Cantos 29-33 is the Apocalypse commentary attributed to the Dominican Hugh of St. Cher (mid-thirteenth century), who writes: "By the ladder [of Jacob] is signified the subject of this book, in which there are seven degrees, for seven are the parts of this book, to wit seven visions . . . The form [of this book] is touched on where it is said that Jacob saw a ladder standing and angels rising and descending on it."

Although the vertical dimension of descent and return is not omitted in Dante's procession (cf. 32.88-90), Hugh's application of Jacob's ladder to the progressive revelations of the seven angels in the Apocalypse renders it horizontally, just as Dante's procession emerges out of and returns to the East; the divine procession comes to meet the pilgrim in Eden (see 28.1-3 and notes), and his path is then incorporated with it as he and Statius join Beatrice and the virtues. Progress and return, at once vertical and horizontal, echo the link between Jacob's ladder and the Exodus (cf. *Mind's Journey,* 1.9), for the Exodus narrates a *crossing* on the horizontal plane: so affording a crucial mediation of the divine scheme of descent and return.

Of course, vertical procession and return are basic to Dante's poem: the pilgrim descends into Hell (assisted, at a crucial juncture, by the descent of the angelic messenger, recalling Christ's sending) and then returns to Heaven, via Purgatory, after his "resurrection" on Easter Sunday (*Purg.* 1.17). This pattern reaches its climax in Eden, where the pilgrim is brought before Beatrice for judgment, in anticipation of Christ's *parousia*, and in the sense that the narrative action of *Purgatorio* is a "return to Eden" after the exile of this life in the "widowed Northern hemisphere"(1.7). Beatrice herself has "descended" (31.107) as Wisdom with her handmaidens, a "second" advent that recalls her first advent (for procession and return in the *Vita nova*, see Durling/Martinez 1990; Martinez 1998; Durling 2001a); and she will reascend with the pilgrim (*Par.* 1.49-54).

The Earthly Paradise also recapitulates the second cantica. Eden's drama of the Fall is anticipated in the reference to the "first people" (1.7) and in the serpent's invasion of the valley (8.94-108; see also 32.130-35); the sevens of Eden echo the seven-storied mountain of purgation, and the seven-based numerology of *Purgatorio* itself (see Additional Note 9). Eden itself "descends" the mountain: in the trees that tempt the gluttons in Cantos 22 and 24, and in the earthquake heralding Statius' release, which fulfills the mountain's purpose. The most significant recapitulation is of the Exodus, mentioned at 2.46, 8.22, 11.13-15, and 18.133-35. These references culminate in Beatrice's reiteration of Christ's advent, his coming to those who were in bondage and captivity in Egypt. In Canto 29, the procession moves between the flash of lightning and its thunder-clap, as if between the *fiat lux* of creation and the thunder of the Last Judgment (Gen. 1.3; Apoc. 8.1, 17.10): as if encompassing the whole relationship of Christ and his bride the Church, from beginning to end, figure to fulfillment, Alpha to Omega.

R.L.M.

TEXTUAL VARIANTS

I list here, with brief comments, passages where I have adopted readings rejected by Petrocchi. It should be noted that nine of these involve decisions about punctuation, which are always editorial: accents and apostrophes indicating contractions exist in no medieval manuscripts, and the division of syntactic units is always a matter of judgment. See the remarks on the text in the Preface.

R.M.D.

1.62. Petrocchi's accentuation of *lì* seems unmotivated; the traditional unaccented form means "there was," as opposed to "was there" (i.e., in that place).

2.44. Petrocchi's reading is *faria beato pur descripto* [would make one blessed if merely described], which makes little sense and has little manuscript support (though it is reported as the reading of *Urb.* by Sanguineti); see Chiavacci Leonardi *ad loc.*

2.108. Petrocchi reads *doglie* [sorrows or griefs], which fits the context less well than *voglie* [desires], also the *Urb.* reading.

5.70. I follow Petrocchi's usual practice in expanding *di* [of] to *d'i* [of the] before masculine plurals (cf. the note on the variant in *Inf.* 11.28).

5.100-102. I follow Momigliano, Sapegno, Mattalia, and Lanza in rejecting Barbi's 1934 argument that because *perdere la vista e la parola* [to lose sight and speech] often occurs as a set expression for "to die," there must be a full stop at the end of line 100. In addition to preserving the logical progression of the passage, discussed in our note, the punctuation preserves the expressiveness of the enjambments (Momigliano in Mazzoni).

6.72. A majority of the manuscripts (including the Trivulziano) read "Mantova" here; Sanguineti gives "Mantoa." See our note on the passage.

7.16. Petrocchi reads *di Latin* [of Italians]; again, I follow his usual rule in reading *d'i Latin* [of the Italians].

8.69. Petrocchi reads *non lì è guado* [there, there is no ford]; without the accent on *li* (see the headnote), the phrase means "there is no ford to it" (i.e., God's counsel).

10.30. Many modern editions (including Sanguineti) give *che dritto di salita aveva manco*, interpreting it, if commenting, variously: as "which ascended less vertically" (implying that the base of the cliff slants), or "which gave least right—i.e., possibility—of ascent" (implying that the base is vertical). The line is one with many variants in the manuscripts; the one we follow gives a sense less tortured than the others. See our notes on the passage and Additional Note 6.

11.68. The past tense, *fe'*, is more appropriate to the context than the present *(fa)*.

11.129. *Là giù* [down there] (also adopted by Sanguineti) seems clearly required by the contrast with *qua su* [up here], lost in Petrocchi's reading, *qua giù* [down here].

12.5. The reading *(buon con) la vela* [sail] (also in Sanguineti) seems better attested than Petrocchi's *(buono con) l'ali* [wings]; also, according to 11.38, wings cannot be moved here and the pilgrim's own are not even said to grow until 27.123.

13.7. As in earlier instances, the unaccented *li* seems preferable.

14.4. Petrocchi's expansion of *che* [that] into *ch'e'* [that he] seems gratuitous; the meaning is perfectly clear without the expansion. See the headnote; in such cases simplicity is to be preferred.

14.20. As in the previous case, expansion of *chi* [who] into *ch'i'* [who I] seems unnecessary, as the meaning is perfectly clear.

22.40. I read *perché* [why] rather than Petrocchi's *per che* [to what]; see our notes on the passage.

22.117. A great majority of the early manuscripts, including *Urb.*, give the reading adopted here, superior in sense to the unsupported *saliri* [ascents].

24.36. The context seems to require *voler contezza* [desire knowledge] (also given by Sanguineti), rather than Petrocchi's *aver contezza* [have knowledge], particularly since *voler* is echoed by the pilgrim's "vaga di parlare" [eager to speak] (line 40).

24.61. The reading we adopt (also adopted by Sanguineti) seems better attested and to make more sense than Petrocchi's *gradire* [step]; it is also supported by "vede" [sees] in line 62.

25.95. The reading *e in quella forma ch'è in lui* [and in that form that is in it] makes nonsense of the passage; see Chiavacci Leonardi *ad loc.*

27.65. Petrocchi and Sanguineti give *toglieva* [took away]. The Trivulziano gives the reading adopted, supported by the use of such verbs as *fendere* and *rompere* in such passages (see the notes to Canto 3, Additional Note 13).

30.67-69. The editorial tradition has a full stop at the end of line 66, beginning a new sentence with line 67 and attaching the terzina to those that follow. Our text attaches lines 67-68 to the *preceding* terzina: the pilgrim can tell that Beatrice is looking at him *although* her veil prevents him from seeing her clearly. That her bearing is *protervo* can be seen from her posture; the difficulty of seeing through her veil thus seems much less relevant to lines 70-72 than to lines 64-66.

30.73. The manuscript tradition is particularly confused about this line. All its branches give readings that imply the repetition of some form of the verb *to be* (*sem* [we are] or *son*[I am]): thus "truly we are, truly we are Beatrice,"or "truly I am, etc.," except for *Urb.*, followed by Sanguineti, which gives quite a different structure: "Guardaci ben, se ben sem Beatrice" [Look at us well, if we really are Beatrice]. To us it seems that the connection of the repetition with other important passages, pointed out in our notes, gives it great authority; we have therefore retained Petrocchi's reading.

30.95. Although only a few manuscripts (including the Trivulziano) have *compatire a me* [compassion on me], it seems superior to Petrocchi's *compartire* [*a me*], used by Dante in 25.125 to mean "to divide"; here it would mean "sharing [with me]" or "taking [my] side"; see Chiavacci Leonardi's note *ad loc.*

31.51. Lanza's argument for the Trivulziano reading seems persuasive: that Petrocchi's *e che so' 'n* [and which are in] gives a form of the verb *to be* that is otherwise unattested in Dante. Furthermore, the passage loses force when the decay of Beatrice's body is placed in a smoothly parallel and, what is more, subordinate clause: the abruptness of the transition to the independent clause is part of the point.

BIBLIOGRAPHY

Reference Works

Battaglia, Salvatore. 1961–. *Grande dizionario della lingua italiana*. 20 vols. by 2000. Turin: UTET.

Enciclopedia dell'arte medievale. 1991–2000. 11 vols. Direttore: Angiola Maria Romanini. Roma: Treccani.

Enciclopedia dantesca. 1967–1983. Direttore: Umberto Bosco. A cura di Giorgio Petrocchi. 6 vols. Rome: Treccani.

Brieger, Peter, Millard Meiss, and Charles S. Singleton. 1969. *Illuminated Manuscripts of the Divine Comedy*. 2 vols. Bollingen Series LXXXI. Princeton, N.J.: Princeton University Press.

Kaske, R. E., with Arthur Groos and Michael W. Twomey. 1988. *Medieval Christian Literary Imagery. A Guide to Interpretation*. Toronto: University of Toronto Press.

Lansing, Richard, ed. 2000. *The Dante Encyclopedia*. New York–London: Garland.

Müller, Gerhard, and Gerhard Krause, eds. 1977–. *Theologische Realenzyklopädie*. 32 vols. by 2001. Berlin-New York: De Gruyter.

Ridpath, Ian. 1993. *Collins Pocket Guide to Stars and Planets*. 2nd ed. London: HarperCollins.

Schiller, Gertrud. 1966–1991. *Ikonographie der christlichen Kunst*. 5 vols. Gütersloh: G. Mohn.

Dante's Minor Works

Convivio. Ed. Cesare Vasoli and Domenico De Robertis. In *Opere minori*. Tomo I/2.

The Convivio. 1995. Tr. Richard Lansing. New York: Garland.

De vulgari eloquentia. Ed. P. V. Mengaldo. In *Opere minori*. Tomo II.

Epistole. Ed. Arsenio Frugoni and Giorgio Brugnolo. In *Opere minori*. Tomo II.

Monarchia. Ed. Bruno Nardi. In *Opere minori*. Tomo II.

Monarchia. 1995. Ed. and trans. Prue Shaw. Cambridge Medieval Classics 4. Cambridge: Cambridge University Press.

Dante's Monarchia. 1998. Trans., with a commentary, by Richard Kay. Studies and Texts 131. Toronto: Pontifical Institute of Mediaeval Studies.

Opere minori. Tomo II. 1979. Milan-Naples: Ricciardi.

Opere minori. Tomo I/2. 1988. Milan-Naples: Ricciardi.

Rime. 1946. Ed. Gianfranco Contini. 2nd ed. Turin: Einaudi.

Dante's Lyric Poetry. 1967. 2 vols. Ed. Kenelm Foster and Patrick Boyde. Oxford: Clarendon.

Vita nuova. 1980. Ed. Domenico De Robertis. Milan-Naples: Ricciardi.

Vita nova. 1996. Ed. Guglielmo Gorni. Turin: Einaudi.

The New Life. 1867. Trans. Charles Eliot Norton. Boston: Houghton, Mifflin.

The *Divine Comedy,* with Commentaries

Alighieri, Pietro. 1845. *Petri Allegherii super ipsius genitoris Comoediam Commentarium*. 3 vols. Ed. Vincentio Nannucci. Florence: Piatti.

Anonimo fiorentino. 1866-1874. *Commento alla Divina Commedia d'anonimo fiorentino del secolo XIV*. Ed. Pietro Fanfani. Bologna: Romagnoli.

Bambaglioli, Graziolo de'. 1915. *Il commento dantesco di Graziolo de' Bambaglioli dal Colombino di Siviglia con altri codici confrontato*. Ed. A. Fiammazzo. Savona.

Benvenuto da Imola. 1885. *Benvenuti de Rambaldis de Imola Comentum super Dantis Aldigherij Comoediam*. 5 vols. Ed. I. P. Lacaita. Florence: Barbèra.

Biagi, E., G. L. Passerini, and E. Rostagno, eds. 1931. *La Divina Commedia nella figurazione artistica e nel secolare commento*. 3 vols. Turin: UTET.

Bosco, Umberto, and Giovanni Reggio, eds. 1979. *La Divina Commedia*. 3 vols. Firenze: Le Monnier.

Buti, Francesco da. 1858-1862 [1989]. *Commento di Francesco da Buti sopra la Divina Commedia di Dante Allighieri*. 5 vols. Ed. Crescentino Giannini. Pisa: Nistri.

Carroll, John S. 1971. *Prisoners of Hope. An Exposition of Dante's Purgatorio*. Reprint of 1904 ed. Port Washington, N.Y.: Kennikat.

Chiavacci Leonardi, A. M. 1994-97. Dante. *Commedia*. 3 vols. Con il commento di Anna Maria Chiavacci Leonardi. (I Meridiani.) Milano: Mondadori.

The Divine Comedy of Dante Alighieri. Volume 1: Inferno. 1996. Ed. and trans. Robert M. Durling. Introduction and Notes by Ronald L. Martinez and Robert M. Durling. Illustrations by Robert Turner. New York–Oxford: Oxford University Press.

Fallani, Giovanni. 1993. *Dante Alighieri, Tutte le opere*. Commenti a cura di Giovanni Fallani, N. Maggi, and S. Zennaro. Rome: Newton.

Gmelin, Hermann. 1954. *Die göttliche Komödie: Kommentar*. 3 vols. Stuttgart: Klett.

Grandgent, C. H., ed. 1933. *La Divina Commedia di Dante Alighieri*. Rev. ed. Boston: D. C. Heath.

Lana, Jacopo della. 1866-1867. *Comedia di Dante degli Allagherii col commento di Jacopo della Lana bolognese*. Ed. Luciano Scarabelli. Bologna.

Lanza, Antonio, ed. 1997. *La Commedìa. Nuovo testo critico secondo i più antichi manoscritt fiorentini*. 2nd ed. Anzio: De Rubeis.

L'Ottimo. 1827-1829. *L'Ottimo Commento della Divina Commedia*. Ed. Alessandro Torri. Pisa: Capurro.

Mattalia, Daniele, ed. 1960. *La Divina Commedia*. 3 vols. Milan: Rizzoli.

Mazzoni, Francesco, ed. 1973. *La Divina Commedia. Purgatorio. Con i commenti di Tommaso Casini-Silvio Adrasto Barbi e di Attilio Momigliano*. Introduzione e aggiornamento bibliografico-critico di Francesco Mazzoni. Florence: Sansoni.

Pézard, André, ed. 1979. *Dante. Oeuvres complètes*. 4th ed. Paris: La Pléiade.

Petrocchi, Giorgio, ed. 1966-1967 [1994]. *La Commedia secondo l'antica vulgata*. 4 vols. Milan: Mondadori [Florence: Casa editrice Le Lettere].

Porena, Manfredo. 1946-1948. *La Divina Commedia*. Commentata da M. Porena. Bologna: Zanichelli.

Sanguineti, Federico, ed. 2001. *Dantis Alagherii Comedia*. Florence: Galluzzo.

Sapegno, Natalino, ed. 1958. *La Divina Commedia*. Milan-Naples: Ricciardi.

Scartazzini, G. A., ed. 1874-1890. *La Divina Commedia*. 4 vols. Riveduta nel testo e commentata da G. A. Scartazzini. Leipzig: Brockhaus.

Singleton, Charles S., trans. 1970. *The Divine Comedy*. 3 vols. Bollingen Series LXXX. Princeton, N.J.: Princeton University Press.

Lecturae Dantis

Lectura Dantis Californiensis. Purgatory. 2001. Ed. Allen Mandelbaum, Anthony Oldcorn, and Charles Ross. Berkeley: University of California Press.

Lectura Dantis neapolitana. Purgatorio. 1989. Ed. Pompeo Giannantonio. Naples: Loffredo.

Lectura Dantis scaligera. Purgatorio. 1968. Florence: Le Monnier.

Lectura Dantis Turicensis: Purgatorio. 2001. Ed. Georges Güntert and Michelangelo Picone. Florence: Cesati.

Lectura Dantis Virginiana: Dante's Divine Comedy. Introductory Readings: Purgatorio. 1993. Charlottesville: University of Virginia Printing Office.

Letture classensi. 1966- . Ravenna: Longo.

Letture dantesche. Purgatorio. 1955. Ed. Giovanni Getto. Florence: Sansoni.

Nuove letture dantesche. Volume quarto: Anno di studi 1968-69. 1970. Casa di Dante, Roma. Florence: Le Monnier.

Nuove letture dantesche. Volume quinto: Anno di studi 1969-70. 1972. Casa di Dante, Roma. Florence: Le Monnier.

Zennaro, Silvio, ed. 1981. *Purgatorio. Letture degli anni 1976-79.* Casa di Dante, Roma. Roma: Bonacci.

Primary Texts

Adelard of Bath. 1903. *De eodem et diverso.* Ed. H. Willner. *Beiträge zur Geschichte der Philosophie des Mittelalters,* 4.

Alain of Lille. 1955. *Anticlaudianus.* Ed. Robert Bossuat. Paris: Vrin.

———. 1980. *The Plaint of Nature.* Trans. James J. Sheridan. Toronto: Pontifical Institute of Mediaeval Studies.

Albertus Magnus. 1890-99. *Opera omnia.* 38 vols. Ed. Auguste Borgnet. Paris: Vivès.

———. 1916. *De animalibus.* Ed. H. Stadler. *Beiträge zur Geschichte der Philosophie des Mittelalters,* 15-16.

———. 1955. *De anima.* Ed. Clemens Stroick. Vol. 7 of *Opera omnia.* Monasterii Westfalorum in Aedibus Aschenbach.

———. 1968. *De natura et origine animae.* Ed. Bernhard Geyer. Vol. 12 of *Opera omnia.* Monasterii Westfalorum in Aedibus Aschenbach.

———. 1999. *On Animals. A Medieval "Summa Zoologica."* Trans. Kenneth F. Kitchell, Jr., and Irwen Michael Resnick. Baltimore: Johns Hopkins University Press.

Alexander of Hales. 1928. *Summa theologica.* 5 vols. Quaracchi: Typographia Collegii S. Bonaventurae.

[Anonymous]. 1949. *La Queste del saint Graal. Roman du xiiie siècle.* Ed. Albert Pauphilet. Classiques français du moyen âge. Paris: Champion.

Aristotle. 1942. *Generation of Animals.* Ed. and trans. A. L. Peck. Loeb Classical Library. Cambridge, Mass.: Harvard University Press.

———. 1983. *Parts of Animals.* Ed. and trans. A. L. Peck. Loeb Classical Library. Cambridge, Mass.: Harvard University Press.

Augustine of Hippo. 1948. *S. Aurelii Augustini Confessionum libri xiii.* Ed. Iosephus Cappello. Turin: Marietti.

———. 1981. *De civitate Dei libri xxii*. 5th ed. 2 vols. Ed. Bernard Dombart and Alfons Kalb. Stuttgart-Leipzig: Teubner.

———. 1995. *De sermone Domini in monte libri duos* post Maurinorum recensionem denuo edidit Almut Nutzenbecher. Corpus Christianorum Latinorum, 35. Turnholt: Brepols.

———. 1960. *Confessions*. Trans. John K. Ryan. Image Books. New York: Doubleday.

Bernard of Clairvaux. 1983. *Obras completas. I. Introducción y tratados.* Madrid: Biblioteca de los Autores Cristianos.

Bestul, Theodore, ed. 1996. *Texts of the Passion*. Philadelphia: University of Pennsylvania Press.

[Bible]. 1965. *Biblia Sacra iuxta Vulgatam clementinam*. 4th ed. Ed. Alberto Colunga and Lorenza Turrado. Madrid: Biblioteca de los Autores Cristianos.

[Bible]. 1989. *The Holy Bible, translated from the Latin Vulgate* [Douay version]. Rockford, Ill.: Tan.

Boccaccio, Giovanni. 1974. *Trattatello in laude di Dante*. Ed. Pier Giorgio Ricci. In vol. 3 of *Tutte le opere di Giovanni Boccaccio*, ed. Vittore Branca. Milano: Mondadori.

———. 1976. *Decameron*. Ed. Vittore Branca. In vol. 4 of *Tutte le opere di Giovanni Boccaccio*, ed. Vittore Branca. Milano: Mondadori.

Boethius. 1957. *Anicii Manlii Severini Boethii Philosophiae Consolatio*. Ed. Ludwig Bieler. Corpus Christianorum Series Latina. Turnholt: Brepols.

Boffitto, J., and C. Melzi d'Eril, eds. 1908. *Almanach Dantis Aligherii sive Prophacii Judaei Montipessulani Almanach perpetuum ad annum 1300 inchoatum*. Florence: Olschki.

Bonaventura of Bagnoreggio. 1955-57. *Obras de san Buenaventura. Edición bilingue*. 2nd ed. 2 vols. Dirigida por Leon Amoros, Bernardo Aperribay, Miguel Oromi. Madrid: Biblioteca de Autores Cristianos.

———. 1953. *The Mind's Road to God*. Trans. George S. Boas. New York: Liberal Arts Press.

Boyle, Leonard E., O.P. 1996a. "'Modi orandi Sancti Dominici': Transkription der Handschrift im Cod. Ross. 3." In *Modi orandi Sancti Dominici* 2:51-67.

Bruni, Leonardo. 1996. *Vita di Dante*. In *Opere letterarie e politiche,* ed. Paolo Viti, 539-52. Turin: UTET.

Chaucer, Geoffrey. 1987. *The Riverside Chaucer*. Gen. ed. Larry D. Benson. Boston: Houghton Mifflin.

Cicero. 1971. *Marci Tulli Ciceronis Laelius de amicitia*. Ed. Paolo Fedeli. Milan: Mondadori.

Claudian. 1922. *Claudian. With an English Translation* by Maurice Platnauer. Loeb Classical Library. New York: Putnam.

Colgrave, Bertram C., ed. 1968. *The Earliest Life of Gregory the Great, by an Anonymous Monk of Whitby.* Lawrence: University of Kansas Press.

Compagni, Dino. 1993. *Cronica delle cose occorrenti ne' tempi suoi.* Ed. Gabriella Mezzanotte. Milan: Mondadori.

Contini, Gianfranco, ed. 1960. *Poeti del duecento.* 2 vols. Milan-Naples: Ricciardi.

Cursietti, Mauro. 1995. *La falsa tenzone di Dante con Forese Donati.* Anzio: De Rubeis.

Dahlberg, Charles, trans. 1983. *The Romance of the Rose.* Hanover, N.H.: University Press of New England.

Daniel, Arnaut. 1978. *Le canzoni.* 2 vols. Ed. Maurizio Perugi. Milan-Naples: Ricciardi.

Durand, Guillaume. 1859. *Rationale divinorum officiorum.* Naples: J. Dura.

De Luca, G. 1951. "Un formulario di cancelleria francescana tra il xiii e xiv secolo." *Archivio italiano della pietà* 1:291-95.

Elliott, J. K. 1993. *The Apocryphal New Testament. A Collection of Apocryphal Christian Literature in an English Translation.* Oxford: Clarendon.

Faral, Edmond, ed. 1924 [repr. 1971]. *Les Arts poétiques du xiie et xiiie siècle.* Paris: Champion.

Friedrich II von Hohenstaufen. 1966. *De arte venandi cum avibus. MS Pal. Lat. 1081, Biblioteca Apostolica Vaticana.Faksimile-Ausgabe.* 2 vols. Graz: Akademische Druck- und Verlagsanstalt.

Grant, Edward, ed. 1974. *A Sourcebook in Medieval Science.* Cambridge, Mass.: Harvard University Press.

Guillaume de Lorris and Jean de Meun. 1970. *Le Roman de la rose.* 3 vols. Ed. Félix Lecoy. Paris: Champion.

Hegesippus. 1900. *Hegesippi qui dicitur Historiae libri V.* 2 vols. Ed. V. Ussiani. Corpus Scriptorum Ecclesiasticorum Latinorum, 66. Turnholt: Brepols.

Hill, R. T., and Thomas G. Bergin. 1973. *Anthology of the Provençal Troubadours,* 2nd ed. 2 vols. Revised by Thomas G. Bergin, with . . . Susan Olson, William D. Paden, Jr., Nathaniel Smith. New Haven: Yale University Press.

Horace. 1901 [1975]. *Q. Horati Flacci Opera.* Ed. E. C. Wickham. Editio altera, ed. H. W. Garrod. Oxford Classical Texts. Oxford: Clarendon.

Innocent III. 1978. *De miseria humanae conditionis.* Ed. R. E. Lewis. Athens: University of Georgia Press.

Isidore of Seville. 1911 [1957]. *Isidori Hispalensis Episcopi Etymologiarum sive originum libri xx.* Ed. W. M. Lindsay. Oxford Classical Texts. Oxford: Clarendon.

Jacobus a Voragine. 1890 [1969]. *Legenda aurea.* Ed. T. Grässe. Osnabrück: Zeller.

John of Salisbury. 1993. *Policraticus*. Ed. X. Keats-Rohan. Corpus Christianorum, Continuatio Mediaevalis, 118. Turnholt: Brepols.

[John the Scot] Eriugena. 1987. *Periphyseon (The Division of Nature)*. Trans. I. P. Sheldon-Williams. Rev. by John J. O'Meara. Cahiers d'études médiévales, Cahier spécial 3. Montreal: Bellarmin.

Justinian. 1877. *Corpus iuris civilis, Volumen I: Institutiones et Digestum*. Ed. Paul Krueger and Theodor Mommsen. Berlin: Weidmann.

———. 1987. *Institutes*. Tr. Peter Birks and Grant McLeod. Ithaca, N.Y.: Cornell University Press.

Juvenal. 1951. *Saturae XIV*. Ed. J. D. Duff. Cambridge: Cambridge University Press.

Latini, Brunetto. 1948. *Li livres dou Tresor*. Ed. Francis J. Carmody. University of California Studies in Modern Philology, 22. Berkeley: University of California Press.

———. 1960. *Il tesoretto*. In Contini 1960, vol. 2.

Livy. 1914 [1964]. *Titi Livi Ab urbe condita. Tomus I. Libri I-V*. Ed. Robert Seymour Conway and Charles Flamstead Walters. Oxford Classical Texts. Oxford: Clarendon

Lucan. 1926. *M. Annaei Lucani Belli civilis libri X*. Ed. A. E. Housman. Cambridge, Mass.: Harvard University Press.

Macrobius. 1970. *Commentarii in Somnium Scipionis*. Ed. James. Willis. Vol. 2 of *Opera*. Leipzig: Teubner.

Malaspina, Saba. 1723. *Rerum sicilianarum libri VI, ab anno MCCI usque ad annum MCCLXXXVI . . . Per Stephanum Baluzium editi, novissima editione*. Leiden: Van der Aa.

Martianus Capella. 1983. *Martianus Capella*. Ed. James Willis. Leipzig: Teubner.

Migne, J.-P. 1844-1864. *Patrologiae cursus completus . . . Series [Latina]*. 221 vols. Paris.

Minnis, A. J., and A. B. Scott, with David Wallace. 1988. *Medieval Literary Theory and Criticism c.1100-c.1375. The Commentary Tradition*. Oxford: Clarendon.

Modi orandi Sancti Dominici. Die Gebets- und Andachtsgesten des heiligen Dominikus: Eine Bilderhandschrift. Faksimile-Ausgabe. 1996. 2 vols. Zürich: Belser.

Monaci, Ernesto. 1955. *Crestomazia italiana dei primi secoli, con prospetto grammaticale e glossario*. Ed. Felice Arese. Rome: Dante Alighieri.

Ovid. 1991. *Metamorphoses*. Ed. William S. Anderson. Stuttgart-Leipzig: Teubner.

Paulus Orosius. 1964. *The Seven Books Against the Pagans*. Trans. Roy J. Deferrari. Washington, D.C.: Catholic University of America Press.

Petrarca, Francesco. 1996. *Canzoniere.* Ed. Marco Santagata. Milan: Mondadori.

Plato. 1937. *Plato's Cosmology. The "Timaeus" of Plato.* Trans., with a running commentary, by F. M. Cornford. London: Routledge & Kegan Paul.

——. 1962. *Timaeus a Calcidio translatus commentarioque instructus.* Ed. J. H. Waszink and P.J. Jensen. Vol. 4 of *Plato latinus,* ed. Raymond Klibansky. London-Leiden: Warburg Institute, Brill.

Pseudo-Dionysius. 1987. *Pseudo-Dionysius: The Complete Works.* Trans. Colm Luibheid. Foreword, notes, and translation collaboration by Paul Rorem. New York: Paulist Press.

Root, R. K., ed. 1945. *Geoffrey Chaucer, Troilus and Criseyde.* Princeton, N.J.: Princeton University Press.

Sacchetti, Franco. 1993. *Le trecentonovelle.* Ed. Antonio Lanza. Firenze: Sansoni.

Segre, Cesare, and Mario Marti, eds. 1959. *La prosa del Duecento.* Milan-Naples: Ricciardi.

Seneca. 1965. *L. Annaei Senecae Ad Lucilium epistulae morales.* 2 vols. Ed. L. D. Reynolds. Oxford Classical Texts. Oxford: Clarendon.

Servius. 1887-1923. *Servii grammatici qui feruntur in Vergilii carmina commentarii.* 3 vols. Ed. G. Thilo and H. Hagen. Leipzig: Teubner.

Silius Italicus. 1996. *Punica.* Ed. Josef Delz. Leipzig: Teubner.

Sordello of Goito. 1954. *Le poesie.* Ed. Marco Boni. Biblioteca degli studi mediolatini e volgari. Bologna: Palmaverde.

Statius. 1906 [1965]. *P. Papini Stati Thebais et Achilleis.* Ed. H. W. Garrod. Oxford Classical Texts. Oxford: Clarendon.

Thomas Aquinas. 1872-1884. *Opera omnia.* 34 vols. Ed. S. E. Fretté. Paris: Vivès.

——. 1950. *In librum Dionysii de divinis nominibus expositio.* Ed. Ceslaus Pera. Turin: Marietti.

——. 1955. *In librum de causis expositio.* Ed. Ceslaus Pera. Turin: Marietti.

——. 1959. *In Aristotelis librum de anima commentarium.* 4th ed. Ed. Angelo Pirotta. Turin: Marietti.

——. 1980. *Opera omnia.* 7 vols. Ed. Roberto Busa, S.J. Stuttgart: Frommann, Holzboog.

Trexler, Richard C. 1987. *The Christian at Prayer. An Illustrated Prayer Manual Attributed to Peter the Chanter.* Binghamton, N.Y.: Medieval & Renaissance Texts & Studies.

Ubertino da Casale. 1961. *Arbor vitae crucifixi Jesu.* Reprint of 1485 ed. Turin: Bottega d'Erasmo.

Valerius Maximus. 1865. *Factorum et dictorum memorabilium libri ix.* Ed. Karl Helm. Leipzig: Teubner.

Vasari, Giorgio. 1966-1987. *Le vite de' più eccellenti pittori, scultori e architettori, nelle redazioni del 1550 e 1568.* Ed. Rossana Bettarini, commento secolare a cura di Paola Barocchi. Florence: Sansoni.

Vergil. 1969. *P. Vergili Maronis Opera.* Ed. R.A.B. Mynors. Oxford Classical Texts. Oxford: Clarendon.

Villani, Giovanni. 1990. *Nuova Cronica.* Vol. 1. Ed. Giuseppe Porta. Fondazione Pietro Bembo. Parma: Guanda.

Wenzel, Siegfried, ed. 1984. *Summa virtutum de remediis animae.* Athens: University of Georgia Press.

Willemsen, Carl Arnold, ed. 1943. *Friderici Romanorum Imperatoris Secundi De arte venandi cum avibus.* Leipzig: Insel.

Modern Works

Abeele, Baudouin van den. 1994. *La Fauconnerie au moyen âge.* Paris: Gallimard.

Abrams, Richard. 1976. "Inspiration and Gluttony: The Moral Context of Dante's Poetics of the 'Sweet New Style.'" *Modern Language Notes* 91:30-59.

———. 1985. "Illicit Pleasures: Dante among the Sensualists (*Purgatorio* XXVI)." *Modern Language Notes* 100:1-41.

Agrimi, Mario. 1966. *Il canto XVI del Purgatorio.* Lectura Dantis Romana. Turin: SEI.

Alfie, Fabian. 1998. "For Want of a Nail: The Guerri-Lanza-Cursietti Argument Regarding the *Tenzone.*" *Dante Studes* 116:141-59.

Ardissino, Erminia. 1990. "I canti liturgici nel *Purgatorio* dantesco." *Dante Studies* 108:39-65.

Arnaldi, Girolamo. 1994. "Il canto 20 del *Purgatorio.*" *L'Alighieri* 35:27-46.

Armour, Peter. 1983a. "Matelda in Eden: The Teacher and the Apple." *Italian Studies* 38:2-27.

———. 1983b. *The Door of Purgatory. A Study of Multiple Symbolism in Dante's "Purgatorio."* Oxford: Clarendon.

———. 1989. *Dante's Griffin and the History of the World: A Study of the Earthly Paradise (Purgatorio Cantos XXIX-XXXIII).* Oxford: Clarendon.

Arnou, R. 1935. "Platonisme des Pères." *Dictionnaire de théologie catholique,* 12.2: 2258-2392.

Ascoli, Albert R. 1989. "The Vowels of Authority (Dante's *Convivio* IV.vi.3-4)." In Brownlee/Stephens 1989:23-46, 255-62.

———. 1990. "'Neminem ante nos': Historicity and Authority in the *De vulgari eloquentia.*" *Annali d'italianistica* 8:186-231.

Astell, Ann. 1994. *Job, Boethius, and Epic Truth.* Ithaca, N.Y.: Cornell University Press.

Auerbach, Erich. 1959. "Figura." In *Scenes from the Drama of Western Literature*, 11-79. New York: Meridian Books.

Aurigemma, Mario. 1965. "Manfredi e il problema delle indulgenze." *Cultura e scuola* 4:540-50.

Ayrton, Michael. 1969. *Giovanni Pisano, Sculptor.* Introduction by Henry Moore. New York: Weybright and Talley.

Bagliani, Agostino Paravicini, and Giorgio Stabile, eds. 1989. *Träume im Mittelalter. Ikonologische Studien.* Stuttgart: Belser.

Baldelli, Ignazio. 1994. "Linguistica e interpretazione: l'amore di Catone, di Casella, di Carlo Martello e le canzoni del *Convivio* II e III." In *Miscellanea di studi linguistici in onore di Walter Belardi,* 2:535-555. Rome: Il Calamo.

———. 1985. "Visione, immaginazione e fantasia nella *Vita nuova.*" In Gregory 1985:1-10.

———. 1997. "I morti di morte violenta: Dante e Sordello." *Dante Studies* 115:111-83.

Barasch, Moshe. 1987. *Giotto and the Language of Gesture.* Cambridge: Cambridge University Press.

Barber, Malcolm. 1994. *The New Knighthood: A History of the Order of the Temple.* Cambridge: Cambridge University Press.

Barbi, Michele. 1934. *Problemi di critica dantesca. Prima serie (1893–1918).* Florence: Sansoni.

Barblan, G., ed. 1988. *Dante e la Bibbia. Atti del Convegno internazionale promosso da "Biblia," Firenze, 26-27-28 settembre 1986.* Florence: Olschki.

Barkan, Leonard. 1975. *Nature's Work of Art. The Human Body as Image of the World.* New Haven: Yale University Press.

———. 1988. *The Gods Made Flesh: The Renaissance.* New Haven: Yale University Press.

———. 1993. *Transuming Passion: Ganymede and the Erotics of Humanism.* Stanford, Calif.: Stanford University Press.

Barnes, John C. 1995. "Vestiges of the Liturgy in Dante's Verse." In Barnes/Cuilleanáin 1995:231-69.

Barnes, John C., and Cormac Ó Cuilleanáin, eds. 1995. *Dante and the Middle Ages: Literary and Historical Essays.* Dublin: Irish Academic Press.

Barolini, Teodolinda. 1984. *Dante's Poets: Textuality and Truth in the "Comedy."* Princeton, N.J.: Princeton University Press.

———. 1992. *The Undivine Comedy: Detheologizing Dante*. Princeton, N.J.: Princeton University Press.

Bauch, Kurt. 1976. *Das mittelalterliche Grabbild. Figürliche Grabmäler des 11. bis 15. Jahrhunderts in Europa*. Berlin: de Gruyter.

Bernardo, Aldo S., and Anthony L. Pellegrini, eds. 1983. *Dante, Petrarch, Boccaccio: Studies in the Italian Trecento In Honor of Charles S. Singleton*. Binghamton, N.Y.: Medieval & Renaissance Texts & Studies.

Bloomfield, Morton W. 1952. *The Seven Deadly Sins: An Introduction to the History of a Religious Concept, with Special Reference to Medieval English Literature*. East Lansing: Michigan State University Press.

Bogdanow, Fanny. 1985. "Robert de Boron's Vision of Arthurian History." In *Arthurian Literature XIV*: 19-52, ed. James P. Carley and Felicity Riddy. Cambridge: D. S. Brewer.

Bologna, Corrado. 1998. Il ritorno di Beatrice. Simmetrie dantesche fra Vita nova, "Petrose" e Commedia. Roma: Salerno Editrice.

Boni, Marco. 1970. "Sordello." *ED* 5:328-33.

Bosco, Umberto. 1966. *Dante vicino. Contributi e letture*. Caltanisetta-Rome: S. Sciascia.

Bottari, Stefano. 1967. "Per la cultura di Oderisi di Gubbio e di Franco Bolognese." In *Dante e Bologna nei tempi di Dante*: 53-59.

Boyde, Patrick. 1971. *Dante's Style in His Lyric Poetry*. Cambridge: Cambridge University Press.

———. 1981. *Dante Philomythes and Philosopher: Man in the Cosmos*. Cambridge: Cambridge University Press.

———. 1993. *Perception and Passion in Dante's Comedy*. Cambridge: Cambridge University Press.

Boyde, Patrick, and Vittorio Russo, eds. 1995. *Dante e la scienza*. Ravenna: Longo Editore.

Boyle, Leonard E., O.P. 1996b. "Der Codex Rossianus 3 und die 'Modi orandi Sancti Dominici.'" In *Modi orandi Sancti Dominici*: 2:31-50.

Branca, Vittore, and Giorgio Padoan, eds. 1966. *Dante e la cultura veneta. Atti del Convegno di studi organizzato . . . dalla Fondazione Giorgio Cini . . . Verona, 30 marzo-5 aprile 1966*. Florence: Le Monnier.

Brownlee, Kevin, and Walter Stevens, eds. 1989. *Discourses of Authority in Medieval and Renaissance Literature*. Hanover, N.H.: University Press of New England.

Brugnoli, Giorgio. 1969. "Stazio in Dante." *Cultura neolatina* 19:117-25.

———. 1998. *Studi danteschi*. 3 vol. Pisa: ETS.

Bruscagli, Riccardo. 1984. "Misure retoriche e morali del canto XIV del *Purgatorio.*" *Studi danteschi* 56:115-39.

Bynum, Caroline Walker. 1995. *The Resurrection of the Body in Western Christianity, 200-1336.* New York: Columbia University Press.

Cachey, Theodore J., Jr., ed. 1995. *Dante Now: Current Trends in Dante Studies.* Notre Dame, Ind.: University of Notre Dame Press.

Cadden, Joan. 1993. *The Meaning of Sex Difference in the Middle Ages.* Cambridge: Cambridge University Press.

Camille, Michael. 1989. *The Gothic Idol: Ideology and Image-Making in Medieval Art.* Cambridge: Cambridge University Press.

Camilli, Amerindo. 1951. "La Bolla giubilare di Bonifazio VIII, le indulgenze per i defunti, e il ritardo di Casella." *Studi danteschi* 30:207-9.

Camporesi, Piero. 1985. *La casa dell'eternità.* 2nd ed. Milan: Garzanti.

Carmignac, Jean. 1969. *Recherches sur le "Notre père."* Paris: Letouzey & Ané.

Carruthers, Mary. 1990. *The Book of Memory: A Study of Memory in Medieval Culture.* Cambridge: Cambridge University Press.

Cassell, Anthony K. 1978. "'Mostrando con le poppe il petto' (*Purg.* XXIII, 102)." *Dante Studies* 96:75-81.

———. 1958. "The Letter of Envy: *Purgatorio* XIII-XIV." *Stanford Italian Review* 4:5-21.

Caviglia, Franco. 1974. "Appunti per la presenza di Stazio nella *Commedia.*" *Rivista di cultura classica e medievale* 16:267-89.

Charmasson, Thérèse. 1980. *Recherches sur une technique divinatoire: la géomancie dans l'Occident médiéval.* Geneva: Droz.

Chenu, Marie-Dominique. 1968. *Nature, Man, and Society in the Twelfth Century.* Ed. and trans. Jerome K. Taylor and Lester K. Little. Chicago: University of Chicago Press.

Cioffi, Caron Ann. 1992. "Fame, Prayer, and Politics: Virgil's Palinurus in *Purgatorio* V and VI." *Dante Studies* 110:179-200.

Cogan, Marc. 1999. *The Design in the Wax. The Structure of the "Divina Commedia" and its Significance.* Notre Dame, Ind.: Notre Dame University Press.

Cohen, Jeremy. 1983. "The Jews as the Killers of Christ in the Latin Tradition, from Augustine to the Friars." *Traditio* 39:1-27.

Contini, Gianfranco. 1959. "Alcuni appunti su *Purgatorio* XXVII." In *Studi in onore di Angelo Monteverdi.* Modena: Società tipografica editoriale Modenese. Now in Contini 1970:459-76.

———. 1970. *Varianti e altra linguistica: Una raccolta di saggi.* Turin: Einaudi.

———. 1976a. *Un'idea di Dante. Saggi danteschi.* Turin: Einaudi.

————. 1976b. "Filologia ed esegesi dantesca." In Contini 1976a:113-42.

Cook, Eleanor. 1999. "Scripture as Enigma: Biblical Allusions in Dante's Earthly Paradise." *Dante Studies* 117:1-19.

Courcelle, Pierre. 1944. "Quelques Symboles funéraires du néoplatonisme latin: Le vol de Dédale—Ulysse et les Sirènes." *Revue des études anciennes* 46:65-93.

————. 1955a. "Les Pères de l'église devant les enfers virgiliens." *Annales d'histoire doctrinale et littéraire du moyen-âge* 30:5-74.

————. 1955b. "Interprétations néo-platonisantes du livre VI de l'*Enéide*." In *Entretiens sur l'Antiquité classique. Recherches sur la tradition platonicienne* 3:95-136.

————. 1957. "Les Exégèses chrétiennes de la quatrième Églogue." *Revue des études anciennes* 59:294-319.

————. 1965. "Tradition platonicienne et traditions chrétiennes du corps-prison (*Phédon* 62 b; *Cratyle* 400 c)." *Revue des études latines* 43:407-43.

————. 1967. *La Consolation de Philosophie dans la tradition littéraire. Antécédents et postérité de Boèce*. Paris: Etudes Augustiniennes.

————. 1984. *Lectures païennes et lectures chrétiennes de l'Enéide. I. Les témoignages littéraires*. 2 vols. Paris: Institut de France.

Croce, Benedetto. 1921. *La poesia di Dante*. Bari: Laterza.

Curtius, Ernst Robert. 1953. *European Literature and the Latin Middle Ages*. Trans. Willard Trask. Bollingen Series 36. Princeton, N.J.: Princeton University Press.

Dales, Richard C. 1995. *The Problem of the Rational Soul in the Thirteenth Century*. Leiden: Brill.

Dante e Bologna nei tempi di Dante. 1967. A cura della Facoltà di Lettere e Filosofia dell'Università di Bologna. Comitato nazionale per le Celebrazioni del VII Centenario della nascita di Dante. Bologna: Commissione per i testi di lingua.

Dante e Roma. Atti del Convegno di studi a cura della "Casa di Dante," sotto gli auspici del Comune di Roma, in collaborazione con l'Istituto di Studi Romani, Roma, 8-9-10 aprile 1965. 1965. Florence: Le Monnier.

Davis, Charles T. 1957. *Dante and the Idea of Rome*. Oxford: Clarendon.

————. 1984. *Dante's Italy and Other Essays*. Philadelphia: University of Pennsylvania Press.

Del Sal, Nievo. 1989. "Guittone (e i Guittoniani) nella 'Commedia'." *Studi danteschi* 61:109-52.

————. 1991. "Cavalcanti in Dante 'comico'." *Rivista di letteratura italiana* 9:9-52.

Delz, Josef, and A. J. Dunston. 1976. "Silius Italìcus, Tiberius Catius Ausonius." In *Catalogus Translationum et Commentariorum* 3:342-48, ed. E. L. Bassett. Washington, D.C.: Catholic University of America.

Demaray, John G. 1974. *The Invention of Dante's "Commedia."* New Haven: Yale University Press.

De Robertis, Domenico. 1970. *Il libro della "Vita nuova."* Florence: Sansoni.

———. 1985. "*Arcades ambo* (Osservazioni sulla pastoralità di Dante e del suo primo amico)." *Filologia e critica* 10:231-38.

———. 1997 "Ancora per Dante e Forese." In Fecondo venner le carte. Studi in onore di Ottavio Besomi, 35-48. Ed. Tatiana Cravelli. Bellinzona: Casagrande.

Derbes, Anne. 1996. *Picturing the Passion in Late Medieval Italy.* Cambridge: Cambridge University Press.

Di Scipio, Giuseppe, and Aldo Scaglione, eds. 1988. *The "Divine Comedy" and the Encyclopedia of Arts and Sciences.* Philadelphia: Benjamin Johns.

D'Ovidio, Francesco. 1901. *Studi sulla Divina Commedia.* Milan: Sandron.

———. 1906. *Nuovi studi danteschi: Il Purgatorio e il suo preludio.* Milan: Hoepli.

Dronke, Peter. 1986. *Dante and Medieval Latin Traditions.* Cambridge: Cambridge University Press.

Durling, Robert M. 1981a. "Deceit and Digestion in the Belly of Hell." In *Allegory and Representation: Selected Papers from the English Institute, 1979-80*:61-93, ed. Stephen M. Greenblatt. Baltimore: Johns Hopkins University Press.

———. 1981b. "Farinata and the Body of Christ." *Stanford Italian Review* 2:5-35.

———. 1985. "A Long Day in the Sun: *Decameron* 8.7." In *Shakespeare's "Rough Magic": Renaissance Essays in Honor of C. L. Barber*: 269-75, ed. Peter Erickson and Coppélia Kahn. Newark: University of Delaware Press.

———. 2001a. "'Mio figlio ov'è?' (*Inferno* X, 60)." In Picone 2001:303-29.

———. 2001b. "Platonism and Poetic Form: Augustine's *Confessions.*" In *Jewish Culture and the Hispanic World: Essays in Memory of Joseph H. Silverman*: 179-89, ed. Samuel G. Armistead and Mishael M. Caspi with Murray Baumgarten. Newark, Del.: Juan de la Cuesta.

———. 2003. "The Body and the Flesh in the *Purgatorio.*" In *Dante 2000: Congress Held at Columbia University, April 8-12, 2000*, ed. Wayne Storey. Yonkers, N.Y.: Fordham University Press. (Forthcoming.)

———, and Ronald L. Martinez. 1990. *Time and the Crystal: Studies in Dante's 'Rime petrose'.* Berkeley: University of California Press.

Eisenhofer, Ludwig. 1932. *Handbuch der katholischen Liturgik.* 2 vols. Freiburg im Breisgau: Herder.

Fallani, Giovanni. 1971. "Ricerca sui protagonisti della miniatura italiana dugentesca: Oderisi da Gubbio e Franco Bolognese." *Studi danteschi* 48:137-51.

————. 1976. *Dante e la cultura figurativa medievale*. 2nd ed. Bergamo: Minerva Italica.

Fergusson, Francis. 1953. *Dante's Drama of the Mind. A Modern Reading of the Purgatorio*. Princeton, N.J.: Princeton University Press.

Ferrucci, Franco. 1990. *Il poema del desiderio. Poetica e passione in Dante*. Milan: Leonardo Editore.

Fido, Franco. 1986. "Writing Like God—or Better? Symmetries in Dante's 26th and 27th Cantos." *Italica* 63:250-64.

Folena, Gianfranco. 1977. "Il canto XXVI del *Purgatorio*." *Giornale storico della letteratura italiana* 154:481-508.

Forti, Fiorenzo. 1970. "Il canto VIII del *Purgatorio*." *Letture classensi* 3:295-322.

Foster, Kenelm. 1957. *God's Tree: Essays on Dante and Other Matters*. Oxford: Blackfriars.

————. 1977. *The Two Dantes and Other Studies*. Berkeley: University of California Press.

Franco, Charles, and Leslie Morgan, eds. 1995. *Dante. Summa Mediaevalis*. Supplement to *Forum italicum* 9.

Freccero, John. 1961 . "Dante's Pilgrim in a Gyre." *PMLA* 76:169-171. Now in Freccero 1986:70-92, 291-99.

————. 1965. "The Sign of Satan." *Modern Language Notes* 80:11-26. Now in Freccero 1986:167-79, 305-308.

————. 1972. "Medusa: The Letter and the Spirit." *Yearbook of Italian Studies* 2:1-18. Now in Freccero 1986:119-35.

————. 1973. "Casella's Song." *Dante Studies* 91: 73-80. Now in Freccero 1986: 186-94, 308-309.

————. 1983. "The Significance of Terza Rima." In Bernardo/Pellegrini 1983:3-17. Now in Freccero 1986:258-71, 316-17.

————. 1986. *Dante: The Poetics of Conversion*. Ed. Rachel Jacoff. Cambridge, Mass.: Harvard University Press.

Frugoni, Arsenio. 1950. *Il Giubileo di Bonifacio VIII. Bullettino dell'Istituto storico italiano per il medio evo e Archivio Muratoriano, no. 62*.

————. 1979. *Incontri nel Medioevo*. Bologna: Il Mulino.

Gardiner, Eileen. 1989. *Visions of Heaven and Hell Before Dante*. New York: Italica.

Gardiner, F. C. 1971. *The Pilgrimage of Desire*. Leiden: Brill.

Garnier, François. 1982-89. *Le Langage des images au moyen-âge*. 2 vols. Paris: Le Léopard d'or.

Gersh, Stephen. 1986. *Middle Platonism and Neoplatonism: The Latin Tradition.* 2 vols. Notre Dame, Ind.: University of Notre Dame Press.

Ghisalberti, Fausto. 1932. "L'enigma delle naiadi." *Studi danteschi* 16:105-25.

Gilson, Etienne. 1939. *Dante et la philosophie.* Paris: Vrin.

———. 1947. *La Philosophie au moyen âge des origines patristiques à la fin du xive siècle.* 2nd ed. Paris: Payot.

———. 1967. "Dante's Notion of a Shade: *Purgatorio* XXV." *Mediaeval Studies* 29:124-42.

———. 1969. *Introduction à l'étude de saint Augustin.* 4th ed. Paris: Vrin.

Gilson, Simon A. 1997. "Dante's Meteorological Optics: Refraction, Reflection, and the Rainbow." *Italian Studies* 52:51-62.

Giunta, Claudio. 1998. *La poesia italiana nell'età di Dante.* Bologna: Il Mulino.

Gizzi, Corrado. 1974. *L'astronomia nel poema sacro.* 2 vols. Naples: Loffredo.

Gmelin, Hermann. 1951. "Die Anrede an den Leser in der Göttlichen Komödie." *Deutsches Dante-Jahrbuch* 30:130-40.

Gorni, Guglielmo. 1981. *Il nodo della lingua e il verbo d'amore: Studi su Dante e altri duecentisti.* Florence: Olschki.

———. 1988. "Parodia e scrittura in Dante." In Barblan 1988: 323-40.

———. 1992. "*Vita nuova* di Dante Alighieri." In *Letteratura italiana. Le opere. Volume primo: Dalle Origini al Cinquecento*: 187-209, ed. Alberto Asor Rosa. Turin: Einaudi.

Graf, Arturo. 1925. *Miti, leggende e superstizioni del Medio Evo.* Turin: Squarotti.

Gregory, Tullio. 1955. *Anima mundi: La filosofia di Guglielmo di Conches e la scuola di Chartres.* Florence: Sansoni.

———. 1957. "Nuove note sul platonismo medievale: Dall'anima mundi all'idea di natura." *Giornale critico della filosofia italiana* 36:37-55.

———. 1958. *Platonismo medievale: Studi e ricerche.* Studi storici, nos. 26-27. Rome: Edizioni di storia e letteratura.

———. 1992. *Mundana sapientia. Forme di conoscenza nella cultura medievale.* Rome: Edizioni di storia e letteratura.

———, ed. 1985. *I sogni nel medioevo: Seminario internazionale, Roma, 2-4 ottobre, 1983.* Rome: Ateneo.

Hamilton, G. L. 1921. "The Pedigree of a Phrase in Dante (*Purg.* VII, 107-8)." *Romanic Review* 12:84-89.

Hardt, Manfred. 1973. *Die Zahl in der Divina Commedia.* Frankfurt am Main: Athenäum.

Hawkins, Peter. 1999. *Dante's Testaments. Essays in Scriptural Imagination*. Stanford, Calif.: Stanford University Press.

Hedemann, Anne Dawson. 1991. *The Royal Image: Illustrations in the "Grandes chroniques de France, 1274-1422*. Berkeley: University of California Press.

Heinimann, Siegfried. 1980/81. "Dante als Bibelübersetzer." *Deutches Dante-Jahrbuch* 55/55:28-49.

Hewson, M. A. 1975. *Giles of Rome and the Medieval Theory of Conception*. London: Athlone.

Hollander, Robert. 1969. *Allegory in Dante's "Commedia."* Princeton, N.J.: Princeton University Press.

———. 1973-75. "The Invocations of the 'Commedia'." *Yearbook of Italian Studies* 2:235-240.

———. 1975. "*Purgatorio* II: Cato's Rebuke and Dante's *scoglio.*" *Italica* 52:348-63.

———. 1980. *Studies in Dante*. Ravenna: Longo.

———. 1983. *Il Virgilio dantesco: Tragedia nella Commedia*. Florence: Olschki.

———. 1999. "Dante's *'dolce stil novo'* and the *Comedy.*" In Picone/Crivelli 1999: 263-81.

Hughes, Robert. 1968. *Heaven and Hell in Western Art*. New York: Stein and Day.

Iannucci, Amilcare, ed. 1997. *Dante: Contemporary Perspectives*. Toronto: University of Toronto Press.

Jacoff, Rachel, and Jeffrey Schnapp, eds. 1991. *The Poetry of Allusion: Virgil and Ovid in Dante's "Comedy."* Stanford, Calif.: Stanford University Press.

Kantorowicz, Ernst H. 1957. *The King's Two Bodies. A Study in Mediaeval Political Theology*. Princeton, N.J.: Princeton University Press.

Kaske, Carol. 1971. "Mount Sinai and Dante's Purgatory." *Dante Studies* 89:1-18.

Kaske, Robert E. 1961. "Dante's DXV and the Veltro." *Traditio* 17:185-254.

———. 1971. "'Sì si conserva il seme ogne giusto' (*Purg.* XXXII, 48)." *Dante Studies* 89:49-54.

———. 1974. "Dante's *Purgatorio* XXXII and XXXIII: A Survey of Christian History." *University of Toronto Quarterly* 43:193-214.

———. 1983. "The Seven 'Status Ecclesiae' in *Purgatorio* XXXII and XXXIII." In Bernardo/Pellegrini 1983:89-113.

Kay, Richard. 1994. *Dante's Christian Astronomy*. Middle Ages Series. Philadelphia: University of Pennsylvania Press.

Kirkham, Victoria. 1992. "Eleven is for Evil: Measured Trespass in Dante's *Commedia.*" *Allegorica* 1:27-50.

Kleinhenz, Christopher. 1977. "Food for Thought: *Purgatorio* XXII, 146-147." *Dante Studies* 95:69-79.

Koonce, B. G. 1959. "Satan the Fowler." *Mediaeval Studies* 21:176-84.

Ladis, Andrew, ed. 1988. *The Arena Chapel and the Genius of Giotto.* New York: Garland.

La Favia, Louis. 1984-86. "'. . . ché quivi per canti' (*Purg.* XII.113): Dante's Programmatic Use of Psalms and Hymns in the *Purgatorio.*" *Studies in Iconography* 9:53-65.

Laing, R. D. 1970. *Knots.* New York: Pantheon.

Lambert, M. D. 1961. *Franciscan Poverty: The Doctrine of the Absolute Poverty of Christ and the Apostles in the Franciscan Order, 1210-1323.* London: SPCK.

Lansing, Richard. 1994. "Narrative Design in Dante's Earthly Paradise." *Dante Studies* 113:101-113.

Le Caron, A. 1928. *L'Office divin chez les frères mineurs au 13e siècle.* Paris: Lethielleux.

Leclercq, Jean. 1952. "Dévotion et théologie mariale dans le monachisme bénédictin." In *Maria. Etudes sur la Sainte Vierge,* 2, 547-78, ed. D'Hubert du Manoir. Paris: Beauchesne.

Leff, Gordon. 1967. *Heresy in the Later Middle Ages. The Relation of Heterodoxy to Dissent c. 1250–c.1450.* 2 vols. Manchester: Manchester University Press.

Le Goff, Jacques. 1981. *La Naissance du Purgatoire.* Paris: Gallimard.

Lieberknecht, Otfried. 1999. *Allegorese und Philologie. Überlegungen zum Problem des mehrfachen Schriftsinns in Dantes "Commedia."* Stuttgart: Franz Steiner.

Leo, Ulrich. 1951. "The Unfinished *Convivio* and Dante's Rereading of the *Aeneid.*" *Mediaeval Studies* 13:41-64.

———. 1962. "Zum 'rifacimento' der 'Vita nuova'." *Romanische Forschungen* 74: 281-317.

Lindheim, Nancy. 1990. "Body, Soul, and Immortality. Some Readings in Dante's *Commedia.*" *Modern Langauge Notes* 105:1-32.

Lubac, Henri de. 1964. *L'Exégèse médiévale. Les quatre sens de l'écriture.* 3 vols. Paris: Aubier.

Maccarrone, Michele. 1950. "La teoria ierocratica e il canto XVI del *Purgatorio.*" *Rivista di storia della Chiesa in Italia* 4:359-98.

———. 1951. "Teologia e diritto canonico nella *Monarchia* III, 3." *Rivista di storia della Chiesa in Italia* 5:7-42.

———. 1955. "Il terzo libro della *Monarchia.*" *Studi danteschi* 33:5-142.

Mackinnon, Patricia L. 1988. *The Analogy of the Body Politic in Saint Augustine, Dante, Petrarch, and Ariosto.* Ph.D. diss. University of California at Santa Cruz. Ann Arbor: University Microfilms, 1989. No. 8905627.

Mâle, Emile. 1958. *The Gothic Image. Religious Art in France of the Thirteenth Century.* Trans. Dora Nussey. New York: Harper & Row.

Manselli, Raoul. 1994. *Scritti sul Medioevo.* Rome: Bulzoni.

Marti, Kevin. 1989-90. "Dante's 'Baptism' and the Theology of the Body in *Purgatorio* 1-2." *Traditio* 45:167-90.

Marti, Mario. 1961. *Realismo dantesco e altri studi.* Milano-Napoli: Riccardi.

———. 1973. *Storia dello stil nuovo.* 2 vols. Lecce: Milella.

———. 1984. *Studi su Dante.* Galatina: Congedo.

———. 1985. "Il pianto di Ugo Ciapetto e il natalizio 'Gloria' nell'unità del XX del *Purgatorio.*" *Giornale storico della letteratura italiana* 142:321-44.

Martinez, Ronald L. 1983. "The Pilgrim's Answer to Bonagiunta and the Poetics of the Spirit." *Stanford Italian Review* 4:37-63.

———. 1989. "La 'sacra fame dell'oro' (*Purgatorio* 22, 41) tra Virgilio e Stazio: Dal testo all'interpretazione." *Letture classensi* 18:177-93.

———. 1991. "Dante Embarks Arnaut." *New England Modern Language Association Italian Studies* 15:5-28.

———. 1995a. "'Nasce il Nilo': Justice, Wisdom, and Dante's Canzone 'Tre donne intorno il cor mi son venute'." In Cachey 1995:15-53.

———. 1995b. "Dante and the Two Canons: Statius in Virgil's Footsteps (*Purgatorio* 21-30)." *Comparative Literature Studies* 32:151-75.

———. 1995c. "Troubadours and Italy." In *Handbook of Troubadours*, ed. F. R. P. Akehurst and Judith H. Davis. Berkeley: University of California Press.

———. 1997. "Lament and Lamentations in *Purgatorio* and the Case of Dante's Statius." *Dante Studies* 115:45-88.

———. 1998. "Mourning Beatrice: The Rhetoric of Threnody in the *Vita nuova.*" *Modern Language Notes* 113:1-29.

———. 2000. "Allegory." In Lansing 2000:24-34.

Masciandaro, Franco. 1970. *La problematica del tempo nella "Commedia."* Ravenna: Longo.

Mazzotta, Giuseppe. 1979. *Dante, Poet of the Desert: History and Allegory in the "Divine Comedy."* Princeton, N.J.: Princeton University Press.

———. 1993. *Dante's Vision and the Circle of Knowledge.* Princeton, N.J.: Princeton University Press.

McCracken, Andrew. 1993. "*In Omnibus Viis Tuis*: Compline in the Valley of the Rulers (*Purg.* VII-VIII)." *Dante Studies* 111:119-29.

McNeill, William H. 1976. *Plagues and Peoples.* Garden City, N.Y.: Anchor Books.

Mineo, Niccolò. 1968. *Profetismo e apocalittica in Dante.* Catania: Facultà di Lettere e Filosofia.

Minnis, A. J. 1988. *Medieval Theory of Authorship. Scholastic Literary Attitudes in the Later Middle Ages.* 2nd ed. Philadelphia: University of Pennsylvania Press.

Monterosso, Raffaello. 1970. "Canzone. Struttura musicale." In *ED* 1:802-809.

Moore, Edward. 1887, repr. 1963. *Studies in Dante.* 4 vols. Oxford: Clarendon.

———. 1887. *The Time-References in the "Divina Commedia."* London: Nutt.

Morgan, Alison. 1990. *Dante and the Medieval Other World.* Cambridge Studies in Medieval Literature 8. Cambridge: Cambridge University Press.

Morrison, Karl F. 1990. *History as a Visual Art in the Twelfth-Century Renaissance.* Princeton, N.J.: Princeton University Press.

Morozzi, Guido. 1987. *Santa Reparata. L'antica cattedrale fiorentina.* Florence: Bonechi.

Muresu, Gabriele. 1983. "La 'sentenza' di Marco Lombardo (Appunti su *Purgatorio* XVI)." *La Rassegna della letteratura italiana* 87:325-51.

———. 1985. "Il bestiario di Guido del Duca (*Purg.* XIV)." *La Rassegna della letteratura italiana* 89:5-26.

———. 1993. "Tra gli arcani dell'Eden." *La Rassegna della letteratura italiana* 97:5-37.

Musa, Mark. 1966. "Le ali di Dante (e il Dolce stil novo). *Purg.* XXIV." *Convivium* 34:361-67.

———. 1974. *Advent at the Gates: Dante's Comedy.* Bloomington: Indiana University Press.

Najemy, John. 1982. *Corporatism and Consensus in Florentine Electoral Politics.* Chapel Hill: University of North Carolina Press.

———. 2001. "Florence." In Lansing 2000:386-403.

Nardi, Bruno. 1914. "Due note al *Purgatorio.*" *Giornale dantesco* 22:237-72.

———. 1944. *Nel mondo di Dante.* Rome: Istituto Grafico Tiberino.

———. 1960. *Studi di filosofia medievale.* Rome: Letteratura e Testi.

———. 1964. *Il canto XV del Purgatorio.* Turin: SEI.

———. 1966. *Saggi e note di critica dantesca.* Milan-Naples: Ricciardi.

———. 1967. *Saggi di filosofia dantesca.* 2nd ed. Florence: La Nuova Italia.

———. 1990. *Dante e la cultura medievale. Nuovi saggi di filosofia dantesca.* Ed. Paolo Mazzatinta. Bari: Laterza.

———. 1992. *"Lecturae" ed altri scritti danteschi.* Ed. Rudy Abardo. Bari: Laterza.

Nardoni, Davide. 1986. *La Colonna Ulpia Traiana.* Rome: Edizioni italiane di letteratura e scienze.

Ortiz, Ramiro. 1925. "La materia epica di ciclo classico nella lirica italiana delle origini. *B*. Reminiscenze ovidiane (*Piramo e Tisbe—Narciso ed Eco—Dedalo ed Icaro*)." *Giornale storico della lettertura italiana* 85:1-93.

Padoan, Giorgio. 1959. "Il mito di Teseo e il cristianesimo di Stazio." *Lettere italiane* 11:432-57.

———.1993. *Il lungo cammino del "Poema sacro."* *Studi danteschi*. Florence: Olschki.

Pagliaro, Antonino. 1967. *Ulisse: Ricerche semantiche sulla Divina Commedia*. Messina: D'Anna.

Palgen, Rudolf. 1967. *L'origine del Purgatorio*. Graz: Sytria.

Panofsky, Erwin. 1957. *Gothic Architecture and Scholasticism*. New York: Meridian Books.

———. 1999. *Hercule à la croisée des chemins et autres matériaux figuratifs de l'Antiquité dans l'art plus récent*. Traduit de l'allemand et présenté par Danielle Cohn. Paris: Flammarion.

Paratore, E. 1968. *Tradizione e struttura in Dante*. Florence: Sansoni.

Parodi, Ernesto G. 1965 [1920]. *Poesia e storia nella Divina Commedia*. Ed. G. Folena and P. V. Mengaldo. Vicenza: N. Pozza.

Pasquazi, Silvio. 1966. *All'eterno dal tempo*. Florence: Le Monnier.

Patch, Howard R. 1950. *The Other World, According to Descriptions in Medieval Literature*. Cambridge, Mass.: Harvard University Press.

Pequigney, Joseph. 1991. "Sodomy in Dante's *Inferno* and *Purgatorio*." *Representations* 36:22-42.

Perkins, Judith. 1995. *The Suffering Self*. London: Routledge & Kegan Paul.

Pertile, Lino. 1994. "Il nodo di Bonagiunta, le penne di Dante e il Dolce Stil Novo." *Lettere italiane* 46:44-75.

———. 1995. "Dante, lo scoglio e la vesta." In *Da una riva e dall'altra. Studi in onore di Antonio D'Andrea*: 85-101, ed. Dante Della Terza. Rome: Cadmo.

———. 1997. "La puttana e la gigante (*Purgatorio* XXXII, 148-60)." In *International Dante Seminar 1994*: 243-72, ed. Zygmunt G. Barański. Florence: Le Lettere.

Perugi, Maurizio. 1978. "Arnaut Daniel in Dante." *Studi danteschi* 51:51-151.

———. 1983. "Il Sordello di Dante e la tradizione mediolatina dell'invettiva." *Studi danteschi* 55:23-135.

Peters, Edward M. 1968. "I principi negligenti di Dante e le concezioni medievali del *Rex inutilis*." *Rivista storica italiana* 80:741-58.

Petrocchi, Giorgio. 1969. *Itinerari danteschi*. Bari: Adriatica.

————. 1984. *Vita di Dante*. Bari: Laterza.

Pickering, F. P. 1970. *Literature and Art in the Middle Ages*. Coral Gables, Fla.: University of Miami Press.

Picone, Michelangelo. 1993. "*Purgatorio* XXII." In *LDV*: 321-35.

————, ed. 1995. *Guittone d'Arezzo nel VII. centenario della morte. Atti del Convegno Internazionale di Arezzo (22-24 aprile 1994)*. Florence: Cesati.

————, ed. 2001. *Dante: Da Firenze all'aldilà. Atti del terzo Seminario dantesco internazionale (Firenze, 9-11 giugno 2000)*. Florence: Cesati.

Picone, Michelangelo, and Tania Crivelli, eds. 1999. *Dante: Mito e poesia. Atti del second Seminario dantesco internazionale (Monte Verità, Ascona, 23-27 giugno 1997)*. Florence: Cesati.

Porcelli, Bruno. 1970. *Studi sulla "Divina Commedia."* Bologna: Pàtron.

Rabuse, Georg. 1958. *Der kosmologische Aufbau der Jenseitsreiche Dantes. Ein Schlüssel zur Göttlichen Komödie*. Graz: Hermann Böhlaus Nachfolger.

————. 1966. "I corpi celesti, centri di ordinamento dell'immaginazione poetica di Dante." In Rabuse 1976a:272-87.

————. 1973. "Les paysages astrologiques de la Divine Comédie." In Rabuse 1976a: 331-47.

————. 1976a. *Gesammelte Aufsätze zu Dante*. Ed. Erika Kanduth, Fritz Peter Kirsch, and Siegfried Löwe. Stuttgart: Braumüller.

————. 1976b. "Die dichterische Funktion der Sterne in der Göttlichen Komödie." In Rabuse 1976a:240-61.

Raimondi, Ezio. 1972. *Metafora e storia*. Turin: Einaudi.

Rajna, Pio. 1960. "Ugo Ciappetta nella *Divina Commedia* (*Purgatorio,* Canto XX)." *Studi danteschi* 37:5-20.

Rheinfelder, Hans. 1966. "Dante's Paternoster." *Estudis romanics* 9:241-49.

————. 1968. *Philologische Schatzgräbereien. Gesammelte Aufsätze*. Munich: Hueber.

————. 1975. *Dante-Studien*. Ed. Marcella Roddewig. Vienna: Bohlau.

Roddewig, Marcella. 1985. "*Purgatorio* V nella esegesi antica e moderna." In *Dante Alighieri 1985. In memoriam Hermann Gmelin*: 31-47, ed. Richard Baum and Willi Hirdt. Tübingen: Stauffenburg.

Roncaglia, Aurelio. 1956. "Il canto VI del *Purgatorio.*" *Rassegna della letteratura italiana* 60:407-26.

Ronconi, Alessandro. 1964. "Per Dante interprete dei poeti latini." *Studi danteschi* 41:5-36.

———. 1965. "L'incontro di Stazio con Virgilio." *Cultura e Scuola* 4:566-71.

Rorem, Paul. 1993. *Pseudo-Dionysius: A Commentary on the Texts and an Introduction to Their Influence.* New York–Oxford: Oxford University Press.

Rossi, Luca Carlo. 1993. "Prospezioni filologiche per lo Stazio di Dante." In *Dante e la "bella scola" della poesia*: 207-28. Ravenna: Longo.

Russo, Vittorio. 1967. *Sussidi di esegesi dantesca.* Naples: Liguori.

———. 1971. *Esperienze e/di letture dantesche (tra il 1966 e il 1970).* Naples: Liguori.

Sarolli, Gian Roberto. 1971. *Prolegomena alla "Divina Commedia."* Florence: Olschki.

Schless, Howard H. 1984. *Chaucer and Dante: A Revaluation.* Norman, Okla.: Pilgrim Press.

Schmitt, Jean-Claude. 1985. "Entre le Texte et l'image: les gestes de prière de saint Dominique." In *Persons in Groups. Social Behavior as Identity Formation in Medieval and Renaissance Europe*: 195-220, ed. R. C. Trexler. Binghamton, N.Y.: Medieval & Renaissance Texts & Studies.

———. 1990. *La Raison des gestes dans l'Occident médiéval.* Paris: Gallimard.

Schreckenberg, Heinz. 1972. *Die Flavius-Josephus-Tradition in Antike und Mittelalter.* Leiden: Brill.

———. 1996. *The Jews in Christian Art: An Illustrated History.* New York: Continuum.

Scott, John A. 1972. "La contemporaneità Enea-Davide [*Convivio*, IV v 6]," *Studi danteschi* 49:129-34.

———. 1977. *Dante magnanimo: Studi sulla "Commedia."* Florence: Olschki.

———. 1990. "Dante and Philosophy." *Annali d'italianistica* 8:258-77.

———. 1991. "Beatrice's Reproaches in Eden: Which 'School' Had Dante Followed?" *Dante Studies* 109:1-23.

———. 1995a. "The Unfinished *Convivio* as a Pathway to the *Comedy*." *Dante Studies* 113:31-56.

———. 1995b. "Una contraddizione scientifica nell'opera dantesca: i 'due soli' di *Purgatorio* XVI.107." In Boyde/Russo 1995:149-55.

———. 1996. *Dante's Political Purgatory.* (Middle Ages Series.) Philadelphia: University of Pennsylvania Press.

———. 2004 [forthcoming]. *Understanding Dante.* Notre Dame: University of Notre Dame Press.

Scrivano, Riccardo. 1970. "L'orazione di Ugo Capeto: Morale, politica e retorica in Dante." *L'Alighieri* 12:13-34.

Shankland, Hugh. 1975. "Dante's 'Aliger'." *Modern Language Review* 70:764-85.

———. 1977. "Dante's 'Aliger' and Ulysses." *Italian Studies* 32:21-40.

Shoaf, Richard A. 1975. "Dante's *colombi* and the Figuralism of Hope in the *Divine Comedy*." *Dante Studies* 93:27-59.

———. 1978. "'Auri sacra fames' and the Age of Gold (*Purg.* XXII, 40-41 and 148-150)." *Dante Studies* 96:195-99.

———. 1991. "Ugolino and Erysichthon." In Sowell 1991:51-64.

Singleton, Charles S. 1954. *Dante Studies I. Elements of Structure*. Cambridge, Mass.: Harvard University Press.

———. 1957. *Dante Studies II. Journey to Beatrice*. Cambridge, Mass.: Harvard University Press.

———. 1965. "The Poet's Number at the Center." *Modern Language Notes* 71:1-10.

———. 1966. "Campi semantici dei canti xii dell'*Inferno* e xiii del *Purgatorio*." In *Miscellanea di studi danteschi*:11-22. Genoa.

Smalley, Beryl. 1964. *The Study of the Bible in the Middle Ages*. 2nd ed. Notre Dame, Ind.: University of Notre Dame Press.

Sowell, Madison A., ed. 1991. *Dante and Ovid: Studies in Intertextuality*. Binghamton, N.Y.: Medieval & Renaissance Texts & Studies.

Spitzer, Leo. 1963. *Classical and Christian Ideas of World Harmony: Prolegomena to an Interpretation of the Word "Stimmung."* Ed. Anna G. Hatcher. Baltimore: Johns Hopkins University Press.

Stefanini, Ruggero. 1992. "Spunti di esegesi dantesca: Due contrappassi (*Inf.* VI e XIX) e due cruces (*Purg.* XXVII 81 e *Par.* XXXII 139). In *Forma e parola: Studi in memoria di Fredi Chiappelli*: 45-65, ed. Dennis J. Dutschke, Pier Massimo Forni, Filippo Grazzini, Benjamin R. Lawton, Laura Sanguineti White. Roma: Bulzoni.

———. 1995a. "Buonconte and Palinurus: Dante's Reworking of a Classical Source." In Franco/Morgan 1995:100-111.

———. 1995b. "Guittone poeta politico." In Picone 1995:165-76.

———. 1996. "Tenzone sì e tenzone no." *Lectura Dantis* 18-19:111-28.

———. 1997. "Fra *Commèdia* e *Com(m)edìa*. Risalendo il testo del poema." *Lectura Dantis* 20-21:3-32.

Stewart, Dana E., and Alison Cornish, eds. 2000. *Sparks and Seeds. Medieval Literature and Its Afterlife. Essays in Honor of John Freccero*. Turnholt: Brepols.

Sturm-Maddox, Sara. 1987. "The *Rime petrose* and the Purgatorial Palinode." *Studies in Philology* 84:119-33.

Tatlock, J. S. P. 1934-35. "The Last Cantos of the *Purgatorio.*" *Modern Philology* 32:111-25.

Thompson, David B. 1974. *Dante's Epic Journeys.* Baltimore: Johns Hopkins University Press.

Toffanin, Giuseppe. 1921. "La 'Foetida Aegyptissa' e la 'femmina balba.'" *Giornale storico della letteratura italiana* 77:147-49.

Toynbee, Paget. 1897. "Dante's Obligations to the *Magnae Derivationes* of Uguccione da Pisa." *Romania* 26:537-554.

Tress, Daryl M. 1999. "The Metaphysical Science of Aristotle's *Generation of Animals* and its Feminist Critics." In *Aristotle: Critical Assessments. II. Physics, Cosmology and Biology*: 330-59, ed. Lloyd P. Gerson. London: Routledge & Kegan Paul.

Tucker, Dunstan J., O.S.B. 1960. "In exitu Israel de Aegypto: *The Divine Comedy* in the Light of the Easter Liturgy." *American Benedictine Review* 11:43-61.

Van Dijk, S. J. P, and J. Hazelden Walker. 1960. *The Origins of the Modern Roman Liturgy: The Liturgy of the Papal Court and the Franciscan Order in the Thirteenth Century.* Westminster, Md.: Newman.

Van Dyke, Carolynn. 1985. *The Fiction of Truth: Structures of Meaning in Narrative and Dramatic Allegory.* Ithaca, N.Y.: Cornell University Press.

Varanini, Giorgio. 1989. "Dante e Lucca." In *Dante e le città dell'esilio. Atti del Congresso Internazionale di Studi, Ravenna (11-15 settembre 1987)*: 91-114, ed. Guido di Pino. Ravenna: Longo.

Verrall, A. W. 1908. "Dante on the Baptism of Statius." *Albany Review* 3:181-203.

Vessey, David. 1973. *Statius and the Thebaid.* Cambridge: Cambridge University Press.

Vickers, Nancy. J. 1983. "Seeing is Believing: Gregory, Trajan, and Dante's Art." *Dante Studies* 101:67-85.

———. 1989. "Widowed Words: Dante, Petrarch, and the Metaphors of Mourning." In Brownlee/Stephens 1989:97-108.

Warner, Marina. 1976. *Alone of All Her Sex. The Myth and the Cult of the Virgin Mary.* New York: Knopf.

Wenzel, Siegfried. 1965. "Dante's Rationale for the Seven Deadly Sins (*Purgatorio* XVII)." *Modern Language Review* 60:529-33.

———. 1967. *The Sin of Sloth: Acedia in Medieval Thought and Literature.* Chapel Hill: University of North Carolina Press.

Wilkins, Ernest Hatch. 1955-56. "Dante's Celestial 'Scaleo': Stairway or Ladder?" *Romance Philology* 9:216-222.

————. 1959. *The Invention of the Sonnet and Other Studies in Italian Literature*. Rome: Edizioni di Storia e Letteratura.

Young, Carl. 1933. *The Drama of the Medieval Church*. 2 vols. Oxford: Clarendon.

Zaleski, C. 1987. *Otherworld Journeys: Accounts of Near-Death Experience in Medieval and Modern Times*. New York–Oxford: Oxford University Press.

Ziolkowski, Jan. 1985. *Alain of Lille's Grammar of Sex: The Meaning of Grammar to a Twelfth-Century Intellectual*. Speculum Anniversary Monographs, vol. 10. Cambridge, Mass.: The Medieval Academy of America.

INDEX OF ITALIAN, LATIN, AND
OTHER FOREIGN WORDS DISCUSSED
IN THE NOTES

Note. The Additional Notes are not included in the indexes.
References are to notes, by canto and line.

INDEX OF PASSAGES CITED
IN THE NOTES

References are to notes, by canto and line.

INDEX OF PROPER NAMES
IN THE NOTES

References are to notes, by canto and line.

INDEX OF PROPER NAMES IN THE TEXT
AND TRANSLATION

Only the actual occurrences of proper names are listed here. In most cases, both Dante's forms and those used in modern English are indexed; the main entry is in English, with Dante's Italian in parentheses. References are by canto and line number.